THE HEROIC CITY

ROSEMARY WAKEMAN

THE HEROIC CITY
Paris, 1945-1958

THE UNIVERSITY OF CHICAGO PRESS — CHICAGO AND LONDON

ROSEMARY WAKEMAN is associate professor of history and director of the Urban Studies Program at Fordham University and the author of *Modernizing the Provincial City: Toulouse, 1945–1975*.

The University of Chicago Press, Chicago 60637
The University of Chicago Press, Ltd., London
© 2009 by The University of Chicago
All rights reserved. Published 2009
Printed in the United States of America
18 17 16 15 14 13 12 11 10 09   1 2 3 4 5
ISBN-13: 978-0-226-87023-6 (cloth)
ISBN-10: 0-226-87023-5 (cloth)

Published with the generous support of Furthermore: a program of the J. M. Kaplan Fund, and the Florence Gould Foundation.

Library of Congress Cataloging-in-Publication Data
Wakeman, Rosemary.
   The heroic city : Paris, 1945–1958 / Rosemary Wakeman.
      p. cm.
   Includes bibliographical references and index.
   ISBN-13: 978-0-226-87023-6 (cloth : alk. paper)
   ISBN-10: 0-226-87023-5 (cloth : alk. paper) 1. Paris (France)—History—1944– 2. Paris (France)—Social life and customs—20th century. 3. Public spaces—France—Paris—History. I. Title.
   DC737.W26 2009
   944'.361082--dc22
                                          2009009146

♾ The paper used in this publication meets the minimum requirements of the American National Standard for Information Sciences—Permanence of Paper for Printed Library Materials, ANSI Z39.48-1992.

To Georgiana and Victoria

List of Illustrations ix
Preface xi

Introduction 1
1. Paris in the 1950s 19
2. The Landscape of Populism 62
3. Public Space and Confrontation 106
4. Spatial Imagination and the Avant-Garde 162
5. Paris as Cinematic Space 204
6. The Left Bank 241
7. Planning Paris 289
Conclusion: Constructing the Paris of Tomorrow 341

Notes 349
Bibliography 377
Index 393

ILLUSTRATIONS

FIGURE 1. Slum district or *îlot insalubre* in 1955   46

FIGURE 2. A vegetable street trader in Montmartre, 1955   52

FIGURE 3. Dockers at the pont d'Austerlitz, June 13, 1950   55

FIGURE 4. Construction of the Maison de la Radio, August 4, 1959   60

FIGURE 5. Jacques Prévert, 1955   72

FIGURE 6. French-fry sellers, rue Rambuteau, 1946   76

FIGURE 7. Avenue Simon Bolivar, Belleville, 1950   78

FIGURE 8. Neighborhood *bal populaire*, place des Abbesses, 1950   87

FIGURE 9. Crowd at the Foire du Trône, place de la Nation, March 29, 1948   93

FIGURE 10. Ridgway Riots, May 30, 1952   125

FIGURE 11. The 1953 May Day march   127

FIGURE 12. Demonstration in support of Abbé Pierre, December 23, 1954   141

FIGURE 13. Tent city along the Seine River, October 1, 1955   142

FIGURE 14. Abbé Pierre with housing prototype, February 20, 1956   143

FIGURE 15. North Africans at La Ville d'Oran Hotel, April 1950   151

FIGURE 16. North Africans gathering at the Grand Mosque, March 9, 1956   155

FIGURE 17. Demonstrators at the place de la République, September 4, 1959   160

FIGURE 18. Îlot 4 and the rue du Château-des-Rentiers, March 8, 1951   174

FIGURE 19. The rue Sauvage, September 29, 1953   190

FIGURE 20. Léo Malet and Felix Labisse, October 31, 1958   194

FIGURE 21. The rue du Château-des-Rentiers, October 28, 1961   197

FIGURE 22. The Deux Moulins redevelopment project, June 12, 1969   202

FIGURE 23. Roger Pigaut and Claire Maffei as *Antoine et Antoinette*, 1947   211

FIGURE 24. Joseph Kosma, Jacques Prévert, Marcel Carné, Jean Gabin, and Alexandre Trauner   227

FIGURE 25. Nathalie Nattier and Yves Montand in *Les Portes de la nuit*, 1946   230

FIGURE 26. Pierre Brasseur and Dany Carrel in *Porte des Lilas*, 1957   234

FIGURE 27. Francis Lemarque and Yves Montand, September 30, 1953   250

FIGURE 28. Scene from *Les Tricheurs*, 1958   263

FIGURE 29. Student rag procession or *monôme de bac*, June 30, 1954   275

FIGURE 30. Student protest, December 10, 1958   284

FIGURE 31. Demonstration for peace in Algeria, October 1957   287

FIGURE 32. The rue du Château-des-Rentiers and îlot 4, June 12, 1969   319

FIGURE 33. The rue Saint Paul in the Marais, December 1942   331

FIGURE 34. Charles de Gaulle and Pierre Sudreau at the "Demain . . . Paris" Exposition, April 17, 1961   342

PREFACE

When I began research for this book, I found that Paris from 1945 to 1958 was a space in between. It was a fuzzy transitional era sandwiched between two extraordinary events: the Second World War, with all its complicated meanings for France, and the 1960s, a period of radical change. The late 1940s and the 1950s were an ignored, little-understood moment that for the most part had gone unexamined. The only trace of it that seemed to remain was in black-and-white photographs dripping with nostalgia for a simpler past, and whose memories, particularly of the wars of decolonization, were too painful to recount. Simply finding the historical evidence of what exactly took place, what actually went on in Paris, was the first priority. The task was made more difficult by my decision to focus on public space and the public domain. The term "public space" did not even come into use until much later. One can look long and hard—and fruitlessly—for the most fleeting reference to this term in government documents, in newspapers, or in the treatises by urbanists in the period under study. Yet the public domain of Paris has been, and continues to be, such a vital arena of historical inquiry, its spectacle so entwined with the way we understand the modern urban experience and with modernity itself, that the investigation of the streets of Paris after the war seemed well worth the effort.

And that effort turned out to be enormous. Traces of the public world of Paris in the 1950s seemed to be nowhere and everywhere at the same time. There was no one library or archive to mine, but seemingly every library and archive. There were no sections of card catalogs straightforwardly marked *l'espace public* or *manifestations populaires* or *fêtes publiques*. Instead, references to public events were hidden away in no end of illogical categories. At times I seemed to be chasing a phantom world recorded only in the most ephemeral references or in dusty boxes of materials no one had ever bothered to organize and catalog. The detective work for this book proved to be the greatest challenge. And yet, just when I would end a day of research frustrated, wandering into a library or bookstore, asking yet again and to no avail whether there were materials on Paris in the 1950s, Parisians of a certain age standing alongside me at the reception desk would chime in that yes, they remembered those years. Then began their recollections and tales of the city, and that world would suddenly appear in all its richness.

And so I made many friends doing research for this book. Complete strangers, Parisians from a variety of backgrounds, were delighted to add their memories and perspectives. Librarians and archivists at a range of institutions dug out photo albums and cartons of neglected materials. Especially important were the massive bound volumes of newspapers that I learned to rely on, page by page, in order to piece together the history of the spaces, places, and events of the Paris landscape. A portion of this research was accomplished off the beaten track—in storage rooms at the offices of the *Revue urbanisme*, for example, which the staff opened for me to rummage through, or in the back rooms of the library at the Musée Social or the Médiathèque musicale de Paris at Les Halles. It would be impossible to recount the number of people I irritated with my dogged insistence on capturing urban space in this bygone era that seemed somehow to have escaped official record. Yet they all patiently added their advice and expertise, and I owe them my genuine thanks for their extraordinary consideration and professionalism. Particularly important was the assistance of the staff at the Institut national de l'audiovisuel, who were immensely helpful in fathoming the world of French television and in locating materials from the 1950s. Although archived, many of the programs were not viewable either because of formatting or because of copyright restrictions. Once again, finding the evidence was the trick. There were also moments of real pleasure in this research. Reading the detective novels of Léo Malet and spending a summer watching films at the Bibliothèque du film are among the most memorable.

Pascal Ory, Danièle Voldman, and Anthony Sutcliffe were the first to help me scope out and frame this research and ask the right questions. I was fortunate to be the beneficiary of the wisdom and insight of Danielle Tartakowsky, Jean-Louis Cohen, and Patrice Higonnet. My colleagues at the Institut d'urbanisme de Paris provided enormous support. I thank them for generously sharing their knowledge and scholarship on Paris, and for introducing me to the extraordinary repository of architectural and urban planning journals that were crucial to this study. My thanks in particular to Annie Fourcaut and Thierry Paquot for their reading of the manuscript draft. Much gratitude goes to my American colleagues Charles Rearick and Vanessa Schwartz for their expertise and perceptive questions, and especially to David Jordan for his extremely valuable evaluation of the manuscript. As editors of *French Historical Studies*, Ted Margadant and Joby Margadant provided vital support with a special issue on twentieth-century Paris. My colleagues and students at Fordham University offer the stimulating academic environment crucial to research and scholarship. The project benefited greatly from a Fordham University Faculty Research Grant. The Florence Gould Foundation and the Furthermore program of the J. M. Kaplan Fund generously provided support for photographs and publication. In the end, the decisions on analysis and the errors in judgment are entirely my own. This book is dedicated to two sisters who were the most formidable influences on my intellectual development, despite the fact that their own educations were quite limited: my mother, Georgiana, and my aunt Victoria. Both refused to accept anything less than advancing intellect, education, and ambition. Both were mesmerized by cities and reveled in living urban lives.

In the summer of 1942, the film director Marcel Carné met with the poet and screenwriter Jacques Prévert in Nice. The two men were seminal figures in French filmmaking in the years before the war. Now in the south of France, evading Vichy and the occupation, both were searching around for a new film project. Paris's legendary "boulevard du Crime," as the boulevard du Temple was known, intrigued Prévert as a possible subject matter. One of the city's grand promenades, the boulevard du Temple had stretched along the boundary between the old Marais on the Right Bank and the outlying faubourg du Temple. Its carnivalesque atmosphere drew *le Tout-Paris* in the first half of the nineteenth century. Packed each night under the boulevard's ancient trees, the crowds imbibed a multitude of more or less moral delights: the theaters and dance halls, circus troupes and farces, the *cabinets de curiosités*, the colorful buffoonery, the political conspirators, the gamblers and pickpockets. The boulevard du Temple evoked the grand spectacle of the streets, and its history overflowed with a thousand alluring tales, especially of the Funambules Theater and Baptiste Debureau, who became the greatest mime of his day; of the legendary actor Frédérick Lemaître, known as the "Talma des boulevards"; and of the fiery poet-assassin Pierre François Lacenaire. Carné left Nice for Paris to scour the Marais's Carnavalet Museum for historic material, and there, amid the engravings and lithographs, he found his film.

Filming for *Les Enfants du paradis* began in 1943 under the watchful eye of Vichy and the German occupiers. This apparently did not prevent the French underground from using the shoot as a cover for their activities, with scores of active Resistance fighters working on the set and Carné fending off the French Milice and the German Gestapo with a variety of excuses. The composer Joseph Kosma and the set designer Alexander Trauner, both Hungarian Jews, worked on the film clandestinely. The boulevard du Temple itself had been a victim of Baron Haussmann's urban renewal projects. It was chopped up and its theaters demolished in 1862 to build the imposing place du Château d'Eau. Those anxious to clean up its image then reconstructed the area as "a platitude . . . a sterile, dead decorative version of itself," in the plaintive words of a critic.[1] Thus the street of the 1940s offered little by way of a backdrop, even if the film could somehow have been shot on location. The Germans carted off the neighborhood's artisan goods, and strict curfews made anything but banal forays into the street exceedingly dangerous. The boulevard's eccentricities were replaced by an oppressive silence. Only the roundup of Jews provided a sort of perverse and tragic antifestival of destitute people parading to their demise. It was left to Carné and his crew to restore the boulevard du Crime in all its drama in the midst of the devastating occupation. Almost 10 percent of the film's budget and three months of work at La Victorine Studios in Nice were dedicated to the lavish re-creation of the boulevard's life, a feat accomplished in the face of wartime shortages, destructive storms that ruined many of the initial structures, and shifts to Paris and then back to Nice during the Allied landings in 1944. Trauner eventually pieced together the backdrop from sets used in Carné's earlier films and contraband materials from the black market.

Yet when we see Carné's boulevard du Crime on film, it is dazzling. Carné slowed down the production process when he heard the news of the Allied landings in Normandy so that *Les Enfants du paradis* would be the first film of the Liberation. And for all else this film evokes, within the context of August 1944 it was a thinly disguised allegory of resistance in a city that can rarely be dominated for long. The silver screen swarms with a multitude engaged in revelry. Over two thousand extras were jammed between makeshift barriers to recapture the boulevard's excitement and pageantry. The entertainers work the crowds with their *parade*, or come-on. The performances are both staged and impromptu. Theater and life are one. The stage set is the city, and the boulevard is a metropolis in miniature. The film's central female character, the enigmatic Garance, played to perfection by Arletty, is the very personification of France—Marianne come to life. Born in Ménilmontant, Garance wistfully remembers her happy childhood in the city's poorest working-class neighborhoods. She refuses to be humiliated. "Myself," she says to Count Mornay in a direct allegory of France's submission to German occupation, "I adore freedom." At the film's end she plunges into the whirlwind along the boulevard du Crime. It absorbs her, and she disappears.

The film serves as an apt introduction to this book. In 1985 the French author Hugo Lacroix mused that "like the Rodin Museum, Marseille's zoo, swimming at Collioure, the *autoroute du Sud*, the Vaux-le-Vicomte chateau, and the Paris Métro, *Les Enfants du paradis* is one of those poles of conversion . . . that is not so much our national heritage as it is our national paradise."[2] This spectacular evocation of the street life of Paris demonstrates perhaps better than any flaunting of sources the significance of the city's public pageantry. The film's title, which translates as *Children of Paradise* or *Children of the Gods*, refers to the city's poor, who occupied the cheap seats high in the balconies of the boulevard du Temple's popular theaters. They were anything but a passive audience. Performing on the boulevard to attract ticket buyers, players were at their mercy. It was this raucous public that decided who was popular, who would find fame, and who would go hungry. Anyone who failed to entertain them was attacked with bawdy uproar and even violence. What is captured so expressively in *Les Enfants du paradis* is public life as theater, or *theatrum mundi*. Melodrama, tragedy, and subversion infiltrate the film's screenplay. The concept has a long tradition. Both the theater and urban space evolved historically as stages of action and drama. The medieval and Renaissance procession, the festival, and the public ceremony were all part of the "publicity of representation" identified by Jürgen Habermas as crucial for creating the space of the city as the privileged eye of power.[3] Social signals were staged. Public posturing and performance were a projection of culture; public behavior, a form of art. They made social encounters meaningful.

Needless to say, the categories of public and civil society changed dramatically during the modern era. New divisions between private and public, between older social codes and new ones, remapped the spaces of the city. Theatrical hyperspace was eventually appropriated by the Paris citizenry as a "theater of revolution" that inaugurated sweeping changes in public space and collective civic life. By the 1830s the virtuoso public performance, the *grand geste*, had become indispensable to romantic sensibilities. Mime Baptiste Debureau and actor Frédérick Lemaître were popular heroes, "men of the people"—stock types of collective urban life. King Louis-Philippe paid homage to this populist theater in his annual procession along the boulevard du Temple to celebrate the *trois glorieuses* cherished by Parisians—the three-day insurrection of July 27–29, 1830. But the unruly crowds in the midst of this working-class enclave made it a risky business. It was indeed the disorder spilling out from the theater balconies onto the rebellious streets of 1848 that threatened the city's elites and prompted them to "renovate" the boulevard de Crime and silence the children of the gods once and for all. The *theatrum mundi* disappeared at the hands of modern bourgeois capitalism and Haussmann's urban renewal. Most scholars point to this moment as a definitive crisis in public culture.[4] Modern public space was organized for the free circulation of money, commodities, and people. It became a capitalist spectacle, a consumable vision of a civic world in which the surfaces of the city lacked any real meaning or engagement and in fact came to stand for estrangement and alienation. The street, the square, space itself became objects, even monuments, disconnected from their social content. The "people" became passive spectators enthralled by the scene. They withdrew from a stage now dedicated to facile leisure and mass consumer spectacle. The individual was suddenly alone in the crowd.

This image of the city as spectacle stands for modernity and determines the way we perceive and represent Paris in the nineteenth and twentieth centuries. It provides a structure to the myriad and complex elements of urban existence and makes them into a comprehensive scene. It has become a commonplace of intellectual history to treat this modern urban space as a central category of social structure and cultural analysis. Social critics from George Simmel to Theodor Adorno, Sigfried Kracauer, and Walter Benjamin have all sought to understand space as an expression of social conditions. Their work provides us with a rich theoretical framework for establishing the spatial foundations upon which metropolitan individuality is constructed, as well as the spatial relationships between the individual and the crowd and among social groups. Paris has been vital to this analysis. The legendary allure of Paris, what made the city special, was its *exterior* quality. Although there was no end of complaining about the disgusting, filthy conditions throughout the nineteenth and twentieth centuries, it was the phantasmagoria of the city's public atmosphere—its streets, cafés, theaters, amusements, boulevards, promenades, and train stations—that attracted so much attention and fascination. Paris became the archetype of modern spectacle.

My purpose is to understand the public realm in Paris during the late 1940s and 1950s—years that lay at the crux of twentieth-century transformation. What happened to the magnetic capital of modernity?[5] How were the public spaces of Paris reshaped by the conflict of the Second World War, the postwar years of rebuilding, and the *trente glorieuses* of modernization between 1945 and 1975?[6] As is well-known, the Second World War cruelly repressed public life. The city's streets, squares, and ceremonial places became heightened metaphorical objects precisely because of the massive disruption of memory and ritual and their sweeping replacement by alien constructions. One has only to think of the newsreel footage of Adolf Hitler standing triumphantly in the summer of 1940 at the Trocadéro and looking out at the Eiffel Tower to sense the explicit, dramatic significance of the city's landscape. That Paris had survived when so many of Europe's other great capitals were reduced to rubble represented something of the eternal, the very core of French identity and spirit. Its endurance alone made the capital a metaphor for the heroic. This image had even more resonance on the streets of Paris, where the anguish and struggle for survival were so apparent.

The experiences of repression, of loss and displacement, of being in exile at home and then liberated, gave the surfaces of Paris intense meaning. By March 1945, when Pathé-Cinéma's three-hour version of *Les Enfants du paradis* premiered at the Palais de Chaillot, it was clear that the price for Garance's dream of freedom had indeed been high. Arletty herself was arrested and briefly imprisoned as a collaborator for her affair with a Luftwaffe officer—this despite her saucy retort that "my heart is French but my ass is international." The boulevard du Temple and the place de la République were the scenes of fierce battles during the Liberation. The Germans controlled the barracks at République, and the fighting went on for three days. German mortars hit the town hall, blasted down the boulevard Voltaire, and plunged into the canal Saint-Martin. At the signal of a huge flag the Forces françaises de l'intérieur (FFI) took up their positions in the doorways and watched as French tanks headed up the rue du Faubourg du Temple toward the Germans, who finally capitulated. Hundreds of wounded were rushed to Saint-Antoine Hospital. The streets were littered with bouquets and makeshift crosses for those killed in combat. At least some of the viewers who had escaped the frigid cold to sit quietly in the dark of the Chaillot auditorium and watch the boulevard's spectacle unfold onscreen had no doubt just fought for its deliverance and staged their own street celebration. The distance of a century must have melted away in their own encounter with the *theatrum mundi* of August 1944. Paris was free. But in 1945 daily life remained a misery. Food, coal, and gasoline were all scarce. A dismayed Carné watched the audience flee during the last thirty minutes of the film's premier in an attempt to catch the last Métro train just after midnight—the only way home. But in *Les Lettres françaises*, Georges Sadoul recalled that in the dark days of that frozen winter of 1944–45, France emerged in Carné's masterpiece, "unscathed—ragged, overwhelmed, desperate, but triumphant in its art . . . with a heartrending confidence that answered our dreams."[7] The film's first run in Paris lasted for over a year and grossed forty-one million francs.

Defining the Public Realm

We should begin with working definitions of the enigmatic concepts of public sphere and public space. Public space is, of course, an arena of lavish representation. While it might be impossible to sort out the exact relationship between the physicality of urban public space and the politics of the public sphere, there are vital links between them.[8] The spaces of the city provide a symbolic context for public activities and a mechanism for carrying them out. It is the specific domain in which civil society takes place. As Mikhail Bakhtin puts it, the public square is the place where history is enacted.[9] It is an assemblage of dynamic elements punctuated by historical events and experiences. We can say, then, that public space is the geography of the public sphere, and I focus on this materiality as well as on the discursive process of producing space. From the perspective of Michel Foucault, ideologies and discursive practices are created in specific *places*.[10] They provide the pictures in our minds when we conceive our identities. Public space materializes the multiple and contradictory meanings held by different social groups. It sets them in concrete and stone. The public domain evolves from social negotiation and conflict. This process operates within and across the physical fabric of the city, and, particularly in Paris, across islands of public usage that are identified by a variety of visual ciphers, histories, and collective manifestations to become polymorphic, overlaid surfaces or strata, or perhaps even webs of meaning. As Richard Sennett has defined it, the public geography of a city is the civic impulse institutionalized.[11]

With the late capitalism of the second-half of the twentieth century, this public domain had changed, as Habermas put it, "from a culture-debating to a culture-consuming public."[12] A number of social theorists persuasively argue that capitalism distorted this robust civic sphere into a glittering shadow of its former self. Late capitalism is prone instead to social atomism and obsessive individualism. The result, according to this school of thought, is an emptying out of the richness and complexity of collective life and public space. Rather than depth of experience, public space is characterized by advertising, public relations, and the engineering of consent. According to the devastating critique of the postwar situationists, the "society of the spectacle" and the *con* of capitalist consumption came to define happiness. They suppressed any possibility of freedom. They were a "freezing of life."[13] This, then, is the spectacle of the city's public atmosphere, saturated with an enticing landscape of commerce and entertainment that the pseudo-citizen passively imbibes. In the strictly regulated and privatized spaces of the late-capitalist metropolis, real political and social power has been surrendered.

Associated with this perspective is the canonical history of the postwar era. The year 1945—Year Zero, as it is often called—is perceived as a divide of extraordinary proportions. It marked a "new beginning" in which modernism and modernization were coopted by the combined forces of corporate capitalist and state bureaucracies in a vast program for the reconstruction and reorganization of France. In the customary historic narrative, which oversimplifies and distorts midcentury culture, the past has been vanquished, leaving France to negotiate the sweeping transformations of the *trente glorieuses*. In the words of Kristin Ross, postwar modernization was "headlong, dramatic, and breathless."[14] Modernist architectural fantasies about creation *ex nihilo* in Paris exactly parallel this imagery. Futuristic clusters of glass-walled skyscrapers and suburban housing estates would replace a decrepit metropolis teetering on the brink of collapse. The nation's capital underwent a relentless dismantling and decentralization beyond the imagination even of Haussmann a hundred years earlier. Modernism's fixation on abstraction and regulation created a vocabulary of timelessness and an unchanging, privatized world of social control. As a result of these entwined historical images, most post-1945 studies of France emphasize the transition to the private consumer utopias of the *grands ensembles* (housing projects) and the retreat from the urban collective sphere.

My argument takes the postwar period and the spaces of the city in another direction. I concentrate on public space and civic engagement and how they interacted to construct a complicated and contentious public topography in the aftermath of war and during the transformative years of the 1950s. The years between 1945 and 1958 saw a transition of extraordinary texture and intensity that energized public debate and the spaces of the city and that determined the forms that late twentieth-century Paris would take. We might say that this period was a high-voltage conduit between the past and the future. My general contention is that, contrary to the traditional narrative of decay, the public spaces of Paris flourished. The city's public landscape was intensified. The streets overflowed with ritual, drama, and spectacle. Public space in Paris—from the *petit quartier* to the city's grandest ceremonial sites—was fluid, polyvalent, pierced with political and social tensions. This perspective makes use of the rich debate about the public sphere that has taken place since the publication of Habermas's *Structural Transformation of the Public Sphere*, and particularly of the cultural and postmodern critique his work has provoked. Rather than focusing on the monolithic, universalistic spectacle of modernism, scholars now point to the complex practices of local and popular culture. Theorists argue that this multifaceted public sphere, rather than being closed by the forces of late-capitalist modernization, has open boundaries. There are subaltern counterpublics that circulate counterdiscourses, actively vie for public power and space, and formulate oppositional interpretations of identities, interests, and needs.[15] The dialectic between normalization and differentiation in space and practice is particularly relevant here. As private space was being increasingly solidified and controlled, public space continued to be liquid and unruly. As technocratic urban planning reached out to impose rationality and uniform composition on the city, the public domain remained ambiguous and unpredictable. It was highly structured by official policy, but it was also a space of serendipity, of freedom of spirit and action. Hugo Lacroix remarks, in his meditation on the meaning of *Les Enfants du paradis*, that for the viewer the film is "paved with interior tensions, with moral crises, of sliding and bending 180 degrees for or against the characters.[16] These social and civic tensions were played out in the spaces of Paris by a multiplicity of publics throughout the period covered in this book. Who could occupy the public domain and how these polyvalent spaces could be appropriated became questions that tested the meaning of urban relations at their deepest level.

These multiform, heterogeneous spatialities mark the late 1940s and 1950s as a crucial transitional period in the twentieth century. It was the bridge between the first half of the century, with all its political violence and class struggle, and the second half, with its modernizing zeal and mass consumer culture. As a result, the chapters that follow deemphasize 1945 as a turning point. Rather than an entirely new "postwar" age, the period from the late 1940s on was shaped by the experiences of the 1920s and 1930s, by the war and occupation, and by the Resistance and Liberation. For this reason, the book frequently refers back to these earlier periods and to the uses of the immediate past in heightened mythic form. This is especially true of the Liberation, which was so effectively used as foundational myth. My analysis also takes the stance that there is no clear distinction between tradition and progress, nor is there any such thing as an "authentic modernity" or "modernism." Instead, there are a variety of modernisms that are distinctive in their complexity. Through a process of creative adaptation, modernism was made culturally specific.[17] The expression of an idiosyncratically French modernism sought the past as well as the future, and this collapsing together of imagery was seen not as a contradiction or a step backward, but as a move forward.

It is not my intention to impose a structured sociological definition on the "public sphere" or on the spaces it inhabited. There can be no single reading of either idea, and indeed the intellectual debate about them is distinguished by the diversity of opinion. Suffice it to refer to the French social critic Henri Lefebvre's contention that "every society produces a space, its own space that has an alphabet, language, signs and symbols of its own. This spatial code is not simply a means of reading or interpreting space: rather it is a means of living in that space, of understanding it, and of producing it."[18] My intention is to apply this perspective on how space is constructed and represented to the material environment of postwar Paris. The network of public spaces in such a flamboyant capital city as Paris is extraordinary in its extent and complexity. It is made up of the streets and squares, the neighborhoods and districts, the Métro stations, the cafés and dance halls, the public buildings, the quays of the Seine—the list goes on. Rather than imposing a rigorous structure on the city's public topography, I have allowed the evidence to take me to what were imagined and deemed to be the most important places. Many of these spaces were already heavily inscribed with historic, symbolic meaning. Forgotten, marginalized spaces emerged as newly significant, while new spaces gained meaning from contemporary events. I make no effort to treat the public spaces of Paris in their entirety—a hopeless task in any case. Nor do I attempt to rationalize or balance treatment across the city's landscape. The book privileges what could largely be called the east of Paris, because without doubt that is where events and discourse about civic life and collective space were most intense. And it privileges the street as public space. The street was understood as a zone of social and political power. For Walter Benjamin, it was a living and working space, the "home of the collective," which he defined as an eternally unquiet, eternally agitated being that experiences, learns, and invents as much as individuals do. "Parisians," Benjamin argued, "make the street an interior."[19] The Parisian street produced the feeling that the whole city was accessible and exploitable. This operational model had particular resonance with regard to the August 1944 Liberation as "retaking the street" and reappropriating the city. The entire period under study was characterized by at times a fun-loving, freewheeling, at times militant pedestrianism through the streets, a powerful "pedestrian speech act" or "walking rhetoric," as Michel de Certeau called it,[20] that transcribed a voracious political and social legibility onto the landscape.

The Decentered Metropolis

The production of urban space is always a battlefield of contending forces, and the Parisian story is a complicated one. One can immediately put forward the seemingly simple supposition that the spaces of Paris evoked the past at the same time as they summoned the future. Traditional uses of public space resurfaced alongside new forms of civic life. Once again, this underscores the bond between pre- and postwar culture. However, this combination of tradition and modernity was a more intricate Gordian knot than might initially appear, and ultimately it defined contemporary French identity. From the outset the thirst for change was accompanied by an almost equally potent sense of regret for all that had been lost. The image of Paris of the late nineteenth and early twentieth centuries was clearly that of a gleaming metropolis made cohesive by a myriad of centralizing influences: the boulevards, the universal expositions, the railroad, the Métro, and the automobile. It had been an unabashed self-reflective display of modernity. But in the confusing and exhilarating late 1940s and 1950s, it was not exactly clear what the future would hold for Paris as either a national or an international capital. The *ville lumière* had been dimmed by wartime catastrophe. It no longer held the position of avant-garde space, whose luminous surfaces and spectacle determined tastes and values. The city's stunning moment of modernity had passed. A prominent center was absent, despite the forces of modernization that had formed the city. There was no essential focal point for collective life, nor were there any primary public arteries that took the place of Haussmann's *grands boulevards*. Nor were the monumental sites of modernity an assumed rendezvous for civic consciousness.

The nostalgia and longing for the older spaces of Paris and their collective life were at their most palpable just when indeed these spaces seemed about to vanish. The rhythms of collective life were shattered not only by the Second World War, but also by the impact of postwar modernization, which threatened to eradicate any vestiges of the city's former life. The wistful remembering reflected the uncertainties and fears about the present; about reconstruction and the *trente glorieuses*, about the cold war, decolonization, and European integration. The impact of everything from mass media and television, fast-paced consumerism, and the new youth culture to promising urban renewal programs on the collective life of the city was profound. These interconnected dynamics constructed a complicated spatial landscape that was destabilizing as well as transformative. They acted as centrifugal forces, breaking down the capital's centrality and cohesion. Paris was a disassembled city. Its spaces were undergoing rupture and upheaval. The mesmerizing imagery of the City of Light was at risk of disintegrating.

The result of these anxieties about disintegration was that long-established collective practices returned with a vengeance. These practices were not vanquished, but instead were reinvigorated and reinvented by the preoccupation with historical memory that was one of the most striking phenomena of French postwar society.[21] But there was a "presentness" to this imagined past. The striking reappearance of customary practices and imagery was not at odds with modern transformation so much as an integral part of it. For Andreas Huyssen, memory discourses such as these are absolutely essential for recovery from trauma and for imagining the future. They permit us to "regain a strong temporal and spatial grounding of life and the imagination in a media and consumer society that increasingly voids temporality and collapses space."[22] The heightened engagement with public life and the spaces of the city in the 1950s was a savoring of the future and a hopeful invention of new forms of social and collective engagement. This intimate relationship between past and future was probably never so dramatic as in the late 1940s and 1950s. The city's spaces revealed the active coexistence of various temporalities that together redefined the idea of modernity and made Paris new.

The Liberation and reconstruction years themselves produced a dramatic and in part revolutionary urban spatiality that was endlessly reiterated as a symbol of a new postwar social contract. Although many would argue this was a short-lived euphoria, it acted as a centrifugal force on the city's topography, fracturing the centralizing influences that had created Paris as the "capital of modernity." The city's working classes were able to incarnate the authentic interests of the nation as a universal class. Out of the puzzle of historic neighborhood-villages the life-world of ordinary people materialized as the hope for a new Paris and a new France. Collective life itself was imagined as primarily an everyday, spatial concept. Kristin Ross argues that an earlier theatrical remapping of social and physical space during the Paris Commune was a form of avant-garde, a "collapsing . . . between high art and popular reportage, poetic and political, the venerable and the vernacular."[23] The same might be said of the *theatrum mundi* of the late 1940s and 1950s in which a variety of actors traversed the mediatized public universe, became visible and invisible, to create a multiplicity of publics and civic dialogues that functioned with richness and complexity.[24] This spatial imaginary created a heterogeneous idea of *place* as a distinctive localized milieu. Its boundaries were porous, its character that of the everyday. There was an intense desire to narrate and visualize the spaces of the city and the ways in which people interacted in them. Novelists and urban observers, film and television directors, and the city's intellectual elites bore down on the city's landscape and focused their collective lenses on its life with a detail and a moral intensity that were unprecedented. The fragmented city was sighted, surveyed, opened up for examination. All of this attention produced novel representations of time, space, and urban practices. The ordinary was heroicized. Anyone could become a celebrity, anything made into a celebrity event. Everyday vernacular places as well as the city's monumental spaces could be appropriated and given new meaning in untold ways. The city's public sphere became a "living" cinema powered by sociopolitical influence, mass media, and the capacity of a plethora of publics to stage their own performances with astonishing imagination and inventiveness.

It is the nature of these kinds of upheavals—experienced partly as threat, partly as liberation—to exhibit dramatic qualities as urban phenomenon. There was a collapsing of boundaries, a dramatic alteration in commonplace understandings of time and space, identity and language. Memory and temporality invaded space. Imagining both the past and the future, commemorating loss, and experimenting with new urban practices and forms were public ceremonies. The practices of public space were sensuous, emotional, and provocative. They relied on alternate forms of expression and subjectivity, the articulation of symbolic codes and representations outside rationalistic discourse. We might call this a *dynamization* of the public spaces of the city as dramatic culture. Rhetoric and posturing, singing and dancing, the inflation of signifiers and liturgy all imbued collective practices with the qualities of performance. It was an overtly modern experience in which media culture intervened to provide a hyperscenographic or even cinematic quality to both new and old forms of collective engagement. The accent was on sensuousness, the theatricality of civic life in the capital and its collective spaces. The heritage of centuries of architecture and urbanism were conceived as the stage on which people, as actors, would display their emotions and behavior, their social identities, their preoccupations, their ambitions, and ultimately their ability to act. This moves us forward to understanding mid-twentieth-century civic culture not as a withered surface version of some former self, but as something made more complex and powerful by the variety of media—photography, film, radio, and television—that created new discursive spaces and practices and new dimensions of the public sphere. The media were instrumental in how the city's life was imagined, formulated, and practiced. They expanded the public domain rather than constricted it, and their presence did not constitute a decline.

Each of the following chapters is meant to act as a lens on public space and collective life in Paris from 1945 to 1958. My purpose is to not only to provide a wide-angle perspective on spatiality, but also to create a cohesive and tangible historic structure to this period of transition. The commonality of vision and thinking is emphasized. A number of terms have been used to capture this mental picture of Paris in the late 1940s and 1950s: nostalgic, poetic, humanistic, communistic, revolutionary, romanticized, and intensely emotive. I have settled on *poetic humanism* and its counterpart, *poetic space*, as the idioms that most closely capture the spirit of this imagined landscape. They invented a sumptuous collective domain that was vivid, daring, highly subjectified, and ultimately heroic.

Chapter 1 begins with a contextual overview of Paris in 1945 and looks specifically at the role of the Liberation as a foundational myth in the spatial theater that followed in the late 1940s and 1950s. The social and cultural imaginary of the fragmented metropolis located the public life of the city in its neighborhoods, among its working people. The vision of Paris was populist. The commonplace was beatified. Chapter 2 examines the narratives that etched the portrait of an archetypal Paris, a mosaic of picturesque quartiers populated by *le peuple de Paris* for whom the street was a vibrant collective space. Through the late 1940s and 1950s, street fairs and dances, parades, student processions, and the May Day and *fête nationale* celebrations contended with endless commemoration ceremonies, star-studded public concerts, and radio shows broadcast live in the streets. More than simple nostalgia, this vision was understood as quintessentially French. It invented, reproduced, and validated treasured images of the city and its people and landscape. It was argued by many of the intellectuals treated in this book that everyday life harbored the capacity for social change. The decentering forces of the everyday gave the collective spaces of the city a rich capacity for invention and upheaval. Its nonrational, subversive qualities provided the ability to imagine in a utopian way. It was a vision explicitly associated with the Liberation and with the possibility of breakthrough into the future. In other words, these populist traditions were not simply nostalgic; rather, they and the atomized world of the neighborhood were propagated as revolutionary.

This fragmented vision of Paris was also linked to a revived municipalism and to the predominance of a left-wing and specifically communist political culture. In fact, decentering was multilayered. The well-known *immobilisme* of the Fourth Republic left the way open for a resurgence of local city politics. However, even unity at the municipal level was disputed by a further fracturing into the political fiefdoms of arrondissements, neighborhoods, and suburban towns. It was at this localized level that communists claimed an independent "right to the city" and set about building a new French society. But it was not just a militant left-wing politics that marked the spaces of Paris in the 1940s and 1950s. A certain style of militant pedestrianism also went with it. Along with strikes and violent protests—of which there were many—there was a collective movement that took place on foot—people walking, marching, dancing, processing in an intense political theater outside the official halls of power. Hundreds of thousands descended into the streets on a regular basis, evoking a multitude of traditional practices and topographies and creating new ones. Public ceremony and spectacle were ways of claiming civic life and citizenship—they were a political instrument.

What all these actors had in common was Paris, the streets and spaces that belonged to them all. "Street life" is a symbol of urban provocation and arousal, provocation that comes from experiences of the unexpected. They make the public space of the city a dynamic, autonomous realm where unwanted truths, independent and uncontrolled attitudes and outlooks, and the reality of exclusion are given free reign. It is this tension or creative collision, as Henri Lefebvre puts it, between the domination of space through private property, the state, and other forms of social power, and the appropriation of space for individual and social purposes that lies at the foundation of this study. The messiness of political practices, civil resistance and violence as spatial strategies, and the conditions under which the spaces of the city could be occupied and by whom are all issues essential to chapter 3. It looks at three examples of the political use of public space. First, strikes and protests over social conditions and the cold war dominated the spaces of Paris in the late 1940s and early 1950s. Secondly, the housing crisis was one of the most contentious political issues of this entire period and spilled out into the public domain, particularly in the mid-1950s. Thirdly, the violent struggle over decolonization that reverberated in the capital ultimately led to the downfall of the Fourth Republic.

The urban explorers and theorists who were instrumental in fashioning the image of Paris in the 1950s are introduced throughout the book. Chapter 4 is dedicated specifically to their engagement with the city and the ways in which their mutual point of focus created a mood of poetic humanism. The analysis focuses specifically on urban sociologists, urban planners, and the 1950s avant-garde. Once again, the commonality of vision in this intellectual cluster is emphasized. These individuals shared a profoundly left-wing grounding inherited from Marxist tradition, the Popular Front, and Liberation as well as from deeply held humanist convictions. Their idealized vision of society was that of a brotherhood of people, a powerful and enthusiastic working class ready to rebuild France. Intellectual elites aligned themselves with the *peuple*, the proletariat, the poor and oppressed. They imagined Paris as a puzzle of enclaves, or îlots, that were pedestrian and particularist in scale. *Flânerie* in the 1950s attempted to capture "real life" and "lived experience" as it took place in the everyday spaces of the city. There was a fascination with uncovering the hidden, decentered places of Paris.

The Paris that was produced in film and television also took part in this vigorous drawing out of the city's fragmented landscape. Chapter 5 is dedicated to these visual media. They offer the most observable evidence of the widely shared fascination with capturing the "lived" city and everyday spatiality, oral speech, and the language that was intrinsic to poetic space. However, film as well as photography and the newer medium of television did not simply reflect perceptions about the city and its public spaces; rather, they all shared in the shaping of those perceptions and the ways in which collective practice was carried out. In the work of critics such as Susan Sontag, visual media are a grammar and an ethics of seeing. They are an anthology of images that explicitly influence the shaping of reality.[25] An analysis of visual media has yet to receive the full attention it deserves for a full understanding of the complex and contradictory experience of urban public territory in the second half of the twentieth century. The photographs of Willy Ronis and Robert Doisneau, the work of filmmakers from Marcel Carné to René Clair, and the film and television documentaries of Jean Dewever and Paul-Henry Chombart de Lauwe (to take some of the most important examples) were instrumental in the production of landscape and collective life in postwar Paris. These visual depictions invented the language and texture of poetic space, of everyday space, and of marginal space, as well as chronicling their transformation. They opened up the city in novel ways and transfused the public sphere with complexity and new meaning.

The public spaces of Paris were filled as well with increasingly influential youth groups, sometimes parading, sometimes rampaging through the city. The postwar generation displayed enormous versatility in acts of defiance, or *détournement*, which are the subject of chapter 6. Their spatial territory was the Left Bank, which was divided into the discrete, separate districts of Saint-Germain-des-Prés and the Latin Quarter. Student strikes and traditional post-exam processions turned into melees, "rites of inversion" in which the ridiculous, the unseemly, and wildness negated the trap of normal existence—and became highly politicized. They were the primal scene of liberated and politically enfranchised French women. They were the terrain of the newly arrived immigrants who signified the painful and violent shift from the French imperium to decolonization. All these *enfants du paradis*—or "wild publics" in postmodern vocabulary[26]—were freewheeling performers in the show. In this role, they broke free of the public discourses controlled by professionals, experts, and state elites and created fertile, contested spaces for new, counterdiscursive practices and uses of the city. Various social groups were successful in appropriating and adding to the endless vocabulary of image and ritual manipulation as effective civic engagement. The city was a visual screen on which everyone became a star, every performance a spectacle.

With some of the worst slums in Europe and with its suburbs partially destroyed by wartime bombardment, the City of Light was actually a sordid place in the late 1940s and 1950s. There was little to recommend it as a vision of the future. Yet it was in the unique circumstance of the war's trauma and destruction that the city was imagined in a new form. The image of Paris was that of France, and the capital lay at the heart of national sentiment. How it would be renovated, how it would deal with its deteriorating infrastructure and housing crisis left by years of depression and war, and how public spaces would be structured were the challenges that confronted technocrats as they pored over the city's maps, plans, and statistical data. The overhaul of vast areas of the central district on the Right Bank and the Left Bank as well as the ringed *zone et fortif* was at stake. However, this study is not concerned with urban design in Paris as a formal discipline per se. Rather, it situates professional urbanists as one set of actors in a broader political drama about the terms of modern collective life. It places them within a public universe in which urbanism and architecture functioned as forms of political and social power. These are the subjects of chapter 7. Urban planning became far more public, more politicized. The French state dominated the public discourse about the capital's future. Urban planning was an attribute of state power and centralization as well as an instrument of social engineering. It was influenced by the heritage of *haussmannisation* as well as by the extraordinary authority of the Congrès internationaux d'architecture moderne (International Congress of Modern Architecture, or CIAM) and its promotion of the modern aesthetic in the reconstruction years. High-modernist visions of urban utopia pointed the way to the future. Yet a variety of competing voices and counterdiscourses, from preservationists to left-wing militants, weighed in on the potentials of the cityscape. The midcentury poetic humanist imaginary produced a body of urban theory and practice that is rarely treated in planning history. Yet it is crucial to understanding French perspectives on the city and the evolution of Paris. It militated against an authoritarian modernist overhaul of the central city, safeguarded the fragmented historic precincts, and produced an alternative ideal—a French version of modernism somewhere between the past and the future. By the end of the period under study in this volume—that is, the demise of the Fourth Republic in 1958—this poetic, humanist point of view was largely purged of its populist social and political muscle and distorted into a nostalgic, touristic vision of an unchanging, picturesque Paris. *Le peuple* were uprooted and displaced to the outer arrondissements and suburbs, where brutal demolition and the construction of modern housing estates completely transformed social and spatial arrangements.

I am not specifically interested in any one instance of these myriad events and movements—any one act in this public drama—or in dissecting its specific elements. My research is not a microhistory of any one aspect. Rather, it is the tumult and fluidity, the hyperbole and multisensuality of public life that are at the base of this study. It is the claiming of space and dialog in public, the inventing and reinventing of usage by a wide range of political and social actors, the use of narrative discourse, allegory, theater, and ritual that provide the thread of analysis. To find this creative capacity, I have followed the lead of Michel de Certeau and given full weight to play, celebration, transgression, and subversion, all of which are by definition transient and instantaneous. They reveal remarkably complex and rich public practices that belie the notion that the "people" of Paris were overpowered by the seductions of the consumer spectacle or modern private bliss and retreated from the public domain. Certainly the city's urban surfaces were intertwined with the contradictions of modernity, with ongoing capitalist formation, and with mass consumer culture. Yet the spectacle was not just one of a mediatized public manipulated by capitalist accumulation. Public culture and spatial appropriation were not limited solely to the official state or capitalist media machines, nor was the public's gaze focused only on the private consumer choices paraded in advertisements and superficial images. At the antithesis of these metaforces were social groups and movements, counterpublics that cobbled together ideas, objects, ceremonies, and language for startling new purposes. Eclectic, ironic, radically zany, at times violent, deeply passionate, and political, the poetic spaces of Paris were, in the words of Jean Vilar, a "theater of the people" that made the city a lavish stage of practice and imagery.

Paris in the 1950s

In 1946 Paris's inveterate *raconteur* and *flâneur* Léon Paul Fargue was commissioned by the Commissariat général au Tourisme to create a pamphlet on Paris that would beckon tourists back after the abyss of war. Fargue was near the end of a long life dedicated to poetry, literature, and loving portraits of the city of his birth. "Finally," Fargue sighed with relief, "we can welcome foreigners back into our hearts overflowing with emotion." With that, the pages of the tour guide begin to reacquaint us with the legendary monuments of Paris in official black-and-white images: the Eiffel Tower, Notre Dame Cathedral, the Arc de Triomphe. Couples stroll along the Seine. The curious browse through old prints and magazines at the quayside bookstalls. Barges meander up and down the river, passing fishermen on the quays as they languidly wait for a nibble. Alongside these iconographic visions of the city, the brochure also captured the other kind of images for which Paris was famous: the *petits métiers de la rue* that one could still see in the years immediately after the war. From the pages of Fargue's travel guide, picturesque street vendors smile into the camera behind carts covered with chestnuts in winter, with ice cream and flowers in summer. Street musicians, open-air artists, and a muscleman demonstrating his strength entertain the crowds. A junk dealer "sells everything and nothing, but freely spouts his opinions to anyone passing by." The pamphlet ends with the enticing promise that "you have only to consult a map of Paris to fulfill your fantasies."[1] Somehow, despite the vagaries of war and the black years of occupation, Paris had not changed. It remained eternally itself. The city's time-honored street spectacle was projected not only in film, most obviously in *Les Enfants du paradis*, but also in official discourse and in the public imagination. It came to represent what Paris *was*, at the heart of its urban experience. Fargue's description was an overtly sentimental, touristic one. But it came to represent a significant aspect of urban identity. Chroniclers turned to the recollection of a reliably unchanging city of the past. They invented a wistful time when the capital's "authentic" generosity of spirit and social peace infused its daily life and landscape—features that would dramatically rematerialize once the tears of war had been wiped away. "Nothing has apparently changed," Fargue intoned. "You can still really sense the down-to-earth spirit and courage of the *petit peuple de Paris*. It's been so long since I've left my refuge to see, to hear."[2] Olivier Merlin, a young journalist for the newspapers *Le Monde* and *Le Temps*, bicycled through a city devoid of automobiles in 1945 to discover a world where "social difference had been abolished; we lived fraternally once again, without violence, without foreign masters, without bombs or camouflage. Never had the Champs-Élysées looked so beautiful: completely cloudless as far as the Tuileries in the far distance." On an early morning ride around the place de l'Étoile, "with not a soul around, I cried out my name along the avenue Foch. I felt as if the familiarity of the sound was an acknowledgment of the right to the city, the right to this imperial esplanade."[3]

These wistful impressions of Paris would continue to resonate across the decade of the 1950s as the forces of change swept across the city until they had become a veritable torrent of evocative adoration about an imaginary place that existed somehow out of time. The hope for a better tomorrow, for the brave new world that would be built from the ashes of war, was intimately mingled with a desire for continuity with the past. The brutal conflicts of the 1930s and 1940s—and, for that matter, even the forces of urban modernization—created a profound longing to return to the familiar, even though it was understood somehow that things could never be the same. The prospect of revolutionary transformation reinforced traditional norms of sociability and the lived environment. *L'Air dans autres temps* was synonymous in everyone's mind with eternal Paris. It was created precisely from the dramatic social and political cataclysms that had overtaken the city. As an aesthetic vision, it was an integral ingredient of urban modernity.

One reason these images of Paris have become so iconographic is that the city did indeed emerge from the agonies of war intact. Unlike so many other European capitals that had suffered the horrors of bombardment,

Paris had surrendered in June 1940 without a struggle. Just after the German military's triumphal parade down the Champs-Élysées on June 18, Adolf Hitler invited the sculptor Arno Breker and the architects Hermann Giesler and Albert Speer to stand at the Trocadéro and feast their eyes on their most beautiful possession. Paris was the Nazi's crown jewel. So intent were the Germans on seducing Parisians and colonizing the City of Light that, at least on the surface, it operated more or less normally during the occupation. Even when the tide turned against the Nazis' New Order, Paris was still spared final destruction. In 1944, rather than hand the city over to Allied forces, Hitler had ordered the city destroyed. Wehrmacht engineers placed explosives around iconographic buildings and sites such as the Luxembourg Palace, the Dome of the Invalides, the Eiffel Tower, and Notre Dame Cathedral. Bombing the city with V1 and V2 rockets was another possibility. But General Dietrich von Choltitz, commander of Gross Paris, refused to carry out the Führer's orders. This decision, more than any other, saved the historic central districts. The joyous scenes of the Liberation in 1944, the street dances, the infectious rediscovery of the public domain became historic because the central city was still standing. Although bleak and exhausted, the view of Paris was a familiar, reassuring site. When the novelist Claude Aveline returned to Paris after the miracle of the Liberation, he realized immediately that it had escaped the war's destruction: "Paris knew none of this. There were some traces of combat, but that's all. And the most celebrated, legendary places, the Concorde, the Invalides, the Latin Quarter, the Luxembourg, the Étoile: they were free and safe."[4] The city's cherished monuments were still standing. Its landscape was recognizable as the nineteenth-century City of Light, the erstwhile temple of modernity. Historians, urbanists, and chroniclers of all points of view agreed that the Paris of the late 1940s and early 1950s was still visually the one magisterially fashioned under the Second Empire. It seemed to reemerge like a romantic vision from the past, symbolizing the nation's endurance just at this moment when it seemed so shattered. All of the elegance and sophistication, the grace and luminous beauty somehow would magically rematerialize. Life in Paris would be gay and confident again.

This visual bubble shielded the reality. The dark years of the war and occupation had been a disaster. They extinguished any notion of a genuine public sphere and isolated Paris from the rest of France almost completely. First of all, Paris was no longer the capital of France, but was reduced instead to a regional prefecture under the control of Vichy's military commanders and ultimately the German authorities. The occupation forces stationed their headquarters at the Opéra, while the German military occupied the Hôtel Mercure on the rue de Rivoli, and the Abwehr, the Hôtel Lutetia on the boulevard Raspail. Members of the municipal council and prefecture were appointed by the German occupying force. The Germans retained ultimate control over the governance of Gross Paris, spinning an administrative and martial web that ensured domination.[5] Some 2 million people hurriedly packed what they could and joined the massive exodus of lost souls heading south in June 1940 while being strafed by Stuka dive-bombers along the roads. It has been estimated that over forty thousand refugees died in their flight from the city. Paris was temporarily drained; only about one-third of its normal citizenry remained, although the numbers rebounded to around 2.5 million by 1941.

Every morning the Germans paraded down the Champs-Élysées in full uniform with military bands playing and flags flying. Huge swastikas hung from buildings and monuments. In a slap in the face to French sensibilities, even the city's clocks were set to Berlin time. Street and direction signs were in German. But scenes of hideous repression—neighborhood hunts and arrests, unmitigated violence and cruelty, the roundup of Jews—were the real public spectacles. According to official statistics, 1,360 Parisians were executed.[6] The persecution of the city's Jews began almost immediately. Beyond the humiliating brutality, the restrictions, and the property confiscations, deportation to the concentration camps began with a week in squalid captivity at the makeshift processing centers at Drancy or inside the Vélodrome d'hiver (Vél' d'Hiv) sports stadium. It culminated in the July 16–17, 1942, roundup or *rafle* of thirteen thousand non-French Jews living in the city, to which were added twelve thousand Parisian Jews who disappeared during the occupation. Young workers were indentured as conscripts in the Service du travail obligatoire (STO) that kept Germany war's industry humming. All commemorative events, demonstrations, processions, marches, public meetings, and displays of the French tricolor flag and patriotic symbols were outlawed—except, of course, those that promoted French-German relations. Nightly blackouts, curfews, and harsh public repression curtailed any and all suspicious activities. Street traffic was restricted. Public transportation was limited by shortages of fuel and electricity. Heating oil was scarce (and the winter of 1940-41 proved to be one of the coldest on record). The city was gray and empty. The bronze sculptures that graced the city's great public spaces were decimated by the Vichy government's policy of melting them down for war production. Statuary and urban embellishment were secreted behind earthworks. As inflation robbed Parisians of any purchasing power, the Germans absconded with everything they could carry and used their authority to claim the city's famed art and luxury goods as their own.

The oppression provoked hundreds, perhaps thousands of individual gestures of public defiance as well as more organized acts of refusal. It is impossible to recount this remarkable history here. Suffice it so say that the graffiti, the jeers and taunting of German officials, the public singing of the "Marseillaise," the distribution of tracts, the surreptitious honoring of key dates in the nation's history, the displaying of the "V" sign for victory, the protest marches and demonstrations constituted an extraordinary and highly dangerous public theater in their own right. The capital was built from a landscape of monuments and national symbols that rallied patriotic sentiment and protest. The intensity of partisan acts forced the occupying powers to continuously increase the presence of the Gestapo and French police forces on the streets. On November 1, 1940, twenty thousand people gathered at the Arc de Triomphe to lay five hundred bouquets at the Tomb of the Unknown Soldier. Groups of people gathered at the statue of Jeanne d'Arc to commemorate Labor Day on May 1, 1941. On July 14, 1941—Bastille Day—the police arrested 1,667 people for wearing the tricolor cockade. But it was food that obsessed the majority of Parisians. Food shortages squeezed life to its limits. Public demonstrations were often simply against the bleak hardship of daily life. Supplies were sparse. The daily food ration was 850 calories per day. Food coupons were guarded with desperation, and public anger exploded in a myriad of localized protests on the streets. The immaculate gardens of the Invalides, the Luxembourg, and the Tuileries were summarily dug up and replaced with vegetable patches. Most people learned inventive ways to get by—the famous *système débrouille*, or Système D—and the fiendish black-market racketeers who hiked prices to exorbitant levels. The *bofs*—shopkeepers who sold butter, eggs, and cheese for outrageous sums—earned a reputation for dishonesty. The injustices only aggravated the suffering and desperation. Families relied on their wits and sold their possessions to survive while Germans and their collaborators ate well, paraded their fine clothes and costly possessions, and enjoyed the nightlife of "gay Paree." Bribery and corruption—always the fiends of war—thrived.

And although Paris was eventually declared an "open city," it did not completely escape destruction. Wartime aerial bombardments came in two waves; first the German invasion in June 1940 and then the Allied attacks that followed. During the German assault,[7] forty-four bridges on the Marne, five on the Seine, and sixteen between Paris and Montereau in the southeast were destroyed. Parisians set the city's fuel-oil depots ablaze to prevent them from falling into German hands. Six of the city's seven synagogues were dynamited in October 1941 by a collaborationist organization. The Germans set fire to the Grand Palais during the final days of the occupation. In the Allied wave, British Royal Air Force bombing began in March 1942. It was concentrated on industrial targets along the fringes of the capital. RAF bombers first struck the Renault factory at Billancourt, the core of the great automobile and aircraft manufacturing district to the west of Paris. The surrounding suburbs were destroyed, and two thousand civilians were killed or injured. The heavy industry and freight railways in the northern suburbs at Saint-Denis, Asnières, Saint-Ouen, and Aubervilliers, the city's port at Gennevilliers, and Le Bourget airport were all destroyed or damaged along with the districts around them. The canal de l'Ourcq was breached and obstructed by debris by the 1944 bombardments. The train yards of the gare du Nord, the vast bus depot, and the warehouse district at the porte de la Chapelle all suffered severe damage in the Allied attempt to paralyze the German war machine. Nearly one thousand people in the northern suburbs lost their lives. The preparations for the Normandy invasion in June 1944 intensified the air attacks. Waves of Allied bombers flew over Paris several times each day. The Basilica of Sacre Cœur was damaged. Over six hundred were killed and almost as many wounded in the bombing raid on April 20. Six days later, Marshal Pétain visited Paris to share its grief and attend a memorial ceremony to the dead at Notre Dame Cathedral. The situation was worse in the suburbs—Noisy-le-Sec, Villeneuve-Saint-Georges, Villeneuve-Triage, Saint-Cyr, Massy Palaiseau, Massy-Verrières, and others—bombed in the last stages of the fighting. Far from the city, these remote districts suddenly felt the hand of global conflict. A total of seventy communes in the Paris region suffered wartime destruction. Some five thousand residential buildings were destroyed throughout the department of the Seine and another thirteen thousand made uninhabitable. Families living in ruined buildings searched desperately for clothing, for coal, for anything to eat just to stay alive.

Liberation

For Parisians, an inkling of the Liberation was first *heard* the evening of August 24 and the morning of August 25, 1944: "As night fell, the church bells, all the church bells of Paris began ringing. In tears, I ran out onto the balcony with my neighbors . . . what joy, this incredible concert of over a hundred church bells ringing out in the warm evening sky. . . . Then suddenly we heard this one bell. It was grave, splendid: the great bell of Notre Dame."[8] The memories recounted by Parisians attest to this perception of deliverance not simply as a momentous historic event, but as one with powerful psychological, even mystical, religious overtones. "All the church bells in Paris started ringing. . . . The bells were ringing out under a sky in which the guns still thunder while the smoke rises from the burning Grand Palais. People are singing the 'Marseillaise' in the street, cheering, and it's delirious."[9] The Liberation of Paris was perhaps the ultimate urban spectacle. It meant seizing and transforming place, a city, civil society in which people lived, congregated, acted. It was a civic moment of astonishing vividness and intensity. The imagery found in contemporary accounts was of a city in the grip of ecstasy. On August 26 a reporter for the daily newspaper *Le Figaro* described the streets:

> As soon as I left the Hôtel de Ville, I was stopped, submerged by an enormous crowd that was everywhere, on the streets, the quays, the avenues, the passage ways. They applauded. They shouted. They stamped their feet. They cried. On one of the tanks, surrounded by the din of motors and smoke, a cat, a minuscule little cat, calmly sat surveying the scene. The crowd roared their approval. That was what this unique day was like: one part exuberant celebration, exalted, delirious, an incredible lightheartedness that poured out in song, kisses, in unbounded joy; the other part, a climate of civil war.[10]

The brief discussion in this chapter focuses on the Liberation as a triumphant reappropriation of urban space and on its mythic status in the reemergence of the public domain. It regards the Liberation as a populist urban movement created not just by the street fighting, which was of course crucial for those who risked their lives, but by ritual, staging, and civic theater, and by public ceremonies that left a long-lasting, contentious legacy. Public ceremony and spectacle became ways of reconstituting civility and citizenship—they were a political instrument. Contemporary perceptions and usages of the Liberation will be dealt with frequently in the ensuing chapters. My purpose here is simply to introduce the event as public performance and as a baseline for understanding its extraordinary and highly idealized meaning throughout the late 1940s and 1950s. In his book *Libération: Fête folle*, Alain Brossard argues that as spectacle, the Liberation took place outside modern time and place, that its tone was more like that of premodern celebrations and the tomfoolery once associated with seasonal cycles or public festivals rejoicing springtime rebirth.[11] Yet one could argue that its appropriation of dramatic spectacle, its plurality, its self-conscious reflexivity and explicit use of celebrity, and its contentious quality all made the performance of the Liberation overtly modern. It was a cultural performance, a metanarrative of action and deeds, a tumult of transgression, hyperbole, hypersensoriness, and iconoclasm in a distinctively modern genre. As a spatial event it translated the public arena of Paris into a theatrical stage abounding with scenes and tableaux. For one participant, Jean Galtier-Boissière, "fighting in the streets is less risky and more picturesque than open campaigning. One comes home to lunch carrying one's rifle; the whole neighborhood is at the windows to have a look and to applaud; the milkman, the green-grocer, and the man in the bistro won't chalk anything up on the slate. If only the cameras were turning, glory would be absolute."[12]

Actually, the cameras were turning. The events were self-consciously documented by observers, photographers, and filmmakers as spontaneous theater in which everyone could claim celebrity. The city's population, eager to capture the event as it took place and as a testament of their role in it, created an enormous photographic record of the Liberation. Neighbors and friends posed with *maquis* fighters in uniform alongside tanks in the streets and in front of barricades and liberated public buildings. The costumes and staging of these photographs were central. The stylized visual composition was meant to accentuate the role of the people—the everyman, the worker who rarely gained renown—in the extraordinary deliverance of Paris.[13] In the Comité de Libération du Cinéma's filming of the Liberation of Paris as it took place, a map of the city was cut into sectors, and twenty film crews, each with a camera, were sent out to capture the events. They followed the battles and barricades through the city. Any staged scenes were cut so that only actual combatants and participants were featured performers in this "reality" cinema.[14] This photographic and cinematic dramatization in fact invented what would soon become the past and made the spaces of the city into an extraordinary stage for the display of the Liberation as a popular urban resurrection. Paris was imagined as a heroic society, a place of extraordinary deeds.

The countless films and photographic images of the Liberation of Paris are an illustrious part of twentieth-century iconography. For the French, this visual text captured August 1944 as a mythic moment of deliverance and national transformation in which the people of Paris had prevailed. The word "Liberation" crystallized into a French achievement, a self-freeing that was translated as the reemergence of the French people. Of course, the degree to which the city carried this off without the help of the Americans and British has been the subject of controversy ever since. Even some contemporary observers were shocked at the boasting that made the Liberation such a self-satisfied legend.

The heavily mediatized nature of the activities and the importance of recording participation in an historic turning point are also clear from, for example, an official Canadian film of the Liberation. In shots of de Gaulle entering Paris and marching down the Champs-Élysées, mobs of journalists film the huge crowds, while the crowds themselves click away with their cameras, photographing friends and family amid the extravaganza.[15] Radio and newsreel planes circle overhead and recording vans push through the crowds while their reporters, mikes in hand, shout out orders to the throng. The media spectacle crisscrossed between journalists and participants. Celebrity was for the taking. Public space became a stage for outpourings of public emotion and zany performances that were impulsive, reflexive, and fame seeking. In the photographer Robert Doisneau's visual portrait of the Liberation, spontaneous rumba lines snake through the streets, young men stripped down to their shorts frolic in the fountains at the place de la Concorde, people dance impulsively—together, alone—and wave, wrap themselves in, parade with the French tricolor.[16] The Liberation was not only a signifier of civic life, but a civic explosion, a moment of tense unity, the relishing of the end of suffering and renewed patriotism. It was a seizing, a dizzying transformation of the everyday. Life was reformed, reformulated in a playful speculation on what might be. It expressed the emergence of spatial form and meaning out of chaos. Jean-Paul Sartre wrote his impressions on "the street, this theater" during the Liberation in a series of articles for the Resistance newspaper *Combat*. Among the many vignettes he described was the blind accordionist on the rue de la Gaité playing tunes from *La traviata* in the midst of the insurrection: "Someone lit a fire at the corner of the blvd. Montparnasse, . . . and just as July 14 had been celebrated before the war, the crowd danced the farandole around the flames."[17]

It was also a moment of vengeance and retribution. In a wide assortment of neighborhood purges,[18] the punishment of Germans and their collaborators was filmed and photographed as evidence of the righteousness of French loyalties. German stragglers were dragged out of buildings and beaten by bystanders. French women caught with German soldiers were publicly stripped and their heads shaved, and they were paraded in humiliation through the streets. Avaricious shopkeepers and *bofs* were rebuked. Locals suspected of collaboration were turned in or gunned down. These acts of community vigilantism were their own form of theatrical tragedy, meant to cleanse the quartier of an ignominious collaboration that was often represented as a type of immorality or pollutant. A citywide hunt for collaborators began. Leading political figures and members of the press were executed or tried and packed off to prison. Trials of collaborators such as the writer Robert Brasillach (who was committed to the Nazi cause) and the police chief René Bousquet (who organized the Jewish round-ups at Vél' d'Hiv), whipped up the calls for retribution—but with mixed results. Brasillach was shot, while Bousquet was let off and continued his career in public life. Despite blatant collaboration, Maurice Papon escaped persecution and served in the Fourth Republic's highest administrative posts. In 1958 he was appointed chief of police in Paris. These deeply ambivalent dimensions—tragedy and farce, austerity set against pleasure and delight, national unity interlaced with civil conflict and the settling of scores—marked the experience as insurgent civic theater.

Parisians faced a desperate, freezing winter in 1944–45. The city was gray, miserable, and forsaken. In American military film footage, the monumental spaces of the city are barren of people and traffic. Only military vehicles and soldiers and a few daring cars and bicycles break the gloom. The Invalides esplanade and the city's parks at Vincennes and Boulogne are covered with army equipment and *kaks*, or American GIs. Shots of the Sorbonne and the Panthéon focus on their stone walls, riddled with bullet holes from the August battles in the Latin Quarter. Makeshift commemorative plaques with flowers and memorabilia decorate mournful sites of combat.[19] The desolation was made even more oppressive by the urban bustle and cosmopolitanism typically associated with these places. Saul Bellow called Paris of the late 1940s "one of the grimmest cities in the world." Many of its greatest monuments, including the Louvre and Notre Dame Cathedral, were neglected, their stone facades cracked and blackened with pollution. Peeling paintwork, fractured stone and stucco, and potholed roads evidenced years of disregard. A feeling left over from the wartime occupation of "disgrace and resentment darkened the famous facades" and contributed to the general "oppressiveness" of the Parisian air.[20] The swollen Seine reached the tops of the quays in the central city and spilled out over the bombed suburban villages, ruining anything that was left. The city's electricity and water functioned only sporadically. The arrival of coal was the only news worth hearing.

This dejected landscape embodied the grief and unfinished mourning associated with the war and occupation. These were the sacrificial spaces of the city, a veritable torrent of suffering humanity spilling out into the public world, a parade of destitution whose presence consecrated the symbolic spaces of an inhuman dystopia. The wartime refugees who were the first pilgrims to the liberated city recalled its bleakness, the gray pallor, the destitution, sadness, and grief. Each morning at 8:15 the trains of prisoners and deportees arrived at the gare du Nord, to be met by distraught crowds: "There were people, so many people. . . . Inside, Red Cross doctors and nurses were everywhere, surrounded by stretchers and wheelchairs. There were barriers that formed a kind of column through which the arrivals would pass. On either side were the crowds of parents and friends hoping that their loved ones would suddenly materialize." The reception centers at the gare d'Orsay, the gare du Nord, the Hôtel Lutetia, Vél' d'Hiv', and the Gaumont Theater were "incredible spectacles of haggard, wasted people garbed in stripped costumes."[21] Destitution and hopelessness took center stage. There were the inevitable queues of needy people waiting for food, clinics filled with pneumonia sufferers, and charity drives for the most desperate. Infant and child mortality rose to alarming levels. The writer Jean-Louis Babelay remembered that "each night, the city's garbage cans were searched painstakingly by legions of poor people. Everything was rubbed, cleaned, checked."[22] Long lines of Parisians snaked around the local *mairie* (town hall) waiting to be issued ration coupons for the equivalent of nine hundred calories a day, and then waited again at local grocery stores with few goods to offer. Rumor had it that the hulls of American Liberty ships landing at the Mulberry harbors in Normandy were bursting with provisions. But the anticipation wore thin. Meanwhile, speculators and black marketers scalped everything from cigarettes to penicillin. The nouveau riche, brandishing heaps of bank notes acquired through illicit traffic, bought up everything from families living on the edge of penury. Furniture, carpets, jewelry, art and stamp collections, luxury clothing, and family heirlooms all changed hands. The malaise deepened. Tempers frayed. Armed robberies became the norm. Fear, pity, and fate were all embodied in the tragic dramas unfolding in the streets.

Yet throughout 1944 and 1945, alongside this public heartbreak and tragedy, the first anniversaries of wartime victory and Liberation were celebrated with immense popular rejoicing. An unending series of celebrations and remembrances marked what are known as the "Liberation years" of the late 1940s. The historian Henri Ruosso argues that the many celebrations of the Liberation and victory "were proof that France was incapable of constructing a unified national memory of the event."[23] The cultural critic Andreas Huyssen makes the point as well that the discourse of turning points from 1945 on can be read as a symptom of multilayered traumatic experiences that always leave something unresolved and in need of further articulation.[24] These commemorations can be understood in this light. August 1944 proved to be just a brief moment of unity. The past was unsettled, and control over the representations and memory of the Liberation was one of the most contentious issues of the postwar years. One could argue that the event took on hegemonic proportions. It was a hyperreal, mediatized experience in time and space that was so liberating, captivating, and multifaceted that it reinforced self-referentiality and became a standard. The endless ceremonies were almost a compulsive mise-en-scène, the revisiting of Liberation events rapidly receding into history and yet still problematic in the present. The structure of repetition was an essential part of their reenactment, and the construction of the Liberation as a founding, if complicated, myth of a new age.

People used street theater to confront power relations as well as to reinitiate customary public life. It was a machinery of communication integral to the social and political struggles shaping the post-Liberation years. Victory parades abounded, each one greeted by cheering crowds. The first postwar May Day parades from the place de la Nation to the Bastille and the first July 14 celebrations were all spectacular urban celebrations. Communist and Socialist Party marches to the Mur des Fédéres at Père Lachaise Cemetery drew multitudes to honor the heroes of the Resistance and Liberation. Armistice Day in November 1944 was a massive celebration. Many of these gatherings were immediately turned into charity events for some desperate group of castaways (of which there were many); for the homeless, the FFI, orphans, deportees, refugees, the wounded, and the dead. The singer and comedian Pierre Dac, who had been one of the most well-known voices on Radio London during the war, performed at a Red Cross benefit at Luna Park in September 1944. Then it was an open-air music-hall extravaganza to benefit prisoners and war victims. At the end of 1944 public performances during the Semaine de l'Absent gathered donations for prisoners of war and deportees. Jazz and symphony concerts and gala performances by American and French stars from Fred Astaire to Maurice Chevalier offered aid to war victims. The festivities and commemoration pouring out from the place de la Bastille, the place de la Nation, the place Jeanne d'Arc, Notre Dame and the city's churches, the Hôtel de Ville, the Champs-Élysées, the place de la Concorde, the place de l'Opéra, the Tuileries and Luxembourg gardens, and neighborhood squares all signaled a vigorous resurfacing of collective life and public space.

The largest, most electrifying celebration marked the end of the war in Europe, or V-E Day, on May 8, 1945. It elicited an outpouring of emotion and fervor. The American journalist Janet Flanner described it as "an occupation of Paris by Parisians. They streamed out onto their city's avenues and boulevards and took possession of them. . . . They paved the Champs-Élysées with their moving, serried bodies. . . . [They] drowned out the sound of the church bells that clanged for peace." Food was scarce, everyone was hungry, but "all anyone cared about was to keep moving, to keep shouting, to keep singing snatches of the 'Marseillaise.'"[25] Writing in *Combat*, Jean-Paul Sartre described V-E Day in Paris as a "provocative carnival . . . tanks and jeeps maneuver in a sea of humanity, carrying hundreds of improvised tourists." The city was a gleaming stage set for the celebration:

> In the middle of the night an enormous tide streamed around the illuminated monuments. Projectors traced the initial of the day in the sky. Flares, airplane vapor crossed above the Opéra flooded in lights and draped in red, above the Hôtel de Ville, above Notre Dame, above all the great squares where the blinding radiance of the projectors dispelled a night five years long. And mobs, mobs everywhere, as if the population of Paris suddenly tripled. All you could see was an enormous mass of people crying, laughing, singing.[26]

The May 14 procession along the Champs-Élysées was a massive victory march for the city's population. Linked arm in arm in long bands down the avenue, parading and singing, the citizenry replicated the entry and occupation of Paris.[27] The anniversary of the Resistance on June 18, 1945, was celebrated with a massive military parade that stretched from the Arc de Triomphe to the place de la Concorde, with thousands of cheering Parisians lining the streets. A month later, the *fête nationale* was saluted with three days of street parades and dances, replete with orchestras, choral performances, and street theater. Their character was spontaneous, irreverent, and disruptive of everyday normalities, a bursting of the personal into the public domain. Normally private people drank themselves into oblivion, grabbed partners and danced in the streets, interrupted traffic and brought their neighborhoods to a standstill. Throughout the late 1940s the symbolic sites of the city—the great squares at the Hôtel de Ville, Châtelet, the Bourse, the place de l'Opéra, and the place de la Concorde—hosted huge choral performances of the "Marseillaise" with thousands of citizens patriotically joining in song for the annual *fête nationale*.

In short, Paris was liberated by ceremonies in a deliberate claiming of public space. August 1944 and the nonstop commemorations that extended well into the late 1940s and early 1950s constituted a vast public movement—a militant pedestrianism—carried out around "mnemonic sites," to use Pierre Nora's term. They created a monumental narrative of the people freeing their city and, by extension, their nation. The Liberation was encoded as revolt and transgression, and as a new beginning. It seemed to open an era when all things were possible. It was fantasy and euphoria repeated again and again through ceremony and ritual. This myth was vivid, provocative, and open to a myriad of social and political interpretations. The experience inaugurated an immediate postwar period that was a mixture of buoyant, utopian optimism amid dire circumstances and calls for national unity amid political retribution. The war and the Resistance had contributed to a revolutionary populism and to a general politicization of urban space, as had the Liberation itself. After years of tight control, the public spaces of Paris were suddenly an arena for encounters once again, where various social classes could interact in unknown, ill-defined, and divergent ways. Public life was an open question. Although everyone was committed to rebuilding the nation, deep political and social tensions remained and even deepened as the war receded into the past.

The Heroic City

The brief itinerary through the metropolis that follows in this chapter hardly does justice to Paris. But it does provide some indication of the complexity and heightened symbolic meaning of its public world. The panorama of its urban imagery is what makes the city such a fascinating historical study. On the one hand, there was the Paris of glittering elegance, of material opulence, the hallucinatory vision of urban beauty that emerged from the catastrophe of war. In his autobiographical *Paris in the Fifties*, the American journalist Stanley Karnow explains that for the young Americans flocking to Europe after the Second World War, "the city, the legendary *Ville Lumière*, promised something for everyone—beauty, sophistication, culture, cuisine, sex, escape and that indefinable called ambience."[28] On the other hand, there was the Paris of misery. The city was a bleak and wretched place. The deterioration that had come from decades of neglect was obvious. State officials seemed to take some perverse pleasure out of cataloguing the atrocious living conditions, congestion, and urban decay. It was a cesspool of miserable social conditions—and, at the same time, a vibrant economic dynamo that offered the possibility of shared affluence and hope for the future. Paris was both wistfully imagined as a puzzle of historic neighborhoods and conjured up as an amorphous monster spreading out over the Seine valley like a cancer. The symbolic dimensions of its landscape were intensified by its status as the capital of a reconstituted nation. Yet it was not that clear, at the end of the Second World War, what kind of reconstituted nation Paris was the capital of, nor exactly how far its political authority actually extended, either in France or internationally. This was indeed a turn about from the city's celebrated status as the avant-garde capital of modernity, the urban pivot around which the French hexagon spun. In the opinion of the historian Patrice Higonnet, although the city remained incomparably beautiful, "it was no longer the mythological focal point of the present and the capital of the future."[29] Paris was trading on past glories. The grand discourse of modern centrality fractured into an enigmatic puzzle of competing images and spatiality.

The centrality of Paris and its monumental spaces was certainly revived. The core of the city was the symbolic site for its reemergence as the capital of liberated France. Official ceremonies at the place de la Concorde, the Esplanade des Invalides, on the Champs de Mars and at the Hôtel de Ville;

parades down the Champs-Élysées; expositions and concerts; and fireworks and floodlights showed off everything Paris stood for, or at least what it hoped to stand for. The greatest spectacle, in the end, was the city itself. Its sweeping vistas and glamorous décor were used as the ultimate urban backdrop for this theater of reemergence. In June 1948 the city staged the spectacular Grande Nuit de Paris. Some 120,000 people gathered at the Champs de Mars for this massive *fête populaire*. The Cirque Bouglione performed under the Eiffel Tower, and there were appearances by Rita Hayworth, Hedy Lamarr, Charles Boyer, Ingrid Bergman, Lana Turner, and Edward G. Robinson. Hollywood's beau monde came in droves to welcome Paris back after the dark years. Yves Montand, Lily Pons, and the Folies Bergères performed musical skits on a vast stage set up in the midst of the fountains at the Palais de Chaillot. After an evening of revelry, a spectacular fireworks display was launched, and the historic monuments along the Seine were floodlit with great ceremony. But the dazzling display could not camouflage the political discord between city hall, the Seine prefecture, and the prefecture of police over control of the city's public spaces. These frictions characterized the entire period under study, from the late 1940s through the end of the Fourth Republic in 1958. What had been originally planned as a civic charity event on behalf of Resistance orphans was transformed into a large-scale professional entertainment spectacle. Staged as part of the celebration of the 150th anniversary of the prefecture of police and sponsored by the popular daily newspaper *France-soir*, all control had surreptitiously been taken out of the hands of the Paris municipal council. A portion of the receipts was redirected to police orphans instead. Traffic on the pont d'Iéna, the quay, Trocadéro, and the "public spaces of Paris" was cordoned off, and the streets taken over by private contractors and the police. Decision-making processes were concealed. Municipal councilors argued directly with the prefect of police: "Where is [sic] the municipal council and the opinion of Parisians in all this?" While they disparaged the extravagant entertainment and pyrotechnics of the *France-soir* spectacle, the fête by the *peuple* on the Champs de Mars was lauded as a stellar success.[30]

The event that probably best symbolized this complicated and contentious reemergence of Paris after the long night of war was the celebration of the city's two thousandth anniversary in 1951. As a machinery of communication, it was a self-conscious display of renewed urban identity, a muscular show befitting the capital of France and the occasion to put on the kind of glamorous spectacle the whole world expected of Paris. The focus on the city's history represented a distinctive notion of civic space and time. The celebration invented a new visual vocabulary enshrining "Paris" as an eternal entity. The newspaper *Le Parisien libéré* gushed that "all this will transport radiant Parisians into the streets in joyous waves, in love with their city more than ever, all this will impassion foreigners who have kept secreted in their hearts memories of their idyll with this old Paris now so young."[31] More than 120 mayors from around the world were invited. The celebration actually generated a 12 to 15 percent increase in tourism over the previous year. It was known in the popular press as the Bi, for "Bi-millénaire," and activities were scheduled from the height of the summer tourist season all the way to December. Hundreds of events took place, from art expositions, passion plays, concerts, and galas to sport competitions and the *grands bals populaires* (open-air dances) held on the first and second platforms of the Eiffel Tower; at the Hôtel de Ville, the Bourse, and the place de la Bastille; on the boulevard du Temple, the rue des Batignolles, and avenue Gambetta; and at Neuilly. Rather than privileging only the breathtaking monumental sites, the Bi-millénaire was spread throughout the neighborhoods, which put on their own celebrations. Shop windows and streets throughout the city were flamboyantly decorated. In May a Grande Semaine de l'Université was organized for the Latin Quarter that featured art and theater expositions, film festivals, dances, and the crowning of "Miss Journal." Shopkeepers on the boulevard Saint-Michel decked the street in a "Paris dans la Renaissance des Lettres" theme. In late June the *grands boulevards* on the Right Bank put on a "1900" spectacle in an attempt to recapture the glory years of the belle époque. Cafés prepared dishes that had been popular at the turn of the century, served by waiters dressed up in period costume. High-fashion boutiques dressed their mannequins in belle époque style. The boulevards were festooned with colored lanterns, and a festival or *kermesse* was staged with local music-hall stars. The quartier de la Monnie in Saint-Germain-des-Prés followed suit with its own theme festival, "De Henri IV à Danton," staged along the Seine between the quai des Grands-Augustins and the place Saint-Michel.

The official birthday commemoration took place on July 8 with the entire city *en fête*. At noon the city's church bells rang in unison in an auditory extravaganza that reiterated the first moments of the Liberation. President Vincent Auriol hosted a military-music festival at the Esplanade des Invalides featuring marching bands and folklore groups. Flags and banners paraded triumphantly before four grandstands of officialdom and tens of thousands of spectators, and then proceeded across the pont Alexandre III and down the Champs-Élysées to the Arc de Triomphe. The symphonic spectacle of military music and national hymns awoke, according to *Combat*, "patriotic shivers and martial emotions" among listeners.[32] It was an inflated, grandiloquent declaration of the city's role as capital of France. The evening events were extravagant. Traditional *bals populaires* took place in the city's main squares and throughout the neighborhoods, followed by a massive fireworks display that drew multitudes to the Invalides and along the banks of the Seine. At the stroke of midnight, "written in the sky were blazing images of Jeanne d'Arc and the Sun King that lit up the quays of the Seine."[33]

The theatrical urban staging and dazzling spectacles of both the Grande Nuit de Paris and the Bi-millénaire attempted to invent urban citizenship and a sense of unity around emotionally compelling representations of Paris and its history. Parisians would come under the spell of a unifying idealism and hope for the future. On the one hand, the events retained the tone of populist performance in their emphasis on music, song, and dance in the public spaces of the city and in the incorporation of *bals populaires* and neighborhood festivals. On the other hand, the professional staging of the urban core also evidenced a compliant theater of modern mass-produced entertainment that functioned as a festive form of social control. The later was associated with the emergence of French state authority in the late 1940s and the shift toward tightened forms of governance. However, the legitimacy of the core of Paris as a dramatic backdrop for narratives of unity and patriotism was in fact not all that clear. The city's ability to foster genuine collective life could no longer be taken for granted. More than anything, the ostentatious boosterism exposed a general apprehension about the city's deflated status, a fear that the shimmering image of modernity had vanished. Indeed, these citywide staged commemorations and celebrations were few in number and had virtually evaporated by the early 1950s. The official Comité des fêtes for Paris continued to organize themed pageants and parades: the Fête des Fleurs of 1953, the Corso des Corporations of 1954, and the 1955 Hommage de Paris aux Provinces Françaises. Although they continued to draw crowds, they became facile touristic entertainment and were finally abandoned on account of their traffic snarls. The gregarious obsession with street life took a turn away from the monumental and away from the iconographic spaces of modernity. As a result, the spatiality of Paris became far less contracted around the boulevards and central districts and far more dispersed across a multitude of sites and public spaces. Although urban centrality did not disappear, it was the decentered, nonunifying spaces of the city that acted as the dynamic theater of "the people" and carried on the hopes of the Liberation. Subversive in quality, it retained the elements of spontaneity and *fête*. Despite the dazzling spectacles that paid homage to the city's reemergence, the reality was that Paris offered problems in plenitude that became the focus of collective action. The streets were more often an agitational theater of protest and strikes, of civil disobedience and social conflict. This fragmented, unrestrained landscape was where the postwar tensions in the metropolis were played out. Understanding them requires that we focus analysis broadly across the city and insinuate our lens into the streets and spaces of everyday life.

The number of people packed into these overbuilt spaces of the capital was among its most striking features. The central districts had actually attained their largest population in 1921 with a total of 2,906,000 inhabitants, and then began to decline. By 1954 the number of residents was slightly lower at 2,854,000, and by 1962 that number had declined even further to 2,750,000. So although its population was no longer growing, what distinguished Paris from other European capitals was its density. With the twenty arrondissements comprising only 10,516 hectares, it was small and jam-packed. The overcrowding had been the focus of ire even in the prewar years. At the 1937 Paris Congress, Georges Sébille, Architect honoraire for the city of Paris, reflected that "the Paris of tomorrow" could only be conceived by understanding the extent of its congestion; the cars, the lack of open space, and above all the ten buildings jammed into spaces meant for two: "And there is the problem of Paris. It's there. It's always there. And it's there that we should direct ourselves in imagining a new Paris." In 1939 the playwright and urban observer Jean Giraudoux remarked that "Paris was a perfect demonstration of human congestion."[34] The situation only worsened in the postwar years. Although population-density figures are notoriously tricky, density in Paris averaged on the order of 380 inhabitants per hectare. In central neighborhoods such as those around the National Archives in the Marais, density reached 493 inhabitants per hectare. These were far higher figures than those for London or even New York (112 and 344 inhabitants per hectare, respectively).[35] The city was completely overbuilt; its housing stock dilapidated. Outside of the two great parks of Boulogne and Vincennes, there was on average only a little more than one square meter of open space per inhabitant in the capital.

The eastern districts had essentially no public gardens at all.³⁶ By 1958 official documents were quoting shocking densities of 800 to 1,000 people per hectare in some of the core districts,³⁷ all crammed into rundown buildings along with thousands of commercial and industrial establishments and an unknown number of offices of every size and variety.

Added to the nightmare of overcrowded housing was the growing volume of road traffic. With gasoline in short supply in the early postwar years, bicycles and rickshaw *vélo-taxis* were everywhere. But by the mid-1950s a vast processions of cars and trucks jammed the roads. *France-soir* put traffic at well over one million vehicles daily. Delivery trucks negotiated their maneuvers with 2CV and 4CV Renaults and Citroëns whipping through the streets. Along with 2,500 RATP platform buses and G7 taxis, they clogged avenues and roadways and paralyzed any hope of moving through the city. Over 600,000 commuters boarded buses daily, along with everyday voyagers threading their way through the city. Another 220,000 motorized bikes, motor scooters, and assorted two- and three-wheeled contraptions competed for road space.³⁸ There were few restrictions, and the heterogeneity of transport subsumed everything from draft animals pulling farm carts to the sleek Citroën DS—a composite image that magnified the transitional qualities of this period. Delivery trucks blocked side streets and alleys. The roads around Les Halles, the Halles aux Vins at Jussieu, La Villette, and the city's other wholesale and street markets were brought to a standstill by the volume of daily loading and offloading of foodstuffs, meats, wines, groceries, and piles of garbage left at the end of the day. The railroad stations were buried in cars and taxis, their horns blaring, their arrival timed to coincide with the arrival and departure of trains. Pedestrians defiantly took their lives in their hands and plunged into a sea of speeding vehicles to cross the roadways. The traditional public spaces of the city, the *grandes places* and *carrefours*, were besieged by traffic. Sidewalks became parking lots. The prefect of police admonished Parisians that "the streets aren't personal garages."³⁹ Newspapers were filled with daily reports of automobile accidents, while satirical editorial cartoons reported on the ongoing battle for control of the roads. Added to this, the use of automobiles for daily commuting between the suburbs and the capital doubled between 1936 and 1954 to reach over 600,000.⁴⁰ On weekends the *portes* in and out of Paris were brought to a standstill by the gridlock. The Paris municipal council promulgated one traffic regulation after another in a vain attempt to control the spreading anarchy. The rue de Rivoli and other main boulevards were turned into one-way streets to relieve the traffic congestion, while the place de la Concorde became a one-directional merry-go-round. The din of car horns and high-pitched buzz of motorbikes enveloped the city in unending noise. The racket was such that the use of car horns was prohibited in 1954—to no avail. But that year the central city's entire transportation system ground to halt when rain and ice from winter storms made roads impassable while the Seine spilled over the quays.

The teeming crowds of people and vehicular uproar seemed utter chaos. But beneath the surface clatter, the spaces of the city actually followed the stark social divisions that were largely the legacy left by Haussmann. The nineteenth century seemed to have definitively fixed not only the image of monumental Paris, but also its social segregation. In 1951 André Siegfried, an esteemed member of the Academie française and an itinerant urban explorer, conjured up a social mapping of the crowded city in his *Géographie humoristique de Paris*. It was based on the subway lines. Siegfried's choice of the Métro as a mapping technique was apropos. Hordes of people streamed underground to hop on what was by the early 1950s a system badly in need of repair. Its initial postwar popularity was a symptom of the continuous gas shortages and surface transportation restrictions. But even as early as 1954, daily Métro commuters reached over one million. The Métro was quintessentially Parisian. It was an emblem of the capital, the "big city," its fluidity and quick pace. Riding the Métro, Siegfried argued, gave a pretty good indication of the *pays de Paris*. Each arrondissement was like a department of France, a sort of individualized *patrie* that a Parisian left at the cost of self-imposed exile. Each Métro station had its own particular type of passenger. A tour through the stops on line 6 (today's line 2), for example, on the Right Bank could provide a *flâneur* such as Siegfried with some sense of the city's social landscape.[41] The western section of line 6, from the place de l'Étoile to Villiers, threaded through the *beaux quartiers* of elegance, wealth, and cosmopolitan sophistication. Class boundaries remained rigid in the 1950s. Every statistical study bore that out. The city's upper crust still lived to the west. On the Right Bank, the 1st, 2nd, 8th, 9th, 16th, and 17th arrondissements were the haunts of the city's well-to-do. In 1951 Siegfried's contemporary, the writer Henri Calet, left his beloved 14th arrondissement and toured the city's "rich neighborhoods," in this case from the rear platform of bus 92: "From Alma, it seems as if you are in a different city: the cars are shinier, the buildings more beautiful, the women too. . . . it's as if existence has a higher price, that it's worth more: even the air seems a little different, finer. There is the illusion of being a stranger, just passing through."[42] Nonetheless, in the early postwar years this vision of elegance and luxury so associated with the Right Bank was conflicted ground. Some of its most iconographic spaces of modernity had been implicated by association with the German authorities. In the surprisingly liberal atmosphere of occupied Paris, there was no end of temptations for the city's glitterati: opening nights at the Opéra; receptions and dinners at the Ritz and Maxim's; or mingling with the German elite at gallery openings. Whether the motives were opportunism, misplaced patriotism, or political ideology, for much of *le Tout-Paris* the line between continuing the city's dazzling spectacle and shameless collaboration was fine indeed. The bourgeois circle of influence was tainted. In the *ouvriériste* ("workerist") groundswell sweeping through the city, bourgeois elites had turned into venal parasites associated with fallen regimes, both Vichy and the Third Republic.

Although the districts around Haussmann's *grands boulevards* had lost much of the bourgeois cachet they enjoyed in the late nineteenth and early twentieth centuries, they were still the focus of the city's entertainment scene. Fifty-three movie theaters and five music halls were already going full blast by mid-1946, jammed with patrons escaping the meanness of daily life. Saturday night filmgoers strolled the boulevards from the Madeleine to La République and canvassed the Gaumont Palace and Pathé movie theaters for premiers. American films inundated Paris immediately after the war. But the French film industry quickly picked up production and grew to enjoy a golden age of poetic realism that garnered immense popular acclaim through the mid-1950s. Movie stars from Jean Gabin and Gérard Philippe to Brigitte Bardot attended film openings and posed for photo ops on the boulevards, with mobs of fans peering through the press lines and flashing cameras. The great music-hall temples, especially the Olympia on the rue Capucines, near the Opéra; the ABC Theater, on the boulevard Poissonnière; the Alhambra, off the place de la République; and the Théâtre de l'Étoile, on the rue du Château d'Eau, were the centers of the capital's music industry. There Maurice Chevalier, Edith Piaf, Francis Lemarque, and Yves Montand all entertained adoring fans.

The Right Bank entertainment spectacle continued just south of the boulevards in the great open-air festivals that marked the Liberation years. The immensely popular Kermesse aux Étoiles (Festival of the Stars) was staged annually at the Tuileries gardens beginning in 1948 and continued to be an unequaled success until 1955. It was hosted by General Jacques-Philippe Leclerc himself and organized by the promoter Alain Duchemin.[43] In 1948 some eighty advertising stands were purchased by private companies for the weekend event. The Tuileries was converted into a vast scenographic theater as Jean Gabin, Gérard Philipe, Louis Jouvet, Jean Marais, Fernandel, and a host of French stage and screen actors greeted a public numbering in the hundreds of thousands. The French president shook hands with Gary Cooper, flown in from Hollywood for the occasion. There was dancing on the terrace of the Jeu de Paume and Orangerie, where young women wandered through the crowds offering product samples in a blend of popular *fête* and commercialized spectacle. The three-day 1953 Kermesse stretched eight and a half miles along the Tuileries gardens and the Right Bank. A cavalcade of stars paraded in front of thousands of adoring fans, with Gina Lollobrigida and Juliette Gréco the crowd favorites. Some 400,000 spectators attended for the chance, as *Paris Match* gushed, "to fulfill the impossible dream: living for a few hours in the company of the stars."[44] However, subversive farce and the capacity of the people to make their own theater were in full evidence. Alain Duchemin hurried past the iron fence around the Tuileries gardens, where public lavatories had been set up, only to find hundreds of people laughing hysterically at the spontaneous spectacle of a line of commodes in full use, the back walls of the cabins having been inadvertently left open.[45]

The western area of the Right Bank was also the nerve center for the nation's economy and for news and trends. In March 1945 the French fashion industry relaunched itself with an exposition of the first postwar Parisian collection at the Louvre—in miniature, using dolls as models. Over 100,000 people came to see the exhibit, although haute couture was far beyond the reach of their pocketbooks. By year's end the rue de la Paix, the rue du Faubourg Saint-Honoré, and the whole voguish district around the place de l'Opéra and the place Vendôme dripped with the fashion and luxury goods for which Paris was famous. The district between the gare Saint-Lazare and the Champs-Élysées was a beehive of business and commerce. An address on the Champs-Élysées or on the prestigious ring of Haussmann's boulevards was the envy of every French company on the hunt for tony headquarters. A full 83 percent of France's publishing and news industry was lodged in the capital, including *Le Monde*, which began publication in 1945. More than half of French banks and financial institutions managed the nation's economy from the well-heeled neighborhoods around the Bourse (stock exchange), the Élysées presidential palace, and the Champs-Élysées. Some 64 percent of French private companies had headquarters there.[46] It was the world of lawyers and notaries, bank directors and company presidents. Yet the city lacked any modern office space for all these rapidly expanding capitalist activities. Although the value of commercial property had revived after the war, there was little new office construction. The old buildings that lined the boulevards were as ill-adapted to the pace of capitalist enterprise as they were to modern housing. Businesses were spreading out into the 16th and 17th arrondissement, retrofitting residential buildings into makeshift office space. If reconstruction meant modernization, the French capital was bound to fall behind without modern commercial districts. Politicians and planners eyed the area around the gare Saint-Lazare on the Right Bank as a possible location for a first-class business center. As an eastern extension of the Champs-Élysées, some pointed to La Défense as the best site for an ambitious new office district. Others looked to the Left Bank around the dilapidated gare Montparnasse as a possible setting for high-rise office towers.

Leaving behind the wealth and glamour of the boulevards and continuing on line 6 to the north—to the place Clichy and the Blanche and Pigalle Métro stations—*flâneur* and guide Siegfried introduced his readers to another Paris. These stops were traditionally known for their nightclubs and strip joints, filled with foreign tourists until dawn. But in surveying "the colors of Montmartre," Siegfried pointed instead to "a curious injection of Arabs and all the picturesque, colorful residents of these famous places." By 1950 there were already well over 200,000 North Africans in Paris and its suburbs. And these numbers hardly took into account the underground population floating in and out of the region. The vast majority were Algerian men working as unskilled labor in the campaign for reconstruction or simply unemployed and living in the cheap hotels and public shelters in the city's worst slums of La Goutte d'Or, the 13th arrondissement, and the northern districts stretching out into the woebegone suburban shantytowns. The presence on the streets and in the cafés and bars of growing numbers of Muslim Arabs provoked ambivalence and shifting perceptions of public space. The end of the Indochinese War brought an influx of Chinese and Vietnamese to the city who tended to settle around the place d'Italie. The exotic had long been considered one of the city's attractions as capital of the French Empire, and the clichéd orientalist image of colorful Arabs with their zouks and Islamic mores and of Chinese markets filled with strange vitals was only beginning to break down with the onset of decolonization. The 1950s would see this older discourse exchanged for a far more violent and chilling public theater in which North Africans in particular were perceived as the city's principal threat. The Algerian War played out on the streets of the city like a malevolent curse. By the spring of 1958 it had escalated into the political crisis that brought down the Fourth Republic.

Finally, the Barbès-Rochechouart station was, according to Siegfried, "the entrance into the immense, dense, fascinating populist Paris of the East."[47] In many ways, the Second World War had moved the heart of Paris to the eastern districts. The working-class neighborhoods of the faubourg Saint-Antoine, Charonne, Ménilmontant, Belleville, Buttes-Chaumont, and La Villette were a geographic cryptogram for the militant populism of the late 1940s and 1950s. It extended out into the great arc of industrial suburbs to the north. The apogee of working-class Paris was what Patrick Fridenson has called the "civilization of the Resistance." It was here where the local Resistance movement was organized and where much of the fighting against the Germans had taken place during the Liberation. The struggle was imagined as an extension of the prewar Popular Front. The *vélos* of Paris, the *gars* of La Villette, and the *métallos* at Saint-Denis emerged from the war vindicated and triumphant.[48] The space of their daily lives was given new meaning by historic events. Although the Resistance movement itself lost momentum once political life began reconstituting around a traditional party structure in the late 1940s, the euphoric ideals it envisioned remained powerful. Prosperity and abundance, sweeping economic and social reform, a new movement of democratization and national renewal, and the right to work, to leisure, to education, and to a home represented the dreams of the future. They were the aspirations of the workers and small-time artisans, the immigrants, the poor living in what the geographer Albert Demangeon described as

> these eccentric neighborhoods par excellence, the habitat of the lower classes. . . . Rochechouart with its workers and small employers, Saint-Vincent-de-Paul where the workers from the neighboring warehouses and abattoirs live, Buttes-Chaumont and Ménilmontant, from where each day thousands of workers descend to the center of the city, Salpêtrière, Gare, Maison-Blanche which still have their alleyways and miserable shacks."[49]

These extraordinary hopes born of the Resistance and Liberation collided with the deplorable conditions and inequalities that weighed on the city's triumphant working classes. The city's reemergence as a capital as of luxury and pleasure was glorious, but for most Parisians the western districts and the *lieux de plaisir* along the boulevards were out of reach and a painful reminder of the bleak conditions haunting the rest of the city. This deeper reality underlay ambivalence about the city's future prospects. The nouveau riche who had connections did well, while the rest of the population was burdened with the inequities only made worse by the war and occupation. While the fashionable neighborhoods in the 7th and 8th arrondissements were awash in splendid apartments, families squeezed into hovels in the eastern districts. Skyrocketing inflation, the rising cost of living, and stagnating salaries (which generally fell between 1938 and 1954) made daily life in Paris grueling for the majority of working people. Rationing of key foodstuffs continued until 1949. Real wages, adjusted for inflation, reached their lowest level in 1949, when earnings were only 54 percent of what they had been in 1937. Any kind of social solidarity remained fragile, pierced even more deeply by the purges and "civil wars" provoked by the Nazi occupation. Whether in the city or in the suburbs, the difficulties were palpable and provoked reaction.

Realizing that the meanness of life extended far beyond the war years is crucial for understanding the social and political conflicts that permeated the capital's public sphere. They expressed themselves in a web of antagonisms between resisters and collaborators, between the proletariat and the bourgeoisie, between the young and the old. Social strains were exacerbated by the passions swirling around the cold war and the painful process of decolonization. Unrest, street demonstrations, and riots riddled the city's symbolic spaces during the late 1940s and early 1950s. Workers, students, and the homeless protested their miserable circumstances. One strike after another evidenced the mounting disillusionment and anger. Communists railed against their purge from the machinery of government in May 1947. The political clashes and strike waves of 1947 immobilized the capital. Riots broke out in 1952 against the visit by the American General Matthew Ridgway. Abbé Pierre launched a public mobilization against homelessness in 1953. The hated Indochinese War and the debacle of Dien Bien Phu in March 1954 brought thousands into the street. Police crackdowns and repression further fueled animosities. Once the Marshall Plan and reconstruction kicked in, salaries and standards of living began to steadily climb.[50] By the early to mid-1950s some working-class families could think about making real purchases and enjoying the first fruits of prosperity. As a result, in the second half of the 1950s Paris was less the scene of social clashes. But by that time the Algerian War was setting up an even more intense civil conflict that would pour into the streets, especially in the disorders of May 1958.

Albert Demangeon's reference to "miserable shacks" was not just literary license. Finding a better life meant first and foremost finding a decent place to live in Paris, which remained an elusive dream for far too many. Housing was the city's foremost crisis. Rent freezes and construction costs had shriveled private real-estate investment for years before the war. The resulting nonstop subdivision and overcrowding of the housing stock covered Paris with decrepit, blighted buildings. Its enchanting cityscape was made up of a vast collection of ancient structures jerry-rigged for gas and electricity, many without toilets, bathtubs, or heat. A litany of official reports and statistics poured out the horrors of living in the City of Light. In 1943 the city's Inspection générale des services techniques de topographie et d'urbanisme (department of public works) carried out an intensive study of the conditions in Paris. Some 800,000 souls were living in circumstances that were at best unhealthy and at worst simply dangerous. There were 200,000 crammed into ancient flats, while another 150,000 found shelter in dreary rooming houses. It was estimated that one-fifth of Parisians lived in attic rooms under the city's well-known mansard roofs, rooms "that were sweltering in summer [and] freezing in winter," or in "humid and obscure" hideaways lost behind the street-level facades.[51] These squalid conditions were aggravated by the wartime attacks against the capital's industrial infrastructure. Poor, gray, and dirty, in some cases reduced to rubble, the industrial districts of the northeast were a muddle of rustic firetraps converted into ateliers and warehouses or some semblance of dwelling for the city's workers and the poor. Despite the wretched conditions, any sort of lodging was a miracle. Over 15,000 people in the 18th arrondissement alone had been left homeless by the war. They shared cramped housing with family or were relocated to temporary barrack camps in the suburbs. By the war's end, some 450,000 people were categorized in government reports as *les plus défavorisés* or *mal-lotis*. By the early 1950s, government reports estimated that over 433,000 people still lived in rented boarding rooms or hovels with a few sticks of furniture in what every observer described as deplorable circumstances. Nearly 100,000 people still remained homeless.[52] From end

FIGURE 1. Slum district or *îlot insalubre* in 1955. © KEYSTONE-FRANCE.

to end, Paris seemed to be as strange hallucination of postwar Europe in crisis, nothing but urban debris.

Worst of all were the *îlots insalubres* (unhealthy pockets or blocks), great swaths of Paris that were identified as breeding grounds for crime, vice, and disease. Slums are constructions of the imagination. They were a stereotype fashioned in the early nineteenth century that conflated "slums" with working-class neighborhoods. As an invented genre, the slum retained an extraordinary hold over social reformers. In 1906 the municipal council had proposed the demolition of six "tubercular districts," the worst of the worst slums. The most notorious was îlot 1 on the Arcis-Beaubourg plateau in the district of Saint-Merri, just north of the Hôtel de Ville. Îlot 2 was behind the

Jardin des Plantes down through the rue Mouffetard on the Left Bank. Also on the Left Bank were îlot 3 at Saint-Michel in the 5th arrondissement and îlot 4 including the notorious cité Jeanne-d'Arc near the place d'Italie in the 13th arrondissement. Îlot 5 was located at the porte de Clichy in the north of Paris, and îlot 6 was the archetypal working-class district of the faubourg Saint-Antoine. The original proposal called for clearing out around 1,500 houses and some 60,000 people. When the project reemerged after the First World War, a full seventeen *îlots insalubres* had been identified.[53] Most of the newly designated slum districts were in the eastern half of Paris. Thirteen were located along the city's periphery. The designation not only imposed a new spatial mapping of the central districts, but, after expropriation and demolition, opened them for private redevelopment and real-estate initiatives in areas covering some 4,200 buildings and threatening the expulsion of around 180,000 people. A small number of clearance projects were carried out in the interwar years and under Vichy. Destruction rained down on sections of îlot 9, in the northern district of Clignancourt (where reported cases of the plague served as the pretext), and in îlots 1, 2, and 4. The worst of the slum housing was cleared away. But the paucity of public housing and the general failure of any kind of robust urban reform measures meant that these neighborhoods formed a long-standing geography of indigence that worsened with each passing year. The *îlots insalubres* took on a diabolical character in public debates about the city. Paris was a dark, malodorous hell swarming with putrid lanes and blind alleys that led to iniquity. Rooting out these fetid rookeries became an obsession of the planners and architects whipping up visions of Paris arising from the ashes like a modern phoenix.

None of these conditions necessarily stopped population growth in the capital. Despite the fact that the *city* of Paris itself was losing residents, in each of the years from 1946 to 1954 the Paris *region* as a whole gained an average of 75,000 people. The well-known postwar baby boom was one important factor in this demographic boost. Throughout its modern history, the city's population had always been fueled by the incessant flood of provincial immigrants making their way to jobs and a new life. But by 1954, for the first time, the number of people born in the department of the Seine exceeded the number of people coming from the provinces. Both the birthrate and the number of foreign arrivals increased, while provincial immigration to the department of the Seine essentially remained stable. But the fact that provincial migration had evened out did not mean that the French, or anyone else for that matter, had changed their minds about settling in the capital and its environs. They simply settled in the outlying suburbs, especially the distant periphery outside the historic first ring of suburban growth and outside the department of the Seine into the neighboring departments extending out through the Île-de-France. This vast Paris region mushroomed in population and area. From 1954 to 1962 125,000 inhabitants were added to the population rolls in the Paris region each year.[54] The sea of humanity flooding into the suburbs thus found a diverse world. The inner faubourgs, the factories and *lotissement* housing of the "red belt," the garden-city projects, the nostalgic rural districts with their ancient villages, and the outer zones of abject poverty and new settlement made up a complex environment that fascinated as well as horrified the capital's observers.[55] They seized upon it as an entirely different universe. It was stigmatized with an endless stream of images and meanings, most of them derogatory comparisons to the tight circle of twenty arrondissements that the shared cultural imaginary called "Paris."

The walls that divided the city from the suburbs were thus both physical and psychological. In the words of the longtime urbanist and Paris observer Albert Guérard, they were "more formidable than Thiers's military fortifications."[56] Until 1943 the *octroi* tax gates still guarded entry into the sacred arrondissements of historic Paris. Automobiles coming into the city paid a gas toll as they passed through. Just beyond, the demolition of the military fortifications or *fortifs*, which had been completed by 1932, had left, along with a buffer zone or *zone non aedificandi*, a ring of about twenty-two miles (some 1,200 acres) divided up in piecemeal fashion. Seven-story Habitation a bon marché (HBM) public housing was constructed there during the interwar years and formed a new barrier. But the leftover open terrain along the edges of the city continued to hold a special allure for Parisians. The magnetism of the *zone* was a combination of nostalgic memories of promenades and open-air cafés and fascination with its tarnished and grubby surfaces. By the 1940s sections of the *zone* were a well-entrenched wasteland of old cemeteries, railroad tracks and sidings, factories, sports stadiums, claptrap wooden houses, miserable shantytowns, and squatter settlements occupied by an indigent population of some 125,000 *zoniers*. Step by step, the land was requisitioned by the public authorities. The grim days of the occupation were marked by the expropriation of the last 260 hectares and the final eviction of the squatters. It was accompanied by a well-organized protest. A

Comité des Zoniers attacked their removal as a double occupation of their territory—first by the Germans, second by a French administration bent on expelling them and using it for their own purposes.[57]

Beyond the *zone* lay the infamous *ceinture rouge* (red belt). A flood of immigrants had found jobs in the heavy industry of the suburbs during the first half of the twentieth century. But this created miserable living conditions in workers' ghettos and shanty districts.[58] Shelter for working-class families in this first suburban ring meant wretched lodging houses, run-down flats, makeshift settlements, and *bidonvilles*.[59] In the infamous *lotissement* housing estates of the interwar years, speculators and laborers themselves had set about constructing every sort of edifice in pursuit of suburban home ownership. They stretched into the present-day departments of the Haut-de-Seine, Seine-Saint-Denis, and Val-de-Marne. These marginalized places made few investments in decent streets, water, sewers, or any other kind of basic infrastructure. The aerial bombardments during the Second World War against the capital's heavy industry made the situation dramatically worse. Suburbs such as Noisy-le-Sec in the northeast and Ivry-sur-Seine in the southwest sustained substantial damage.[60] Families lived in temporary barracks that at best were "experiments" in postwar housing design, and at worst were little more than refugee camps. In all of the suburban industrial districts hit by the bombardments, squatters took over abandoned structures or partially damaged buildings in an effort to find shelter and piece together their lives.

But even the dreadful conditions did little to stop the stream of people looking for work and a chance to make it in Paris. By the mid-1950s, 7.5 million people—more than 17 percent of the French population—lived in the 435 square miles of the officially designated *agglomération parisienne*. By the end of the decade, the population was approaching 8 million. Some 60 percent of Parisians already lived in the suburbs. Thousands wrestled with commutes averaging one and two hours a day on the few local trains. In 1954 some 650,000 people commuted into Paris daily from the suburbs, while another 560,000 commuted between jobs and home in the suburban districts without ever entering the city. Fifteen cities around Paris contained over 50,000 inhabitants each. The largest was Boulogne-Billancourt in the west, with 94,000 residents hemmed into a dense and decaying urban core made even shoddier by the wartime bombardments. In the north, Saint-Denis had a population of 80,000, while neighboring Asnières had 78,000.[61] Suburban communities spread farther and farther out in the Seine valley to some 264 communes extending into the departments of Val-de-Oise, Yvelines, Essone, and Seine-et-Marne. The most distant settlements were made up mostly of new migrants. This unforgiving wilderness was the antithesis of the capital's reputation for sophistication and urbanity: ancient buildings, limited running water and electricity, virtually no services or infrastructure, and few schools. Working-class slums along the suburban periphery became a byword for spatial and social marginalization. By the end of the 1950s, 400,000 people still eked out their survival in rented hovels lost in isolated suburban slums far from Parisian glamour.

Reconstruction

It is precisely the paradox of this period that despite these horrendous conditions, the public life and landscape of Paris were attuned to the rhythms of a rich urban economy. The city's dense mosaic of industrial and commercial activities, the street markets and workaday world that made the landscape of the capital so readable, reappeared in the late 1940s and early 1950s with an intensity and elation that mark them as dramatic and overflowing with social and political meaning. The vast crusade for reconstruction and modernization was perhaps the most dominant theme of postwar France. The zeal for repair and renewal was palpable everywhere and shared across social and political spectrums. Reconstruction began with the city's infrastructure. Roads, railroad tracks, bridges, canals, and public utilities were rebuilt. Each success was heavily publicized; a storefront display along the Marne River in late 1944 proclaimed, "Since the reconstruction of this bridge, coal tonnage destined for the Paris region has quadrupled in 15 days."[62] Businesses reopened. Both the automobile and the aircraft industries were nationalized in 1945, and the city's manufacturing was jump-started with Marshall Plan aid. Then the French "economic miracle" kicked in and further stimulated production. The accent was on productivity and efficiency. By 1954 the French economy had essentially recovered. Average national income and consumption rose by over a third between 1949 and 1958. Eager Parisian shoppers crammed the markets and stores of the city with gusto. Every new automobile model and the displays of television sets, refrigerators, and washing machines in store windows attracted crowds of eager consumers. Jobs were plentiful and paychecks ready to be spent.

The Paris region reached its zenith as an industrial and commercial powerhouse during the early 1950s. Within the city itself, industry and public works employed 720,000, just about half of the 1,443,000 industrial jobs found throughout the metropolitan area. Jean Bastié estimated that around 300,000 people were working directly in production in the Right Bank districts. The Right Bank was the city's industrial dynamo. In "Physiologie de grands boulevards," the novelist Armand Lanoux describes an "early-morning flood of men and women on foot, on bicycle, by bus or subway, descending from Batignolles, Saint-Ouen, Clignancourt, Pantin, La Villette, Lilas, and the Butte onto the *Grands Bouls*" and the surrounding neighborhoods.[63] Another 100,000 were employed in production on the Left Bank, and over 200,000 were working along the city's periphery.[64] Altogether the Paris region employed around 20 percent of all French industrial workers in 1954. Three industrial sectors predominated. First was all of the diverse manufactures that fell under the umbrella of the "mechanical" industry. They employed half a million people in the Paris region, and of these 150,000 were directly involved in automobile manufacture. The second sector was made up of the ready-to-wear fashion, haute couture, perfume, gold, and jewelry of the luxury-goods industry. Nearly 200,000 people were employed producing Paris's fineries and perfumes. The third sector was the publishing industry, with 80,000 workers.[65] The chemical and electric industries also employed vast numbers of Parisians. There was virtually no unemployment, and indeed foreign workers, the majority from North Africa, streamed into Paris in search of jobs. In good part, the spectacle of public life was this reemergence and expansion of manufacturing production and the urban culture created around it.

The fact that central Paris had been spared any damage worked to preserve its traditional commercial and artisanal economy. The number of French artisans probably reached its twentieth-century peak in 1948.[66] The reconstruction years were marked by an effort to jump-start the city's economy through an informal, enthusiastic alliance between this substratum of small-scale businesses that dominated the central districts and the large companies of the industrial periphery. The furniture of the faubourg Saint-Antoine, the hats and shoes made in the faubourg Saint-Martin, the ready-to-wear garments and shoes of Belleville, Ménilmontant, and Charonne, the leather goods of the Bièvre, and the ceramics and glass along the rue de Paradis stocked the city's great department stores and the boutiques of the quartier de l'Opéra. Just to the north of Les Halles were the garment districts that wound from the rue Saint-Denis, where each evening prostitutes appropriated public

FIGURE 2. A vegetable street trader or *marchand des quatre-saisons* in Montmartre, 1955. © KEYSTONE-FRANCE.

space to ply their trade, up to Sentier. Thousands of *petits métiers* specializing in everything from gloves and lingerie to artificial flowers, knickknacks, umbrellas, and precious jewelry animated local neighborhood spaces, along with small metalworking and electronic shops. Work was still done in the interior courtyards of buildings and on the sidewalks. Armenians, Greeks, Jews, and Italians labored alongside provincial French in a flourishing job market. Prisoners of war and conscripted workers returning to Paris added their names to the trade registers and opened new businesses. Small-time artisans floated in and out of commercial success, depending on their acumen and personal acquaintances. They were vital to the internal structure and physiognomy of the neighborhoods.

Joining them along the *rue marchande* in every district was the myriad of commercial purveyors and local markets that specialized in everyday needs. In the mid- to late 1950s, 20 percent of all French commerce was centralized in the Paris region, where some 150,000 commercial businesses plied their trade. There were 80,000 located in the central city, most of them traditional specialty shops selling everything from the city's famous handmade luxuries to the predictable neighborhood bakery.[67] There were also 1,200 chain stores and the newer self-service groceries that made a splash in the postwar years. Families did their shopping with the city's four thousand (mainly women) *marchandes des quatre-saisons* in the ancient enclosed markets of the place de l'Aigre and the marché Saint-Germain, and in the street markets along the rue de Ménilmontant in eastern Paris, the rue Lepic around the place Clichy, or on the rue Mouffetard and the rue Daguerre on the Left Bank, to take just a few of the better-known examples. After years of food shortages, the ritual Saturday market day was itself sheer spectacle, drawing mobs of consumers and onlookers. The butcher and poultry shops, fish stalls, bakeries, and open-air vegetable stalls were an extravaganza of sights and smells. The *petits métiers de la rue* were an informal economy of barbers, quacks, fortune tellers, knife sharpeners, caners, bric-a-brac peddlers, street singers, and entertainers. Street vendors sold chestnuts, garlic, wines, and regional specialties. *Bergers des champs* with their herds of goats still wandered the streets selling cheese in the years after the war. The cycle of trade and market fairs was vital to these neighborhood economies. Their reappearance in the reconstruction years was a celebration of bounty, a feast of food and material well-being that chased away the painful scarcity of the wartime years. They were laden with precious food, produce, and goods not seen in years. The crowds at the scrap metal and ham fairs on the boulevard Richard Lenoir in the faubourg Saint-Antoine were enormous. The neighborhood ateliers were emptied as workers and their families jammed the booths, buying up anything and everything available. Neighborhood committees organized commercial festivals to attract consumers. Window displays and holiday decorations decked the local streets. Sales events with such themes as "Two Merry Weeks," "Deadly Sins," and "Fables of La Fontaine" sweetened the allure of buying. Altogether, they constituted a vernacular economic culture built around informal localized networks catering to growing demand.

The Seine and Marne rivers and the city's canals were still vital commercial arteries in the late 1940s and early 1950s. They were lined with working docks and warehouses engaged in the ceaseless task of provisioning the capital and exporting its merchandise. The squat *Magasins généraux* stood guard over the Seine. On the Right Bank, just east of the city, the docks at Bercy were the entry into the world of the wine trade. Wine was big business, dominated by large-scale companies such as Gévéor and Vins du Postillon. Bercy remained a world apart, protected by ferocious customs agents and a ten-foot-high grating. It consisted of a secret labyrinth of bungalows and warehouses where merchants negotiated along streets named Médoc, Mâcon, Chablis, and Beaugency. Flanking Bercy, the quai Henri IV and the bassin de l'Arsenal were commercial ports surrounded by heaps of sand and cement, workshops, boatyards, and sheds. The district around them housed some of the city's most important companies, especially the Compagnie générale de navigation Havre-Paris-Lyon-Marseille (HPLM), the largest inland navigation company in France, with its three thousand employees and vast boat repair facilities. From the Seine barges piled with wheat, sugar, salt, coal, and construction material trekked through the locks from the Arsenal to the canal Saint-Martin and then up through the bassin de La Villette to the canal Saint-Denis and the canal de l'Ourcq. In *Paris insolite* (1954), urban observer Jean-Paul Clébert described a landscape of "factory chimneys, glass roofs, suspended bridges, gasometers, streams of flickering lights, flat houses and high houses, business and administrative buildings spread out along the quay alongside private properties, bonded warehouses, staircased sentry boxes for the watchmen."[68]

Over nine million tons of merchandise was transported into Paris each year, using the *petite ceinture* or circular rail connection to move between the main railroad stations and then offloading goods into a multitude of local warehouses. The ancient food market at Les Halles, the "guts of Paris," which eluded all efforts to destroy it, functioned only as a shadow of itself during the war, the black market dictating what trade there was. The urban reforms promulgated under Vichy in 1943 had once again called for its removal, as had the French government's Conseil économique in 1949. Nonetheless, the reconstruction years brought back the familiar spectacle of smells, the clamor of rowdy dealers, *musclés*, *mandataires*, and wisecracking deliverymen bringing in the *cargos de la route*. Crates loaded with fruits and vegetables were crammed into the stalls. Tables overflowed with fish, cheeses, and meats, an assortment of hanging sausages and hams swinging

FIGURE 3. Dockers at the pont d'Austerlitz on the Seine River, June 13, 1950. © GERALD BLONCOURT/RUE DES ARCHIVES.

through the air. Merchants and clients negotiated the confusion while the poor rummaged through heaps of garbage to get what they could. Water poured out everywhere through spigots, buckets, and hoses. Cats and rats proliferated. The smell of *frites* in hot oil permeated the atmosphere. Clients picked their way through the puddles, over the crates and produce, and out through the maze of bistros that surrounded Victor Baltard's glass pavilions. Although Les Halles was well beyond its limits, the messy, sumptuous assortment of provisions that appeared after the lean years of war gave it renewed meaning for everyone.

Although the boulevard de Sébastopol separated them, the quotidian work of Les Halles and the Marais were by their nature joined. Their relationship was symbiotic. The ancient buildings of the Marais housed a dense network of industries, commercial establishments, and sweatshops kept humming by a diverse immigrant population. Socially and ethnically it was a heterogeneous locality. It was to the Marais that Parisian *flâneurs* ventured for Sunday promenades to see the exotic blend of people, languages, and customs packed into the dilapidated streetscape. From the Marais, the rue Saint-Antoine wound toward the place de la Bastille and the faubourg Saint-Antoine. In the late 1940s and early 1950s, the place de la Bastille was one of the most animated sites in the city, a whirlwind of movement and urban flux. Once gasoline became available again, thousands of automobiles circled the July Column. The sidewalks were packed with people. As public space, it was the site of a never-ending stream of *fêtes foraines* (loosely translated as "fun fairs"), outdoor markets, street hawkers and entertainers, clowns, and musicians. The place de la Bastille led into the furniture-making district of the faubourg Saint-Antoine. Carpenters, upholsterers, and joiners lived and worked on the rue du Faubourg Saint-Antoine and its web of alleyways and cul-de-sacs. The Germans had carted off much of the district's furniture during the occupation, and the lack of wood and materials just after the war further hindered production. Despite the desperate need of families restarting their lives, by 1949 the market for traditional French furniture was actually waning. Nevertheless, the ongoing street parade of workers loaded down with tables and massive armoires and transporting hulking furniture to waiting stores still took place daily. The competition between the showrooms along the rue du Faubourg Saint-Antoine was fierce. Illuminated signs advertised rock-bottom prices, while window displays gleamed with furnishings. Slick sales agents in double-breasted suits lured clients in while "pickmen" set up deals for clients directly with manufacturers.

The real heart of industrial Paris lay in the outer arrondissements and peripheral zones to the northeast. The rue du Faubourg du Temple was the world of metalworking and machine shops, foundries, and scrap and sheet-metal depots. It was the principle activity of the 11th arrondissement and

much of the eastern districts. Metalworking was traced in the street names—
the cour de la Fonderie, the rue des Taillandiers, the cité de l'Industrielle—as
well as in the union halls and health clinics for the *métallos*. Jammed together
in dilapidated buildings, spewing out pollution and waste, the industries of
the eastern neighborhoods were racked by spectacular fires and gas explosions that brought firefighters out en masse. Machine and metalwork shops
and small refineries lined the canal Saint-Martin all the way to La Villette
and pont de Flandre. This Parisian dynamo represented a full 35 percent of
the French mechanical industry. La Villette was known most famously for
the visceral atmosphere of its two worlds, the cattle market at the porte de
Pantin and the slaughterhouses at the porte de la Villette. There, the canal
Saint-Martin joined the bassin de la Villette, the center of the city's waterway
system. The canal de l'Ourcq and the canal Saint-Denis stretched it into
the suburbs beyond. The heavy odor of salt and sugar followed the barges
up through the locks on their way to the *Magasins généraux* in Aubervilliers.
Here were found the two large-scale sugar refineries of François and Leb-
audy-Sommier; the food processing plants of Damoy, SOPAD, and Nutrop;
the Grands Moulins flour mills at Pantin; the myriad beverage-processing
units; and silos and warehouses, along with virtually every sector of the food
industry—a vast cartography of urban provisioning.

Here began the great arc of large-scale industry that swung from Saint-
Ouen and La Plaine Saint-Denis to La Courneuve, Aubervilliers, and Pantin.
The imagery was both legendary and notorious. Food and butchering, chemical plants, automobile and aircraft factories, metalworks and ironworks, oil
refineries and gasworks, aluminum, leather, paper, soap, and perfume plants,
varnish, dye, tallow and lubricant makers, textile mills, and paper and publishing enterprises, joined a profusion of ancillary manufactories and workshops. This dense industrial landscape followed the railway lines and the
three highways stretching out to the north. Some 33,000 people worked in
various sectors of the chemical industry (44 percent of the French sector),
from perfume to pharmaceuticals to the manufacture of abrasives. Another
11,000 worked in the district's rubber manufactories. The André and Bata
companies led shoe manufacturing. Érard, on the rue de Flandre near the
bassin de la Villette, employed around two thousand workers to make musical instruments. The Lang printing works close by on the rue Curial and the
vast printing plant of the magazine *L'Illustration* at Bobigny led the capital's
printing industry, which employed thousands; Lang alone employed 3,000

people.[69] Toxic fumes and pollution spewed out across a maze of factories, sheds, dilapidated hovels and lodgings, warehouses, railroad tracks, and disgusting wastewater channels. The canals and the Rouillon, Crould, and Montfort streams were putrid sewers that wound through Aubervilliers and Saint-Denis and eventually emptied into the Seine. Here were the industrial guts of Paris. It was a landscape that captured both the energy of economic renewal, the hopes for the future, and the weariness of social despair.

The Left Bank of Paris was a far less industrial landscape. But in the southeast, in the 13th arrondissement from the gare d'Austerlitz to Salpêtrière, La Gare, and Maison Blanche, a complex of manufactories, refineries, warehouses, and assorted factories composed an industrial cartography of extraordinary dimensions. By the mid-1950s the district was already facing decline. Behind Austerlitz on the boulevard de la Gare (Vincent-Auriol) was the giant Say sugar refinery and the Lombart chocolate works. Close by were the gas works on the avenue de Choisy. Alleys lined with miserable shanties disgorged their inhabitants into the industrial badlands lining the tiny Bièvre River that zigzagged from the Seine to Butte-aux-Cailles. The breweries, starch and shoemaking factories, tanneries, and laundries of *la Bièvre* emitted an array of odious smells and pollution. Just adjacent, along the southern periphery, the great automobile and aircraft manufacturers were found:[70] Panhard at the porte d'Ivry and SNECMA on the boulevard Kellermann (both in the 13th arrondissement). Citroën, at the quai de Javel, in the 15th arrondissement employed 18,000 workers in 1950. This industrial landscape merged into the suburban towns of Ivry, Vitry, and Choisy-le-Roi. To the west, the huge Renault plant at Boulogne-Billancourt on the Seine in the 16th arrondissement employed between 36,000 and 42,000 during the reconstruction years (figures for 1948–52). Over 80 percent of French automobiles were made in Paris. Humming factories churned out the Renault 4CVs and eventually the Citroën DS, which became emblems of the 1950s. Factoring in workers and their families as well as shopkeepers and local inhabitants who provided services, it has been estimated that some 200,000 people relied on the Renault plant for their livelihood.

Paris in the 1950s was, in sum, a vast industrial and commercial combine hitting its stride in the great campaign for reconstruction and modernization. This reality is often missed in histories of post-1945 France. The apogee of working-class, industrial Paris was reached in the years of reconstruction and modernization after the Second World War. But in the minds of France's technocratic elites, the dawning of this new postwar era required disassembling the capital's colossal economy. Paris was too big. It had siphoned off development from the rest of the country. Its industrial districts and suburbs were an unremitting geography of filthy squalor, social instability, and political unrest. It is easy to forgive anyone looking at the evidence from the 1950s for failing to see either the economic achievements taking place in this landscape or the extraordinary public culture they represented. State documents in particular form a veritable mountain of formulary slurs and evidence against the capital that would justify its relentless dismantling. Rather than promote any further expansion of this urban vampire sucking dry the country's growth and potential, the Ministère de la Reconstruction et de l'Urbanisme (MRU) and the Commissariat Général du Plan insisted on the decentralization of the city's industrial might to the provinces. There it would balance the country's economic development according to the rationale principles of *aménagement du territoire*. The groundwork for this discourse was laid in the 1940s and 1950s. Its implementation began in the early 1950s with only fifty-five "industrial decentralization operations" and then picked up steam during the second half of the decade with four hundred operations.[71] Private businesses took advantage of government subsidies to relocate to provincial cities where they could construct modern plants. Felix Potin, Nutrop, and Damoy led the parade out of Paris in the late 1950s, and the large-scale state-owned automobile and aircraft factories followed. Most of this deindustrialization impacted the city's traditional chemical, automobile and metalworking plants, its leather and food-processing plants in the city's old industrial districts, and the great industrial ribbon from Saint-Ouen through Saint-Denis to Pantin in the north. Many of these establishments were no longer competitive and simply died away as a result of modernization and the changing tastes of consumers. The city's ancient industrial infrastructure—its port, the canals and railroad lines, the great La Villette complex, the Bercy wine market, and the Halles aux Vins at Jussieu were all out of date. One after the next government decision was made against renovating them, opting instead for demolition.

By 1958 among the most significant visual images in the city were of demolition and reconstruction. Most of the renewal projects took place in old industrial areas and especially in the *zone* that ringed the city. Old railroad yards and wholesale market depots were the first to be dismantled. Ancient garages, workshops, dilapidated factories, and blighted slums were bulldozed down or left abandoned in a painful landscape of destruction. Warehouses

FIGURE 4. Construction of the Maison de la Radio in the 16th arrondissement, August 4, 1959. Architect: Henry Bernard. © RUE DES ARCHIVES/AGIP.

and market halls were torn apart and carted away. Neighbors gathered to watch demolition crews drag down walls of ancient brick and disassemble crumbling apartment houses and cottages. Thousands of jobs were lost, and hundreds of thousands were displaced. But it was a moment of great hope for the future. Paris was being recreated as a dynamic city of material well-being and wealth, of prestige and modern glamour. Huge cranes and building equipment hung over the cityscape in a great ring around the old historic center. Bulldozers and trucks roared into action. Vast cleared, open areas of the *fortifs* and outer arrondissements were the scenes of humming construction activity. The skeletons of new apartment blocks rose upward across the skyline. Paris's first "skyscraper" of twenty-one stories, "exactly the height of Notre Dame," was going up on the rue Croulebarbe in the 13th arrondissement.[72] Newsreels and television reports witnessed the city's metamorphosis, tracking around the outer districts to report on the newest construction projects. Fresh air, light, gardens, and green spaces would surround modern apartments fitted with the newest home luxuries and appliances. Flabbergasted slum dwellers, belongings in hand, passed through the door into domestic utopia and modern middle-class lives. To the north near Le Bourget Airport, the "City of the Future" was blooming in the fields at Sarcelles. Advertisements gushed over the finished apartment complexes of Sarcelles Lochères, Sarcelles Les Paillards, and Sarcelles Les Hirondelles. Suburban *grands ensembles* emerged at Créteil, Massy-Antony, and Poissy. It was an advance guard of things to come. By 1955 sites along the Seine were moving toward renovation. The sassy new Maison de l'UNESCO was taking form on the place de Fontenoy as a symbol of the city's modern role on the world stage. The site for the ultramodern NATO headquarters at the porte Dauphine was cleared and readied for construction. The old wine warehouses at Jussieu on the Left Bank were falling to the demolition crews to make way for a new Faculty of Science of the University of Paris. The architect Henry Bernard's designs were revealed for the Maison de la Radio to be built on the cleared quai de Passy, while architects excitedly hovered over preliminary sketches for the Maine-Montparnasse renewal project and for La Défense. The capital of France was rebuilding, reemerging in new form, and so was the country itself.

2 The Landscape of Populism

After the fall of France and the ignominy of occupation, national unity was portrayed as an imperative that overrode all differences. The immediate past remained unsettled and conflict-ridden. Retribution was meted out with ferocity. The purges and high-profile trials of collaborators kept the fires of hatred smoldering. Yet in response to the trauma France had suffered, the bitterness and deep divisions, all sides trumpeted a common patriotic rhetoric. According to the historian Michael Kelly, the more strongly internal conflicts raged, the more intensely national unity was affirmed: "French post-war elites demonstrated a remarkable unanimity on one central point: the need to rebuild the nation."[1] However controversial its memory was, the Liberation gave legitimacy to the notion of transcendence. This patriotism, as well as the future of France for that matter, was translated as progressive and revolutionary. In this call for a French renaissance, the key concept was "the people," a mythic term that provided the vocabulary with which to imagine an all-encompassing French identity. The "people" meant all working people, all the ordinary people who had suffered through the black years of adversity and who would now join together to create a new France. The images of a threatening proletariat, the persistent hatreds were all sidestepped for a glorified conception of the French as progressive, hopeful, and civilized. Their victory in the Resistance and in the Liberation of Paris had proven their mettle and their national loyalty.

This vast national community was imagined from a perspective that was at once spatial, cultural, and historic. It was a portrait composed of a wealth of urban sites and geographic locations. In Paris the rhetoric was instilled with an organic, naturalized portrait of a people embedded in their quartiers in what amounted to a mythic urban folklorism. It found expression in the reinvigoration of the traditional forms and scenes of public life, especially at the level of neighborhood. This is where the *peuple* could be found. The local neighborhood or quartier (the terms were used interchangeably) was traditionally the location, the cultural nexus, of social consciousness and everyday life experiences. It was also the physical space on which the city's working-class past was inscribed, traceable in the memories, stories, and myths of its public history. We could say that the quartier was a spatial pictogram of meaning and of collective imagination. After the war, revalorizing this most intimate of public spaces seemed the first priority. It was the glue of urban society and created a moralized landscape imbued with a renewed sense of consolidation and constructedness.

Until the end of the 1950s, a working, proletarian Paris remained embedded and localized in these long-established urban territories. Some were iconographic, legendary places and metaphors for urban insurrection, while others were barely known. All were part of the city's flourishing industrial and commercial economy. Many of these neighborhoods have since become historicized tourist districts, and it is worth mentioning the most important of them to remember the extent of this productive working-class world. Beginning in the historic core, they included the 1st, 2nd, 3rd, and 4th arrondissements on the Right Bank, especially the neighborhoods of Les Halles, the Marais, and Sentier. Sections of the 5th and 6th arrondissements on the Left Bank around the rue de Buci and the rue Mazarine, from the Contrescarpe down the rue Monge and the rue Mouffetard were all archetypally working class. Moving outward, the neighborhoods of the faubourg du Temple, the canal Saint-Martin and around the railway stations in the 10th arrondissement, the faubourg Saint-Antoine, the Bastille and République, the districts of Charonne and Nation in the 11th arrondissement, and the 18th, 19th, and 20th arrondissements, which included Belleville, La Villette, and Ménilmontant, formed a broad proletarian band that covered the entire east and north of the city. Farther east along the working waterway of the Seine was Bercy in the 12th arrondissement, and to the south, the districts of La Gare and Maison-Blanche, the Bièvre, and the Buttes aux Cailles in the 13th arrondissement. To these were added Batignolles in the northwest and Grenelle and Vaugirard to the south. The expression "people of Paris" also included the inhabitants of Aubervilliers, Bagneux, Gennevilliers, Ivry, Montreuil, and Saint-Denis in the suburban ring around the capital. According to traditional perceptions of social space in the city of Paname, these *quartiers populaires* were a puzzle of working villages. The boundaries of these neighborhoods, and of the even smaller îlots, were fluid, determined as much by custom and practice as by official delineation. Each functioned as a subculture known to the people who lived there, but also characterized and invented in guidebooks, histories, and literature. The narrative created a heterogeneous idea of "place" as a distinctive localized milieu. It was imagined as organic, particularistic, a miniature representation of the world. Neither trivial nor routine, these spaces of everyday "lived life" were understood as dynamic and creative. This was close to Bakhtin's claim that judgments, values, and behavior emerged organically out of the terrain of the everyday. In making this quotidian world a meaningful place, people engage in an ongoing process of practical doing and change.[2] It made the territory of the everyday a restlessly creative zone that promoted not just continuity, but also rupture and transformation.

Up to the Second World War, the centrality of Parisian topography had been a well-established fact. All of its cherished monuments and public decor, its grand boulevards and monumental squares, the sweeping vistas of political power along the Seine had given a unity to urban space and made the city an arena of the modern. These forces of spatial coherency had broken through and opened up the disjointed muddle of localized spaces and cast aside any nostalgic yearning for them. The historian Evelyne Cohen argues that even during the 1920s urban writers were far more interested in the madcap "crazy years" in the *beaux quartiers* and the avant-garde scene on the Left Bank. The proletarian neighborhoods that had spread through vast sections of the north and east remained unfamiliar worlds only imagined from the descriptions of Émile Zola. It was only in the 1930s that authors such as Léon-Paul Fargue, Robert Garric, Daniel Halévy, and Jules Romains turned once more to the *quartiers populaires*.[3] What is striking is that the catastrophe of war and the beginning of postwar modernization gave renewed life to this older discourse. The dazzling reputation of the City of Light had been tarnished. The classic representations of bourgeois modernity were now outmoded or, even worse, tainted with defeat and occupation. The privileged spaces that fashioned Paris into a modernist geography disintegrated. Instead, the *Paris des camarades* was forged in opposition to these leanings. Paris was imagined once again as *lived spaces*—a montage of village environments synonymous with a folkloric, almost homespun native soil that mitigated the cold spectacle of the boulevards.[4] These were decentered spaces that fractured the consolidating forces that had dominated Parisian history since the mid-nineteenth century. It was in this fractured landscape that "the people" would reappear to reinvigorate traditional forms of collective life and produce new ones. They would be the machinery of patriotism and progress.

Reviving the memory of these backwaters and neglected places, bringing them to light, became a cultural obsession. Urban observers plunged into the *bas quartiers* to discover their authentic qualities and picturesque charm. A plethora of books were reissued, published posthumously (in the case of Fargue) or for the first time, as if Paris were being discovered anew: Henri Calet's *Le Tout sur le tout* (1948) and *Les Grandes largeurs: Balades parisiennes* (1951), Léon-Paul Fargue's *Le Piéton de Paris* (1939, reprinted 1951) and *Les XX arrondissements de Paris* (1951), the reissue of Louis Cheronnet's *Paris et qu'il fut* (1951) and *Paris, mon cœur* (1952), and Albert Fournier's *Métiers curieux de Paris* (1953). A flood of publications in 1954, from Jean-Paul Clébert's *Paris insolite* to Gosselin Lenôtre's *Secrets du vieux Paris*; Claude Henri Rocquet's *Paris des rues: Les Petits métiers de Paris*; and Francis Jourdain's *Paris* and *Les Parisiens tels qu'ils sont*, kept up the tradition of *flânerie* in search of the city's soul. Photographers added a visual element to this narrative. Izis's *Paris de rêves* (1950), Willy Ronis's *Belleville-Ménilmontant* (1954), and Robert Doisneau's *Instantanés de Paris* (1955) were among the best of the pictorial records. These are but a few of the chronicles and photographic portraits that were produced as an invented discourse about the city. Some of these chroniclers, such as Fargue or Cherennot, were dyed-in-the-wool traditionalists intent on seeing the historic beauty of Paris even in the most dilapidated old districts. Others were writers and sentimentalists, journalists, or social reformers bent on uncovering the social life that went on there. Whatever their purposes or proclivities, these urban observers shared an almost ethnographic inquisitiveness, a new angle on the local that searched out the genuine, authentic Paris and its people. They produced the images and stories and the invented landscapes of populism and transformed urban *space* into *place* hedged in by social consciousness. Urban commentary exuded an evocative sentimentalism, an emotional bonding, and a sense of resurgence that marked it as a vital part of the poetic humanist genre. This spatial imagery had cogency despite the city's drabness, the atrocious slums that most Parisians lived in, and their poverty and deprivation—all of which were only too real.

Those who sought the simple magic of the city in the late 1940s and early 1950s dug deep into an historic treasure trove of characters haunting the streets. This vision of Paris was produced from a long heritage beginning with Sébastien Mércer and in which the naturalism of Zola held particularly strong sway. The novelist Armand Lanoux (later a winner of the Prix Goncourt) explored the city's revered social landscape on a variety of sentimental journeys. In "Physiologie de grands boulevards" (1954), Lanoux introduces the reader to old Alphonse, a junk dealer at the Saint-Ouen flea market, and Louise, a ragpicker who sings comic opera at the top of her lungs on the rue de Maubeuge. They exude the innocence of *la France profonde*, and indeed Lanoux's writings were by and large suffused with folkoric *images d'Épinal*. It is through these two characters "out of Dickens" that Lanoux chooses to introduce the local *zinc* (bar) from where the street scene along the boulevards is inspected.[5] In *Physiologie de Paris*, also published in 1954, Lanoux explains that in Belleville (that native soil of Paris) certain "urban races" survive: "They are archetypes only thought to exist in literature. The Saturday-night drunk, the hard-slapping shrew, the street urchin puffing on his smoke on the way home from school, the virtuous sister who raises the brood are preserved here in a living serial drama." At night the only people on the street are classic characters: bike cops and beat cops, sharks and provocateurs.[6] It was above all these working-class districts in the east to which this poetic sense of distinct place and culture was ascribed. The historian Jean El Gammal remarks that they were infused with an atmosphere of nostalgia and sentimentality in the late 1940s and 1950s.[7] In Jules Romain's *Portrait de Paris*, published for the city's two thousandth anniversary in 1951, Catholic social reformer Robert Garric wandered the city to summon up the mythic world of the "people of Paris." Their neighborhoods had

> charming names: Ménilmontant and Charonne, Bercy and Montrouge, les Gobelins, La Villette and Grenelle, Montmartre, Belleville. What cities within the city! What closed little worlds, so distinct, their streets and neighborhoods with such intense personalities. Some are animated and noisy, with an eccentric cheeriness; the cries of the street peddlers, the songs of the shopkeepers can still be heard. And others seem shadowed by sadness.... To live in one of these neighborhoods is to penetrate little by little into the unique sensibility of those who live there, to understand their habits, their memories, the pride of their traditions and their past.[8]

Guided by social Catholicism, Garric had created the Équipes sociales movement in 1920 to educate the working classes. He began the first study circle at Belleville. In his "friendly *flânerie* in the streets, remembering, listening, trying to hear the voice of the people," Garric evoked Belleville and

> its great, endless street, so varied and lively, its church, the memories of the Commune, its cinemas and theaters, its blazing cafes, and this ardent, mixed up sense of a crowd that is just as ready for merrymaking as for a meeting. It is on these streets, on the high terrace of the Buttes Chaumont, one of the most beautiful sites in Paris, in these dwellings, where if we listen, without speaking, if we remain silent, we can hear the voice and catch the heart of the people.[9]

In this populist ode Garric portrayed a concrete, tangible image of Parisians living in their own milieu. Although bathed in naturalism, this imagery clearly imparted the edifying moral that the quotidian, workaday world was a valiant one. This passion for discovering the quintessential qualities of ordinary neighborhood life was a voyage in search of the truth. It was an invented ethnographic exploration, an unearthing that would affirm the true qualities of Frenchness.

The pictures invented by urban observers like Lanoux and Garric border on the anachronistic and almost repeat the stereotypes of Eugène Sue in *Les Mystères de Paris*, published in 1841. Here was a taste of the piquant, the exotic, that made venturing into these districts tantamount to a voyage into the interior of an alien land. It was an exploitation of the mysterious and labyrinthine picturesque. These writers constructed, in the words of André Wurmser, who reviewed three of the publications on Paris in *Les Lettres françaises* in 1952, "a halo of false charm" and "magical evocations of the scenery of our childhood like one of those insipid historical novels." Wurmser was incredulous about "the beauty and charm of Paris" that could be found in the city's ancient neighborhoods: "These heartrending, charming houses of tuberculosis," he snidely remarked, "are admired today by amateurs . . . who stroll by them, but don't have to live inside."[10] Yet this mixture of fiction and reality transposed the moral dilemmas of the times onto the city's landscape. They reflected the uncertainties of the present and the fears of loss. The scenes invented by urban observers of conviviality and neighborhood fidelity and the salt-of-the-earth qualities of the working people were the converse of the actual civil strife that had fractured the public domain in the 1930s and 1940s. The purges that marked the early postwar years threatened to destroy the familiarity and trust normally associated with quotidian existence. The timelessness and humanity evoked in the city's neighborhood landscape pacified the isolation, mistrust, suspicions, and fear that had dominated the spaces of the city. These were depictions of the majority of everyday people as *les bons Français*. Genuinely patriotic, they had remained steadfast through the dark years and shared in the community of suffering and resistance. The world of quotidian existence is made harmonious, eternal. Parisians had reconquered the spaces of their public lives. Their physical presence in the streets, their resurgence as an enduring icon reactivated an intimately familiar memory of the city as home. Robert Garric described the "people of Paris," recruited from every corner of the country: "They have their gatherings, their holidays . . . their music, their songs, their newspapers. And Paris is the melting pot, it absorbs them all."[11]

Hence this outpouring of urban writing and imagery was more than just musings about a bucolic past. As an invented discourse it functioned entirely within the present as a cognitive urban mapping. The way to discover this eternal humanistic world was by walking through it. "There are hundreds of kilometers to explore," Jean-Paul Clébert declared eagerly as he set out on his itinerary to discover the unknown *Paris insolite*: "each street, alley, impasse, cul-de-sac has its personality, its own life, each is an îlot of houses, hovels, sheds, and chicken coops, its closed universe, its bistros, storeowners, its prostitutes, its inhabitants, habits and customs, that have nothing to do with their neighbors, and its architecture, its own spirit, its opinions, its work."[12] Space is transparent and legible from within. Clébert's intent was to traverse and illuminate this fragmented landscape of distinctiveness. The urban biographer Henri Calet also journeyed into the interior of eastern Paris, where he had spent a part of his youth. In *Le Tout sur le tout*, Calet described an "immense village of streets . . . descending, snaking, with country names . . . rue des Pavillons, rue du Soleil, rue de l'Ermitage, rue du Guignier, rue des Soupirs, rue des Rigoles, rue de la Mare, rue des Cascades. . . ."[13] This naming of streets, which pervaded virtually this entire genre, functioned to restore memory and place, to shift the public gaze from the grand boulevards down into the neighborhood districts and to equilibrate the city's geography around a far more decentered axis. In *The Arcades Project*, Walter Benjamin noted this strange power of names, spaces, and allegorical signification. There is a peculiar voluptuousness, a sensuality in the naming of streets.[14] They revealed the neighborhood's secrets. Spatial sites and their symbolic objects juxtaposed and provided continuity between the past, present, and the future. They illuminated the teeming activity, the cacophony of places and spaces, the "what took place here" at the heart of Paris's vast collectivity and rendered perception richer.

Inventing the Populist Landscape

Although riddled with political tensions, this mythic landscape of a self-actualizing Rousseauian people persisted from the late 1940s through the mid-1950s to provide the moral landscape upon which national unity could be imagined. In this invented topographical discourse, the public spaces of the city—that is, the streets and alleyways, the bistros and markets, the local festivals and street dances—were the places associated with their world. The interior of the workplace or home is rarely invoked. Instead, the street becomes a type of collective domestic interior. We catch a glimpse of *les Parisiens* in movement, strolling after dinner or dancing in the neighborhood square, on their way to work, crossing Sébasto to Les Halles, and traversing the boulevards and river quays. The street space claims existence when it is filled with human life. The interactions between human beings and between social groups were conceived as space filling. On summer evenings, families claimed a space on the sidewalk for a candlelight dinner and the chance to chat with neighbors. Saturday night meant the *accordéon musette* at the local café or dance hall. On Sunday afternoons families and couples promenaded along the boulevard or in the nearby park. Among the most well-known evidence for this poetic spatiality was that produced by the photographer Robert Doisneau. Even a superficial reading of his Parisian portraits evidences the absorption with the commonplace, with neighborhood life, and also with the apprehension that this authentic Paris would vanish. For Doisneau, Paris was moving because it was threatened, provisional, ephemeral. His intimate black-and-white photographs captured daily life in the everyday spaces of the city: men play pétanque in the park, old men gather around a table on the sidewalk for cards, children stage a roller-skating race, and religious processions parade through the quartier on feast days and to celebrate marriages and first communions. Street vendors provide a continuous carnival atmosphere in Doisneau's vision, selling everything from hot chestnuts, french fries, and sandwiches to cigarette lighters and flowers. Delivery carts and wagons disgorge their contents onto the sidewalks in an animated streetscape that shifts with the daily and weekly rhythms of exchange.[15] The local church or charity bazaars known as *kermesses*, the *fêtes foraines* and open-air dances that celebrated local holidays and the *quatorze juillet* were legendary and awaited with immense anticipation. These neighborhood scenes were powerful and unique. As part of the machinery of working-class cultural production, they obscured France's social and ideological struggles and diverted attention away from the shame of occupation. The city's citizens were unified, reassured of their human bonds. The sense of social connection implicit in these renderings was remarkable. The images became fixed metaphors for the noble quality of the small-scale environments that made up Paris. Firmly embedded in the political and social vision of the early postwar years, they immortalized the idea of neighborhood public life and attempted to naturalize the *popolo* as part of the vernacular landscape. Endlessly objectified and moralized, these images of the people were rooted in the *pays* of Paris as a textual allegory for the resurgence of an eternal city.

Two influential urban explorers were perhaps most responsible for inventing this populist spatial dynamic and the entire working-class topos: Jacques Prévert and Willy Ronis. Their portraits in poetry, song, and photography bathed the working-class districts of Paris in the glow of poetic humanism. Of the two, the poet, playwright, composer, and screenwriter Jacques Prévert was perhaps more identified with the Paris of the late 1940s and 1950s than any other individual.[16] His life and work were in essence Parisian. Prévert was born into a straitlaced bourgeois family and raised on the rue du Vieux-Colombier in Saint-Germain-des-Prés. His austere grandfather Auguste Prévert was director of the city's main charity office on the rue Monge. Over the course of his childhood, Jacques accompanied both his father and grandfather into the city's northern districts to visit the misery and poverty of the capital. From La Chapelle to La Villette, from the canal de l'Ourcq to the canal Saint-Martin, from Ménilmontant to the Buttes-Chaumont, he observed firsthand the traditional street scenes of working-class Paris in the first half of the twentieth century in all their richness, complexity, and misery. Revealing the mysteries of these unknown places and artistically rendering the spectacle of the street in the city's poorest neighborhoods became his passion. And in the parlance of the day, even the city's poorest slums were identified as "working class." Prévert shared this humanist point of view with sociologists studying the common people, who will be treated in a later chapter. The purpose of both was to give voice to the voiceless and expose the conditions in the city's marginal places. The familiar images of burly workers and artisans, the rowdy street kids, the elegant Japanese footbridges and barges of the canal Saint-Martin, the old haunts of the "children of paradise" along the rue du Faubourg du Temple all became part of the drama and melancholy of Prévert's poetic landscape. As a *flâneur*, he fed on sensory data. Assessing Prévert's extraordinary popularity during the 1940s and 1950s in *Les Lettres françaises* in 1956, when Prévert was rising to the level of "national poet," the journalist René Lacôte argued that he was a rare case "of poetic genius defined by the marvelous connection between the poet's sensitivity and popular sensitivity."[17]

The experience of Prévert's youth also provoked a political reaction to the searing social injustices all too evident in the city's landscape. He attacked the deliberate ignorance of conditions for the working classes laboring in the capital's industries. He decried the absence of "the people" from the city's artistic whirl, whether theater, film, or literature. Prévert's writing was antiestablishment and consciously scandalous, bent on creating a new universe that defied official versions of the truth. He was a familiar figure among the avant-garde gathered at the bistros of Montparnasse in the 1920s and the golden triangle of cafés on the place Saint-Germain-des-Prés in the 1930s. Although never an official member of the Communist Party, Prévert was immersed in the prewar blend of surrealism and anarchism. His Groupe Octobre (1932–36) was a theatrical agitprop troop that staged caustic buffoonery and social satire and was often called upon for performances at Communist Party political rallies in Paris. His writing was insolent and unruly, eternally rebellious, with a candor and simplicity that belied its underlying power. And for those reasons, Prévert left Paris in June 1940 with thousands upon thousands of others, by Métro, on foot, by truck, bus, and even riding on the back of a cannon, along with his longtime allies Joseph Kosma and Brassaï. They were followed into exile in the south of France by Marcel Carné, Alexandre Trauner, and a coterie of shaken artists.

Two factors were critical to Prévert's influence and popularity in the 1940s and 1950s. First was his relationship with the film director Marcel Carné and the screen actor Jean Gabin, as well as the series of tour-de-force films that resulted from their artistic alliance. This troika had already worked together on two important prewar films, *Le Quai des brumes* and *Le Jour se lève*. Prévert

FIGURE 5. Jacques Prévert, 1955. © ROBERT DOISNEAU/RAPHO.

provided the surrealist avant-garde style, Carné the gritty realism of the streets, and Gabin the portrayal of the archetypal working-class Parisian in a series of films that were among the most popular of the 1950s. The second was the publication in May 1946 of his first anthology of poems, *Paroles*, with a cover photograph of wall graffiti by Georges Brassaï. Patched together by René Bertelé from Prévert's newspaper articles and reviews, cabaret songs, and scribblings on the backs of envelopes and bistro tablecloths, it was an overnight sensation and catapulted Prévert from the literary margins to make him the idol of a new generation. As in many of his poems, Prévert creates an aesthetics of emotion in "La Rue de Buci maintenant" that captures the somber occupation mood in the normally vibrant market street of Saint-

Germain-des-Prés. The city's upset and grief are not repressed. Emotion and compassion reign in Prévert's vision of the world:

> Where has it gone
> The crazy little world on Sunday morning
> Who has lowered this awful dusty veil
>
> And the irons on this street
> This street once so happy and proud of being a street
> like a happy girl and proud of being naked
> Poor street
> Now abandoned in the neighborhood
> Itself abandoned in an empty city
> Poor street
> Gloomy corridor leading from one dead spot to another dead spot
> Your lonely, skinny dogs and your gross war wounded
> who are so skinny themselves. . . ..[18]

Even before its publication, copies of *Paroles* were passed hand-to-hand through the underground as a form of resistance to the occupation. The week of its official appearance in Paris, 5,000 copies were immediately snatched up, and over the next few years over 100,000 copies were sold. It was followed in 1951 by the publication of *Spectacle*. Prévert's *parole*—as poetry, oral literature, song lyrics, and film dialogue—authenticated the informal language of the everyday and provided a sense of linguistic consciousness. It was the spoken idiom of the people of Paris, found in the spaces of their city. In the poem "Et la fête continue," from *Paroles* (put to music by Joseph Kosma and Yves Montand), he evokes the atmosphere of a local *zinc*:

> Standing by the bar
> At the stroke of ten
> A tall plumber
> Dressed for Sunday on Monday
> Sings for himself alone
> Sings that it's Thursday
> That there's no school today
> That the war is over

> And work too
> That life is so beautiful
> And the girls so pretty
> And staggering by the bar
> But guided by his plumb line
> He stops dead before the proprietor
> Three peasants will pay and pay you
> Then disappears in the sun
> Without settling for the drinks
> Disappears in the sun all the while singing his song.[19]

The language of the people was conventionally marginalized as puerile and uneducated. Their everyday lives were deemed repetitive and meaningless, outside formal history. With Prévert, this universe became heroic. The *petit peuple* are brought on to the stage of public life along with their grammar and speech, their aesthetic. A deep humanity returns to the surface of the city.

Just as Prévert gave voice to the people of Paris, Willy Ronis pictured them. Ronis, along with Henri Cartier-Bresson and Robert Doisneau, was one of the most well-known photographers of Paris in the 1950s. The work of all three men became famous during the heyday of photojournalism immediately after the war, before television became widespread. Millions of people still learned what was happening in the world through the images in illustrated periodicals such as *Paris Match*, *France-soir*, and *Point de vue*. Ronis's photographs of Paris in the 1950s are not as renowned as those of Doisneau. However, his work followed an independent, idiosyncratic course and perhaps reveals a more intense visual inquiry of the city's ordinary life and its public spaces. Born at the foot of Montmartre in 1910, Ronis learned photography in his family's modest portrait studio on the boulevard Voltaire. His work was heavily influenced by the new ways of looking at and using the photograph pioneered by avant-garde artists such as László Moholy-Nagy and the Surrealists. He eventually spent a long career out on the streets pursuing an independent creative course and spearheading the genre of photo reportage.[20]

As the child of Jewish immigrants, Ronis had an acute awareness of marginality and the dispossessed and was an unswerving champion of the city's working class. His objective was to visually portray the more fraternal society found in the social life of the *quartiers populaires*. His photographs of the city's strikes, social movements, and street life were quickly bought up by magazines such as the communist weekly *Regards*. With the fall of France, Ronis found Paris a dangerous place for a Jew. In a hazardous crossing into unoccupied territory in southern France, he met up with Jacques Prévert and his troupe of exiles in Nice and eventually joined Alexandre Trauner at Tourette-sur-Loup during preparations for *Les Enfants du paradis*. After the war Ronis returned to Paris, and like many left-wing artists and intellectuals of his generation, became a fellow-traveler in the Communist Party, of which he remained a member until 1965. He joined the Groupe des XV, an association dedicated to promoting French photographic style, and along with Doisneau and Georges Brassaï signed on with the Rapho agency (whose name, incidentally, was coined by Henri Calet). Ronis became one of its premier photojournalists, winning the Kodak Prize in 1947 and the Gold Medal at the 1957 Venice Biennale, among a cavalcade of other honors that spanned the decade.[21]

Ronis created a visual chronicle, almost a memory board, of *Paris profond*. He focused his lens on anonymous people recognizable in ordinary space: strollers along the quai Malaquais, shoppers at the marché d'Aligre, *le titi parisien* (street urchins) playing on the buttes of Belleville, lovers kissing on the passage Julien-Lacroix, Christmas shoppers on the rue de Mogador. For Ronis, the city only existed in its human, livable dimension. His public spaces are articulated through human presence and social exchange rather than through physical artifice. This aesthetic makes Ronis's photographs among the principal archives of the city's life from the 1930s through the 1950s. The photographer becomes a self-actuated passionate *flâneur* sharing the same spaces and gaze as his subjects. It is there, looking at his images, that we chance upon the fragments of lived experience, the daily routines of work, café life, shopping, promenades, street dances, and *fêtes foraines* that defined this particularistic urbanity. It is an expressive ethnophotography, a voyeuristic peek into an intimate, forgotten world. Ronis's compositions bathe the instantaneous moments of the everyday in a sheer unpretentious honesty. His dictum was to honor his subjects, to reclaim the integrity of the working-class world of the quartiers. The ordinary is made touching, extraordinary.[22] These were not impromptu shots. The seemingly random social and spatial formations were purposeful compositions. Ronis constructed a mise en scène or staging of the action in which everyday urban life becomes performance. Ordinary people leading ordinary lives become unsuspect-

FIGURE 6. French-fry sellers, rue Rambuteau, 1946. © WILLY RONIS/RAPHO.

ing celebrities framed in half-real, half-surreal beauty. The quality is dramatic, hyperscenographic. In his well-known shot of the Sèvres-Babylone intersection taken in 1948, the simply act of a woman crossing the street is transformed into visionary drama by the black-and-white textures and the conscious framing of the action around the street awning in the foreground.

Ronis composed french-fry sellers at work on the rue Rambuteau (1946), smiling, backlit in sunshine, nearly beatific in features. The gaiety of a *fête foraine* on the boulevard Garibaldi (1947) spills out from a merry-go-round packed with laughing people. These images exude the discovery of the angelic beauty, the nobility, and the goodness of ordinary people that was the hallmark of poetic humanism.

The districts of Belleville and Ménilmontant were the object of Ronis's extended focus from 1947 through 1951. The districts, little known and certainly little photographed, were only then being rediscovered by urban observers. The images were published by Arthaud in 1954 as *Belleville Ménilmontant*, with an introduction by the novelist Pierre Mac Orlan (author of the fictional *Le Quai des brumes*, set in Montmartre and made into a film by Carné and Prévert). The volume offers what appears to be a nostalgic vision of the twin *quartiers populaires*, almost suspended in time. But Ronis had little patience for nostalgia. Rather, his creative impulse was to portray the immediacy of the city's life. The urban artifice of public spaces, streets, and stairways become the indigenous theater of the Bellevillois and the Ménilmuche that Ronis captures in his ethnoreportage. In his introduction, Mac Orlan describes the quality of Belleville and Ménilmontant as a "poetic of authenticity" that is revealed "in song and careful observation, and by Ronis's camera."[23] It is deeply sensuous and emotional. This poetic power is found in place-names, in evocative faces on precise streets, the particularities of the urban environment that take on life in Ronis's black-and-white images. He fixes his gaze on the public world of street sellers and singers, of local markets, of busybodies peering out their windows, of May Day parades and celebrations, of neighbors chatting and children playing. The butte of Belleville and its angular stairs form a constant stage of human action. The power of these images lies in their accuracy and ordinariness. This collective life of the streets, the energy and vigor of ordinary people, threads together the physical setting. Ronis's gaze transmutes them into scenes of simple, exquisite beauty. The city's surfaces become a field of psychological and social intimacy.

The works of Prévert and Ronis are among the principal images stamped on our vision of Paris during the 1950s, and they portray the complex urban imaginary of the period. Passionate wanderers, the two men left behind the elegance of the boulevards and the endless flux of modernism and instead haunted the back streets of the capital, looking for the authentic expression of Paris. Like Prévert, Ronis defined his art as an imaginative language that

FIGURE 7. Avenue Simon Bolivar, Belleville, 1950. © WILLY RONIS/RAPHO.

transmuted reality in what he called the "poetry of the streets." Both their photographs and their poetry exude a moral sensibility. They created a sentimental, humanist aesthetic of working-class Parisians, honest and genuine, naturalized in their own neighborhood landscape. Despite the harshness of modern urban life, the spaces of the city are still sites of childlike play and collective pleasure, intimacy and sociability. The public domain is collectively and individually readable as an extension of the self. The lived environment of Paris became marvelous through their eyes. Although the charms of these poems and photographs are obvious, they are also rooted in a transformative posture. If Paris was, in the words of Mac Orlan's introduction, "a museum of nuances,"[24] its particularist qualities were not relegated to an inert and rose-colored past. They were fashioned in the currency of the present. Both Ronis and Prévert sought a transcendent vision in which the ordinary, the mundane sameness, of the urban landscape was in fact a freeing up, an embrace of life. Their work projected newness, provocation, and disruption in the midst of what appeared to be commonplace, in a fashion close to that espoused in the situationist *dérive*. In his 1956 article in *Les Lettres françaises*, René Lacôte described Prévert's work as "exalting with an intense direct power the sentiment of revolt, or *de fronde*."[25] The heightened sense of everyday language and imagery and the dramatic sensuousness of public space as collective experience formed an idiom of social worth and self-expression, and they involved an intense political consciousness.

Festival as Utopia

In *Rabelais and His World*, Mikhail Bakhtin pointed to the ceaseless battle between official and unofficial sociocultural forces, the latter identified with the popular or folk-festive culture of the people, the eternally living element of unofficial speech and unofficial thought that appears under specific circumstances.[26] Without a doubt, collective leisure and entertainment practices in this tradition of neighborhood *fête* or folk festival (much of it so eloquently captured by Prévert and Ronis) returned with a vengeance in the specific circumstance of the war's end in 1945. Street dances, circus and acrobatic performances, *fêtes foraines* and festivals, bands, choirs, and parades—a whole range of populist spectacles took over the streets. The triumph of the working classes intensified popular culture as a field of collective identity and action. In the supercharged atmosphere of the Liberation and reconstruction years, cultural practices in the plebeian districts became a form of collective public theater. Rather than a rational disciplining of the self, the public spaces of the city were associated with self-expression in subjective acts of emotion. The boisterous, disruptive, libidinous qualities of song, of the *fête* or carnivalesque, were associated with a living populism and the capacity for change and transformation. It was a language of fearlessness in which everyone participated. For Bakhtin, "the carnivalesque crowd in the marketplace or in the streets is not merely a crowd. It is the people as a whole, but organized *in their own way*, the way of the people. It is outside of and contrary to all existing forms of coercive socioeconomic and political organization, which is suspended for the time of the festivity."[27] This was professed as a prolongation of the Liberation: life turned inside out, a subversion that jolted people out of the norm and into other potentialities. It was generally nonviolent, yet all manner of unexpected things could happen. These festival qualities of popular activism dramatized both the quest for patriotic unity and the profound social hopes that sprang up in Paris in the wake of the Liberation's deliverance. The widespread ludic festivities represented freedom, fraternity, and the dream of a happier life for an entire people. Much of it was widely covered on radio and television and by mainstream newspapers, which added to their scenographic performance qualities. Stardom and celebrity awaited just outside the door, in the streets, in the squares, in the dance halls and cafés. Yet at the same time these practices of celebration and *fête* were also expressive of postwar social and cultural tensions. They captured the struggle between official and unofficial voices, the shifting visibility and invisibility of social actors on the stage of the city's public spaces.

In the French cultural imagination that emerged from the 1930s through the 1950s, merrymaking was at once both ordinary and profound in its significance. The entire corpus of Jacque Prévert's work, for example, privileged festivity, *fête*, and frolicking, both personal and collective. The *fête* is proletarian, and the street is its privileged site. It is always ordinary working people, for example, whom Prévert imagines at the center of revelry. In "Grand bal du printemps," Prévert writes that "people are the ones who create fun / conjure it with their hands make it alive with their laughter pay for it in cash parade through it their loves their wives their children // People create fun / others just pretend."[28] This exhilarated expression of life's energies in the spaces of the city had a particularly complicated range of meanings after the Second World War. It was part remembrance of custom, part hope for the future. The "people," the working classes, the "nation," and the young performed and cavorted in the quest for legitimacy. Joyful and renewed, they would join in common celebration of Liberation and a new world. Eating and drinking together, singing and dancing, marching, and the parodies embedded in fooling around and farce were imagined as the "real" acts of collective life. They were an embodiment of the common people and acted to express their political militancy, their ultimate victory, and their capacity for transformation. This idealized vision conceived of

Paris as a magical arena and stressed the inseparability of people from the spaces of their lives.

Collective song in particular represented this quixotic voice of a people refound and politicized. It signified the sensuous, unofficial-speech quality of folk theater and had tremendous symbolic power. Song was a speech act, a form of expression associated with public space and the discourse created in it. It was part of what Bakhtin constituted as the heteroglossia of the public square, a utopia in which every socioideological language develops spontaneously, and no narrative or story conflicts with another.[29] Hearing and making sound placed people at the center of spatial events. It was participatory and collectively unifying. Song was a potent site of memory, a mechanism for education and mobilization. The geographer Paul Rodaway argues that the sensuousness of acoustic space makes it deeply humanistic. It flows outside the normal visual systems imposed by architecture and the physical fabric of the city and makes space hypersensorial. The auditory codes and different timings of the soundscape in the street—its complexity and intermittency—cause people to act and interact in different ways.[30] In other words, music has the capacity to be disruptive and subversive.

Music had always echoed through Parisian streets, and it has enjoyed a long history as political protest and community practice. The *chansonnier* selling songbooks and sheet music was a stock figure of the street scene and enjoyed a peak of popularity under the Third Republic. One-man bands clanged their tunes through the neighborhoods. Open-air concerts and impromptu singalongs by amateur neighborhood choruses in bistros and local public squares were traditional features of the working-class world. In 1936 Paris was home to over a hundred amateur choral societies.[31] Political or labor-union activities in the neighborhoods were also structured around ritual music and celebration: buying May 1 lilies, the open-air dance parties of the *fête nationale* on July 14, and renewing party membership each January were accompanied by the working-class *goguettes* or singing societies at the local bistro. Much of this was in decline during the first half of the twentieth century when war, depression, and the grind of commuting to work broke down older practices. The *people* seldom performed; rather, they consumed music as a *public*. Music became an industry fashioned by the stars of Paris's music theaters and by radio and film.[32] Ultimately, according to theorists such as Theodor Adorno and Max Horkheimer, the modern world became obedient to capitalist culture and the entertainment industries that replaced the tradition of vernacular amusements. They exercised iron hegemony.

What is most striking, however, is the reappearance of vernacular song performance in the aftermath of the war. Street performers, along with street singing, dancing, and open-air concerts, acted as a momentary symbolic code of social unity and an evocative vision of urban cohesiveness. Michel de Certeau described walking in the city as a "chorus of idle footsteps" and likened all the modalities of walking—trying out, transgressing, suspecting, and respecting—to song.[33] In the milieu of symbolic public spaces, we might describe this as a militant pedestrianism, with song as a collective speech act. In his recollections of the 11th arrondissement, one Parisian, Lionel Mouaux, recounted that circles of people immediately formed around street singers, quietly listening, singing along, and then buying their sheet music. Lily Lian, one of the city's last street singers, recalled "selling pounds" of sheet music on street corners in late 1944 and 1945 and singing with the crowds at the Mur des Fédérés outside Père-Lachaise Cemetery, the Barbès-Rochechouart and La Motte-Picquet Métro stations, at the place de l'Opéra, and on the Champs-Élysées.[34] Among Lian's corners were the gates of the Renault and Citroën factories in the suburbs. During the lunch hour, thousands of workers streamed out to accompany her in rounds of "Le Chant des partisans," "Le Petit vin blanc," and "On boit l'café au lait au lit."[35]

Neighborhood choirs, accordion groups, and brass bands were reconstituted with an intensive schedule of competitions, street parades, and concerts. It was a sonorous engagement between people and the physical environment of neighborhood. Life in 1947 was still weighed down by restrictions, privation, and the war's tribulations. Yet at Montreuil, in the woebegone suburbs still reeling from wartime bombardments, Sundays meant the appearance of the local fifteen-member uniformed L'Espérance brass band parading through the streets. The 10th arrondissement of Paris, which included the districts around the gare du Nord, the gare de l'Est, and the canal Saint-Martin, sponsored a full calendar of community festivities, foremost among them musical entertainment. Their amateur musicians of the Harmonie municipale du 10ème arrondissement offered fifteen street concerts in the summer of 1947, while a fifty-member volunteer symphony orchestra and a theater group organized a winter schedule of performances. All of these community associations were headquartered at the town hall, which promoted their 10th arrondissement as the "birthplace of song and the artistic center of the capital; *Spectacle vivant* [or live performance] is the life of the 10th." In a slam at skyrocketing government fees and taxes that were "killing the tradition of *spectacle vivant*," the mayor's office vowed to patiently persevere in reviving them in "all their past brilliance."[36] It is tempting to translate the concept of *spectacle vivant* literally as "living spectacle," a description that exemplifies the dramatic temperament of neighborhood public life in the war's aftermath. The neighborhood spaces of Paris became an ongoing community musical theater. Radio music shows such as *Ploum ploum tralala*, launched in 1945, with its title melody, "On chante dans mon quartier" (music by Rolf Marbot and lyrics by Francis Blanche), proliferated, and their tunes were immediately incorporated into community public performance: "Ploum ploum tra la la / Voilà c'qu'on chante / Ploum ploum tra la la / Voilà c'qu'on chante chez moi" (That's what I sing / That's what I sing at my place).

In this rhapsodic musical discourse, the people emerged from the wartime debacle powerful and militant. The traditional imagery of the working classes as wretched, irrational, and insurrectionary, cut off from civilization in despicable slums reminiscent of Zola, had been dissolved by wartime struggle. Instead, they were sane, loyal, conscientious, rational, and naturally good, in the Rousseauian sense of the term. They dignified their past and shouldered their historic mission. They were moral and idealistic, and they shared a spirit of fraternity and solidarity. This political aspect of song was particularly critical for the Communist Party, which emerged from the war as the most popular and triumphant "voice" of the people. The lusty communal singing of the "Marseillaise" and the "Internationale" was a hallmark of communist political activity. A January 1946 editorial in the communist daily newspaper *L'Humanité* on the reappearance of street singers disparaged the ban on street music during the black years of occupation as too frivolous

> for the hardness of war, work, and the austerity. It was in singing that the sans-culottes emerged victorious at Valmy. I have never heard such joyous music as in Spain where we fought for nearly three years.... Song expresses the rebellious spirit of Paris. The indignation against the "munichois," against the Nazis, and the traitors streamed out from song. That's why we were deprived of it. They feared the song of the French people.[37]

The Parti communiste français (French Communist Party, or PCF) championed the revival of working-class song and dance such as that practiced by *sociétés orphéoniques* and neighborhood music societies, by accordionists and brass bands. A reporter for the communist daily *L'Humanité* painted a rosy picture in January on the place Wagram in the working-class district of the 17th arrondissement, which, despite freezing temperatures, was filled with "seamstresses and shopgirls, students, bicyclists, housewives with flutes in their arms, people at their windows," all there to sing with the popular vocalist Saint-Granier and his accordionist. "It's difficult to choose between the amateurs who take their turn at the microphone. The cobblers and carpenters sing as they work. . . . I vote for the subway driver. And suddenly, despite my voice, I find myself singing along with the chorus, me too! An excellent idea, this 'singing in my neighborhood.'"[38] The romanticized imagery was superimposed over far more complex and politically conflicted postwar realities. Yet in this theater of memory, archetypal *Parisiens*, entertaining themselves in simple ways despite the difficulties, were immediate, genuinely well-meaning, and optimistic. Their bonhomie was the stuff of legend.

Even at the heights of musical stardom, the reemergence of the people of Paris was celebrated in song. The historian Jean-Louis Robert points to a privileged moment of "Paris songs" around 1950, reaching an apogee of ten songs about the city in 1951.[39] Edith Piaf (born in Belleville) and Maurice Chevalier (born in Ménilmontant) were of course the established stars of the genre. But they were compromised by their concerts in Germany to "cheer up" French prisoners of war, an episode Chevalier justified in Marcel Ophuls's epic *The Sorrow and the Pity*. Young stars such as Yves Montand and Francis Lemarque took over the tradition of Paris popular songs in the 1950s. In this musical vision of the times, the secure everyday world of the Parisian *vélo*, the artisan, and the *midinette* emerged from the war not only unscathed, but victorious. They were actors in history. In Yves Montand's "À Paris" (by Montand and Lemarque), "Depuis qu'à Paris on a pris la Bastille / Dans tous les faubourgs et à chaque carrefour / Il y a des gars et il y a des filles / Qui sont sur les pavés sans arrêt nuit et jour / Font des tours / Et des tours / À Paris" (As soon as you hit the Bastille in Paris / No matter where you go / There are guys and gals / Nonstop on the streets day and night / Cruising / Cruising / In Paris). Montand himself was the personification of this Parisian populist imaginary: he was the working-class guy, the *gars*, who had achieved fame and fortune through hard work and talent. From a fiercely communist family, he long remained a member of the French Communist Party. In his 1952

"Rendez-vous avec liberté" (by Renaud and Philippe-Gérard), "Les quais de Paris chantent / . . . les murs de Paris chantent / Le sang qui coule / L'espoir des foules / Et leur grand cœur / Et l'histoire/ Dont les leçons enfantent / Les victoires . . ." (The quays of Paris sing / The walls of Paris sing / Blood flows / The hope of the people / And their great heart / And history / Whose lessons bring forth / Victories). In October 1953 Montand's show at the Théâtre de l'Étoile opened with an unpublished poem by Jacques Prévert and ended with an emotional rendition of "À Paris" and a finale encore of Prévert and Kosma's "Falling Leaves." The performance was an absolute sensation and established Montand as the most popular star on the French music scene. More than one-third of his songs were stories of the *les petits gens* of Paris, many of them emotional renditions of Prévert's and Lemarque's lyrics.[40] The 1951 popular song "Paris en fête" (by Henri Bassis and Kosma) asked "Qui veut que le Peuple règne / C'est Paris / Celui que les bourgeois craignent / Qui du monde porte enseigne / C'est Paris! C'est Paris!" (Who wants the people to reign / It's Paris / What the bourgeois fear / What the world knows / It's Paris / It's Paris).

For the people of Paris to outwardly manifest themselves and their political culture, they became, to use Robespierre's phrase, their own spectacle. They sang, danced, and marched to music and paraded in an outburst of collective theatricality. It was a mass performance, an emotive outpouring that continuously reappropriated public space. Dance halls and *bals populaires* carried on this vernacular musical entertainment as a vital form of neighborhood sociability. From the late nineteenth century on the dance halls and taverns of Paris and its suburbs were symbolic institutions of social integration and democratic urban life for the *classes populaires*.[41] They enjoyed three privileged moments of extraordinary success: at their origin in the 1880s, during the Popular Front, and again from 1945 to the end of the 1950s. For a dozen years after the war, the historian Marie-Claude Blanc-Chaléard argues, "the success of the *bals* and the *guinguettes* was enormous."[42] The most popular were on the rue de Lappe, the narrow alley near the place de la Bastille that for decades had been the meeting point of the fearsome Apache hooligans, small-time gangsters and pimps. It was the street of the *bals musettes*, the traditional dance halls with Italianesque accordion band and music kept alive by the immigrant community from the Auvergne who lived in the surrounding neighborhood of La Roquette. In the war's aftermath, the rue de Lappe was a gathering place for young people crowding into the Balajo, the Bousca, the

Boule Rouge, the Barreaux Verts, the Bal des Familles, the Musette, and the Petit Balcon on weekends to enjoy traditional dances such as the *valse* and the *java*. The proletarian *guinguettes* (local taverns with dance floors and musical entertainment) and *bals musettes* around the edge of Paris in places such as Montmartre, La Villette, and Belleville, and along the Marne River, were also renowned entertainment spots. The novelist and poet Blaise Cendrars captured the atmosphere in the eastern suburbs in 1949: "a tavern, jazz, a dance, a crowd all night, with little bridges, little lakes, arbors decorated with Venetian lanterns, stone paths as in Buttes-Chaumont."[43] The popularity of both the *bals musettes* and the *guinguettes* were enormous during the Liberation years and the early 1950s.

The Parisian Colette Bouisson remembered that "after four years of immobility an explosion of dance shook the city. There had never been so many evenings of dance, places to dance, clubs, studios, get-togethers, parties . . . here the waltz, there the tango or even the charleston, while from neighborhood to neighborhood there were outbursts of bebop."[44] Neighborhood associations organized open-air dances. In order to attract clients, local cafés organized *bals* that usually included amateur singing contests. Accompanied by a singer and accordionist, people spontaneously broke into dancing in the streets and around Métro stations. The cellar clubs and streets of Saint-Germain-des-Prés vibrated with swing and bebop. All functioned as spaces of transparency and impulsiveness, made even more potent by the political meanings of Liberation and the triumph of the *classes populaires*. Public dancing, especially bebop and the jitterbug, was the ultimate expression of a freeing, a liberating of the civic body. Like *fêtes foraines*, dance halls and *bals publics* were places of inversion and experimentation, of misbehavior and acting up, of breaking from the routines of weekday work—places where people of all backgrounds and every shade of reputation bumped elbows and more on the dance floor. Even in the late 1950s, the *bals* continued to be one of the main institutions of sociability and youthful play. In Michel Déon's 1958 novel *Les Gens de la nuit*, young friends find a *bal musette* called Chez Auguste near the place de la République, where they dance to accordion music played by a blind albino. Although the atmosphere of some thirty couples crammed together on the dance floor is stifling, filled with smoke and the smell of alcohol, they can distinguish "the *petits employés* who, in the evening, dress in sweaters and loud shirts with unbuttoned collars in an attempt to look classy in front of their girls."[45] In her book *Les Gens du passage* (1959),

FIGURE 8. Traditional neighborhood *bal populaire* at the place des Abbesses, 1950.
© L'HUMANITÉ/KEYSTONE-FRANCE.

Clarisse Francillon recounts daily life along the passage Prévost in the 13th arrondissement. The shy heroine, Denise, is pushed into attending the Bal Wagram by a girlfriend, where Denise meets a pharmacist who will become her boyfriend. They watch as the crowd elects the "prettiest legs in Paris." The Salle Wagram is packed with young people; "a cloud of dust envelops the crowd, paper streamers hang in their hair."[46]

The *bals populaires* and general celebration associated with three events—the anniversary of the February 6, 1934, political clashes, the May 1 Labor Day, and the July 14 *fête nationale*—were perhaps the most anticipated and, for our purposes, the most politically charged within the context of the war and reconstruction years. They were fundamental to urban political revelry. The shared memory of reconciliation associated with them was crucial to the formation of national community around a united citizenry. The ritual commemoration of the defeat of "the attempted fascist coup d'état" in February 1934 and the traditional May Day festivities sanctified the memory and myth of revolutionary Paris and assured, as Jean-Pierre Bernard has put it, that "the future would be a mirror of the past."[47] This invented memory harked back to a golden age, to the historic moments of working-class solidarity against the evils of fascism. Each July 14 celebration after the war was an occasion to relive the Liberation and celebrate the people and their deliverance. It was saluted with massive street parades and dances, complete with orchestras, choral performances, and street theater. The celebrations were represented as a reemergence of the traditional open-air festivities and political spectacle associated with Parisian revolutionary culture. For the 1948 *fête nationale*, some five thousand Parisians gathered at a glimmering place de la Concorde for a performance by the city's beloved music-hall and radio stars, foremost among them Yves Montand and Georges Guétary; the "French can-can"; and a giant *bal populaire* that made the square, according to the Christian Democratic newspaper *L'Aube*, "truly into a scene of harmony and popular rejoicing."[48] Newspapers were among the most important promoters and chroniclers of these electrifying events. They created the public narrative, embellished the celebrations, and gave them shared meaning. Radio and newsreel coverage molded them into media spectacles. The Union Nationale du Spectacle and the communist newspaper *L'Humanité* organized open-air extravaganzas at symbolic hubs of working-class life: the place de la République, the porte Saint-Martin, and the porte Saint-Denis in the northern districts. Enormous crowds listened to the People's Choral Society of Paris and the Choral Society of Suresnes sing and recite from the historic texts of the French revolutionary tradition. Dancers from the Opéra Ballet performed "revolutionary dances" in full costume.[49] Musical performances such as these consecrated the public realm and acted as theatrical devices for inaugurating patriotic citizenship and reviving populist collective traditions as well as the myths of fraternity and solidarity. A veneer of harmony reigned in the *quartiers populaires*. The proximity of space and the familiarity of these iconographic moments, the sense that they occurred amid the plain everyday realities of working-class life, gave the urban landscape the texture of populist theater.

The largest *bals populaires* to celebrate the *fête nationale* were at the Bastille, the place Voltaire, and the place de la République. Support for these events came from a variety of sources ranging from city hall to neighborhood firehouses and businesses, newspapers, and local school budgets. In this sense they were deeply embedded not only in social community, but in the political life of the city. In 1949 for example, the Paris municipal council sponsored the major *bals traditionnels* at the place de l'Hôtel de Ville, the place de la Bastille, the place de la Nation, the place Armand-Carrel, the place Victor-Basch (at the Alésia-Maine-Châtillon intersection), the place Gambetta, and the place Voltaire. As well as hosting these citywide events, complete with fireworks, the municipal council's Commission des Fêtes donated over two million francs to arrondissements and quartiers in need of public subsidies to pay for their local revelry,[50] although a small entrance fee usually helped to offset costs. The neighborhood versions sponsored by the local firehouse were the occasions for vast street parties that were legendary in their extent and enthusiasm. Consequently, no one centralized spectacle dominated the reverie. Instead, the merrymaking was spread out across the spaces of the city in a multiplicity of decentralized locations. All of them featured live music, usually a small orchestra installed on a temporary platform in the main square decorated with traditional Venetian lanterns, with the space around given over to dancing. Their character was spontaneous, the inversion of everyday normalities, a "bursting" of the personal into the public domain. Normally private people grabbed partners and danced into the streets, interrupting traffic and bringing their neighborhoods to a standstill. Whatever their size, they were populist festivals, celebrations fraught with political overtones.

Collective action was tempered by this reversion to public rituals that were deliberately traditional in their structure, décor, and social comportment, and yet reiterated endlessly the moment of carnivalesque rebellion of the Liberation itself. This juxtaposition of tensions—a ritualized calling for both social harmony and social revolution, looking back to the past and ahead toward the future—charged these events with intense meaning. They were a form of magic theater. Describing the 1945 *fête nationale*, *L'Humanité* affirmed that "we have found once more the paper lanterns, the canopies, the garlands and flags, the little platforms on the square, the neighborhood orchestras and accordion players, with couples dancing and drinking in the street... and the floodlights and fireworks after all these years of blackouts!" But the festivities represented more than just merriment, because "one sensed in the popular joy of this July 14 a new republican fervor and an affirmation of the vitality of a people who want with all their hearts and energy to rise from the ruins and construct a new France, strong and happy."[51] In 1950 neighborhood businesses and civic organizations inaugurated a week of *fête nationale* celebrations in Montparnasse that culminated in the "Nuit du 14 juillet." From the carrefour de Rennes to the carrefour de l'Observatoire, the neighborhood was strewn with colored electric lights, Venetian lanterns, and patriotic decorations. The bistros sponsored live music and dancing, especially at the carrefour Vavin, where the liveliest action took place.[52] Mobs of people descended on Montparnasse for the festivities. What is significant about this revelry is its *extent*. To refer to Bahktin once again, the folk festival of the crowd must be concrete, sensual, a visible form of their mass and unity. It provides them with a sense of historic immortality, the uninterrupted continuity of their becoming and growth. The festivities are the victory of the future over the past, the victory, Bakhtin argues, "of the people's material abundance, freedom, equality, brotherhood."[53] Bakhtin's point of view captures exactly this performance quality and utopian hope for French rebirth as it overflowed in the public spaces of the city. Neighborhood after neighborhood, suburban town after suburban town fell under its spell and sponsored celebrations that were actively reported in the media as a sign of renewed vitality. The merriment was couched in traditional custom, but transmitted in the spirit of progress and commitment to the future.

Much like the week-long neighborhood bash in Montparnasse, the galas and celebrations organized by suburban municipalities and by philanthropic societies raised money for needed projects and were symbols of local boosterism. The reports in the newspaper *L'Avenir de la banlieue de Paris* (which served the suburban ring south of Paris) for 1954, 1955, and 1956 give a good indication of the extent of this revelry.[54] The May 1954 Springtime Festival at Plessis-Robinson featured a cavalcade of song, dance, sporting events, and open-air theater. Folklore and ballet troupes, judo, gymnastic and trapeze exhibitions, dancing, and a grand ball attracted such enormous crowds that organizers were forced to turn people away. In June 1954 Choisy-le-Roi organized a Fête des Gondoles that featured a procession of amateur events, all serenaded by the volunteer Choisy Music Band. At Cachan the June 1954 Grand Kermesse des Écoles to support the *colonies de vacances* (summer camps) demonstrated the local political squabbling over these events and their money-making importance. The city's centrist administration lauded the charity bazaar as the most successful and lucrative ever attempted. Local musicians and comedians entertained the crowds. An evening concert and community dance was attended by nine hundred paid entrees. In a settling of scores, the success of the 1954 *kermesse* was distinguished sharply from the "dismal failure" of 1947 organized by the communists, although "they ceaselessly use support for public schools to attack the mayor and for political propaganda." At Clamart the local Commission des fêtes and the mayor clashed over support for a springtime festival on the place de la Mairie. The mayor sided with local businesses sponsoring the reverie as an alternative to the traditional *fête foraine*. On the other hand, the commission (packed with traditional *fête foraine* backers) washed its collective hands of the whole matter and refused to "take responsibility for any accidents that might occur." However, both the commission and the mayor's office could agree on the authorization of a *fête champêtre*, or country fair, organized by the Association des combattants prisonniers de guerre de la Seine, that was predicted to draw some thirty thousand to forty thousand people to a local park site. The justification was the business it would bring in for local tradesmen.

These few examples among a host of others make it clear that local event committees and city halls in the suburban townships were responsible for organizing substantial entertainment to rival that produced by their neighbors. Part city boosterism, part fund-raising for schools, part money makers for local business, they also represented community spirit and collective play. They were infused with a sense of civic showmanship from a multitude of angles—onstage, in various sport, music, and dance competitions, in costumed parades, and on the dance floor. The organized entertainment was usually a combination of amateur groups and professionals that showcased local talent and local public sites, from municipal halls and sports stadiums to central squares and city halls. These municipal spectacles essentially mediatized suburban public space and the collective activities that took place within it. They are signs of the spatial splintering and the intensely decentralized nature of urban spectacle in the 1950s. And they were not just slipshod local talent shows. A February 1955 municipal gala organized by Issy-les-Moulineaux drew not only the local community, but thousands from neighboring communes and "even from Paris" to hear Tino Rossi and a host of other legendary entertainers in its "acclaimed Salle des fêtes." In April of the same year, Le Kremlin-Bicêtre organized an evening dance at the municipal hall that was featured live on the radio program "Ce soir, on danse . . ." and included entertainment by the famed accordionist Étienne Lorin. At Antony, the springtime festivities featured Miss Europe 1955, the award-winning and immensely popular entertainment group Arc-en-Ciel from the Renault factories, and a host of local amateur performers. The municipality of Plessis-Robinson organized the Île-de-France Music Festival in June 1955, which allied a wide range of official organizations from the Comité officiel des fêtes de Paris to the Fédération des musiques populaires de Seine et Seine-et-Oise. Plessis-Robinson's favorite sons, backed by the Plessis-Robinson amateur choir, publicized the event on the Saturday-night broadcast of the popular television show *Télé-Paris*. The festival featured concerts and musical events at the principal public spaces of the township. An official parade snaked through the streets from the main place des Martyrs de la Résistance to the local sports stadium, where an enormous concert ended the afternoon. The entertainment continued throughout the evening with gala performances by a host of singers and stars and ended with a massive fireworks display.

As the ultimate in this kind of populist theater, the carnivelesque *fêtes foraines* were the object of veritable cult worship. Urban carnivals as civic celebrations proved much longer-lived than might initially have been expected. As a modern form of amusement they reached their heyday during the reconstruction years immediately following the Second World War. They were vast parties whose subtext was clearly about control over the spaces of the city. The Paris historian and observer André Warnod listed five major *fêtes foraines* traditionally celebrated in Paris: on the Right Bank, the Foire du Trône on the place de la Nation, the Fête à Montmartre, the Fête des Buttes-Chaumont, the Foire du boulevard de la Villette; and on the Left Bank, at the place Denfert-Rochereau, the Foire du Lion de Belfort.[55] Smaller versions of the *fête foraine* were held on a regular basis throughout Paris. At their prewar height in 1928, some thirty-eight fairs were celebrated throughout the year, although the next year, in response to growing complaints, the prefecture of police limited the annual calendar to thirteen fairs. For the first postwar 1946–47 fair cycle, the prefecture of police authorized thirty-two fairs "to be held at their traditional sites throughout the city, including the boulevard Saint-Michel." The number increased to forty-five in 1948. By 1950 the prefecture of police had authorized fifty-three fairs on the schedule. The largest number of fairs, nine for the year, each averaging three weeks in length, was scheduled in the 11th arrondissement. The Fête de la Bastille, for example, contained more than four hundred stalls.[56] The inner arrondissements of eastern Paris tended to hold the fairs around the July 14 national holiday, while the outer arrondissements of the northeast associated the carnival atmosphere of the fairs with the August commemoration of the Liberation. The fair circuit continued into the working-class suburbs beyond the city's borders with, for example, the Fête Foraine des Quatre Routes, held at the vast intersection in the center of La Courneuve between 1944 and 1960. No fairs were scheduled for the 1st, 6th, or 8th arrondissements, and only one for the 7th, where "tourists and Parisians who

FIGURE 9. The crowd at the Foire du Trône, place de la Nation, March 29, 1948.
© KEYSTONE-FRANCE.

loved the history and stunning panorama of the capital would have considered a *fête foraine* on the Esplanade des Invalides a sort of sacrilege."[57]

To take perhaps the best-known example, the Foire du Trône was an annual post-Lenten celebration shared by all the working-class neighborhoods of the eastern districts.[58] It was integral to "growing up" in and experiencing the particularity of neighborhood social rites, a passage associated with folkloric tradition and the carnivalesque frivolity of street life. The fairs were privileged sites of escape and transgression from the daily routine of the workplace. In the immediate postwar years, they were rich with the more complicated meanings of diversion from the war and its privations and the reemerging vitality of the people. Stretching from the place de la Nation down the avenue du Trône and up the rue des Pyrénées to the park at Vincennes, the fair was a month-long carnival of amusement rides, games, sideshows, and caravans, with their cavalcade of curiosities and gastronomies. In the years after the war, three different circuses—the Zanfretta, the Lambert, and the Fanny—lined the avenue du Trône. The fair celebration and the reenactment of its precise rituals were guarded as a local entitlement. The crowning of Esmerelda was a custom specific to the Foire du Trône and was traditionally carried on until 1939 and the wartime ban. It was revived with the first postwar fair in 1946, when the new Esmerelda and her cortege of floats and musicians paraded from the place de la République down the boulevard Beaumarchais, around the place de la Bastille, up rue du Faubourg Saint-Antoine, and on to the place de la Nation. These were mammoth public events that swept over neighborhood space and life. They were a reenactment of the right to the city.

The battles for and against the *fêtes foraines* were already endless by the reconstruction years. Although embraced as a symbol of the city's reemergence, not everyone appreciated the farcical aesthetics and the mobs that poured into the streets. For some, especially local residents who had to put up with all the noise and aggravation, they were a public menace. The character of the *fêtes foraines* was open-ended, threatening. As the descendants of Carnival, seen particularly in the seedy ambience that increasingly dominated their runs, the fairs were signs of inversion, of the grotesque and unseemly—features that made them suspect for those Parisians interested in questions of propriety and moral renewal. The music, loudspeakers, amusement rides, fair booths, and congestion that had in the early twentieth century been signs of a mesmerizing urban modernity were now an infuriating, infernal din. An amateur documentary film of the 1954 Foire du Trône captures the creepy sideshow atmosphere of leering clowns and barkers, cheap rides, and shooting galleries.[59] The lurid qualities and social mix of the *fête foraine* in particular provoked public fears about the savagery and volatility of collective space. The transient *foraine* families and the crowds were deemed socially marginal and dangerous to the community—a breach in the interior quality of neighborhood space. They were described as a "resounding sham," "the plagues of Paris," and "an intolerable torment."[60] They threatened public hygiene and were a menace to traffic. Even neighborhood businesses began lining up against them for driving away customers. The only arguments in their favor seemed to be their contribution to the local school budget and that they were a fairly acceptable hangout for young people.

Despite the criticism, the tradition was not easy to suppress. Populist images of Paris are filled with renditions of the traveling carnival shows and their celebratory street atmosphere. In Jacques Prévert's *Parole* (1946), the joyful fun of the *fête foraine* is spontaneous, vital, a collective merriment that is the stuff of life:

Happy as the trout climbing the torrent
Happy the heart of the world
On its waterspout of blood
Happy the barrel-organ
Bawling in the dust
With its citrus voice
A popular tune
Without rhyme or reason
Happy the lovers
On the Russian mountains
Happy the russet-haired girl
On her white horse
Happy the brown boy
Who waits for her smiling
Happy this man in mourning
Standing in his skiff
Happy the fat dame
With her paper kite
Happy the old fool
Smashing plates. . . .[61]

Henri Calet, the chronicler of *Paris populaire*, captured the spellbinding pleasures and sheer size of the annual fall Fête du Lion in his *Le Tout sur le tout* (1948). The great lion statue on the place Denfert watched over a cavalcade of traveling entertainers almost every weekend. But the annual *fête foraine* was a spectacular affair. A profusion of the strange and bizarre displayed in sideshow stands mixed with the Folies Cubaines and the Sirènes de Paris, with their dance of the veils. Entrance marquees titillated fairgoers with exhibitions of the "Human Passions" and the "Debauchery of the Big City." Acrobats, fire-eaters, strongmen, and escape artists entertained the crowds. Miss Liliane performed her snake dance on stage with two lions. The Cirque Fanny shared the place Denfert with the Grande ménagerie africaine and an immense boat ride on the site of the present-day RER railway station that swung fifty screaming people in a high arc above the crowds.[62] In Jacques Baratier and Jean Valère's commercially produced documentary film *Paris la nuit* (1956), crowds jam a kaleidoscopic *fête foraine*, wildly enjoying the amusement rides, midway games, and entertainment. Couples dance the night away at a *bal*. Families, children, and young lovers are entranced by the extravagant panorama.⁶³ The *fête foraine* was one of the most enduring features of neighborhood life and its public spaces, and it remained so throughout the 1950s. For most people, these fairs represented postwar reconstruction and revival, and the reappearance of stability, well-being, and pleasure. In a *Les Actualités françaises* newsreel from March 1951 entitled "Springtime in Paris," Yves Montand walks along the Seine and watches children playing hopscotch in the street while he croons about "le printemps dans mon quartier." He ends at the midway rides of a *fête foraine*, singing the joys of "la fête de dimanche" before he is mobbed by young girls begging for autographs.⁶⁴ Promenading the fairs and ending the day at the local café with neighbors and friends was an essential ceremony that commemorated the well-being of public space. But the carnival spirit of an alternative universe filled with the unexpected remained. A motley display of inversion, irregularity, and satirical clowning seethed just below the surface.

There was an edgy quality to this conscious performance, this reappropriation of the spaces of the city by the people. In the postwar context singing and dancing, bazaars and *fêtes foraines* were all reintegrated into the popular imagination as part of the time-honored visual and sensory seasonal cycles of the city. The uses of the past were magnified. This sense of the nostalgic reappearance of ludic, carnivelesque art forms was intense enough to cause some people to invoke the fairs as obsolete vestiges that had outlived their time and purpose. But this public criticism hid the deeper meanings of these populist festivals and spatial rituals. Rather than simply fleeting and meaningless, or for that matter nostalgic, they were a theater of becoming in which the power of the people was given free rein. They were *other than* everyday life, and yet they were *in* everyday life. In his *Critique of Everyday Life* (1947), Henri Lefebvre listed the *fête foraine*, along with the café, radio, and television, as among examples of the work-leisure dialect. They hold real content and yet retain an illusory form: "Here we enter a humble, restless microcosm, extraordinary and vulgar. And apparently cheap."⁶⁵ The fooling around, the unruly spatial performance was an autonomous realm; it was ungovernable. Adored as entertainment, the fairs were incorrigible scenes of provocation and arousal. In the context of the postwar era, they could also be read as a rebellion against the absurdity of the cold war and the atomic bomb, which threatened to wipe out existence at a moment's notice. But more than mere defiance, the intent of this nervy theater was to revolutionize the everyday practices and spaces of the city and to inscribe them with new meaning. Festival and play laid the outlines for a new kind of society, a counternarrative to the utopian dreams for a new France in official reconstruction discourse. They harked back to France's revolutionary heritage and to the broad project of creating a new civilization. It was the "reign of mirth." The *fête* became a fixed part of a postwar cosmology that attributed this revolutionary, transformative capacity to the French people themselves. In other words, far more than just nostalgic revelry, populist street entertainment and festivals were permeated with contemporary counterrhetoric and practice.

Magical Urbanism

Perhaps no other event captured this subversive, transformative quality of the *fête* than the legendary Fête de l'Humanité, the prewar working-class celebration that drew all of eastern Paris and its suburbs into great festivals of public solidarity. Once the war was over, *L'Humanité* immediately sponsored the reappearance of the Fête de l'Humanité in September 1945 and again in 1946. Media outlets from newspapers to radio and film newsreels were the primary chroniclers of these events and helped to produce them as narrative and visual spectacles. Over a million people streamed from the subway stations into the Reuilly hollow in the Bois de Vincennes (where the event was held annually until 1956) singing the "Marseillaise," the "Internationale," and the "Chant des Partisans." "It is the people, singing!" *L'Humanité* raved.[66] In its re-creation of the ceremonial procession through the city, the movement en masse to the park was as significant as the event itself and was featured prominently in the militant Cinéfrance documentary *Fête de l'Humanité 1946*, in which cars and trucks decorated with "Fête de l'Hum" posters parade, along with a flood of revelers, through the streets to Vincennes.[67] Much as in the tradition of the World's Fairs, these people's expositions aspired to a utopian vision of urbanity and were christened the worker's capital city. The 1945 festival constructed "a real city," entered through a sparkling silver triumphal arch beribboned in red, white, and blue. Fairgoers then promenaded down the "Champs-Élysées de la fête," flanked by "perfectly aligned" booths and stalls. The 1946 fair was hailed as the "the second city of France." The triumphal boulevard was lined with colossal statues of the heroes of French democracy. Marching bands, clowns, food, and games imparted a carnival atmosphere. The Communist Party booth featured can-can dancers in costume. During the course of the day, fairgoers were treated to a traditional music festival and a colorful "parade of flags of the democratic nations." In both the 1945 and the 1946 festivals, a massive stage guarded by trumpeters was the scene of a theatrical reenactment of the "Resistance, Victory and Liberation" with full chorus and ballet. Then a "streets of Paris" set formed the backdrop for a 1946 performance of the "return of the free press after the Liberation," complete with newsboys hawking copies of *L'Humanité* and other left-wing newspapers. A satirical presentation of "restrictions, recovery, and the struggle against the black market" featured dancers costumed as meat, vegetables, and dairy products. Finally, Maurice Thorez, André Marty, Jacques Duclos, and other French and Spanish Communist Party officials climbed the platform to whip up the crowds with fiery speeches and a collective singing of the "Marseillaise." Parachutists dropped from the sky, giant boats floated into the stage. By evening, a star-studded regalia of singers and dancers performed on the fully illuminated platform (a "fantasy" after years of black-outs) draped in tri-colors. And then the festivities broke into a myriad of *bals publics* with accordionists, to be followed by a massive fireworks display.[68] This was magic theater, a paradise made by all. It was an extravagant glorification of the people of Paris and their urban world. The PCF pronounced; "the Fête de l'Humanité is now the Fête de Paris." It was a sign of the "immense fraternal community of more than a million men." The people were liberated from work and daily struggle, from the penury of life. Here they set in motion their authentic and creative powers and fashioned a new urban realm.

This extension of play tactics did not preclude lashing out at political enemies. The September 1949 Fête de l'Humanité included a rambunctious "massacre game" in which contestants could finish off dolls representing Jules Moch, Paul Ramadier, Robert Shuman, and Charles de Gaulle. Despite police threats to banish the festival from Vincennes for such an outrage, the Communist Party's annual celebration continued to draw upwards of 100,000 people during the early 1950s. De Gaulle's Rassemblement du Peuple Français (RPF) countered the Fête de l'Humanité with its own festival at Vincennes. The Fête de la Jeunesse, du Travail et du Sport, held annually in October from 1947 to 1953, included information booths from the city's most important manufacturers (Renault, Citroën, SNECMA, EDF, and SNCF, among others) as well as entertainment. Although the September 1947 Fête de l'Humanité drew over a million participants, the Fête de la Jeunesse drew an estimated 70,000 people. The fair was undercut by a suspicious series of calamities (road debris, broken Métro trains, unplugged loudspeakers) blamed on "communist sabotage."

The children of paradise had returned to claim the spectacle. The framework for their urban utopia was the creative power of play, satire and farce, sabotage. In the utopian New Babylon constructed by Constant and the situationist movement in the late 1950s, fun would be the new normality. Constant's urban mirage was built on inversion and disorientation, a deliberate confusion of spatial hierarchies.[69] The revolutionary idea of pleasure and collective play underlined the entirety of situationist values. In commenting on the work of Johan Huizinga on the relationship between play and seriousness, Guy Debord argued for "the transitory, the free domain of ludic activities . . . as the only field of real life." It was by making play a fundamental moral, Debord believed, that the real construction of urbanism, in the largest sense of the term, would be possible.[70] The "real city" of the Fête de l'Humanité was gay, melodious, and festive. It exuded a civic infatuation with the imagery of a people rising up, on the march, claiming the future. All this activity suggests not merely a reappropriation of space, but a making over of the city in the populist image. Street renaming and embellishment and celebrations of collective fraternity and play escaped from hegemonic political and economic structures and fashioned a transformative spatial domain.

In *The Practice of Everyday Life*, Michel de Certeau argues that the names of streets are part of a broader discourse of "local authority" that creates habitability outside prevailing functionalist discourses. It creates a poetic geography that eludes systematization. Spatial topoi are instead organized on superstition, legend, memory, and dreams.[71] They embellish local topography with fantasy, with recollections and stories. The inscription of the memory of the Resistance and Liberation on the streets of the city was one of the most palpable localized counter-urbanistic discourses of the early postwar years in Paris. The process began from the moment of the Liberation and continued to reverberate through the 1950s. The Liberation of Paris immediately became the stuff of localized place and memory at the level of neighborhood—largely in place of official citywide or national commemoration. Makeshift memorials at sites where individuals had been killed by the Germans or had died in the Liberation of Paris were fabricated immediately after August 1944. Local Liberation committees and the *parti des 75,000 fusillés*, as the Communist Party called itself, were in the vanguard in honoring fallen martyrs. The communists had been the driving force behind the Liberation on the streets of Paris, and they understood the movement as a grass-roots insurrection. They treated the spaces of the city as text upon which the heroic history of the Resistance and Liberation would be written. For example, in the days following the Liberation, the communist section of the 9th arrondissement between the gare Saint-Lazare and the gare de Nord circulated two hundred flyers requesting local residents to come forward with information on anyone arrested, deported, or killed during the occupation or sacrificed in the Liberation of Paris so that they could be honored.[72] The walls of buildings, sidewalks, and trees in the neighborhoods where fighting had taken place were decorated with the names of the dead, inscribed on small pieces of wood along with written testimonials, photographs, and flowers in a spontaneous display of public sorrow and witnessing. In keeping with the fashioning of the Liberation as a populist revolt, the memorials were embedded directly into the urban landscape where the events had actually taken place.

These early testimonials could be interpreted as forms of magic theater or even graffiti that represented "the 'primitive' energy of the everyday life of the 'masses'" in the sense meant by Cobra founder Constant, writing in 1948.[73] The streets would become sacred sites. These gestures collapsed both mythologized space and lived space into one. The unauthorized and fractured nature of decision making turned them into forms of provocative populist urbanism. They transformed urban topography. They were discrete formulations of urban utopia in which the act of renaming became the framework for setting in place a new society. On October 21, 1944, the Communist Party organized solemn local corteges and ceremonies during which eighteen streets in Paris were renamed for fallen heroes. The selection of those to be honored as martyrs was determined entirely by the space and politics of neighborhood. *L'Humanité* reported that in the 11th arrondissement, where severe fighting had taken place, forty thousand were in attendance for the renaming of the rue Jean-Pierre Timbaud, a local *métallo* and militant communist hero killed during the war.[74] The ceremony was presided over by the communist mayor of the 11th arrondissement, along with officialdom from the local metallurgy union and the Confédération générale du travail (General Confederation of Labor, or CGT). In sum, the "glorious week of August 18–25" was commemorated in a splintered fashion, at the level of the streets that figured in discrete events. It revealed a creative, expressive zone that intertwined temporal and spatial allegory as well as the capacity for creative rupture.

The abundance of improvised shrines and street renamings pointed to the fragmentation of political power and the degree of autonomous place-making enjoyed by the arrondissements and neighborhoods in the first months after the Liberation. The process became more formalized by 1945, when the Paris municipal council began to recoup its authority. Neighborhoods seeking a commemorative street-name change were to formally apply to the municipal council, which would then make the final decision and organize official acts of tribute and remembrance. The council's general resistance to the penchant for spontaneous, unofficial street renaming at the neighborhood level was a sign of the latter's provocative self-determining quality. But it was difficult to ignore the emotional longing to inscribe experiences in the urban landscape, or the power of local Liberation committees and their communist activists. In July 1945 in particular, the Paris municipal council took up a steady stream of nominations accompanied by formal testimony of the heroism in question. To honor the battle for the 10th arrondissement that had raged at the place de la République, the Prince-Eugène barracks were renamed for Jean Vérines, the commander of the Republican Guards, killed in 1943. Most of the streets along the canal Saint-Martin were rechristened for local Resistance heroes.[75] Enormous crowds watched the official inauguration of the place du Colonel Fabien near the canal Saint-Martin, named after the communist Pierre Georges (or Colonel Fabien). A plaque bearing his name and an account of his heroic exploits also graced the Barbès-Rochechouart Métro station. With the help of the ambassador to the Soviet Union, the place de la Villette was rechristened the place Stalingrad in honor of the Red Army victory.[76] In 1946 a local committee at the place Stalingrad petitioned the municipal council to support a further commemoration with the planting of a Liberation-Victory tree.[77]

In the political heat of the Liberation, a ritual purging of the city's spaces of any reference to collaboration was initially nearly as important as honoring the dead. The avenue Victor-Emmanuel III was one such street name chosen to be removed; it was renamed for the American President Franklin Roosevelt in order to wipe out any urban reference to a country (Italy) that had "fallen under the chains of fascism."[78] Under the German occupation's "dejudaizing," the rue Henri Heine in the 16th arrondissement had become the rue Jean-Sébastien Bach. After pressure from the street's residents, the municipal council cleansed the street of the Nazi nomenclature and rechristened it for the "anti-Prussian" poet Heinrich Heine, while a street in the 13th arrondissement named for Georges Prade, a former member of the municipal council and among the most well-known of Nazi collaborators, was purged and given Bach's name instead. The boundary between remembering and forgetting was unambiguous, although the political interpretation of historical personalities was clearly subjective and ideological.

These local "revolutionary" initiatives to invent a Liberation tableau in the spaces of the city were largely victorious. They are normally interpreted within the rubric of invented memory. Certainly, the city's spaces acted as the text of collective memory. But they were also instruments of social and political power and affected the construction of the urban realm. Especially in working-class neighborhoods and suburban towns, these "spaces consecrated to the blood of martyrs" effectively acted as claims to political entitlement and communal liberty. The streets were sanctified. They were a catalyst for change. Renaming and the placing of symbolic objects set in motion quotidian spaces and triggered their transformative capacity. Name changes were a linguistic *détournement* that demolished past imagery and instead invested surroundings with personality and subjectivity and with the emotive, violent struggle of the streets. The magic of proper names for streets, according to Benjamin, is that they are "conceptually unburdened and purely acoustic." They are bare formulas that can be filled up with feelings.[79] Renaming produced a new layer of spatial consciousness and the outline for a transformation of urban life in what amounted to a radical and fragmentary urbanism. It was devised from distinct topographic fragments onto which events were inscribed.

Some indication of the deep meaning and urbanistic qualities of these renaming rituals can be gleaned from two areas of the city that played instrumental roles in August 1944: the place Saint-Michel in the 5th arrondissement, and the 14th arrondissement. The place Saint-Michel was the site of one of the first and most important Resistance barricades during the Liberation. After the events the emotional outpouring by residents was such that the mayor and president of the local Liberation committee of the 5th arrondissement were compelled to sponsor the hanging of temporary wooden plaques on the place Saint-Michel around which people could leave mementos and express their grief and respect. However, the socialist municipal councilor Henri Vergnolle proposed a far more grandiose memorial: the erection of a monumental column at the place Saint-Michel (along the lines of the Bastille column commemorating the 1830 Revolution) that would include the names of the fallen and bas-relief scenes of the battles on the streets of Paris.[80] Memorializing the Liberation was interpreted as monumental urban design. In the same sense, local Liberation and worker's committees also proposed the erection of two monumental columns at the porte d'Orléans in the 14th arrondissement to commemorate the entry of Leclerc's divisions on August 24 and the entry of de Gaulle on August 26. The 14th arrondissement had been the scene of some of the most vicious fighting in August 1944, and the debates about how to commemorate various sites in the district were heated. The local Liberation committee was responsible for the placing of twenty marble plaques on building facades throughout the district. It had independently voted, for example, to rename the rue de Vanves for one of its municipal councilors, Raymond Losserand, a well-known militant and Resistance hero executed by the Gestapo. Because "his memory will always remain alive for the population of the 14th arrondissement," the municipal council was left with little choice but to agree to the proposal. When local residents in the 14th decided to rename their rue de la Voie-Verte for a local hero, Père Corentin, who had been killed by the Nazis, the Commission du vieux Paris finally stepped in. It insisted that the rue de la Voie-Verte was one of the most venerable in Paris, that its name be retained, and that in general all of the city's revered street names be left untouched. As a matter of honor, the argument over the rue de la Voie-Verte pitted those councilors who could claim *résistant* status against those who could not. Communist supporters of the name change taunted its principal opponent, François Latour, "If you had been in the Resistance, you would have known Père Corentin."[81]

Renaming was a radical and magical transformation of the street effected by those who lived on it. The *peuple* were capable of freeing themselves and inscribing their experiences in the topography of their neighborhoods. It was not simply the presence of these names that counted, but their visibility and absorption into the texture of the civic landscape. The ceremonies were often part of commemorative anniversaries of, for example, the war's end in May 1945, when *La Vie ouvrière* reported that "commemorative plaques for the heroes of the barricades blossomed" amid the massive crowds, the singing, and the observances.[82] Both at the place Saint-Michel and at Barbès-Rochechouart, the staging of plaque ceremonies included officers and members of the FFI in full uniform, speeches and music, and the placement of bouquets in what were combinations of funereal and festival rites attended by thousands of local residents. Ten streets were inaugurated in the northern district of Gennevilliers and five in Saint-Denis. The local population of Gennevilliers began their commemoration of the Liberation at the place de la Mairie (which had been rechristened the place Jean Grandel, after a Resistance hero), then marched in tribute to the cemetery and its monument to the dead, to the gasworks that had been the scene of the last battles of the Liberation, and then to the cenotaph to British war pilots. At Saint-Denis residents gathered before the commemorative inscription to local militia killed during the Liberation, then marched to the place de la Résistance and on to other scenes of the fighting, each in turn marked by a memorial plaque.[83] Largely under the influence of the Communist Party, the Liberation was memorialized as a glorious urban insurrection carried out by the *peuple de Paris* in their neighborhoods.

Yet these gestures were saturated with political tensions. As the centralizing forces of the Fourth Republic under de Gaulle's leadership began to triumph, the municipal council resisted any further changes to street names or existing space. In the case of the place Saint-Michel, for example, rather than continuing the call for a monumental column, the local mayor of the 5th arrondissement instead acceded to the Seine prefect's insistence on funding far less obtrusive commemorative marble tablets. Even the text inscribed on them had to be approved by the prefecture.[84] These were no longer simply neighborhood decisions made in the zeal of Liberation, but instead reflected the cementing of an official history. The historian Gérard Namer has called Sunday, August 19, 1945 (the first anniversary of the Liberation), the "day of the plaques" that consecrated the landscape of the uprising through official ceremonies and the placement of commemorative tablets throughout the city. The carefully choreographed citywide ceremonies were overseen by the Conseil national de la Résistance (National Council of the Resistance, or CNR) and de Gaulle's government. At the Parc des Princes, the crowd paid homage to the fallen and heard political speeches and music by an American military band. Russian performers interpreted songs of the Red Army. It was a carefully selected historic imagery that suppressed debate and attempted to unite collective memory across invented points of reference. The eventual inauguration of the newly named avenue du Général Leclerc in the 14th arrondissement was deliberately fixed by the municipal council for the anniversary of de Gaulle's appeal to the French nation of June 18, 1940, with Charles de Gaulle's brother, Pierre, as master of ceremonies. The communists staged a counter-demonstration at the mayor's office in the 14th arrondissement. As the vectors of memory became increasingly associated with official interpretation and Gaullist symbolism, local Resistance fighters were promised that their martyrs would be venerated by the plaques mounted and the names affixed to the streets, stadiums, parks, and squares in the modern neighborhoods that would blossom along the city's periphery. The inscribing of local memory was absorbed as part of French state urban planning schemes and would follow the working classes out to the suburbs. Further debate was to be suppressed in favor of rationalized technocratic mapping.

But, according to Namer, this official narrative lacked both the legitimacy and the intimacy of the local rituals. Instead, what marked the commemoration of the Liberation was the extreme dispersion of the ceremonies and the theatricalization of local commemoration.[85] It was a map of the new urban world, a measure of passion and instrumentality at the most localized and self-directed level. Street naming and celebrations, the local festivals and performances, the singing and dancing that reemerged with such intensity at the end of the Second World War were mnemonic sites that triggered social remembrance and association with free action and subversion. They were, in other words, a form of avant-garde collective engagement on the boundary between neighborhood and city, between tradition and novelty, both rooted in and an inversion of the everyday. They were a practical action in the lifeworld of the neighborhood, exemplary instances of how people escaped from the definitions and systems of control that the dominant culture endeavored to apply to them. They acted as a seamless continuation of the Resistance aura and the Liberation, a stage in the struggle for political legitimacy that underlay the fragmented landscape of the capital. Not just nostalgia, they were deeply intertwined with the possibility of thinking about and voicing the future and its visionary hopes. In this sense, they formed a parallel public sphere, which in this case illuminated and exposed social class and populist culture in entirely modern ways. It also formulated a magical urbanism: an idiom and a set of practices that together constituted an alternative vision of Paris.

3 Public Space and Confrontation

In the fifteen years after the war, from 1945 to 1959, the eastern part of Paris was characterized by an intense political militancy derived from the Resistance and Liberation. August 1944 was construed as the "triumph of the people" and the hope for a utopian social republic. The dark days of the occupation were swept away, and suddenly real revolution seemed possible. On the masthead of Albert Camus's daily newspaper *Combat* was printed the motto "From Resistance to Revolution." But for the vast majority of people, this was not a call for insurrection. It exactly captured the hope of carrying the spirit of the Resistance and Liberation struggles into the rebirth of France. It was a commitment to far-reaching social transformation and a new kind of society. The *Renaissance française* would be built from a common core of humanistic, progressive values. These were idealistic ends. Every facet of people's lives seemed open to discussion and reform. Collective behaviors were intensified. Everyday life was politicized. Amid severe social conflict there was a passionate yearning for unity, for community, and for securing an invigorated sense of French identity. That the factory and work remained vital to this enterprise was clear in the February 1945 creation of *comités d'entreprise* (participatory work councils) that were meant to bring far-reaching changes to the heart of the postwar economy. But workplace reform was now part of a broader debate that included the city's massive housing crisis and how the new material culture of the budding "economic miracle" would be shared. These were the new terrains of militancy. There were intense working-class ambitions around the new prosperity and an improved quality of life, the right to housing, leisure and education, culture and sports. There was deep infatuation with the idea that these would be distributed equitably for the common good. Democratization of all spheres of life would make Paris a model of social harmony and patriotic renewal. In 1946 the working-class newspaper *Syndicalisme* reported on visionary designs for Paris that included sports parks on the city's periphery, swimming pools and public baths, fountains with great jets of water, and lawns and shade trees surrounding modern apartments outfitted with every comfort. It was "the great work of social peace" that would restore the dignity of France and its workers.[1]

The public spaces of Paris were the sites of confrontation over these social ideals. The questions of *accessibility* and right to the public domain were decisive for the representation and interpretation of the future of Paris. After years of tight control under the occupation, the public spaces of the capital were suddenly the arena for encounters once again, where various social classes and political groups could interact in known and unknown, defined and undefined ways. The surfaces of the city became a multilayered, pluralistic zone of publics and counterpublics. Public space was fluid, permeable, and endlessly contested.

The Fourth Republic was hounded by unrest. The late 1940s and 1950s were marked by a dispersion of political power across the spaces of Paris. The diversity of protests, marches, parades, and riots—of radically different natures, both traditional and new—suggest the complexity of this decade of transition. These pressures from the street, heightened by mass media, were far from Habermas's rational public sphere. They formed what Bakhtin called a "grotesque symposium" that breaks down the dogmatism of official, authoritative speech.[2] The street was the space of power and legitimation for those excluded from accepted public discourse. Scenes and actors shifted; they could be ebullient, and then at other times threatening. Sometimes they were peaceful; other times, violent. They were phenomena of space and time, linked to specific moments of political crisis and to transitory appropriations of an evolving cartography of symbolic places and trajectories. In response, security forces defended the state apparatus and attempted to curtail the public sphere and maintain order. Each public formed a picture of the city according to its own interests, a mental topography of paths of flight and pursuit, of spaces of freedom and surveillance, of confidence and fear, of domination and subordination. This chapter looks at three specific movements that depict the contested geopolitics of public space and the permeability of its boundaries. First, the scores of protests, staged largely by the communists, in the context of reconstruction and the cold war; second, the housing protests, especially those of Abbé Pierre in 1953; and lastly, the political struggles created by the cancer of the Algerian War. Together they evidence the multiplicity of distinct public discourses, the overlapping scenes and spaces of collective action and contestation that permeated the capital.

Decentering Collective Power

The war and occupation made Paris a city unquestionably of the Left. The main beneficiary was the Communist Party, under the guidance of Maurice Thorez. Between 1944 and 1956 the culture and politics of communism in the capital reached an extraordinary zenith. The communists' role in the Resistance and Liberation was lionized. A new generation of scholars is rewriting the history of the French Resistance and questioning the hegemonic sway of the Communist Party over the movement.[3] Yet there is no doubt that Communism was a *de rigueur* force in the capital, a chic ideology of astonishing influence in the years after the war. It was almost an autonomous power in Paris—a counterstate—guarding its fiefdoms in the north and east, relying on a legion of militants and launching offensives at will against the French state and bourgeois society and against the American colossus. The PCF had its own newspapers and literary forums and controlled the most important intellectual publications in Paris, foremost among them *Les Lettres françaises*, the major publishing outlet for the intellectual Left and managed by Louis Aragon. The intellectual beau monde of the Left Bank adopted the language of revolutionary politics and was the PCF's most vocal champion. The party's seduction reached out to capture the flashy world of artistic and media stardom with a long list of fierce advocates, from Picasso to Gérard Philipe and Yves Montand. They put their signature to communist and pacifist petitions, including the 1950 Stockholm Appeal against the use of atomic weapons, and marched in the streets along with the party's rank and file. In the late 1940s and early 1950s the party's evening daily *Ce Soir* (also under the directorship of Louis Aragon) and the official communist organ *L'Humanité* each enjoyed a daily readership of 450,000 devotees. The party produced its own advertising and campaign films and had its own public-relations agency, youth festivals, film premiers, conferences, and publications. It could rely on a full 30 percent of the vote in municipal elections in the early postwar years and controlled the suburban ring of industrial towns that surrounded the capital. The party's stronghold remained the working-class districts of the 11th, 13th, 18th, 19th, and 20th arrondissements, 55–60 percent of which still voted communist in 1956.[4] In the mid-1950s the communists still controlled twenty-seven municipalities in the Paris suburbs, six of which were in communes with more than fifty thousand inhabitants: Aubervilliers, Drancy, Montreuil, Nanterre, Saint-Denis, Vitry-sur-Seine.[5] The suburban population tended to increase most in these towns, and the newcomers blended easily into districts marked by party solidarity and working-class sociability.

Yet the party drew its appeal and power to mobilize not so much from these votes or from strict ideology, but from its historical legitimacy and its claim to represent the true France. The communists laid claim to universality. For all practical purposes, they were willing to domesticate their opposition and rallied to the defense of the nation and the newly formed Fourth Republic, participating in coalition governments until the onset of the cold war led to their expulsion in 1947. But at the level of principles and public promotion, they were unshakably bound to a view of France's postwar government as "bourgeois." The Fourth Republic and de Gaulle's RPF were seen as unscrupulous and self-seeking, sworn enemies of the people and incapable of representing them. And there was absolutely nothing ambivalent about the party's perspective on Paris. Theirs was a comprehensive critique of existing urban society. Paris was really two cities: the corrupted and vilified bourgeois society in the western districts and the proletarian world of the eastern neighborhoods. This equivocation between political participation and genuine hostility led the party to stress its proletarian identity and its separateness.[6] It offered a coherent social and political model for these working classes—referred to broadly as *le peuple* or *les petits*—and fought for their hopes and dreams for the future. Based on this imagery, the party represented not merely class interests, but the French people as a whole. Even more important for the uses of public space, between 1944 and 1956 the Communist Party was the principal force of political agitation and protest in Paris. And there were plenty of glaring contradictions in the *trente glorieuses* to fuel frustration and political militancy.

For all the joy of freedom and hopes of the Liberation, for all the talk of a French renaissance, Paris was a dreary, dirty place with few comforts. Heating costs had skyrocketed. There was a chronic shortage of food, which was still rationed in the late 1940s. Official quotas offered each adult the equivalent of 900 calories a day in August 1944 and 1,500 in May 1945. Bread was more severely rationed in 1947 than during the worst hours of the "Fritz" (Germans), and the hunt for milk was still a nightmare. All of this meant long, frustrating queues at local markets. Parisians made ample use of the black market and hoarded ration tickets. Resentment was fueled by the reality that there were three sets of quotas: one for the poor, another for the rich, and yet another for the occupying American and British forces. Even when quotas on basic foodstuffs ended, soaring inflation made them shockingly expensive. In 1947 even the public outcry over the out-of-control rat population, which threatened public health in the working-class districts, went unheard.

Yet for all these difficulties, housing still remained the fundamental crisis facing the city's people. A 1948 law began to free up rents, but it still protected those (mostly the elderly and the well-off) who already had somewhere to live. Anyone looking for shelter faced housing costs that jumped sixfold between 1948 and 1956. Finding any sort of dwelling in Paris was a virtually hopeless task that involved a procedural jungle, myriad contacts, and the likelihood of payoffs for even the nastiest of abodes. This contrast between the dreams of a better life and the reality facing young families is one of the most enduring features of this entire period. After years of deprivation, millions of Parisians strolled through mesmerizing expositions on reconstruction, habitat, decorative arts, and urbanism. They drooled over the displays of modern kitchen appliances, washing machines, and sleek furniture designed by Charlotte Perriand at the 1947 Exposition internationale de l'urbanisme et de l'habitation. Attendance at the 1951 Salon des arts ménagers alone reached well over one million.[7] The tempting peeks at the future made the difficulties all the harder to bear. Shysters sold lists of apartments "soon to be available." Young couples scoured public auctions and the black market for basic furniture that cost a fortune. For thousands of people in the capital—but especially in the northern and eastern neighborhoods—sordid living conditions became the norm. In 1944 the working-class newspaper *Syndicalisme* launched an editorial on housing conditions that asked why workers toiled in factories with the most modern, efficient machinery and yet went home to hovels: "We want to see the instruments of liberation. Where is the clean airy kitchen attached to healthy living spaces? Where is the bathroom, the washing machine, the indirect light that softens the view . . . ?"[8]

Beyond the immediate injustices palpable at the level of everyday life, the *trente glorieuses* more generally caught the traditional working classes in its wake. Gains in France were real, and total wages increased regularly, with all wage earners experiencing an improvement in their purchasing power. Yet these positive indicators hid the widening inequality in wages and standards of living. Reconstruction and modernization favored the most qualified and talented. Those with the training to wade into the new industries and the expanding service sector were highly competitive, and their incomes rose accordingly. This was particularly true for the new managerial and employee classes, or *cadres supérieurs* and *cadres moyens*, as well as of skilled workers. Workers in traditional industries faced stagnating salaries and saw their standard of living decline relative to these gains. Even worse, by the mid-1950s many of these manufacturing activities were no longer profitable. They faded from the scene. Those Parisian companies that did remain viable were being banished to the provinces in the government's decentralization programs. The result was that income inequalities and social hierarchies were exaggerated. In 1949 real salaries were at their lowest point for the entire period between 1913 and 1954, and 50 percent lower than they had been in 1937. Although they did begin to increase after 1949, by 1954 they had still not reached their prewar levels.[9] The city's working classes, who were the PCF's traditional political base, found themselves facing a tightening job market and declining purchasing power just when consumer goods were dangling in store windows and mass culture was offering a new way of life. In a 1956 study of the working classes, the respondents in an opinion poll indicated that the cost of living, housing, and fears about the future were their most immediate problems. When asked whether their lives had improved over the last five years, over 50 percent replied in the negative.[10] Between 1956 and 1964 the real income of managers in France increased by 39.5 percent, that of employees by 32 percent, and that of skilled workers by 25 percent, yet for minimum-wage earners the increase was just 3.8 percent. While the *cadres* were busy buying cars and domestic goods for their homes, food was still consuming nearly 60 percent of the budget of working families. The minimum wage, or SMIG, was increasingly divorced from economic reality, which by 1952 was already trailing 35 percent behind the cost of living.[11] Traditional representations of the flourishing *trente glorieuses* thus hide deep social tensions. The inequalities were most palpable at the level of everyday life. Despite the dream of a good life for all, prosperity and access to consumption were far from democratic. There were plenty of reasons to join the Communist Party, to organize strike movements and descend into the streets in protest. The public spaces of the city were volatile, chimerical. All things seemed possible.

In the somber atmosphere of the postwar era, the PCF fought against these injustices. It was the defender of the people. In the words of Pierre Nora, "No other political party or group created a universe so thoroughly mapped out, so reassuring, so full of signs and markers, so warm, protective, or comforting."[12] The solidity of its moral and revolutionary appeal was striking, and it was both nostalgic and avant-garde in orientation. Paris was imagined and idealized as a topography of localized populist neighborhoods—unified in a revolutionary genealogy that had carried through to the Liberation. Through a universe of ingrained rituals, ceremonies, historical references, cultural postures, and codes, the party invented the framework for a republic of the people, a countersociety that claimed the public spaces of the city as its own. The proletarian Paris of the northern and eastern districts was lionized as the territory of communist militancy. It was a base, a training ground, a space of withdrawal and regroupment. In May 1952, when police flooded the rue de Ménilmontant looking for a local PCF official, the neighborhood immediately defended its terrain against the hostile invasion.[13] The PCF was the *true* Paris in this cult of *Paris populaire*. In 1945 the communist *L'Avant-garde* conjured up the magical street naming that turned the rue de Ménilmontant and the surrounding neighborhood into a lyrical topos of working-class political culture:

> Ménilmontant Street, Belleville Boulevard, a working-class neighborhood of Paris sings the melody of its life and touches the heart of our people. Hermitage Street, Enverges Street, Maronites Street, poetic names where freedom, happiness and justice have always been passionately defended. And the young will continue the fight: the Commune, February 1934 and the Resistance. There is a mark of nobility at Ménilmuche.[14]

This was the poetic landscape made so poignant by Jacques Prévert and Willy Ronis. Although these stereotypes came under some criticism by the Left, the party generally supported them. They were an emotional appeal to memory and symbolism, to the rituals of the street. A cornucopia of local observances and celebrations created an informal communist or *ouvriériste* sociability and territory in neighborhood space. This expressive discourse reached back into historic practices and traditions to knit back up the unraveled fabric of urban civic practices. It was on this foundation that the people would surge toward a future of their own making and lead the renaissance of France. This mythic imagery succeeded in politicizing virtually every aspect of collective life.

This hypnotic vision was reproduced in the localized power of the arrondissements, the number of communist mayors who controlled them, and the unique character with which each and every neighborhood was imbued. The experience of the Resistance and the Liberation itself had taken place largely at the level of urban neighborhood. Partisan loyalties were defined within the restricted context of quarter, arrondissement, and suburban town. The experience effectively politicized municipal governance. Before the war, mayoral seats in local city halls in the arrondissements were largely honorific positions held by aging local elites. In the aftermath of the deliverance, they were controlled by local Liberation committees made up of young activists from the Resistance, who were emerging as the new political leadership. By February 1945 communist mayors controlled the working-class enclaves of the 3rd, 10th, 11th, 14th, 15th, 18th, 19th, and 20th arrondissements, as well as nearly half of the city's assistant mayoral seats.[15] Raymond Bossus, originally from Charonne and one of the leaders of the August 1944 insurrection, dominated municipal politics in Belleville and Ménilmontant. Marcel Cachin, a party chief, was elected deputy and municipal councilor from La Goutte d'Or in the 18th arrondissement. An assortment of neighborhood communist newsletters—*Le Phare du Ve, Le Patriote du VIe, La Voix du XVIe*—enjoyed avid readership and popularity. The party's influence even spread to better-off areas of the city and the core central districts. This localized municipalism in Paris was mirrored in the working-class suburbs. The historian Jean Girault makes the point that after the Liberation, the local municipality became an essential component of the "red suburbs" and the most effective political tool of the Communist Party. In 1945 fifty of the eighty municipalities in the department of the Seine were controlled by the communists. For the first time in the long, sordid history of the exorcised margins, communist mayors of towns such as Saint-Denis and Aubervilliers, filled with a newfound municipal pride, were powerful political figures in their own right. The most illustrious leaders of the Communist Party—Charles Tillon, Ambroise Croizat, and André Marty—were elected from Paris and its suburbs.

During the war years, mayors and municipal councils were directly appointed by local Vichy officialdom. The stain of collaboration and consequent purges offered the opening for thoroughgoing electoral and administrative reform at the local level. In the first election after the war in April 1945 (and the first in which women voted) municipal councilors were chosen by arrondissement. But, inspired by the ideas of Henri Sellier, one Communist

Party member, Georges Marrane, proposed to the Comité parisien de la Libération a complete overhaul of the city's administration. The Paris municipal council would be dissolved altogether in favor of autonomous municipal councils for each of the twenty arrondissements. They would be twenty separate "cities" with independent powers and would see to local affairs just as the municipal councils did in the suburban towns. The Paris region as a whole would then be administered by an elected representative assembly. Marrane argued that not only was the Paris municipal council hopelessly inept, but each of the arrondissements was different, with different problems that only a local mayor could hope to understand.[16] Although the communists tried repeatedly to push through this idea of local autonomy between 1945 and 1947, the proposition ultimately failed. However, it spoke to the decentralized sense of work, living, and politics in the *quartiers populaires* as a universe of possibilities, legitimized by wartime resistance and by the promises of reconstruction. The difficulties of war and occupation had already required ingenuity and resourcefulness. The subculture of daily privation and "ersatz" living inadvertently cleared the way for the transformation of everyday life. This quotidian localized environment was the zone of immediate experience and symbolic representations, a place of social action, initiative, and invention. It was in this dispersed, autonomous geography that the communists would build homes, new public schools and daycare centers, parks and sports arenas, and fulfill the hopes of the Liberation.

In October 1947, in the newspaper *Paris Centre*, the Communist Party sections of the 1st, 2nd, 8th, and 9th arrondissements insisted that "Paris should be administered by its elected" and flaunted their accomplishments: day-care centers and schools opened, a new neighborhood square renovated, a sports field outfitted with lights, an inexpensive restaurant launched. The party championed worker management and the renovation of Les Halles.[17] The PCF also produced its own media campaign, including a 1947 promotional film entitled *À la conquête du bonheur*. After paying homage to the *résistants* and deportees who gave their lives in the war, the film recounts the reforms enacted by various communist municipalities in the suburbs. Alongside the paucity of city and state aid, ineptly meted out, the local examples are inspiring: the health clinics at Villejuif and Gennevilliers are portrayed as model facilities, the day-care center at Bezons rings with children's laughter, thousands of healthy lunches are served at school canteens, the trade school at Gennevilliers graduates skilled workers, and free wood is distributed to the elderly for heat. The campaign film captures volunteer "shock troops" organizing to provide temporary shelter for the homeless at Ivry and constructing a bus-stop shelter at Noisy-le-Sec.[18] These images portray a mythical French people, recognizable for their modesty and courage, busy making their lives and mobilizing locally in their quartier to construct a brave new world. In the same way, the communist municipal council of suburban Malakoff boasted in September 1947 about the ultramodern health clinic, the prenatal care facilities and nursery schools, and the town's *colonie de vacances*.[19] The most triumphant programs were carried out in Saint-Denis, one of the main bastions of the *banlieue rouge*, which was heavily damaged by wartime bombardments. The communist municipality set out a visionary program of public housing and urbanism under the architect André Lurçat. A member of CIAM and the modernist movement, Lurçat was an active member of the PCF in the years after the war. In stark contrast to the housing paralysis in Paris, Saint-Denis had already begun construction of the cité Paul Langevin public-housing project as early as 1946. Nursery schools were opened and a *colonie de vacances* inaugurated for the city's children. Paris and its suburbs had fractured into self-actualizing localized spaces of practical doing and accomplishment. Through hard work, *les camarades* would share in prosperity as never before and lead the transformation of France.

The Spatial Logic of Class

In the same sense, the PCF had every intention of taking to the streets and fighting against the injustices so palpable on the landscape. The spaces of Paris, as the capital, were unquestionably a national terrain of visibility and political power. Its topography overflowed with emblematic sites, with tradition and ritual. The extraordinary influence of the Left and especially of the Communist Party in Paris made the struggle for control over this public sphere passionate and highly volatile. The overt *ouvriérisme* found its expression in the civic spaces of the city. Its claim to spatial and political legitimacy called upon history and memory, rite and celebration, dramatic posturing and performance, and violent struggle. *Ouvriérisme* was a staging of transgression, hyperbole, and iconoclasm. It turned the streets of Paris into an ongoing political pageant, an insurgent civic theater that continued the revolutionary legacy and the outpouring of the Liberation. The immediacy and influence of the capital's public spaces was made even more unequivocal by newspaper and television coverage. The reporting of street demonstrations on television newscasts is a particularly risky terrain for historians to maneuver. Radiodiffusion télévision française (RTF) was government controlled. News broadcasts remained exceptionally conformist and followed government policy on the legitimacy of spatial access and use of the public domain. Ostensibly tolerated rituals such as the May Day and July 14 parades and the student *monôme du bac*, or rag parade, received privileged coverage by visual media, while more explicit political demonstrations and strikes rarely appeared on either film newsreels or television sets. When they did, the narrative and visual sequence tended to portray first the gathering, then the inevitable breakdown into violence, and finally the successful crackdown by police forces.[20] Highly popular photoessay magazines such as *Paris Match* tended to follow the same logic. Taking into account these significant biases, the combination of newspaper and visual coverage can nevertheless provide a fuller picture of political activity on the streets of Paris. They also provide valuable insight into the ways in which visual media were appropriated by protesters themselves for their own purposes. The city's topography was heightened as a multilayered, fluid political landscape occupied and enriched by an assortment of political voices.

Through the mid-1950s political demonstrations in Paris were generally prohibited, so participants in overt protests risked incendiary confrontations with law enforcement. The communists also walked a fine line between opposition to the bourgeois Fourth Republic and cooperation in the "battle for production" and the reconstruction of France. Up to 1947 they held ministerial positions. Hostility was restrained. As a result, a myriad of cultural practices served as a proxy for political struggle. Benign neighborhood social events and time-honored ceremonies and anniversaries were occasions for reasserting political power in the street. They were strategies of action and representation. This tactic relied on the reinvention of the memory of place and the political rituals that had formed the framework of neighborhood life before the catastrophe of the war. For the Left (especially the communists), the founding myths of Paris were the 1789 and 1848 Revolutions and the 1871 Paris Commune. This ideal of the people manning the barricades was rediscovered in the Popular Front and in the Resistance. Indeed, the myth of the Liberation was that Parisians had emerged from the oppression of the *années noires* and would regain the liberty of the prewar years. This historic past provided coherence and legitimacy and wreathed the working classes, the true *people*, in the city's revolutionary heritage. In October 1944 the Communist Party invited Parisians to commemorate the deaths of Paul Vaillant-Couturier, Henri Barbusse, and the martyrs of the war and Liberation with a time-honored march to the Mur des Fédérés at Père Lachaise Cemetery. One of the first political demonstrations after the Liberation and attended, according to L'Humanité, by over 250,000 people,[21] it inaugurated a cenotaph to the Left's martyred heroes. The ceremony immediately reactualized the symbolic place and glorious memory of working-class struggle and placed the communists in the forefront of political expression in the streets. The PCF even took charge of the capital's Armistice Day celebration at the Arc de Triomphe on November 11, 1944, which went on without de Gaulle or any other official government representation. The May 1 Labor Day march to the Mur des Fédérés in 1945 celebrated the victory of the communists in the municipal elections, while the traditional May 27 march in commemoration of the *fédérés* of the Paris Commune honored wartime deportees. It drew hundreds of thousands. The performance quality of these events and the staging of wartime tragedy were apparent in the spectacle of deportees, who marched in their "odious blue and gray costumes, head shaved, with grave faces . . . the women wore their miserable dresses, but their faces showed they had refound Paris, fraternal emotion and the shared élan of a people."[22] Huge crowds laid wreaths on the tombs of "the heroes of the Commune and their descendants, the martyrs of the Liberation" in a fusion of political imagery. They proclaimed, according to the Confédération générale du travail (CGT) labor-union newspaper *La Vie ouvrière*, "their faith in the France of yesterday and tomorrow by their willingness to act, to work together for the immediate reconstruction of the country."[23] A July 31 pilgrimage organized by the Socialist Party to the Mur des Fédérés and the Panthéon to commemorate the assassination of Jean Jaurès also drew tens of thousands. What distinguishes these parades, pilgrimages, political festivals, and commemorations is, first, their quantity, and second, the tens of thousands, in some cases hundreds of thousands, of people who took part. The sheer number of events and the exceptional levels of participation in public ceremonies far exceeded those in the years before the war. This massively claimed "right to the city" was associated with a people's arrival at power and the ceremonial posturing that went with it. Armistice Day, the commemoration of the May 8 wartime victory and of the historic leaders of the Left, and the homage to the Resistance and to wartime martyrs and returning prisoners of war were all conceived as spatial and political spectacle.

The annual May Day and July 14 marches and the commemoration of the February 1934 political crisis (which was interpreted as a defense against a fascist coup d'état) were the most sustained political theater through the mid 1950s. The most sanctified route for these parades was between the place de la Bastille and the place de la Nation. This topography was pierced with historical meaning and political possibilities that were magnified in the context of the immediate postwar period. The May Day caravan from the Bastille to the place de la Nation organized by the PCF privileged the heritage of revolutionary Paris with the slogan "May 1, 1934—May 1, 1946 at Paris." Led by top communist and socialist officials, huge masses of people marched through the streets on foot and on bicycle, carrying banners, insignias, and placards celebrating the "fête de l'espoir" and "rénové." The parade route was turned into a huge open-air traveling carnival and political rally. These were expressions of solidarity, national sovereignty, and a people allied in the great work of reconstruction. Enormous placards heralded the *manifestation populaire*. They led a procession of highly stylized banners and floats that carried on the tradition of constructivist street decor. Folkloric groups and populist organizations displayed their streamers, flags, insignia, and badges in a festival of civic right and spatial appropriation.[24]

Such was the moral authority of the working classes at the war's end that processions veered out of this archetypal working-class territory of eastern Paris to appropriate official sites of political power in Paris. In the case of the July 14, 1946, parade (the first after the war), the French state's official military pageant shifted from its normal trajectory down the Champs-Élysées to the place de la Bastille, where it joined ranks with the victorious working classes. The parade's destination was the old place de Grève, the time-honored square in front of the Hôtel de Ville that would be ceremoniously "conquered" by the city's people. *Les Actualités françaises* filmed the historic procession in all its patriotic regalia. The clip begins with quintessential shots of the city's great monuments floodlit at night—a glorious site in itself after years of wartime darkness. The appropriation of historical imagery is arresting: wax figures depicting French Revolutionary heroes introduce images of the celebration. The procession of the "Armée nouvelle" begins at the place de la Bastille, in honor of "the first cry of freedom by the French people." The public pageant is led by a grandiose *défilé populaire*: men and women, many of them dressed in traditional costumes, march amid a sea of flags, banners, and elaborate floats. Soldiers and colonial troops file by in ceremonial ranks and tanks parade in a staging of French military might. And "for the first time," workers from the armaments factories join the official procession along with Resistance cells now triumphantly on display with their leaders. In a similar celebratory appropriation of official political space, *Les Actualités françaises* captured the 1947 May Day parade as it wound from the place de la République to the place de la Concorde.[25] These film images reveal a self-conscious arrival at power and sovereignty, with all of the posturing and monumental ceremony that goes with it. Hundreds of thousands of people lined the parade routes in a reiteration of the Liberation's retaking of the city. The people of Paris were the main actors in this public theater of the street that included its own dramatic conflict. The latter celebration took place just a few days before the expulsion of the communists from government. According to *Combat*, the communist contingents in the parade were cheered wildly, while the Socialists were admonished for their lack of political unity.[26]

The start of the cold war and the expulsion of the PCF from government in 1947 radically intensified this political drama playing out on the streets of the capital. Communist ministers were summarily dismissed from Paul Ramadier's government on May 4. The PCF was driven out of a number of mayoral seats throughout its base in the city's working-class districts. The mayors of the 11th and 20th arrondissements were dismissed. Mayors in the 3rd, 13th, 18th, and 19th arrondissements were later sacked, along with twenty-five communist mayoral adjuncts.[27] Political protests were subject to more and more restrictions. In the midst of the November 1947 strike waves, they were banned altogether for the first time since the Liberation. Commemoration parades became the only political activity negotiable with police authorities, and even political speeches at these events were officially barred. The parades became a form of subversive art and political masquerade. In 1948 alone the party organized nine commemorative corteges that rallied from 100,000 to a million participants.[28] Especially along the hallowed ground from the Bastille to the place de la Nation, the parades were among the few authorized opportunities for the Communist Party and labor unions to flex their political muscle in public space without recourse to dangerous civil disobedience. As political theater the marches were "messy" paradoxical political events, both conservative and radical in content. They acted as a mechanism of political protest, yet did not ostensibly threaten to undermine the country's fragile stability. The throngs on parade through the working-class stronghold were popular *fêtes*. They were political festivals that triggered social remembrance and association with free action and subversion. They were a form of mockery, derision, and subterfuge. The "play-acting" of revolution and the performance of social roles could be genuine or spurious, valid or phony. One could make the argument that this visual narrative created a mythology, a hyperreal spectacle that was an illusion of reality and actually hid social relations. But as a type of militant pedestrianism, it acted ostensibly as a claim to accessibility in the public sphere. This practical theater of protest was saturated with complexity and contradiction. Led by Communist Party and labor leaders, workers proudly carried their union and factory banners along with posters proclaiming the political slogans of the moment. There was a free intermingling of festival and protest, of the playful and the serious. The parade became a political prank. Ice cream vendors and street merchants selling souvenirs worked the crowds along the parade route in what increasingly took on the atmosphere of a carnival or *fête foraine*. In newspaper metaphors used to describe the processions, the crowds surge, stream, and flow. There is a sense of fluidity in space, of sensuousness and provocation that the historian David Glassberg links to a thinly veiled sexual imagery.[29] The crowds seethe with political passion and righteousness. The festivities end with fiery speeches by left-wing luminaries at the place de la Nation. The 1948 and 1949 marches commemorating February 1934 both drew some 25,000 spectators. In 1951 the event still attracted a crowd of 20,000, according to the police count. The multiplicity of cortèges, marches, and symbolic demonstrations of power in the streets of the city infinitely appropriated and reappropriated the spaces of the city. They wound along hallowed routes and acted out the reemergence of the *peuple* as a political and civic force, forming a topographic bond imbued with a sense of political rebelliousness and social power.

One reason to interpret this political spectacle as more than pretense is that it was not unaccompanied. The multiplicity of industrial actions, walkouts, and demonstrations kept the streets of Paris in an habitual state of agitation. Protests against persistent penury and unfair food rationing, against low wages and salary disparities between Paris and the suburbs, against rising prices and shyster opportunists, fueled the battle for spatial and political legitimacy. For example, in both 1949 and 1950, wounded war veterans staged protest marches at the capital's official sites of political power, moving down the Champs-Élysées from the place de la Concorde and the Opéra. Giving voice to their demands for more public aid, they rolled makeshift wheelchairs and handicap pushcarts in front of television cameras for full effect as crowds watched. In November 1946 a crowd estimated at 100,000 converged on the slaughterhouse at La Villette to protest rising prices and demand the immediate arrest of the "meat gangsters and muggers of La Villette." Danielle Tartakowsky points to the ritualistic forms of these protests, which harked back to the atmosphere of a *fête champêtre* or even "carnivelesque forms inherited from the Popular Front."[30] They were, in other words, doubly coded festivals in which play erupts into political threat. The most important followed a specific pattern of populist spectacle that accentuated their incendiary and arousal qualities: an angry, emotionally incited crowd moving toward riot, the party or labor unions channeling passions into disciplined protest, the breakdown into violence, the bloodshed or, even worse, deaths, with the aftermath of more protests and funeral marches. In September 1948 ten thousand workers in the SNECMA plants walked out on strike. Masses of picketers fought with police in front of company headquarters on the boulevard Haussmann. February and March 1950 saw strikes at the Renault factory, by public transport workers, then by the city's gas and electricity employees. Bomb explosions rocked the Paris branches of the North European Commercial Bank and the Bank of Worms. The success during August 1953 of the massive public-sector strike waves over retirement and promotion benefits surprised even union officials. The spontaneous groundswell of protests during the traditional month of vacation paralyzed Paris as well as the rest of France and demonstrated the people's apprehension about bread-and-butter issues. Enormous crowds of striking workers blocked entrances to the city's railroad stations and held outdoor meetings. They took over post offices and public buildings. Thousands jammed the Bourse de Travail on the rue du Château d'Eau near the place de la République. The army was brought in to maintain public order and carry out essential public services. For weeks the spaces of Paris looked as though they were under siege.[31]

The most politically charged and violent postwar demonstrations were the massive strike movements of 1947, the Ridgway riots of 1952, the brutal battles of July 14, 1953, and the anticommunist protests of 1956. The 1947 strike waves were instigated by a cabal of social and political tensions. The working-class standard of living had risen at the Liberation to around 60 percent of its prewar level, and then to 80 percent in late 1945. By May 1947 it had fallen back to half the prewar level.[32] People were putting in longer hours with little possibility of achieving any real gains. The refusal by the socialist prime minister, Paul Ramadier, to respond to this emergency and instead to freeze wages infuriated workers and aggravated social hostilities. Protest marches organized by labor unions converged on the Champs-de-Mars in a demonstration of their power and discipline and to defend "their right to life, the Republic, and democracy." Wildcat work stoppages demanding pay increases broke out in a variety of industries. In April workers in the Say Sugar Refinery in the 13th arrondissement went out on strike. Then it was the turn of the workers at the Grands Moulins flour mills, and next the city's laundry workers. The strike at Renault in April was the largest. Then, on May 4, Maurice Thorez and the communist ministers were expelled from Ramadier's government. The PCF reacted to its marginalization by calling the rank and file out of the factories and into the streets. Workers in the aeronautic and automobile plants joined the Renault strike. Yet despite the inflammatory rhetoric and tense standoffs, the strike waves that hit in November 1947 still retained their customary tone and practice. Led again by workers in the Renault factory, nearly all of the metallurgical industry went out on strike to demand 25 percent pay increases. By November 22 front-page headlines in *L'Humanité* reported 70,000 workers on strike, with 30,000 young *compagnons* on the march to a massive rally at Vél' d'Hiv'. They filled the streets around the stadium, appropriating a space already filled with police by breaking into traditional songs of insurrection amid clashes. One worker and former *résistante* was killed and hundreds wounded in a pitched battle with anticommunists around the Salle Wagram, near the place de l'Étoile. Military reservists and riot squads were called out to protect the National Assembly and patrol the streets. Appropriating revolutionary imagery, young workers from the Citroën plant were described as arriving "still covered in blood from the blows they received in the magnificent afternoon battle against the police, against the mobile guards launched by the enemy of the people." They battled "for a young, happy and strong France." Workers occupying the Citroën factory held off police while singing the "Marseillaise."[33]

The strident calls for an end to social injustices that reverberated across Paris were rolled into anti-American and cold war hyperbole. Communist demonstrations against the Marshall Plan ended in violent clashes, while parades against "coca-colonisation" spilled into the streets. The PCF intensified efforts to block what they derided as American militarism not only because of the wars in Indochina and Korea, but also to prevent the rearming of the German Federal Republic. Fear of German military rearmament was widespread on the Left and was equated with the rise of Nazi Germany. In 1950 violence broke out along the Champs-Élysées during a communist protest against *Le Figaro*'s serial publication of a memoir by the former SS officer Otto Skorzeny. Camera crews climbed onto automobile rooftops to film the police charges into the crowds and the ensuing fracas as protesters tore apart the bistro chairs and tables to use as projectiles.[34] The January 1951 visit to Paris by Dwight D. Eisenhower, dubbed the "General of German Rearmament" by the Left, was welcomed with a call for patriotic strikes and protests by the Paris section of the PCF while thousands marched for peace down the Champs-Élysées. The arrival in Paris of German Chancellor Konrad Adenauer (accompanied by General Hans Speidel) in late November 1951 brought more street protests and violent clashes. Although the march was banned, tens of thousands paraded along the triangle between the place de la République, the place de l'Opéra, and the gare Saint-Lazare. More than seven thousand police were massed along the Champs-Élysées. Street fighting and smaller public protests took place in the northern and eastern districts, interrupting traffic, with cars horns blaring in support or in annoyance. Thousands were rounded up and arrested.

Although politically marginalized, the PCF continued to wear the mantle of patriotism by launching a powerful version of the peace movement in the capital's streets. It was a single-issue campaign meant to mobilize the French nation and distinguish it as independent from U.S. imperialism and acting in the best interests of the future. Because the socialists were aligned with Atlanticism, the communists essentially monopolized what proved to be an immensely popular movement against atomic weapons and the cold war. The years 1948 and 1949 saw some seven peace demonstrations organized by the communists and the Union de la jeunesse républicaine française (Union of Young French Republicans, or UJRF) on the interior boulevards. The centrality of the location marked them as essentially national in context. They were meant to sway French public opinion against the cold war, as was the PCF's 1949 World Peace Congress in Paris. The Stockholm Appeal launched by Frédéric Joliot-Curie and the communist-sponsored World Congress of Partisans of Peace in March 1950 sped up the momentum. The campaign collected millions of signatures demanding the banning of all atomic weapons as a crime against humanity. The peace movement was played out at the PCF's populist base. Peace rallies were held regularly in various public venues such as the Stade de Buffalo and the Salle Wagram, in suburban factories and communist-held municipalities. In 1951 local peace conferences were organized in twenty-nine locations in the communist-dominated arrondissements and suburban towns. *L'Humanité* called them "dozens of popular little assemblies in the street, laboratories, apartment buildings and places of work."[35] At the Veteran's Day celebrations in the 15th arrondissement on November 11, 1953, the communists called for the neighborhood's women, "all the mothers worried over the threat of war," to rally against the rearming of Germany, the Bonn Accords, and the Treaty of Paris.[36] Initially none of these activities seriously challenged police-regulated access to public space, nor did they risk violent engagement or a destabilization of the streets. However, the atmosphere changed when the PCF began to launch a more aggressive policy of confrontation. In this, they could rely on the myth that "the Parisian proletariat are ready and quick, prepared to descend into the street at a moment's notice from the Party."[37]

General Matthew Ridgway was targeted when he was named to replace Eisenhower as the head of NATO. He was branded a war criminal by the communist press and accused of ordering the use of bacteriological weapons in the Korean War. When Antoine Pinay's government banned a peace demonstration in Paris on May 28, 1952, the PCF decided to counter with a massive protest. The narrative description of the worst day of protest and rioting from *L'Humanité* exudes the sense of fluidity and sensuousness, the fierce struggle for command of the streets that was the heritage of the Revolution:

> The streets of Paris around 6 in the evening, under a drizzle that began to fall at the end of the afternoon; a huge snarl-up at the crossroads empty of traffic cops, who had been called to the rescue by a police already on the defensive. The place de la République, black with helmets and under the helmets, pale, very pale faces. At that moment, at the factory gates, the mouths of the subways, at the bus stops, groups began to form, and then suddenly signs appear, signs saying "Ridgway Get Out!," "Go Home!," "Americans Go Back to America," "We Want Peace!" Signs held up on solid poles, long thick poles. The police aren't reading the signs. They just look at them. Nothing can stop this clamor that swells out to engulf passersby, and other groups, waiting for this moment, [to] join in the demonstration. People applaud at the windows. This is how it is everywhere in Paris, to the north, south, east, and west. In a hundred

FIGURE 10. Demonstrators and police on the streets of Paris during the Ridgway Riots, May 30, 1952. © BETTMANN/CORBIS.

different places, irresistible columns have taken charge. The police are beaten. The street belongs to the people of Paris.[38]

The tactic of the communists and their followers was to use the Métro to spread out and attack police units from a variety of places rather than confronting them head-on in battle. The Métro was a Parisian icon, an extension of working-class maneuverability and swiftness. Demonstrators emerged at the boulevard Magenta, the rue du Temple, the rue du Faubourg du Temple, the avenue de la République, the gare de l'Est, the gare Saint-Lazare, the place des Victoires, and the place de l'Odéon.[39] The image invented by the communists was of a people with quick reflexes, intelligent and fast, against whom a plodding police force had little hope: "Baylot only knew how to respond with the mad rage of his units, who took their revenge on the loners, on prisoners. They unleashed themselves on the North Africans with ignoble racist sadism."[40] A contingent of two thousand descended from Aubervilliers by Métro and fought police in the gare du Nord in a scene of complete confusion. As the clashes tore apart the main hall, windows were smashed and shots rang out amid fleeing commuters. Some twenty thousand demonstrators took part in the protests and riots, with one of their number left dead, two hundred wounded, and hundreds arrested, among them the Communist Party secretary, Jacques Duclos.

After the Ridgway riots, all demonstrations and street theater in Paris, including the traditional February, May Day, and July 14 marches, were forbidden unless police had no choice but to concede territory to demonstrators. In 1953 the PCF, labor unions, and an assortment of neighborhood and suburban organizing committees, supported by a host of intellectuals and media personalities, defiantly went ahead with plans to commemorate May Day and July 14 in "defense of liberty." *L'Humanité* called for a "vast protest" against the prohibition that "unmasked the fascist character of the government."[41] The pressure forced police authorization of a May Day march limited strictly to the traditional Bastille-to-Nation route. In a show of unity, officials from the Union des syndicats de la région parisienne, the CGT, and the PCF, as well as a variety of left-wing organizations, marched along with some sixty municipal councilors and parliamentary deputies in a parade of some 22,000 people. The police were ready to head off any repeat of the Ridgway riots and immediately cracked down on groups massing anywhere outside the faubourg Saint-Antoine. For the July 14 parade, the PCF plans featured veteran and youth organizations as well as women's groups, who would march alongside representatives of the arrondissements and suburban towns in defense of long-established public rights and territory. *L'Humanité* publicized the plans as a mobilization of the *peuple*. The appeal would be made all the more passionate by the violence and deaths that ended the day (see "The Presence of Undesirables" later in this chapter). The official reaction was to ban further marches along the Bastille-to-Nation route and to push the traditional commemorations even further outside the city in an unprecedented suppression of political and populist uses of public space. The 1954 May Day commemoration was authorized strictly for the Reuilly meadow in the Bois de Vincennes with police cordoning off access to the place de la Nation. After thousands defiantly marched in a *spectacle-manifestation* on July 14, 1954, *L'Humanité* announced triumphantly, "It is impossible to ban July 14. The unwarranted banning of the traditional parade from the Bastille to Nation, and of all patriotic and republican protests on July 14, has not stopped Parisian men and women and the people of the laboring suburbs from celebrating this date, known the world over as the symbol of freedom

PUBLIC SPACE AND CONFRONTATION | 127

FIGURE 11. The 1953 May Day march. © GERALD BLONCOURT/RUE DES ARCHIVES.

and the nation." The police restriction was attributed to the planned visit to Paris by John Foster Dulles, who was blamed for attempting to break down peace negotiations in Geneva on the war in Indochina. The descriptions of the parade, local dances, and fireworks were laced with calls for peace.[42]

The clampdown was unmistakable in the repressive tactics for the ninth commemoration of victory in the Second World War at the place de l'Étoile on May 8, 1954. In the late 1940s victory tributes had been the most populist, emancipatory events in Paris. Instead, every official effort was now made to maintain security and control. The commemorations would be restored in "all their dignity"; "only" the French president, a small number of government ministers, along with veteran representatives would participate. Two lines of police barricades would ensure total control over the area and "access to the plateau of the Arc de Triomphe by the public would be rigorously prohibited."[43] *Paris Match* reported the preparedness of prefect of police, Jean Baylot, who was ready with squadrons of CRS and mobile guard units, radio communication, and air surveillance.[44] The security was so tight even de Gaulle objected. He complained at a press conference, "I will be at the Arc de Triomphe, but I will be alone, without a cortege. . . . I ask that the people be there. I ask that veterans be there."[45] For the most part, de Gaulle and the RPR kept a low profile on the streets of Paris. The capital was not their political fiefdom, and flashy public displays generally brought immediate reaction by the Left. When the RPR did engage in commemorations and rituals, such as, in 1945, the Day of the Flags (March), the Fête de Jeanne d'Arc (May), or the commemoration of Armistice Day, they were oriented around the capital's monumental spaces, especially the Invalides, the place de la Concorde, and the Champs-Élysées. In any case, the 1954 victory ceremony at the place de l'Étoile did take place under an onslaught of police and without the typical crowds. Photographs of the event expose the emptiness of space, the sense of a ceremony inside a stark void. In contrast to the massive populist celebrations that marked these anniversaries in the immediate post-Liberation years, the official 1954 ceremony was distinguished by its attempted closure of the public domain and the banishment of Parisians deemed too dangerous to play a role.

These attempts at repression were undermined by the war in Indochina and the shock of Dien Bien Phu, which reverberated through the city's symbolic sites with particular ferocity. Just a month earlier, in April 1954, a ceremony honoring the defenders of Dien Bien Phu at the place de l'Étoile attended by Prime Minister Joseph Laniel and René Pleven was suddenly broken up by thousands of protestors screaming for their resignations. An attempted getaway by members of the government was foiled when massive crowds surrounded their automobiles. Although the media generally favored facile depictions of ceremonies venerating war veterans, this time *Paris Match* photographers snapped away as police attempted to quell the momentary panic and push back the mobs. By the next month Dien Bien Phu had fallen. Despite every effort to maintain security, the May 8 victory celebration by General de Gaulle at the Arc de Triomphe was interrupted when veterans from the Corps expéditionnaire d'Extrême-Orient, along with extreme right-wing groups incensed by the defeat, attempted to smash through the police barricades. They rallied around a paratrooper draped in a regimental flag. Somehow, some two thousand protesters broke through police lines. The ensuing violence was filmed live by television crews as it moved around the Champs-Élysées. Baylot watched the live broadcast from his command post and used it to direct the crackdown and reestablish public order.[46] The event itself and its convoluted reporting were illustrative of the spatial and visual interaction taking place around civic life and the ways in which it produced meaning. The event was also symptomatic of the political complexities. Complaints about the disturbances provoked by the Dien Bien Phu disaster poured in from Second World War veterans, especially from the 9th Colonial Infantry Division:

> On May 8, 1954, we were celebrating our victory . . . we were the first to battle in this ungrateful land [Indochina], we were heartbroken by this terrible defeat. . . . I saw these men sobbing with their heads in their hands, not with rage, certainly not, but with shame, because for us the word "Honor" will remain in our hearts until death. . . . But why May 8, 1954? Why?[47]

How can we read this explosion of political militancy and violence in the spaces of Paris? The range of disputes and the intensity of the clashes made the public domain a volatile, multilayered expression of reconstruction and cold war tensions. Yet these episodes did not ostensibly threaten the fragile national unity fashioned from Liberation, nor did they reach insurrectionary proportions in the capital until the crisis of decolonization. For all its aggressiveness, the public imaginary of the reconstruction years was constructed as much around patriotic loyalties as it was around rebellion. This sense of national endurance and continuity of political culture was essential in a period riddled with change and crisis. Activism and unruliness were formulated around traditional rituals that regenerated symbolic public spaces and political combat—at times ruthless—without disintegration. This spatial topos was also deeply intertwined with the possibility of thinking about and voicing visionary plans and hopes for the future. Ironically, all actors claimed to represent patriotic sentiment and the new France. National identity and the future lay as much in a mythic concept of the heroic *people* as it did in state apparatus. The rebirth of state hegemony that took place in the late 1940s and early 1950s did not extinguish this myth or the localized cartography that sustained it. Protest marches, demonstrations, and battles with police were understood as legitimate and patriotic appropriations of civic space. Power was in the streets. These diverse locations of French identity and wearing of the national mantle worked to fracture political struggle across a multiplicity of spatial trajectories and topographies, and across a multiplicity of publics. Political and social clashes were carried out with a spatial autonomy and fluidity that belied any privileging of traditional official sites. They took place through thorny negotiation with the forces of repression. The battle for control over these fragmented public spaces and for control over the memory and history of what took place there defined the postwar reconstruction years. Filmed and reported in the press, they were media events that illuminated and exposed social class and populist culture as an intense political theater spread across the capital.

By the mid-1950s the great moment of communist supremacy in the capital was beginning to wane. The aura of revolutionary cachet that had radiated out from the political culture of the northern and eastern arrondissements no longer captured the city's imagination. The evening communist daily *Ce Soir* disappeared in 1953 and *L'Humanité* began to lose readers. The lavish commemoration ceremonies honoring the Second World War and Liberation had become worn spectacles. The streets of the city remained intensely politicized, but these rituals either disappeared or were appropriated by French state officialdom anxious to promote itself in public. For the communists, Khrushchev's 1956 de-Stalinization speech, the troubles in both Poland and Hungary, and then the brutal suppression of the 1956 Hungarian uprising in Budapest all had ramifications on the local level. In a reversal of fortune, angry crowds led by René Pleven, Georges Bidault, and Antoine Pinay marched up the Champs-Élysées in November in a nighttime protest carrying placards against the "Soviet Assassins" and turning left-wing newspapers into torches.[48] The Communist Party headquarters at the rue de Châteaudun crossing in the 9th arrondissement was attacked by angry mobs. This symbolic site of communist power was irreverently renamed the place Kossuth by the municipal council. In protest against this outrage, the PCF moved its headquarters to the place du Colonel Fabien. Even the Fête de l'Humanité was banned by a municipal council vote in 1957. Enraged fellow-travelers and much of the intellectual scene on the Left Bank broke with the party, while the Soviet model held little attraction for the younger generation. By the late 1950s mass consumer culture was also breaking down proletarian and neighborhood identity as well as the communist counternarrative of national unity.

It was too early to draw the curtain down completely on the city's left-wing populism. By the 1959 municipal elections, the PCF could still lay claim to 29 percent of the vote in Paris and even more in the suburbs, where the *ceinture rouge* remained a communist fief. Marches and protest demonstrations continued to resound in the spaces of the capital across the decade. They endlessly reiterated political ritual and the spectacle of insurrectionary allusion, a symbolic taking of the streets. The end of October and the beginning of November 1957 brought a "week of social agitation" with crippling strikes and demonstrations. But the slow, irreversible erosion of communist support was clear. Protests and street demonstrations themselves were turning away from the *ouvriérisme* of reconstruction toward the tragic crisis of decolonization and the Algerian War. The public spaces of the city were pierced by new, far more dangerous political trajectories.

The Housing Crisis

The world of the lower classes in Paris has always had a bad reputation. The historian Daniel Roche, for example, discovered an eighteenth-century public discourse that, although laced with descriptive accuracy, conveyed "an instinctive recoil of horror . . . the intimate life of the people is encamped in a décor devoid of culture."[49] It is interesting to examine the public outcry over housing and slum conditions after the Second World War from this longer historic perspective. There was certainly no doubt about the misery. In 1946 the mean age of buildings in Paris was eighty-three years. The building stock suffered from perennial neglect. Some half a million families lived in *garnis*, cheap boarding rooms fitted with the bare minimum of comfort—a bed, a chair, and a table.[50] The housing crisis formed one of the most important public debates of the late 1940s and 1950s. It preoccupied the entire spectrum of intellectual and political thought and produced a cottage industry of research and surveys. A torrential outpouring of official statistics and inquiries as well as journalistic reporting attempted to capture the extent of the problem and the overwhelming wretchedness. Newspapers, magazines, and intellectual journals featured investigations of the ghastly conditions found in the most blighted districts of the city. Images of these pitiful dwellings were sensationalized in film and on television. Yet the housing crisis was subject to contradictory readings that resulted in drastically different interpretations. As a public debate, it was multifaceted, heavily moralized, and steeped in political and social tensions.

The MRU, assorted other state ministries, and the Seine prefecture all sponsored studies of the city's *îlots insalubres* and the notorious *ceinture rouge*. The reports outdid each other in condemning these areas as social cesspools threatening the nation's survival. In official discourse the *quartiers populaires* and the everyday reality of working-class life were equated with slums. They were spatial and temporal voids between a modern future to be built and an urban past to be destroyed. The dogmatic language and use of statistical research techniques made these official descriptions tantamount to truth. Any authentic public dialog was deemed superfluous. In 1943 an intensive study of the conditions in Paris carried out by the Inspection générale des services techniques de topographie et d'urbanisme estimated that 150,000 people lived in furnished boarding rooms "in a promiscuity that breeds all sorts of bad behavior."[51] A 1946 government report entitled "Struggle against Slums" laid out the consequences of the unhealthy living conditions in the city's mean districts with an early nineteenth-century social reform moralism and fear of crime, vice, and contagion. The working classes appear as a wretched and irrational human phantasmagoria. Their rundown neighborhoods were "places for the propagation of infectious diseases, laboratories for murderous epidemics, agents of moral degradation, destroyers of family life . . . even if there are some proper activities, they are done in isolation and undermined by degenerative factors such as hunger, alcoholism, intellectual instability, and amorality." The degraded housing conditions were threatening French renewal and the birth rate. A vast study of housing in Paris completed in 1948 by the Seine prefecture concluded that "order is practically impossible, to say nothing of hygiene or elemental decency. Family life in this atmosphere of degeneration and promiscuity is lamentable."[52] Proof of unwholesome conditions was provided by the statistical rates of tuberculosis; the age and bleakness of housing; the lack of sanitary facilities, gas, water, and electricity; and population-density rates. It was a perennial litany of simplified, rationally standardized measurements of the urban condition. *Pour la vie*, the review of family studies, gave evidentiary confirmation that in buildings with a lack of these comforts and insufficiency of space,

> health was compromised, mothers were exhausted, any new birth is considered a catastrophe. . . . When young married couples have to live with parents or with foreign persons, who doesn't know instances of separation and disunion? And this doesn't even speak of promiscuity, when people live on top of one another in minuscule apartments (for example Paris, the City of Light) and the dramas provoked by these situations. . . . We must absolutely furnish families an indispensable framework for their normal development; it is a vital issue for the country.[53]

In a 1953 *enquête sociologique* in the district of Pantin along the canal de l'Ourcq northeast of the city, the Ministère de l'Équipement commissioned photographic documentation as evidence of conditions. The images are portraits of urban dystopia. Ruined buildings boarded up, shacks pieced together with abandoned materials, and pools of putrid water depict a state of savagery. Young families and children caught in the camera lens amid jerryrigged electrical wiring, dripping water pipes, exposed sewers, rotting beams and plaster, and windowless shacks on the verge of collapse summon up images of the worst nineteenth-century slums.[54] These were scenes out of Zola's novels. But the families being photographed are without agency. They are robbed of their status as *le peuple*. They are incapable of maintaining a proper quality of life. They are elements of material wretchedness, part of a despicable decor to be cleared out.

Despite the appalling conditions, government authorities actually did not have any real urban planning or housing policy. Between 1948 and 1952 the local Office public des habitations à loyer modéré (public housing office, or HLM) received 85,000 applications for housing. It was able to fill only a few thousand of the requests and predicted the same meager availability for 1953 and 1954, when the number of applications would continue to flood in. In the face of desperate need, a total of only 12,000 lodgings were constructed in Paris between 1944 and 1954, according to official statistics. Around 40,000 were built in the Seine department outside Paris.[55] Year after year public financing for housing was either blocked or reduced still further. In the meantime, the MRU focused on ultramodern housing archetypes by architectural luminaries that were, for all practical purposes, relegated to either experimental sites or small public-housing projects around the capital. The French state essentially followed a laissez-faire course, which left the housing market to the vagaries of the established construction industry and private real-estate interests. The decision by the MRU chief, Eugène Claudius-Petit, to continue rent control in Paris through legislation in 1948 was justified by the anxiety over maintaining order and "social peace." But it seemed destined to set ever more solidly in place the vicious circle deterring any property investment in the capital. Building owners had little reason to repair existing housing stock, which fell further into decay. By the early 1950s the housing situation had become a full-blown, well-publicized national emergency, one that was particularly severe in the Paris suburbs.[56]

Although the grid of official interpretation privileged statistical analysis, infectious disease and immorality (and then offered utopian solutions to this crisis), those in left-wing discourse narrated and visualized the experience of human suffering. Shelter for working-class families meant wretched rooming houses, makeshift settlements, and *bidonvilles* (shantytowns). Desperate squatters took over vacant apartments and bombed-out houses, and then ended up in collisions with police. High densities and shocking infant mortality rates destroyed any semblance of family stability. Tubercular parents were forced to spend months in sanatoria. The housing crisis was caused by slumlords who raised rents to exorbitant levels for pathetic hovels and regularly threw families out into the street if they were unable to pay. In the shoddy rooming houses that functioned as homes for thousands, families were forced to split up because owners refused to accept children or because the sordid rooms had no heat or even the means "to heat a baby's bottle."[57] In the press, the spotlight was on life stories about identifiable disadvantaged households and individuals. The measurement of the housing crisis was particularistic, contextually situated, personal. "Who offers lodging," the self-help community at Montreuil asked, "to the family with five children, whose father was a war prisoner and has struggled for seven years to find a place to live and is still in the two small rooms where the air streams up from underneath the cracked, bare flooring, where the stairwell barely supports anyone attempting to climb it but the rats?" "What do you say," it continued, "to a worker who, after two months of unemployment, is thrown out of his wooden shed because he hasn't paid his rent and his landlord profits from the situation by pointing to the clause that allows him to demand 75,000 francs for breaking the contract?"[58] There are few statistics in this discourse. The tragic descriptions and narratives about the truth of the housing crisis stretched across the 1940s and 1950s in emotional, heartbreaking portrayals that resonated with the general public and illuminated a solid working people and their struggle with misery. In this discourse the *peuple* are victims, but they are not without power. They maintain their Rousseauian goodness and their courage in the face of misfortune. They have the capacity to defend their interests and act on their own behalf.

In general, the Left was suspicious of the state's revolutionary housing schemes as utopian fantasy and a pretext for inaction. The immediate need for decent housing set them against the grand-scale designs for the future city that were pouring out of the MRU. Reacting against the dazzling Première Exposition de la Reconstruction organized by the MRU in late 1945, *Syndicalisme* decried "the refined luxuries, the prodigious displays of sumptuousness, the superficial modernism without any consideration of the extremely urgent needs of slum dwellers and workers without decent homes." In setting out an agenda for the next exposition, "we would like to see a very important special section reserved to modest homes that should nevertheless be outfitted with practical comforts."[59] *La Vie ouvrière* went further in its critique of the Exposition: "We can't go astray with these unreal utopian solutions. Not taking into account the financial and material resources of our country, ignoring the limits the current regime puts on solving the housing problem is to perhaps increase desires ... and deceive public opinion."[60] In September of the same year *La Vie ouvrière* contemptuously exposed construction priorities in the city. Near the gare de Courbevoie, the luxurious "American" Prado bistro and bar was undergoing complete renovation for tap and swing dancing and "*zazous* frolicking." There was no glass for windowpanes or materials to rebuild homes, but the Prado was installing an enormous glass facade that looked out onto the street. The Seine prefecture had capped the budget for reconstruction work, but thousands of francs were being poured into luxury makeovers: "The moral: the shameless waste of building materials, black-market trafficking and the employment of workers 'unavailable' for the homeless. The disaster victims of Courbevoie demand an explanation."[61] Lowering construction costs through prefabrication, refurbishing buildings damaged by bombardments, making use of existing housing stock through renovation, requisitioning private flats and *chambres de bonne*, and supporting self-help housing projects were all among the practical solutions offered by the Left as an alternative to the private housing market or the official dreamscape of modernist prototypes.

The communists in particular launched a dramatic attack against the shameful living conditions the working classes were forced to endure. So critical was this issue that an analysis of elections during the early 1950s found a direct correlation between dissatisfaction with housing and Communist Party votes.[62] During the 1952 municipal elections, the PCF compared the Pleven government's hefty military financing of the "American war" in Korea and the war in Indochina to its paltry investments in housing. Campaign advertising jabbed directly at the rank and file's sorest wound: "Badly Housed, without Housing at All! Make the municipal elections an immense protest by the real victims of this crisis!"[63] From their seats on the Paris municipal council the PCF railed against the state's denial of sufficient funding for new public-housing projects. The communist Maurice Collin reminded his colleagues of

Eugène Claudius-Petit's caustic remark that "'France is not a milk cow with an inexhaustible udder.' In other words," he translated, "if you want a place to live, count on yourselves." If France could not solve its housing problem, it would lead to catastrophe. Collin needled the Seine prefecture to study the low-cost housing projects being completed by communist municipalities at Aubervilliers and Argenteuil.[64]

The housing crisis was exploited very successfully by the PCF, especially after the party's expulsion from government in 1947 and return to opposition. In 1951 the raconteur and novelist Jean-Pierre Chabrol began a series for *L'Humanité* entitled "Paris Stories" that mounted to a *flânerie* by taxi through the city to explore the social landscape. It employed the humanist, life-story technique typical of the counternarrative to state rationalist discourse. In one episode, the archetypal Parisian concierge leads the reader into a poor neighborhood in the city's northern outskirts: "There are neighborhoods in Paris where the silence must thwart the sleep of Monsieur Claudius-Petit, that minister of ruins and grand constructor of *amerilôques* chateaux." Concierge Madame Douillard is listening to the entreaties of a man at the door asking for a place to live:

> He says his prayers but knows he hasn't a chance; ". . . even a small room? An attic? An old office even, I'll take anything." He stops himself from yelling, "I'm not a beggar. I work hard, honestly. I have a wife and children. . . ." "You are the tenth one since the beginning of the week," Madame Douillard answers his pleas.

But she knows how hard life is in this poor neighborhood;

> she senses it around her . . . the growing anger against the rising costs, the misery, the preparation for war. She has already collected one hundred and twenty signatures in the little notebook she has been given in the petition drive for the Pact of Five. It's already full! "Even if people say that the ministers have invited Adenauer, the head of the Nazis, to Paris, only a few years after the Liberation. It's not possible!"[65]

Throughout the winter months of 1953, *L'Humanité* featured an ongoing series of articles on housing and slum conditions in Paris. Interviews with families barely surviving in sordid hovels were followed by scathing criticism of the

Seine prefecture. The housing crisis was blamed on the Americans and the cold war, which siphoned off funds needed to build homes. In the miserably cold winter of January 1953, a group of shanties illegally sitting on land over an ancient mushroom cavern in Nanterre disappeared into a black abyss of vapors. When asked why they were living there, the inhabitants responded, "We knew it was risky, but at least it was a roof over our heads!" "US Go Home!" the article ended; "We want to build for the French, not for the occupiers! More money for houses, not for guns."[66]

In retaliation against the PCF's withering criticism, the prefect of the Seine defended the government's record by arguing that the housing crisis could be solved if monies didn't have to be poured into the French defense budget to counteract international communism. The crisis was brought on by people's refusal to spend more of their salary on where they lived. It was caused by strikes in the construction industry and by architects.[67] Responding to the government's cold-war campaign warning against a "French Soviet republic," the well-known socialist mayor of Sceaux, Édouard Depreux, wrote in the newspaper *L'Avenir de la banlieue de Paris* that

> these anticommunist advertising slogans have little influence on families living in cellars, attics, slums, on young families waiting in vain for six or seven years for housing, on dozens of thousands of workers condemned to a mediocre standard of living. Freedom, in the name of which they should mobilize against dictatorship and totalitarianism . . . has little meaning to them. To be free requires having a minimum of well-being and comfort.[68]

As evidence of the mounting public pressure, in 1953 the MRU officially changed its name to the Ministère de la reconstruction et du logement (ministry of reconstruction and housing, or MRL). Yet little changed beyond the symbolic. Writing in an article entitled "Our Houses and Our Cities" in a special issue of *Esprit*, the sociologist Paul-Henry Chombart de Lauwe reproached this

> "happy country," France, which displays the splendors of Paris for tourists. . . . But leprous neighborhoods, stinking alleyways, and shantytowns are judiciously hidden away because of the taboo about housing. Hundreds of thousands of families live in hell in cheap hotel rooms, in sheet-

metal huts, in one-room hovels. And at the same time, there are men of goodwill, truly sincere, who say that the problem of housing is not that bad, that it will pass in two or three years.[69]

Public outrage over the tragic plight of the homeless in Paris was finally galvanized by what one author has called Abbé Pierre's agitprop campaign.[70] The Catholic priest Henri de Groués, known by his Resistance pseudonym Abbé Pierre, worked among the vagrants and squatters in the notorious *zone* surrounding the city. Groués joined the Resistance and eventually worked for the legendary Vercors *maquis*. Captured and imprisoned by the enemy, he escaped, crossed the Pyrenees into Spain, and finally reached Algiers. In 1946 he was elected to the National Assembly on the Christian Democratic Mouvement républicain populaire (MRP) ticket and adroitly used his political connections to fund his community projects. His Emmaüs self-help community grew from the youth hostel he established in 1947 in an old house in Neuilly-Plaisance, in the suburbs east of Paris. Its "pilgrims" quickly shifted from weekend and overnight backpackers to homeless vagrants and families desperate for shelter. The roots of Emmaüs lay in the notions of Christian humanism and social welfare in which much of centrist political ideology was absorbed at the war's end. By 1954 more than a hundred families lived at Emmaüs in a series of self-constructed apartments and dwellings made from prefabricated lumber frames set on cement foundations with tin roofs. They were paid for with the meager proceeds derived from ragpicking and recycling programs organized on a community-wide basis. The Emmaüs community was built illegally, without the required MRU construction permits, dependent for protection on Abbé Pierre's celebrity and influence.[71] Offshoots of Emmaüs were established at suburban Neuilly-sur-Marne, at Pontault-Combault, and at Plessis-Trévise. The workers in and around his colonies were invariably communists or sympathizers who participated in such rituals as the Fête de l'Humanité and the annual May Day procession from the place de la Bastille to the place de la République. To display his solidarity with them, Abbé Pierre himself regularly appeared in the parades and also took part in demonstrations denouncing the Marshall Plan, NATO, and Coca-Cola.

In what became a foundational allegory for the housing movement, during the night of January 6–7, 1954, just after the French Chamber of Deputies had refused to allocate funds for emergency shelters for the poor, a baby died of cold in the abandoned shell of a city bus that served as his family's home in Neuilly-Plaisance. The commercial media was instrumental in exposing this tale of the excluded, which normally would have gone unseen and unnoticed. It is an account of human misfortune meant to be emotional in content. The incident was not an anomaly. Seventeen Parisians were found frozen to death in one frigid night that winter. Then, in early February 1954, the worst cold wave in memory struck the city. Over the course of a week, the severe weather claimed the lives of some one hundred Parisians, among them infants and elderly trapped in ramshackle unheated tenements. In another emblematic account, the police found a woman sprawled dead on the boulevard de Sébastopol, an eviction notice from her landlord clutched in her fist. The morgue was crammed with the frozen bodies of homeless *clochards*, and the hospitals were filled with the sick and shivering.

Incensed by the tragedies, Abbé Pierre launched a public campaign on behalf of the homeless and poor. He wrote an open letter to the minister of construction and housing, Maurice Lemaire, inviting him to the funeral of the poor dead infant who came to symbolize the human tragedy of the housing crisis. He wrote to *Le Figaro* and on February 1 appealed to Parisians, via a broadcast on Radio Luxembourg, to assemble each night at the place du Panthéon in a great rescue campaign.[72] Thousands of people in their automobiles showed up ready to hunt the city for the homeless freezing on the streets. Abbé Pierre demanded the opening of shelters and funding for emergency housing. The radio, daily newspapers, and magazines took up his call with nonstop features on the housing problem, the human drama of the slums, and the misery of the homeless. *Les Actualités françaises* featured "A Night with Abbé Pierre" in local movie theaters. The visual narrative begins with images of bitter cold and the frozen Seine, with homeless families lying in the streets and sitting over grates for heat. The scenes are followed by shots of Abbé Pierre visiting the destitute and of his claptrap *cité d'urgence*, made up of sheds, old trailers, and pieced-together huts. The last sequence is almost pure social sponsorship, with Abbé Pierre at the Panthéon asking for help and people answering his call, contributing blankets and clothing.[73]

A tireless promoter, Abbé Pierre spoke from church pulpits, in the streets and bistros, over the radio, during theater intermissions, even in nightclubs. He wangled a spot on the radio quiz show *Double or Nothing*, breezed through a series of questions on international affairs, and won 300,000 francs. He climbed the stage at the Gaumont Palace and, with a spotlight silhouetting his profile against the white screen, confronted an audience of thousands waiting to hear his appeal. The images of Abbé Pierre and his self-help community electrified public opinion. Through the mass media and through television broadcasts and films produced about Abbé Pierre beginning in 1954 and continuing for some years after, the public essentially consumed what Roland Barthes called a bright display of Christian charity. It collectively gazed "at the shop-window of saintliness" and responded to the ideal of good works.[74] Abbé Pierre's radio broadcasts from Neuilly-Plaisance initiated an "insurrection of kindness" that drew reporters from newspapers and national magazines such as *Paris Match* and *Elle* intent on doing photo spreads on the community of ragpickers who had pricked the national conscience. In February 1954 *Paris Match* published exposés that included Grouès's life story and a panoply of photographs on homelessness and his good works in the capital. Many of them displayed families finally finding a roof over their heads: "Having become in one night Star no. 1 of film, radio, music hall and television, this shock-priest leads his monstrous parade with the faith and marvelous candor of Saint Francis."[75] The grotesque images of the dispossessed exposed the contradictions of the *trente glorieuses*, placed the housing crisis front and center on the public stage, and succeeded in completely subverting official discourse.

The French responded to all these mediatized entreaties with unprecedented compassion and generosity. The plight of the homeless exploded into broad daylight, and public opinion was mobilized. Within two weeks of his call of February 1 on Radio Luxembourg, more than one billion francs poured into Abbé Pierre's coffers. Local aid committees were organized. The Hotel Rochester on the tony rue de la Boétie near the Champs-Élysées offered space for a drop-off center for blankets and coats. The area was jammed with people bringing donations. A tent was set up on the rue de la Montagne Saint-Geneviève for collecting and distributing sleeping bags to the dispossessed. Money, clothes, hotel rooms, and office and storage space were donated. Marches and mass meetings were staged. The press was flooded with reports on the appalling state of French housing. *Le Monde* related the details of the suicide of a young mother who killed herself so that her family would have more room in their thirty-square-foot hovel.[76] Caught up in the campaign, Métro supervisors converted three unused stations into a dormitory for the destitute, while the French railways reopened a closed wing of the gare d'Orsay as a storage depot for donated supplies. Neighborhood

FIGURE 12. Demonstrators gather in front of the Hôtel de Ville to march in support of Abbé Pierre's housing campaign. Photograph by Stephanie Tavoularis, December 23, 1954. © BETTMANN/CORBIS.

city halls were opened to welcome the homeless at night. Day after day the popular press showcased feature articles on the community outpouring.

The result of all this media coverage was the emergence of the marginalized and homeless from the hidden recesses, the otherness, of the city's spaces. Invisibility was replaced by a moving forward onto the public stage in a spectacle of poverty. Press depictions of the *compagnons* eking out an existence at Emmaüs followed the poetic, sentimental images of the working poor taking up responsibility for their condition and sharing the burden of reconstruction. The illumination of the destitute made clear that they were neither drunks nor vagrants, but good French working families—the virtuous poor. Their moral fiber was upright, and they were capable of a transformative posture, of affecting the construction of the urban realm. The short 1954 promotional film on Abbé Pierre and Emmaüs focused on the power of celebrity and its political entitlement, with politicians and housing officials trekking out to Neuilly-Plaisance in deference to the self-help colony, where

FIGURE 13. Tent city for the homeless erected along the Seine River by Abbé Pierre. Photograph by René Henry, October 1, 1955. © BETTMANN/CORBIS.

workers handed out copies of the issue of *Paris Match* featuring Abbé Pierre. The film laid bare the poverty that haunted the prosperity of the *trente glorieuses* with the poignancy and dramatic naturalism that marked the visual perspective of these years. Emmaüs is presented as a world that taps into the innate fraternity and camaraderie found among the *peuple*. The community of workers builds a shelter as a celebration of collective fraternity. It is a *geste d'humanité* celebrated with a song and the ceremonial handing over of the keys to a waiting family, who open the door to their new home.[77]

More than just good works, this self-help housing movement amounted to a radical urbanism. It demonstrated passion and instrumentality at a localized, self-directed level. The space of exclusion was transformed into a space of freedom, and the poor were set in motion to reimagine and fashion their urban realm. The margins of the city become a magical arena of urbanistic design. Hundreds of barrel-shaped barracks (dubbed "igloos") were set up

FIGURE 14. Abbé Pierre helping to install a low-income housing prototype designed by Jean Prouvé along the Seine near the Alexandre III Bridge, February 20, 1956. © RUE DES ARCHIVES/AGIP.

at Noisy-le-Grand modeled after emergency shelters designed in 1945. In an embarrassing slap at the sluggish MRU bureaucracy, under Abbé Pierre's direction the ragpicker-builders designed and built a complete model for an efficiency home in six weeks. With the help of a public loan, they adopted the avant-garde housing blueprints of the architect Jean Prouvé for an emergency shelter development at Plessis-Trévise that was completed in two months.[78] In a signal of their populist political authority, in August 1955 Abbé Pierre and his crew of ragpickers were filmed by film and television crews setting up a *cité d'urgence* of tent shelters in the center of Paris, amid the traffic on the pont Sully and the quai Henri IV. The images spotlight a family setting up house inside one of the shelters, with the good wife and mother tending to her family and the children tucked contentedly in bed.[79]

Paris Match continued its coverage of the housing drama with a 1954 follow-up report on the poor couple who had lost their infant to the cold. The narrative construction exudes populist poetic humanism. Paul and Lucette had met at a July 14 *bal populaire* at Boulogne-Billancourt. He worked at the Renault factory; she was a laundress. They had been thrown out of their two-room apartment by an unscrupulous landlord. Paul first heard of Abbé Pierre at the factory, and the family found shelter in the converted bus at the Emmaüs community at Neuilly-Plaisance. By mustering all their pitiful resources, Paul was able to buy the motorbike he needed to commute to the Renault factory. But tragedy struck the young family with the death of their infant, Marc-Petit, on that cold January night in 1954. And Lemaire did indeed attend the funeral for the baby. He walked solemnly behind the horse-drawn funeral carriage along with Abbé Pierre and his *compagnons* in civic atonement for the tragedy. The sad procession wound through a miserable landscape of hovels gathered below the mammoth gas tanks of the cité des Coquelicots at Neuilly-Plaisance. But at the narrative's conclusion, after terrible heartbreak, Paul and Lucette receive the keys to one of the first homes in the emergency-housing village of Plessis-Trévis: three rooms, a kitchen, a bathroom, and a garden. "Thanks to Abbé Pierre," the *Paris Match* article concludes, "the baby coming in the spring will be born in a real home."[80]

The end of Claudius-Petit's tenure as reconstruction minister in 1953 is usually seen by scholars as the key moment in the struggle for housing. In this interpretation, state officialdom instinctively responded to the mounting crisis and initiated a comprehensive policy of construction. However, in retrospect it is clear that although 1953–54 was indeed the turning point, Abbé Pierre's campaign was the key impetus for change. People from a variety of backgrounds joined together in common cause to create a highly mediatized counterpublic sphere. Under increasing pressure, the government launched construction of thousands of emergency housing units in the *zone verte* (as the *zone* was then called) just outside the city limits. The marginal, forgotten spaces of Paris emerged into public view and claimed a right to social justice. The French parliament voted to subsidize low-cost housing to the tune of hundreds of thousands of francs, and it inaugurated a series of measures aimed at expanding the stock of modest housing options: the reinstitution of the wartime 1 percent charge on employers to finance lodging for their workers; a design competition, known as Opération Million, for durable, low-cost family homes; the LOGECO program to stimulate the private construction of reasonably priced residences; and the Plan Courant, which offered generous loans (up to 80 percent of cost) for would-be homeowners. The winner of the Opération Million competition, the architect Georges Candilis, conferred with Abbé Pierre in the design and construction of a hundred buildings for the poor at Bobigny, Blanc-Mesnil, and other communes around Paris. The February 7, 1953, "Lafay Law" permitted the construction of residential estates in the *zone* through a new system of expropriation. The measure provided the first hope of relief from the housing crisis. In response, in December 1953 and January 1954 the municipal council approved a construction program for 4000 housing units on seven different sectors of the *zone*. This shift in government housing policy was triggered by the social tensions evident on the streets of Paris. It was a reaction to passionate public protest and to the magical urbanism carried out in the fragmented, marginalized spaces of the city. The large-scale public-housing projects eventually put into place from the mid-1950s on were meant to quell this social conflict and to counteract the enormous influence of the communists and of Abbé Pierre, whose campaigns on behalf of the working classes received overwhelming support.

The Presence of Undesirables

In 1949 *Le Parisien libéré* reported on the general attitude toward the growing number of North Africans on the streets of Paris: "'They are liars, thieves, lazy' ... this, without much interest in the fact that Moroccans are outstanding workers in the most laborious jobs (in foundries for example), that the quasi-totality of Tunisians in Paris live a perfectly normal life, that 30,000 Algerians who have long lived in the capital have regular and honorable employment." Having said this, the newspaper went on to chronicle the dolorous conditions that the 1,500 to 2,000 new arrivals each month found in ""verminous slums" such as La Goutte d'Or, "in hovels in Gennevilliers, Argenteuil or Boulogne-Billancourt where boards and pieces of carton take the place of windows, where they hang out and are squeezed into the most lamentable conditions, where a pair of shoes is a luxury for those who dreamt only a month before of a brilliant return to their country, their fortune having been made." The paper estimated that some 80,000 to 90,000 North Africans lived in these conditions—if they weren't homeless, living on the street, hounded by constant police surveillance.⁸¹ Some indication of the perceived threat Arabs posed to the city's public life can be gleaned from a 1948 portrayal from the politically conservative newspaper *L'Aurore*, which along with the *L'Époque* reported frequently on the new peril:

> North Africans are, in Paris, specialists and record holders of the nighttime attack. More precisely, the Arab is the thief who awaits a late passerby on the corner of the street, attacks him, and steals his watch. The reality of the Arabs swarming Paris is that this city is today one of the least safe in the world between sundown and sunset. Of the 105,000 North Africans in the Paris region, 80,000 are unemployed. They are lodged in atrocious boarding houses on the rue de la Charbonnière or in Grenelle with ten other of their fellow religious. They are tubercular and syphilitic.⁸²

The presence on the streets and in cafés and bars of groups of Muslim Arab men provoked a mix of exotic images and dread: "The provincial or tourist who wanders the streets at certain hours between La Chapelle and the place Clichy registers a picturesque image in the presence of more and more North Africans, gathered in groups on the sidewalks of the boulevards or regularly sitting in the establishments of Montmartre." And "the streets of Paris seem to be less safe than the exterior boulevards in 1900!"⁸³

One reason for this alarmist discourse was that the population of North Africans in the Seine department had jumped, according to official statistics, from around 45,000 before the war to over 100,000, especially after the borders were opened to Algerian immigration with the September 20, 1947, law establishing "continuity" between France and the department of Algeria. However, including the underground floating population, estimates of the number of North African immigrants in the city and suburbs were much higher by the mid-1950s. They were the ultimate outsiders, excluded from the public sphere and the spaces of public life, perceived only as a menace. The vast majority were Algerian men, with a much smaller number of Tunisians and Moroccans—all looking for work in the city's industries. The newcomers arrived in the capital with high hopes but often completely without resources, falling rapidly into the worst of conditions. A study by the Institut national d'études démographiques (INED) estimated that some 60,000 North Africans—60 percent of their official numbers in Paris—remained unemployed.⁸⁴ Those who did find work most often labored in heavy industry and in construction, where their jobs were low paid, temporary, and seasonal. Jean-Pierre Chabrol's 1953 "Paris Stories" series for *L'Humanité* explores the obscure, clandestine places of these undesirables. Chabrol arrives in the 2nd arrondissement on the rue Grénéta near Réamur-Sébastopol, where he describes the "despicable lairs, for the price of gold, where a third of Algerian workers attempt to live with their families. We already know about the shameful boxes, without windows, without furniture or beds, constructed for them like cages under cramped stairways, and for which they pay three to six thousand francs a month." The Sunday of his visit, the water in the building is turned off and the poor renters are left to beg for water in the streets.[85] The Algerian War (1954–62) massively increased the number of exiles and added large numbers of women and children who were escaping the crisis. By the late 1950s official estimates put the number of cheap rooming houses, cafés, bars, and assorted establishments exclusively serving the North African population in Paris at well over two thousand.[86]

The settlers were mainly clustered in the fleabag hotels, boarding houses, hostels, and streets of La Chapelle and La Gotte d'Or in the 18th arrondissement, around La Villette in the 19th and 20th arrondissements, and around the cité Jeanne d'Arc in the 13th arrondissement. Thousands found work and lodging in the inner ring of northern suburbs at Clichy, Levallois, Gennevilliers, Aubervilliers, and Saint-Denis. As early as in 1945, the geographer Jean Gravier (who would make his career cataloguing the dreadful conditions in Paris) described the tenements in places such as Saint-Denis as "a sordid concentration camp for immigrants."[87] West of Paris they gathered in the slums of Puteaux and Nanterre and around Boulogne-Billancourt. They moved outward from the 13th arrondissement into the suburbs of Vitry and Choisy-le-Roi. Although the inhabitants appeared to be nomadic, their migration generally followed a traditional pattern. Immigrant settler communities acted as a buffer. Newcomers sought out contacts from their old neighborhoods in Algeria who might provide lodging, aid in finding work, and a *communauté de douar* (village community). The state's Service des affaires musulmanes, the Seine prefecture, and the prefecture of police issued a series of official reports aimed at surveying and controlling disruptive immigrant populations. Identifying their place of origin and religion was the framework for the construction of discrete social and ethnic characteristics. For example, according to the "Étude de la population nord-africaine à Paris et dans le département de la Seine,"[88] completed by the prefecture of police in 1955, nearly all of the four thousand Algerians in the northern district of La Villette were Kabyles from the capital city of Algiers and neighboring Tizi-Ouzou. They found work in the Lebaudy and François refineries or in La Villette's foundries and metallurgical works. They congregated in the some 150 Algerian bars, cafés, and markets in the neighborhood, establishments never frequented by the local working-class population. The report's findings thus reinforced the boundary between native Parisians and the new immigrants. In both La Goutte d'Or on the Right Bank (home to nearly four thousand North Africans) and the slums of the 13th arrondissement on the Left Bank (another three thousand), immigrants were mainly from the cities of Tizi-Ouzou and from Bougie (Béjaïa). In the 13th arrondissement, they gathered in the cafés on the rue Nationale and the rue du Château-des-Rentiers. In the suburbs, the situation was much worse. Police estimated that some four thousand migrants in Gennevelliers were crowded into sordid shelters, shacks, and cellars, much of which was clandestine. The *bidonville* of La Plaine in Nanterre was infamous. There, over eight thousand North Africans found refuge in assorted claptrap housing, blockhouses, and squatter camps on rotting wastelands. Sanitary conditions were abominable. Indeed, the term *bidonville* itself was first used in the 1950s during the French protectorate in Morocco to describe poor neighborhoods where the roofs of makeshift housing were cut out of metallic fuel containers or *bidons*. It then came into general use to depict *indigènes algériens* who were blamed for the physical decline of metropolitan areas. In the series "Capitals of Suffering" (1957), the *L'Humanité* reporter Raymond Lavigne descended into the abyss of the Nanterre *bidonville* to find life stories of utter misery and unremitting danger. Djemila's broken-down wooden hut went up in flames with his wife and children inside. They were saved, only to find themselves living in a condemned basement so humid the children were sent to a sanatorium, while his wife awaited the birth of a fifth child. The interviews are a litany of sorrows.[89]

Early on, the prefect Roger Verlomme acknowledged the growing humanitarian crisis in Paris and outlined the government's efforts to alleviate it. Public shelters or *foyers* reserved for North Africans were opened in Batignolles and Malesherbes in the 17th arrondissement, in Gennevilliers, and in Nanterre. By the mid-1950s there were five in Paris and thirty-four in the suburbs. A North African dispensary was created at the Franco-Musulman Hospital in Bobigny. Soup kitchens were pressed into service. But whether it was a question of public aid or the reality of their social marginalization, what characterized the condition of North African immigrants was spatial segregation. They remained in their own wards, their own bars and cafés, strictly divided from the normal life of the neighborhood they inhabited. In the long, passionate public debate over housing conditions in Paris, only rarely were North African immigrants included among the dispossessed. In what was essentially an extension of the colonial regime, North African immigrants labored to reconstruct France without taking any part in the country's life. In *Les Deux bouts*, the novelist Henri Calet visits an Algerian construction worker named Ahmed Brahimi, a veteran of Leclerc's famous 2nd French Armored Division who took part in the 1944 Normandy landing. Calet follows him on his daily commute to the chic district around the place de l'Étoile, where he labors on a construction project for luxury apartments costing over two million francs each. "What is curious about Ahmed," Calet dryly remarks, "is that although he builds houses with his own hands, he has been more or less homeless since he came to France." For two months after his arrival in Paris in 1952, Ahmed passed his nights going from one bistro to another, and then wandered the streets until work started in the morning. Since "nearly all the hotel owners refuse to rent to Muslims . . . even if they are well dressed," he finally found one room to share with ten other Algerian immigrants.[90]

Government reports accounted for these conditions by explaining that Algerians were generally from rural villages and little prepared for life in the modern spaces of the capital, a convenient fiction (despite the data showing that most were from Algiers, Tizi-Ouzou, and Bougie) that hid the underlying official strategy of racial containment and exclusion. According to the 1955 police report, the influence of Islam furthered the chasm, as did the dense living circumstances of the immigrant population: "It appears almost impossible for the moment to imagine the assimilation of North Africans into a purely secular [*laïque*] society."[91] In a continuation of fears about hygiene and contagion in the *bidonvilles*, North Africans were believed to carry deadly diseases, especially tuberculosis. They remained excluded in Paris, speaking Arabic, wearing traditional clothing, retaining Islamic cultural practices and their own sense of the public sphere. The most important public gathering places for Algerians were the neighborhoods of La Chapelle and La Goutte d'Or, especially the triangle formed by the rue de la Charbonnière, the rue de Chartres and the boulevard de la Chapelle. This was the heart of the "Parisian Medina," the Trois Chats, as they were known. It was dominated by the open-air Charbonnière market, by the network of Arab bars and cafés, and the social life of the street. In his *Paris insolite*, Jean-Paul Clébert described the atmosphere in 1952:

> You know you are entering the Arab bistros of La Goutte d'Or and La Chapelle by the odor of kef. The men sit silently smoking on benches along walls of cracking plaster, steadily sipping water or tea in between their cigarettes, not even bothering to crumble their pastille or crush the tobacco in their pockets that they roll by pinching, and then put carefully on the table, spreading it out on three pieces of Job Noir cigarette paper.[92]

The "oriental market, a sort of souk," as it was referred to in the press,[93] attracted thousands of North Africans from throughout the metropolitan region, especially on weekends, drawn by its informal economy of cheap clothing, food, and wares. It was an illicit space, one of the centers of the black-market trade, with everything from American military stockpiles to goods stolen throughout the region to drug traffickers. For years after the war, the market was tacitly ignored by the authorities. Around it were assembled some 72 cheap hotels and 127 cafés, most of them run by immigrants from Tizi-Ouzou and Bougie and serving the local immigrant population. The hotel-café was the public arena of ethnic life and sociability as well as an expression of cultural heritage. Much as in nineteenth-century Paris, it acted as a transformative, mnemonic site: a passage between private and public life, between the collective practices of the village and the modern city. With their phonograph music, singing, and dancing, the Arab cafés of the rue Nationale, for example, "had the allure of *guinguettes*," according to Jean-Paul Clébert.[94] Young men spilled out into the streets around their favorite haunts in an expanding circle of public sociability. Sundays were the only times immigrant workers had to venture out from work into the city. Like other Parisians, they strolled the boulevards, met in cafés, and went to soccer matches, bicycle races, and films, especially Egyptian films near the gare de l'Est. As North Africans came increasingly to dominate neighborhood public life in places such as La Goutte d'Or, the former residents fled the area. The animosity between North African and Parisians was mutual. In what the 1955 police surveillance report referred to as a "vicious circle,"

FIGURE 15. North Africans gathered in front of La Ville d'Oran Hotel, where furnished rooms were rented to immigrants, April 1950. © KEYSTONE-FRANCE.

their presence on the landscape provoked fear and anxiety—to which their reaction was defiance and further isolation.[95]

All North Africans (including Moroccans and Tunisians) were considered guilty by association and were under constant suspicion of terrorism and collusion with the revolutionary Front de libération nationale (FLN). Police surveillance, raids, and roundups were the norm given the overt intolerance and bigotry spurred on by daily newspapers and xenophobic fears of criminality and foreignness. The Service des affaires indigènes nord-africaines on the rue Lecomte scrutinized every aspect of North African life in the capital. The function of certain spaces in the metropolis is to isolate and make invisible. La Goutte d'Or became this kind of acknowledged heterotopic territory. The paramilitary attack against it was a mark of the deepening crisis of decolonization. In December 1947 police agents, accompanied by journalists, staged a *grande rafle* (raid) at La Goutte d'Or, surrounding the neighborhood and taking into custody some one hundred individuals who were carted off to police headquarters on the quai des Orfèvres. The roundups of suspicious Algerians continued through the winter.[96] The 1955 police report acknowledged 4,405

Algerians arrested in 1952, then 5,143 arrested in 1953, and 5,471 arrested in 1954. The increase signaled the worsening of relations. Algerians constituted 25 percent of those arrested for murder, 35 percent of those apprehended for violent behavior, 54 percent of those arrested for violent theft, 54 percent of those arrested for armed robbery in public, 52 percent of those arrested for shooting, and 60 percent of those arrested for carrying weapons.[97] In early August 1955 the Fête de l'Aïd El Kébir brought another round of violence at La Goutte d'Or. Here the volatile character of *la fête* was stripped of sentiment and interpreted instead as an assault, an attack against the French nation itself by fanatic mobs. Police intervention in the market on the rue de la Charbonnière was met with attacks by some 1,500 to 2,000 protestors. Hundreds of young Algerians rampaged through the neighborhood, attacking passersby, damaging stores, and throwing bricks at automobiles. Police and the Paris prefecture retaliated by permanently closing down the infamous black-market bazaar and cordoning off the neighborhood to all but locals with identity papers for the next week.

The escalating crisis in Algeria made the sense of the imminent threat North African immigrants posed to the city's public domain explosive. The mounting calls for Algerian independence or separatism were treated as despicable treachery. The traditional Algerian People's Party was outlawed. To take its place, Messali Hadj's radical Mouvement pour le triomphe des libertés démocratiques (movement for the victory of democratic freedoms, or MTLD) opened its headquarters on the boulevard Saint-Michel. As the Algerian nationalist movement began to appropriate the capital's symbolic sites of protest, the state's repressive apparatus was intensified. The appearance of Arab and Muslim delegations at the United Nations in Paris in 1951 was the occasion for a general prohibition of any North African political activity. The rally planned at Vél' d'Hiv turned into what the newspaper *Franc-tireur* termed a "police roundup reminiscent of the sad measures of Chiappe-Tardieu-Laval." Squads of police and CRS units raged through the area, setting up roadblocks around Vél' d'Hiv. Thousands were hunted down and arrested.[98] An illegal rally in the Salle Wagram led to a thousand arrests and violent confrontations with police on the place des Ternes. Increasingly politicized, Algerians protested against the prohibition of the newspaper *Algérie libre* at the headquarters of the Société nationale des entreprises de presse (SNEP) on the rue Réaumur the same year. In what had become a too-frequent finale, the protest ended in violent confrontation with police that left wounded on both sides, and then more arrests. The MTLD and its supporters attempted to claim the symbolic space of the Champs-Élysées for a march in support of their leader, Messali Hadj, in May 1952. A political demonstration at Vél' d'Hiv in December of that year led to a second police raid in the area that ended with violent confrontations and three thousand taken into custody.[99]

Algerian delegations also took part with increasing regularity in the traditional May Day and July 14 processions from the place de la Nation to the Bastille, usually under the protective wing of the Communist Party. In general Algerian immigrants during the period 1945–54 were seen as laborers necessary for reconstruction. Although the communists maintained a discreet distance from MTLD-organized protests, nonetheless Algerians were treated with respect as workers. Their political groups were welcomed at the time-honored public pageants, but they marched separately from the main contingent and always under police surveillance. The traditional commemoration of February 1934 from the Bastille to the place de la Nation in 1951 brought some twenty thousand people into the streets. But the most notable feature in this working-class spectacle was some six thousand Algerians marching under the banner of the MTLD. During the May Day march the same year, the appearance of separatist MTLD flags led to riots on the rue Ledru-Rollin. Hundreds were arrested and sixty-eight wounded. Ironically, the police had attempted to prevent trouble by arresting in advance some 1,600 Algerians who were coming into Paris from the suburbs. The huge protests against the arrival of the American General Ridgway in May 1952 brought Algerians along with the PCF out into the streets in record numbers. The one death reported during the riots and skirmishes with police was that of an Algerian on the place Stalingrad.

By far the most violent and deadliest incident took place during the *fête nationale* celebration on July 14, 1953. Although the march from the Bastille to the place de la Nation was the traditional opportunity for the PCF to flex its political muscle, the throngs on parade through the working-class stronghold were part of a popular *fête* and were tolerated if they followed the time-honored pattern approved by the police. It was a political festival, with workers marching behind union and factory banners along with floats, folkloric groups, and marching bands. What sparked confrontation was in part the changing economic atmosphere. By the mid-1950s, reconstruction was winding down. Employment opportunities in the Paris region began to dry up even though industrial productivity remained high. Competition for jobs, especially those taken by North African immigrants, sharpened racism. Always precarious, jobs for the marginalized Algerian community dropped precipitously, especially during the winter months, and became an increasing source of discontent.[100] This combination of economic pressures and the growing crisis of the Algerian War effectively split North African "undesirables" off psychologically and politically even further from any pool of working-class solidarity. Tensions between nationalist paratroopers and Algerians had already put previous marches on edge, with insults flying on both sides. Impassioned by their own crusade for freedom, the Algerian contingents were increasingly segregated from the main processions. Where they had once been welcomed as comrades, North Africans were now eyed with bitterness and suspicion in the fading *ouvriériste* imaginary.

In pouring rain, the march passed before the reviewing stands, where stood Marcel Cachin (a deputy and municipal councilor from La Goutte d'Or), Jacques Duclos, and Communist Party notables, and then began to disperse under the watchful eyes of law enforcement. But the contingent of Algerians, five thousand to six thousand strong, continued to rally for the MTLD under the Trône column, demanding freedom for Messali Hadj and chanting for Algerian independence and an end to colonialism. When police rushed in to break up the gathering, the inevitable violence broke out. It went on for nearly an hour. Bistros on the place de la Nation were ransacked, and police cars were set ablaze; Cachin and Duclos were rushed away from the bloody scene. Police and CRS forces charged the rioters. The melee ended in seven dead (six Algerians and one French) and some one hundred people wounded, many of whom were police. Crowds milled around the disaster; according to *Le Parisien libéré*, "a woman sat dumbstruck on the bandstand where the orchestra was set to play for the July 14 ball, next to the piano, which was miraculously untouched."[101] The tragedy was a turning point for the capital. The outpouring of shock and emotion reverberated through the neighborhoods as people descended into the streets. With demonstrations banned, the protests took a variety of alternative forms: localized cortèges against police brutality, the gathering of signatures for letters of protest, public moments of silence. Makeshift memorial plaques with the names of the victims, who had died "for liberty," appeared spontaneously on the streets once more as people reached into the immediate past of the Liberation for commemorative practices. On June 21 a massive meeting was organized by

FIGURE 16. The crowd of North Africans gathering in front of the Grand Mosque on March 9, 1956. © BETTMANN/CORBIS.

the Communist Party at the Cirque d'Hiver in the 11th arrondissement to demonstrate the city's "anger against those responsible for this reactionary and racist crime at the place de la Nation." The PCF called for work stoppages throughout the city's industries. Thousands waited in line to view the bodies at the Grand Mosque on the Left Bank, and more than twenty thousand people marched from the Maison des Métallos to Père Lachaise Cemetery for the burial services.[102] But the events only ended with more repression. Arrests continued. The prefect of police, Maurice Papon, resuscitated the old Brigade nord-africaine, a police unit specializing in the repression of North African activities and rechristened it the Brigade des aggressions et violences (BAV). The new name sardonically laid out the outfit's mission. The public spaces of the city were entered into the topography of colonial war. Paris was well on its way to Charonne.

As Algeria exploded, so did the streets of the capital. The war and struggle for independence in 1955 and 1956 provoked immediate reaction. Algerian workers demonstrated in La Goutte d'Or against the state of emergency declared in Algeria in July 1955. Bands of young men, joined by students, headed for the main railroad stations, where they staged protests by blocking train traffic.[103] The 13th, 18th, and 19th arrondissements became sectarian combat zones when the MTLD split between those who remained faithful to Messali Hadj and the powerful new FLN. Terrorism and frequent assassinations by one side against the other became the new public spectacles, with the dead and wounded counted up and carted away by police authorities.[104] The spaces of the capital turned into a geography of fear—of the collapse of empire and the decline of France, of violent clashes and terrorism, of plots by zealot Algerian nationalists. The reaction was increased surveillance, more retribution, and severe repression.

On March 9, 1956, the National Assembly was set to deliberate on the granting of special powers to the government to quell the violence in Algeria and restore French authority. "As if by some mysterious order," according to *Le Parisien libéré*, massive numbers of Algerians throughout the Paris region "deserted their workshops and construction sites to affirm their solidarity with the rebels in North Africa."[105] The morning strike movement called by the FLN along with the Mouvement national algérien and its charismatic leader, Hadj, was followed by a call to prayer at the city's Grand Mosque. The result was massive crowds (ten thousand, according to press estimates), made up mostly of young men, that quickly transformed into a political demonstration. They marched along a novel political route from the Mosque off the rue Daubenton past the Jardin des Plantes. Unable to advance along the quays of the Left Bank to reach their final destination of the Palais Bourbon (which was defended by thousands of CRS forces) the protesters attempted to cross the pont Sully to the Hôtel de Ville. Screaming slogans in Arabic and waving the green and white flag of Algerian independence, they threaded their way through a tangle of trucks and automobiles with horns blaring in anger and aggravation. When some 2,500 of them were rounded up and taken away by police, the crowds reacted with violence, rampaging through the streets, ransacking boutiques and automobiles, and harassing passersby. Clashes between police and demonstrators intensified throughout the afternoon, leaving a trail of destruction and debris in its wake along the quai Henri IV and the quai de la Rapé. Clots of traffic came to a standstill, with innocent bystanders caught in the fray. After a last siege at the Hôtel de Ville, the riots finally dissipated by the end of the afternoon.

The reaction in the municipal council was immediate outrage. Calling the protestors "assassins and thieves," members from a swath of political persuasions indulged in a xenophobic stupor and castigated the prefect of police for his moderate strategy in the face of "10,000 men parading through the streets of Paris, slapping the face of the nation and demanding separation from it." When the communist Camille Denis attempted to defend their right to "demonstrate their desire for peace and freedom for their country," he met with loud ridicule.[106] To add to the threat, the rioters were identified as "minors." The image of the young Arab male played into the fear of juvenile delinquency and gangs of *tricheur* troublemakers, of thievery and criminal behavior. The May 1957 assassination of Ali Chekkal, vice president of the Algerian Assembly at the Stade de Colombes, did nothing to calm anxieties, nor did the arrests of FLN leaders at Clichy and Saint-Ouen. The topography of Paris seemed to be exploding into pieces as a corollary of the Algerian conflict. The political meaning of the fractured symbolic landscape was grotesquely exaggerated as adherents from all sides battled for control of the capital.

The Italian urban observer Alberto Arbasino reflected on the anxiety and agitation of the summer of 1957 as the capital awaited the annual *fête nationale* celebrations:

The place is swarming with paratroopers. . . . They have taken possession of the city. . . . They are amassing in Paris for the great Sunday morning parade down the Champs-Élysées; 14,245 men, 123 planes, 60 tanks, 32 cannon, 377 military vehicles, 415 horses, and they are taking advantage of their free time in their occupied capital.

The Fourth Republic was in a hopeless position, with the threat of a military coup to save French Algeria all too real: "Each time they arrive at a *bal prolétaire*, the paratroopers are welcomed with enthusiasm as good saviors of a nation in difficulty."[107] The Right appropriated the western districts of monumental Paris for their defense of France and Algeria, from the Champs-Élysées to Notre Dame. In March 1958 a massive protest march by the Syndicat général de la police wound from the prefecture to the Palais Bourbon in a test of the government's legitimacy, while right-wing groups staged a relentless stream of demonstrations in support of French Algeria and in "homage to Jeanne d'Arc." The Left relied on its splintered neighborhood landscape in the eastern districts for the defense of "republicanism." A day of national protest and strikes against the war in Algeria was called by the PCF on October 17, 1957. Thousands marched through the streets from

Saint-Denis to the Latin Quarter in a reiteration of the decentered political cartography that dominated the city. Three hundred people wound down the rue Mouffetard shouting "Peace in Algeria!" In Batignolles as in most places the protesters combined their calls for peace with those for an end to misery. In the 13th arrondissement, the infamous slums around the rue Nationale attempted a protest that was swiftly broken up by police.[108] A general strike was called on October 25 the same year. Once again, demonstrators took to the streets for marches and meetings.

By May 8, 1958, in the midst of the national political crisis, *Le Figaro* reported on yet another traditional celebration taken over by the passions and urgency of the moment. V-E Day, or the May 8 victory in the Second World War, which had been honored in the past with such enthusiasm, "was no longer celebrated as a *fête* in the hearts of men because it costs too much blood and too many tears." The traditional commemoration march down the Champs-Élysées drew only a small crowd, many of them tourists and foreigners, largely indifferent in a "melancholic" atmosphere of grey skies and rain. Only the street vendors offering their souvenirs broke the mood.[109] Rather than a popular *fête*, the parade had become a grandiose display by a government on the edge of collapse, with motorcades of black cars bringing in President René Coty and his entourage, the Republican guard on horseback, colonial troops in their regalia. It was the war in Algeria, far more than the one that had been fought fifteen years previously, that was on the minds of Parisians. The superficial pretension of state power at the May 8 victory parade drew few patriots and did nothing to hide the atmosphere of national emergency. It was eclipsed by strike movements, work stoppages, "committees of resistance," protest marches, and right-wing military demonstrations that furled out across the public landscape of the capital. The spaces of Paris became a polymorphic political tableau depicting the downfall of the Fourth Republic.

Crowds of French *colons* (colonials, many of them students) and a coterie of French army officers stormed the French Government-General building in Algiers on May 13, where General Jacques Massu of the brutal 10th Paratroop Division became head of a newly formed Committee of Public Safety against the *fellaghas*. They demanded that Coty do the same in Paris. Right-wing activists mobilized in preparation for a military seizure of power in Paris. The Association des anciens combattants (army veterans' association) staged a march from the Tomb of the Unknown Soldier at the Arc de

Triomphe down the Champs-Élysées to the place de la Concorde. It was led by Jean-Marie Le Pen and Jean-Maurice Demarquet, outfitted in paratrooper berets, carrying regimental flags, and shouting "To the Chamber [of Deputies]!" and "French Algeria!" The event provoked comparison to the February 1934 march, when extreme right-wing demonstrators tried to cross the Seine and storm the Chamber of Deputies. As the protesters crossed the pont de la Concorde, they were stopped by riot-police barricades and a wall of CRS vans. The ensuing violence left a trail of wounded as protesters dodged police lines and continued their protest on the rue de Rivoli and the place de l'Opéra. Faced with a looming military coup, President Coty asked de Gaulle to become premier, under the condition that he rule by decree for six months and submit a new constitution. After de Gaulle's press conference on May 19 declaring he was ready to take the reins of government, thousands of young men took to the street in support of his investiture. A May 29 march began at the rue Solferino, then moved to the Champs-Élysées past the Arc de Triomphe and the Tomb of the Unknown Soldier, where demonstrators observed a moment of silence and sang the "Marseillaise." They then moved on to the place de la Concorde.[110] Violent street battles took place on May 30 on the Champs-Élysées between supporters of de Gaulle and communist militants.

On May 28 the Left struck back. That morning Pierre Pflimlin resigned as premier, leaving a power vacuum that only de Gaulle was capable of filling. Led by Pierre Mendès-France, François Mitterand, and Edward Daladier, some 120,000 to 150,000 demonstrators descended onto the streets of Paris in a great unity march. According to *Le Figaro*,

> The place de la Nation, the avenue Trône, the cours de Vincennes were everywhere overflowing with delegations. Workers, women, young men massed on the boulevards and adjacent streets, responding to the call of a newly organized left-wing alliance, the Comité d'action et de défense républicaine, that was joined by the communists, the CGT, the Union of Socialist Left, and no end of progressive and pseudo-communist groups.[111]

Under surveillance by police and CRS units, they marched by professions, by trades, by veteran associations, carrying their flags, banners, and signs to the place de la République, where they sang the "Marseillaise" and the

FIGURE 17. Demonstrators protesting against the referendum on Algerian independence during Charles de Gaulle's speech at the place de la République, September 4, 1959.
© GERALD BLONCOURT/RUE DES ARCHIVES.

"Chant du départ" and shouted "Vive la République!" Prominent left-wing intellectuals and media stars marched with them, led by Jean-Paul Sartre, Simone de Beauvoir, and Gérard Philipe. It was one of the largest demonstrations of the postwar era.

Demonstrations and protests continued throughout the working-class districts on June 1. In the 13th arrondissement, crowds marched from the rue Jeanne d'Arc to Gobelins. Five thousand marched from the gare Saint-Lazare to the Louis-Blanc Métro station, thousands from the rue Saint-Antoine through Saint-Paul to Les Halles, from the gare Montparnasse to the gare Austerlitz, from the Latin Quarter down the rue Mouffetard. *L'Humanité* reported these events as a "Popular Front" against fascism. In a series of dazzling editorials, the former *résistante* and journalist Nelly Feld took her rhetoric and imagery directly from populist memory. The images are a replay of the Liberation, with young men and women smiling, being photographed, self-conscious and aware that they are participating in an historical event. The people of Paris mobilized with flowers, with their placards and flags. There was a sense of enthusiasm and resolve.

> From Nation to République. By hundreds of thousands we have marched. Paris, heart of the nation, rises to defend the Republic. The sounds of the Marseillaise and the Chant du Départ thunder through the city. . . . And the place de la République, already black with people, erupts into song with the cortege. In the center, the statue of the Republic applauds. She applauds the dozens of hands held high, all around her pedestal. The circle squeezes up around her. Then a "Marseillaise" resounds the likes of which is rarely heard. I look at the dates inscribed on the pedestal of the statue: 1792, 1793. I imagine that this is how they sang in those times—with this fire, with this enthusiasm, an enthusiasm that filled their hearts. The great joy of feeling strong, because we are united, because we are so strong.[112]

But the loyalty to republicanism, the passion and ritual, did nothing to alter the course of events. By June 1 de Gaulle was invested as the head of government, with full powers. He presented the new constitution at the place de la République to a jubilant crowd. "Once again," André Malraux cried, "the meeting at the Republic is with history, and with General de Gaulle."

4 Spatial Imagination and the Avant-Garde

With the war's end, intellectuals, architects, and urbanists, along with the professional *cadre supérieur*, streamed back into Paris from the south or from Algiers. After the Liberation, they took Paris by storm, reclaiming intellectual life and continuing a public conversation about the nature of the modern city that had gone on since the nineteenth century. The deterioration of Paris had been the topic of endless discussion throughout the 1930s and 1940s. It was bleak, worn down by disrepair and by economic and political crisis, and now it was beyond the capacity of urban planners or social reformers to save. The last great gathering about the city before the war was the Paris Congress, held in 1937 in conjunction with the Exposition Internationale des Arts et Techniques. Le Corbusier and CIAM erected a huge tent outside the fairground to display a futuristic "radiant city" of glass towers on the Right Bank from the gare de l'Est to the rue de Rivoli. It was a visionary solution to what ailed Paris that attracted a steady stream of avid enthusiasts and horrified critics. The 1943 Salon des Urbanistes provided yet another chance to condemn the evils of Paris, although this time the solutions proposed were far more conventional. The battle continued to rage through the occupation, swinging back and forth between preservationists defending the city's historic "beauty" and modernists ready to sacrifice it all in the name of the future.

But by 1945 the terms of the debate had changed. The apocalypse had happened. The turning point of the Liberation opened up the possibility of a moral and social revolution. The future was now, and responding to the capital's complicated legacy and lived experience held the possibility of transformation. These were, after all, the original "spaces of modernity." This was the city of Baudelaire and Zola, of Marcel Poëte and Louis Aragon, and a host of avant-garde predecessors who had breathed in and shaped its ambience. The intellectual and artistic elites who surfaced in Paris after the dark years had at their disposal a rich heritage of urban prospecting and *flânerie*. Some of the city's most well-known observers were passing from the scene. Two literary giants, Jean Giraudoux and Paul Valéry, passed away at the war's end. Léon-Paul Fargue died in 1947. The preservationists of the Ligue urbaine et rurale, men such as the historian Bernard Champigneulle, faded from view. Intellectuals discredited by their collaboration with the Vichy government were extirpated in disgrace. The right-wing mouthpiece *La Nouvelle revue française* was banned. The Resistance-inspired Comité national des écrivains (CNE) drew up a blacklist of writers vilified for their Vichy sympathies. The journalists Georges Suarez and Henri Béraud were shot in late 1944 after they were found guilty in the first of the purge trials. Robert Brasillach was executed in February 1945. The writers Lucien Rebatet and Céline were found guilty but were eventually released. Others, such as Jacques Prévert and Marcel Carné, seemed to have crossed the great divide from the prewar years into a new world ready to be born. The occupation and purges that followed cleared the way for new voices. They emerged among the technocratic young turks of Vichy's National Revolution, from the Resistance and the experience of Liberation, from a new generation of avant-garde.

Besides, in the superheated intellectual atmosphere of the Left Bank, there were plenty of opportunities for passionate discussion about Paris. A vindicated and profoundly left-wing political grounding was supported by a milieu of Parisian intellectuals aligned with or along the margins of the Communist Party, often working together at their CNRS offices, thrashing out policies on the editorial boards of the leftist literary reviews *Les Lettres françaises*, *Les Temps modernes*, *Argument*, *La Pensée*, and *Esprit* and meeting at Left Bank bistros. In the decade following the war Louis Aragon became one of the most powerful figures of intellectual Paris. He was secretary general of the Resistance-inspired Union nationale des intellectuels and a member of the Central Committee of the French Communist Party. The old-guard surrealists around Aragon haunted Le Select, Le Dôme, and La Coupole in Montparnasse. Aragon and Paul Éluard were the dominant figures in a tight circle of Left Bank fellow-travelers, along with Claude Roy, Edgar Morin, and Frédéric Joliot-Curie. The regular communist gatherings in Marguerite

Duras's apartment on the rue Saint-Benoît and the party cell on the rue de Rennes in Saint-Germain-des-Prés were a catalog of Parisian intellectual glitterati of the 1950s fantasizing about revolutionary worker activism. For their part, Jean-Paul Sartre, Maurice Merleau-Ponty, and Emmanuel Mounier worked along the edges of communist sympathies. Sartre and Simone de Beauvoir held court at the Café de Flore. Merleau-Ponty presided over his inner circle a block away at the Rhumerie Martiniquaise. André Malraux worked from his regular bistro on the rue du Dragon. A familiar figure in Saint-Germain-des-Prés, Albert Camus was working as a journalist, initially dividing his time between *Combat* and Gallimard, writing *La Peste* (1947) and fighting off admirers. Lucien Febvre and Fernand Braudel were inaugurating the Annales school at the École pratique des hautes études with money from the Rockefeller Foundation. Roland Barthes held a research appointment in Paris at the Centre national de la recherche scientifique (CNRS) during the 1950s and was writing *Mythologies*, his tour de force on the empire of signs. The autumn book sale of the Comité national des écrivains was among the most spectacular and brilliant literary events of the Paris season. Thousands attended with the hope of spotting *les intellos* and media luminaries that made the event an annual leftist ritual. In 1956 *Les Lettres françaises* (which originated as a CNE review) published a map of the booths at Vél' d'Hiv so that fans could easily locate their favorite cerebral idols. Michel de Certeau was working on his doctorate at the Sorbonne, where Jean-Luc Godard was also a student; Maurice Agulhon, Michel Foucault, and Emmanuel Le Roy Ladurie were at the École normale supérieure; and Guy Debord and his band of followers were drifting through the city. Postwar Paris was a ferment of intellectual avant-gardism.[1]

The purpose of this discussion is to weave together the intertwining threads that created a general field of public discourse, a pattern of understanding and perception about Paris and about urban spatiality that was shared by these intellectual and artistic elites. Movements as diverse as social Marxism, Catholic reformism, technocratic rationalism, surrealism, and progressive patriotism all contributed to French perceptions of the modern urban experience. Although it may seem as though individuals were separated by insurmountable ideological barriers, they often shared cultural assumptions that went far deeper than their differences. Urban modernity allows for a myriad of itineraries. The labyrinthine windings of Parisian topography and questions of social class, subjectivity, and rational reform played themselves out across this field of understanding in manifold ways. But a perceptual coherency places these intellectual elites firmly within the milieu of mid-twentieth-century Paris and the quest to find the relationship between space, culture, and society. French cultural theory is now something of a cottage industry, and the work of renowned theorists such as Henri Lefebvre and others in this chapter who dominated the Paris intellectual scene has been brilliantly mined by specialists. Other urban observers considered here are perhaps less well recognized. My purpose is to find the intersection of these voices, the common vocabulary that was used to articulate the spatial dynamics in the Paris of their time. This contextualizes the aesthetics of everyday life, the spatialities and temporalities of the capital that were produced as a field of knowledge during the postwar period.

We can begin by saying that what all these urban observers shared was a common framework, one often articulated as humanism. In his analysis of the cultural and intellectual rebuilding of postwar France, the historian Michael Kelly argues that humanism "provided the ideological adhesive for French national unity, a precious and fragile field in 1944, and defined the parameters of what was thinkable, or at least speakable." Humanism was expounded explicitly. Its characteristic preoccupations were with "Man, the Individual, Society, Culture, Science, and History."[2] It was more a field of consensual understanding and values than a rational construct. In the context of a shattered nation, this utopian discourse held enormous power. It brought together intellectuals from a variety of backgrounds, from the religious to the secular, the technocratic to the Marxist. It was a way for all French to relate to one another. Humanists endorsed the ideal of human brotherhood. They shared a sentimental sympathy for ordinary people in a vision that was mythic and emotional in content. Throughout the late 1940s and 1950s, this ideological framework produced an ethnographic vision of the city's population and spaces that was close to the folk tradition of *images d'épinal*, lending a poetic, sentimentalized quality to the humanist point of view. The traditional *quartier populaire*, with its informal, effortless sociability and street life, was naturalized as the social space indigenous to Paris and to its morally good people.

These images were laced together from a number of intertwining standpoints. First, the Resistance and Liberation were the prelude to the zenith of French working-class politics and culture during the early postwar years. The proletariat incarnated the authentic interests of the nation. Their Paris was *the* Paris of the late 1940s and early 1950s. Broadly speaking, it was not so much a militant vision of the working class as a notion of a brotherhood of people, that is, of workers and ordinary people who were wage earners of all sorts. Secondly, intellectuals attempted to take up responsibility for the rebuilding of France and openly ally with this populist community. They took their cues from the militancy in the streets, from the strikes and demonstrations, the *ouvriérisme* that resounded in the spaces of the capital. Coming together in a renewed, progressive patriotism was a theme familiar from the Resistance that continued through the reconstruction years. Joining the Communist Party was one way for many prominent left-wing intellectuals to struggle on the same side as the class of the future. The new elites would help to nourish and improve the lot of working Parisians and give voice to the silenced and ignored. The result was a humanistic vision of this victorious, collective urban milieu that took hold of intellectuals from a variety of ideological sensibilities and backgrounds. Inspiration could be found among the progressive, archetypal Parisians of the street. Even scientific investigations of the city echoed this heroic imagery. The vernacular space of the city—the experiences of the everyday and the outpouring of public life—was the arena of social reconciliation and unity. Third, tradition and modernity were not juxtaposed. The historicity of every element of space and landscape established meaning and distinctiveness. The human scale of the neighborhood, the social interactions, the improvisations and festivities that took place there gave everyday life its own authentic, unstructured aesthetic.

The result was the construction from the 1930s through the 1950s of a distinctively French approach to urban planning and to Paris. This vision of a mosaic of *petits villages*—the natural and traditional spaces of community for the *classes populaires*—was a far cry from that proposed by the modernist mandarins attached to CIAM, or that envisioned by many technocratic social reformers. High modernism envisioned a city no longer encumbered with its history, its idiosyncrasies, its everyday culture. Urban topography was imagined as cleared, vacant space, waiting to be filled with a monumental morphology—new buildings and new notions of both the public and private domain. Space was abstract, objective, and measurable, qualities often encapsulated in the term "site." Despite this normative vision of modern postwar transformation, there was in reality no one single version of modernism. Rather, there were a variety of modernisms that were debated within and adapted to local contexts. It was in fact this multiform quality that continually twisted and refashioned the notion of the modern city. French intellectual elites were mesmerized by the richness of neighborhood collective life that was lived in the streets and spaces of Paris. They plunged into a world of images and sensations that was peopled by whom they imagined to be modern, self-actualizing, valiant individuals who found their strength in collective existence. The landscape of Paris was poetic, humanistic, almost sheathed in a golden dust.

The Populist Currents of Urban Sociology

An extraordinary intellectual debate took place in Paris in 1951 at the Deuxième semaine sociologique, sponsored by the embryonic CNRS and its first research laboratory, the Centre d'études sociologiques (CES). The theme was *villes et campagnes*. It was a pageant of the intellectual avant-garde that would swing inquiry toward a more critical and applied appraisal of society, the economy, mentalities, and history. Among the participants were the historians Lucien Febvre, Fernand Braudel, Ernst Labrousse, and Louis Chevalier. The sociologists were represented by Georges Friedmann, Alain Touraine, Georges Gurvitch, Henri Lefebvre, and Paul-Henry Chombart de Lauwe. The architect Robert Auzelle, the geographers Marcel Roncayolo and Jean Gottmann, and the economists Alfred Sauvy, Jean Fourastié, and Charles Bettelheim led the effort toward a multidisciplinary conversation on the problems facing a rapidly changing France. The Villes et campagnes conference reopened the public debate on French cities and exactly captured this key moment of urban transformation. The backdrop was the clash between the rural world, where true French identity lay, and the urban one. Ernst Labrousse began the event with a presentation that posited urban life as a "conquering civilization." Given what the gathering described as the "permanence of the rural milieu as a distinctive social characteristic of France," was there any way to save it? Fernand Braudel answered that the "rural world was not always lost." Its distinctive qualities were profound and resilient. The challenge was to find a policy that would reconcile the two worlds—that would, in the words of Alfred Sauvy, "ruralize the city and urbanize the countryside."[3] It was an imagery that had resonated among technocrats and intellectuals during the Vichy years (see chapter 7). There remained, however, the particular "problem of Paris." The capital, according to the historian Lucien Febvre, was "the urban monster *par excellence*.

Because of its astonishing grandeur, at the local level, this city of Paris has grown and developed so excessively with so many problems that I've never seen anyone, up to today, consider this situation viable."[4]

Auzelle voiced anxiety about the traumas caused by reconstruction and rapid urbanization, for which "it was difficult to see remedies." In an interview published in 1986, Alain Touraine described this early postwar French sociological thought as carrying the weight of the French defeat and as "anxious and somewhat pessimistic" about the changes the country faced.[5] Modernization was certainly not new to France. But the difference was the accelerated pace of change, which threatened to overwhelm the French way of life. This apprehension was associated with urbanization and a conquering modern rationalism. The *trente glorieuses* were shifting the terrain of everyday existence out of recognition. It was an overwhelming specter. The experience of Paris was traumatizing. It siphoned off the vitality of France. There was little to be said for it beyond the brutal commutes, dreadful housing, and oppressive daily grind the growing population was forced to suffer. For the intellectuals assembled at the Villes et campagnes conference, reconstruction was accelerating these trends with a frightening intensity. Modern postwar life promised to disrupt traditional communities, create an increasingly chaotic urban environment, and push people further into the grip of "mass culture." How had it come to this? The technocratic and intellectual elites who had emerged from the war and who now sat together in this conference in March 1951 had no intention of repeating the mistakes of the past. Their motivations were shame over the catastrophe that had befallen France and, springing from that, both a renewed patriotism and a belief in recovery. Yet there was anxiety about the country's future role. Humanism provided them with a guide through this thicket of difficulties and with a form of heroic self-affirmation. And Paris was the terrain on which they would carry out their vision of universal brotherhood and cooperation.

Although experts were eager to help, little was actually known about the working classes staging their street theater or about their genuine needs and aspirations. Urban studies or urban sociology proper did not even formally exist in France before the war.[6] Its progenitors were Maurice Halbwachs and Marcel Mauss, both disciples of Émile Durkheim. The work of this second generation of Durkheimians provided French intellectuals with a massive interpretive framework. But in the context of postwar reconstruction, reliance on this theoretical corpus proved unsatisfactory. A variety of intellectual voices called for demystification and genuine familiarity with the working classes, for an understanding of their real world, the reality of their lives, in order to improve their prospects through reform. Progressive thinkers could no longer be cut off from ordinary Parisians, for it was they who were leading the way forward. This shared desire to actually know what was happening to the "workers" in postwar France, both in their daily lives and in their work environment, and then to bring this knowledge to planners and decision makers who could implement reform, constituted one of the major intellectual motivations behind all postwar sociology. Social scientists simply had to come to grips with the contextual aspects of everyday life and space from the perspective of the people who lived it. There was a quality to it of human solidarity and emotional union born from the Resistance and Liberation.

Tony Judt makes the point that there was also an aspect of intellectual "slumming" and condescension in this newfound humility and desire to help the working classes.[7] The task was made easier by the heroic vision of the worker that dominated in these years. Self-actualizing, moral, and good, with a saintly glow that symbolized the soul of France, *le peuple* were infinitely approachable. Despite this idealized vision, there was a genuine desire among thinkers from a variety of ideological casts to find common cause and a unity of spirit with the working classes.

The new role of the sociologist was to take the pulse of French society and organize a system of social knowledge that could influence the rapid transformation taking place before their eyes. Georges Gurvitch, the director of CES and convener of the Villes et campagnes conference, acknowledged that it was up to teams of experts such as themselves to launch social studies and offer tangible reform and policy guidelines. As a result, a host of geographic and sociological studies appeared about Paris immediately after the war and through the 1950s. Some of it was a continuation of inquiries carried on before the war, such as Demangeon's exacting analysis *Paris: La Ville et sa banlieue*, which first appeared in 1934 and was republished in 1949. The geographer Pierre George and his research team published their findings on the Paris suburbs in 1950, and the historian and demographer Louis Chevalier completed a series of population studies of Paris for the INED and, by the end of the decade, for the Institut national de la statistique et des études économiques (INSEE). Chevalier dedicated some of his courses at the Collège de France to urban sociology, and his *Le Problème de la soci-*

ologie des villes (1958) was the first major review of the discipline. Chevalier thought that urban sociology based on scientific and statistical analysis was by its very nature "associated directly or indirectly to public responsibility."[8] He insisted on the importance of "working with the administration" to accumulate the data necessary for understanding the social composition and the diversity of France's cities—an approach, by the way, that did not make use of American methodologies, which "[left] important problems in the dark."[9] Instead, Chevalier evoked Halbwachs's analysis of collective memory and the "stones of the city" in articulating the permanence of the Parisian milieu, the "very particular form of sensibility, intelligence, spirit" specific to the capital. Statistical and social science research required scrutiny at the level of the quartier and its everyday life. There, sociologists and public administrators would come to understand "the workers of Paris, the children of Paris," who Chevalier believed would benefit from public aid.[10]

Sociologists became interactive, descending into the streets to study ordinary people in their own world and the workings of their neighborhoods. The class prejudices of elitist theoreticians who deigned to speak on behalf of the lower orders they disdained would no longer be tolerated. Sociology would be based on genuine fieldwork, on sympathy and respect for the sociologists' subjects. A new emphasis on subjective meaning and "insider knowledge" would reveal the ways in which people reflexively negotiated their life-world. Working-class behavior, gestures, language, and social relations became the material of investigation. This approach was a defense of autonomous popular culture, with its own collective space and practices. Chevalier's work is especially evocative of this interplay between analysis and imagination that invented a naturalized, ethnographic spatial landscape. His population studies and his better-known *Classes laborieuses et classes dangereuses* (1958) were based on exacting scrutiny of the *pays* of Paris that assumed a geographic determinism. Chevalier argued that Parisian civilization exhibited different characteristics depending on the quartiers. The criminality in Montmartre differed from that in Belleville. In his *flânerie* through Paris, Chevalier found poetry and pleasure, and an innate sensuality in urban civilization that pervaded every aspect of life. His intimacy with urban space produced as much passion as scientific analysis.[11]

All of these intellectual trends were crucial to the thought of the sociologist Paul-Henry Chombart de Lauwe. He had been a student of Halbwachs and was also heavily influenced by Mauss. Like a number of French intellectuals, Chombart discovered the French working classes during the war, as a member of the Resistance, and in the post-Liberation years of reconstruction. It was this new awareness that moved him to switch his sociological and ethnographic training from Central Africa to the *classe ouvrière* in Paris. As with many of these midcentury social reformers, Catholic thought played an instrumental role in the construction of Chombart's social humanism. His ideas were clearly guided by Pierre Teilhard de Chardin; by Catholic social action movements such as Robert Garric's applied-research "Social Teams" in the northern districts of Paris, in which Chombart participated before the war; and by the questionnaire methodologies of the Dominican cleric Louis-Joseph Lebret's Économie et Humanisme movement, founded in 1941, with which Chombart maintained contact.[12] Their shared Christian humanism was not ideological, but instead found its inspiration in concrete projects for democracy and social justice. Vichy's call for moral regeneration initially offered the possibility of a spiritual rebirth for the nation. This ideal helps explain why Chombart became involved in the Vichy regime's Uriage Leadership School. It was there that he began to outline his ambition of "remaking contact with France" and learning the reality that the working classes faced, not just from a disinterested empirical point of view, but because of "our affection for them and our desire to help them."[13] It was also at Uriage that he began to assemble his young team of researchers to carry out the study of a *grand cité*.

Disillusioned with Vichy as it become more collaborationist, in 1942 Chombart joined the Allied troops in North Africa and served as an RAF fighter pilot. With the war's end, he returned to the Musée de l'Homme and was eventually hired by the new CES as one of a number of unconventional scholars largely ignored by French academic elites. In 1949–50 Chombart set up the Groupe d'ethnologie sociale at the Musée de l'Homme to study the behavior of the working class in the metropolis of Paris. Although French sociology remained largely wedded to specifically productivist models, Chombart's interest was centered on the relationship between work and the needs and aspirations of the working-class family in terms of lodging, space, transport, and consumption—the conditions of their daily lives. Taking the local working-class community as a framework, his research team analyzed the shift from traditional urban neighborhoods to new forms of modern habitat and their impact on families' psychosociological welfare. In other words, in the Chombartian universe, material conditions did not dictate social phenomena and the city. Instead, urban morphology itself—that is, the spaces and practices of urban life—reflected or represented society as a whole. Reading the urban landscape was the best way to understand this framework of social and economic relations. The result was Chombart's *Paris et l'agglomération parisienne*, published in 1952, a two-volume tour de force in the interdisciplinary study of urban community that utilized interview techniques, a panoply of social and economic statistics, cartography, and data on housing, disease, violence, and juvenile delinquency.[14] For Chombart, only urban social science methods such as these could provide the essential knowledge, the documented basis from which public authorities could meet the needs and aspirations of the city's working population.

Chombart's findings delineated the differences between bourgeois and working-class conceptions of social relations. His research specifically distinguished the rhythms of everyday collective life in the eastern neighborhoods of Paris from those of the *beaux quartiers* in the western part of the city. While the bourgeois emphasized individuality and isolation from the urban milieu, the worker looked for the social connections essential for survival. Collective practices were mapped onto the dynamic spatial arrangement of daily needs, the comings and goings of women and children, the pattern of commerce and services, the going to and returning from work that together created the intimacy and sociability of everyday neighborhood life. *Pensée populaire* was elaborated in public places, at markets and fairs, and in family homes. The basic unit of community life functioned in tangible, multifaceted spaces that changed with the rhythms of daily existence. It was this rich collective experience, imperceptible from the exterior, that tied together the working-class community and offered families stability, shared memory, and social cohesion. The connection between home and neighborhood was fluid and open. The barriers guarding privacy were porous. The need to share outlooks and experiences, to share the joys and pains of life, was more important than preserving independence.[15] The Chombartian view of this world gave it a rational social consciousness. It was obvious to postwar sociological thinking that the neighborhood was a natural social unit closely knit by internal ties and hidden away in the vast metropolis of Paris.

Paris et l'agglomération parisienne included meticulous geographic profiles of the decentered spaces of the city. The level was the arrondissement, a specific sector, or an îlot. Although the arrondissement may have begun as an arbitrary administrative boundary, it was interpreted as having evolved into a "living unit." At the next level down in the spatial hierarchy, the landscape of social life was situated in discrete "familiar spaces" that represented a true quartier. To focus even more intently on each neighborhood, the *petite îlot* represented a natural unit whose boundaries and style of life were palpable.[16] The sociologist Jean-Pierre Frey has pointed to the commonalities between Chombart's social mapping of the Paris landscape and that of the urbanist Gaston Bardet (see the next section in this chapter), who had created highly detailed diagrams of the city's fragmented social morphology before the Second World War.[17] Both Chombart's and Bardet's underlying objective was to understand the life of the quartier and the ways in which its inhabitants interacted informally to create a sense of community and spatial organization. They shared an organic, naturalist conception of the lived environment. The analysis invented a picture of how people appropriated place to their needs and aspirations and portrayed the spatial representations and practices that shaped milieu. This information could then be used by planners whose objectives were to renovate Paris and create new suburban communities around it. Most important, this vision of the traditional working-class quartier and îlot acted as a counterpoint to descriptions of depraved urban slums or *îlots insalubres*, code words for clearance and removal. Chombart's lens magnified the viability and hidden beauty of social life in precisely these forsaken areas. It became the rallying cry for his efforts to prevent the wholesale destruction of neighborhoods such as the rue Mouffetard, the Marais, or the rue Nationale.

This shift in discourse can best be examined in the 13th arrondissement on the Left Bank. It was one of the city's densest industrial districts, packed with the city's old flour mills and the Say sugar refinery, the railroad and industrial networks around the gare d'Austerlitz, gas works and factories, the automobile plants of Panhard & Levassor and SNECMA, the starch and shoemaking workshops, and the breweries, tanneries and laundries along the Bièvre River. And it was suffering a decline that was rapidly finishing off the city's traditional manufacturing sector, leaving miserable slum conditions in its wake. Claptrap buildings in a maze of ancient alleyways and sordid lanes offered shelter for working-class families, immigrants, and the poor. The entire area was in an advanced state of decay. The sector known as La Gare, situated behind the gare d'Austerlitz between the boulevard de la Gare (now the boulevard Vincent Auriol) and the boulevard Masséna, was identified as part of *îlot insalubre* 4 on the city's official register of slum districts. It contained

FIGURE 18. View of îlot 4 and the rue du Château-des-Rentiers, March 8, 1951. © COLL. PAVILLON DE L'ARSENAL, CLICHÉ DUVP.

some of the most notorious *cours de miracles* in the city: the cité Doré and in particular the militant cité Jeanne d'Arc, where political protests in 1934 had reached insurrectionary proportions. The confrontational atmosphere meant they were slated for slum clearance without delay—among the few partial projects carried out in the interwar years. The rue Nationale and the axis of the rue Jeanne d'Arc, the rue de Patay, and the rue de Tolbiac were the district's main arteries. All of these blighted areas were delineated by city officials according to a well-established discourse on social hygiene and public health: rates of tuberculosis and contagious diseases, alcoholism, infant mortality, housing conditions, and "intellectual instability and immorality."[18] The closure of the old Ivry gas works in particular had left the area in a state of advanced neglect, represented by the bleak, dejected rue du Château-des-Rentiers.

It was to La Gare that Chombart's young research team went to discover the social spaces of the working classes. Nearly fifty thousand people lived in the neighborhood, which according to their study, "has a bad reputation: there is a homeless shelter on the Château des Rentiers, a cité Jeanne d'Arc peopled by ragpickers, seedy dance halls that offer cheap wine, houses of prostitution." Miserable shanties and abandoned depots left to ruin were interspersed with vacant property, putrid canals, and railroad lines. North African immigrants lived squeezed together in cheap rooming houses, along with new arrivals from Vietnam and the rest of Asia. Algerian bars attracted the police. Wandering through the district in 1954, the writer Jean-Paul Clébert called it a "neighborhood fertile in tip-off meetings, a region littered with shelters, clinics, poor houses, philanthropic good works, Nicolas Flamel on the rue du Château-des-Rentiers, Le Corbusier—the A.S. skyscraper called the White House—rue Cantagrel."[19] Chombart's team set to work studying the area's history, demography, and density, and the quality of its lived environment: its public spaces, its circulation and transportation patterns, its workforce, its commerce and local economic life, its recreation and entertainment activities. The mix of data was mapped in a sociopsychological cartography that located distinct quartiers and îlots and graphically distinguished every aspect of the area's everyday life with diagrams and maps filled in with patterns of lines, shading, and contoured shapes. The vision was organic, immediate. The results gave a stunning portrait of La Gare as a dynamic "little city" with a diverse social life, and it delineated the specific needs of the community.[20]

Chombart and his team were crucial to the postwar development of French urban sociology. Their research was a product of a left-wing Catholic social reform movement that was open to social science methods, especially the neighborhood surveys of British social reformers in London and the urban ecology approach of Anthony Burgess and Robert Park in Chicago. As a spatial imaginary, it mapped collective practices to a heterogenic ideal of "place." Their investigations were also illustrative of the interactional posture of French urban sociology and the close bond between research and the state. Chombart's relationships with Auzelle (who had been in the same military unit as Chombart and became a top official at the Ministère de la construction et de l'urbanisme) and to Paul Delouvrier (a companion from the Uriage Training School) were instrumental in establishing relationships with the state planners who would carry out indispensable reforms. The research for *Paris et l'agglomération parisienne*, done in association with Auzelle's Centre d'études de la Direction générale de l'urbanisme (study center on urbanism) at the MRU, helped to sharpen the diagnostic tools for state urbanists faced with reconstruction and the renovation of slum districts. A series of grants from the MRU, the Commissariat général du Plan, and the District de la région parisienne also allowed Chombart to establish his research laboratories: first the Groupe d'ethnologie sociale, then the Centre d'études des groupes sociaux (created in 1955), which became the Centre de sociologie urbaine in 1958–59. Chombart's work, in other words, was grounded in the politics of ameliorating the urban conditions he found so deplorable. His lens on Paris and its everyday spaces had the effect of valorizing the particularities of working-class life in the eyes of state technocratic planners.

There is a touch of romanticism in Chombart's work about a people left outside traditional sociological discourse. His portrait of their collective lives has an artificial, nearly idyllic quality. Yet his aim was to shine the light of empirical research on these unknown, outcast social spaces, to improve them, and to integrate them into the life of the city and ultimately into a unified French society. For Chombart, the science of urbanism was less a matter of invention and more a matter of discovery. It aspired to respond to the needs and hopes of all levels of the population and all social groups.[21] Over time, however, Chombart and his team became disillusioned with the increasing dismissal and marginalization of their work, both by public administrators and by French academic elites. By the early 1960s Chombart's work was being criticized as sociology for state planners, without intellectual merit. Perhaps more important, the social humanism of the Liberation and reconstruction years was rapidly receding into the past, and with it went the poetic expression of neighborhood as an intrinsic cultural and social morphology.

Marxist sociology offered the most powerful alternative to the Catholic social reformism of the 1940s and 1950s. Marxists remained steadfastly antagonistic toward American social science methods as a threat to French cultural values and because it used psychological and statistical research in place of class analysis. Yet the Marxist approach to the city generated a critique of the everyday that was also spatial in orientation and specifically French in conception. It was an indication of how significant the milieu of the Liberation and reconstruction years was to the formation of French intellectual life. The most well-known and prolific French Marxist thinker of this period was Henri Lefebvre.[22] Although his career spanned sixty years and a wide range of pursuits, what interests us here is the narrower task of situating Lefebvre's life and work within the intellectual setting of the late 1940s and 1950s. During the war, Lefebvre worked for the Resistance in the south and eventually took refuge in the Pyrenees, where he helped organize local Resistance groups along the Spanish border and eventually achieved the rank of captain in the FFI. He also began field research on peasant life and folklore in the town of Campan that would eventually lead him away from traditional philosophy into sociology and provide the impetus for his doctoral thesis, published as *La Vallée de Campan: Étude de sociologie rurale* in 1963. By the Liberation, Lefebvre was in precarious straights. In 1947 he arrived in Paris, where he was tapped by Georges Gurvitch to join CNRS to study rural sociology. He remained there—barring a year of suspension for his communist links—until 1961.

Compared to philosophy, sociology was a political safe haven for Lefebvre. He was the main exponent of a French nondogmatic, humanist version of Marxism that was wholly consonant with the intellectual climate in Paris during these years. Its sensuous, emotional content in fact appealed to the social and Catholic democratic Left more than to the Communist Party. His interest was in the struggle against alienation, the possibility of human self-realization and the fulfillment of "total man." Although Lefebvre never explicitly wrote on Paris, the text of immediate interest is his 1947 *Critique of Everyday Life*, which became the philosophical source book for much noncommunist Marxist thinking of the 1950s and 1960s. It eventually became the first volume of three published under the title *Critique of Everyday Life* (1947, 1961, and 1981). Written from August through December 1945 during the heady days of Liberation and published by Grasset in February 1947, the original volume had the aura of humanist optimism and belief in social transformation characteristic of these years. The imagery is heroic. "In the enthusiasm of the Liberation," Lefebvre wrote in the introduction to the second volume, "it was hoped that soon life would be changed and the world transformed. More than that: life had already been changed; the peoples were on the move, the masses were in a ferment . . . the proletariat was no longer an oppressed class." *Critique of Everyday Life* situates itself at a moment in which intellectuals descended from the heights of theoretical abstraction to become active participants with the people: "To talk about alienation was no longer possible, no longer permissible."[23] The book was a call to action. Rather than focusing on the family as had Chombart, Lefebvre saw everyday life as the heart of social practice in the modern world. Precisely because it was insignificant, uneventful, and overlooked, Lefebvre argued that the everyday was the site where essential human desires, powers, and potentialities were formulated, developed, and ultimately realized. It is in the space of the everyday that we confront the social world and a common culture. It is a fluid present, a perpetual becoming that gives the quotidian its radical character.

For Lefebvre, Marxism was ultimately a critical knowledge of the everyday. From this point of view, the *esprit* of the working-class neighborhood was built around the thousand and one manifestations of worker social behavior and community. Even the worst slum districts sustained intense social practice, created largely from the solidarity and mutual aid necessitated by privation. Lefebvre called for a critique of these human needs, which Marxism had insufficiently illuminated,[24] in much the same vein as Chombart. Under modern capitalism, everyday existence has been undermined and devalued by the enchanted theater of consumer capitalism. But Lefebvre was optimistic that the empowerment and fulfillment of "total man" or "whole man" was possible if one revived natural social formations such as the festival and collective play. Everyday life, he postulated, was a *theatrum mundi* in which human beings "play a role." Acting extended reality and explored what was possible.[25] It was up to the committed Marxist to look for such a transfigured social existence in the seemingly trivial deeds and gestures of the everyday, and more specifically in the theatrics and festival that intensify and magnify everyday practices. It was there that a true art of living and a genuine humanism could be found. In other words, everyday life is revolutionary. This mise-en-scène in the spaces of the city, the collective celebration, playfulness and laughter, is transformative; it provides a glimpse of a fully realized social world. The *Critique* combined the influences that lay at the heart of Lefebvre's humanism: a fear of loss, a note of nostalgic sentimentality for community and the pastoral villages of Lefebvre's youth in the Landes, and his rural-folkoric studies of Campan during the war. The everyday is a blend of poetic space and the metaphysical space of the Hegelian school Lefebvre had explicitly chosen for his conception of Marxism. Ultimately, it is the space of both individual and collective transformation.

Lefebvre would of course go on to expound much further on the relationship between the city, everyday life, and modernity. But the 1947 essay—written in the postwar atmosphere of celebration, unbounded hopes, and the militant pedestrianism spilling out into the streets—contained the core of the many themes he returned to throughout his career. He shared with his intellectual contemporaries an outlook derived from the experience of surrealism and political avant-gardism, the war and the Resistance, the study of rurality and ethnographic folklore, and a deeply committed humanism.

Superimposed over the everyday spaces and streets of the city, especially in Paris, this perspective made the public arena the ultimate site of creativity and the imagination. The influence of *Critique of Everyday Life* was imported into the situationist movement by way of Constant Nieuwenhuys and the founding of the 1948 Cobra, an avant-garde group. Their initial fascination, which they shared with Lefebvre, was with an urban environment that could activate new conditions and new situations. Lefebvre, Guy Debord, and Constant met in Debord's *chambre de bonne* on the rue Saint-Martin, drinking tequila and talking late into the night about the commonalities in "moments" and "situations," about a new postwar architecture and urbanism. They would be devices for radical thinking, for fracturing urban space, for a celebratory urban theater of provocation. For both Lefebvre and the situationists, the *dérive* (drift) revealed the growing fragmentation of the city. In his interview with Kristin Ross, Lefebvre recounted his view of Paris as a once-powerful organic unity that was fragmenting into a puzzle of places, each with its own physiognomy.[26] It is the street that acts as the fundamental and original element of modern urban life. It is the medium of meeting and exchange, of real relations and practical everyday life. This actualizing disorderly space is where a consciousness of life in movement, its reality and its unfulfilled possibilities, can be attained. The trivial was magic.

Urban Planning and Humanist Discourse

Although far less well-known, the urban theorists working in Paris during and after the war echoed this same intellectual vision of the decentered metropolis. Beginning with Marcel Poëte and continuing with Auzelle, Gaston Bardet, and Pierre Lavedan, the work of the urbanists forms the basis of the following discussion. Among the most prominent thinkers about the urban experience, they constructed the language and texture of a distinctively French humanist perspective on the city and were instrumental in articulating a vernacular spatial topography in Paris. And the challenges seemed overwhelming. The capital was awash in intractable problems that went from the immediate needs of reconstruction to the tragic housing crisis, the never-ending nightmare of vast slum districts in the city, and the suburban anarchy engulfing the surrounding region. The spatiality and built environment of the capital formed among the most significant public debates of the entire period from the 1930s through the 1960s. Three different conferences on the future of Paris were held in 1942 and 1943 alone. Its redevelopment was under intense scrutiny in René Mestais's 1943 plan for the "transformation of Paris," André Thirion's 1951 and then Bernard Lafay's 1954 planning reports, and Jean Gravier's 1947 *Paris et le désert français* (see chapter 7). The debate played itself out in a mass of government documentation and propaganda among proponents on one side or another. In the process, a generation of engineers and technicians working for the city of Paris, the departments of the Seine and the Seine-et-Oise, and the French state were trained in professional urban planning and design techniques. They provided a remarkable coherency to the understanding of French *urbanisme* at midcentury, from the 1930s through the 1950s and beyond. But in 1945 architects and planners spun their dreamscapes in a staggering atmosphere. The war acted as a purge, an opportunity to finally realize the urban designs that had once been only fantasies. The impossible could suddenly be accomplished.

Within the city of Paris itself, the most pressing issue was the severe disrepair of the built environment that was behind both the housing crisis and the vast slum districts. Everyone agreed that Paris needed renovation. Exactly what kind was guided by a shared humanist point of focus. The approach produced a kind of ameliorated *haussmannisation* that took into account a far more nuanced sense of the richness of the capital's urban life and the authenticity of its neighborhood-village qualities. This concept was developed by the first generation of urban professionals working between the two world wars, many of them in reaction to the damage done by the Second Empire's authoritarian vision of the City of Light. For Marcel Poëte, professor at the Institut d'histoire, de géographie et d'économie urbaine housed at the Bibliothèque historique de la ville de Paris (where he taught the first courses on the history of Paris), the capital had developed according to an organic logic that had to be respected: the *beaux quartiers* were in the west, the working-class districts in the east, and the industrial suburbs in the north; the Right Bank was the city's business center, and the Left Bank its intellectual center. The historic heart of Paris was on the Île-de-la-Cité, its extremities, the railroad lines that stretched into France. It was a living entity, a multicellular organism with an historic form that set the pattern for the future. The functional mold of the core would simply spread out to the periphery. The historian Evelyne Cohen, among others, points out that Poëte's vision of Paris was an application of the Bergsonian principle of *élan vital*.[27] To rediscover the city's urban heritage, the particularity of its neighborhoods, and its vernacular spaces and architecture was to rediscover the essential qualities of Frenchness. As chief librarian at the Bibliothèque historique, Poëte had purchased over three thousand of the photographer Eugène Atget's turn-of-the-century architectural and topographical views of "Old Paris" as an inventory of the city's vernacular landscape. Based on this data, the study of the city's sites, and sociological investigation, Paris could be made modern without sacrificing its distinctiveness.

It would be difficult to overestimate the influence of Poëte on the development of French urban theory and on the city of Paris. He was the equivalent of Louis Mumford in the United States and Patrick Geddes in Britain. Poëte's vision stimulated lively discussion among the French intelligentsia about how the history and memory of the city is invented and sustained and, from this, how the city becomes a complex, living entity. Poëte's perspective on urban history was continued by his students at the École des hautes études urbaines (which he founded with Henri Sellier in 1919), most of whom went on to play key roles in the formulation of what the French called *art urbain* and the development of Paris. Among them were the historian and urbanist Pierre Lavedan and Gaston Bardet. Lavedan's publications on urban planning—beginning in 1926 with *Qu'est-ce que l'urbanisme?*, his imposing *Histoire de l'urbanisme* (the first volume published in 1941), and the 1952 *La ville contemporaine*—became the standard texts for a growing cadre of professional urbanists. His introduction to *Qu'est-ce que l'urbanisme?* evoked Poëte's conception of the city as a complex "living organism" and referred to Mauss's understanding of social morphology as enveloping "everything that serves the functioning of collective life." This same concept, according to Lavedan, could be used as the basis of urban planning.[28] The work of Raymond Unwin in England on garden cities and Unwin's notion of the variations and individuality of city form were also essential to Lavedan's intellectual repertoire. His interpretations of the city's planning heritage would have particular significance during the 1950s. As editor of *La Vie urbaine* (founded by Marcel Poëte in 1919), director of the Institut d'urbanisme de l'Université de Paris from 1942 until 1964, professor of architectural history at the École des beaux-arts, and member of the Commission du vieux Paris, Lavedan wielded enormous influence in planning circles and played an increasing role in the decisions made by both the municipality and the state about the future of the capital. He disapproved of Haussmann's work as excessively concerned with aesthetics and power, as "political, we can even say *policier*" (italics added).[29] Lavedan opposed Le

Corbusier's utopian conceptions as well. The genius of French rationalism, of which he remained an ardent enthusiast, was in its suppleness. Like his contemporaries, Lavedan believed that geography determined urban place, and his points of reference were rooted in spatial topography and the natural elements of site. A city's evolution could be translated through its physical form and the durability of its plan and street layout. He argued that planning should be based on scientific diagnostics and thorough knowledge of a city's history. Along with Chevalier and Chombart, Lavedan shared the belief that these strategies would illuminate the particularities of place and social morphology that had evolved in the ancient villages of the capital. In a narrative imagery matching that of Chevalier, he concluded that "the inhabitant of Montmartre is something other than a citizen of the 18th arrondissement, while the man of Batignolles, of Belleville, or of Auteuil is no less attached to his quartier though it may not have any noble artistic titles."[30]

Lavedan's contemporary Bardet was among the most well-known urbanists writing at midcentury. Because of his Catholic spiritualism and close association with Vichy, his career in France faltered by the early 1950s. Much like Chombart's, Bardet's work was progressively discredited and ignored by the modernist wave sweeping the *trente glorieuses*. However, Jean-Louis Cohen has described Bardet as a major figure in twentieth century French urbanism. His work has recently been rediscovered as an essential influence on the pattern of French urban thought. Following in the footsteps of Poëte (both his mentor and father-in-law), Bardet accumulated a vast knowledge of urban history and *art urbain* and was one of the French theorists best schooled in contemporary Anglo-Saxon and German approaches to urban planning. Mumford's *The Culture of Cities* and Geddes' *Civic Survey* had a profound impact on his intellectual development.[31] Teaching at the Institut d'urbanisme de l'Université de Paris, Bardet's purpose was to formulate a "New Urbanism" through meticulous research on the social topography of Paris. Pedagogically, his approach led to the creation of the Atelier supérieur d'urbanisme appliqué (applied urban planning studio), in which students such as Auzelle and Jean de Maisonseul began the design analysis of the Marais that proved crucial to that district's ultimate renovation (see chapter 7). The workshop also participated in projects with Lebret's Économie et Humanisme movement, which advocated the practical study of urban conditions in order to determine the needs of the population and implement more humanistic forms of development.

Bardet approached the city from the Bergsonian perspective of *élan vital* or as an organic entity in continuous evolution. The purpose of urban life was not to facilitate traffic or commerce, but to multiply the possibilities for individual self-realization and association between people. His masterwork, written in 1943–44 and published as *Le Nouvel urbanisme* in 1948, created a spatial hierarchy of the capital's life, from the metropolitan scale of 500,000 to 1,500,000 families down to the "patriarchal" scale of 50 to 150 families. The urban landscape was broken up into discrete microzones. Given the intensity and alienation of the modern metropolis, the level of neighborhood or quartier offered the best chance for the flowering of communal sociability and civic life. It balanced the relationship between the individual and the community. Although theorists of the garden city, such as Ebenezer Howard in England and Clarence Perry of the Russell Sage Foundation in the United States, had approached this understanding, Bardet argued that their knowledge was largely theoretical. Instead, in the same vein as that of the French sociologists, his research on Paris was applied and interactive. It attempted to provide scrupulously detailed evidence of neighborhood space as a living, feeling phenomenon that could be used by urban planners to solve the problems of the modern city. Bardet defined the parish or quartier as about a thousand families grouped around their public space and public institutions—school, church, markets, and shops. It contained all the elements necessary for collective life. The larger city around the neighborhood offered sites of work and pleasure, but like Chombart, Bardet argued that it was only at the village scale that a sane and happy social life could blossom.[32] By imagining the metropolis as a federation of neighborhood cells and providing them with their collective needs, urban life would take on its authentic "organic" and "spiritual" form.

Here again the influence of prewar social Catholicism was clear. Catholic values attributed the utmost fulfillment of individuals to their life in the community. Even if Catholic intellectuals did not wholeheartedly endorse the politics of the Vichy Regime, they could find sympathy for its ideal of moral order and its accent on family and community. Conservative elements within the church saw the German victory as punishment for the sins of the selfish, secular Third Republic. This consensual rhetoric on morality, social order, and spiritual community meant that Catholic thinkers could be found guilty of tacit support for Vichy's National Revolution. The marginalization of Bardet himself is clear evidence of this view. After the Liberation, Bardet was shunned by the MRU and by the Institut d'urbanisme, and by 1947 he had left France altogether. The core of his teachings continued, however, to inspire his students, who began their professional work in Paris just after the war. In fact, by the early postwar years this type of progressive Catholic social reformism, including Emmanuel Mounier's personalist movement, built around the journal *Esprit*, had clearly swung into the camp of the Left. It had become part of the mainstream and found willing listeners among the technocrats filling the ranks of the state bureaucracy and the professional cadre carrying out the reconstruction of France's cities. Writing in *Esprit* in August 1945, when the Liberation was about to offer utopian prospects to the urbanists, Bardet argued that the real, authentic public life of the city could be found at the level of the quartier, where the puzzle of houses and ordinary small shops and the network of streets created a living entity with its own unique character. The center of this *physionomie sociale* was the public monument, which "creates the quartier" and provides it not only with a spatial structure, but with a neighborhood spirit. The purpose of the new urbanism was to create this kind of material and social form.[33] It could be done by focusing on a complex, organic neighborhood fabric centered on its public space rather than on rationalist zoning formulas.

Bardet's conceptions were a clear indication of how far urbanists had come from Haussmann's grand-scale monumentalizing of the capital. A patchwork of imagined spaces—quartier, îlot, *cité satellite*—replaced the brutal topography of Haussmann's boulevards. They became the essential elements in imagining urban transformation, operational categories for sociological study and urban planning. Chombart argued that the îlot was the only geographical category in which the multiple elements of social life could be precisely studied and mapped.[34] It was a compact space nearly invisible to the city around it, and its public life was oriented around an internal maze of streets, courtyards, and public space. This was not a voyage into nostalgic preservationism. In fact, the "regressive, narrow-minded" cultural vision of the prewar years that had given the preservationists such power over the Paris municipal council was renounced. The policy of privileging the capital's "beauty" and its "picturesque" historic central districts while ignoring the spreading cancer of the slums was judged an ill-fated blunder. Even the Ligue urbaine et rurale, one of the city's most powerful lobbying groups, begun by Raoul Dautry and Jean Giraudoux in 1926, refused to "defend the past in such a jealous, egotistical, and sterile manner." Writing on behalf of the organization in 1945, the architect Marcel Raval defined a "new French humanism" to be accomplished by creating modernized neighborhood places that took into account the rich temporality and spatiality that made Paris so distinct and enviable as a city: "Only the winds of renovation can transfigure these sites, houses, hotels, châteaux that are too often nothing more than structures without souls, sordid and transparent shells."[35] The mental mapping by residents was accomplished through a familiarity and informal sociability born of everyday life. The rhythms, activities, and exchanges within the îlot's public space were essentially an extension of the self. Multiplied across the neighborhood, they created a collective reading of space that was subjective, intuitive, and humanistic.

This humanist discourse around the îlot was carried through from the 1930s to the mid-1950s by architects such as Auzelle, Michel Roux-Spitz, and Georges Sébille. Auzelle was perhaps the quintessential model of a deeply humanistic architect-urbanist. He not only carried on scholarship at the Institut d'urbanisme, but also dedicated himself to an applied urbanism that was a "conscious organization of space"—a view reflected in the title of his 1962 *Plaidoyer pour une organisation consciente de l'espace*. A student before the war of both Poëte and Bardet, Auzelle pleaded for a reconsideration of planning that took into account the particularities of place and its everyday uses. That did not mean he opposed the modernism of CIAM's Athens Charter. Auzelle admired both Auguste Perret and Le Corbusier for their courage in rebelling against aesthetic custom and offering new theoretical structures. However, he deplored the bitter, oversimplified dispute between the proponents of modernist formalism and the preservationists of the traditional vernacular cityscape. And he hated what the automobile had done to the street.

Using the language of progressive Catholic circles, both Auzelle and Sébille sought a third way: the transformation of historical, sociological, and geographic insights into modern planning techniques. The way forward was to follow the lead of Poëte and Bardet. In the late 1930s and early 1940s, Auzelle and Sébille proposed the îlot as the groundwork for the new concept of *rénovation*. In his contribution to the influential 1943 urban testimonial *Destinée de Paris*, Auzelle began with the statement that "Paris is in part built on a fragmented culture." He argued that it was the "built îlot that currently predominated in Paris."[36] Quoting Sébille, he defined it as "a complex element, the intermediary between the house and the city." It was delimited by public streets. Neighborhood public life was organized around distinctively shaped, articulated spaces. This perspective was a result of his association with Chombart, with whom he frequently "discussed ethnology and anthropology,"[37] as well as the influence of Bardet's notion of "cities within cities." Rather than simply understanding it as an urban parcel, the street and the *cours* or public square were articulated as the elemental spaces of collective life. In 1939, in *îlot insalubre* 16, in the Marais between the churches of Saint-Gervais and Saint-Paul, Auzelle and Sébille proposed building renovations rather than complete demolition, the conservation of ancient roadways, and if necessary, the clearing out of *bâtiments parasitaires* (parasitic buildings) to "open up" the local landscape of traditional public courtyards and squares.[38]

By the war's end in 1945, Auzelle was in charge of a number of reconstruction projects being carried out by the newly established MRU, and in 1948 he was named director of the study center for the MRU's Direction générale de l'urbanisme et de l'habitat. His *Technique de l'urbanisme*, published in 1953, was instrumental in opening up the debate about urbanism to the larger public. In 1947 Auzelle enlisted Chombart for a diagnostic study of the suburban development of La Plaine at Clamart in the department of Hauts-de-Seine north of Paris. The evaluation would "take the pulse" of *place* and social environment for state planners, who would then use it to thread the distinctive character of the neighborhood into their redevelopment schemes. Around fifty of these diagnostic studies were done under Auzelle's guidance between 1950 and 1955, particularly within the context of his collaboration on Chombart's momentous investigation *Paris et l'agglomération parisienne*. They included Auzelle's use of the *maquettoscope*, which added a telescopic lens to aerial photography in order to take highly detailed images of the built environment, infrastructure, social and commercial networks, and topography of sites under renovation. According to Auzelle, these kinds of multifaceted site studies were the key to successful urban redevelopment and the reenergizing of local collective life.[39] Swooping down on the city as if to catch it unawares, the aerial sequences sited, surveyed, and opened the city for examination. In many ways they shared the same visual perspective as the commercial films produced about Paris in the 1950s (see chapter 5).

The renovation of La Plaine at Clamart from 1947 to 1952 was one of the most eloquent counterstatements to the eventual policy of *grand ensemble* suburban housing complexes. His design took into account the social needs of community and neighborhood as well as existing architectural volumes, views, and the natural environment. An unpretentious permeability existed between the street and the interiors of homes. A complete range of some two thousand new dwellings were constructed in a series of *îlots urbains* that were oriented toward the streets and modeled after his vision of the garden city. New construction respected the scale of existing historic structures. A greenbelt threaded through the new district, linking playgrounds, the commercial center, schools, and church. Strict traffic regulations limited the types of vehicles allowed access to the all-important network of community lanes and roads that represented neighborhood spatiality and sociability. Developing his methods through the 1950s, Auzelle carried out a diagnostic study of "sector 7" of the infamous *zone* surrounding Paris that would be developed under the Lafay Law for the construction of housing estates. The area from the porte de Pantin to the porte des Lilas was subjected to excruciating analysis of topography and soil quality, historical evolution, population, and social and community services. The result was a plan that privileged neighborhood groupings or îlots composed of different housing blocks ("some low, some high") centered on a community complex of public services, school, and church.[40]

Auzelle's work exemplifies the attentiveness to temporality and distinct spatiality that characterized an alternative French vision of modern urban planning at midcentury. It was distinguished by the deep relationship between urban planners and sociologists and the way they interacted in their research. Urbanists shared a social-reformist orientation and a humanist approach that steered away from monumental designs for the capital and instead fractured the space of the city into îlots, or naturalized neighborhoods of lived experience. In other words, *urbanisme* was translated as social reform—or, perhaps more exactly, as the opportunity to redeem a population shattered by war and mounting daily struggle. It was in many ways an extension of the reformist or social municipalism of the 1930s, which was based on the notion of a social contract and new social rights through expert knowledge of the city. This discourse ennobled the working classes and what were perceived as their indigenous collective spaces. Taken together, this reading of Paris created an influential planning corpus that largely eschewed the *tabula rasa* of modernist universalism and instead attempted to invent a particularist vision of a progressive, twentieth-century capital. Modern urban planning would be assimilated into the city's historic cultural geography. Planners imagined Paris as a timeless web of vernacular districts, historic buildings, and monumental stage sets. Here lay the creative tableau upon which France would press forward into a modern renaissance and regain its glory. The city's historic places were to be protected and its quality of life enhanced by rejuvenating neighborhoods both in the central city and in the suburbs. Just as the îlot acted as the wellspring of social life in the city, the *cité-jardin* was to be the basic social unit of the suburbs. Twentieth-century urban planning and social reform would revive the magnetism of *la ville lumière* and represent the unique character of French modern.

The Avant-Garde

This third section of the chapter looks at the shared visions of Paris among the postwar avant-garde, specifically from the perspective of the lettrist movement, which would eventually evolve into the Situationist International (SI), and of the writers Léo Malet and Henri Calet. The literature on the SI in particular is distinguished by its quantity and its exceptional quality, and it is not my intent to go over such well-cultivated ground here. On the other hand, the brilliant urban reportage of Malet and Calet is far less well-known.[41] Rather than focusing with exactitude on the œuvre of each, my purpose is to situate these actors or, even more pointedly, these *wanderers* as they crossed and crisscrossed the spaces of Paris along with Auzelle, Chevalier, Chombart, Prévert, and Ronis—each of them carrying out their urban mapping, pointing their cameras and their *maquettoscopes*, recording the layers of meaning in the city's spatiality, and creating a common portrait of an idiosyncratic, naturalized urban topography. They shared an ethos of descending into the streets to discover the city's soul. Together their narrative imagery infused Paris with a moral aesthetic that was humanist, populist, and ultimately poetic.

There is no doubt about the continued influence of the prewar avant-garde movements and especially of surrealism on postwar intellectual and artistic elites. In the case of France, the aesthetic continuities across the Second World War may be more interesting than the ruptures, especially in relation to experiments in urban space. In fact, cultural historian Pascal Ory argues that it is a mistake to see surrealism as a movement of the prewar years. The real victory of surrealism dates from the Liberation, when the generation that had shared a youthful phase of surrealist avant-gardism came into their own as the new elites.[42] Prévert, Lefebvre, and Raymond Queneau were the cultural celebrities of the late 1940s and 1950s. Surrealism encouraged them to confront life, reality, and the urban nexus from a capricious, radical trajectory. The surrealists imagined Paris spatially. The monumental spaces of modernity, the *grands boulevards*, the cafés and shopping districts, the flamboyant and monumental face of the capital were cast off as touristic, effete, without spontaneity. Instead, the surrealist itinerary wound through the populist, ordinary spaces of the city in neighborhoods such as Les Halles, Saint-Paul, and Saint-Merri. It was there that individuals could situate themselves and find a sense of identity, meaning, and value. The experience of space piqued the imagination and insight into the self as well as the surrounding city in a "topography of subjectivity."[43] Personal identity and destiny are manifested in the encounter with the urban setting. The streets and spaces of Paris are arenas of possibility, of individual metamorphosis, of emotion and play.

The postwar movement that most closely followed in the footsteps of the surrealist urban wanderer was the lettrists, which formed around Debord and Jean-Isidore Isou in the 1950s. As Isou shouted at the January 8, 1946, Paris premiere of Tristan Tzara's play *La Fuit* at the Vieux-Colombier Theater in Saint-Germain-des-Prés, "Dada is dead! Lettrism has taken its place!" Isou saw the Lettrists as a youth movement that would carry on a post-Dada avant-garde art for the new age. The promise that "12 million young people will hit the streets in the lettrist revolution!" was scrawled onto the walls of the Left Bank.[44] The movement's stomping ground was Saint-Germain-des-Prés, and its experimental landscape was Paris. The inflammatory antics produced by this antecedent of the SI around both its artistic production and infighting were its own form of street theater. In April 1950 they disrupted Easter Sunday mass at Notre Dame by posing as priests chanting condemnations against the church and exhorting parishioners to "exalt in a land where God is dead."[45] The founding document of the Lettrist International, the first to break away from Isou's group, was duly signed at Aubervilliers by Debord and a few followers, shoved in a bottle, and thrown into "the sea" (the canal). They disrupted a Charlie Chaplin press conference at the Hôtel Ritz in October 1952. They painted graffiti on the city walls. Members of the group produced a "spoken" news bulletin lasting for two or three hours from a bench on the place Saint-Sulpice. Provocateur allies of Debord rained stink bombs and sneezing powder on the audience trying to fathom a showing of *Hurlements en faveur de Sade* at the Ciné-Club du Quartier Latin in June 1952. This was precisely the kind of clownish Left Bank agitprop theater that subverted the society of the spectacle. Debord and his band snubbed the existentialist scene at the Tabou and the Rose Rouge nightclubs to find more unpretentious, cheaper haunts: the Mabillon and Old Navy on the boulevard Saint-Germain, the Chop Gauloise on the rue Bonaparte, and especially the Café Moineau on the rue du Four. There they could merge into the inspired zone of the ordinary.

The lettrists pushed the notion of *flânerie* forward by roaming through Paris in what they called the *dérive* or drift. To demystify the spectacle of mass consumer culture, Debord and his band descended into the streets of the working-class neighborhoods of Paris to explore the ludic culture that survived there. Debord was fascinated by the dramatic urban social geography of Chombart and his *Paris et l'agglomération parisienne*. Chombart's dissection of Paris revealed astonishing subtleties in the uses of the city and the indigenous social associations at the level of the neighborhood. During the summer of 1953, the lettrists went on "heroic expeditions" through the alien microzones of Paris.[46] They drifted through the Chinese neighborhood behind the gare de Lyon, to the "beautiful and tragic" rue d'Aubervilliers and the district of La Plaine, through the 13th arrondissement to the rue Sauvage (which they described as "one of the most moving nocturnal perspectives in the capital," "more alive than the Champs-Élysées"),[47] on to the Saint-Paul

FIGURE 19. The rue Sauvage, September 29, 1953. © COLL. PAVILLON DE L'ARSENAL, CLICHÉ DUVP.

section of the Marais, across to Les Halles—and then slipped back across the Seine to the Arab bar on the rue Xavier-Privas and to their headquarters on the "continent" Contrescarpe and the cafés of Saint-Germain-des-Prés. In his 1953 "Formula for a New Urbanism," in a naming ritual not unlike that which took place after the Liberation, Ivan Chtcheglov (writing under the pseudonym Gilles Ivain) discovered the mysteries of the city's signs and billboards:

Center for Functional Recuperation
Saint-Anne Ambulance
Café Fifth Avenue
Prolonged Willingness Street
Family Boarding House in the Garden
Stranger's Hotel
Wild Street

And the swimming pool on the Street of Little Girls. And the police station on Rendezvous Street. The medical-surgical clinic and the free placement center on Goldsmith's Quay. The artificial flowers on Sun Street. The Chateau Cellars hotel, the Ocean Bar, and the Coming and Going Café. The Epoch Hotel.[48]

Street names and signs become a magical cryptography of neglected backwaters. Texts on this activity were published in *Naked Lips* in 1955 and 1956. Debord's 1959 film *On the Passage of a Few People through a Brief Moment of Time* included depictions of their "drifts" through the sinuous spaces of the city, searching for eccentricity and the exotic, for play, for the erotic, for any signs of freedom and refusal. The sublime was found in chance encounters, in dubious characters and forbidden pleasures. In his 1950 pictographic tour of "Saint Ghetto des Prêts" (Saint-Germain-des-Prés), the lettrist Gabriel Pomerand described a place seething with legend and possibilities in every chance encounter; every moment, word, building, person revealed an opening into a secret utopia. "Saint-Germain-des-Prés is a ghetto," he wrote; "Everyone there wears a yellow star."[49]

Debord was fascinated by the deviant characters that inhabited these emotive spaces. Drinking and drugs, carousing and run-ins with the police, wandering the streets with slogans painted on their clothes, his band of followers was itself a living example of *détournement* (diversion). In his seminal article on situationist space, Tom McDonough points out that as a practice of the city, the *dérive* "reappropriated public space from the realm of myth, restoring it to its fullness, richness, and its history."[50] But the lettrists were hardly alone on these expeditions. The Liberation in August 1944 was of course the ultimate model of appropriation and street theater. Debord and his band were joined in the course of these pre- and post-Liberation years by a youth pageantry of costumed *zazous* sporting yellow stars in dangerous wartime resistance, existential beatniks in black roaming Saint-Germain-des-Prés, and partying students dressed in the bizarre garb of the *mônome de bac*. Weird styles and gestures, the farcical manipulation of symbols, and playful carnival rites made up a subversive theater in the setting of the street. Play and the festive produced novel environments. All manner of unexpected, dangerous, potentially creative things could happen.

The perpetuation of this inspired bond between social marginality, the avant-garde, and the everyday theater of urban space was remarkable. Jean Vilar, the director of the Théâtre national populaire (TNP), dreamed of demystifying French drama and moving it in a democratic direction. Writing in *Esprit* in 1949, Vilar declared, "The pimps, the whores, sailors, workers, students, concierges, bus drivers, drunkards, tramps, neighborhood shopkeepers, the pretty young girls on the street, all mixed inside the theater are better for our dramatic literature than the Saint-Sulpicien, the orthodox Marxist, or the committed literati and the ex-prince of the black market."[51] By midcentury the conventional *flâneur* had transmuted into another, more subversive figure—that of the vagabond-seer who alone possessed the marginal vision that transgressed boundaries and turned them into thresholds. Vilar's materialization of the all-seeing tramp haunting the city's streets in Marcel Carné's 1946 *Les Portes de la nuit* produced this way of seeing. "Revelation about life in a city," according to Jean-Paul Clébert, one of Paris's greatest urban observers in search of the strange, "is . . . reserved for the initiated, for very rare poets, for the very numerous vagabonds, each of them drinking it in according to their mood and their emotional capacity. And to conquer it you have to be truly a vagabond-poet or a poet-vagabond."[52] The avant-garde reached into an ethnographic index of extraordinary Parisian street types to create scenes of subjectivity and sensuality, of intuitiveness. Paris was less a European cultural capital than a disjointed, quotidian theater of the exiled. The everyday spaces of the city were the terrain of marginality, deviance, and subversion.

This was also a confrontation with individual psyche, a compulsive, dreamlike search for the self. The lettrists mapped out what they called a "psychogeography" of Paris based on their surreal, mixed-up drifts. A collage was made of a torn-up city map in an intuitive cartography of space that was subjective, disjointed, undisciplined. Their diagrammatic experiments led to the publication in 1957 of *The Naked City*. The title was based on Jules Dassin's American detective film *The Naked City* (1948),[53] which Debord held in high regard. In fact, the similarities between the detective genre and Debord's psychogeographic collage of Paris, in which he hopes, as he writes in his 1955 "Introduction to a Critique of Urban Geography," to capture "the sudden change of atmosphere in a street within the space of a few meters, the sharp division of a city into zones of distinct psychological climates," are unmistakable.[54] The parallels are clearest in relation to the narrative maps of Paris in Léo Malet's detective series *Les Nouveaux mystères de Paris*, written between 1953 and 1959. Malet is considered one of the founders of the French *roman noir*, the detective fiction that was the literary analog of the *film noir* so appropriate to the mood in France in the 1940s and 1950s. Although the series won the Grand Prix de littérature policière in 1948 as well as the prestigious Grand Prix de l'humour noir Xavier Forneret in 1959, it initially achieved only limited popular success. A play on Eugène Sue's *Les Mystères de Paris* (1841), each novel in the series takes place in one of the arrondissements of Paris. The setting is urban. The spaces of Paris are the central characters of these novels, and Malet adored exploring and exposing their incongruities, their life and death. His visual and anthropological perspective attempted to capture the authentic essence of urban life in much the same way as did the early situationists, or Chombart or even Auzelle. All attempted to penetrate the superficial urban spectacle and grasp an authentic humanity and the spaces of truth.

Malet lived most of his life on the edges of society and experienced firsthand the marginality and disconnectedness the lettrists attempted to capture in their *dérives*. He knew the reality of the city's mean streets below the mystifying spectacle of capitalism, especially in the 13th arrondissement, where the new arrival from Montpellier at first found refuge in a vegetarian hostel on the rue de Tolbiac. It was not far from where, in 1926, he was found by the police, destitute, sleeping under the pont Sully.[55] Malet was the vagabond-seer come to life. He was inspired by a mélange of influences that included an early interest in anarchism. Employment in a series of low-

FIGURE 20. Novelist Léo Malet and illustrator Felix Labisse with their book *Les Nouveaux Mystères de Paris,* October 31, 1958. © RUE DES ARCHIVES / THE GRANGER COLLECTION, NEW YORK.

paying jobs helped him survive: dishwasher at Félix Potin, factory laborer, telephone operator, newsboy, cabaret singer. These experiences would find their way into his novels in pointillist detail. In the 1930s he discovered surrealism and found himself in the frequent company of André Breton, Paul Éluard, Alberto Giacometti, and Louis Aragon. Imprisoned in Germany after the June 1940 invasion, Malet was released in 1941 and returned to Paris and the Left Bank. In 1952, desperate for a scheme that would earn him money, he came up with the idea for a series of hardboiled thrillers starring the *detective de choc* (ace detective) and *flâneur* extraordinaire Nestor Burma, owner and sole operator of the Fiat Lux Detective Agency. Burma's adventures begin during the Second World War and continue through the 1950s. In an autobiographical twist, he is, like Malet, a former left-wing idealist and anarchist. Malet planned to have the character solve a crime in each of the city's arrondissements, and fifteen of the twenty books were written.

Despite all the recognizable Parisian landmarks in these novels, there is no one prominent center. Malet avoids the monumental capital in search of the authentic life of the city, the lived experience revealed in the microscopic, anthropological gaze of Nestor Burma. The urban fragments, the objects and details, that typify the spaces of the city gain significance in an atmosphere of a trivial, everyday actuality. Burma's *flânerie* is little more focused than the wanderings of the lettrists. True to his surrealist proclivities, Malet allowed the story to take form as Burma strolled through the landscape, acting as a surrogate for readers. In his notes on the *flâneur*, Walter Benjamin noted the figure's performance as detective. The role presented a "plausible front, behind which, in reality, hides the riveted attention of an observer who will not let the unsuspecting malefactor out of his sight."[56] In tracking down clues and duplicitous characters, Nestor Burma paces the city's streets hunting for the details, the unusual, instantaneous moments in the life of these urban places that will reveal the truth he is seeking. The precision of his gaze is investigatory, almost photographic.

Both Debord and Malet attempt to lay bare the social body of the city. Their urban landscape was feminine, ripe with sensuous, hidden qualities. Malet's lyric descriptions are atmospheric and at times erotic, first because in detective novels the city is always feminine, and secondly because the poetic sentimentality is emotional and bittersweet. Debord too (and, for that matter, Chevalier and Chombart as well) explored his passion for the city and searched out the emotional feel of its streets, uncovering its secrets. Both Malet and Debord splinter the map of Paris into fragments. They search for tiny clues: Malet to solve a crime and Debord to transform urban life. And for both, the fragmented spaces of the city can be experienced only by a situated subject in a discrete period of time. The perception of place is distinct, particular to a localized urban milieu. Malet's descriptions are exact; they shape a topographic drama. Each arrondissement and neighborhood is illuminated by the particularities of its landscape and its buildings, by the continuity of its streets and spaces. Simple facts, bits of local lore, and fleeting images are not merely inert, but take on the character of lived life. They are the snapshots that reveal the disjointed patches or "unities" of atmosphere the situationists were searching for.

The situationist mapping of their detective-style drifts through *The Naked City* was taken from the diagrams rendered by the CNRS researcher Louis Couvreur for Chombart's *Paris et l'agglomération parisienne*. Debord was dependent on the social geography of Chombart and on the humanist townscaping prevalent among urbanists. For Chombart and the situationists alike, the quartier is the basic unit of urban structure. It possesses a distinct character and is the site of social life. Writing on their drift through Les Halles, for example, fellow-traveler Abdelhafid Khatib mapped out the area in emulation of Chombart's spatial-sociological techniques.[57] The nuances of space and atmosphere—or the *ambiance*, as Khatib put it—must be discovered by the observer in the social practices, the behaviors and speech, and the social rites of the community. The evolving situationist conception was of a transfigured urban space with the maximum degree of communality and interchange, free dialog and play. Human interaction was conceived as space filling. In the October 1955 issue of *Potlatch*, the lettrists presented this solution to the problem of urbanism in Paris: the city's squares, rooftops, Métro, renovated footbridges, and passageways should all be opened at night as new spaces for play and social participation.[58] These would be the mechanisms for a breakthrough into self-actualization and authentic existence. The aesthetics that represented these "unities of atmosphere," or îlots, in the urbanist vocabulary, were the eclectic blend of historic, pedestrian, and expressive structures that had grown up over time. Much of this language and discourse was intrinsic to the universe of French sociology and urbanism. Chevalier, Chombart, Bardet, and Auzelle all shared this narrative and visual imagery. Public space was filled with an abundance of temporalities and visual expressions. It was organic, perpetually changing, brimming with possibilities and situations, and revolutionary in content.

This approach to Paris was shared by Malet, whose urban narration and character depictions are deeply humanist. Nestor Burma is a breed of sleuth who relies on his intuitive awareness of the human condition and his populist links. Malet humanizes faceless city dwellers and restores the experience of place. In the 13th arrondissement, the Lettrist International championed the preservation of derelict streets such as the rue Sauvage behind the gare d'Austerlitz as an example of authentic, quotidian Paris untouched by the mesmerizing spectacle of the modern city. It was located in the dingy slum

FIGURE 21. The rue du Château-des-Rentiers, October 28, 1961. © COLL. PAVILLON DE L'ARSENAL, CLICHÉ DUVP

of La Gare with the remains of its cité Jeanne d'Arc—otherwise known as *îlot insalubre* 4. In drifts through the district, the lettrist René Crevel renamed the miserable rue du Château-des-Rentiers the rue du Taudis-des-Chomeurs (the slum of unemployed) in an unearthing of the "what took place there." His fellow drifter Ralph Rumney remembered sleeping at a shelter "in the neighborhood of Léo Malet's youth."[59] It would have been easy for them to bump into Chombart's young research team poring over the area, collecting data for their sociological study.

Burma, as Malet's alter ego, wanders through La Gare in what is considered one of the best novels of the series, the 1956 *Brouillard au Pont de Tolbiac*.[60] The action takes place in an interminable, penetrating fog "that took possession of the neighborhood" and signified the cast-out, forlorn atmosphere of the locale. The irony of its despair and poverty is caught in the street names that Burma recites, and then inverts: "The 13th arrondissement is full of streets with charming, picturesque names, generally deceiving. The rue des Cinq Diamants, there are no diamonds; the rue du Château-des-Rentiers, there is mainly the Nicolas Flamel shelter; the rue des Terres au Curé, where I've seen no priest." In this linguistic *détournement*, Malet fractures the mystique and decomposes the space. He is there to investigate the death of his old anarchist friend Albert Lenantais, who, having barely survived a German concentration camp, had descended into the morass of ragpicking on the passage des Hautes Formes on the edge of La Gare's cité Jeanne d'Arc. It is a pitiful alleyway; the neighborhood is grimy and cheerless. "Too much misery, crap, misfortune," Burma sadly remarks. But he falls for the exotic gypsy Bélita Moralés, a poor flower seller who lives on the *passage* by her wits and any other means. When he loses her, he searches the streets: "It's been said that we walk the streets in search of something, a piece of bread, a shelter, a little love." He merges into the neighborhood and dives into a local café to escape the cold and fog and to find solace: "The typical noise at the bar: the brouhaha of conversation, the clink of glasses and the racket of the pinball machine manhandled by a guy who has no intention of losing and throws himself into it despite the ringing tilt bells. A jukebox begins to play and the voice of Georges Brassens singing 'Gare au gorille' suddenly overpowers the uproar." It is miserable and poor, but Burma has found the quartier's sociability, its passion. He discovers the soul and the sometimes cruel, sometimes kind urban condition. It is a poetic *noir* story that echoes the melancholy and heartbreak of

Carné's *Les Portes de la nuit*. It is also a search for authentic urban life in the forgotten places of Paris; the expressive, fragmented spatial topography whose ordinariness was the antonym of the capital's glamour and spectacle. In the last scene Burma finds Bélita on the pont de Tolbiac, only to have her die in this arms—killed by the murderer he has been searching for. "If you want to avenge something," Burma says to the police inspector, "you should avenge this gypsy, a girl forgotten by everyone."

Much like Malet, the *flâneur* Calet was mesmerized by what he imagined as the city's populist, poetic landscape. Calet dominated the urban literature on Paris during the 1950s. His career spanned a variety of media, from newspapers to novels, radio, and television. He grew up in a Paris of misery and narrowly escaped being imprisoned for theft. Calet was an outsider, a nonconformist. But mostly he was an itinerant urban traveler, someone who lived "a walking life" exploring the streets of the city and discovering its ordinary people. After the war and months in German captivity, Calet returned to Paris, where he wrote most frequently for *Combat* and worked on a book he conceived on the twenty arrondissements of Paris. It was published by Gallimard in 1948 as *Le Tout sur le tout* to immediate acclaim, followed in 1951 by *Les Grandes largeurs*. Calet's writing about the city is passionate and autobiographical. With the war behind him, he wanders a landscape of melancholy and tenderness, of sentimentality and love, and of memory.

> I know this city in depth; I take her apart stone by stone and rebuild her somewhere else. That's what I do when I'm away from her.
>
> Paris twelve months of the year, Paris changing, Paris during the four seasons, Paris in miniature, Paris every day, Paris in a bird's flight, Paris in a windowpane, Paris in the morning, Paris in the evening, Paris in the moon, Paris in song, Paris in a rainbow, Paris in a hundred thousand pipes, Paris frosted blue, Paris rosy, Paris translucent, Paris sweating, Paris in snow, Paris in a bride's veil, Paris in the evening toilette, Paris adorned with its stars, Paris in everyday dress, Paris wrapped in scarves of mist, Paris poor, abandoned, uninhabitable, bombarded, Paris rich, Paris shirttails in the wind—
>
> I am suited to this city, it's perfect, it's my size. I see it in all manners. It's an intimacy devoid of secrets. Paris in its nightgown, Paris naked. . . . It is life and death between us (life for her, death for me).[61]

His language play is a form of eroticism. His words evoke the color of voices, the textures of out-of-the-way places, the fluidity and rhythm of the city. The language he uses is commonplace and populist in tone—spoken prose. Rather than just banal, this speech is emotional and central to writing as a *flâneur*, digressing, wandering here and there, rapidly creating scenes and vignettes. Calet watched for the gesture, the local slang, the insult or shout that leveled with life and revealed the truth. It provoked the deepest inherited recollections and familiarity of the *peuple*. Going back to his old neighborhood in the 14th arrondissement, on the rue Marthe—which had been rechristened the rue Georges-Pitard, after a victim of Nazi atrocities—Calet runs into his old coal deliveryman on the street. They immediately recognize each other and begin chatting about their lives in the space of the commons. It is the stuff of spontaneous sociability and bonhomie.

Like Malet and Debord, Calet is an archaeologist of spatial meaning, digging though the layers of perception and revealing the multiplicity of perspectives to embellish a sense of place. The writing stays on ground level and embraces the daily drama of the capital. Calet loses himself in his *dérives* through the city, digressing and splintering his stories as he comes upon chance encounters and finds the diminutive, unseen urban world. Michel Schmitt argues that Calet's notes for the 7th arrondissement (which would eventually find their way into many of his books) are written in the form of a fragmented psychogeography or speech act, in the vein of situationism. Each page is a constructed situation that blends space, time, and observation.[62] In the early 1950s Calet used a variety of media to illuminate his own psychogeography of the everyday. A 1952 weekly radio show produced by him and directed by Jean Kerchbron, *Huit quartiers de roture*, illuminated life in the common working-class neighborhoods of La Villette, Amérique, Combat, pont de Flandre, Saint-Fargeau, Belleville, Père Lachaise, and Charonne. The same year the two produced a television film entitled *Quelques quartiers de Paris* that explored Bercy, Grenelle, and La Villette. They were one among many visual lenses turned upon the city.

In May and June 1953 Calet published a special investigative report in *Le Parisien libéré* on the people of modest circumstances in Paris and its suburbs. The set of articles was published in 1954 by Gallimard as *Les Deux bouts*. Calet's approach was nearly ethnoanthropological. The daily life and personal habits of his interviewees and their construction of a *Paris utilitaire* are described in the analytical pointillism of social research. In one vignette

Calet follows Paul Roy, who lives with his wife, Geneviève, on the rue d'Assas in the 6th arrondissement and works at the Halle aux Vins along the Seine at Jussieu in the 5th arrondissement. The daily itinerary and activities of this archetypal Parisian worker are captured in exquisite detail, revealing his life as genuine, if not heroic, and indisputably linked to the urban landscape. Each morning at 7:50 A.M., he bikes up the avenue de l'Observatoire, the boulevard Saint-Michel, and the rue des Écoles to the Halle aux Vins. At 10:00 he starts his job filling bottles with wine, apéritifs, and digéstifs. At noon, he lunches at the museum in the Jardin des Plantes with a clientele that is half wine-market employees and half students, and then takes a promenade around the gardens or along the quays of the Seine.[63] The mundane, taken-for-granted routine is made into poetic narrative. Calet planned to plunge even further into the everyday spaces in a report for *Le Parisien* in which he would explore the city "arrondissement by arrondissement." Much as was the case with Chombart, each of his creative media allowed him to discover the city's spatial imaginary. He is both an investigative reporter and novelist, inventing a "fiction of the everyday" that stitches together the little stories, the fabric, of spatial history and the setting of time and place.[64] He illuminates the lives of "all those who form this mass we find at the Métro entrances, on the stairs of the railroad stations, in the markets and sports fields, in the squares, at the entrance to factories, on the bus platforms, on the suburban trains."[65]

Not all these intellectuals and urban observers shared the same perspective or strategies. The architectural historian Simon Sadler has pointed out that the situationists actually had little real sympathy for the underprivileged residents of the rue Sauvage or along the canals of Aubervilliers that they used as revolutionary sites of future power. The lettrist wanderings through the streets in a drunken stupor did not make for empathy. And they certainly did not share in the sentimentality of poetic realism. Yet a humanistic "fiction of the everyday" was invented as a foundational imaginary among a wide variety of *les intellos* and the avant-garde. They were the inventors of a fractured urban landscape, of the slums and forgotten corners of the city. In their passionate wanderings, their attempt to demystify modern urban spectacle by looking in the cracks and crevices for signs of authentic life, in their valorization of the everyday populist world, the situationists shared with sociologists, urban planners, and urban observers a subjective, humanist perspective specific to the 1950s. It was vernacular and political. The drift is the street reclaimed. The practice of space is active sociological and psychological observation,

FIGURE 22. The rue du Château-des-Rentiers and the "Deux Moulins" redevelopment project, June 12, 1969. © COLL. PAVILLON DE L'ARSENAL, CLICHÉ DUVP

where the essential nature of urban existence can be rediscovered. In this Rousseauian universe, the ordinary people of Paris are good. They have reason and emotion, and they are moral. The *peuple* are a living force and the ordinary spaces they inhabit are the source of radical change. Paris is made heroic in the invented discourse of social humanism.

Ironically, intellectuals discovered the quotidian world of these forgotten districts just as they were about to disappear. By the mid-1950s urban space seemed to be increasingly in flux and was undergoing seismic shifts. Demolition rained down on La Gare in the massive slum clearance projects that transformed the 13th arrondissement. Interiorized small-scale neighborhoods and îlots would no longer be tolerated. The rue Sauvage disappeared altogether. Léo Malet's rue du Château-des-Rentiers and the rest of the sordid cité Jeanne d'Arc were destroyed. The crumbling Ivry gas works was cleared away. The old courtyards and alleyways and the decrepit housing were replaced with a *cité moderne* in the sardonically named Château-des-Rentiers and Deux-Moulins redevelopment projects. New schools, playgrounds, supermarkets, and commercial centers, and a modern police station, graced the district. Modern high-rise residential towers designed by the architects Marc Leboucher and Albert Magot appeared on the boulevard Masséna, at Les Olympiades, and on the rue Nationale. Public space was transmuted into "open space" and pleasant landscaping in the interior of residential complexes. The transformation of the quartier was recorded by Chombart's student Henri Coing, who carried out his well-known sociological investigation of La Gare or *îlot insalubre* 4 in the early 1960s.[66] The makeover of La Gare and the rue Nationale were then recounted in Norma Evenson's *Paris: A Century of Change* (1979) to become the archetypal case study of the city's destruction at the hands of modern urban planning.[67] The particularist, decentered world that Chombart, Bardet, Debord, Malet, and Calet had each discovered was ravaged, its geography merged into a monumental, unified vision of the modern city in the "reconquest of Paris." But from the reconstruction years through the 1950s these spaces were imagined as decidedly vernacular and working class. The militant and potentially threatening proletariat was initially absorbed into the French national fold not as members of a modern middle class or broad middle stratum, but as authentic representatives of the *peuple* living in the time-honored puzzle of villages and everyday spaces that made up the capital. The seamless new structures of modern identity and the social homogenization around privatized values did not take place as rapidly or as effortlessly as is often described. In the middle years of the century, the spaces of the city remained fractured, deeply humanistic, and subversive in the intellectual imagination.

5 Paris as Cinematic Space

There are many reasons the cinematic presentation of Paris is so important to the analysis of public space. First, the years after the Second World War are considered part of the golden age of French cinema. The industry produced an abundance of both high-quality and popular Saturday-night films. The French flocked to the "seventh art" as one of the most important forms of entertainment and information. Some 2.5 million Parisians went to the movies each year. According to a 1953 survey, on average they saw three films each month.[1] Paris had almost four hundred first-run, second-run, art, and experimental movie houses spread throughout the city, and this number remained more or less stable over the decade. Beyond the great movie palaces on the Champs-Élysées and along the boulevard des Capucines and boulevard des Italiens, going to the movies was also a populist amusement. In a cartography that reiterated urban decentering, the exterior boulevards from the place Clichy to the Barbès Métro station—that is, the streets in the northern and eastern working-class districts—were packed with movie theaters: thirty-one in the 18th arrondissement, eighteen in the 19th, and twenty-six in the 20th.[2]

The depictions of Paris in the visual arts and photography were already voluminous by the early twentieth century. Because its reputation as the bustling city of enchantment was so well established, it became a virtual geography on the silver screen almost immediately. Some fifty film titles alone referred to Paris and its pleasures, especially those of the night: *Paris est toujours Paris, Paris canaille, Paris music-hall, Paris palace hôtel, Adieu Paris, C'est arrivé à Paris, C'est la vie parisienne, Mademoiselle de Paris, Rires de Paris,*

Plaisirs de Paris, Femmes de Paris, Boum sur Paris, Moineaux de Paris, Gamins de Paris, Rencontre à Paris, Soirs de Paris, Nuits de Paris, Paris coquin, Quatre jours à Paris, Paris chante toujours.[3] Film spectators were placed squarely in a Paris that was visible and effortlessly knowable. The diversion these fantasies provided from the grim reality of daily life explains their popularity, and French film companies were only too happy to produce them. Yet at the same time, the seventh art lurched into what were invisible, enigmatic places in the metropolis and provided a visual legibility to the poetic humanism and populism of the age. These were urban mysteries, crime and gangster films, from classics such as *Quai des Orfèvres, La Traversée de Paris, Paris nous appartient, Casque d'Or,* and *Le Silence est d'Or* to Jacques Becker's adaptation of Albert Simonin's novel *Touchez pas au Grisbi,* the suspense thriller *Du Rififi chez les hommes, Voici le temps des assassins,* and *Bob le flambeur.* The list is endless. Paris was depicted and delivered from the screen to the audience over and over again. The visions invented were a crucial factor in the way people conceptualized the city's spatiality. There were a multitude of poetic realist films that portrayed the social landscape such as *Sous le ciel de Paris, Antoine et Antoinette, Le Café du cadran, L'Air de Paris,* and *Lettre ouverte.* They juxtaposed human crises and emotions with social interaction and bridged the gap between everyday life and the built environment—all from a centripetal point of view. This visual narrative was a means of generating new spatial knowledge and was essential to how urban life was imagined and how urban territory was negotiated. Movies are an integral constituent of the urban environment.[4] By the mid-twentieth century a vast accumulation of bodies, gestures, urban surfaces, and types of movement were being filmed across the capital. Film cameras caught a kaleidoscope of crowds and processions; cars, buses, and trucks rushing by on the boulevards; monumental architecture; and pleasure spots. It recorded speed, noise, and the fluidity of the city, cutting back and forth across space and time.

The new medium of television, which was just being introduced in France in the late 1940s and 1950s, reiterated and deepened this cinematic vision. The Allied forces took control of the television transmitter on the Eiffel Tower during the Liberation in August 1944. It was handed over to government-controlled Radiodiffusion nationale in October 1945, which then worked to inaugurate programming over the next few years to become Radiodiffusion télévision française in 1947. Over the course of the 1950s, a second transmitter on the Eiffel Tower (one of which was eventually destroyed in a January 1955 fire) and technical advances such as kinescope, as well as a new television studio at Buttes-Chaumont, helped to expand capabilities. The first news broadcast took place on June 29, 1949, and by 1950 the noontime *Télé-Paris* program was being aired with local information and interviews with the city's glitterati. The launch of Eurovision in June 1954 and the Europe 1 network in January 1955 gave RTF access to a new body of taped and live broadcasts that considerably extended the television season.[5] Nonetheless, it was a slow beginning, and the television audience was small. Parisians across a wide political spectrum shared an initial mistrust of the new medium as culturally corrupting and banal. And a television set remained far beyond most people's means. The Galeries Lafayette department store displayed models such as the Grammont television set for a price of 10,000 francs, to say nothing of the 4,000 francs required for television service.

In the early years, television was much more of a communal activity set up in public places. Parisians watched television like a film audience, in cafés or standing outside store windows where sets were installed. Among the first live television broadcasts was a variety show from the Théâtre des Champs-Élysées in June 1947. In 1948 viewers were treated to coverage of the Tour de France arriving at the Parc des Princes and Christmas Eve services from Notre Dame Cathedral. On New Year's Eve 1951, crowds gathered in front of the Rex Theater on the boulevard Poissonière to watch grainy black-and-white images of Maurice Chevalier performing inside on television sets installed on the sidewalk.[6] Like hundreds of thousands of other Europeans, in June 1953 Parisians stood mesmerized, watching the coronation of Elizabeth II flickering on television screens in cafés and shop windows or at a neighbor's house. It was many people's first major television experience. "It was THE great day for television," reported *Paris Match*.[7] The event provoked a rush to rent or buy television sets and set up service.

As the standard of living improved over the course of the 1950s, consumers opened their pocketbooks to acquire the magic box along with other signs of leisure and recreation. By 1955 there were 142,000 television sets in use in the Paris region, and by 1958 that number had more than doubled to 370,000.[8] Although the number of viewers remained small, the switch in the early 1950s to live, on-location broadcasting made Paris a visual stage set for television productions. Like film, it produced, opened up, and mediatized the city's landscape, fracturing it into a multitude of local spaces and situations and into a montage of images. But television was even a more populist medium than film in the 1950s. Its descent into the streets relied far less on professional actors and, in an early version of amateurish "reality" programs, more on the city's ordinary people. The unexceptional members of urban society were made into celebrities. They were given agency in the spaces of their lives. Television would thus be instrumental in the way the city's landscape was produced, communicated, and visually grasped.

The Paris of Poetic Realism

In the late 1940s and early 1950s, much of French cinema followed the public's desire to forget the cruel realities, the penury and misery, of recent experience. Film after film retreated into sumptuous costume dramas adapted from literature and boulevard theater into screwball comedy, stereotypic yarns, and heroic Resistance adventures—anywhere but the troubles of everyday life. Neither economic scarcity nor the post Liberation purges nor the war in Indochina appeared on the silver screen. While Italian cinema marched bravely forward into neorealism, the French remained content with the rose-colored distractions offered by films such as *French Cancan*, by the cinematic giant Jean Renoir. Comedian Fernandel with his toothy grin and thick Marseilles accent enjoyed a major comeback, making multiple films each year in the 1950s. Heartthrob Gérard Philippe soared to fame in 1947 as a lovesick adolescent in *Le Diable du corps*. He played the hero in countless romantic dramas that appealed to the generation that came of age during the war. Well-known prewar stars—Arletty, Sacha Guitry, Tino Rossi, Maurice Chevalier, and Pierre Fresnay—were arrested for "soft" collaboration during the Liberation. Most were released while their cases were being considered, and they resumed their careers.[9] Despite the resentment their goodwill tours in Germany aroused, Maurice Chevalier and Tino Rossi once again broke into song in a cavalcade of filmed musical comedies. The time-honored image of Paris as spectacle filled the need for these frothy and entertaining diversions quite nicely. Particularly enticing were cinematic peeks into the beau monde of the Champs-Élysées or the rue Royale, whose lifestyle few Parisians could enjoy at the war's end. Filmgoers were titillated by campy descents into the delights of *Minuit Champs-Élysées*, *Scandale aux Champs-Élysées*, *La Dame de chez Maxim's*, and *Le Chasseur de chez Maxim's*.

The early 1950s were the years of studio productions in the French film industry. This was in part a response to the scarcity of resources. Electricity, coal for heat, and celluloid film were all precious commodities, and they could all be economized on upon sound stages. But studio films were also a mechanism for quality control; that is to say, rather than relying on the exigencies of on-location sets, filmmakers fabricated highly stylized and perfected productions in the tradition of prestigious, high-gloss French cinema.[10] Protected by the strict regulations and censorship of the Centre national du cinéma (CNC) and conventional training at the Institut des hautes études cinématographiques (IDHEC), the film industry became a closed-circuit corporate system dominated by the privileged elites who reemerged after the war: Marcel Carné, Jacques Prévert, René Clair, René Clément, and Julien Duvivier. It was this prewar avant-garde of the golden age of French filmmaking, transmuted by the war into an entrenched coterie, that provided the continuity of poetic vision. This poetic realism was endlessly reproduced through the studio and star system, by sophisticated decor and lighting, complicated camera angles, brilliant dialogue, and the use of literary adaptation. Its appeal derived from a unique combination of feeling, sentimentality, and social criticism. Relying on this formula, French film production has often been criticized as being overly intellectual, almost mechanical. It was only the young turks of the *nouvelle vague* in the late 1950s that finally transformed French filmmaking and with it the vision of Paris.

This is in part what makes the cinematic presentation of Paris so useful to this analysis. It was invented by filmmakers and presented to the public as urban artifice. Working in the studio was a response to the theatrical tradition of French cinema and insured complete creative control to fabricate Paris and the thousand cinematic stories of its streets. A visual urban theater was fashioned through emphasis on formal visual beauty, on music and decor, atmosphere, and on an ensemble of actors rather than close-ups of isolated stars.[11] However, film directors also used a combination of studio sets and location shoots that together merged into a distinct urban imaginary that coincided with poetic realist, or humanist, sensibilities. "When will the cinema go down into the street?" Marcel Carné famously asked.[12] The city ceased to be simply background. Instead, urban life itself became the focus of cinematic study. The films were encoded with cues that stood for "social reality." In the hands of poetic realist directors, Paris became the stage on which the lives and labors of ordinary people were played out in an atmosphere of everyday humanity. There was a close resemblance between the view of the photographer-filmmaker and that of the wanderer, and a correlation of urban life with the street.

Directors such as Marcel Carné and Valéry Jahier had long called for a socially committed cinema. These roots lay in the 1930s and the experience of the Popular Front. Indeed, the term "poetic realism" was first used cinematically to describe Pierre Chenal's *La Rue sans nom* (1933), an allusion once again to the magical, populist qualities associated with the street. The avant-garde Groupe Octobre (1932–36) included individuals directly involved in filmmaking: Jean-Paul Dreyfus-Le Chanois, Joseph Kosma, Jacques Prévert, Jean Renoir, and Alexander Trauner. Ciné-Liberté (1936–37), which was directly linked to the CGT and the Popular Front, absorbed members of the defunct Groupe Octobre and produced a number of *ouvriériste* documentary and educational films. This social urban imaginary was made even more vital by the Resistance and the Liberation and the triumph of the working classes at the war's end. Historians have often condemned the French film industry for its lack of vision and its reversion to prewar cinematographers and stylistic forms. But poetic realism remained successful because it reflected a heroic vision of Paris and its populist spaces in the late 1940s and early 1950s. The degree to which it mirrored its times is striking. The quotidian world of working-class neighborhoods formed a renewed circle of nobility and legitimacy. Even those insightful films that attempted a more "socially realistic" portrayal of the city at midcentury, and which were often quite political, remained within this genre of populist or poetic realism. That is to say, they offered a stylized vision of the city that reinvented familiar places and characters and made them wholesome and valiant—in a word, heroic.

The theater was the metaphor for visualizing cinematic urban space and collective practices in these films, whether in the neighborhood, the street, or an individual building. More than just architecture and built environment, Paris is lived space. It is an urban scenography, a social spectacle, in which performances by formulaic individuals symbolized the "people" and their essential humanity. In other words, poetic realism created a social fantasy in the city's public domain and the pursuits and encounters that took place there. The pervasive use of aerial or long views that captured the iconographic visions of Paris, the crowd sequences filmed from eye or ground level, and the animated street scenes underscore the significance of urban spatiality in this film genre. We are placed at the intersection of various personal journeys through Paris, each of them emblematic of city life. The heroes go in search of their souls, find joy or tragedy, and live out their daily heartbreaks and pleasures. They are enclosed in an atmosphere that is poignant and metaphysical. The city's spaces are a transcendental fabric that holds more than mere appearances. They could easily be described as psychogeographical in the situationist sense of searching for valid experience and the self in the milieu of the street. Fate, hubris, pathos, bravery, tragedy, and joy are all at work in the landscape. It is not the external spectacle that matters as much as the search for truth. The city surfaces are emotional, psychological, filled with pervasive moods and moral parables. There is optimism, yet paradox and uncertainty. In this respect both film and still photography brilliantly captured the mood of the city as it recovered from war and faced a modern transformation in the second half of the century.

We can look at some of the masterpieces that "produced" Paris in the late 1940s and 1950s as a means of understanding this visual invention of the city's landscape. As a genre they are poetic humanist documentaries, journeys of ethnographic discovery that uncovered the courage and innate decency of the *peuple* in their urban milieu. Jacques Becker's *Antoine et Antoinette* (1947) is one of the best examples of this quotidian poetic naturalism that situated Paris socially and topographically in the reconstruction years.[13] The film was an enormous popular success and won the award for Best Psychological and Romantic Film at the 1947 Cannes Film Festival. It offered a living tableau of the *petit peuple* and their neighborhood in the 18th arrondissement. Becker saw himself as a *cinéaste social* and had already worked as an assistant director, along with Le Chanois, on the Communist Party's propaganda film *La Vie est à nous* (1936), with its stories of everyday life. His sympathies with the party were of long standing, as was evidenced in his filming of combat scenes in *La Libération de Paris* (1944). The Antoine and Antoinette of his film are a young working-class couple confident about their lives despite the lack of decent housing and the scarcity of just about everything else. They are the epitome of reconstruction optimism, a modern version of the *sublimes ouvriers* that reflects the insistent tug of the past as well as the seductive lure of the future.

Antoine (Roger Pigaut) is a skilled paper cutter in a book-publishing factory. Antoinette (Claire Maffei) works at the Prisunic on the Champs-Élysées. They inhabit a working-class world of hopefulness and human decency. The film portrays their efforts at self-improvement and their clever grasp of the newfangled technologies of the postwar world. In an almost documentary

FIGURE 23. Roger Pigaut and Claire Maffei as the title characters in Jacques Becker's film *Antoine et Antoinette*. Production Gaumont, 1947. © GAUMONT.

style, Becker takes us through a series of quotidian urban scenes filled with humor and bonhomie: the working-class couple at work, in the Métro, at home, at dinner where they share what food they have, at the bistro with friends, at the soccer match, at the park. Their freedom of movement across the city, the multiplicity of spaces they traverse, mark postwar conceptions of modern urban experience as fluid and self-assured. The dialog is simple and sincere, the characters virtuous. The film is an affectionate fantasy of neighborhood solidarity and sociability. Antoine and Antoinette's family is their quartier. Their private lives spill out into the public domain. Chance conversations and face-to-face encounters, friendship and daily support are everywhere. There is no anonymity or alienation to plague urban existence. A kind local grocer slips Antoinette a free can of sardines to take with her vegetables. Her neighbor steps in to protect her against the advances of the lecherous petit-bourgeois *bof* who mistreats his women employees. Their love and bravery in the face of postwar troubles land the couple a winning lottery ticket. The plot revolves around the precious ticket that is found, lost, and then found again in a happy ending filled with the promise of material well-being. In the film's last scene Antoine jubilantly rides off on the motorcycle he has long coveted, with Antoinette in the sidecar beside him. Despite the rain clouds, despite the housing crisis and hardship, all turns out well.

Becker's film is a mild sociological study of Parisian working-class mores, behavior, and aspirations that conformed to all the rules of populist poetic realism. His style was known for its precision, its dedication to authentic, documentary-style conception in almost artisanal terms. His depiction of Parisian life reiterated the *ouvriériste* viewpoint of French social scientists in their quest to "take the pulse" of postwar realities. The movie is an ethnographic research project. It illuminates a working-class urban experience that had largely been out of sight, ignored, and treated with contempt. And it found that the traditional neighborhoods and quotidian public spaces of Paris were the arena of the city's magnificence. It was here that the innate nobility and humanity of the French could be found, and where the resurgence of urbanity and civic life was most evident. The film produces the working classes in their own surroundings with an exact attention to behavior and interpersonal relations, to the rituals of sociability and the uses of urban space. This was not simply a reiteration of cinematic codes of the prewar years. It was a universe of understanding, a postwar populist conviction that captured filmmakers and photographers as well as sociologists and ethnographers, and of course the public at large. Film particularly leant itself to this poetic narrative about the nobility and heroism of the quotidian. Antoine and Antoinette's desire for a good life embraces material abundance, decent living conditions, good relations with their neighbors in peace and security. The film endows these desires with a symbolic meaning that makes them something more. The young French couple was making history in the modest arena of their quartier. Their individual lives were the story of family, class, and nation.

It is interesting to note that the film appeared in late 1947, a year of rampant inflation and a precipitous drop in the standard of living. While filmgoers enjoyed the fragile illusion of *Antoine et Antoinette* in their neighborhood theaters, strike waves and pitched street battles reverberated through the city. A film review by Roger Boussinot in *Action* remarked that Antoine and Antoinette "were not unionized, made no demands . . . they are the conventional bourgeois dream of good workers . . . the likable domestic pets of a society that presses on them all the weight of injustice." What proof did Boussinot offer for the illegitimacy of Becker's notion of "realism"? In the fight scene, when Antoine finally clobbers the lascivious grocer, the couple's tiny apartment is demolished. The neighbors gather to cheer Antoine on, but no one rushes to save their belongings. "This is idiotic!" groused Boussinot. "Any worker knows only too well the value, the cost in work, of each object not to show any upset when some creep destroys all his neighbor's possessions."[14] All of these early postwar films were rigorously reviewed by a budding series of specialized film periodicals. Cosponsored by the PCF and two Resistance movements and hosted by *Les Lettres françaises,* the film review *L'Écran français* was perhaps the best in terms of quality, style, and openness. But all of them, including *Action,* kept a keen eye on the visual invention of the victorious working classes. Regardless of the criticisms, the Communist Party took advantage of the film's success by staging a promotional campaign comparing the lives of two hundred young working-class couples in its weekly magazine *Regards* and naming the CGT women's group *Antoinette.* And Becker replied to Boussinot's caustic critique that his intention was to give filmgoers

> an exact as possible impression of the ATTITUDE of the men and women of the Parisian working class. . . . Neither the cinema nor the theater has ever paid homage to certain precious qualities that are often encountered among workers . . . kindness, emotional restraint, hospitality, they are capable of loving with true passion, incapable of the "fake pretensions" of the bourgeoisie. They possess an instinctive "breeding" ("education") . . . workers are more profoundly "gracious" than the bourgeoisie in their social relations. . . . This kindheartedness that French workers share between them, the sincerity of their love, this graciousness that they almost constantly exhibit, their "optimism," this "wholesome" optimism that has its origins in "wholesome" hearts, this is what I wanted to show in my film.[15]

Becker lays out a social landscape from the vantage point of a poetic humanist. The quotidian spaces of the city become the stage in which human—that is, psychological and moral stories—are played out. More than just backdrop, Paris becomes an extension of individual self-awareness. Examining the everyday lives, the lived experience, of average people in the various microcosms of Paris was a device for probing French society at a moment of extraordinary change. It portrayed the insider's knowledge that was key to understanding the symbolic and subjective meanings people utilize to comprehend their world.

Julien Duvivier's film *Sous le ciel de Paris* (1951) is perhaps the epitome of this poetic humanism.[16] In this particular film, Paris was clearly the star, and the plot explored the experiences and moods of the city. The film opens with a panoramic aerial sequence (shot by the cinematographer René Corbeau) along the Seine, with its iconic architecture and monuments. This is unmistakably Paris, and the perspective promises to capture the city's totality of experience. One film critic commented that it was like watching the city's life from atop the Eiffel Tower. From this altitude, Paris is comprehended as a living cartography to be explored. However, the film scholar Edward Dimendberg has made the point that this type of grandiloquent aerial opening raises suspicions and might be better grasped as anxiety that the "city had been eclipsed and its concentrated centers rendered inconsequential." The palpable absence of a single prominent center, despite the recognizable landmarks, and the continual motion of the camera "hint at a decisive shift" in identity.[17] Although Dimendberg is referring to film noir's portrayal of American cities, the same sensation is evident in Duvivier's film. Filmmakers visually echoed the city's fragmentation and the consequent trepidation that the monumental identity of Paris had vanished.

Swooping down on the city and gradually dropping, the camera fractures the landscape by following the exploits of a group of six individuals across the capital—this time over the course of a single day, during which they each discover "their destiny." The film has a sociological, investigatory quality. The roles were played by unknown young actors, which added to the sense of realistic documentation. This social tableau of everyday heroes ranged from the poor to the wealthy, the young to the old. Duvivier's camera is a voyeuristic peek into their lives. The camera lens adopts the gaze of the *flâneur* as a means of knowing. However, in this case the *flâneur* is invisible, outside the space he peers into and observes through his device. Duvivier's position provides him an extraordinary ability to take "visual possession of the city" and invent its phenomena.[18] The visual narrative is deeply humanistic in its vivid recognition of the "faceless" in the urban crowd. It was this "human quality" that critic Boussinot pointed to as representing classic French filmmaking.[19] An old women living in misery begs for food for her cats. A worker named Hermenault takes part in a strike at his factory. Georges Forrestier, a medical student, is trying to pass his exams. His girlfriend, Marie-Thérèse, lives the high life as a fashion model. A newcomer, Denise Lombers, arrives from the provinces in search of "love, fortune, and glory." For all of them, Paris is filled with both opportunities and delusions. The film is a story of their journeys—a sociopsychological mapping. The plot stitches together a spatial narrative from their individual bits and pieces that is embedded in the city's landscape. It is a voyage of personal discovery and destiny—from Notre Dame to the Eiffel Tower, from the Bastille to the Opéra, the bridges on the Seine and the quays of Bercy and Auteuil, the streets of Ménilmontant and Montmartre. The viewer follows along to explore the landscape of Paris produced in this cinematic montage.

Duvivier presents a mobile, vigorous place streaming with human and vehicular traffic. Horse-drawn wagons and bicycles weave between taxis and automobiles hurtling through the streets. Traffic jams, with their inevitable accidents and blaring horns, border the Seine. Crowds pack the rue Mouffetard on market day. Students jam the Latin Quarter while shoppers stream in and out of department stores. Boats and barges travel the river. The photo shoot at the Trocadéro fountains, with fashion models draped in elegant dresses and dripping with jewels, is the epitome of prosperity, while the unwanted elderly rummage through garbage and eat at soup kitchens. A fisherman discovers a body floating in the Seine—"the third this year," the police inspector remarks, presumably killed by the film's mad sculptor, who slits the throat of an innocent woman along a gloomy street. The fleeting scenes reinforce the geography of the film as fragmented spatial pieces.

Sous le ciel de Paris attempts to map the moods and drama of the city by traversing it. The shifting of scenes from one place to another is enormously effective in conveying emotion and psychological drama. The individualized psychogeographies are experiments in understanding divergent experiences. This film and others like it explored the speed and intensity of the modern city, the perpetual movement and circulation of people, goods, encounters, and events. They captured the bizarre juxtapositions and strange coincidences, the simultaneity of experience. The boundaries between interior space and public space remain permeable. We see and hear the tensions and antagonisms, the sheer quantity, the brilliance as well as the indifference, the hopefulness and fears—in other words, the kaleidoscopic flow of contemporary life through the capital. It is where destiny plays its hand. Particularly evocative are the expeditions or pilgrimages, many overtaken by unexpected events inevitable in the city's life. They are journeys of discovery. The viewer is asked to descend from the heights of aerial panorama and penetrate the city's streets and buildings, to see beyond the surfaces to the feeling and humanity of the city's thousand ordinary stories. Little Colette (Marie-France) runs away from home to avoid being punished for getting bad grades in school. She embarks on a trip down the Seine and under the pont Neuf to Australia (the Île Saint-Louis) and New Zealand (the quays of Bercy) with a young boy who captains their small vessel. Suddenly abandoned on the quay, lost and afraid, she wanders through the alleys of Bercy as night approaches, only to meet the mad sculptor Mathias, who has murder in his eyes. Because she befriends him in innocence, Mathias spares her life and accompanies her back across the Seine to her home on the rue Mouffetard. There the miserable old woman who has been rejected by everyone fulfills her destiny by helping the frightened child find the courage to confront her parents. Colette's journey through Paris and her chance meeting with the strangers who haunt the streets have given her the maturity to face her fears and her responsibilities.

We take a similar pilgrimage across Paris in Le Chanois's *Sans laisser d'adresse*,[20] released in January 1951, which won the Golden Bear Prize at the Berlin Film Festival the same year and was also warmly welcomed in the Soviet Union. Le Chanois (whose real name was Jean-Paul Dreyfus; Le Chanois was his wartime pseudonym) was from a Jewish family in the 9th arrondissement of Paris. He was an early member of Prévert's band of young followers who met together in Prévert's apartment on the rue Dauphine, and an enthusiastic member of the Groupe Octobre hanging out in the cafés of Saint-Germain-des-Prés during the 1930s. It was through Prévert's influence that Le Chanois was introduced to the capital's populist universe. He wrote productions for the Fête de l'Humanité, attended the May commemorations of the Paris Commune at Père Lachaise Cemetery, and took part in the Groupe Octobre's agitprop theater. By 1933 Le Chanois had became a member of the Communist Party. He was part of the Resistance during the war, then later organized a French cinematic underground cell attached to the CGT and worked clandestinely both in the provinces and in Paris.[21] Like Prévert, Le Chanois was an author, a poet, and a songwriter as well as a cinematographer. His films exuded the populism of the poetic realist style. They are portraits of the contradictions, optimism, and doubts about the postwar world. Le Chanois's "tender, sensitive, charmingly funny" portrayal of everyday petit bourgeois family life "without pretension" in the 18th arrondissement in *Papa, maman, la bonne et moi* (1954) is perhaps the better-known of his two populist films.[22] Here we have a good-humored caricature of the average French family, *Paris profond*, that takes the pulse of life in the fragmented cartography of the city's neighborhoods.

In *Sans laisser d'adresse*, the actress Danièle Delorme plays a young mother arriving in Paris at the gare de Lyon to find the father of her child, who has left her in Chambéry "without leaving an address." Thérèse has no money or support, but she meets a benevolent taxi driver, Émile Gauthier (Bernard Blier), who takes it upon himself to solve her predicament by piloting her around Paris in his no. 85 Renault G7 in search of Forrestier, her absent lover. The hunt, set to the music of Joseph Kosma, forms the pretext for an extraordinary tour of the city and its neighborhoods. The character of Émile functions as an up-to-date *flâneur*, a proxy and guide for the film's viewers. In his 1946 tourist guide of Paris, Léon Paul Fargue argued that the best kind of contemporary *flânerie* in Paris was by taxi.[23] And indeed Émile's taxi spins around the place de la Bastille, where an open-air orchestra leads a local *fête*. From the rue Ravignan in the 18th arrondissement to the rue de l'Abbaye in the 6th, Émile and Thérèse drive from destination to destination in search of Forrestier, at one point following a tour bus loaded with visitors craning their necks left and right to see the "beauties of Paris." They stop at a bistro at Barbès and at the Club Saint-Germain, where Juliette Greco sings. Émile attends a union meeting at the Mutualité on the rue Saint-Victor in the 5th arrondissement. In a symbolic gesture of working-class solidarity, he dons a jacket and tie and steps up to the tribune to become union treasurer. The film was quotidian theater, threaded with the common language and humor of populist sociability, with the slang of the street. The characters exude a natural simplicity and goodness.

Paris appears as a collection of quartiers that are emblematic visual codes for populist space. Film was a medium for discovering the city's fragmented spatial imaginary and portraying the human drama in a public domain filled with instantaneous moments and quotidian possibilities. Le Chanois's film constructs a landscape of familiarity and spontaneous social and verbal exchange. The streets are a place of face-to-face contact. Émile's assorted clients, the neighborhood denizens who guide their search for the wayward father Forrestier, the street sweepers, the hospital nurses, the railway workers all come alive in a scenography of everyday urban existence. In certain ways, it was the visual analog to the melodrama and spatial discovery of Louis Malet's detective Nestor Burma stalking the streets in search not of cads, but of criminals. The scenes are atmospheric and psychogeographic.

On the rue de la Saïda in the 18th arrondissement, the duo come upon a sordid square and a forlorn HBM public housing project. Émile describes the people from all walks of life who have found shelter in this *caserne* (barracks). Among them is Forrestier, and it is his wife and child who answer Thérèse and Émile's knock at the door. Hopeless and disheartened, Thérèse flees. She contemplates abandoning her baby on a quay overlooking the Seine. Émile and his comrades launch their fleet of taxis through Paris in search of her—to the boulevard Diderot, to the place de la Nation, the rue Chalon, to Bercy—in what Jacques Krier called in his review of the film "a new 'Battle of the Marne,' so moving, in order to save a poor girl who no longer believes in happiness."[24] Émile's comrades share an elemental fraternity and optimism. Thérèse is rescued by the simple goodness and humanity of the *peuple de Paris*. For both characters, their chance encounters through Paris have been a voyage of personal discovery. The taxi driver navigates the urban landscape as an extension of himself. The film ends with a smiling Émile bathed in an angelic light that echoes Ronis's working-class photographic portraits. Like Ronis, Le Chanois produced a tableau of the common people—their heroism, innate compassion, and bonhomie. Patrons sitting in local movie houses across the working-class districts watched stylized, valiant versions of themselves. It was an easy visual palliative for the struggle taking place in the streets.

Television Hits the Streets: Paris En Direct de . . .

Television opened up the public spaces of the city for viewing as no other medium had ever done. It created a new visual collage of images that represented reality and was absorbed collectively as contemporary values. Its aesthetic was increasingly based on live and on-location broadcasting that created the illusion of instantaneousness, of simultaneity, of dramatizing the ephemera of the city's everyday life. Entirely under the control of the French state, live television coverage was certainly not extended to the strikes and demonstrations, the pitched battles with police, the round-ups of suspect Algerians that rocked the streets in the 1950s. Homelessness and poverty made no appearance on television screens. Instead, the new medium broadcast a prosaic spatial imaginary. With their parades, live music, and street dances, July 14 celebrations were in particular a source for live news coverage. The annual Kermesse aux Étoiles was televised annually from the Tuileries gardens beginning in 1949. Television captured the sporting events and the movie stars and celebrities who sought the camera's glare and mingled with fans. However, television shows and reporting did not simply record events, but dramatized and indeed produced them. For example, the commotion over a holdup on the rue Vaneau in March 1945 was shown on television just two hours after the incident, spectacularizing what would ordinarily be considered a commonplace crime. The discovery of old gold coins during the demolition of a building on the rue Mouffetard was broadcast in real time, cameras panning the normally mundane street packed with shoppers and gawkers. In 1956 RTF staged a mock air attack on Paris under the pretext of testing the city's air defenses. The effect of all this was to create the impression of simultaneity, of immediacy, of a scenography of the ephemeral in public space and the illusion of participation and voyeurism.

The development of French television and especially this type of live on-location reporting was most clearly associated with the arrival in 1952 of Jean D'Arcy as director of broadcasting at RTF. D'Arcy was anxious for television to create its own aesthetic and style and saw it ultimately as a populist medium. He recalled in his autobiography that "we were delighted with photos of *bidonvilles* or the northern districts topped with television antennas. This was the sense that we had of our mission. Not at all of misery or pauperism, but the desire to bring to people the opportunity to dream, to escape, which they had much more need of than the public today."[25] He quickly changed the orientation of the early line-ups from film reruns and prerecorded theatrical shows to live programming and on-location transmissions. Television became an open window on French life as D'Arcy's seven teams of reporters with their cameramen and equipment in tow descended into the streets, into factories and mines, into parks and museums, anywhere there was something to see. For the 1952 *Semaine franco-britannique* citywide event, four equipment teams loaded down with eleven cameras tethered by cable to production trucks descended into the streets to capture "a true image of contemporary life in Paris and of the Parisians," which were mixed and transmitted live via the Eiffel Tower and a local transmitter in Lille to television screens across the United Kingdom.[26] Images of the public spaces and sites of the city were scrutinized by the camera's gaze and spread out all over the country. This produced a disjointed and chaotic montage of places and situations. Paris was made visible and mediatized, made instantly accessible to discovery and exploration.

From the mid-1950s television shows such as the Sunday evening *En direct de* . . . transported viewers to sites throughout Paris from an insider's tour of the Panthéon, to the International Boat Show on the Seine, to the inauguration of the UNESCO headquarters on the place Fontenoy. Some sense of the growing quantity of these on-location shows and their broadening coverage can be gleaned from descriptions in weekly television magazines. A tour of the "horse sculptures" of Paris took viewers to the city's monumental parks and especially to the Luxembourg gardens, where neighborhood denizens of the Boul' Mich' were interviewed during the show. The popular program *Ce soir à Paris* went on location to various sites from the fabulous Moulin Rouge to the shadowy Rôtisserie de l'Abbaye basement club of Saint-Germain-des-Prés, while *Les Actualités françaises* went to hear rock 'n' roll at the Club Saint-Germain-des-Prés. The series *Visite à . . .* took viewers on a musical tour of the Île-Saint-Louis and to the gardens of the Palais Royale. *Les Actualités françaises* spent "Twelve Hours at Les Halles" in 1952. Some of these locations were normally off-limits to the general public. In February 1959, for example, *En direct de . . .* went to the Hôtel de Ville and entered the historic reception rooms, covered with Aubusson and Gobelin tapestries, where viewers "would be received like Queen Elizabeth of England."[27] Live broadcasting invented a censored, televised style of touristic spatiality. Moreover, it produced a highly stylized, almost ceremonial portrait of modernity and the prosperity associated with postwar reconstruction and the *trente glorieuses*.

Television created new discursive spaces and new dimensions of the public sphere in which ordinary people became media celebrities. French radio programming had already led the way with on-location programs such as the overwhelmingly popular *On chante dans mon quartier* (also known by its theme song, "Ploum-ploum"), which began broadcasting in December 1945. Hosted by the celebrated singer Saint-Granier, each day at 12:30 P.M. the program visited a city or neighborhood in Paris and invited amateur singers to compete in a song contest, with the local crowd acting as the background choir. *On chante dans mon quartier* was a product of the Liberation and the reappropriation of public space that was so critical to the city's renewed sense of freedom. It was followed by a number of other radio music-contest and game shows that went on expeditions through the streets of the city. Television built on this form of populist participatory spatiality. Even more, unlike relatively passive film viewing, on-location television programs created reciprocal practices. There was always a possibility of "audiences" being seen and performing. In January 1951 the newspaper *Paris-presse* sponsored a televised treasure hunt called "La Course aux Étoiles" from "under the four iron feet of the Eiffel Tower." Devoted readers found clues in the newspaper that would reveal the location of various "star emblems" hidden on the grounds of the Champs de Mars. The winner would not only find himself or herself fêted on television, but would also receive the grand prize of a Philips television set worth 72,000 francs.[28] This multilayered, mediatized space (a televised contest with the winner receiving a television, on television) was reiterated in game shows broadcast live. France's first popular television game show, *Télé-match*, began broadcasting on Thursday evenings in 1954. Created under the guidance of Jean D'Arcy, the series went out into the public spaces of Paris, *en direct de* . . . , to give the city's ordinary people, the man or woman in the street, a chance to win money and prizes. Its host, Pierre Bellemare, described the show's extraordinary success: "The streets were black with people when we went out. The popular enthusiasm was amazing."[29] Like an early version of reality television, some contestants on *Télé-match* became momentary celebrities in their own right and were brought back on the program by popular demand. Although the contestant Georges Lacœur lost the game on the history of Paris to Brigette Bar, he resurfaced on *Télé-match* as a tour guide through his neighborhood in the Marais. Lacœur discussed his amateur *flânerie* to explore the ancient alleyways, the old hotels, and the rustic buildings, and with the show's camera team in tow he pointed out to viewers the "oldest house in Paris." What is played up in this form of celebrity is the connection to ordinary lives and ordinary spaces. The normally powerless could be heard and seen. In 1958 *Télé-match* was at the Buttes-Chaumont for a *pétanque* contest. Although Jo Arama, a former *pétanque* national champion who worked as a *bof* in Les Halles, lost the contest, he returned on the show to give viewers tips on their *pétanque* game.[30]

For the July 14 festivities in 1959, Bellemare was on the place d'Italie with microphone in hand, followed by his team of cameramen. Passersby were randomly chosen to answer game questions presented live in the television studio for a prize of 20,000 francs. By August the show had developed a "treasure hunt," with co-host Jacques Bénétin and his television team wandering through Paris to ask unsuspecting ordinary people to identity mysterious objects.[31] Televising and making celebrities of "real people" in Paris was the ultimate expression of populist sensibilities. Putting ordinary people on display was a successful form of entertainment because they were viewed through the lens of decency and admiration. The image of the threatening proletariat, of the teeming and uncultivated hordes, was discarded for that of a people naturalized and at home in the spaces of the city. The television camera acted as voyeur, saturating the screen with Parisians' reasonableness, intelligence, and generosity of spirit. The film characters Antoine, Antoinette, and Émile Gauthier could easily appear in the crowd. The lens focused on and opened up the spaces of their lives to reveal the moods and drama of their everyday world. Their dramatic performances depicted the thousand ordinary stories of the street and gave the *peuple* the veneer of a spontaneous, immediate agency.

From 1957 to 1960 Jean-Claude Bergeret and Jacques Krier produced a series of fourteen short documentary films for television called *A la découverte des français*. Their purpose was to explore the new medium of television as a form of popular education. The films were meant to showcase the research of Paul-Henry Chombart de Lauwe and his team at the Groupe d'ethnologie sociale at the Musée de l'Homme. Chombart acted as the consultant for the series, the objective of which was to show the structures of social life written in the landscape in both the provinces and the capital. Chombart knew Jean D'Arcy well and like him was anxious to experiment with the new television medium as an instructive tool. As a whole, the series composed a panoramic view of everyday life in the urban neighborhoods and provincial villages of France during the 1950s. Much like Jacques Becker's commercial films, they were a visual device—a voyage of discovery—for understanding national life during the *trente glorieuses*. Although the Communist Party is often associated with opposition to television as an American corruption, in a 1994 interview Jacques Krier explained:

> We were men of the Left. I was a communist. The others weren't, but they were still very left-wing. This was the generation of the Liberation. We were very politicized, and politicized on the left. We had many common opinions, especially a very strong ethic concerning television, an ethic of public service. This was an absolute value that we shared.

The social groups presented were archetypal and easily identifiable: workers, salaried employees, miners, peasants. There is a sense of ethnographic curiosity about these shows. Jacques Krier humorously admitted, "We went to find the French like filmmakers in search of the natives."[32] It was, in other words, a form of sociological fieldwork. The effect was a voyeuristic look into a micro–social world in which the theater of the everyday was put in motion. Each film presented a specific collectivity along with the families and individuals that inhabited it. Their everyday practices, social relations, and forms of public engagement were made visible. For Paris, the areas chosen were the slum district of Moulin de la Pointe in the 13th arrondissement and the rue Mouffetard in the 5th arrondissement. Two other films in the series dealt with the Paris suburbs: the Café du Beau Site and La Butte à la Reine.

In the first film in the series, a taxi brings us to the rue du Moulin de la Pointe, a small street in the 13th arrondissement slum of Maison Blanche. There we meet the Spinoza family and their newborn infant, Serge.[33] We watch as the neighborhood women knit baby clothes for the new member of the neighborhood while children play in the "authentic" traditional courtyard. In the Chombartian understanding of urban space, the courtyard is a social unit, its own miniature îlot with its own life. It was precisely in these diminutive, hidden public spaces and the family homes that surrounded them that *pensée populaire* was elaborated. Neighborhood functions in tangible places that change with the rhythms and temporality of daily existence. The women do their washing, sweeping, and cleaning in the courtyard; Monsieur Spinoza works on his scooter there with Serge as he grows up. Having aggravated the neighbors, the children find refuge in the home of the local fireman to watch children's shows on the new television set. Families attend the neighborhood cinema and promenade along the avenue d'Italie on Sunday afternoons. We see men playing pool and sharing drinks at the *zinc* in a friendly neighborhood bistro. The men work in the local automobile factories, while the women find jobs in the leather industry of the Bièvre.

Poverty, high infant mortality, and a tumbledown housing stock with cramped rooms that lacked running water, gas, and electricity defined Moulin de la Pointe as slum no. 13 in official discourse. Indeed, Pierre Sudreau's Commissariat à la construction et à l'urbanisme had pronounced only two of the neighborhood's buildings viable. The rest "were in a state of deplorable dereliction" and would be razed.[34] The visual narration attempted to literally "show" how this assessment obscured and distorted the spatial forms and social conditions of the neighborhood. The life stories reveal the neighborhood's human strength despite the sordid conditions. The film's narrator assures us there is a "delicacy of life," a solidarity and independence that is often characteristic of the *peuple*. It can be found in the "heart of each home" and makes these people proud of their neighborhood and their lives, with little desire to leave. More than simply being photographed, the roles in Chombart's documentaries were acted by local residents who were then taped at the film's end discussing with Chombart and his team their participation and the presentation of their quartier. The last installment in the series was a round-table debate among all the "actors" who had contributed to the neighborhood portraits.

The case-study documentary functioned as a visual representation of Chombart's sociological research and an opportunity to act out his ideals as a form of televised populist instruction. The inhabitants of this slum do not live in a state of chaos and degeneracy, nor are their children born delinquents. They have tactics and specific skills that enable them to decipher and negotiate their environment. Their lives are organized around socially shaped spaces. Material conditions are difficult, but, according to Chombart, "social life is extremely active and warm-hearted. People seem happy, which the film portrays well."[35] An interview with the local barber attests to neighborhood solidarity. He recounts that they have all spent the last twenty years watching Serge grow up. And so we meet Serge as a handsome young man in a leather jacket who courts his bride-to-be, Anna, on his motorcycle. The entire neighborhood prepares for their wedding, and they march in full regalia through the courtyard to the church to exchange vows. The Serge and Anna of Chombart's sociological study have much in common with Jacques Becker's Antoine and Antoinette. Both couples represent a youthful postwar generation, optimistic about their future despite the difficulties they face. They are modish and independent. Although clearly working class, they lack the traditional proletarian disposition of their parents. Yet they remain attached to their neighborhood roots. Despite every effort to find housing in the beloved rue du Moulin de la Pointe where they have grown up, there is nothing. The young couple are forced to leave behind their friends and family for an HLM apartment in the suburbs.

What happened when people like Serge and Anna, alias Antoine and Antoinette, moved out of the natural habitat of the quartier? In the series's next film, *La Butte à la Reine*,[36] the Levavasseur family moves from the 13th arrondissement as part of the slum-clearance operations to a new apartment building in the suburban *cité-jardin* of La Butte à la Reine. They have waited two years for this apartment, with its modern amenities, clean whitewashed walls and balcony, and views of the countryside. Their children are mesmerized as the kitchen appliances, purchased on credit, arrive. The apartment is a visual depiction of the habitat norms that became standardized in public housing as the "F" category system, especially the "F3" or 170-square-foot three-room flat, with well-equipped kitchen and bathroom and open to light and air.[37] It was considered the summit of rational planning. Despite the fact that Monsieur Levavasseur will commute an hour to work by train into Paris, "their life has been transformed—a new mentality is born. The family has joyously moved into their apartment and into the future." But there are problems. The old neighborhood in the 13th was *sympathique*. In La Butte à la Reine there is little chance to meet the neighbors until they are faced with a flood in the building. There are hardly any local shops, and the prices are too high. Most women travel back to Paris, to the Uniprix at Denfert Rochereau, for food and provisions. But there is little connection between the old city and the new *cité-jardin*. Despite hopes for a collective experience, the new inhabitants began building fences with "private property" signs around their building, which is renamed a *résidence*. Suburban life privatizes and territorializes the Levavasseur family. They have been ripped away from the natural sociability and support system of working-class neighborhood life in Paris. The sense of community accommodation, their roots and true identity, have all been lost.

All of these films and television shows displayed optimism and enthusiasm as well as ambivalence and apprehension about the future and the impact of the *trente glorieuses*. The complicated textures of a disassembled city are made visible. The viewer has time to gaze at the splintered physicality and spaces of Paris, their vitality and persistence. We find traces of memory and the familiar in this cartography. And yet, more than just made observable, vernacular spaces and sociability were *produced* as national pageantry in 1950s film and television. This was where the soul of the nation could be found. These images constructed a fictionalized, mediatized dream of urban community after years of civil conflict. Chombart's television documentary was a lyrical, aestheticized construction of Paris that left more than enough room for illusion. The imagery was arresting. Life was graceful, full of feeling, hopeful even in want. The presentation of social cohesion was so intensely poetic and idealized that even the actors in Chombart's version of neighborhood life in *La Rue du Moulin de la Pointe* gently chastised the research team for ignoring neighborhood conflicts and tensions.[38] The documentary's imaginary magnified the hidden beauty of social life in these forgotten slum districts, creating its own stereotype and exaggerating community cohesion. In *La Butte à la Reine*, the production team of Bergeret, Krier, and Chombart began by admitting that the term "solidarity" had been overused and was not meant to discount the hardship in slums like Moulin de la Pointe. Nevertheless, they emphasized that "human warmth" existed in working-class neighborhoods despite their obscurity and appalling difficulties. Fraternity and solidarity were lived experiences.[39] The tone was emotional, poignant, and expressive of a collective dimension that stood outside material conditions. Urban space was a trope for overheated humanistic ambitions.

Popular films, documentaries, and television programs did not impose a single overarching vision. But we can say that the humanist perspective played a significant part in how the public sphere was identified and produced and in imagining what took place in the spaces that accompanied it. A set of visual codes and characteristic sites was invented by film and television to stand for this intensely lyrical humanist idiom. Regardless of the visual genre, urban space is depicted with the same conscious consistency. Paris was a visual setting saturated with emotional, psychological, and social meaning. The films were exquisite tales of urban struggle that were based on a postwar socioethnographic perspective that professed to understand the French as they really were. Neither the silver nor the television screen presented unnerving scenes of the street protests or the rioting, strikes, and crisis of decolonization taking place in the streets of Paris. Even the production of destitution and urban squalor retained a fantastic and fatalistic quality. The *peuple* suffered in these films, but they patiently endured and remained faithful to French values.

Portraits in Film Noir

Paris may have been an alchemical mix of power and possibilities, but the irony of these years is that it was also a place of disillusion and false hope that was best captured in so-called film noir or noir realism. These crime thrillers, detective stories, *policier*, and *polar* used stark lighting, unusual angles, and black-and-white composition to create a dark urban realm. Their subject matter was a somber social realism, violence and loss, and ambivalence about the moral universe. The protagonists realize too late that they are victims of fate and of the roles they have chosen.[40] Marcel Carné's 1946 production *Les Portes de la nuit* is one of the great icons of this genre.[41] It was also filmed entirely in the studio. The clarity of Carné's vision was, of course, already well-known. He was the master portraitist of *Paris populaire* in the forgotten corners of the city, away from the monumental capital. The son of a furniture maker in the faubourg Saint-Antoine, Carné was orphaned and raised by an indulgent grandmother in the Batignolles district of the 17th arrondissement. His personal image of the city's poor industrial neighborhoods garnered popular acclaim in the 1930s with masterpieces such as *Hôtel du Nord* (the canal Saint-Martin), *Jenny* (the canal de l'Ourcq), and *Le Jour se lève* (the working-class faubourgs). It was also Carné's film depictions that produced the most influential and popular imagery of "the people" that reemerged during the Liberation and euphoric years that followed. They were marked by the tension between a gritty realism and a romanticized metaphysical dimension beyond that represented on the screen. Carné's style of populist realism made everyday people into heroes, often of the tragic kind. They were embodied by the actors Jean Gabin and Yves Montand. Everything about their screen personas labeled them as typical working-class Parisians, a social type identified by gestures, language, clothes, and milieu. Carné sketched their portraits, while the screenwriter Jacques Prévert gave them voice. It was

FIGURE 24. Joseph Kosma, Jacques Prévert, Marcel Carné, Jean Gabin, and Alexandre Trauner. © CINEMATHÈQUE FRANÇAISE.

a team that emerged from the communist and surrealist avant-garde movements of the 1930s and was committed to fashioning working-class art and a more humanist future. Their vision of the working classes was lyrical and metaphysical, yet set on the surfaces of the city in the concrete social milieu of the city's industrial neighborhoods. The people of Paris were indivisible from their spatial environment. Even in tragedy, Paris was magical. Its appeal was irresistible. The portrayal was closest to that of Zola in its dramatic naturalism and depiction of the urban landscape. According to Carné, "The star of *Les Portes de la nuit* would be neither a Marlene [Dietrich] nor a Gabin, but a working-class neighborhood in the capital during the sad winter that followed the magnificent summer of the Liberation."[42]

The film was an urban adaptation of Prévert's ballet *Le Rendez-vous* and a deliberate revival of the poetic realism that had been banned during the occupation and that now served the emotional rapture and despair of the postwar years so well. Once again, the team included set designer Alexandre Trauner, composer Joseph Kosma, and cameraman Roger Hubert—all from *Les Enfants du paradis*. But the circumstances had changed. Although Prévert had played little role in the Resistance, he was deeply affected by the Liberation and the subsequent purges. The publication of his first book, *Paroles*, in 1946 met with immense popular acclaim, and he was ready to exert his newfound status on the film team by merging the classic themes of tragic love and heartbreak with the all-too-real tragedies found in the city's spaces just after the Liberation. The scene was Carné's own Barbès-Rochechouart Métro station near the gare du Nord and the *Paris populaire* of the 18th and 19th arrondissement. At a time when the Barbès station barely functioned, precious resources (according to the critics) were used to construct Alexandre Trauner's cinematic stage set, populated with a universe of Parisian stereotypes constructed long before the war: street hawkers and paperboys, vagabonds and locals, street singers and accordionists wandering amid commuters racing for the train. Carné and Prévert's characters are controlled by a hidden fatalism, and the itinerants who frequent the city embody this theme of destiny. Jean Vilar plays the role of Fate, who is disguised as a tramp haunting the streets at Barbès-Rochechouart. His portrayal of the vagabond-seer who watches the inevitable tragedy of the city's life play itself out is one of the most evocative superimpositions of cultural meaning on to the cityscape.

It is at the Barbès Métro station that the *résistant* and proletarian hero Jean Diego—Yves Montand, in his first film—chances upon Fate, who foretells that the young man will meet and fall in love with "the most beautiful girl in the world." The young Montand had met Prévert in Provence in 1948 and introduced the film's title song, *Autumn Leaves*, with lyrics by Prévert and music by Kosma, which immediately became a popular hit. Although the film itself was a commercial flop, it served as a vehicle for Montand's stardom, thanks in good part to Kosma's brilliant musical adaptation of Prévert's poetry. The visual quality of poetic realism was particularly arresting, but its musical and performance dimensions were just as essential to its achievement and linked it to French theatrical tradition. Kosma himself was one of the most influential forces in French popular culture, providing the music to Prévert's *parole* and writing a host of film scores that included *Le Crime de Monsieur Lange* (1936), *La Grande illusion* (1937), *Les Enfants du paradis* (1945), and even Le Chanois's *Sans laisser d'adresse* (1951). He chose to work with Prévert "to express man's anguish before the menace of the modern world, which seemed inhuman."[43] This ethic marked his scores as ideal for a film genre of romantic tragedy, melancholy, and regret.

In the film, Fate's prophecy comes true, and Jean Diego meets Malou (Nathalie Nattier), who has left an unhappy marriage and found her way back to the working-class neighborhood where she was born and spent her youth—"although," she tells her war-profiteer husband, "it is too simple for you." Diego and Malou interact in a disturbing exposé of the city's postwar persona. The film laid bare the misery and tragedy of the northern working-class districts between the Barbès station and Aubervilliers in the autumn of 1945: the hunger and cold, the shortage of coal and electricity, the squalid housing, the fiendish tone of the black market, the neighbor accused of collaborating "at Drancy." The interpretation of the industrial landscape of warehouses, murky canals, and railroad yards is sinister and forbidding. The city is shrouded in eternal night and populated by ruthless scoundrels, *femmes fatales*, frauds, and traitors. Malou's father was accused by his neighbors of collaboration, and her brother worked for the Milice. While they live in comfort, children steal wood for heat, and the destitute scour through street garbage. An atmosphere of malaise and hideous cruelty permeates the gloom. Only Diego and his Resistance friends show any humanity. Diego is a promethean image of the average working guy who has stayed the moral course through the Black Years of the war. The film exalts the sacrifices made by these ordinary people. Although Diego and Malou inhabit a moribund landscape, they magically transform it into a

FIGURE 25. Nathalie Nattier and Yves Montand in Marcel Carné's *Les Portes de la nuit*, 1946.
© RUE DES ARCHIVES/COLLECTION CSFF.

terrain of startling shape and beauty. A dreamy sexual desire pervades the atmosphere. But tragedy awaits the young lovers. The doomed Malou is shot by her dejected husband and dies in Diego's arms. A bittersweet melancholy permeates the atmosphere in this sad depiction of the future after the euphoria of the Liberation. The city's spaces were chimerical, elusive, and untrustworthy.

Perhaps Carné and Prévert had touched the aching, hidden pain of the city too deeply. The film was skewered by critics and the public: it was too expensive, it took too much electricity, it was too long in the making, too pessimistic and psychophilosophical. Georges Altman, reviewer for the communist *L'Écran français*, described "these *nouveaux mystères de Paris* [italics mine] as a new and violent vision of a Paris mired in privation, rotten with its black market, withered in its unfriendliness."[44] Despite the caustic disparagement, the defenders of the film argued that its vision of Paris and its somber, forgotten places rang true. Carné, according to even negative reviews, had recreated Paris with "rigorous exactitude." The combination of studio and location shots had created "a mythic city, a poetic portrait of a city that is closer to reality than a documentary." Prévert, Trauner, and Carné had recreated their eternal Paris:

> The boulevard Barbès of "Les Portes de la nuit" is the boulevard du Crime of "Enfants du paradis." The throngs descending the stairs into the Métro is the same as that crowding the entry of the Funambules Theater. Stairs and gates, alleyways and streetlamps, railroad tracks, luminous canals in the night, once again we soak in the atmosphere of Paris. Once again, the setting, the mood fills us with wonder and seduces us.[45]

It would be difficult to argue that the film portrayed "life as it is led" in any naturalistic way. Ginette Vincendeau argues that the achievement of poetic realist films such as *Les Portes de la nuit* was to create authentic characters connected to their environment who, despite the artificiality of the sets, possessed the capacity to stand for reality.[46] This was due in part to the accumulated visual recollection of Paris, which began most importantly with Zola, and in part to the evocative sets and lighting or atmosphere that permeated the screen. But the film also depicted the tensions between accepted perceptions of Paris as the capital of modern splendor and the disregarded spaces that pierced a far more decentered geography. The depiction of this dark and dreary postwar reality captured the moral unease, the anxiety over ruin and loss, that permeated a troubled city.

Both Carné and Prévert continued to create a Paris imbued with the dramatic and aesthetic vision of poetic realism, although by the end of the 1950s they had fallen out of favor with a public that was turning its attention to the more complicated imagery of the *nouvelle vague*. Carné's *L'Air de Paris* (1954),[47] starring Jean Gabin as the "papa" for the young men at his gym and Arletty as his tough wife, was an ardent portrait of working-class life and ambitions. Following the hopes of the young boxer André (Roland Lesaffre), Carné takes us on a tour of Paris: the boulevard de Grenelle, the Île de la Cité, the Île Saint-Louis, Baltard's sheds at Les Halles, a wretched hotel populated by North African immigrants where the hotel manager profits by jamming his "dirty clients" together "five people to a bed." Guided by the songs of Francis Lemarque and Yves Montand, the city is a theater of life for young André. But his flirtation with the wealthy bourgeois world of his girlfriend ends in heartbreak. The social differences are too difficult to surmount. He is rescued from despair by Gabin and brought back into the warm fold of his working-class roots.

Prévert followed *Les Portes de la nuit* with a series of Paris films that reiterated his populist imaginary: *La Seine a rencontré Paris* (1957), *Paris mange son pain* (1958), *Les Primitifs du XIII* (1958), and the incomparably nostalgic *Paris la belle* (1958). Although stylistically striking, both Carné's and Prévert's film projects late in the decade lost much of their defiant, rebellious quality and instead projected a simpler, sentimentalized portrait of a Paris that existed only in wistful memory. Prévert's deliberately black-and-white world, where "the bad are on one side, the good on the other," where "the rich are almost always malicious, the poor almost always generous of heart," had less relevance as the war and reconstruction years faded into the past.[48] His detractors increasingly took him to task, while admirers spent more and more time defending his vision as an authentic, populist poet. Carné's vision was criticized as passé, one reviewer comparing his portraits of Paris to the ubiquitous images on postcards. The scenes of working-class life were too beautiful, too sensuous and luminous: "It's terrific. But it is not enough to make a film," and not enough to take seriously even when you add the boxing gym.[49]

The darker reality of Paris was also taken up in a variety of 1950s *policier* films and gloomier *noir* portraits of the city's life. Filmmakers were preoccupied with the decayed and ruined urban landscape, and their visual narratives entered the public debate about the city's spaces and its future. The films discussed here chart the ways in which the screen probed urban blight and the layers of detritus that dominated much of the capital's landscape. René Clair's *Porte des Lilas* (1957) is a poignant portrait of poverty and exile in the northeast working-class districts of the city.[50] In the ironic *détournement* of street naming, the porte des Lilas brought to mind springtime and the *guinguettes* on the city's outskirts. But for all the nostalgia about the surrounding environs and their enchantment, the edges of Paris also formed a ferocious zone of social injustice and conflict. There was long-standing anxiety about the mysterious badlands, the *terrain vague*, that enveloped the city. The decentered urban landscape seemed to shatter along its margins into areas of exile and oblivion. Film brought to the surface the spatial antipode or inverse of the centralizing spaces of the monumental capital. The porte des Lilas created by the film's set designer, Léon Barsacq, constructed partially in the studio and enhanced by lighting, was a derelict landscape of urban misery shrouded in rain and snow. Dilapidated housing, dreary mud streets, railroad yards and smokestacks, rubble, and the notorious *zone* compose the bleak cinematic landscape. The film mirrored the wretchedness of the neighborhood's reality. Contemporary reports described the porte des Lilas as a maze of shacks, garages, and tool sheds, ill-kept gardens with their rabbit and chicken cages, gypsy wagons, and broken-down trucks. Here lived an erstwhile community of ragpickers, scrap merchants, chair caners, beggars, panhandlers, and all those who make their living in the classic informal economy of the indigent. To alleviate what was designated as slum conditions, the city of Paris had already begun constructing 336 emergency housing units for the poor at the porte des Lilas. By the mid-1950s Robert Auzelle was carrying out his site studies of the *zone* between the porte de Pantin and the porte des Lilas in preparation for redevelopment.

But rather than reiterating the grotesque underworld that dominated the public's imagination about slums, the film crafts a very human visual rendering. The neighborhood vagabond Juju is played by the actor Pierre Brasseur, who also starred as Frédérick Lemaître in *Les Enfants du paradis*. Juju shares a dingy apartment with his mother and sister, who pick rags and sell them at the local flea market. In his only film role, the folk singer Georges Brassens plays a destitute musician who croons his mournful songs at the local bistro where customers chase away the monotony of life. Young boys on the edge of delinquency harass the neighbors and carouse in the street. The only outsiders who dare enter this miserable domain are a dangerous criminal and the police chasing him. Yet despite the misery and meanness of life, Clair presents the neighborhood as a noble community with its own practices and tactics for survival. They make do with the simple pleasures of song and camaraderie. Their solidarity diminishes the misery, and they organize to defend themselves against the criminal in their midst. The film offers a cinematic glimpse into an unknown world of destitution outside the bounds of affluence and urban sophistication. Juju provides the film's psychological portrait. He is unsightly and unkempt, yet despite his pitiable condition as neighborhood vagrant, moocher, and butt of local jokes, Juju is not what he seems. He is a man of gentle character and noble heart, a version of the all-knowing, all-seeing vagabond, a mythical presence on the streets of Paris. Juju befriends all those around him, including his beloved Maria (the starlet Dany Carrel), the café-owner's daughter, whom he whirls around the dance floor at the July 14 *musette*. It is the only relief from the grueling dullness of their lives. The film is drenched in loneliness. In Clair's soft, drifting

FIGURE 26. Pierre Brasseur and Dany Carrel in René Clair's *Porte des Lilas*, 1957. © RUE DES ARCHIVES / THE GRANGER COLLECTION, NEW YORK.

melancholy, the two friends, trapped in hardship and isolation, make plans to flee the ravages of a disenchanted urban world: "When you are rich, Juju," asks Maria, "will you take me to the Midi?" For both of them, the polished, egotistical killer who has hidden out in this forgotten neighborhood offers the only excitement. He is the epitome of the arrogant bourgeois martinet. His haughty remark that "money is always easy to find" is aimed at Juju and hits him like a bullet to the heart. Despite Juju's altruism and his compassion for those around him, he ends by destroying Maria's happiness, illusory as it may be, and murdering the criminal to defend her. He is an aesthetic reflection of the social outcast suddenly captured by the camera and made visible on the surface of the city.

In *Les Lettres françaises*, the critic Georges Sadoul pointed to the film's underlying humanity, "the confidence in men, even the most fallen. Tenderness and emotion fill the air of this porte des Lilas."[51] Clair's objective was to reveal a hidden world and create a cinematic realism that was "more striking than reality itself"—hence the studio version of the seedy neighborhood, the heavy use of slang, and the visual spectacle of poverty. Clair argued that the slang and mannerisms of this unknown place were one of the film's principal characters.[52] He adopts the role of an ethnologist embarking on a voyage of discovery to a strange land. Working-class behavior, gestures, language, and dialogue became the material of visual investigation. The written language of Léo Malet and Henri Calet are brought to life. The film was nominated for an Academy Award and won the Danish Bodil Award for Best European Film. Nevertheless, *L'Humanité* accused Clair of being a petit-bourgeois anarchist with a romanticized view of the twentieth century—tender and sentimental. *L'Esprit* took him to task for too much "emotional populism" and sentimental *flânerie*. No doubt there is an exoticism, a purely cinematic pantomime of the forgotten world of poverty that Clair imagined.[53] Yet the extreme stylization infused Paris with poetic melancholy and gave this disregarded urban landscape a powerful sense of nobility and classic tragedy—or, perhaps even more to the genre's point, a sense of fatalism. The characters are mythic archetypes, the scenarios literary, almost ethereal in quality.

The expressive visual presentation and implied social criticism in Clair's *Porte des Lilas* was close to that in the renowned documentary on the *terrain vague* just to the north, Jacques Prévert and the photographer Eli Lotar's documentary *Aubervilliers* (1945).[54] Combining both surrealist and realist sensibilities, Lotar had already produced powerful photographs of the abattoirs at La Villette and an evocative series entitled "Somewhere in Paris" as early as 1929.[55] The uneasy images in both series evoke the harsh environment along the margins of the city that fascinated the avant-garde. By the 1930s Lotar had turned to documentary film. Twenty minutes in length, *Aubervilliers* is a jarring exposé that reiterated this same vision of the city's edge. Passing through the porte d'Aubervilliers in 1952 and in part reacting to the film, the urban commentator Jean-Paul Clébert remarked that the "poetry and horror of the *zone* had a great many times been decried, inspected, photographed, filmed, reconstituted in studio, exported for foreign countries as national heritage (French culture and taste), utilized for literary, artistic, moralistic, political ends and forced under the nose of the indifferent by all of the describers of the social fantastic."[56] As a marginal space, Aubervilliers offered a spectacle of dissolution and entropy. It was an alien life that contradicted the splendor of central Paris. Prévert spoke the poetic commentary for the film. The music, performed by Germaine Montero and Fabien Loris, was by Joseph Kosma, whose forlorn "Gentils enfants d'Aubervilliers" was especially poignant:

> Sweet children of Aubervilliers
> Sweet children of the proletariat
> Sweet children of misery
> Sweet children the world over
> Sweet children of Aubervilliers

Aubervilliers was just one of four Prévert films playing in theaters in 1946, among them *Les Enfants du paradis*. Montero regularly gave Prévert song recitals in Paris at the war's end, often accompanied by Kosma on the piano. In other words, *Aubervilliers* came in on the coattails of Prévert's extraordinary popular success. Commissioned by the communist minister of aviation, Charles Tillon, who was also mayor of the industrial town of Aubervilliers, the film's political purpose was to wholly disgrace the town's previous mayor, Pierre Laval, who had been condemned to death and executed by firing squad in October 1945. One of the most hated collaborators in France, he was blamed for the appalling conditions in Paris's proletarian suburbs. The film's premiere, which took place in a local movie house in Aubervilliers in March 1946, was presided over by Tillon himself. We are visually introduced to the squalor along the northern margins of the City of Light. Children dive into a heavily polluted canal. Dead animals and garbage float by while factories spew their toxic waste into the watercourse. We meet a Portuguese laborer named Joseph, a living embodiment of Juju, who hangs his bread from the ceiling of his crumbling shed to protect it from rats. Pathetic old couples live in squalid lean-tos amid the war's debris. The portraits sink to the bottom of heartbreak. The shots and lighting focus on their cheerless, worn faces. An interview with an old woman living in degradation reveals she was once the recipient of the "French Family Medal" and had won first prize in a baby competition—both honors signed by the president of France, she wistfully recounts. As a young man, her "baby" had been lost in the war and her family home bombed, leaving her only its ruins for shelter. A respectable working-class family with six children lives in penury in the bombed out remains of a decrepit building. Their brood will become the cigarette-smoking adolescents captured going bad, setting fires along the banks of the Seine. The film is proof positive of Prévert's poetic humanist vision. Part political propaganda, part a classic Dickensian portrait of squalor and suffering, the visual spectacle magnified his sense of tragedy and fatalism. Audiences reacted with tears and applause to *Aubervilliers*, so much so that it was only shown during the week so as not to offend sensibilities during the weekend fare of light cinematic entertainment.[57]

Film as an analytic tool of urban discourse, in this case about disabused, threatening spatial residues, is also clear from Jean Dewever's *La Crise du logement* (1956),[58] which received the Prix Lumière in the year it opened. It offers a very different visual reading of the capital from Lotar and Prévert's *Aubervilliers*. In a swipe at Lotar's film, Dewever argued that he refused to "aestheticize" misery and instead insisted on an exacting, documented portrayal of misery. The camera takes viewers through the worst badlands of the 1st and 4th arrondissements in the center of Paris. The film was actually shot in 1953, when the degradation was palpable. Tumble-down condemned buildings still in use line the rue de Louvre and the rue de la Grande-Truanderie. A family of four lives in a twenty-square-foot room in a pathetic boardinghouse. Disgusting alleyways filled with trash and rats depict a dystopian city of dread and decay. Despite his emphasis on objective documentation, Dewever played on emotions by panning the dingy streets' new commemorative plaques honoring the death of a neighborhood *résistant* in the Liberation of Paris and the republic's motto of *liberté, égalité, fraternité*. The conditions along the margins of the city, in the *bidonville* of Noisy-le-Grand, where some of the scenes were shot in the face of local hostility, are even worse. The outskirts are chilling, lethal, made up of makeshift shacks and wagons, with lines of corrugated metal shelters along mud alleyways. The purpose of Dewever's twenty-five-minute elaboration of spatial dystopia was to mobilize public opinion about the dreadful housing crisis that gripped everyday life in the capital's *îlots insalubres* and urban edges (although RTF deemed it too offensive and refused to show it on television). They are spatial gaps, temporal voids—hidden, sordid scraps that defame the landscape. Official statistics on their deficiencies blaze across the screen: the absence of electricity, water, gas, plumbing. Repeating the traditional discourse inherited from the urban hygienics movement, the squalor causes psychological problems, disease, tuberculosis, alcoholism, divorce, and revolt. People walk the dreary streets like automatons. Rather than tragic, as in the poetic humanist imaginary, these images are repulsive. Paris is an antisocial, immoral city where abnormality and alienation reign. Dewever's film presents the solution to this terrifying problem as annihilation, wiping these districts off the map. The city would be made normal through modernist redevelopment schemes and a rational plan of *aménagement du territoire*. Although admitting its importance, critics panned the film's conventional revelations, which by 1956 had already been exposed by Abbé Pierre's campaign.[59] But *La Crise du logement* was just one in a parade of documentary films that visually laid out the French government's stance with respect to Paris's intractable slums. Roger Leenhardt and Sydney Jezequiel produced *Paris et le désert français* in 1956, and Dewever filmed a second documentary entitled *Des logis et des hommes* in 1958.

The minister of construction and urbanism himself, Pierre Sudreau, jumped into the fray with an ORTF television series broadcast in November and December 1958 and entitled *Problèmes de la construction* (see also chapter 7). Each episode was dedicated to a specific aspect of housing and urban planning. The broadcasts expanded on official discourse and on Dewever's imagery and indeed used some of the footage from his films. In the November 6 "Interview with Monsieur Pierre Sudreau," the slums are portrayed as catastrophic,[60] shapeless pockets of chaos and disorder. The shots of Glacière in the 13th arrondissement broadcast to television viewers show hundred-year-old buildings, "without water or sanitation, without social services or schools, without gardens or social equipment," being summarily demolished. The violence of the act is blatant. Of the thirteen hundred people living in Glacière, one thousand were being evacuated. There is no social sympathy in these presentations for what has been lost. Although the rue du Moulin de la Pointe captured in Chombart's television documentary is not far away, in these later broadcasts there is no poignant humanism, no encounter with fate to be found along the mean streets. At Ménilmontant, viewers see "some of the worst conditions in Paris" and then watch as ancient buildings are burned down under the watchful eyes of firefighters. Any possibility of renovation or step-by-step evolution toward basic comforts was viewed with complete pessimism and pushed aside by arguments for modern standards of living. The government stood by a scorched-earth policy to completely raze the malevolent, filthy blight that had infected Paris for too long. In its place, the film displays a utopian world of modern housing estates that will welcome the erstwhile inhabitants of the city's shattered slums. The new quartiers will have work, services, commerce, a market three times a week, schools, and youth and cultural centers.

All these films—whether television documentaries, theatrical short films, or full-length commercial entertainment—were haunting visual dramas. Together they demonstrate film's deep engagement with urban space and its fundamental and very specific role in the discourse about the city. The medium produced a series of visual codes and fictional spatial forms that stood for populist, working-class Paris. A decomposed spatiality, the ruins and festering places hidden away from the spectacle of modern urbanity, saturate the screen. Clair and Lotar both used the camera's lens to construct these marginalized wastelands along the edges of the capital as a moral, humanistic landscape. Dewever and Sudreau visually denounced slum districts as open drains of malefaction, disease, and social anarchy. In stark contrast to either of these imaginaries, Jacques Tati's classic film *Mon oncle* also reached movie houses in 1958.[61] The film was released during the collapse of the Fourth Republic in mid-May, and by then French filmmaking was marching decidedly toward other genres, whether in comedy or the *nouvelle vague*. Tati's films displayed a humor and exteriority in their presentation of space and landscape that was far from the drama of poetic realism. First of all, *Mon oncle* was Tati's first color film. Secondly, his films were less emotional and without dramatic dialogue. Rather, they were a militant satire on the transformation of the *trente glorieuses*, featuring explorations of its spatial dynamics and a clownish resistance against modern urban utopia.

The dramatic upheavals in the urban landscape captured in *Mon oncle* were filmed at three different locations between September 1956 and February 1957: buildings designed by the architect Henri Vicariot that were under construction at Paris's new airport at Orly, the HLM apartment blocks rising up at Créteil at Pierre Sudreau's behest, and La Victorine studios in Nice. Tati despised Sudreau's destruction of Paris. In a 1958 interview on the making of *Mon oncle*, he pointed "to the intelligence of the German general who, despite Hitler, saved Paris from destruction, and now we are in the process of destroying it. . . . We are systematically knocking down everything that gives it charm and personality."[62] The film's scenario is built around the radical contrasts between two different forms of urban life: modern suburbia and the shabby old neighborhood of traditional existence. "What I am defending," Tati explained in a 1958 interview with *L'Humanité*, "is the *petit quartier*, the tranquil corner against roads, highways, aerodromes, all the uniform organization of the modern city."[63] In *Mon oncle* the pittoresque *petit quartier populaire* invented by humanist discourse is still visible. But the stage set that was built into the place d'Armes of suburban Saint-Maur to depict the *sympathique* îlot was no longer heroic. Rather, it was a sentimental myth about to disappear. The pulverizing forces of modernization and urban renewal were well under way. In place of the myth is the vast system of consumer objects, the sterile homogenization and abstraction of modern architecture that become Tati's cinematic subjects. Paris would be liquidated altogether in Tati's later film *Playtime* (1967), replaced by an entirely prefabricated world. Everything looks like everything else. In the inverse of Dewever's visual reading of space, it is this modernist utopia that produces disorientation, alienation, and unfeeling automatons dedicated to the capitalist machine.

Tati's defense of particularity and place echoed the intellectual and avantgarde visions of the city through the 1950s. It was a counternarrative to the urbanistic eradication spearheaded by modernists such as Bernard Lafay and Raymond Lopez, and ultimately to the plans of Pierre Sudreau. Tati's visual mapping of neighborhood geography and the ways in which his central character, Monsieur Hulot, interacts with the two spatial worlds in *Mon oncle* are close to the situationist definition of *détournement*, a sort of impish fun or grown-up stunt. A number of film critics have pointed to this association between Tati's films and Guy Debord's *Society of the Spectacle*, and it is no surprise that Debord himself was an admirer of Tati's work.[64] Hulot (played by Tati himself) is a comic everyman, just another nobody in the populist tradition. He bumbles about in an ancient, ramshackle tenement building. Motley packs of stray dogs, mischievous schoolboys, chattering neighbors, and bicycles and carts weaving in and out among street vendors' stands mark the public domain that passes under Hulot's attic window. It is spontaneous, convivial, entirely irrational, and inefficient. The distracted street sweeper does everything but sweep. The chain of images is constructed as a set of interruptions and coincidences. The local bistro, Chez Margot, is the center of social life. Private lives spill out in full view in the squares and streets. Everyday life is filled with emotional, human potential. It is the visual depiction of the îlot, the social *unité* imagined by the humanist intellectual tradition. But despite Tati's comic defense of this perceived world, and perhaps his situationist proclivities, the vision had faded into a rose-colored nostalgia by the late 1950s. Canaries sing, and the street is perpetually filled with music. In reviewing the film, *La Vie ouvrière* argued that the dilapidation and clumsiness of the old neighborhood portrayed in *Mon oncle* was "an element of decor, of folklore. It is never catastrophic. . . . In fact, the quartier is not as nice as that. The old buildings won't resolve the housing crisis. The moral and physical health of young kids playing freely isn't always what Tati thinks it to be."[65] The humanist imaginary had disintegrated.

6

The Left Bank

In August 1946 the communist UJRF organized a "March for the Future" dedicated to the young people of France. It mobilized some 200,000 Parisians in a long, cheerful caravan from the place de la République to the Palais de Chaillot. They were led by a banner emblazoned with the slogan "Struggle and Reconstruct for a Better Future" and escorted by a sea of tricolor flags, and the newspaper *L'Humanité* reported that the "magnificent spectacle was an image of strength and hope." Miners, construction workers, carpenters, *midinettes*, and *métallos* joined in the march with "thousands of young" campers, athletes, skiers, basketball players, mountaineers, folklore groups, and marching bands to celebrate the future. "Those who write that the young are corrupt, those who find their evidence in bars frequented by degenerates," the article goes on to admonish, "should come to look at these genuine representatives of 'young French elites.'"[1] Probably no subject received more passionate attention during the reconstruction years than the question of France's young people. And probably no group was more visible in the public spaces of Paris, especially on the Left Bank. The programs of the Liberation and the early Fourth Republic promoted education and youth organizations as essential to the work of national renewal. A Direction des mouvements de jeunesse et d'éducation populaire was created at the Ministère de l'éducation nationale. Improving popular taste and appealing to young people as the future of France were the impetus behind the creation of such highly successful groups such as the Ciné-Clubs. The Paris municipal council endlessly debated the need for more schools, sports facilities, parks, and recreation centers for the city's young people. The future seemed a battle for the hearts and minds of the generation reaching adulthood during the 1950s and for their younger brothers and sisters of the baby boom, growing up behind them. The quandary over whether France was really ready to accept these first postwar adolescents was dramatically played out in the public spaces of the city.

This chapter takes up the question of this young generation, their presence in the public domain, and their influence on perceptions of urban spatiality. It argues that the visibility of young people in Paris produced new spatial and temporal forms associated with "youth" both by habitual use and by metaphor. Youth was a psychological landscape. It was a style of avant-garde public performance. The Left Bank enjoyed a prodigious heritage as the city's cultural and intellectual incubator, and it had always been the heart of bohemian student life. It was divided into two distinct worlds: the Latin Quarter, with its celebrated university institutions, and Saint-Germain-des-Prés, with its celebrated café and nightlife. What is interesting about the Left Bank in the late 1940s and 1950s, however, is that both Saint-Germain-des-Prés and the Latin Quarter became renewed sites of resistance, a new frontier of cultural production for a generational identity somewhere between childhood and adulthood. This youthful category, its fashion and music, its politics, its range of public practices, invented a topos or place that complicated and overlapped older discourses about class. It was locally based, territorially defined. Like social class, youth formed a counterpublic and a counterspace that challenged optimistic perceptions about reconstruction and the future of France. Youth as a spatial itinerary was also imagined as disorder, as a threat that heightened anxieties about urban decomposition and fed into the political unrest of the time. The power and complexity of this cultural concoction of "teenager," "youth," and "student" were extraordinary. These identities were exercised in a multiplicity of ways in the spaces of the Left Bank as avant-gardist and highly politicized public theater.

The Left Bank was already a site of furious ideological controversy during the interwar years. In the political storms of the 1930s, rival left- and right-wing factions distributed tracts, delivered speeches, demonstrated, and fought pitched battles with police along the boulevard Saint-Michel. The bistros of Montparnasse were a combat zone of surrealists, communists, and fascists, partisans on all sides of the Spanish Civil War. As the black years of occupation settled over the city, the mood on the Left Bank grew somber and bleak. But student opposition was unrelenting. On October 30, 1940, students gathered before the Collège de France to protest the arrest of the physician Paul Langevin, and a year later they gathered at the Sorbonne in a vigil for hostages executed by the Nazis. Responding to a tract entitled "Étudiants de France," on November 11, 1940 (the anniversary of France's victory over Germany in the First World War), thousands of lycée and college students defied the ban on public assembly and marched in protest down the Champs-Élysées to the Tomb of the Unknown Soldier. The Germans acted swiftly to quell this dissent. A number of protesters were killed and wounded, and 123 were immediately arrested and sent off to concentration camps. In fact, the organized Resistance, which also began in the fall of 1940, was to a real degree a "youth movement"—some of the most serious fighting during the Liberation took place in the Latin Quarter and along the Boul' Mich'. A number of student organizations were born in the murky, clandestine world of the underground.[2] The Bataillons de la jeunesse, or Young Communists, and the Jewish Communists were among the first to organize Resistance activities; both organizations were led by teenagers. The Défense de la France was a college student movement that published a clandestine newspaper from the basement of the Sorbonne, while the Volontaires de la liberté was organized by lycée students in April 1941. The Forces unies de la jeunesse patriotique (united forces of patriotic youth, or FUJP) attempted to unify these isolated resistance cells and attach them to the CNR, and even wrote a "youth charter" of reforms to be promulgated at Liberation. Those carrying out actual acts of sabotage and violence paid a heavy price. In the spring of 1942 thirty-four young Parisians were rounded up by the French police and put through two highly publicized show trials. One doomed woman was sent to the guillotine, and twenty-three men were executed by firing squad. In June 1944, before the Gestapo abandoned Paris, they executed thirty-five Parisians whose average age was seventeen. Another forty-two young people were shot in August in the Bois de Boulogne, many of them members of the underground Organisation civile et militaire de la jeunesse and the Jeunesses ouvrières chrétiennes de l'Île-de-France. Their courage and their deaths at the hands of the Gestapo were recounted before the municipal council by a citizen's committee of the 16th arrondissement in December 1945 in an effort to memorialize their sacrifice with a monument at the site where they were killed.

Alongside these overt acts of organized resistance, surreptitious public activities carried on by young people in Paris were abundant in number and invention; laying wreaths for fallen comrades; dropping tracts and pamphlets in Métro stations, on buses and in stores; destroying German street signage; heckling of German officials; writing graffiti; and flaunting symbols of French patriotism. Many of the people arrested for these infractions were teenagers. Daring public performances and engaging in activities aimed at "shocking respectability" were unrelenting forms of opposition that were especially associated with the Latin Quarter, which refused, according to occupation officials, to be "won back from Jewish influence and Gaullist trickery."[3] After the June 1, 1942 decree compelling Jews to identify themselves with yellow stars, students and young people paraded along the boulevard Saint-Germain-des-Prés sporting the infamous badges decorated with personalized inscriptions. In June 1943 students ended their exams with a traditional *monôme du bac*, processing through the streets of the Latin Quarter and singing traditional student songs laced with political lampooning. They then staged a sit-down demonstration at the Panthéon until the police arrived. In the general scuffle that followed, oppositional political tracts spontaneously appeared throughout the neighborhood.[4]

Clandestine *surboums* (surprise or impromptu dance parties), covert swing dancing, and listening to Radio London music broadcasts were also youthful acts of rebellion. Swing was adopted as political parody to become the countermusic to official military marches and folkloric hymns. The craze was most closely identified with the rebellious and very public *zazous*. *Zazou* style defied accepted fashion norms. Young men swaggered through Paris sporting pompadour hairdos and garish zoot-suit jackets. Young women strutted along beside them in tight-fitting turtleneck sweaters, short pleated skirts, and flowing long hair. Dark glasses, umbrellas, striped socks, wartime wooden-soled shoes, and a slang peppered with English were all essential to this rebellious masquerade. Their contemptuous attitude mocked the New Order. The historian Paul Yonnet likens the *zazou* movement to the Paris Commune. It was a cultural reformulation and a preview of things to come, a youth movement based on clothes and music, a lifestyle that battled custom and collective constraints. The movement was a challenge to the older generation (in this case, that of *pétainistes*) and ultimately an affirmation of urbanity and civic life.[5] Their hangouts were the Champs-Élysées and the Latin Quarter. They paraded the Boul' Mich' and the boulevard Saint-Germain-des-Prés flaunting conspicuous yellow stars on their chests emblazoned with the words "swing," "*zazous*," or "J3s," as they were often called, after the name of the ration category for thirteen- to twenty-one-year-olds.[6] Their idols were the singer Johnny Hess, whose hits included "Je suis swing" and "Ils sont zazous," and the singer-actress Irène de Trébert, with "Elle était swing" and "Mademoiselle Swing." They were played on BBC radio in a direct slap at Nazi-controlled Radio-Paris. Hess ridiculed the moralists of the New Order and their absorption with racism: "Black music and hot jazz / Are not our thing / Now to be hip / You have to swing / Za zou, za zou, za zou ze."

In the aftermath of the war and Liberation, young people dominated the public spaces of Paris, flooding into the streets in an explosion of freedom. Public festivities were rites of inversion in which the ridiculous, the unseemly, and the wild negated the trapped sense bred by living in wartime. A new generational dissonance fed into the complexities of traditional social and class divisions. The Liberation changed everything for the *zazous*. American merchandise, American swing, and American films became the rage. The *zazous* rummaged through the flea market at Saint-Ouen for American clothes sent by relief agencies and sold for almost nothing. The J3s sported crew cuts and khaki pants in emulation of the *kaks*. American military-issue Ray-Ban sunglasses became a fashion craze. Once the curfews were lifted, young people savored the freedom of the streets at night, even if it meant freezing on street corners outside jazz clubs in Saint-Germain-des-Prés. Hélène Brunschwig was in the Latin Quarter in late August 1944, "where on every street corner there was dancing. It was incredible to see all of Paris dancing the tango, the waltz . . . the bebop, the rumba."[7] Public space became a zone of spontaneous mood and invention. Taking to the street in jam sessions and general free-for-all dancing was a mechanism of public empowerment that expressed a right to the city. Musicians set up shop in the young crowds' favorite haunts, particularly the Latin Quarter, Saint-Germain-de-Prés, and around the place de la Bastille, where dancing went on spontaneously in the streets and around Métro stations. The *bals publics* thrived as spaces of youthful energy and sexuality. They were open-ended and unpredictable, a ridicule of officialdom and hierarchy, a violation of decorum and proportion. More than just a pressure valve allowing young people to let off steam, all of these acts of youthful rebellion were liminal phenomena, a continuous projection of the Liberation. They were a ritual performance, a subversive clowning that sets in motion a freeing up, making possible novel configurations of ideas and social relations.

Saint-Germain-des-Prés

Despite the noisy youthful effervescence that spilled into its streets, Saint-Germain-des-Prés retained its enigmatic intellectual quality in the 1940s. The avant-garde had already migrated from Montparnasse and taken up residence in its cafés in the years before the war. In 1939, Léon-Paul Fargue described the place Saint-Germain-des-Prés, with its ancient abbey church, as one of those places in the capital where you felt the most "up-to-date, nearest to current trends and the men who have their finger on the pulse of the country, the world, Art." For Fargue, "the place lives, breathes, throbs, and sleeps by virtue of the three cafés more famous today than the institutions of state: the Deux Magots, the Café de Flore, and the Brasserie Lipp."[8] It was in the Café Flore and the Deux Magots that the beau monde of avant-gardism and left-wing intellectual culture—Marcel Carné and Jacques Prévert, André Breton and Pablo Picasso, Jean-Paul Sartre and Simone de Beauvoir—shared tables and conversation. The Brasserie Lipp on the opposite side of the boulevard Saint-Germain-des-Prés was the nerve center of right-wing intellectuals. They even co-opted the Left Bank name in their Rive Gauche lecture group, which met at first in the Vieux-Colombier Theater and later at the Bonaparte Cinema on the place Saint-Sulpice, or they met at the Rive Gauche bookstore on the boulevard Saint-Michel. The rival factions generally inhabited the same Left Bank space, just as they shared the same publishers—Gallimard and Grasset. In general, the Left Bank suffered fewer of the injustices inflicted by the occupation on other areas of the city. The district was cheerless and deserted, the food markets bare. The cafés remained open with the usual clientele, now escaping flats made frigid by the fuel shortage. Life went on. The Germans never set foot in the command center of left-wing intellectual life, the Café de Flore.[9] Most of the avant-garde who remained in Paris chose either to keep their heads down and continue working, or to negotiate with the regime in a way that avoided moral abrogation. But the superficial security of the district hid the troubled road of Parisian intellectuals to either collaboration or resistance.

It was the intimate parish quality, the cheap flats and bistros, of Saint-Germain-des-Prés that made it a cultural scene on the frontier between the bourgeois capital of the Right Bank and the old literary and art colonies of Montparnasse. The district was nostalgically portrayed by poets, novelists, and sentimentalists as a cherished quotidian village of working people, of courtyards and craft shops clustered around its church. Some of the old elites still clung to their mansions along the quiet streets. But even the most dignified of the district's buildings were showing their age, and the more mundane structures were just shoddy and ramshackle. In the early postwar years Boris Vian wrote a *Manuel de Saint-Germain-des-Prés* and drew the perimeters of the island, "with its insular nature," that was taking shape as a youthful mecca: from the quai Malaquais and the quai Conti down the rue Dauphine to the rue de l'Ancienne-Comédie and then to the rue Saint-Sulpice, the rue du Vieux-Colombier, and the rue des Saints-Pères.[10] Cheap and ordinary, the district's socially heterogeneous quality and idiosyncrasy by comparison to the glitter on the Right Bank gave it an air of refuge, freedom, and avant-garde chic. The beau monde of would-be intellectuals shared the public spaces and bistros with vagrants and the poor, with North Africans looking for work, with a working-class subculture simply going about its daily life. In other words, they settled into precisely the populist world that French sociologists and urbanists were so intent on discovering.

It might have been a bohemian hangout, but there was little to suggest that Saint-Germain would become a zone of musical novelty. It was the cabarets of the Right Bank, such as Chez Agnès Capri on the rue Molière and Chez Gilles on the avenue de l'Opéra, and the celebrated theaters and musical halls on the *grands boulevards* that captured the imagination of musical devotees, even during the occupation. But the early postwar years brought a fracturing in the city's cultural geography. The music and entertainment scene shifted toward the Left Bank, where an avant-garde of young entertainers was introducing new musical forms. They performed on the Right Bank only after they became famous. Immediately after the Liberation, Henri Leduc, the flamboyant impresario of Montmartre and Saint-Germain-des-Prés, opened Le Bar Vert on the rue Jacob, the first cabaret to play American music. Claude Luter and his jazz combo set up the first basement club in the Hôtel de Lorient in May 1946 on the rue des Carmes. The basement *boîtes* and sidewalks of Saint-Germain-des-Prés pulsated with the sounds of a growing revelry of jazz musicians and devotees. The basement clubs formed an underground spatial realm. Music was appropriated as the voice of a new generation and its transgressive, antiestablishment urban order. The clubs competed for the favors of American jazz greats. When Duke Ellington played the Club Saint-Germain-des-Prés in 1948, more than a thousand admirers jammed into the narrow rue Saint-Benoît to catch a glimpse of their idol.

Dizzy Gillespie and Miles Davis followed. The Vieux-Colombier countered with Sidney Bechet. For the writer Olivier Merlin, their horns trumpeted the "pure spirit of Paris."[11] The French acceptance of American cultural forms was certainly problematic, and would become more so as the cold war and the 1950s advanced. But it was clear that the young people emerging from the shadow of war were fascinated by American music, American film, and American popular culture.

At the same time, in clubs such as La Rose Rouge, Le Quod Libet, and L'Échelle de Jacob,[12] the entertainers Boris Vian, Francis Lemarque, and Juliette Gréco (the darling of the existentialists) created their own style of poetic, spoken Left Bank music. One Parisian, Anne-Marie Deschodt, remembered that her musical education had been "honorable" up to 1947, when she "became old enough to go out alone," left behind the Edith Piaf records in her family's apartment, and headed for a jazz festival in the streets of Saint-Germain-de-Prés to hear Vian, Jacqueline François, and Gilbert Bécaud.[13] The district's avant-garde soundscape was disruptive and rebellious. The vocal group Frères Jacques was a good example of the innovative musical combinations of jazz, French *yé-yé*, and early rock 'n' roll emanating from the Left Bank during the post-Liberation years. The group's originator, André Bellec, participated in both the Vichy regime's wartime Chantiers de jeunesse (youth work camps) and the postwar Travail et culture movement (TEC). The four "brothers" of Frères Jacques mixed song, humor, dance, and mime in a colossally successful cabaret act that was both folkloric and novel in content. The Frères Jacques were the headliners at La Rose Rouge and emblematic of the club's reputation as a laboratory of musical experimentation. There the poetry of Jacques Prévert, the music of Joseph Kosma, and the verse of Raymond Queneau and François Mauriac sung by Juliette Gréco, Léo Ferré, and the Frères Jacques captivated their audiences. The genre functioned as a paradigmatic resource, a medium for the constitution of an alternative youth identity and engagement. The nightclub became the emblematic social space, the training ground in which the parameters of youthful rebellion could be tested. They were a place of *bricolage*, of improvisation, and of seditious performance.

Prévert's populist language and lyrical style, the open defiance of his *Paroles* and its humor, matched the libertarian mood of young men and women, the *zazous* and students emerging from wartime captivity. His poetry was the bebop or the boogie-woogie of the written word and existentialism for a generation for whom the philosophy meant living to the fullest a life of personal freedom. Prévert had been a mainstay of the Saint-Germain scene since before the war, where he lived (on the rue Dauphine), launched his Groupe Octobre amateur acting troop, and began writing song lyrics. Prévert was everywhere in Paris at the war's end. In the spring of 1945 the singer Germaine Montero gave a Prévert recital at the Athénée Theater accompanied on the piano by Kosma. In June the ballet *Le Rendez-vous*, created by Roland Petit and written by Prévert with music by Kosma, was staged at the Sarah Bernhardt Theater. At the end of 1945 his play *L'École buissonnière* was staged in Paris, and five radio programs hosted by Robert Scipion were devoted to Prévert and his opus. In 1946 four films for which Prévert had written the screenplay—*Aubervilliers*, *Les Enfants du paradis*, *Sortilèges*, and *Le Voleur de paratonnerres*—were in movie houses at the same time a recital of Prévert and Kosma's music was being given at the Pleyel Theater. In her autobiography *The Prime of Life*, Simone de Beauvoir described the extraordinary position held by Prévert among the artistic elite gathered at Saint-Germain-des-Prés and the Café de Flore: "At the time, their god, oracle and mentor was Jacques Prévert, whose films and poems they worshiped, whose language and wit they sought to emulate."[14] By 1954 the periodical *Positif* published an editorial acknowledging that "the real world is beginning to look a lot like that imagined by Prévert." Claude Roy acknowledged that

> everywhere in Paris it seems we find Prévert. Just as of a landscape, we say "It's a Corot," or of a street corner on Montmartre, we say "It's an Utrillo," we find Prévert in a conversation on the street, in the smile of a flower-vendor, or a taxi driver's belting out his songs. He is with us in his films, his poetry, his music, the long monologues he weaves about life and everyone's passing days.[15]

The singer and songwriter Francis Lemarque also personified this politically engaged French style of music and spoken word that sprang from the spaces of Saint-Germain-des-Prés. His performances headlined on the cabaret circuit at La Rose Rouge and L'Échelle de Jacob, while his plays were staged at the neighboring Théâtre de l'Humour and the Théâtre de Poche. Lemarque traveled in Prévert's charmed circle in Saint-Germain-des-Prés and through him met Yves Montand, who commissioned a multitude of his Paris ballads. Many of Lemarque's songs evoked the working-class neighborhoods of Paris,

FIGURE 27. Francis Lemarque and Yves Montand along the Seine, September 30, 1953.
© GERALD BLONCOURT/RUE DES ARCHIVES.

the world of *guinguettes*, *bals musettes*, and young bands of teenage hoodlums. Although he never became a Communist Party member, his work was committed to the Left and the avant-garde pacifism that dominated the Left Bank milieu. Lemarque performed regularly at Communist Party galas and youth festivals. In the mid-1950s he embarked on a series of major international tours to communist countries, from China and the Soviet Union to North Korea. His anti-war classic "Quand un soldat" rocketed to fame in 1953: "When a soldier leaves for war / With a shiny weapon in his pack/ . . . Leaving perhaps to die / To war to war / It's a strange little game / That no one loves / But always / When summer arrives / They go . . . those who will die." When the Soviets launched the Sputnik satellite in 1957, Lemarque immediately celebrated this coup de grâce against the United States with "Soleil d'acier" (Lemarque and Castella, 1957): "A flaming sun of steel / Passes over and wakes me / It rises in the sky to explore the universe."[16] His performances at the legendary Olympia in 1958 with Paul Anka as the headliner were among the high points of a long and successful career as one of the most Parisian singer-songwriters to emerge from the Saint-Germain-des-Prés scene.

La Rose Rouge was only one in a circuit of nighttime haunts on the streets of Saint-Germain-des-Prés. Each cultivated its own brand of entertainment and stars, its own enthralled groupies, its own rituals. Music was used as a form of spatial mapping. The battle raged between the clubs that remained loyal to traditional jazz and those, such as the Tabou and the Caveau de la Huchette, that became "bebop havens," with boogie-woogie and jitterbug dance exhibitions that spilled out into the street.[17] Police were called in to intervene regularly throughout the 1950s when the jam sessions, concerts, and party scenes on the place Saint-Germain-des-Prés got out of hand. There was a spontaneity and libertarianism to these performances that combined a carnival formula with youthful transgression. It had its own cultural pastiche. The lettrist Gabriel Pomerand recited "letter poetry" in the middle of the night at the Tabou. The strategy of provocation, of undercutting accepted norms, was applied to raffish cabaret skits and beauty contests immersed in sexual play and innuendo. The Miss Tabou and Miss Vice contests were amateur strip teases, while the election of Apollo at the Tabou was the occasion for young men in briefs to show off their muscles. In *Mythologies*, Roland Barthes remarked on the spectacle and erotic power of these notorious amateur striptease contests, noting that their very awkwardness gave them unexpected sensual and seditious qualities.[18] Chicago night required gangster costumes, while western night meant women in saloon-girl getups. They were a form of mockery, of confrontational charade. The rest of Paris saw these youthful agitators as bent on outrageous, vulgar farce. They excited a mixture of scandal and envy. *Le Tout-Paris* arrived to imbibe the depraved ambience and pose for the paparazzi.

Although the clubs inevitably took up residence in some long-forgotten cellar, the cafés, streets, and public spaces of Saint-Germain-des-Prés themselves became emblematic of the new youth culture. The Café de Flore, the Deux Magots, and the Brasserie Lipp formed a golden triangle of existential cool and sophistication. The Chop Gauloise on the rue Bonaparte and Chez Georges on the rue des Canettes were cheaper alternatives that were still within sight of the glitterati. For hip young people reaching adulthood in the reconstruction years, existentialism meant an unrestrained freedom from the black years and a new confidence in the future, despite difficult times and hard choices. They searched for self-awareness and intensity of experience. Existentialism was a form of philosophical and personal rebellion. It was a seizing of intellectualism, a dramatic transfusion of the public sphere. As a radically new system of values, it was practiced as a lifestyle, an image-act, an "offensive," to use Simone de Beauvoir's term, in a spatial theater carried out in the streets, cafés, and nightclubs of Saint-Germain-des-Prés. The movement was instrumental to the way the Left Bank was produced, and it revolutionized the city on behalf of a new postwar generation. Its followers were legion. The city's avant-garde elites, from Camus and Merleau-Ponty to Gréco and Vian, were held in its sway.

The district was also the haunt of American tourists and modish young expatriates anxious to brush up against *la vie de bohème* and the avant-garde scene.[19] Joining them was a new generation of American black and Latin American writers, artists, and musicians. Richard Wright and James Baldwin moved with ease in the world of Saint-Germain-des-Prés. Jorge Amado enjoyed the charmed friendship of Sartre and de Beauvoir. The bistros presided over by the literati, the experimental film festivals and theater premiers, the dance parties and soirées, the avant-garde publications and esoteric magazines found in trendy bookstores, functioned as an exhilarating form of spatial theater. It was the heyday of the film clubs in Paris. Students and young people gathered at the Ciné-Club d'Avant-Garde, the communist Ciné-Clartés at the Lux-Rennes, and the Ciné-Club du Quartier Latin to see the latest films or experimental œuvre. This last was the hang-out of Jean-Luc Godard, Eric Rohmer, and François Truffaut. It was at the Ciné-Club du Quartier Latin that Guy Debord's *Hurlements en faveur de Sade* was first previewed in 1952. The tiny Théâtre de Poche, the Vieux-Colombier, the Huchette, and the Noctambules mounted bare-bones improvisational productions. The bookstores on the rue de l'Odéon were hip meeting grounds for readings and discussion. The new La Hune bookshop alongside the Café Deux Magots launched avant-garde exhibitions. The most prestigious publishing houses were within a stone's through of the abbey church; Gallimard, Le Seuil, Émile-Paul, and Flammarion were among the most important of these. Sartre's *Les Temps modernes* and Emmanuel Mounier's *Esprit* both had their offices in the neighborhood. These revues were as much literary-political movements as businesses, and their weekly staff meetings were opportunities for passionate debate. Every word of muscular left-wing publications from *Combat* and *Les Lettres françaises* to *Les Temps modernes* was poured over and discussed endlessly. Every move by Sartre and Simone de Beauvoir in their Saint-Germain-des-Prés haunts was avidly scrutinized in the press. They became celebrities in a mythic public theater carried on daily in which any number of disciples could take part.

Sensationalist newspapers such as *Samedi-soir* and *France-dimanche* published lurid accounts of the district's night spots and its would-be existentialists. In May 1947 *Samedi-soir* catapulted Saint-Germain-des-Prés into the spotlight with a front-page photo of the "existentialists" Roger Vadim and Juliette Gréco (in tight slacks) in a basement club. The photo was accompanied by the instantly taken-up catch phrase "This is how the troglodytes of Saint-Germain-des-Prés live." "It is in their basement refuges," the in-depth scoop began, "that existentialists waiting for the atomic bomb drink, dance, love, and sleep." In September 1951 *Les Actualités françaises* ran a televised news report titled "L'existentialisme à Saint-Germain-des-Prés" that featured the complete symbolic panorama.[20] The camera pans the great open square shared by the abbey church, the Deux Magots, and the Café de Flore, where a young American couple on their honeymoon takes in the sights. Throngs of young people mill around the bistros. Juliette Gréco strolls nonchalantly past the outdoor tables, which are packed with gawkers. Jean-Paul Sartre is spied at the late-night jazz scene at the Club Saint-Germain-des-Prés. The film is filled with young *zazous* turned existentialists in beatnik black with their scooters and broken-down Renaults, promenading the streets and congregating in the cafés, meandering through the bookstores and neighborhood groceries, and above all in the basement jazz clubs. Young couples jam the dance floors showing off their wildest jitterbug and bebop acrobatics while others line the walls puffing on cigarettes, drinking, and swinging to the music. Sunglasses, bare feet or sandals, and svelte black signify these hip, cerebral trendsetters. "Ah," the film commentator ends, "and so this is existentialism!" The repetitive, stereotypic quality of these mediatized images speaks to their role as a visual code for the unconventional and for understanding the new, liberated postwar world.

The director Jacques Becker captured this new Paris in the 1949 film *Rendez-vous de juillet*, which was an immediate sensation and also won the film critics' Prix Louis Delluc. The subject was the "unknown zone" of the "unknown" young generation,[21] the J3s growing up during the war and its aftermath. In an almost photojournalistic montage, we follow the adventures through Paris of a troop of friends, played by unknown actors starring in their first film. The sequence of scenes shoots back and forth between their individual stories. The characters traverse the film and the public spaces of the city. The effect was the creation of a public domain of simultaneity, vitality, and mobility. The young Parisians glide down the Seine in a used American amphibious vehicle driven by their *zazou* buddy. They haunt the Café Lorientais and descend into the basement clubs of Saint-Germain-des-Prés. The jazz of Claude Luter is their religion. They attend classes on the Left Bank and act in its theaters. At night they stroll through the streets on their way to dance parties. They smoke American cigarettes and talk on the telephone endlessly, to the chagrin of their bourgeois and petit-bourgeois parents, who press them to get "real jobs." But life is good; the future beckons. They follow their own ambitions. Roger plays trumpet in a jazz combo and dreams of owning a movie theater, while Thérèse pursues an acting career in an avant-garde drama. Lucien studies ethnography at the Musée de l'Homme and tenaciously searches for funding to become an explorer in Africa. When his friends cave in to family pressures, he castigates them for not "following their dreams." But these individual stories are not as important as the visualization of the Left Bank itself. In a review in *Combat*, Jacques Chastel argued that the Paris of *Rendez-vous de juillet* "is the first Paris in the cinema that actually resembles that of Parisians" in the exactitude of its presentation of daily life and behaviors.[22] The motif is material well-being and the modern, hip universe of early postwar Paris. These young people are the hope for a better society. There are archetypes of the future. Despite obstacles, despite the typical calamities of adolescence they face, Becker's film is explicitly optimistic about their prospects. They move through the streets and public spaces of the city with confidence and aplomb. In this urban choreography, they pass from the war and its disillusion to fantasies about the future and thence to the tangible realities of ambition and experience.

This mental image of postwar Paris has become so familiar that it is easy to forget how transgressive and nonconformist this youthful street theater was. The free-spirited unruly style was an affront to the "return to order," the straitlaced, moralizing sensibilities of reconstruction. In his memoir *Paris after the Liberation*, the British historian Antony Beevor remarks that the tight-fitting black sweaters and slacks of Saint-Germain's young women provoked shock and acrimony in the *beaux quartiers* of Paris: "On the Right Bank, a girl wearing trousers risked having things thrown at her."[23] The dancing, music, and indigent lifestyles were associated with moral corruption and unbridled sexuality. Sex and the social in Saint-Germain-des-Prés were signs of warping and deviance, of subversion. However, what the troglodytes had was pastiche and free play. Part fascinating, part shocking, the performance landscape of Saint-Germain-des-Prés contributed to the image of youth as deviant, exotic, celebratory, and entertaining. It was antiestablishment. Vian captured the sense of burlesque political theater in "La Java des bombes atomiques," written after the March 1954 explosion of the first American H-bomb on Bikini Island and recorded by the French singer and actor Serge Reggiani. A member of the Resistance, Reggiani returned to Paris at the war's end and starred in his first feature film, *Les Portes de la nuit*, as Malou's brother; His bad-boy image made him all the rage among young music enthusiasts.

> My uncle, a well-known handyman
> Made on his own
> Some atomic bombs
> . . . Making an "A" bomb
> . . . Is like making a tart
> The question of the detonator
> Amounts to a quarter of an hour
> . . . As to the "H" bomb
> There's no big difference
> . . . Knowing the results are the same
> All the heads of state
> Came to visit him
> . . . And, when the bomb exploded
> Of all these personages
> Nothing remained

The vulgar antics and buffoonery of improvisational theater in the cabarets and the cafés had the quality of resistance and release, the sense of alternative realities. Saint-Germain-des-Prés was a space of *bricolage*: a cheerful and cheeky cobbling together, an expressive assemblage of bits and pieces that mocked the traditional urban realm. The result was carnivalesque, kaleidoscopic, and ultimately subversive. The celebratory, slapdash practices of public space carried forward the groundbreaking realization that the notion of proper place could be broken down, that lived experience could be transformed. Public space could be reclaimed and altered.

While Becker's depiction of the new generation of the Left Bank reproduced the optimistic hopes of the early reconstruction years, Léo Malet's *Les Nouveaux mystères de Paris* captured the more deviant and cynical violation of accepted norms and the more multifaceted spatial meaning of Saint-Germain-des-Prés as it evolved over the decade. A return once again to his detective series provides perhaps the finest entrée into the divergent territories of the Left Bank. Malet knew it better than any other area of Paris. He lived and worked in the 5th and 6th arrondissements as well as farther out in the 13th and 14th arrondissements. Among his many métiers, Malet was a poet, singer, and songwriter in the Saint-Germain-des-Prés night spots and in 1929 opened and entertained in his own basement cabaret on the rue des Grands-Dégres. By 1935 he had joined the avant-garde Groupe de la rue du Château, which held court at the Café de Flore. Around their table could be found Yves Tanguy, Henri Filipacchi, Jacques and Pierre Prévert, and Marcel Duhamel. June 1940 and the German occupation forced a momentary hiatus in the avant-garde scene. But after his release from a German prison in 1941, Malet returned once again to his intellectual home in Saint-Germain-des-Prés. His *flânerie* through the district took him to the cafés and clubs, the bookstores, the back-alley "improv" stages, the radical newspapers and small publishers, the chic art galleries. It was there that he discovered Dashiell Hammett, Raymond Chandler, and American detective novels and attended events such as the June 1946 Grande Nuit de la Série Noir.

Malet's 1955 *La Nuit de Saint-Germain-des-Prés* featured all the places of which he had intimate knowledge, and many of his friends and acquaintances appeared in its pages. His ace detective Nestor Burma identifies the troglodyte phenomenon in the basement clubs

> by the nostalgic signs or something like that. The descents into the basement in the middle of the night, the dismal sound of sirens, the attempts to neck with the neighbor across the landing or discover certain of her secret charms. They try to relive the good times. Then the journalists turn up and start spreading stories, and so it goes. That's how the hip quartier was launched.

Burma follows a hot trail to the fictional Cave-Bleue on the passage Dauphine, where he takes in the scene:

> The path leading to the famous Cave-Bleue was littered with obstacles. First you stumbled against the trash bins awaiting the garbage men under the entry to the passage Dauphine. Then you twisted your ankles on the infernal jagged pavement that makes this type of place so charming. That's not all. The worst is still ahead: getting into the basement. In front of the squat door, above which the Cave-Bleue was scrawled in chaotic writing on a wood plank flanked by two bizarre lanterns, a packed crowd was massed, shouting and pushing like a pack of animals. It was raining on everybody, but as if that wasn't enough, from time to time, from a window on one of the floors above, the contents of a pail of water, in the best-case scenario, added its own drama, accompanied by the curses of the dispatcher, who just wanted to get a little sleep. Two leathery women, originating from the New World, more or less contemporaries of Abraham Lincoln, already victims of one of these extra waterfalls, find all this very funny and exciting, and scream at the top of their lungs for another sprinkling. Usually you don't have to wait.[24]

Burma descends into the smoke-filled basement-inferno, which is jammed with regulars of "both sexes in different conditions, from the latest bohemian to the wealthy filmmaker, the waiting-to-be-discovered starlet and the aging tourist in search of novel sensations." The racket and jazz music are ear-splitting. He arrives just in time to see the first round of the Miss Poubelle contest: "Three girls suddenly appear from who knows where and jump onto the tables, where they strike a pose. Camera flashes explode. The three graces are in bizarre getups. Leeks, turnips, carrots and other vegetables of doubtful freshness have replaced Josephine Baker's bananas. The bracelets and crowns of the candidates are made of food tins." The audience votes with their raucous applause, and a pretty blonde makes it to the elimination round, to be held in a few days. In *Micmac moche au Boul'Mich'* (1957), Malet features a cabaret scene at the site on the rue des Grands-Dégres between the boulevard Saint-Germain and the quai de Tournelles where he and his wife Paulette had launched their Cabaret du Poète Pendu. Nestor Burma finds himself in the now-fictional Chez Colin des Cayeux nightclub in the broken-down building. The basement is a showcase for the club's Middle

Ages theme, carried out with "troubadours ... apparently of masculine sex" and a medieval striptease act by a young student.[25]

For the communists, Saint-Germain-des-Prés as the new territory of aspiration was an entirely corrupted one. The boozing and reverie, the open sexuality, the drugs, and the outrageous behavior all signified the seduction waiting to hypnotize impressionable young people in the spaces of the city. Even Jacques Becker's optimistic *Rendez-vous de juillet* came under withering censure in the communist press. The Young Communist newspaper *L'Avant-garde* asked incredulously why Becker "portrayed this handful of corrupted youth, without making clear they have nothing to do with the millions and millions of young people who struggle in the factories, the fields, or the universities?"[26] The category of youth itself was viable for the communists only within the traditional nexus of class struggle and the myth of resistance. The *sublimes ouvriers* were always young; they never aged. Their heroic image of young French proletariat leading the country forward in revolution had little to do with the wild nights staged by spoiled bourgeois kids in Saint-Germain-des-Prés. The image of youth fell into one of two categories: it was an abstract representation of the good and courageous or the bad and degraded, and the spatial dichotomies were clear. Becker's cinematic invention *Antoine et Antoinette* provided the communist ideal of splendid young French living in traditional working-class districts. It was for these brave young proletariats that the PCF continued its struggle for schools, sports facilities, and proper cultural activities. *L'Humanité*, for example, described a performance of "authentic popular theater" on New Year's Day, 1953. The Worker's Revue took place in the Metallurgist's Hall on the newly renamed rue Pierre-Jean-Timbaud in the 11th arrondissement. The evening's combination of professional and amateur entertainment included a play by Jean Cazalbou on the 1936 factory occupations and the Popular Front. "These kinds of one-act plays," reported *L'Humanité*, "are easy for small amateur groups and the young and are absolutely necessary to our people's fight."[27] The communist student newspaper *Clarté* sponsored traditional *bals populaires* in the Latin Quarter. Mixtures of *fêtes populaires* and "Youth Nights" were held regularly throughout the late 1940s and 1950s in the hope of attracting students and young workers. The first "Youth Night," held in December 1944 at Vél d'Hiv, featured the music-hall stars Josephine Baker and Charles Trénet, accordion music, and the traditional choir singing militant anthems.[28] But by the mid-1950s these events were already fading into wistful nostalgia.

The communist condemnation of nonconformist adolescent behavior focused on a single source: Americanization. The anti-American polemics of the communists were well-known throughout the late 1940s and 1950s and became particularly virulent as the cold war intensified. While sultry young rebels modeled themselves after the American stars Elvis Presley and James Dean, young communists adored their French idols, Yves Montand and Gérard Philippe. Existentialism itself was associated with the depravity infecting France from across the Atlantic. Sartre's ambivalence toward the United States only fueled communist skepticism about his philosophy. Nowhere did the Yankee distortion of the future have more dire consequences, according to communist dogma, than in the seduction of France's youth in the Latin Quarter and Saint-Germain-des-Prés. The Left Bank was, according to the communist student newspaper *Clarté*, the "hunting ground for those who would make our country a colony."[29] In *Paris rouge*, Jean-Pierre Bernard argues that "this ideological and cultural battle between the Good and the Bad took place right in the middle of Paris, often along the frontier of the boulevard Saint-Germain."[30] On one side, the Latin Quarter was associated with struggling students aiming to better themselves and their social condition through French higher education. On the other side, the sleazy world waiting in the cafés and smoky basement *boîtes* of Saint-Germain-des-Prés was identified with a decadent French bourgeoisie under the influence of the American opiate. In his erstwhile memoirs, the lettrist Jean-Michel Mension recounted the psychological border between the Latin Quarter and Saint-Germain-des-Prés that was marked so indelibly in the city's spaces. The Café Dupont-Latin in the Latin Quarter "was the port, or the beach, before the great departure; and you had to cross the Boul' Mich'—leave the Latin Quarter, was the way we put it—and make the voyage from the Dupont-Latin to the Mabillon: that was the initiation. Most people got lost, got drowned, on the way over."[31] Thus the public sites of this cultural struggle were quite specific, and they were largely cafés and jazz clubs: the Mabillon, the Bonaparte, the Huchette (Cave de la Huchette), the Kentucky, and the Vieux-Co (Club du Vieux-Colombier).

The golden days of Saint-Germain-des-Prés were actually short-lived. The district's exotic denizens were quickly turned into the city's foremost tourist attraction. By 1953 the scene had dissolved into a bogus carnival overdiscovered by journalists and invaded by busloads of rubbernecking tourists in search of the cool. *Les intéllos* were ambushed for interviews and fled their bistros in search of the comforts of solitude and ennui. Sartre, de Beauvoir, Gréco, and Prévert all departed. Claude Luter and his jazz combo left for a road tour of France with a series of "Nights in Saint-Germain-des-Prés" concerts. In the words of the journalist Stanley Karnow, the district's avant-gardism rapidly congealed into feigned sophistication by dilettantes and poseurs.[32] The overmediatized landscape became a parody of itself. No end of pseudoexistentialists turned up for the rapidly disappearing and definitely passé jam sessions, beat poetry readings, and wild dancing. Posh art galleries, antique dealers, and chic restaurants followed the smart set into the district of hip. By 1958 a television special on "nostalgic music" was already bringing viewers to the Caveau de la Huchette, "the last of the fabled caves of the Latin Quarter."[33]

Les Tricheurs

Two films of the late 1950s that depicted the degeneracy of Saint-Germain-des-Prés and its rapid decline elicited an outpouring of public debate about the consequences of placing the future in the hands of this new generation and the threat it posed to the public spaces of the city. These were Marcel Carné's *Les Tricheurs* (1958) and Eric Rohmer's *Le Signe du lion* (1959).[34] *Les Tricheurs* (translated for export as *Youthful Sinners*) won the Grand prix du cinéma français in the year of its release, despite the fact that for many it hardly represented the "expression of French thought" that was the requirement for the coveted prize. But such was the anxiety over disaffected youth spending their nights in *caves* and their days in existential despair that the film's subject was deemed vital for public discussion. Its release in October took place just after the extraordinary political crisis that ended the Fourth Republic and the September referendum that set up the Fifth Republic, with de Gaulle at its head. Wayward teenagers and gangs of violent juvenile delinquents wandering the streets were urban similes for a badly shaken and politically volatile nation. The customary spaces of Paris seemed to be disintegrating under the weight of France's changing fortunes, its bloody process of decolonization, and the mutations of the *trente glorieuses*. There was no doubt as to the controversy the movie stirred. Filmgoers lined up outside theaters to see Carné's version of *le mal de la jeunesse*. He found himself defending the film's portrayal of youth against public outrage. In an interview with *Le Monde*, the director explained that his purpose was to make a realistic film about young people in Saint-Germain-des-Prés: "I have personally known Saint-Germain-des-Prés for the past twenty years, and I can tell you that these young people exist and they were there on the spot. We asked for their advice, they taught us their slang, and they created part of the dialog." These disaffected young men and women, he maintained, were "for the most part students who had abandoned their studies. They were habitués of [the café] Bonaparte, very different from the cafés of the Latin Quarter. . . . Their greatest fault is an absence of courage. They lack guts and live from day to day. They refuse to feel until something finally gets through to them."[35] Carné believed that although they were completely apolitical, underneath their haughty attitude lay the cold-war reality that the atomic bomb could "liquidate" existence at any moment. They were victims of their time.

The term *tricheurs* quickly came into common usage to depict a 1950s generation lost in immorality and ennui. In Carné's film they slide precipitously down a slope from freewheeling adolescent independence to tragedy. Although nostalgia for the poetic populist imagery of the Liberation and reconstruction years still gripped the public, by the late 1950s Paris was flooded with the spatial textures of a new, volatile style of modernity. There was a breakdown of urban coherence, a raw degradation and obsession with the sexual and riotous turmoil taking place in Saint-Germain-des-Prés.[36] The public domain became polymorphic, riddled with new tensions and complexity. The film's unknown actors featured Jacques Charrier (who later married Brigitte Bardot) as Bob, a middle-class *banlieusard* from the 15th arrondissement. Bob is studying for the École normale but is seduced by Saint-Germain-des-Prés and abandons his education. He finds himself embroiled with two young women: a wild working-class girl living on her own (Pascale Petit, who was "discovered" working in a hairdresser's shop) and a young lady (Andréa Parisy) of aristocratic lineage who throws riotous parties in her family's luxurious home. Every social class is implicated in this "quasi-documentary" crisis of youth and spatial dynamics that dealt

> with the description of a milieu. . . . This is no longer the era of the literary cafés of 1934 (that Carné-Prévert operated in), nor that of the old postwar philosophy called "existentialism." The action begins at Le Bonaparte, which had been a quasi-provincial little bistro, but today is the hangout of young "bands" with their records, jazz, whisky, dance, the "parties," revolt, and despair.[37]

The city surfaces are emotional, psychological, filled with sensuality, provocation, anxiety, and fear. The film takes viewers on an invented tour of Saint-Germain-des-Prés as a debasing urban influence; to the place Saint-Germain-des-Prés, the swinging record shops, and the "existential" cafés, to the wild music and dancing at the Caveau de la Huchette, to the cheap flats and dance parties. Its emblematic spaces were made even more notorious by the intense coverage surrounding the film. One caustic movie reviewer quipped that the filming on location at Saint-Germain-des-Prés had at least helped everyone in the neighborhood eat well in the weeks that followed.[38]

Music, alcohol, and fast living are the mantras of Carné's band of youth, which, as one of the girls puts it, is "for freedom in all its forms." "Especially sexual," another chimes in. They share "the same cafés, the same records, the same guys." When Bob reveals he is looking for a proper girl, his friends ridicule him for being bourgeois. The party scene features a parade of threats, from homosexuals and pretty boys, free sexuality, and drunkenness to the careless destruction of property. In her rebellion against her working-class family "from another time," that "understands nothing—and I can't explain," the heroine, Mic, abandons any idea of becoming a teacher for the seduction of a Jag (that is, the sports car) in her brother's garage. Any sense of working-class nobility has been squandered on slavish desires. For her, existentialism means immediate gratification. She has "gone bad" and hooks up with the film's juvenile delinquent, Alain (Laurent Terzieff). A classic hooligan in jeans, leather jacket, and pompadour, he lacks either morals or feeling. Money and material things are Mic and Alain's only ambitions. Malaise and a bored cynicism darken the urban atmosphere. The film's two heroines pay dearly for their hedonism; Chlo becomes pregnant, and Mic dies racing her beloved sports car. In the final scene of this morality tale about youthful excess, Bob walks along the boulevard Saint-Germain-des-Prés, stunned by the turn of events, only to see a new group of youngsters on motor scooters planning their *surboum* with cigarettes and alcohol. He leaves Saint-Germain-des-Prés for a "life of more courage."

Carné produced a frightening image of youthful corruption and urban disintegration. In it the optimism of *Paris populaire* has been exchanged for the image of an unforgiving place where youth and the future are out of control. The film elicited an outpouring of public discussion for and against these antisocial *tricheurs*, who they were, and where they could be found in the city. In December 1958 the Centre catholique des intellectuels français

FIGURE 28. Scene from the film *Les Tricheurs* by Marcel Carné, with Jean Paul Belmondo, Pascale Petit, and Laurent Terzieff, 1958. © RUE DES ARCHIVES / THE GRANGER COLLECTION, NEW YORK.

led a public debate about Carné's film at the Palais de la Mutualité, one of the traditional Left Bank assembly places for meetings and protest rallies. In a reiteration of the Left Bank's mental divide, students from the Latin Quarter testified that their own lives had little to do with the screen images or with Saint-Germain-des-Prés.[39] Taking advantage of the film's notoriety, the magazines *L'Express* and *Réalités* both launched investigations of "teenagers" and juvenile delinquency. In imitation of live television coverage, their investigative reporters went on location, descending into the streets, stalking the city's cafés and dance halls in search of the characters depicted in Carné's film. Their interviews were clearly skewed toward the magazine's readership, but they took the form of a quasi-field study of a generation and their unruly urban territory, heretofore hidden from view. At the Bal de la Marine on the quai de Grenelle, the thirty-two-year-old reporter Jean Cau described for the readers of *L'Express* sultry young men outfitted in white shirts with collars up and black leather jackets, with ducktails "greased and coiffured with love." The girls, all of them in identical cotton blouses and full skirts, giggle, chitchat together, and chew gum. Gau's subjects are from Montrouge, in the suburbs, where they work or are apprenticed in factories and small workshops. Their response to his questions about politics and the war and to the query "Have you done your military service?" is utter lack of interest. He has more success when asking about relationships and sexuality at the bar on the rue des Canettes. But even here a feigned tedium reigns as he peppers his interviewees with "How many people are you sleeping with?" and "Do you believe in love?" "From the 'Trois Maillets' to 'La Huchette,' to 'Kentucky,'" Cau searches out these would-be *tricheurs* and finds instead young French people "waiting for Godot" to solve their problems. But as in Samuel Beckett's play, he has doubts whether either Godot or France will come to their aid.[40] In a special 1959 report in *Réalités*, the customs of *les jeunes* in the public spaces of the city were investigated with an almost voyeuristic curiosity—especially their unguarded sexuality. A hidden cartography of youth is exposed and mapped out. On Saturday evenings they invaded Saint-Germain-des-Prés, especially the bars on the rue Mabillon and the rue du Four. They are caught together in groups or as couples wrapped around each other in the Jardin des Plantes, on the Left Bank streets and along the river quay. There was little difference, according to the report, "between the behavior of a young bourgeois in his jacket and a young worker in his shirt."[41] Reporters "go live" to porte d'Ivry in search of gangs of disaffected youth. Once a group of young men is located who admit to gang membership and to taking part in "rumbles," the interrogation begins. They have all seen Carné's film but refuse to identity with it. The silver-screen *tricheurs* have money and cars—they are from a fictional 16th arrondissement and don't work. The young men get "pissed off" every time someone labels them. Everyone imagines that all you need is a black jacket, but in fact the situation at porte d'Ivry is far more difficult. To the reporter's question about how many gangs they are in, the men answer that most guys are communists. "The class struggle isn't wrong," they argue, but their gang is more like a family.[42]

The films and press coverage about teenagers and juvenile delinquency toward the end of the 1950s and into the 1960s reflected the French apprehension over public space in Paris and its disruptive, dangerous qualities. Public places were claimed as the domain of a new generation that acted out their entitlement through novel practices. Saturday night for young people had traditionally meant dancing at neighborhood *bals populaires* on the rue de Lapp, the Bal Wagram, or at a dance party in someone's flat. Evenings at a local bistro were opportunities to watch sporting events on television, especially *le catch*, or wrestling. But more and more young people were simply hanging out in the street. Saint-Germain-des-Prés was certainly not the only site of youthful rebellion, although it specifically symbolized the arrival of the postwar hip generation. In this new social geography, groups of teenagers on the streets or screaming by on Vespa scooters and in old jalopies could be found in the *beaux quartiers* as well as the *quartiers populaires*. The Saturday flea market at Saint-Ouen was alive with young people searching for Levi's 501 jeans, cowboy shirts, and belts. They jammed into record stores and bistros listening to the irrepressible gyrating rhythms of early French rock and the latest American hits. The first French rock 'n' roll records were cut in June 1956 by Henri Salvador and Baptiste "Mac-Kac" Reilles. The former used lyrics by Boris Vian, while the latter was a pillar of the Saint-Germain-des-Prés scene. Henri Salvador publicized his first recording in a public concert in front of Notre Dame Cathedral just after its release. Salvador also appeared on *36 Chandelles*, France's most popular television show, in October 1956 in a live broadcast from the porte Saint-Martin.[43] The city's music halls, especially the Olympia and the ABC, were scenes of screaming, unrestrained young women and wild disturbances during rock concerts. Music was a customary populist practice in the streets of Paris, and "teenagers" claimed its disruptive, subversive qualities as their own. Police were called in to control the crowds when Lionel Hampton played at the Palais de Chaillot in 1953. A concert by Louis Armstrong in July 1955 was followed by a melee. Bill Haley's *Rock Around the Clock* was the number 1 hit in 1956. His arrival at the Olympia in October 1958 provoked an hour of mayhem and substantial property damage.[44]

By the end of the decade, the public psychosis over youth gangs—the *tricheurs* and *blousons noirs*, as they were alternatively called—terrorizing a variety of urban places had reached unprecedented levels. Any sense of the city's fixed authenticity, of its customary spatial imaginary, seemed to be evaporating into a geography of fear. The *zazous* and J3s of the immediate postwar years had transmuted into something far more threatening.[45] Although the label *tricheurs* had been popularized by Carné's film, the production of a wider vocabulary of meaning with such terms as *blousons noirs*, *blousonnets*, *voyous*, *teddy boys*, and *jeunes voyous* pointed to more serious social deviance and urban violence. All of these expressions conjured up images of hooliganism and juvenile delinquency. In the novelist Michel Déon's portrait of youthful ennui, *Les Gens de la nuit* (1958), the main protagonist walks onto Saint-Germain-des-Prés's rue Saint-Benoît to find a crowd watching "two big guys in leather jackets," one "a mulatto with shaved head," livid with rage and savagely beating up their victim.[46] The summer of 1959 was dubbed the "summer of the *blousons noirs.*" The media hype over this new social type was one of the principal reasons for the discourse of apocalyptic doom in the hands of a young generation. Lurid front-page headlines depicted rumbles between rival gangs on the streets of Paris with an arsenal of gruesome weaponry: metal tubes, whips and chains, brass knuckles, bludgeons, and bleach guns. Over the summer the police took some five hundred adolescents into custody. The only actual violence occurred on July 22 in the 15th arrondissement on the Square Saint-Lambert between the local gang and their rivals from the porte de Vanves. It resulted in twenty-seven arrests and became the most often used example of the frightening gang violence normally associated with the asphalt jungle of New York. Although a July 28 fight in the same area was not much more than a noisy shoving match, the press treated it as dangerous unrest. For one judge in the Paris juvenile court system, it was the city's *terrain vague* that created the opportunity for this kind of misbehavior: "It is the *fête foraine*, the movie theater, the *bal*, the pinball machines in cafés, especially foosball."[47] The time-honored public places that had represented urban sociability and Parisian populism were now a menacing urban abyss that required continual surveillance.

This apprehension about the invasion of customary spaces was shared by the city's municipal councilors and corroborated by an official 1959 police report on the *blousons noirs*.[48] It was meant to counteract the media exploitation of juvenile delinquency and calm public fears by providing a law-and-order panoply of statistics on arrests and violent behavior. But it verified that between 1956 and 1959 the number of juveniles taken into custody grew to an unprecedented 9.4 percent of all arrests. The report gave an account of the new urban phenomenon of "black jackets" whose dress and behavior, the police report declared, were downright obnoxious as well as threatening. But it rarely ended in significant violence or confrontations with the police. Wearing Levi's jeans, riveted belts, and black leather jackets, crowds of mostly male adolescents hung out at certain places in the city: *fêtes foraines*, kermesses, public dances and cafés, squares and intersections, and Métro station entrances. They arrogantly took over public spaces, hassled passersby, caused no end of uproar with their rude conduct, and pestered and followed young women. The police report insisted that these were not local kids but misfits from elsewhere in the capital—ciphers for the classic "other" or "outsider," who staged their theater in quartiers where they were not known. The depraved misfit or outsider as public menace was reiterated in 1959 municipal council debates on the "summer of the *blousons noirs.*" Members told of their own encounters with "vagabonds between Clichy and Pigalle, in the *fêtes foraines*, in front of sleazy billboards, in front of garishly lit bars, and where prostitutes and homosexuals hang out and, sorry to say!, prey on the young." They admonished police to "step up surveillance of movie theaters, *fêtes foraines*, and all the other places of pleasure."[49]

A 1959 newspaper article succeeded in identifying between sixty and seventy gangs occupying a realm of illicit spaces and terrorizing various neighborhoods. Émile Copfermann's research located about eighty youth bands made up of some ten thousand teenagers throughout the Seine department.[50] The police accused reporters of paying local teenagers at the square Saint-Lambert to stage a rumble they could film for sale to the French and foreign press. In a "Geography of Youth Gangs in Paris," the magazine *Aux Écoutes du monde* singled out the Trocadéro gang, composed of young men from good families in the 16th arrondissement, as particularly "brilliant." Their hangouts were the clubs along the avenue Henri-Martin. Their nightly *surboums* were crashed by rival bands and ended in violence and vandalism. The Neuilly gang hung out at Mamy's Bar on the rue de Washington.[51] More typically, the reaction to these young rebels revealed persistent fears about working-class culture. The 1959 police report, for example, identified most of them as working class or lower middle class, from modest but not miserable social circumstances.[52] The well-organized Bastille gang allied with those at Montreuil, Clignancourt, Bagnolet, and Nation in forays against their archrivals, the Ritals. Their brawl on the place de la Réunion in the 20th arrondissement brought out the police. The Saint-Denis gang was led by a particularly precocious eighteen-year-old who laid out a strategy of public attacks against taxi drivers, firefighters, and people collecting family-benefit payments. The Maisons-Laffite gang specialized in attacks against women, while others went after North African immigrants and homosexuals.[53] Commentators pointed to the *terrain vague* of the city's periphery and the *zone* as an infernal nest of dangerous *blousons noirs*. In the December 1959 Paris municipal council debate on the problem of the *blousons noirs*, the 20th arrondissement around the porte de Montreuil and, even more specifically, the low-income public housing projects on the rue Félix-Terrier were identified as trouble spots. When a local journalist who had published a typically exaggerated description of delinquency on the street was invited to see for himself, he refused to go for fear of retribution.

This imaginary landscape of violence perpetrated by teenage troublemakers was a sign of heightened anxieties about urban life and a society that had gone off course. The explosion of adolescent misbehavior was blamed on a variety of influences: immorality, the breakdown of family and schools, American "young rebel" films, the new consumerism, adolescent physiology, and so on. For Copfermann, the *blousons noirs* were the sign of a moral crisis, especially the crisis of conscience brought on by the Algerian War and the abandonment of moral values for the immediate gratification of consumerism.[54] As evidence, Copfermann cited the growing number of reports in *Le Monde* and other newspapers of urban violence and street gangs. The communists on the municipal council whipped up the reproach, arguing that juveniles were only emulating the state-sanctioned police violence against Algerians and war protesters in the streets of Paris. Gangs were also associated with postwar public-housing projects in Paris and with the first migrations to the *grands ensembles* in the Paris suburbs. Modern architecture and urban planning were deemed the culprits for social problems. "Modern housing projects without any kind of supervision or recreation for children," claimed the communist city councilor Raymond Bossus, "are worse than slums because they favor the sprouting of these bands."[55] It was an opportune moment for communists to point to their long-standing commitment to a socially conscious urbanism and to their support for public projects in the neighborhoods, schools, youth centers, and sports facilities that were viewed as the antidote to delinquency.

This anxiety-ridden vision of Paris as the epitome of the cruel big city with all its problems of juvenile delinquency, poverty, and social malaise was presented in Eric Rohmer's film *Le Signe du lion* (1959). Rohmer was among the young turks of the New Wave, and this first film under his direction has a decidedly different tone from the poetic realism of Carné or the optimism of Becker. Instead, it captures the darker, more cynical mood spreading through the spaces of Paris by the late 1950s. The film opens with the classic shots of monumental Paris: a *peniche* (barge) meanders down the Seine, car traffic streams along the quays and bridges, the dome of the Invalides appears. Finally the place Saint-Germain-des-Prés comes into view, where a group of young friends is spending the evening in a café. "You have the most beautiful view of Paris," one of them remarks as the camera pans across the panoramic nighttime skyline. The film recounts their daily lives, their drunken parties, their music, and ultimately their independence from societal and familial constraints. Like many of Rohm's films, *Le Signe du lion* was semi-improvised and shot on location on a shoestring budget. One scene captures the July 14 celebrations on the place Saint-Germain-des-Prés. Strung with colored lights, the space has been converted into a giant *bal public*. Throngs of young people and tourists jam the cafés and join revelers dancing in the street to a live orchestra. The waiters snake through the mobs, their trays held high. Smoking, drinking, anticipating amorous encounters, the street party is an arousing carnival of youth. Anything goes. The film's hero, Pierre (Jess Hahn), a music student, describes himself as an American "from everywhere" in his effort to charm a new acquaintance.

But the film paints a dismal portrait of a Saint-Germain-des-Prés that had crumbled under the weight of its own duplicity. The tale turns dark and foreboding. Despite the festive atmosphere, life is not easy. Pierre loses his inheritance and is left penniless and alone. Unable to pay his bills, the film recounts his rapid descent into penury and homelessness. It is the topographic tactics Rohmer uses to depict Pierre's fall from hopeful violinist to *clochard* that is most enlightening. Once again Paris is on view. With an acute sense of irony, the tragic figure of Pierre lumbers through the stunning spaces of the capital. From the central districts to the periphery of Nanterre and back again, the film excoriates the city, exposing it as a bleak, cruel-hearted place. Rohmer transmutes the figure of the *flâneur* into a hopeless and estranged drifter, tramping the streets until his shoes have worn out. Pierre searches in vain for anyone to help him. The city's famed sociability and street life have turned sour. People have no compassion. He rummages through garbage at Les Halles. Despondent, he watches young people in the cafés of Saint-Germain, in the Luxembourg gardens, along the rue Mouffetard. Shot after location shot displays the youthful, idyllic atmosphere of the Left Bank in summer. But the cool sophisticates are oblivious to his desperation, and Pierre bursts out that he "hates Paris." The incident marks his rage toward the city around him and his mental breakdown. In a final scene, shot in the streets of Saint-Germain-des-Prés, a drunken, crazed Pierre becomes street entertainment for the tourists. They surround him, their cameras clicking to capture the spectacle for family back home. Both Pierre and his tourist audience become theater for the neighborhood's young people, who walk by shaking their heads in amusement.

Although Pierre is saved in the end, Rohmer's film is a relentless portrait of descent, not only of Pierre, but of Paris itself. The film's two failed drifters (Pierre and his hobo pal) probe along the boundaries of the vagabond-seer. Their decline into aesthetic negativity and deviant antics provokes the seer's transgression and inversion of order. But the creative impulse, the sensuality and psychogeographic intuitiveness that permeated the poetic rendition of the vagabond figure has crumbled. For the most part the film depicts Pierre and his hobo friend as drunken fools in a spatial theater gone wrong. Rohmer's film is a corrosive observation of an unfeeling metropolis at the decade's end. This descent into hell is mirrored in Michel Déon's *Les Gens de la nuit*. A member of the young right-wing literary Hussards, Déon's political trajectory differed radically from Rohmer's or, for that matter, from Carné's in *Les Tricheurs*, but they shared a merciless vision of hedonism in Saint-Germain-des-Prés. Pessimism and cynicism invaded the spaces of the city. In Déon's morality tale of wayward youth, two friends are claimed by the district's pernicious influence: the drug addict Gisèle sets in motion Maggy's suicide on the rue Saint-Benoît. Maggy's broken body lying dead on the pavement draws a crowd of shaken onlookers. The novel's protagonist watches with a glass of liquor in hand as a pool of blood engulfs her face and hair; the narrator intones, "The girls were pale, the men silent. Everyone knew Maggy." But the end of this lethal public theater is quickly reached. Once Maggy's remains are removed by the police, the hotel manager cleans the sidewalk. Sports cars whiz by on the street; couples once again walk by arm in arm. By evening Maggy's suicide is no longer a topic of conversation.[56] The self-absorbed whirl of drinking and drugs, parties and sex, carries on. A stroll through Saint-Germain-des-Prés described by the American journalist Janet Flanner in 1958 was an equally chilling exposé of a cruel city: "a stabbed Algerian lay dying in a pool of blood on the sidewalk before Lipp's brasserie in St.-Germain-des-Prés, with a crazy old flower vender shuffling in the gore and offering his faded bouquets for sale, as if it were all a scene from a Surrealist picture."[57] The image of avant-gardism had indeed changed.

The Latin Quarter

Against the fast living and degeneracy of Saint-Germain-des-Prés stood the image of the Sorbonne and the long history of struggle in the Latin Quarter. The two districts were distinct, if not diametrically opposed in character.

The Latin Quarter proper in the 5th arrondissement was the city's traditional student district and center of bohemianism. Its character had long been determined by the life of the university. In the years before the state's decentralization programs scattered French higher education to the Paris suburbs and various provincial capitals, the Latin Quarter enjoyed an unrivaled monopoly on intellectual life. Its bookstores, avant-garde cinema and theaters, and its cafés were the ultimate image of urbane scholarly cool. To be a student, to yearn for the life of the mind, was to live and study in the Latin Quarter. In the 1950s the imposing Sorbonne stood on the rue des Écoles as the country's most illustrious educational institution. Around it was gathered a wide fan of faculties and universities, from the elite École normale superièure on the rue d'Ulm to the Faculty of Medicine on the boulevard Saint-Germain-des-Prés, the Faculty of Law on the rue Saint-Jacques, and the École des mines on the boulevard Saint-Michel, as well as a host of colleges and institutes. Further east in Saint-Germain-des-Prés were the École des beaux-arts on the rue Bonaparte and the Fondation nationale des sciences politiques, or Sciences Po, on the rue Jacob.

None of this was new territory. It was the traditional educational landscape of the Left Bank, a discrete zone with its own distinctive mores and temperament that was separate from the rest of the capital. What had changed was the growing number of young people who identified with its life. The French university system was already following a more open policy in the years after the First World War. Secondary education was made free in 1930. Between 1920 and 1935 the number of university students grew from around 21,000 to more than 32,000. The Second World War and the occupation crimped the flow of students into the Left Bank. But after the Liberation, young men and women anxious to restart their lives enrolled in Paris's institutions of higher education in record numbers. Well over 53,000 students were already waiting to begin the 1945–46 academic year. They continued to flow into the Left Bank districts throughout the 1950s and mainly into the Faculty of Letters lodged at the Sorbonne. By 1960 the total number of students had swelled to 77,800.[58] Many were members of petit-bourgeois families who were sending their children to university for the first time. They represented the dream of social mobility in the new France of the postwar years. But the universities were ill prepared to welcome them. The Sorbonne was built in 1890 to welcome about 1,000 students. In 1956 20,000 were enrolled. The amphitheater for the first-year philosophy class held seven hundred seats for the 2,480 registered students. The Sorbonne library had seating for a total of 422 students. The Faculty of Science was the worst off, with antiquated equipment and a paucity of classrooms and laboratories for overwhelming numbers. The physics, chemistry, and biology wing could accommodate 400 students but was faced with 5,000.[59] The only respite in this litany of woes was the new Faculty of Medicine on the rue Saints-Pères, which opened in early 1954 after long delays. There were plans for a magnificent new university building at the Halles aux Vins at Jussieu. The wine warehouses there had been partially destroyed during the 1944 bombardments. The location next to the Jardin des Plantes seemed a perfect setting for a state-of-the-art Latin Quarter university. But negotiations dragged on, with large-scale wine merchants such as Dubonnet refusing to move across the Seine to Bercy.

The jazz clubs may well have been groundbreaking territory; but they were also a needed diversion from these conditions and from the general penury of student life during the reconstruction years. Masses of young people, many of them without regular incomes, descended into the Latin Quarter, hopes in hand. At first their living conditions were dreadful. Even regular meals were a luxury, and there were student protests against the government's food restrictions as early as 1944. Students swamped the city's few social-welfare offices looking for a place to live, medical services, and restaurant passes. They hunted the broken-down buildings on the rue Lhomond and the rue Tournefort and around "la Mouff" for *chambres de bonnes*. The Contrescarpe behind the Panthéon was a worker-student ghetto of dilapidated garrets straight out of *La Bohème*. Given the general housing crisis, even rooms in the cheap hotels or pensions on the Left Bank were scarce. The newspaper *Combat* investigated student conditions in the Latin Quarter for the opening of the 1950 academic year. It found overwhelming need at the offices of the Comité parisien des œuvres en faveur de la jeunesse scolaire et universitaire (Paris aid committee for students) on the rue Soufflot. Mobs of students crammed the stairway seeking help finding housing, medical services, and meals. *Combat* calculated living and education costs at well above what most students could hope to afford. Buying books was out of the question.[60] Well aware of the appalling conditions, the authorities increased food rations and meal tickets and opened the first student restaurant in the Mortier barracks at the porte des Lilas in December 1947. By the end of the 1940s there were fifteen university restaurants in Paris. But the numbers of students far exceeded what their kitchens could serve: "At the door of all the restaurants, whether on the boulevard du Port-Royal, or at Saint-Geneviève, or at the École des mines, lines of students queued up at meal hours and sometimes . . . for nothing."[61] The early 1950s saw the opening of a series of state-of-the-art cafeterias. The Prince served a thousand meals a day, the Beaux-Arts turned out eight hundred, and the Mabillon was a modern showcase of dining services offering students some six thousand meals a day. Its opening in 1953 was hailed as a major event. Nevertheless, the flood of students outpaced the meals. Five years later, during the fall *rentrée* of 1958, the Union des jeunesses communistes (union of young communists, or UJC) newspaper *Clarté* declared food to be the number 1 problem for students, especially after the price of a meal was raised from 85 to 100 francs at the university restaurants.[62]

As far as emergencies went, the only thing that topped nourishment was housing. The authorities estimated that some twenty thousand students at any one time were looking for accommodations. Unscrupulous landlords regularly took advantage of their distraught pleas for lodging. The rental price doubled and tripled for the classic *chambre de bonne* with two to three students crammed into rooms meant for one. In Henri Calet's urban reportage in *Les Deux bouts*, a student named Louis Gilbert lives "in a narrow room that was more like a hallway at the Hotel Montaigne on the rue de la Sorbonne, where all the renters were students, where all the doors were open all the time." The cheap rooms were "without air, without water, without gas, without electricity, without heat," reported *Clarté*.[63] In 1956 the Comité parisien des œuvres en faveur de la jeunesse scolaire et universitaire recommended that the prefecture reestablish its policy of requisitioning *chambres de bonnes* throughout the Left Bank for student use. Worst off were students coming from the crumbling French empire, especially Morocco and Tunisia. Most of the four thousand colonial students enrolled in the French university system were in Paris. They met a cold reception in the Latin Quarter. The aid committee had little choice but to acknowledge the reality of segregation and buy cheap rooming houses where they could be lodged. In her memoirs the historian Annie Kriegel noted 130 Moroccan students boarding on the rue des Écoles and the rue Bonaparte, Vietnamese students in hotels on the rue de l'Observatoire, and Réunion students on the rue Saint-Sulpice.[64]

If home was a garret, all the more reason to find life and friends in the cafés. The Left Bank bistros served as living space for everyone from Simone de Beauvoir to the poorest student. Since heat was a fiction in many a flat, the drinks and potbellied stoves in neighborhood bistros were an immediate draw in winter. Students shuffled between classes and the tables at a favorite haunt where they pored over textbooks. When the weather turned warm, the outdoor café scene was a baroque theater of student collectivism. "Depending on the hour," according to a reporter for *Réalités* magazine describing a bistro behind the Panthéon in 1959, "you can find everything: couples after a movie, the neighborhood communist cell, the corner grocer, students, make-believe students, future starlets, future *licenciés* (graduates). And music 'of any kind.'"[65] The public scenography was shared with Armenian bistros around Saint-Severin church and the North African cafés on the rue Galande. In *Génération*, Hervé Harmon and Patrick Rotman recount the geography of lively watering holes in the Latin Quarter. Le Champo on the place Paul-Painlevé across from the Sorbonne was claimed by the Union des étudiants communistes (communist student union, or UEC), as a sort of annex to the nearby UEC *Clarté* bookstore. The southernmost cafés were the Mahieu and the Capoulade at the end of the rue Soufflot. Across the place du Luxembourg was the Luco.[66] The celebrated canteens of Saint-Germain-des-Prés such as the Café de Flore and the Deux Magots were beyond the budgets of most students, reserved for special pilgrimages to see the intellectual mandarins who mesmerized their followers in the 1950s.

The public sphere in Paris during the 1950s was a multilayered medium of expression that absorbed both spatiality and temporality. Traditional practices resurfaced in dramatic, hypersensory form. In the case of student activism, a mélange of folkloric rituals initially provided the foundation for a maturing political consciousness. Political protest often took place within the context of the *monôme de bac*, the time-honored student rag procession at the end of the infamous *baccalauréat* examinations required as the first diploma of higher education. The modern version of the ritual dated from 1893 and the appearance of the first post-exam *bal des Quat'z-Arts* at the École des beaux-arts. When police intervened in the affair to bring the drunken carousing to a halt, two thousand students staged a giant *monôme* at the place de Sorbonne. By the 1920s it generally consisted of a traditional parade led by the students and brass band of the École des beaux-arts, which had the quality of a ludic rite that had already seen its best days. But the war and its aftermath reinvigorated the *monôme* with an edgy, politically disputatious quality. During the occupation, students gathered after exams near the Panthéon and serendipitously paraded in small groups along the

THE LEFT BANK | 275

FIGURE 29. A traditional student rag procession or *monôme de bac* celebrating the end of the *baccalauréat* turns into a demonstration along the boulevard Saint-Michel, June 30, 1954. © KEYSTONE-FRANCE.

rue Soufflot and the boulevard Saint-Michel or up the rue Lhomond, singing and chanting, improvising the lyrics with political slogans and slurs, and handing out clandestine communist and Gaullist tracts.[67] The custom of the *monôme du bac* was then renewed as a public protest against the dreadful student conditions in the early postwar years. For the most part it was viewed sympathetically by the broader public, or even as a charming revival of Left Bank mores and amusement. But the *monôme* was a carnivalesque zone of hidden volatility and discontent. Dressed in traditional costume, students were transformed into merry pranksters parading in a farcical, provocative procession. In his analysis of popular festive forms, Bakhtin noted that "folly is an inverted wisdom." In the case of the *monôme*, the spoof of learning was "an expression of criticism and deep distrust of official truth." It was "a language of fearlessness, a language with no reservations and omissions, about the world and about power."[68] By the mid-1950s the nonsensical performance had taken on an even more politicized form. It activated hidden possibilities. The call to "form a *monôme*" became the incendiary spark that ignited student resistance in the Latin Quarter. Rather than naive or nostalgic, the increasingly aggressive and violent escapades were a crucial framework for the evolution of political action. It was a conduit from traditional student revelry to deliberately articulated protest against educational conditions, and then in its most powerful form to a student movement against both the war in Indochina and the Algerian War. The student occupation of public space became modern rather than archaic. No longer a parody of youthful foolishness, it had been transfigured into a more transparent political dialog, a more intentional form of collective action in the public arena.

During the early reconstruction years, student politics were largely inspired by the communist Resistance. Student leaders either had served in the fight against fascism during the war, or in the case of the youngest among them, intended to carry on the fight when they reached adulthood in the postwar years. The Left Bank was a bastion of communist intellectual muscle. Many young *francs-tireurs* found camaraderie around the communist newspaper *Action* and the Left Bank Communist Party cell on the rue Saint-Benoît. The Communist Party's UJC and UEC were prominent hubs of student political solidarity. The École normale supérieure on the rue d'Ulm was the inner sanctum of a young generation of communist intellectuals that included Michel Foucault, Emmanuel Le Roy Ladurie, Louis Althusser, and Pierre Bourdieu. Despite the idealized imagery of Left Bank existentialism and political activism, the conditions suffered by even the most prominent of young intellectuals were in reality miserable. Their memoirs are filled with accounts of their poverty and daily struggle. The communists understood the dreadful student conditions on the Left Bank as a mirror of the state of affairs for the working classes in general. During the 1947 strike wave, the communist student newspaper *Clarté* took up the question of whether the Latin Quarter was "a world apart:" Since the Middle Ages the Latin Quarter had been considered a distinct little community, closed to the center of the capital: a community with its own rules, customs, and history. But the tragic experience of the occupation and the Resistance, which united young students and workers in combat, the difficulties of daily life, the worry about tomorrow, have broken down the walls of the Latin Quarter. And now, . . . are we going to close in on ourselves, jealously guarding our intellectual "isolation," or, on the contrary, are we going to openly breath in the winds of change that are crossing the nation?

The Latin Quarter was the terrain of class struggle, the battle zone against rival Trotskyites, against the American imposter, and against French colonial repression. Communist youth organizations were at the forefront of demonstrations against American imperialism and French colonialism throughout the 1950s. Students and young people were everywhere in the protests and riots against General Ridgway in 1952, including the clashes on the rue des Écoles and the carrefour de l'Odéon. The young Resistance fighter and seaman Henri Martin, tried and incarcerated for his propaganda against the war in Indochina, became a communist symbol of heroic youth. The campaign to have him freed became a cause célèbre, with petitions, songs, leaflets, and graffiti dedicated to Henri Martin as a sign of resistance. In yet another layer of emblematic street naming, communist municipalities in the Paris region proclaimed "Henri Martin" streets. The communist magazine *Regards*, Sartre's *Les Temps modernes*, and *Esprit* all joined the campaign.[69] Once again, at the end of the decade, a 1958 special issue of *Clarté* on the Latin Quarter described an illustrious history that included "the polytechniciens on the barricades of '48, the Communards shot in the Luxembourg gardens . . . Jaurès joining Hugo in the Panthéon . . . the student strikes, the protests on the Boul' Mich'."[70]

Despite intense engagement by the PCF and its youth organizations, as the 1950s wore on the power of the Resistance and revolutionary communism waned for the majority of struggling students. The decade was generally an era of more moderate "student syndicalism." The Union nationale des étudiants de France (national students' union, or UNEF) emerged as the most popular student organization in France. It was recognized as the legitimate political voice of the majority of students, with about eleven thousand members in Paris in 1950.[71] Its headquarters on the rue Soufflot that joined the boulevard Saint-Michel and the Luxembourg gardens to the Panthéon acted as the focal point for student activism in the Latin Quarter. Its leadership largely ignored raucous political divisions for a national unity platform in keeping with the atmosphere of the reconstruction years, and with the hint of political apathy among rank-and-file students. The Communist Party had relatively little influence over its policies, many of which were centered on democratizing the university and improving educational conditions. But virtually every political persuasion found shelter under its wing. The majority of French political parties established a student section. Thus, along with left-wing Catholic movements, the Jeunesses Socialistes, and the communist UJC, the UNEF shaped the opposition to the government's paltry support for university education and the conditions of student life. However, it would be incorrect to consider student dissent to have been limited just to these issues. Student action was heavily informed by the general atmosphere of political struggle during the 1950s and by the agonizing crisis of decolonization. The UNEF gained a distinguished reputation on the Left for its early condemnation of the French war in Indochina and eventually for its stance against the Algerian War.

Between 1947 and 1958 there were nine major student strikes and protests in Paris. The most important, and most successful, protests took place in 1947 and 1953. The June 6–7, 1947, student movement coincided with mounting cold war tensions, the ouster of the PCF from government, and the unrest that ended in the strikes and "great fear" of the autumn. Food and coal shortages, inflationary price spirals, and the deteriorating conditions of daily life produced near desperation and panic. For students, the misery was all the worse. Their protests centered on a planned government cut in student subsidies at the same time university inscription fees were to be increased. Demanding the right to a free public education, this first UNEF-led student strike of the postwar years paralyzed the university and ultimately forced the Ministry of Education to back down. It was an indication of the growing demographic and political power of "students" as a postwar category of understanding. The framework of political dissent followed a prescribed mental topography and known rituals that were generally tolerated by the police as long as they remained within tacitly accepted spatial boundaries. Strikers first prevented entrance into the Sorbonne. Then the crowds amassed at the UNEF offices on the rue Soufflot and marched down the boulevard Saint-Michel and back up to the starting point on the rue Saint-Jacques and the Sorbonne.[72] The trajectory symbolized the civic right of student protest and entitlement to the public space of the Latin Quarter. Even a certain level of ritualized violence in traditional clashes with police within this privileged zone was deemed acceptable. However, these customary practices rapidly broke down when students attempted to escape the constraints of the Latin Quarter. The Cité internationale universitaire, for example, along the border of the 14th arrondissement between the porte d'Orléans and porte de Gentilly, was a terrain newly claimed by students and defended in their interests. Violence there was far more insidious and the reprisals swift. During the 1947 strikes police faced off against students armed with pieces of scrap iron and water cannons.[73]

Student challenges to more official sites in Paris were perceived as direct threats both to the capital and to the Republic. In November 1948 communist students attempted to stage a memorial "march to the Étoile" to commemorate the November 1940 protest against Nazi occupation down the Champs-Élysées to the Arc de Triomphe by five thousand university and lycée students. Although this 1948 march was one of numerous commemoration ceremonies staged during the late 1940s, it was interpreted as an ominous danger: first because of the growing antagonism to the communist presence, and secondly because the agreed-upon sanctuary of the Latin Quarter had been breached. Youth groups' prospects for asserting their presence beyond the tightly controlled and partitioned space of the Latin Quarter depended on their ability to "jump scale" and expand their spatial range.[74] The boundaries around the Latin Quarter were perceived as impermeable by the state apparatus and its security forces. The cortege began at the traditional gathering point at the Sorbonne and continued down the boulevard Saint-Michel to the boulevard Saint-Germain-des-Prés, where the battle with waiting police units ensued. Not to be dissuaded, protesters reassembled and headed for the place de la Concorde singing the "Marseillaise," the "Chant des partisans," and the "Chant du départ." The police gave chase, and the students scattered, using whatever means they had to make it to the Arc de Triomphe. Their numbers having dwindled to hundreds, they once again clashed with police at the avenue George V.[75] This ritual restaging of the public protest and repression of the occupation associated the government of President Vincent Auriol with fascism. The use of the symbolic space of the Champs-Élysées and the Étoile pointed to the broader—in this case communist-led—student engagement in postwar politics that broke free of the established confines of the Latin Quarter.

In March 1951 the UNEF called for a student strike in the Latin Quarter to protest cuts in student social security. On March 16 a stream of several thousand students marched up the boulevard Saint-Michel to UNEF headquarters on the rue Soufflot, where they listened to speeches berating the government. Shouting for the resignation of the minister of education, the crowds once again attempted to break the cordon around the Latin Quarter. They headed for the Chamber of Deputies via the boulevard Saint-Michel and the quai des Grands-Augustins, where they were blocked and assaulted by police. The clashes and street fighting between law enforcement and five hundred to six hundred students stunned the Latin Quarter. Smashed windows and cars littered the street. The crowd was pushed by police up the boulevard Saint-Germain to the place de l'Odéon. The fight reached its height on the corner of the rue Saint-Dominique and the rue de la Bellechasse when some six hundred students tried again to reach the Chamber of Deputies. Breaking out of the agreed-upon zone of student protest, about half the crowd reached the assembly and disrupted traffic until the police regained control. The atmosphere of violent inversion and defiance opened the way to a more general breaking of the rules by onlookers. When students pelted police with coins along the boulevard Saint-Germain-des-Prés, a horde of homeless vagrants suddenly appeared amid the melee, scrambling to pocket the sudden treasure lying on the street.[76] The taking of collective action in the spaces of the city was multidimensional—messy, fluid, and boundless in its capacity for invention.

The December 15, 1953, protests against cuts in the education budget were far larger, and ultimately far more successful. They followed the ritual route from fiery speeches at the UNEF offices on the rue Soufflet, down the boulevard Saint-Michel. Despite "absolutely no provocation," according to the socialist student newspaper, they were charged by police at the rue des Écoles in what the paper termed "traditional scenes of violence." These clashes were particularly brutal. Protesters were hemmed in by police barricades on the boulevard Saint-Germain-des-Prés and the rue des Écoles in an attempt to constrain the melee to customary spatial territory. Lines of city buses filled with shocked passengers waited along the edges of the violent clash until traffic could be reestablished.[77] The media coverage of these events in the streets of the Latin Quarter were a key ingredient in visually encrypting symbolic sites such as the courtyard of the Sorbonne, the Boul' Mich', and boulevard Saint-Germain-des-Prés. It reinvested power back to the localized level. A wounded and bloody Jean-Marc Mousseron, president of UNEF, became a media martyr, asserting student demands during radio and television interviews from the hospital emergency room. The protests and violence ignited a storm of protest by politicians from every side as well as by the Socialist and Communist Parties and the Conseil général de la Seine. The minister of the interior, Léon Martinaud-Deplat, and the prefect of police, Jean Baylot, were accused of overreaction and police brutality. The left-wing newspaper *Libération* reported the Latin Quarter closed to traffic and under a "state of siege," with the National Assembly across the Seine to the place de la Concorde and down the rue de Rivoli under police control:

> Such is the spectacle organized by the prefect of police. Why? Because thousands of students protested along with their professors on the boulevard Saint-Michel—and with a good part of the National Assembly—to obtain a budget commensurate with the needs of national education, above all places to work, rooms to live in, restaurants to eat in, scholarships to study, and decent treatment for their professors.[78]

But the struggle for control over urban space pitted students against a police force determined to put a stop to the threat of unruliness and disorder. In response to the accusations, Baylot justified the repression with the need to maintain traffic circulation along the boulevard Saint-Germain-des-Prés and defend the National Assembly from protesters. The National Assembly itself finally voted unanimously to condemn the brutality used against students during the demonstration. Even more, the Ministry of Education conceded and increased university funding.

The June 1954 *monôme du bac* fed into the controversies swirling around the Latin Quarter as an uncontrollable, rowdy stage for student struggle. The festivities were clothed, literally, in the farcical masquerade of Carnival, with the Beaux-Arts marching band masked in false beards and wearing bowler hats, striped shirts, and black tights. They entertained some three thousand would-be *baccalauréats* at the foot of the fountain on the place Saint-Michel. "In another time," reported the *Le Parisien libéré*, "the students would be looking to scandalize the bourgeois . . . but now the festivities are harmless. Following established custom, students sang under the good-natured eyes of the police." When an on-call fire engine was surrounded by heckling students, firemen jokingly responded by spraying them with hoses. The band led the crowds up the Boul' Mich' to the rue Soufflot and played a concert under the windows of the UNEF headquarters. But the frivolity and lightheartedness of the festivities concealed the subversive quality of the Latin Quarter's collective realm. Nothing could be taken for granted. The entertainment was suddenly interrupted by hundreds of students rioting through the streets, breaking windows, torching cars, and molesting bystanders. A bus was set ablaze on the boulevard Saint-Germain-des-Prés. When a beloved local street singer refused to perform at the "rites," he was sprayed with talcum powder. Fights broke out between police and a diehard group of some two hundred young people in front of the gare du Luxembourg. Ten police and fifteen innocent bystanders were hurt. *Paris Match* condemned the free-for-all *monôme du bac* with graphic photographs of the fighting and damage. Baylot reacted by promising that "the street would no longer be left to badly brought up children."[79]

Held midway through the decade, this 1954 march was indicative of the transitional path between folkoric ritual and modern student action. The staging of a farcical village *fête* shifted into agitational theater and then into vandalism and violence as forms of defiance. This dialectic between the structure of ritual and the antistructure that was embedded within it is what made public performances such as the *monôme* so dynamic and potent. The twisting of the traditional into spontaneous street action could easily be described as *détournement*. Given the spreading lettrist and eventually situationist message on the Left Bank, the notion of employing prankster art and festival for subversive ends aptly characterizes the role of the *monôme* rite. It was a transformative site in which traditional student identity transmuted into modern political form. As evidence of this provocative quality, the municipal council engaged in a semantic debate about the *monôme* in July 1954, comparing it in particular with the UNEF-sponsored protests in December 1953. Some argued that the *monôme* processions were a good-natured habit, that they were "peaceful" and should be tolerated as long as they remained within their prescribed spatial boundaries. From this perspective, the repression of the 1954 *monôme* was deemed "police brutality." Other, irate municipal councilors berated the "spontaneous" gatherings, the "rioting" and disorder that extended to the quays of the Seine, the cars sprayed with talcum powder and pelted with stones, the infiltration by "foreigners" into the Left Bank, and the fights with police. They were a threat to the public and warranted direct police action. Still others saw in the *mônome* a justifiable demonstration, or *manifestation*, of student dissent.⁸⁰ This unsteady concoction of meaning epitomized the growing fears of disintegration that permeated discussion about the surfaces of the city. Spatial practices in the Latin Quarter were no longer predictable, but instead had fractured into a heteroglossia of indefinable incidents.

As a formula for student expression, the *monôme* disappeared by the end of the decade, replaced by the *manif*. The transition between the two forms of action had always been fluid, with UNEF, communist protests, and the *monôme* all sharing ritual practices and spaces. Although the historian Jean-Yves Sabot shies away from calling the students of the 1950s a "reconstruction" or "cold-war" generation, he describes them as an intermediary cohort that acted as a bridge between archaic student practices and modern political ones. The moderate UNEF suited their mainly consensus sensibilities and their emphasis on Left Bank student conditions. Although many of the problems of everyday life in the Latin Quarter were in the process of being resolved by the mid-1950s, the grievances about student subsidies, access to student restaurants and housing, and educational reform still ignited ferocious protest. In March 1956 five thousand students staged a demonstration march down the Boul' Mich' to commemorate the death of a professor killed in a tragic laboratory accident blamed on poor equipment. They gathered at the place de la Sorbonne and marched in cortege to Jussieu and the site of the proposed Faculty of Science, for which the ground was yet to be broken.⁸¹ As students, they still imagined themselves as something of a distinctive caste occupying the protected territory of the Latin Quarter. In May the same year, after fleeing their exam rooms, some three thousand students shouting the ritual call "Formez le monôme!" marched down the boulevard Saint-Michel, interrupting traffic. Waiting police columns charged the marchers, who threw everything from cheese to bottles of ink at their adversaries. The result was dozens hurt and over one hundred arrests.⁸² Even when their protests broke out of this domain into broader spaces of resistance, traces of customary student identity and ritual were retained. Only the communists attempted to recast students in the image of an oppressed working class. But it was clear by the closing years of the decade that these Latin Quarter strategies were unlikely to withstand the escalating police repression. However, this transitional student cohort did, Sabot argues, lay the groundwork for a generation of future *enragés* who reached the age of about twenty between 1954 and 1962.⁸³

FIGURE 30. Students protesting the lack of professors and government funding for education, December 10, 1958. © RUE DES ARCHIVES / THE GRANGER COLLECTION, NEW YORK.

The UNEF itself did not possess sufficient unity or influence to absorb the complexities of the student movement as it evolved over the decade. In a mirror of French society as a whole, the political idiom of student protest was increasingly fractured by the polemics of the cold war and decolonization, and ultimately by the Algerian crisis. The old guard within the UNEF insisted on maintaining its national unity stance. But the generation informed by the Resistance, by the miserable living conditions of the early postwar years, and by the opening salvos of the cold war was giving way to younger leaders. The organization splintered into battling clans and lost its privileged position as a semiofficial student mouthpiece able to negotiate with government authorities. Its "majority" radical faction increasingly distanced itself from *mônome* practices and from Mousseron (who led marches in support of French Algeria through the Latin Quarter). Instead, the UNEF allied with the powerful French labor unions in support of Algerian independence and then with the illegal Union générale des étudiants musulmans algériens (union of Algerian Muslim students, or UGEMA). The reality was that young male students were directly impacted by the military call-up to fight in Algeria. Student protesters and action committees often spearheaded by various communist groups and the UNEF were increasingly likely to join with Algerian demonstrations in the streets.[84] The Left Bank became a pacifist, antiwar stronghold. In 1955 the new radio station Europe 1 began playing Algerian protest songs that were banned on all other stations. Boris Vian's antiwar *Le Déserteur* (Vian and Berg, 1954) became the neighborhood anthem. Sung by the Algerian singer and songwriter Mouloudji (a regular of the Saint-Germain scene), it warned the president of France to stuff his war:

> Mr. President
> I am writing you a letter
> That maybe you will read
> If you have the time
> I've just received
> My call-up papers
> To leave for war
> Before Wednesday night
> Mr. President
> I don't want to go
> I'm not on this earth
> To kill poor people
> This isn't meant to annoy you
> But I have to say
> Wars are insane
> The world has had enough of them
>
> Since I was born
> I have seen brothers die
> I have seen fathers leave
> And children cry

> Mothers have suffered too much
> While others prosper
> And live at ease
> In spite of the mud and blood
> There are prisoners
> Whose souls have been stolen
> Whose wives have been stolen
> And all their loved ones gone
> Tomorrow, first thing in the morning
> I will close the door
> On the smell of these dead years
> I will take to the road

Yves Montand, a longtime communist, entered the political fray with an adaptation of the old pacifist song *Giroflé, Girofla*: "How beautiful are your barley fields / Girofle, girofla / In your orchards, fruits abound / Good times are here / Do you hear the forge whirring? / Girofle, girofla / The cannons will mow them down."

In heated municipal council debates after the strikes and protests in support of Algerian independence in March 1956, Jean Legaret, a moderate, railed against the "ten thousand North Africans who—to the indignant astonishment of Parisians—swarmed into the streets" and warned the council that it was "the young who were protesting: young people were at the quai de la Rapée and in the Latin Quarter." Outraged municipal councilors admonished the prefect of police for not protecting public colleges and lycées from infiltration by pro-Algerian elements. *Le Figaro* had reported that the lycée Voltaire and other schools were the scenes of gatherings by students and teachers to organize a "popular front" in support of victims of police repression. "We do not want to see," declared the Gaullist Pierre Devraigne, "the *drapeau des fellagha* [guerilla flag] in our schools and lycées, or in the auditorium of the Mutualité, along with demands for money for these so-called victims of police repression." In a pointed retort, the left-wing opposition invited student groups to the symbolic site of the Mutualité for a meeting to demand an immediate cease-fire in Algeria.[85] Communists led student demonstrations in the Latin Quarter against the Algerian War on the PCF's day of national protest on October 17, 1957. The historian Philippe Robrieux, a participant in the antiwar demonstrations, recalled that marching down

FIGURE 31. A demonstration for peace in Algeria by the Union des jeunesses communistes de France in Belleville, October 1957. © GERALD BLONCOURT/RUE DES ARCHIVES.

the Boul' Mich' in protest against the disbanding of the Algerian students' UGEMA "signified 'taking the Latin Quarter.' The Boul' Mich' symbolized possession of the historic heart of the 'Quartier.'"[86] In a symbol of Left Bank solidarity, the march crossed the boundary between the Latin Quarter and Saint-Germain-des-Prés, winding from the boulevard Saint-Michel along the boulevard Saint-Germain-des-Prés to the rue de Seine and the rue de Buci market. The political crises of the late 1950s was breaking down older spatial formulations and formulating new ones.

The political crisis of May 1958 that sealed the fate of the Fourth Republic brought hundreds of thousands of young people and students out into the street to take possession of the Boul' Mich' and the Latin Quarter and to participate in demonstrations throughout the capital (see chapter 3). It is the very dissimilar, often oppositional practices by this "1950s generation" during the explosive month of May that warrants passing attention here. They substantiate the fluid, polyvalent, unpredictable quality of public life in this transitional decade and the dispersion of political power across the spaces of the capital. The new generational category of "youth" and its range of public practices fractured older discourses about class, populism, and the meaning of the people of Paris. A space of resistance and contestation, the Left Bank was itself contested terrain. On May Day students marched down the rue Mouffetard to Gobelins to protest the execution of the student and freedom fighter Abderhamane Taleb, who was branded a "terrorist" in Algiers. Fervent about the cause of an independent Algeria, the cortege stood in stark contrast to the folkloric celebration on May 11, when the Paris Université Club (PUC) celebrated its fiftieth anniversary with a 1900s-themed masquerade ball in the streets of the Latin Quarter, with the Frères Jacques and Monsieur Hulot himself as celebrity hosts. The redoubtable Beaux-Arts brass band provided music. By month's end, on May 28, the massive unity march in defense of the republic from the place de la Nation to the place de la République brought out some 150,000 demonstrators, many of them young people. Students by the thousands assembled at the gare de Lyon and then separated into their various associations to take part in the demonstration. At first watching apathetically along the sidelines on the rue du Temple, a group of *blousons noirs* in blue jeans and black jackets finally joined in, screaming "Peace in Algeria!" and "De Gaulle to the gallows!" at the top of their lungs and racing through the crowds. The trajectory of supporters of de Gaulle and the Algerian War the next night was far different. On May 29 thousands of young men took to the street in support of de Gaulle's investiture as head of government. Oriented toward the capital's official spaces, they marched down the Champs-Élysées past the Arc de Triomphe to the Tomb of the Unknown Soldier. That same night there was a massive street party and concert on the place Saint-Germain-des-Prés. CRS mobile guard units were called out to deal with the thousands of young people and the infernal din of their music.[87]

7 Planning Paris

In an editorial in the *Revue urbanisme,* the chief of the MRU, Raoul Dautry, declared 1945 to be "the year of urbanism." The gusto of his declaration reveals the passion with which urban planning was debated at the war's end. Paris was treated to a series of exhibitions meant to showcase the modern urbanism that would wash clean the lugubrious and unhealthy conditions that had plagued the capital since the nineteenth century. They were an immense success. After years of deprivation, thousands of Parisians came to see the displays, eager to see the future. The Première Exposition de la Reconstruction was organized by the MRU from October 31 to December 31, 1945, at the gare des Invalides. In the cold, depressing winter, just a few months after the war's end, Parisians passed through the entrance gawking at a gigantic photomontage depicting the vision of a reconstructed city superimposed over smoldering ruins. The exhibit was just an early glimpse of the MRU's dazzling picture of modern housing and urban life. The crowds were tantalized by miniature model communities under glass featuring prefabricated single-family homes equipped with every convenience. The first prototypes were already being constructed in the suburbs at Noisy-le-Sec. A huge, multicolored, electrically wired map of Paris laid out the site of each *projet d'aménagement.* At the press of a button, each zone lit up, to the delight of exposition-goers. A year later, on June 14–July 21, 1946, the Exposition des Techniques Américaines de l'Habitation et de l'Urbanisme at the Grand Palais was even more impressive. The exhibits featured American mass-production techniques, building tools, and equipment from bulldozers and scrapers to finishers for roadwork. Photographic murals and documentary films introduced the French to the American way of living. Fully equipped American homes with names like the Arcadia, the Woolaway House, and the Jeep were built by the MRU at model villages at Noisy-le-Grand and other Paris suburbs. The exposition was a sign of the American material culture and Marshall Plan aid that would arrive in thundering waves throughout the reconstruction years. From July 10 to August 17, 1947, Paris hosted another exhibit, the Exposition Internationale de l'Urbanisme et de l'Habitation. Nine European countries displayed the revolutionary urban-planning techniques that would rebuild a shattered world.[1] The entrance to the Grand Palais was decked out in monumental metal tubular scaffolding, displaying the new urban aesthetic, while the interior exhibits were arranged in ultramodern modular format. The exposition catalog laid out the conviction that "Lodging is . . . the most essential human necessity. It responds to the needs of the body as well as to the spirit, to the needs of the individual as well as the family, to the needs of the nation and society as a whole: It is the clearest sign of the level and quality of civilization."[2]

The prefect of the Seine, Guy Périer de Féral, ceremoniously presented the official urban plan for Paris at this 1947 international exposition. An enormous relief map was displayed that outlined all the work to be accomplished to improve the capital's quality of life. Since 1943 the Inspection générale des services techniques de topographie et d'urbanisme (public works service) had been carrying out intensive studies of conditions in Paris as preparation for urban renewal projects. Each neighborhood had been the subject of detailed research. Huge three-dimensional scale models of refurbished neighborhoods were set up for display, with special "before" and "after" slum clearance models of îlot 16 in the Marais, îlot 11 in Ménilmontant, and îlot 2 along the rue Mouffetard. Urbanistic magic would transform these pedestrian, dilapidated neighborhoods into modern fantasylands. Architecture and urbanism was heralded as transformative of habitat, of urban life, and of France itself. The ambience was inspired. It was precisely the apocalyptic visions, the struggle to design utopia as a remedy for healing the social and cultural fracturing of France and the wounds of war, that marked these public displays as significant and placed them within the context of what Manfred Tufari has called a theatrical imagination. Images of dystopia and utopia, of decline and renewal, were constructed around the capital as the laboratory and showcase for this heroic experiment in reinventing the modern city.

There was an air of pure fantasy about all these plans and designs, all this prophetic conjuring up of a magnificent future. Nothing could have been further from the reality outside the ceremonial tubular entrance of the Grand Palais. Resources were scarce, and urban renovation schemes—even housing—were far down the list of national priorities. Yet the circumstances engendered a far-reaching public discussion about Paris as the landscape of utopia that expanded into a debate about the nature of modern urban life. Paris was a city designed to impress. Restoring it as the capital was tantamount to restoring the nation. It was to be a showcase for reconstruction and the new France. This planning discourse about Paris, the meaningful metaphors and emotionally laden visual imagery, was complicated, riddled with ironies, anxieties, and confusion. On one hand, it pointed to a deep yearning to recapture French virtues in the capital's traditional landscape and architectural forms. It sought the path trodden as much as the future that beckoned. The style has often been referred to as a moderated Haussmannization, or *haussmannisme amélioré*. To call it that is to immediately suggest the enduring legacy of Haussmann's reconstruction of Paris under Napoleon III and his master-planning techniques.[3] The fateful formula of French state authority and large-scale public works for fashioning a modern "City of all the French," as Haussmann put it, remained the dream of many a French urbanist. Looking out over the dilapidated, dreary landscape of the once glittering City of Light, a growing corps of frustrated urban planners were still guided by Haussmann's *grande croisée*, his network of boulevards, his open vistas and broad public spaces, his monumentality and rationalist vision. In his review of the 1947 Paris exhibit at the Grand Palais, C. Eyraud, the director of the Services d'architecture et d'urbanisme à la préfecture de la Seine (architecture and urban planning services for the prefecture of the Seine), wrote that "many have criticized Baron Haussmann and often with reason. . . . But it is worthwhile remembering that he had the prescience to understand what Paris would be like in the years to come. It would be difficult to imagine what the situation would now be if the medieval city had been conserved intact, without the wide avenues that were realized."[4]

The French then glanced back to their nineteenth-century modernist roots. On the other hand, they also looked forward to a twentieth-century modernist movement that had arrived triumphant as the alternative, the potential reality of the postwar age, ready to shape a better world. A new generation of international architects working under the auspices of CIAM claimed the legacy of modernism. The 1943 publication of the Athens Charter contained the resolutions of the Fourth Congress of CIAM and was both a manifesto and a utopian vision of the modern city. Even more, it was an "injunction to think right," according to Le Corbusier's expression. CIAM's militants tended to mark public space as homogeneous and universal in quality. For these professionals, the city and its spaces were abstract, objective, and measurable. Modernists recomposed urban topography as a structured and utopian scene—a fantasy stage set for the theater of contemporary life. Everywhere, "disorder was replaced by functional order; diversity by serial repetition; and surprise by uniform expectancy."[5] The radical authority of high modernism during the reconstruction years was astonishing. It treated both wartime destruction and the historic decay of the city as obsolescent. Its radical rejection of both, its practical functionality as a reconstructive form, offered an entirely new cultural vision, a new mechanism for reuniting the nation and creating a new kind of society. The convergence of this postwar modernist creed with the reemergence of France from the long night of war gave urban planning a militant, revolutionary quality.

Whether modernism was envisioned in the nineteenth- or twentieth-century version, it was seen as a way to domesticate change and reconstitute the civic life of the capital. It was a mechanism for healing the social fracturing that had torn apart the nation and led to its defeat. Only the power of the French state seemed capable of intervening in the chaos on behalf of the nation and offering a utopian capital as a symbol of a reemergent France. State elites produced an uncompromising official urbanist discourse, socially brutal in tone and often violent in practice. Especially with the institution of Vichy's *dirigiste* (state interventionist) policies, local authority was steadily undermined and responsibility for the capital aggressively co-opted by state technocrats. For this reason, the chapter begins with a discussion of Vichy's plans for Paris. This official structure was then appropriated by the MRU at the war's end. With remarkable moral righteousness, professional urban planners and *techniciens* in the service of the French state wrested control of Paris and its region away from the narrow-minded local politicians who were blamed for all that had gone wrong.

But the state technocrats who all stood hungrily over the "problem of Paris" were just one set of actors in this battle over the terms of modern urban life. Despite their every effort, they did not entirely monopolize public debate. A myriad of counterdiscourses contributed much to the form Paris would take in the future. The vision of the capital's spatial pattern represented different social and cultural ideals, as well as ideals of political power. Both the political Right and the Left proclaimed the city as the terrain of the future. Municipal authority swung from Vichy to the communist-led Resistance to the Gaullists. A tradition of social-democratic and reformist municipalism fed into the experience of Resistance and working-class solidarity. A robust localism fractured the city's landscape into a multitude of cohesive, intensely politicized neighborhood-villages. City officialdom clashed with state technocrats and a handful of Seine prefects over futuristic visions of the capital. The fiery enthusiasts of Paris planning from all sides were writing, campaigning, and lobbying political elites. Reports and recommendations rolled off the presses at lightening speed, only to be met by a barrage of criticism and censure. The plans for Paris passed through a gauntlet of political negotiations and endured numerous revisions and iterations. The entire city, from its most prestigious monuments down to its most rickety shacks, was studied, measured, and analyzed. Each of these actors and each peak moment in this aesthetic drama espoused a different vision of the city's future. Paris was imagined as a panorama of traditional French grandeur or of modern postwar French society. It was an insatiable urban omnivore. The housing crisis, the eradication of old neighborhoods, the preservation of the city's picturesque beauty, and the loss of traditional public space were all argued over and deliberated. For some, the annihilation of historic Paris was the objective; for others, the past was the gateway to the future.

Taken together, the debates about Paris created an influential planning corpus that largely eschewed the tabula rasa of modernist universalism and instead attempted to invent a particularist vision of a progressive, twentieth-century capital. It acted as the theoretical anchor, the taproot, for the renewal projects carried out in the 1960s and after. More than simply *haussmannisme amélioré*, it was part of a broad-based humanist, poetic imaginary that defined the mid-twentieth century. French urban analysts shared a deep conviction in an urbanism that was more humane, in a collective experience that was prosaic and poetic, and in an urban aesthetic that was expressive and vernacular. It was a powerful counterpoint to high-modernist doctrine and essentially prevented any twentieth-century repetition of grand-scale urban renovation in the capital's central districts. Instead, modern urban planning would be assimilated into the city's historic cultural geography. In his review of the 1947 exhibit, Eyraud clarified that despite the efficacy of Haussmann's vision, the 1947 Paris exhibit's prodigious maps were not meant to represent reality for the entire city, but for each îlot, "in order to exactly draw out the character of each block of houses, the available sites, and the exact nature of the population that lives and resides there."[6] The fractured landscape of *petites villages* lived on.

But it did not necessarily mean that *le peuple*, as heroicized in poetic humanist discourse, lived on with them. By the end of the 1950s Paris was imagined as a historicized web of vernacular streetscapes, heritage buildings, and monumental stage sets, all cleared of their meddlesome working classes. The city's center was transformed into a *zone cristalisée* that succeeded admirably in promoting tourism. The poetic vision of the capital was largely stripped of its social and political militancy and became something of an antecedent to postmodernism. An unchanging, nostalgic Paris was the ultimate tourist destination, its particularist spaces guarded with a vengeance. This posture grossly exaggerated the division between the adored inner arrondissements and the forgotten edges and suburbs that surrounded them. If grand-scale modernist planning schemes were abandoned in the heart of Paris, they were applied with a shocking vengeance in the outer arrondissements and throughout the region.

Vichy and the Plans for Paris

One of the most remarkable meditations on planning and design in twentieth-century Paris appeared in 1943 under the title *Destinée de Paris*, written for the city's two thousandth anniversary, edited by the historian and preservationist Bernard Champigneule, and published by Chêne. Some of the city's most preeminent apologists contributed articles. Marcel Raval, architect and luminary of the Ligue urbaine et rurale, attacked the inept and self-serving political elites of the Third Republic, "imbued with the imbecilic myth of French superiority and interested above all in courting electoral favors." While foreign capital cities experimented with new urban planning techniques, Paris became open terrain for the greed and vagaries of private financial interests. Munich, Nuremberg, Lübeck, Bern, Bruges, and Anvers had all seen their historic districts restored while model worker cities took root in their suburbs. In the meantime, "France has done little but nourish old superstitions and enlist a pitiful egoism in urban matters."[7] Above all, *Destinée de Paris* was a ringing protest against the modernist vision of the future articulated by Le Corbusier at the 1937 Exposition Internationale des

Arts et Techniques and in his *Destin de Paris*, published in 1941 by Fernand Sorlot, which was closely allied with the Vichy regime. These two publications acted as counterpoints in the loud public battle over the capital's landscape. For Le Corbusier, Paris was more than a city; it was a world, a metropolis for modern times where individual freedom and spirit were the essence of cosmopolitanism. Paris was at the core of French destiny.[8] Le Corbusier's notorious Plan Voisin (reworked continuously from 1925 on) demolished a vast swath of territory on the Right Bank from the gare de l'Est to the rue de Rivoli and replaced it with eighteen uniform 700-foot-high freestanding towers "to have air, light and greenery all around us again."[9] By the 1930s his design included a network of superhighways and a vast elevated expressway running along the rue de Rivoli–Champs-Élysées backbone. In the hopes of currying favor with Vichy, *Destin de Paris* exchanged slum districts for a mesmerizing vision of high-rise apartment buildings to welcome a thousand inhabitants per hectare and the principles of zoning that would efficiently lay out the city's functions: 245 hectares for an historic zone, 452 hectares for a new administrative zone, 500 hectares for urban artisans, 120 hectares for commerce, and so on. Le Corbusier's plans evolved into a radicalized version of Haussmann's modernization, and he indeed saw them as the contemporary embodiment of the grand scale of French tradition.

The contributors to *Destinée de Paris* threw down the gauntlet against the frightening supremacy of this modernist vision of the future. Champigneulle defended Paris because "cities are the mirrors of their epoch. They are the image of a civilization. If France wants to initiate the great intellectual and moral reforms on which our future depends, then it should portray a clear and noble face and treat the French landscape with deference."[10] Historic Paris was the noblest face of France. In this conceptualization, urban space and architecture were the essential structures in which social identity, culture, and memory in Paris were inscribed. In another essay, Pierre d'Espezel took readers on a loving tour of Parisian geographic, historic, and sociological idiosyncrasies. Each of them, each neighborhood, all the riches of the natural topography, was essential to understanding and shielding the city's character and beauty from hegemonic modernist designs. In his 1945 "Incarnation de l'urbanisme," Gaston Bardet added his voice to the rising clamor against the "megalopolis" and the brutality of internationalism.[11]

Well-known Paris devotees such as Champigneule, Raval, René Héron de Villefosse, and George Pillement, all of whom had led the fight to safeguard the city's historic districts for years before the war, continued through the 1940s to promote preservationist formulas. They found good cause with the new Vichy regime. For Vichy, the city as a cultural and sociopolitical artifact represented all that had led France to catastrophe. According to the new government's Commission d'étude de la région parisienne (study commission for the Paris region), the physiognomy of Paris was "banal, chaotic, even inhumane." In February 1942 Marshal Pétain addressed the commission's inaugural session: "Over the past sixty years, due to the failure of authorities who neither planned, nor demanded, nor acted in time, the Paris agglomeration has continued to spread out in disarray over the surrounding countryside, widening the circle of misery and ugliness that surrounds the city, saddening the heart and the mind."[12] As Robert Paxton has argued, "Vichy moved France significantly toward the technicians' vision: urban, efficient, productive, planned, and impersonal."[13] Technocratic planning was one of the great victors of the age.

For the first time in France, the regime imposed a national agenda on urban planning. All large cities in France were finally to produce comprehensive land-use plans under Vichy's Law on Urbanism of June 1943. It was an attempt to control the frenzied growth spreading across the Seine basin as well as around all of the country's major cities, a goal that had initially been articulated in legislation instituted at the end of the First World War in 1919 but toward which little progress had been made. It was finally accomplished within the context of the wartime occupation as a canvas upon which to devise a new vision for France. The Vichy years succeeded in substantially expanding the role of the Seine prefecture and ultimately state authority over the capital's future. Responsibility for Paris was taken over by the Vichy Ministère de l'intérieur, the new Délégation générale de l'équipement national (state delegation on national infrastructure, or DGEN), which was established to handle a broad sweep of urban responsibilities from slum clearance, urban planning, and redevelopment to housing construction, as well as by a Conseil national de l'urbanisme (national council on urbanism).[14] The interwar professional cadre of the "Paris school" of urban and regional planning was directly incorporated into this expanding administrative machinery. France's first generation of professional urban planners—individuals such as Gabriel Dessus, Pierre Gibel, Henri Giraud, André Gutton, René Mestais, André Prothin, and Pierre-Armand Thiébaud—had all built their careers studying and arranging the puzzle of the Paris region. A number of them had attended the Institut d'urbanisme de l'Université de Paris (IUUP) and completed their studies under Henri Prost, France's leading architect-urbanist of the interwar years. They worked together in the dizzying array of public agencies and survived almost intact from the mid-1930s through the Vichy years and into the 1950s to lay out the future of the capital and its surrounding suburbs.[15] The combined influence of this midcentury technocratic corps of professional urban reformers explains in part why planning for Paris remained so remarkably consistent, from the designs worked out by Prost and his students at the IUUP in 1935 through the 1959 Plan d'urbanisme directeur. They moved urban planning toward a scientific professionalism that disdained any association with the capital's fractured localism or with the political twists and turns of midcentury France. The rationalization and modernization of Paris was their ultimate mission. Their work depended on analytical research of urban conditions, mapping and cartographic study, specific definitions of housing, and habitat norms: density and public health, building quality and condition, availability of domestic goods and services, and the amount of ground covered by buildings. These became the standard measures of quality of life by a technocratic cadre that achieved official power through the newly forming network of state planning agencies.

Despite this seeming professional neutrality, Vichy's approach to the city was clothed in moralistic ambitions for the renaissance of traditional France. It reimagined the decaying monster of Paris as a capital worthy of French greatness. Urban revival was a concocted brew of *passéiste* (backward-looking) traditionalism and technocratic modernization. What was worth saving in Paris, according to the Commission d'étude de la région parisienne, was "the heritage made from the beauty of work by old artisans and the historic souvenirs necessary for the spiritual and moral life of the population."[16] Charles Magny, Vichy's prefect for the Seine department, was a lifelong advocate of the "beauty of Paris," an ideal that had emerged in the first years of the twentieth century and found its aesthetic expression in built heritage and the preservation of the past. Although the preservationists were divided between those who fought for the picturesque legacy of pre-Haussmann Paris and those who wanted to continue Haussmann's tradition, they unanimously rejected high modernism as antithetical to the French capital. The insipid monotony of towers, especially in American cities such as Chicago, as well as the vision of Le Corbusier became the antipode to the traditional visual fantasy of Paris. The historian and preservationist Louis Hourticq wrote with the approval of *L'Architecture française* (one of the quasi-official mouthpieces for Vichy's urban principles) that "like topography, history guides the urbanist. It counsels prudence more than audaciousness. In a city with its own tastes and traditions, newness is rude and aggressively shocking. It would be ridiculous to introduce into the historic center of Paris a 'rational' building . . . [and] completely insensitive to construct one of these modern carcasses."[17]

Vichy was preoccupied with restoring the monumental image of the capital, and its plans for Paris were prodigious. They were largely the work of René Mestais, head of the Services techniques de topographie et d'urbanisme, and his team of urban planners. A darling of the preservationists, Mestais had been involved with planning the city's future since the 1930s and was largely responsible for the land-use plan first presented at the 1937 Paris Congress, held in conjunction with the Exposition Internationale des Arts et Techniques. Along with the Services d'architecture et d'urbanisme attached to the Seine prefecture (whose director was Maurice Baudot), they produced voluminous studies on Paris, its history, and its landscape, including comparative research on the evolution of Europe's capital cities since 1870 as a basis for understanding the development of the French capital.[18] It was an effort to rectify the lack of attention given the city in the years before the war and to lay down the principles on which Paris, in Baudot's words, "could breathe better, be better built, and, in a word, live better."[19] Their results were presented in May and June 1943 at two conferences dedicated to Vichy's new Law on Urbanism. The more important of the two was the Salon des Urbanistes, hosted by the prefect of the Seine, Guy Périer de Féral. It was a remarkable display that featured extensive presentations, maps and graphs, statistical tables, and photographs that captured the city's debilitated state and set out the vision for the future.

True to the French state's urban planning heritage, the work of Haussmann was presented as the model of achievement. A new grand cross of "magisterial arteries" in the heart of Paris would replace the blighted areas of the Right Bank and assure the flow of transportation over the next century: the east-west axis would stretch through a modernized faubourg Saint-Antoine, and the north-south axis would run from Les Halles and the rue de Rivoli to the gare de l'Est.[20] To round out this purification of the Right Bank, the cultural necklace of the Bibliothèque nationale, the Conservatoire national des arts et métiers, and the Archives nationales would all be expanded. Altogether, some 120 different projects were to be carried out throughout Paris. New streets would be opened up, existing ones widened, access to the renovated railroad stations improved, and new train lines to the suburbs opened. The markets at Les Halles would be transferred outside Paris. Périer de Féral presented Vichy's commitment to transforming the newly acquired *zone non aedificandi*. Wartime legislation had facilitated its complete annexation and expropriation. Maps and photographs of the great ring that girdled Paris laid out its long history, its sordid state, and its glittering future. Schools and sports complexes, gardens and public promenades would grace the new "green belt" carved from the circle of Thiers's old fortifications and field of fire.[21]

But the great aesthetic emblem of the "Renaissance of Paris" as the "grand salon of Europe" would be the 55-yard-wide *boulevard périphérique*, which would surround the city with a new monumentality and open the Île-de-France to its natural splendor. When lit at night to reveal the great entrances into Paris, it would appear as a glowing magisterial crown around the capital.[22] The *boulevard périphérique*, the brainchild of Mestais, was a traditionalist patina, a Beaux-Arts vision of the Haussmannian boulevard as the quintessence of urban renewal and innovative design. Here lay the creative tableau upon which France would press forward into a modern renaissance and regain its glory. State planning would revive the magnetism of *la ville lumière* that symbolized the unique character of French modern. Mestais predicted that "with all collaborating in the *'Renaissance de Paris*,' France will become, as yesterday, the *second country* of all men."[23]

For all its seeming emulation of Haussmann's work *tout court*, Mestais's plan was a compromise. The renovation of specific îlots became the operational unit for planning and design. These interiorized districts were topographic evidence of vernacular tradition and history and the counterpart to the idyllic rural village. It was these rustic patterns inherent in urban life that Vichy sought to rediscover underneath the fetid slums and industrial squalor. It was tantamount to uncovering true France. And Vichy had inherited the witch's brew of *îlots insalubres* to be cleared and redeveloped. In his presentation to the 1943 Salon des Urbanistes, Maurice Baudot explained that while seventeen years of Haussmann's projects had displaced 350,000 people, the new slum clearance programs called for the number of expropriated to reach 500,000.[24] Yet Vichy's focus was not bent on wholesale slaughter, but on a carefully chosen "clearing out" that would honor the "old places" and "conserve them for a living usage." A new *superintendance* of buildings would be instituted, "analogous to that of the ancien régime, which assured down through the centuries a unity of views [and] the employment of local materials, and reconciled the boldness of the new in a harmonious way."[25]

The city's working-class population would be dispersed, and Paris would be opened to the healthy benefits of the countryside. Vichy's new agencies produced a land-use plan based on the sweeping incorporation of the 1934 Prost Plan with the city of Paris itself. It included the departments of the Seine, Seine-et-Oise, and Seine-et-Marne, and five cantons in the department of the Oise as the new, official Paris region. The area extended to a general radius of thirty-seven miles from the center of Paris and was composed of 1,305 separate communes. Here charming cottages and apartments would await the thousands of slum dwellers relocated from the central districts to "city-villages" surrounded by parks and open space.[26] A technocratic, neo-rural pastiche would be imposed upon the discredited, republican visions of the capital. Families would find social harmony and utopian existence in a "greener" setting. The well-developed social-reform themes of sport and health were crucial to Vichy's renewal of the working classes and the citizen body. Numerous designs were done for gymnasiums and sports centers, many of them featured in the pages of *L'Illustration* magazine, because "refreshing the body, training muscles, extending the chest cavity, [and] calming the spirit lead to the physical and moral balance of our regenerated citizenry."[27] To make way for this utopia, the diseased industrial viscera of Paris would be thinned out by decentralizing factories to the provinces. "What will the Paris of tomorrow be in terms of its population density and its industrial infrastructure?" Baudot asked. "What type of wise and prudent policy of deconcentration and industrial decentralization should we have? How will provincial life be reconstructed and reborn, and how will Parisians find themselves affected? How will this return to the land create the conditions for restraining the capital's population?"[28]

The Reconstruction Years

Vichy's DGEN was essentially perpetuated with the establishment at the Liberation of the MRU, led first by Raoul Dautry and then by Eugène Claudius-Petit. The technocratic elites who led Vichy's drive to reform Paris merged almost seamlessly into the new regime. Politics were banished from their discourse, questions of collaboration turned aside. The first priorities in recruiting candidates for the MRU were technical knowledge, experience, and intelligence. There was simply no question for these reform-minded experts but to continue the modernization programs that would benefit all Parisians, regardless of political proclivities. But given the zealous militancy of the Liberation years and the pretense of an administrative cleansing, this ostensible continuity was veiled. The MRU immediately renounced Vichy's "regressive, narrow-minded" cultural vision. But the discourse and policies remained the same. A new discipline, a rational ordering of the city would heal not only the ravages of war and occupation, but also the social frictions that had led to the country's ignominious fall. This would require an overarching state power and vigilance. The MRU and its technocrats shaped their image of Paris from a sweeping regionalist, even national point of view of *aménagement du territoire*. This whole state logic veered sharply away from the freewheeling localism of the city's municipal elites and their understanding of a fractured landscape of quartiers. The conflict between the French state and the city of Paris sharpened intensely in this moment of utopian postwar hope.

When the Paris municipal council was reinstated in 1945, it did not receive any independent jurisdiction over the planning of Paris. The prefect of the Seine and the prefect of police, both appointed by the state, were the highest-ranking municipal officials. Although any city plan needed the tacit approval of the municipal council before it could be instituted, nothing could be done without the endorsement of the MRU. Central to understanding the political clashes that would ensue within this officialdom was that the municipal council had virtually no independent financial authority. Its pinched budget relied on the state Ministries of Finance and the Interior and their largesse, or lack of it, in funding appropriations. Loans, subsidies, and bonds all required state authorization. Given the postwar political tensions, easy agreement was highly improbable. While state technocrats brandished a professionalized urbanism as their primary weapon, municipal authorities called upon their democratic political base for support. Each accused the other of arrogant indifference and ineptitude. The municipal council was hardly eviscerated by the looming presence of the state in the city's affairs. The power of the Resistance and the PCF was extraordinary in postwar Paris, and they dominated urban politics. They, along with the socialists and moderate Mouvement républicain populaire (MRP), could pack the municipal council chamber at the Hôtel de Ville with stalwart representatives. In fact, the commitment to far-reaching social transformation and a new kind of society was as intense at the local level as it was in the halls of state power. From the point of view of the communists, urban reform was already being carried out daily under their municipal patronage throughout the capital's neighborhoods and suburban towns. Such was their success that the PCF was pushing for autonomous councils for each of the twenty arrondissements, which would see to the arrondissement's own local affairs (see chapter 3). The imposition of state authority over Paris and over this resurgent left-wing localism tasted of cruel disdain, and the reaction against it was visceral.

In August 1945 the MRU called upon the Seine prefecture to reflect on how the land-use plan set out by Mestais might be adapted to the new postwar circumstances. Various preliminary studies were undertaken between 1946 and 1948 and reported to the Paris municipal council by the Seine prefect, Marcel Flouret. Flouret had been appointed directly from the government in exile in Algiers and been responsible for cutting off the power of the city's local liberation committees after August 1944 (eventually he became head of both SNCF and EDF). Newly installed in the Hôtel de Ville, he battled local Resistance leaders, with their nerve centers in the various arrondissements, for control over the capital. It was Flouret's plan that was presented to the public in July and August 1947 at the Exposition Internationale de l'Urbanisme et de l'Habitation at the Grand Palais. As the spokesperson for the newly established French government, Flouret argued that the urban planner's role was not just to deal with the day-to-day problems of living in the city, but to present a vision for the future and to "prepare our Capital for the role it will play in Europe and the world of tomorrow." "If we are not careful," Flouret intoned, "in twenty or thirty years, London, Berlin and the other European capitals, which experienced such cruel destruction during the war, will be rebuilt, while Paris, which by some miracle escaped the storm nearly intact, will become the most backward of capital cities." It was a moment for public debate. "That is why, despite the tortured hours we have traversed and the lack of investments, land-use planning shouldn't be considered a pointless exercise. It is an opportunity to toss around ideas, to listen to opinion, to come up with the best solutions."[29]

Despite the call for "tossing around ideas," the plan essentially continued the vision that had been articulated since the early years of the twentieth century and codified under Vichy in 1943. On the one hand, official state policy embraced modernism as a tool for political authority and centralization. The ideals articulated by CIAM and Le Corbusier inhabited a momentary pinnacle as both revolutionary avant-garde and doctrinal mouthpiece for the reconstitution of the nation. On the other hand, the policy looked backward, to the heritage of French state tradition, as much as to the future. The building programs of the seventeenth- and eighteenth-century French monarchies were honored as models of authoritarian urban policy, their order and visual power hailed as successful urban design. Versailles was held up for its grandeur of planning, as were the royal squares in Paris, the place Vendôme and the place des Vosges. The rue de Rivoli was cited for its rhythm, nobility, and rigorous order. The Second Empire was considered the last great moment of urban planning in Paris. Writing in 1951, Pierre Lavedan noted that "if Descartes were to judge Haussmann's work, he would recognize its reasonableness."[30] Not only were these paradigms of state power, they were nostalgic images of French glory at a moment of national remorse and tragedy—an effort to reawaken French *élan vital* in the Parisian landscape.

In fact, state elites did not wholeheartedly embrace CIAM's modernist principles for urban planning. They looked just as frequently to a French rendering of urban form that preserved an indigenous physiognomy and specificity of place. Reconstruction and the reality of postwar planning often meant the reappearance and repetition of local urban form. In his work on architecture and reconstruction in France, the urbanist Anatole Kopp called this a "reasonable modernization" that forged a compromise between the old and the new.[31] Flouret's reincarnation of Mestais's vision had the same attention to sweeping vistas, to rationalizing the landscape, and to modern circulation schemes and a loop highway that would open up the city. It also retained an ingrained humanistic perspective that privileged the particularities and idiosyncrasies of place. Flouret argued that

> it is to satisfy the needs of the great human community of the city that the streets, public buildings, gardens, and houses are constructed and maintained. It is to satisfy the needs of the modest community of the family that housing is built. In studying these communities—large and small—we will come to understand our priorities and the projects to undertake. In sum, urbanism in general is neither an architecture nor a geometry, but a social problem of the most important kind. In the same

way, construction is a human problem. This is precisely what has led us today to abandon the construction of vast edifices advocated before 1939 in which families disappear and individuals lose themselves in barrack life. The texture of a city is far from homogeneous.... Alongside the millions of people, a multitude of small communities exist that possess their own characteristics and their own particular psychology. It is essential to take them into account.[32]

Although modernist planners typically envisioned the urban landscape as virgin space waiting to be filled with monumental morphology, Flouret pointed to other sources for understanding place: "The special mentality of each community has many sources, but one of the principal [ones] is the genre of life created by the work that sustains families." In a language matching that of Chombart de Lauwe, his study of Paris planning went on to call for for research on the needs of families—the old, the young, adolescents, and adults—especially in terms of public space and infrastructure: "What are these needs that we can quality as *psychological*" for gardens, open spaces, public promenades, for public demonstrations and various activities, for sports and recreational facilities?[33]

Flouret's plan marked something of a bridge from the Paris articulated under Vichy to the modern Paris taking shape in the minds of postwar state technocrats during the 1950s. They were resolute in using the apocalyptic moment of Liberation as the springboard for modernizing France and its capital. The public agencies in charge of planning the Paris metropolitan area—that is, the Comité d'aménagement de la région parisienne (CARP), the Service de l'aménagement de la région parisienne (SARP), and the Direction des travaux de la ville de Paris—were all put under the jurisdiction of the MRU. The *culture parisienne* of the Institut d'urbanisme de Paris and many of its members, such as Pierre Gibel and André Prothin, were now in the service of the Fourth Republic.[34] Their ability to survive professionally was remarkable. An explosion of official working groups, task forces, and research teams investigating the state of affairs in Paris let loose a barrage of technical evidence on the horrendous conditions that had amassed. One after another state edict and regulation thundered out orders to eliminate them. Prothin, the state director of urbanism, espoused a new functional segregation and zoning to "restore the natural rhythms and calm of the city." The urbanist, in Prothin's estimation, had to "fight the waste, the inhuman and miserable ambience. The hours lost . . . on poorly designed public transportation trying to get from work to housing spread through the suburbs: the waste of time driving to find nature."[35] In the official narrative, urban and regional planning were interpreted as rationalizing the urban landscape through functional zoning, through highway expansion and a systemization of "circulation and transportation," and ultimately through a policy of dispersion and suburbanization.

Gibel, the director of SARP, was charged with continuing the effort to plan the Paris metropolitan region. In justifying the state's sponsorship, he raised the wise spirit of the social reformer Henri Sellier, quoting his concerns before the Conseil général de la Seine that the communes and municipal administrations in the Paris region could not, on their own, possibly make the sacrifices and carry out the master planning that would ensure the public good.[36] Gibel's official report was filled with futuristic road maps that crisscrossed the Île-de-France and opened up the region to efficient circulation flows. Such a grand-scale vision of regional planning could be undertaken only by urban professionals under state auspices. The city of Paris itself was left a stark void in these visual diagrams. It would be emptied of people, industry, and commerce. The citizens of Paris would find a better life in the modern residential complexes planned throughout the suburbs, which would be "filled with everything necessary for a humane life." "For the good of the country as well as the good of the working classes," wrote Gibel, the new Paris plan would take into account working-class social needs, the communities and neighborhoods that had taken root amid the chaos, and new housing, schools, hospitals, public services, roads, and public transportation. It would be a *plan directeur* (master plan) that would design a better future through public works.[37]

In his study of urban policies in the Paris region, the sociologist Jean Lojkine makes the argument that the state's attempts to undermine the local power of the Paris municipal council and the Seine general council required nationalizing urban problems and mobilizing popular opinion around the state's cause, a process that had begun in the interwar years and continued with fierce intensity within the context of post-1945 reconstruction.[38] The city's future was put in step with the Commissariat général du Plan's decentralization policies. Rather than promote any further expansion of the squalid Paris monster gorging on the country's growth and potential, the MRU and the Commissariat insisted on dispersing the city's aircraft, chemical, and armaments industries to the provinces, where they would rebalance the country's modernization according to the rational principles of *aménagement du territoire*. During the war, the DGEN had taken the first initiatives toward solving the problem of industrial decentralization. Gabriel Dessus coordinated a series of studies by various experts, including the historian and geographer Jean-François Gravier, who was asked to reflect on the economic condition of the Paris region. His conclusions were presented in November 1947 to the MRU and CARP and then famously published as *Paris et le désert français*. Gravier's views were highly influential in government circles. The first edition included a preface by Raoul Dautry. Gravier's suppositions were also vigorously supported by Eugène Claudius-Petit, who took over from Dautry at the MRU in September 1948. "After the long night of oppression," wrote Claudius-Petit in 1945, "the light harshly glares upon the sores of our worn out society, the ugliness and rot of our suburbs and worker cities, the filth of our factories and their anachronism."[39] Gravier's remedies for these alleged sores were also overtly hostile to Paris. He railed against the Parisian "cartel" that was responsible for the demographic frailty of France and the disintegration of its regional life.[40] He called for an immediate moratorium on all construction in Paris and its suburbs for the next ten years. Furthermore, he recommended the demolition of 75,000 slum buildings, which would not be replaced, in order to reduce the city's population. Gibel's plan for Paris essentially echoed Gravier's vision. Rather than praising the postwar population growth of Paris as a sign of regeneration, he blamed it for emptying the provinces of vital talent. The war offered the opportunity to remodel Paris rationally and adapt it to the currents of modern life. For Gravier and the technocratic planners at the MRU, this meant destroying the capital's supremacy for the benefit of a more just equilibrium across the French nation. It would be a salve for national wounds.

Despite the impression given by official state discourse that somehow the monster of Paris could magically be tamed, the population of the Seine basin continued to swell. So did all the accumulated problems that went with it. More and more residents were added to the region's population roll each year, and the numbers inched upward toward eight million by the end of the 1950s. The Paris share of the French population actually increased slightly from 16.6 percent to 17.8 percent. Given the fact that the state claimed all decision-making authority over the Île-de-France, promoted a decentralization policy that would rob Paris of its economic vitality, and yet failed to solve even the most pressing problems of public infrastructure and housing, the municipal council could do little but throw up its collective hands in frustration. The reshaping of Paris was on everyone's minds, but the state's plans were quickly exposed as overtly anti-Parisian. The whole territorial logic of *aménagement du territoire* was stacked against the capital. Gravier's *Paris et le désert français* in particular was deplored. Gravier further infuriated local elites by suggesting that even the traditional commercial activities of the old districts be transferred out to the new green belt. In the 1947 municipal elections, the tone of the city's political leadership changed dramatically. The communists were ousted from power. In a stunning victory, the Gaullist RPF gained an absolute majority on the municipal council, now presided over by Pierre de Gaulle, who represented the 5th, 6th, and 7th arrondissements of the Left Bank. Yet regardless of the shifting political sands, the state's humiliating decentralization policies were a lightening rod for opposition. To make matters worse, the state's emphatic denial of bonds or subsidies for municipal improvements left the city bereft of any real resources to invest in public assistance programs, schools, hospitals, roads, or even housing. In the vitriolic battles that raged between the state and the city between 1946 and 1958, the municipal council received only 51 billion of the 121 billion francs in state funding it demanded.[41] It was hardly enough to make a dent in the intractable problems that seemed to be accumulating exponentially. Even the investment priorities set out by the municipal council were scrutinized and altered by state officialdom. In November 1948, the council passed an official resolution protesting the intolerable interference of the state into the affairs of Paris. Again in 1950 the council formally stood up against the cabal of state officialdom that blatantly disregarded Parisian interests.

The state's plans for Paris were further elaborated in June 1948 with a "communication" by the new prefect of the Seine, Roger Verlomme, that reached the level of a "draft project" in March 1950. The report began with an official bow to the built heritage and extraordinary richness of the city's life. Respecting them would require a sensitive and progressive evolution and "ordering" of the city that would not radically modify its physiognomy. Limiting building heights and protecting archaeological sites were offered as proof of sincerity. That said, the project was driven by the state's policy of dispersing the city's teeming masses, along with their muddle of trade and industry. To replace the fragmented and defiant *quartiers populaires*, a rational cartography was set in place that conceptualized the city as a cohesive whole. Six zoning districts were laid out for the center of Paris. Among them were two separate districts for "business" and "commercial activity" as well as zones for industry, warehousing, and transport. These delineations more or less conformed to the traditional spaces of productive activity and did not radically alter the landscape. Yet they were underpinned by an emerging economic vision in which state-of-the-art commercial and business services would make Paris a capital of Europe.[42] The proposal also embodied the growing enthusiasm for regulating space through functional zoning. Not surprisingly, Verlomme's plan was soundly rejected by the municipal council.

In 1951 the political firebrand André Thirion attempted to shake things up with an alternative plan that resolutely affirmed the capital's centrality and preeminence. Thirion was a former surrealist, communist, and member of the Resistance who had made his way into the municipal council on the Gaullist RPF platform. Under his leadership, the municipal council set up its own Commission spéciale d'aménagement de Paris, and its members launched a public campaign on behalf of the city. Its report lashed out at "the committees, filled mainly with technicians and functionaries, who may be distinguished, but are irresponsible and who can dictate in Paris what would be impossible in a lowly village without the agreement of its elected mayor." It was intentionally provocative and deliberately modern in orientation—a daring vision of the future. The report excoriated the decentralization directives that would drive Les Halles, La Villette, the gare Saint-Lazare, and the Renault and Citroën plants out of the city and condemned "everything in the plan that in the most literal sense of the word blows Paris apart."[43] Instead it extolled Paris as "the capital of a great nation" and went on to plead that "the attraction Paris has over men and over events is due directly to its legitimate authority and the weight of its history. And given this grandeur . . . no one has the right to commit the monstrous error of diminishing, for any reason or in any sphere, this remarkable city." The city's historical legacy would be saved from the havoc wreaked by planned inner-city thoroughfares and road improvements: "The absolute respect for the sites, monuments, and even the character of those places representing the long history of Paris . . . has led us to propose the complete abandonment of the large number of road projects planned for the districts of Saint-Germain-des-Prés, the Marais, and the Opéra."[44]

Many of Thirion's proposals were inspired by American planning techniques and by the principles laid out by CIAM. An underground tunnel from the boulevard Saint-Germain-des-Prés to Les Halles would traverse the central districts without disturbing them. The city's outer corona of boulevards (which basically follow lines 2 and 6 of the Métro on the site of the old *fermiers généraux* toll wall) would be widened and modernized. The municipal council fought the state's downgrading of the planned triumphant *boulevard périphérique* to an *allée-promenade*. Thirion's plan reinstated it. Calling Paris a great industrial and commercial center, the plan anticipated the expansion of its economic life rather than its diminishment. It recommended the clearance of a vast swath of central Paris to erect a new business district bounded by the place de la République, the gare Saint-Lazare, and the gare du Nord. The ideal was not far from that proposed by Le Corbusier in the 1941 *Destin de Paris*. The area's residents would be moved to the rebuilt outer neighborhoods and arrondissements, as well as to the suburbs, where they would find a better life in modern apartment complexes offered as a vision of domestic bliss.

The hostile reaction of the communists on the municipal council to Thirion's plan was immediate and fierce, particularly because of the personal animosity between Thirion and his former colleagues among the party's leadership. The RPF was attempting to deport the working class from the capital and reserve Paris for the privileged: it was the inevitable red scare, a "bulldozer operation" that was nothing more than a continuation of the social exile launched by Haussmann.[45] The communist municipal councilor Maria Doriath rebuked the government: "You don't want to build in Paris because you are afraid of the Parisian workers, the workers of the Commune, the workers of the Liberation."[46] In large part the communists opposed grand-scale modernist planning—especially that proposed by state functionaries—as little more than vain promises. Although erstwhile urbanists conjured up no end of utopian designs, little was actually done to solve the intractable housing crisis or to improve the deplorable slum conditions working people were forced to endure day after day. The opposition assailed the RPF's plan for "its complete indifference to the hundreds of thousands of miserably lodged families who make up the poorest, most forgotten people."[47] The communists offered their own plan, which removed the railroad stations to the suburbs and linked them together with three new "express subway lines." In their place, thirty thousand new residences would be constructed in a reoccupation of the central city. Thirion's plan was narrowly defeated in May 1952 by a vote of thirty-six to thirty-three, and the plan for Paris went back to committee.[48]

Achievement of any vision for Paris floundered. Negotiations between the state, the city, and suburban collectivities were refracted through a fierce political lens. Authorization for infrastructure and public housing projects was underhandedly delayed or blocked by the state's anti-Parisian policies. Political opinion on the draft plan for Paris shifted from seeing it as too modest to calling it overly ambitious. To confuse matters even further, the municipal council partially approved a conciliatory document that laid out three zones for Paris: a residential and commercial zone covering the center of the city, an industrial zone to the east, and a warehousing zone. In a March 1952 plenary meeting meant to hash out further concessions, Prothin, who was head of the MRU's Direction de l'aménagement du territoire, offered four zones in place of the municipal council's murky three. Prothin was a zealous advocate both of zoning as a way to escape the inefficiencies and disarray of the city and impose modern rationality, and of state directives to carry it out. His first zone was an "official Paris" in the 1st and 7th arrondissements that would be composed of government buildings, palaces, ministries, and embassies. A second zone would comprise business and financial activities in the 9th and 10th arrondissements, from which the area's residents would be expelled and the ancient housing torn down. A university zone would continue on the Left Bank, and a residential zone along the periphery rounded out Prothin's streamlined, rationalized tableau. The old slaughterhouse and meatpacking district at La Villette, the wine market at Bercy, and the Halles aux Vins on the Left Bank at Jussieu—and above all, Les Halles—would be either renovated or torn down and moved to modern facilities in the suburbs.

C. Eyraud, the director of the Services d'architecture et d'urbanisme à la préfecture de la Seine, refused to be taken in by this scheme "to make Paris more pleasant and more organized." He defended the city's mélange of housing, commerce, and industry as its heritage. The municipal council's plan for a vast "mixed zone" in the central city with two adjacent zones for large-scale industry and for warehousing along the periphery conformed to tradition. For the same reason, the municipal council refused to give up the great industrial plants, including the Citroën auto works. It was exactly this kind of self-protective, retrograde thinking that Prothin held responsible for the "ugliness of cities," which was a consequence of "narrow particularism, of spatial disorder and a total absence of general directives." Prothin cavalierly shot back that this would succeed in "creating modern slums." "We have to think in terms of the future," he insisted, "a future that is better. We have to create a firm attitude on this, and in this way, command."[49]

The MRU's CARP insisted on more technical precision in delineating the functional zones that would carry Paris into the future. The municipal council retreated to its Commission spéciale d'aménagement de Paris to prepare a response. It again offered its simplified diagram of three zones, with a massive residential and commercial sector covering nearly the entirety of central Paris. But as a compromise, this last was then subdivided into the state's more rationalized official Paris, business Paris, and intellectual Paris. It was a useless attempt to satisfy all parties. Thirion's scheme for a central-city business center, which had created such a "violent and acerbic" backlash, was banished to La Défense, where "a monument of comparable dimensions to that of the Arc de Triomphe will carry through the triumphal panorama from the Louvre to the Saint-Germain embankment."[50] The commission agreed that the city's wholesale markets, especially Les Halles, had to be broken up and moved outside the central districts. Then, in 1954, the Conseil général des bâtiments de France and the Conseil de l'ordre des architectes entered the fray, rebuking the state for abandoning the preservationist policies that safeguarded the city's built heritage and picturesque village landscapes. CARP defended its position that "harmony is never found in disorder and confusion, but in the perfect adaptation of functionalism."[51] Urban planning for the capital set off in opposite directions. Political rivals tore up the city's map and bickered over piecing it back together. The contest raged between the abstraction of urban space as entirely functional and its preservation as humanistic; between a unified, rationalized metropolis and a fractured, particularist one. The municipal council staged another unsuccessful revolt to wrest control away from the state. In March 1954 a commission set up by the municipal council president, Édouard Frédéric-Dupont, a political moderate, aired its long-standing grievances against a brutally autocratic prefecture that "directs, administers, [and] manages the City of Paris" in direct violation of the French constitution's promise of independent municipal jurisdiction. It set out to amend the city's administrative statutes, which were "unjust, outmoded, and humiliating," and recommended reinstituting election of municipal councilors by quartier as the only way to reclaim local power.[52] Hopes of designing the capital's future languished under the political standoff.

As part of its reporting on Abbé Pierre's campaign, in January 1954 *Paris*

Match published an extensive interview with Le Corbusier. Year after year, the article dismally reported, the same atrocious housing conditions exist in Paris: "All the architects know it has become practically impossible to touch Paris. Parisians and their assemblies simply refuse. They act as if it will be a holocaust for their city if it does not keep its features of one hundred or a thousand years ago." When Le Corbusier proposes destroying the slums of the north and east of Paris and replacing them with a modern, clean, practical city, his ideas are welcomed with cries of horror. "Oh! The beauty of certain streets in Paris! Perhaps they are not seeing clearly, the filthy buildings in a state of collapse, the broken windowpanes, the ragged kids, the misery . . . and this they say is atmosphere! Poetry!" For Le Corbusier, this is a perverted taste for the old and dirty. The reality in this "monster of Paris" is that children die of cold, of misery, of tuberculosis. "Paris," Le Corbusier declared, "is killing itself."[53]

Reconquering Paris

At the end of 1954 the new president of the municipal council, Bernard Lafay, repeated the litany of proposals for the city and then intoned, "In sum, we are at an impasse. The reality is that Paris has no land-use plan and we are completely illegal."[54] A doctor by profession and member of the Resistance, Lafay was one of the most important leaders of the municipal council during the 1950s and one of the most dedicated to urban planning. First elected in 1945, he served on the council until his death in 1977. His diverse political trajectories carried him as a centrist from a representative of the 17th arrondissement to various ministerial portfolios under both the Fourth and the Fifth Republics. The pinnacle of his local political influence came in the mid-1950s, when non-Gaullist centrists such as he were able to take advantage of the change in political winds and suddenly make their mark on the city's future. The great age of communist power had peaked and begun its slow decline. At the same time, the old Radical Party finally crumbled, providing Lafay the opportunity to help build the Rassemblement des gauches républicaines (RGR) movement as a springboard to city power. In collaboration with the architect Raymond Lopez, Lafay wrote what is considered to be the definitive report on planning in Paris during the 1950s. It was originally presented as an official municipal council report and then published in 1954 in brochure format for general distribution by the Comité du nouveau Paris as

"Solutions aux problèmes de Paris."[55] It was promptly christened the Lafay Plan. Regardless of the version or name, the report launched a more audacious, dynamic approach toward planning the city and its far-flung region that would culminate in the 1959 Plan d'urbanisme directeur. If the first half of the 1950s was characterized by a bewildering miasma of false starts and general state obstructionism, the second half of the 1950s was marked by a much stronger hand.

The Lafay Plan was clearly inspired by the modernist movement and by American planning theory. Raymond Lopez was a member of the postwar generation of modernists for whom the ideals of the Athens Charter and of CIAM were a religious conviction. He had first gone to the United States on a Delano Fellowship in 1935 and then returned again in 1956. Profoundly influenced by the work of Mies van der Rohe and the designs of influential American firms such as Skidmore, Owings & Merill, Lopez would eventually be involved in designing some of the most daring projects on the Paris landscape, including the aluminum-framed offices of the Caisse centrale d'allocations familiales (family benefit fund) building in the 15th arrondissement, the Maine-Montparnasse Tower, and the flashy Front-de-Seine project that converted an old warehousing district into a model of modern urban renewal. Lopez reached the height of his influence in the late 1950s and 1960s. As chief architect in charge of the French Service des bâtiments civils et palais nationaux and professor at the École nationale des ponts et chaussées, with a vast architectural firm on the boulevard Raspail employing over one hundred architects, he was perfectly placed to carry out his modernist utopian vision.

Calling Paris "the most damaged city in France," Lopez condemned both the municipal council and the city's inhabitants for their incompetence. The first was too politicized; the second simply had "no real interest in the city upon which their physical, economic and social life entirely depends." Their minds were vacant. They were oblivious to the hideousness around them. Abbé Pierre's crusade and the housing protests, the calls for urban renewal from every quarter, the communist protests and neighborhood projects, all either escaped Lopez's purview or were ignored as futile attempts by the uninformed. The complex experiential knowledge and the magical urbanism of local citizens were all disregarded. He acidly predicted there would never be "crowds of men, women, and children parading the boulevards carrying banners, the way we see in England, marked 'We want our Town-Plan.'" As to intellectuals, Lopez dismissed them as mesmerized by their own *images d'Épinal*: "'Paris, Greatest City in the World'—'Paris, Capital of the West'—'Paris, City of Light'—etc., etc., and thinking that all is well in the world because we have built Notre Dame—because we took the Bastille—because we have our place de la Concorde—because we promenade down the Champs-Élysées." Lopez metaphorically shook his head in shame at a city where "the last chances of survival diminish each day, where street alignments lack any regularity, where îlots close themselves in on all sides; where the last open spaces are carved up, and where all hope of saving the situation is in vain even if new construction is accelerated."[56] It was difficult to paint a bleaker picture. The disassembled city was a catastrophe. Paris had fallen under a curse. More chaos would only ensue without a *plan directeur* that envisioned the whole of the urban region. It was up to the French state and the architect to rescue the capital from its own demise. They represented the common interest and shared a civic-mindedness that would rise above the poisonous stew of squabbling local bureaucracies, private interests, and politics.

"Solutions aux problèmes de Paris" was replete with comparisons with American cities and heavily illustrated with American planning techniques as well as with Lopez's high-modernist designs. Although there was some grousing about "making Paris into a new Chicago," in general the municipal council heeded the siren call of modernism by the mid-1950s and consciously referred to American examples as symbolic of their progressive spirit.[57] And yet, at the same time, the plan harked back to the capital's long history. Lafay placed the modernist vision for Paris neatly within the context of the city's design heritage. Using Gaston Bardet's theories of urban historical development, Lafay conjured up forerunners in the Bellarmato Plan, the Plan des Artistes, and the urban renewal of the Second Empire. Lopez also viewed CIAM and Le Corbusier's modernist imaginary as successors to Haussmann. "Paris," he affirmed, "is going to live through a new Haussmannian era over the next fifteen years of intense urbanization and intense construction."[58] Collapsing together French tradition and modernism was not seen as a contradiction.

The result was that the agenda set out in the Lafay Plan was a compromise, the product of a cacophony of voices in a noisy public debate. The plan, at once traditional and modern, essentially invented two cities. The core of central Paris was preserved in its historic monumentality. Admitting defeat by the forces allied in defense of the historic districts, Lopez argued that it was useless to try any radical transformation there. The architects Claude Charpentier and Michel Holley, both close associates of Lopez and highly influential in their own right, referred to the historic districts at the city's heart as the *polygone sacré* and the *triangle sacré*. They would not be touched. The Lafay Plan abandoned the long-held dream of continuing Haussmann's *grande croisée*. No further boulevards or highways would be driven through the historic districts; no vast campaign of modernization would be attempted. The intensity and breadth of this protectionist defense of the city center was astonishing. It included preservationists, communists, intellectual elites, the Paris municipal council, and the local governing coalitions in the central arrondissements. Even the Athens Charter had inscribed the "historic city" as a specific zone where picturesque sites, monumental vistas, and the historic built environment would be protected. Increasingly Le Corbusier had turned toward a preservation and reification of the city's great historic monuments that would be accentuated with aesthetic urban backdrops. Notre Dame, the Arc de Triomphe, Sacré-Cœur, the Eiffel Tower, and the Louvre all survived his theoretical obliteration of the historical districts. The architect and geographer Maria Gravari-Barbas argues convincingly that Le Corbusier saw them not as "heritage" per se, but as a necessary part of the capital's fantasy machine and monumentality.[59] The Lafay Plan was simply putting this modernist strategy into practice.

The plan certainly offered a program of road construction that surreptitiously extended inside the *triangle sacré*. It may have been sacred, but the city center was choking in traffic and congestion. Subterranean tunnels under Châtelet, Saint-Augustin, and Concorde would provide efficient transportation arteries without disturbing the historic landscape. A long transverse artery was proposed that would cover the canal Saint-Martin and link the place de la Bastille with the gare d'Austerlitz and beyond. Much of the debate in the late 1950s also focused on the state's attempt to extend the planned *autoroute de sud* at least to the place Denfert-Rochereau in the 14th arrondissement, if not to the place d'Italie. But the municipal council adamantly fought all of these proposals, especially the proposed southern highway's "mutilation of the Montsouris Park" at the porte d'Arcueil. In December 1957 it finally adopted the categorical proposition of the communist Albert Boisseau that "the municipal council is opposed to any intrusion of highways into Paris." A vast alliance of strange bedfellows fell under the city's spell. They turned a blind eye to the grim shabbiness and instead saw only beauty and elegance. In 1957 Albert Guérard, the author of *L'Avenir de Paris* (1929) and now at the end of a long career reflecting on the city, wrote in the *Revue urbanisme* that what Paris demanded of its urbanists was "not little repairs day by day, but total reconstruction." And yet, as much as he admired Le Corbusier and his disciples and the temptations that modernism held for a rational plan, for decent streets and parking garages, for central heat in homes, for gardens and sports parks, "I just refuse to sacrifice the historic personality of Paris. . . . Restraint and grandeur: Paris is "stamped with restraint . . . a restraint of beauty."[60] Writing in the same issue, architect and preservationist Albert Laprade described Paris as a person, "with blue and red blood flowing through its veins," with a beauty so intense, with its river, its wealth of magnificent edifices, its ancient houses and historic heritage, its diverse neighborhoods, that "all this influences the spirit, the behavior, the sensibility and humor of its inhabitants."[61]

By 1956 the center of Paris was zoned for three specific functions: administrative, commercial and banking, and intellectual. These were the prestigious cosmopolitan activities that were signs of "class,"[62] the means by which Paris would boost itself into the league of modern European capitals. Majestic government buildings, swank office space and corporate headquarters, luxury boutiques and department stores, chic apartments for elite cadres, hotels, restaurants, and tourist services would conquer the streets. The core of Paris was reinvented for the consumption of culture, history, and tourism, and for the sophisticated governmental and commercial roles befitting its stature. Negotiations were ongoing over a new commercial *pôle* near the gare Montparnasse. The offices spreading over the 16th and 17th arrondissements would be joined by an entirely new business district at La Défense. The momentum behind this mental picture was clearly the competition posed by West Germany, the creation of the Common Market, and the broad economic pressures of the *trente glorieuses*. By 1959 and the final emergence of the Plan d'urbanisme directeur, the ideal of Haussmann's *grande croisée* had been brought back to life as a vast open-air esplanade, a *cruciforme de prestige*, that stretched along its north-south axis from the gare du Nord to the Seine, and along its east-west axis from Vincennes to Saint-Germain-en-Laye. The Seine would emerge as topographic spectacle, protected from encroachment by strict building regulation. This *zone cristallisé* would be enveloped and secured by an outer circle of modernized boulevards that retraced the old boundary of the *fermiers généraux*, which in the 1950s was often called the *perimetre sacré*. Despite the fact that this schema had appeared in a number of plans, especially André Thirion's 1951 municipal council proposal, the ring of thoroughfares was so closely associated with Lopez that it was also nicknamed the *rocade Lopez* (Lopez beltway).

Underneath this master-planning rhetoric was a whole series of social effects that had powerful aftershocks on the public sphere and its spaces. It predictably depended on an erasure of *Paris populaire*, a sweeping out of the people who lived in the central districts. The artisan and industrial working classes, their ateliers, factories, and warehouses, and their dilapidated apartment buildings, which had long formed a populist landscape, were excluded from this new centrality. Their generalized vilification as "slums" justified urban-renewal projects that exiled the supposedly wretched inhabitants to the suburban margins. The vernacular, poetic landscape was reinvented as a sterilized historic shell through which tourists could wander at their leisure as *flâneurs*. Their gaze lingered over features of the landscape and built environment that were visually objectified and recognizable from endless reproductions in photographs, film, and the media. The territory of the everyday as a creative zone vanished from view. Instead, the topography of Paris formed a system of ciphers and signs that were other than normal, out of the ordinary, and that cut the viewer off from ordinary experience. The tourist could safely venture anywhere in a timeless romantic Paris littered with visual imagery. The central districts were made into a consumable scenography, a decorative past, that had been tamed and controlled by the removal of their uncontainable, provocative elements. The self-actualizing Rousseauian people who inhabited this world disappeared as actors in the public drama, transformed by technocratic planners into passive slum dwellers or pieces of a decaying social economy. Under an increasingly tightening system of surveillance, they were viewed by the late 1950s as dangerous insurgents and public threats and associated with riots, violence, and with the geography of fear. Their elimination was justified as a matter of national survival and rebirth. These stereotypes abstracted the city's working classes as alien and dispensable, or at least suffering from backward qualities to be rooted out by technocratic elites. The dissident, populist spatial dynamic invented by urban observers was stripped of its potency and instead made quaint and nostalgic. The notion of the *peuple*, naturalized in distinctive neighborhood places, was exchanged for one in which they could be extracted from space and moved to the suburbs. This process of spatial cleansing would return Paris to its former beauty.

Beyond the barrier of the *rocade Lopez*, the Lafay Plan argued for a radical program of modernization in the outer arrondissements and surrounding suburbs. They were subject to the new trinity of zoning, automobiles and highways, and large-scale residential compounds and *grands ensembles*. The experimental concept of large-scale residential construction went hand in hand with the ideal of domestic mass consumerism and privatized family life. The design of the new neighborhoods in the outer arrondissements was to be intentionally audacious and utopian in scale.[63] The buildings would be sufficiently high to liberate 50 percent of the terrain as open space. The drawings in the Lafay Plan reveal high-rise apartment blocks set amid pristine gardens, with the rational circulation patterns and broad avenues that stamp them as modernist dreamscapes. To begin the makeover, Lafay had pushed through the February 7, 1953, "Lafay Law," which permitted the construction of residential estates on the *zone* through a new system of expropriation. The measure opened the way for the modernization of the outlying districts. In December 1953 and January 1954 the municipal council immediately approved a construction program for four thousand housing units on seven different sectors of the *zone*. Each sector was handed to an architect to design, among them Robert Auzelle. The vast majority of their proposed renderings took the shape of high-modernist residential estates. High-rise towers and bar-shaped residential complexes jutted up from a greenbelt landscape in parallel lines or at right angles in a strictly rationalist formula. The visionary designs were replete with parks and recreational facilities, and then surrounded by a *boulevard périphérique* that was linked to the *rocade Lopez* by radial highways.[64]

Paris was then divided into three separate precincts that rigorously followed its historic ring pattern and accentuated the boundaries between them. The core central city inside the *rocade Lopez* was enveloped by a circle of modernist residential estates themselves cinched in by the vast sunken belt of the *boulevard péripherique*. Clearing the central districts of the working classes and the poor, resurrecting the boundaries of the old *fermiers généraux* and the fortifications, and relying on state authority to create a new centrality: as daringly modern as the plan was, it could not have been more conventional. The modernist high-rise blocks along the outer perimeter created a veritable wall around the city that coordinated with its concrete moat of the *boulevard*

FIGURE 32. The rue du Château-des-Rentiers and îlot 4, June 12, 1969. © COLL. PAVILLON DE L'ARSENAL, CLICHÉ DUVP

péripherique. In the words of Norma Evenson, "the circular motorway reinforced the image of Paris as a walled city, replacing the old line of defenses with an impenetrable barrier of high-speed vehicles."[65] Beyond them were an industrial and warehousing belt, the discarded suburbs, and the mushrooming *grands ensembles*. To avoid further sprawl, the Paris region was limited to the already built areas, and the population growth stabilized. This resulted essentially in a no-growth policy that would unify, contain, and control the metropolis.

This vast campaign to "Reconquer Paris" was launched in a media blitz that rivaled wartime propaganda in intensity. A flood of public-planning documents, architectural texts, and media coverage laid out the crusade, which corresponded with the appointment in May 1955 of Pierre Sudreau as the new Commissaire à la construction et à l'urbanisme for the Paris region. This position as regional czar for housing and urban planning was attached to the Seine prefecture with the objective of coordinating the development of a Paris region that now spread over 389 communes covering a territory of eight hundred square miles in the Île-de-France and included more than 7.5

million people. Sudreau's rising star was interpreted as a provocation by the municipal council, which saw it as further evidence of the state's strong-arm tactics. Sudreau had been a member of the Resistance and had been deported to Buchenwald in 1944. He was one of a number of young experts who found themselves in positions of political power after the Liberation. Situated in the moderate political center, he was named the youngest under-prefect in France and then became prefect of the Loire-et-Cher before assuming his post in Paris. In his 1956 article "Reconquête de Paris," Sudreau attacked the dismal record of failures, the "million poorly housed people, the thousands of acres of slums that were the sad balance sheet in 1955, and just in the department of the Seine."[66] The blame was laid at the feet of an incompetent local officialdom and an unmanageable city. Like countless administrators before him, Sudreau called for demolition of the infamous slum districts. Given their population density, the only realistic solution was to transfer at least one-third of their population, around sixty thousand inhabitants, either to new housing estates along the city's periphery or to *grands ensembles* in the suburbs.

The symbol of this new era in planning Paris was the Centre de documentation et d'urbanisme (CDU), created by the Seine prefecture in April 1957. It was installed in the newly renovated Hôtel de Sens in the Marais, smack in the middle of the most infamous and controversial slum district in Paris. It was to be an intellectual incubator for dialogue and fresh ideas on urban and regional planning. But ultimately the CDU's mission was to create a Plan d'urbanisme directeur for Paris and to propose a program of operations that would be carried out under the auspices of Sudreau and the Seine prefecture. The campaign was promoted in two issues of the 1957 *Revue urbanisme*, dedicated to "Propos sur Paris" and "Paris et sa région," by urbanists who had worked throughout the twentieth century to devise the capital's future. Sudreau introduced the first issue with an article titled "At the Hour of Europe" that connected the conquest of Paris with French entrance into the Common Market and openly measured it against the resurrection of Berlin and West Germany. The task for Sudreau was imperative, because "it is no longer a matter of being the capital of a country, but that of a continent."[67]

The CDU carried out yet another survey of the capital. Based on its empirical findings, it was decided that Paris could have an ideal population of no more than 2,300,000. A team of architects and planners led by Raymond Lopez and Michel Holley then launched a massive investigation for the CDU of the building stock and spaces of Paris. Under their supervision, some forty students from the École des beaux-arts fanned out across the city for weeks to document conditions and collect statistical evidence. Only the central districts of *Paris cristallisé* escaped their investigation (although the team did venture into Les Halles, which was treated like a carcass). The study was meant to technically ascertain which buildings could be condemned and which could be conserved. "It was a detailed and precise inventory on all the sites to reconquer," the prefect Émile Pelletier told the municipal council.[68] The diagnostic criteria were a mechanism for imposing spatial uniformity and regulation. The verdict for each edifice and space was decided upon with stinging rationality, based on traditional gauges of disease and hygiene, valuation of "norms of comfort," and economic measures such as unemployment. The figures provided a narrow field of vision that in no way captured the social phenomena or the places they presumed to typify. The sites designated for demolition included not only the *îlots insalubres*, but new districts identified as *mal utilisés* based on appraisals of their optimum exploitation. Old railroad and boat yards, depots, and warehouse and industrial areas were prime candidates for clearance. The decision was made to demolish all buildings over one hundred years of age and with fewer than four stories—that is to say, the construction most associated with the city's industrial detritus and with its ancient slums. Buildings less than fifty years old could be conserved.

Based on this research, Lopez created a far-reaching plan for the redevelopment of the capital. It was showcased at the Hôtel de Sens in 1957, along with public meetings and presentations, as evidence of the CDU's leadership in setting out the future. Lopez's vast map of Paris was fastened to the wall of the Hôtel de Sens reception hall in a modernist reenactment of Napoleon III's rolling out of the map of Paris for an enthralled Haussmann, who stood ready to carry out his vision. The building stock and areas of the city that were judged viable and would escape the wrecking ball were marked in black and gray. Badly or under-utilized sites, slum districts and the old *îlots insalubres*, blighted areas littered with ancient warehousing, refineries and tanneries, metal and machine shops, and industrial plants all formed a vast swath of yellow across the map covering enormous sections of the north, east, and south of the city. They included some 1500 hectares of land, nearly one-quarter of the city's territory, where more than ninety thousand people lived. All these areas were condemned and slated for slum clearance. By 1958 the key neighborhoods were designated by the state as *zones à urbaniser en priorité* (ZUPs) to facilitate expropriation and development. Urbanism became a synonym for social exclusion. Much of the area marked for destruction was along the northern and eastern periphery, places that had escaped Haussmann's wrath and had long formed an ancient but livable haven for the working classes, poor and unskilled laborers, the elderly, and North African immigrants. Here is where "disorder" was most evident. Belleville, Ménilmontant, Bastille-Roquette in the north, Gobelins and the Bièvre valley in the south, and the populist Butte-aux-Cailles district, which was considered insufficiently *cristallisé*, were all on the list for modernist overhaul.

For the prefect Jean Benedetti, a new period in the history of urbanism had begun. In his estimation, the first stage had involved an *urbanisme d'alignement* based on the street, the second had been an *urbanisme d'îlot* based on the neighborhood, and the third would now be an *urbanisme d'ensemble* guided by the principles of the Athens Charter. As a modernist prescription, *urbanisme d'ensemble* was a strictly formal, comprehensive, and unified vision of a capital city. It was a strategy for centrality and state power, and as such was an explicit attack against the urban vernacular and its sense of localized space. "The essential idea that marks the rupture with older conceptions," according to Benedetti, "is that the urban framework is no longer defined by the street but by the arrangement of construction, which is itself guided by functional considerations, by the need for architectural unity."[69] The Lafay Plan as well announced that the principle of the îlot as an independent unit had to be abandoned. No longer would urban planning be oriented around the creation of nearly autonomous "modern little settlements." The designs that had been laid out for Paris since the 1930s had produced "too much fragmentation" among the neighborhoods. Although the Plan d'urbanisme directeur portrayed the street as the traditional public space of the city, it argued that "the pestilence of the streets, especially the noise," required that Parisians find repose in residential complexes surrounded by gardens and open space. Planning would integrate neighborhoods within a broader vision of the metropolis that included housing, open space, and transportation networks.

In November and December 1958 Pierre Sudreau took to the airwaves as part of the promotional blitz surrounding the new plan for Paris in a series of five ORTF television presentations titled *Problèmes de la construction*. Shown in the months after de Gaulle's investiture as president, the series was meant to mobilize the French around the new policies of the Fifth Republic.

In the November 27 episode, "The France of Tomorrow," Sudreau narrated a childlike cartoon sketch of the past in which housing and the street were the essentials of urban existence. It smacked of professional condescension, intimating that the city's inhabitants were not sufficiently expert to understand the spatiality of their lives. But the automobile had changed everything, according to Sudreau. As images of Parisian traffic jams flashed across the screen, he explained that "space no longer exists, pedestrians have no functional space . . . people need to get away from the fatigue of industrial, urban life." This required a great work of urbanism, an urbanism that is "as much art as science, and is both sociology and economy."[70] Unity of conception and unity of command were essential. The November 20 show, "Aménagement de la région parisienne," was broadcast from the CDU's new headquarters at the Hôtel de Sens. Calling Paris "an immense vacuum cleaner that empties out the rest of France," Sudreau and Benedetti repeated incessantly that the first priority was to "return order" to the region. The visual narrative was totalizing and centralizing. To bolster the television performance, Raymond Lopez explained his diagnostic study and displayed his vast map of Paris for television viewers, adding his vision of a "noble" city fulfilling its role as a great capital. In place of wretched districts, the series laid out a chimerical model of the *unité d'habitation* surrounded by a vast ring road and a network of highways. The street and the public square would no longer play a functional role in the life of the neighborhood and were banished from this modernist utopia. Instead, open space, light, air, gardens, schools, shopping centers, and services would be the guiding principles of the everyday. Rapt viewers watched as a parallel fantasy world of modern neighborhoods materialized on their television screens. It would transform their personal habits and household organization, their life-world, as well as the meaning and spaces of both the private and public domain. The twelve- to fifteen-story residential towers and bars, the *grands ensembles* and *cités nouvelles* in the suburbs, Sudreau explained, are meant to "liberate open space, green space" and to rationally organize a Paris region that was "too vast, too impenetrable."[71] There was a simple credulity about these imaginary pictures. Modernism was the antidote to all ills. All suffering was denied; life became faultless, ideal. Space was static rather than fluid. The construction of Paris and its environs became the new form of spatial spectacle. It provided descriptions that could easily be read as explanations and therefore as solutions to what was unanimously identified as a disgrace.

These images were also overtly anti-Parisian and decentralist in conception. Draconian formulas restricted any further growth within a sixty-mile radius of Paris. The future population of the region was to be stabilized at no more than nine million inhabitants. The construction of industrial buildings larger than sixteen hundred square feet (five hundred square meters) was prohibited, and public subsidies were offered to those companies willing to relocate elsewhere in the provinces. By 1960 nearly 780 industrial decentralization operations had already been carried out, 230 of which were in the city of Paris and the remainder in the suburbs and wider region.[72] By 1956 the number of jobs lost in the Paris region had mounted to 45,000; by 1960 it had reached 100,000. Those industries left in the city were banished outside the *boulevard péripherique*. In 1955 and again in 1958 office construction in Paris was restricted, and the state moved toward displacing the capital's cultural and educational supremacy. Work began on a regional planning document, known as the Plan d'aménagement et d'organisation générale de la région parisienne (PADOG), that would in Sudreau's words "erase the colossal error of the last half-century of allowing Paris to be encircled by concentric zones of misery and revolt."[73] The PADOG instituted a no-growth policy that would decongest the city and more equitably balance development throughout the Île-de-France according to the rational principles of *aménagement du territoire*. It was eventually approved in 1960.

The plans represented a usurpation of local prerogatives and further inflamed the rivalry between the city of Paris and the French state. They were a direct attack on the humanist narrative that had predominated in midcentury. In an "extraordinary session" in late October 1959, the municipal council debated the emerging Plan d'urbanisme directeur de Paris with the prefect of the Seine, Émile Pelletier, and Sudreau. Both men had just been elevated to prestigious positions in de Gaulle's new government, Pelletier as minister of the interior and Sudreau as minister of construction. The rise of Sudreau as Commissaire à la construction et à l'urbanisme in Paris and then to a ministerial post roiled municipal councilors as they watched their independence disappear. It was a bad omen, a thinly veiled effort by state political elites to disenfranchise the city and its fearsome counterpublics. Janine Alexandre-Debray, a political independent, pleaded against rational zoning, arguing that "Paris is a puzzle, a harmonious puzzle . . . my concern is that cutting Paris up into strictly drawn zones will eradicate its diversified and harmonious character." Auguste Lemasson, a communist, called the plan's rejection of any further mass production in Paris for what it was:

> It's the deindustrialization of Paris to the profit of business, offices, and residences for the wealthy classes. . . . If you amputate manufacturing industry from Paris, one of its liveliest, most important, most varied, most productive sectors, you will unhinge its economy. The disruption in local business will be extraordinary, to say nothing of the impact on working-class families who cannot tear themselves away from the neighborhood so easily. You have to think of the human impact here. But apparently that counts for nothing.

Indeed, the impact on the local population that had to deal with the state's abstract reasoning about rational urban planning could be profoundly cruel. Exuding the aura of official authority, Sudreau shot back with a merciless political card: "Paris is a monster . . . the government has decided not only to apply but to intensify its policy of decentralization in all directions—industrial, technical, scientific research, university. If the majority of the municipal council is against this policy, then you can make your voice heard. But our plan simply conforms to state policy." Not persuaded by the interloper's haughty confidence, one councilor, Roger Pinoteau, went on to recount the extraordinary tribulations facing entire neighborhoods singled out as condemned slums. The brutal declaration was an assault on everyone living there and left them with no civil or commercial recourse:

> And the Administration tells us—and with such magnificent bearing!— that if you want to improve the environment of most artisans then the wheel of misfortune will inevitably crush a certain number of them. And there you have it! It is in the name of these small artisans that I stand up against this Moloch administration that will obliterate the small number without the slightest guarantee of improvement for the majority. And who's to say that the victims won't in fact end up in the majority![74]

The Plan d'urbanisme directeur de la Ville de Paris was finally adopted by the municipal council in 1962 and achieved final government sanction in 1967. It became the foundation on which urban planning and spatial redesign were carried out for the city of Paris for the entire period from 1960 to 1974. The conceptions that guided it were the result of an intense, multifarious public dialogue carried on throughout midcentury. For all its seeming robustness, the Plan d'urbanisme directeur was actually conformist in character. The document was the result of a multitude of compromises and counterdiscourses carried on among powerful interests from the local political level to the heights of state technocracy. Preservationists, municipal elites, urban planners, state technocrats, and political leaders from both the Left and the Right weighed in on the potential for the future and on the nature of the urbanizing process. This vast public debate worked toward establishing a French vision of urbanity immersed as much in the past as in the future. The threads of nineteenth-century-style urban reform, of social municipalism as well as Vichy designs, of the principles of CIAM and 1950s American-style planning techniques, were woven through it in a marriage between past and future that was certainly less than harmonious. Yet despite repeated calls for revolutionary thinking, this complex fabric created more of a continuum in French urban discourse than a real breakthrough. The plan did not radically alter the pattern of urban growth that had been taking place in Paris for over a century. It was a clear indication that despite its totalizing revolutionary discourse, technocratic modernism was as multihued and as infused with contradictions, with the weight of heritage and political negotiation, as any other intellectual and aesthetic movement. For the political scientist James Scott, for example, the most important barrier to thoroughgoing high-modernist schemes has been representative institutions through which resistance can make itself felt.[75] In the case of Paris, these institutions were localized and imbued with a poetic humanist vision that acted as a counternarrative to the state's authoritarian designs. The result was that planning preserved the fragmented city and yet applied a monumental urban and regional vision. Both urban scales were incorporated into the utopian imagination. The central districts and their neighborhoods were reified, prized, and protected as historic precincts that embodied the particularity of French culture and identity. By the late 1950s planning accented a superficial rendering of local urban form that preserved the city's customary physiognomy and specificity of place, even as real local political power and the city's working-class material existence were undermined. It succeeded in inventing the central districts as a historicized *zone cristalisée* devoid of content. In other words, Paris was transformed into a modern tourist mecca.

The ring pattern that had long guided urban growth remained intact, and the two barriers that traditionally separated the city from its suburbs were kept in place. Outside them, a utopian program of modernization was applied to the suburbs by a growing cadre of state technocratic agencies. Between January 1955 and June 1958 nearly 200,000 standardized lodgings were constructed around Paris. Most of them were incorporated into small construction projects of no more than one hundred to two hundred apartments. But above all it was the early *grands ensembles* of the 1950s— the futuristic Sarcelles designed by Jacques Henri Labourdette, the nine thousand residences of Massy-Antony, the five thousand at Mont-Mesly à Créteil, the architect Émile Aillaud's 2,837 apartments at Les Courtilières at Pantin-Bobigny—that produced a futuristic antimodel of the picturesque inner districts. They were designed and built by the modernist architects and large-scale construction and engineering companies favored by the state's technocratic machinery. The *grands ensembles* were meant to fulfill all the aspirations of quality of life, of social mobility and material abundance, that were such a crucial part of the reconstruction years and the *trente glorieuses*. They would control suburban sprawl, solve the housing crisis, and guide the French into a new way of living. At first the pioneers who moved in to these apartments found them miraculous. As young families, dreams in hand, opened the door onto their new lives, there was a sense of overwhelming joy and hopefulness. And indeed, that optimism was shared by French planners and urban reformers who had toiled over the city's intractable problems and the acute housing crisis for decades. Finally, solutions had been found, and new theories were being applied. As the bulldozers and construction equipment rolled out, Paris was entering into an age of great transformation that seemed to be discarding the worst without risking the best of its heritage.

The Politics of Preservation: The Marais

The most important and most divisive questions about the city of Paris had to do with the vast slum districts that pockmarked the historic districts. The two most important immediately after the war were both in the Marais: *îlot insalubre* 1 at Saint-Merri (the ancient plateau Arcis-Beaubourg) and especially the infamous *îlot insalubre* 16 in the southern part of the Marais bordering the Seine between the churches of Saint-Gervais and Saint-Paul. They came to represent the tortured controversies over urban planning, and over French identity, in the midst of war and then reconstruction. Îlot 16 in particular was at the crossroads of some of the most important experiments in urban renovation and design in the capital. No other area in Paris exhibited so well the collision between official narratives and counternarratives, between aesthetics and social relations. Its renovation was the product of a messy, contentious public debate. And perhaps no other area so vividly displayed the weight of humanist urban theory and practice at midcentury, its ironies, and its eventual transformation from populist to tourist allegory.

The Marais bore an impeccable heritage as one of the oldest and most illustrious districts of Paris. Besides the two churches of Saint-Paul and Saint-Gervais, a covey of aristocratic townhouses dating from the sixteenth to the eighteenth century, including the once elegant Hôtel de Sens, graced its sinuous streets. Yet the Marais was a palimpsest, a place that reflected many histories. Besides its Renaissance heritage, the district had a long and distinguished working-class history. Sandwiched between the old place de Grève and the working-class neighborhoods in the 3rd and 12th arrondissements, the Marais was an overtly populist world. It was a nearly perfect representation of the poetic humanist sensibility: a distinct quartier, a *pays de Paris*. A lavish quotidian theater took place in its streets, markets, and public spaces. Well into the 1950s the Marais constituted a buzzing industrial and trading complex. Thousands of the city's workers descended onto the rue Pavé, the rue Malher, the rue de Sévigné, the sidewalks of the rue Saint-Antoine, and the rue des Francs-Bourgeois to take up their posts at pharmaceutical companies, the textile and ready-to-wear garment trades, and the manufactories of *articles de Paris*: jewelry and art objects, toys and costumes, fancy goods, aperitifs, and food delicacies. The Communist Party's first headquarters was located there, on the rue Sainte-Croix-de-la-Bretonnerie. Lively, politically tinged cafés and dance halls and long-established trade-union offices lined the streets. In Léo Malet's *Fièvre au Marais* (1955), Nestor Burma follows a suspect on foot through the Marais and visits a foundry, of which there are "a baker's dozen" in the neighborhood:

> The atelier was situated at the back of the courtyard. Even from the passageway, a strong odor of copper metal stuck in your throat. From the open door, you could see massive silhouettes working over a blazing forge, violently luminous, streaked with violet and dark red flashes. The crackling was wild.
>
> One of three workers raised his head as we went in, then, pointing

to the boss, went back to work. He wore black welder's goggles to protect his eyes from the metal sparks flying from the cauldron worked by the colleagues he oversaw. It was on top of a coffer sitting tilted on the ground, gripped in place by huge wing screws. Growling and smoking, the liquid seemed like a diabolical cracking punch that, inside, took the form of the molds.

In such a scene, the three men looked fantastic. Girded in thick leather aprons, they wore asbestos gloves and boots into which they jammed their trouser legs. Thus dressed, they wandered around their realm. Any hayseed would take them for Martians.[76]

The network of ateliers and commercial establishments was kept humming by a diverse immigrant population, particularly its poor Ashkenazi Jews from Eastern Europe. The Pletzl around the rue des Rosiers and the neighboring art nouveau synagogue on the rue Pavée were a thriving center for the city's Yiddish-speaking community. This "ghetto" was described in the 1939 wanderings of Léon-Paul Fargue as enclosed "by the rue de Roi-de-Sicile, the rue Ferdinand-Duval [otherwise known as the rue des Juifs], and the rue Vieille-du-Temple." Its center was "on the corner of the rue des Ecouffes and the rue des Rosiers, where the Speiser bookstore, the meeting place for Jews from all over the world, is located":

> Sickly children and mangy cats hang around the stagnant debris in the gutters. The odor of fritters, of meat and leeks, trails down from above. Silhouettes bedecked in ringlets cross the narrow street in search of syrup liquors and turnovers in the bookstore-restaurants.
>
> In the morning wrinkled, bearded old men evoke a blend of curiosity and fear, of great *promenadeurs* weighed down and pensive, whom one thinks of as smart and roguish, who at the same time have the air of nostalgia, of guarding secrets, of venerable merchants who have emerged from some museum headed for the synagogue, like chiefs, and the Jewish proletariat of the rue des Rosiers look at them with envy and astonishment, because they are wise and rich.[77]

Rounded up in the July 1942 *rafle*, the Marais's Jewish community was decimated in the Holocaust. Only 3 percent of the area's prewar Jewish population returned from the death camps after the war.

Drastically distorted by this destruction of its traditional inhabitants, the Marais reemerged as the spectacle of a new foreignness in the late 1940s and 1950s. Sephardic Jews, especially from North Africa, settled on the rue de Rosiers and the surrounding streets. Promenading the Marais in 1952, the writer Henri Laborde described a

> veritable mosaic of people.... You come upon curious types of men who immediately make you think of North Africa, [or] Central or Eastern Europe. Many of them retain their national styles of dress, language, habits, and costume long after they arrive. Crossing the rue Pavée, the rue de Turenne, or the rue des Tournelles, you often see groups of men with long beards and sidelocks, like Levite prophets going to the neighborhood rabbinical school or synagogue.... The spectacle is worth a stroll, to get a better sense of the original characters of this neighborhood and to mingle in the life of its workshops and markets.[78]

In *Paris insolite*, Jean-Paul Clébert described the district of Saint-Paul as a "surrealist worksite, the image of a kind of postwar social fantastic in the heart of the Cité."[79] The Marais was also emblematic of the bounty of reconstruction. The Carreau du Temple was a garment emporium jammed with merchants and their clients. The open-air Sunday bazaars and the Marché des Enfants-Rouges were among the city's liveliest street displays, attracting streams of shoppers and onlookers.

Although it might have attracted adventurous locals, the Marais of the 1950s was certainly not the tourist destination it would eventually become. It was a working-class and petit-bourgeois domain. But it was also rotting. A litany of horrors spilled from official typewriters about the dreadful conditions despoiling the capital's historic jewel. By the 1940s the notorious and controversial fourteen hectares of *îlot insalubre* 16 was decreed a disaster: a densely packed, overbuilt slum falling into complete ruin. Its official boundaries were the rue François-Miron, the rue Saint-Antoine, the rue Saint-Paul, the quai des Célestins, the quai de l'Hôtel de Ville, the rue de Brosse, and the place Saint-Gervais. It comprised 403 buildings and a resident population of 10,480. The official statistics on density were meant to be mind-boggling: planning documents claimed that on some streets they rose to 1,800 to 2,000 individuals per square hectare, while the average for Paris was around 300. The official discourse fixated on the crumbling in-

FIGURE 33. 25 rue Saint Paul in the Marais, December 1942. © COLL. PAVILLON DE L'ARSENAL, CLICHÉ DUVP

frastructure and its exploitation by an uncaring population that had sunk into depravity. The crumbling stock of edifices had long been partitioned into cheap lodgings. Illegal squatter workshops found refuge in the decaying remains of once elegant Renaissance townhouses. Hodgepodge sheds and ateliers were squeezed into the maze of dismal courtyards and dead-end alleys with no thought given to issues of hygiene and safety. Building collapses and fires occurred with frightening regularity. Few of the buildings had running water, heat, or lavatories. The lack of facilities kept the neighborhood's few public baths well frequented. The rate of tuberculosis was double that of the capital as a whole. The health and sanitary conditions of îlot 16 were among the worst in Paris, and it was killing off the French people—more than enough justification for demolition. At the 1943 Salon des Urbanistes, René Mestais opened his presentation on the study of the *taudis* (slums) completed by the Services de topographie et d'urbanisme with a commentary on the dire consequences for France of îlot 16:

> Here you are in îlot insalubre no. 16. You enter into this slum. There is no place for a bed. There's nothing more than a pallet up against a wall. It is in thousands of places similar to this that the uprooted and itinerant of the French provinces come to fail. En masse, the Lorrains, Vosgiens, Savoyards, Auvergnats, Bretons, Limousins, Berrichons, and Normands, rich in good health, have come here to die over the last two centuries, stricken by one of four social curses: tuberculosis, alcoholism, syphilis, cancer. Fifty-two of every hundred deaths are attributed to [these diseases]. We are grief stricken by the sad spectacle of these hovels where so many men have passed away without ever knowing what it was to live.[80]

Mestais mentioned nothing about the impact of these conditions on foreign immigrants. The implication was that the French nation itself was systematically being destroyed by a ghastly urban environment that swallowed up all hope.

The Marais was in such a shocking state of deterioration that pulling everything down appeared the only sensible solution. Two different projects were considered by the city's planning office during the 1930s, both of them inspired by modernist proclivities for a radical clearing out of the detritus of disease and dereliction. The first, in 1936, recommended the complete demolition of the area and the construction of public-housing estates, with open squares around the most important monuments. The second, in 1939, was still based on the slum-clearance and modernist principles of Le Corbusier but respected more of the traditional urban fabric and reoriented the renovated infrastructure toward the Seine. The departmental prefecture even considered using the area cleared out along the river for a vast administrative building adjacent to the Hôtel de Ville. In 1941 yet another plan anticipated knocking down the entire area in favor of a series of vast gardens. The preservationists immediately opened fire against these planned assaults. Both the Ligue urbaine et rurale and the Commission du vieux Paris (the two most powerful protectionist organizations in the city) argued that if restored to its Renaissance glory, the Marais could resurface as one of the city's most revered historic areas. They demanded the repair and conservation of the district in its authentic form, with its labyrinth of streets, courtyards, and ancient buildings. The preservationists had just lost the battle to save the old Saint-Lazare prison on the rue du Faubourg Saint-Denis, which they had planned to refurbish as a museum to the French Revolution; now they were adamant about preventing the annihilation of the Marais. It became a cause célèbre, a symbol of resistance against wiping out the historic beauty of Paris. They were joined in the struggle by a cavalcade of urbanistic luminaries, from Albert Laprade, Georges Pillement, and Robert Auzelle to Marcel Raval, Robert Danis, Auguste Perret, Marcel Poëte, and Louis Chevalier.

In 1939 Auzelle and Georges Sébille, on their own initiative, proposed an alternative vision for îlot 16 that cleared out all the buildup and *bâtiments parasitaires* while conserving the ancient streets and opening up the traditional public courtyards and squares of the neighborhood. It was an application of the humanist design principles that Auzelle was perfecting in Gaston Bardet's Atelier supérieur d'urbanisme appliqué at the Institut d'urbanisme (see chapter 4). The proposal was a compromise between the modernists' ideal of zealously sanitizing the entire area and the preservationists' dogmatic defense of historic buildings. The goal instead was to harmonize the îlot as a contiguous complex. Above all, the particularities of the landscape were to be respected. Regardless of the political passions that fueled this debate, Auzelle's humanist perspective would be called upon time and again by all sides as the most viable solution. The historian and arch-preservationist Georges Pillement, for example, even included Auzelle's full project in his *Destruction de Paris* (1941) as the best example of an alternative urbanism.[81] Auzelle's urban theory was also prominently featured in the landmark publication *Destinée de Paris* (1943), much of which was dedicated to saving the Marais.

In September 1941 Vichy set out the conditions and timetable for expropriation with indemnities in the *îlots insalubres* of the central districts. Evictions and demolitions picked up speed. Armed force would be applied if the neighborhood's population opposed expulsion. The social, and indeed racial, engineering could not have been more blatant. The small-scale businesses that had grown like meddlesome weeds in the manicured French gardens of this former Renaissance enclave would be ripped out. This was a direct attack on the working classes—the wretched slum dwellers defined in official discourse—who inhabited the area. Even more certainly, the notorious 1942 roundup and deportation east to the death camps was the most efficient way to remove the Jewish laboring community and rid the villainous slum of "disease." A Bureau d'aménagement des îlots insalubres was created especially to carry out the crackdown in îlot 16, where 143 buildings were torn down.[82] Ridding the Marais of its fetid rookeries along with its poor Jewish community and restoring its Renaissance grandeur was perfectly in keeping with Vichy perspectives on the city. From a lair of poor and foreigners, the district would become the realm of "artists and intellectuals."[83]

The ambition was to reinvent the Marais as it looked in the seventeenth century under the Turgot Plan, at the height of its aristocratic standing. The task was given to three architects: Albert Laprade and Michel Roux-Spitz, both known for their high-quality classic designs, and Robert Danis, chief architect for historic monuments in France. As eventually outlined by the prefect of the Seine, Guy Périer de Féral, in a 1944 special issue of *L'Architecture française*,[84] the renovation plan for the Marais actually looked much like that proposed by Auzelle in that it envisaged demolishing much of the decrepit building stock while retaining the most important monuments and the basic substructure of streets and public places. To create a more hygienic environment of light and air, the magnificent Renaissance gardens of the aristocratic hotels would be reconstituted and made public. In yet another reference to the past, Robert Danis imagined something of an historic garden city, with low buildings surrounded by green spaces. The verdicts on demolition or reconstruction of historic structures would be rendered on a case-by-case basis. But the most significant, such as the Hôtel de Sens and the Hôtel d'Aumont, were to be restored. Although the plan envisioned some widening of the streets along the periphery, the interior of the îlot would be respected.

Housing would be reserved for "members of the Institut [de France] and ... intellectuals in general, as well as ... writers and artists. All trade and all industry should be prohibited." Although a few artisan workshops and food emporiums would be tolerated, the only commerce that would be truly welcomed was antique shops and bookstores. The only novel elements to be introduced in the district also accorded well with Vichy's reformist sensibilities: a sports stadium on the rue St. Paul and a green belt along the quai de l'Hôtel de Ville.

There was more going on here than just battles over legacy buildings and monuments in the Marais. Throughout the 1930s and 1940s preservation legislation in Paris had been reinforced piece by piece. By 1933, 157 historic structures in the central districts were classified as protected.[85] Thirty-four of the most historic buildings in the Marais were added to the two already classified under the 1913 preservation law, even though many of them were in deplorable condition. Vichy's 1943 Law on Urbanism further strengthened preservation by establishing a protective perimeter within 1,640 feet (five hundred meters) of monuments, archaeological sites, and important public buildings. Clearly, progress had been made. Yet the debate about design and planning could not have appeared more convoluted, more driven by competing agendas. These seemingly disparate threads can be drawn together by means of the poetic humanist imaginary. The mental picture of preservation was evolving toward a more integrated understanding of îlot and quartier shared by midcentury urban observers. A vision of the "historic district" was being calibrated as a key ingredient in the cultural imagination of Paris. It involved ambience and charm as much as it did any one individual building worth saving. The vocabulary of understanding was explicit. In 1941, for example, preservationists addressed a petition directly to Marshal Pétain that called for saving "the *poetic* and medieval atmosphere" (emphasis added) of the Saint-Gervais neighborhood.[86] Urban renewal required sensitivity toward the picturesque qualities associated with the city's enchanted landscape. The approach increasingly conceived of urban space as a historicist stage set on which the drama of urban life unfolded.

Élie Debidour, of the Commission du vieux Paris and the city's general inspector for the Services de protection historique et esthétique de Paris, addressed the reformist Musée Social in 1943 regarding his opposition to the proposed demolition of the "tubercular district" of the Marais: "It is undeniable that a great part of the picturesque and interest in the Marais stems from its commercial animation. What makes its life so curious, so amusing, is the activity, the mélange of classes, the best artisanal features." In a slap to Vichy's version of a past filled with Renaissance treasures, and pointing to the Saint-Gervais neighborhood in particular, Debidour argued that "it would be imprudent to implement an exaggerated *passéiste* zoning that assaulted life in the name of history." A taste for the past, he warned, "can risk unjustifiable sacrifices and fall into the artificial."[87] In *Destinée de Paris*, Pillement wrote that "what is regrettable in the Marais is not the destruction of such-and-such edifice, however irreplaceable, but the disappearance of the *atmosphere* that makes Paris charming and still survives in certain neighborhoods that evoke the most glorious, the darkest, the most tragic and the happiest episodes in our history" (emphasis added).[88] One cannot help but call to mind Arletty's plaintive cry of "Atmosphere! atmosphere!" on the bridge over the canal Saint-Martin in Marcel Carné's *Hôtel du Nord*. The preservationist camp had leapt from the defense of historic monuments to the evocation of an invented urban ambience, emotional in content. It was, Pillement argued, these *îlots pittoresques* that the state and the city should protect rather than demolish.

In 1943 the process of hounding the population out of the neighborhood and tearing down buildings was stopped. Without alternative housing for the displaced, and facing bombardment and the stringencies of war, Vichy's urban renewal ground to a halt. By the Liberation, the city was left with an area teetering on the edge of physical collapse. The heat of the immediate postwar purges and retribution caused Vichy's Renaissance dreams for the Marais to be thrown aside, at least rhetorically. In an ironic reversal of Vichy policy, the buildings expropriated during the occupation were used in 1945 to house prisoners and deportees returning from Germany and the camps. The continued lack of resources left the Marais in limbo for years after the war, as it did all of the *îlots insalubres* in the city center. Prefect Roger Verlomme argued, in the first postwar assessment of the situation, that a middle ground had to be found somewhere between the aggressive modernist plans for complete clearance and the preservation opposition to any demolition whatsoever. He called for a "complex and delicate balance between aesthetics and hygiene" in considering the area's future. Innovative modern planning techniques would go hand in hand with safeguarding the area's picturesque qualities.[89]

As a model of what could be done, Michel Roux-Spitz offered an architectural motif consistent with the distinctive visual imagery associated with the capital, the so-called City of Paris design. It was presented in the pages of *L'Architecture française* and attempted to introduce a vernacular modernism usable for construction in the historic districts. Along with Auzelle and Sébille, Roux-Spitz had been instrumental in formulating the îlot as the basis of urban composition. The City of Paris style was meant to be built within this spatial context. Based on a sober classicism, traditional materials, and simple facades, the buildings would harmonize with the *vieux quartier*.[90] Offered at a reasonable price, the orthogonal stands of discrete three- and four-story row houses of different sizes abutted the street. The interior courtyards and alleyways that had made for such a warren of dereliction were prohibited, to be replaced by gardens and green space. Lastly, strict regulation would protect the newly invented historic district and educate the popular classes about aesthetic values. The designs avoided "tasteless" decoration, prohibited the balconies that had served as stashes for laundry lines and coal bins, and offered sensible interiors with modern kitchens and bathrooms where families could gather and live decently.

But even though the plans were based on the humanist imaginary of îlot and renovation and called for repairing the best of the housing stock in the Marais, it was still assumed that less than half the population would continue to live there. The rest would be removed to the modern housing projects planned for the suburbs. In *Les Parisiens* (1967), even the historian Louis Chevalier refused to see the Marais as a legitimate working-class social unit or quartier: "The Marais represented an entity in the originality of its built environment, but not in human terms." It was incontestably an authentic *pays parisien* until the end of the nineteenth century but had since fallen into disgrace. Despite its monuments and historic landscape, despite the "hallucinating" survival of the area's ancient pathways, history had not looked kindly on the Marais, and few Parisians other than the preservationists concerned themselves with it.[91] And for them, the poor were expendable in the effort to "save" the neighborhood. As an example, socialist Henri Vergnolle, president of the municipal council in 1946–47, suggested moving all of the city's most important historic monuments and buildings into one of the old districts, for example the Saint-Gervais district in the Marais, where they would constitute a *quartier des vieilles pierres* (neighborhood of ruins), a sort of *carnavalet de plein air* (outdoor museum). This monumental handing over of one of the *îlot insalubre* to the preservationists would allow the rest of the central city to be redeveloped.[92] Although the Marais was among the city's most venerable working-class districts, it could be sacrificed. It was an irony born of humanist compromise. The communists on the municipal council remained adamantly opposed to the plans for the neighborhood as yet another attempt to conquer working-class terrain and banish its inhabitants to the outskirts. The indemnities offered to the dispossessed became a hotly contested political issue. The PCF accused the police of terrorizing families in îlot 16 by periodically rounding them up at the police commissariat and pressuring them to leave the miserable lodgings they inhabited. But the die had been cast.

The municipal council eventually approved the idea of a "Cité internationale des arts" for îlot 16 that would attract foreign investment and act as a sort of modern Medici villa for Paris. In 1952, as part of the ongoing negotiations with the municipal council, André Prothin, the state's Directeur général de l'aménagement du territoire, offered a zoning plan that would extend the "university zone" in the 5th arrondissement across the Seine into the Marais. It was not a question of purging all of the artisan and commercial activity, Prothin argued, "but of freeing up the old *hôtels* of those activities that can be advantageously replaced by libraries, cultural, and study centers. They would guarantee the conservation of the buildings and provide a dignified framework for the growth of the University of Paris." Once the slums were cleared out, new housing would be offered to professors and students. To safeguard the neighborhood's picturesque streets and public spaces, only artisans offering high-class goods, antique dealers, interior decorators, high-fashion boutiques, and bookstores would be welcomed. The Marais would be cleared of automobile traffic and reoriented toward the banks of the Seine and the Latin Quarter. The once distinguished district would emerge from its isolation and come to life as a vital part of the larger urban fabric. This kind of planning "would allow Paris to conserve and put to good use one of its oldest and most evocative neighborhoods, one that lovers of France have not been able to fully appreciate because of what currently exists there."[93] The reference to tourism was unequivocal.

The task of designing the restoration for îlot 16 remained largely in the hands of Albert Laprade through the 1950s and early 1960s. Trained at the École des beaux-arts, Laprade remained loyal to French architectural and urbanistic proclivities rather than to the modernism offered by CIAM. He had been involved in the debates over the Marais since well before the war. He and the architect Jean-Charles Moreux had originally offered their own counterdesigns for the district in the pages of *L'Illustration* in 1938 and 1941, including an early call for *façadisme*, the inspired suggestion that buildings might be destroyed if their facades were saved. A practitioner of humanist urbanism, Laprade argued that "reconquering" Paris was achievable without wiping out the historical fabric. The most difficult and urgent task in Paris was to "liberate the îlot" by clearing out the detritus and showcasing the original urban typography. Like Auzelle, he argued for renovation, for planting trees, for new construction that harmonized with existing infrastructure. In a 1957 article entitled "Aménagement des quartiers historiques,"[94] Laprade offered two examples of this design approach for îlot 16, both of which evidenced the mounting ironies of poetic humanist discourse by the end of the decade. Although the choices offered effectively saved the Marais from wholesale demolition, they were far less about the beauty, mystery, and insight found among *le peuple* and far more about reifying the built environment. It was a form of historicist remembering that favored social elitism and a touristic gaze. The first example was the site of the old cemetery of Saint-Gervais, where many of the master artisans of the Middle Ages and Renaissance lay. The area was cleared of the working-class squatter structures that had been accumulating over the tombs since the early nineteenth century. Under Laprade's guidance the space was transformed into an urban garden, with the renovated buildings around it enjoying the view and "complete calm." In the second example, the dilapidated buildings surrounding Saint-Gervais Church were demolished to make way for a corner garden and children's crèche. The aesthetic purpose, however, was to open up the view of the church's flying buttresses and peaked roofline.

From these battles over *îlot insalubre* 16 came a new idealization of the historic district. This vision was not intrinsic to the Marais, but was the product of a broad-based, multifaceted public dialog and conscious visual invention. The 1961 Festival of the Marais that opened the district's renowned aristocratic townhouses for public viewing attracted large crowds and mobilized Parisians into believing the district was worth saving. The CDU carried out a massive statistical, architectural, and topographic study of the Marais in 1961 and 1962, on the basis of which its future would be designed.[95] The architectural inventory resulted in a listing of 56 buildings of "very great quality," 121 buildings listed as historic monuments, and 526 buildings deemed of "very great interest" worthy of protection. In addition, more than 1,000 structures belonged to a category of "buildings of accompaniment or atmosphere" that were vital to the district's perceived environment, scale, and harmony. Buildings and gardens were renovated, facades cleaned, courtyards and sinuous streets cleared. Various cultural institutions set up headquarters in the 102 landmarked palaces and townhouses in the Marais, helped by their purchase and restoration by the city of Paris.

In 1962 a new national preservation law, christened the Malraux Law, permitted the registering of entire districts as protected landmarks, or *secteurs sauvegardés*. They were defined as areas or complexes of buildings whose preservation was desirable for either historic or aesthetic reasons. The Marais was classified as a *secteur sauvegardé* in 1964, the first such area in Paris and the largest in France. The Malraux Law defined the Marais in terms not only of its architectural beauty, but also of its ambience and tone, its shabby quaintness. It reemerged as a space of historicism and ultimately of middle-class tourism. The "right to the city" was grossly curtailed and became more and more an elitist prerogative. The district was produced as an architectural and atmospheric museum, a visual fantasyland. The more Paris changed under the impact of modern urban planning, the more the Marais and neighborhoods like it were depicted and defended as staying the same. The value and readability of public space was associated with wandering through a visual landscape caught in a moment of time. This imaginary was static and rigidly conformist. The process of reification constructed an acceptable past and cut entities off from their own history. The *peuple* and their magical place making were banished from these sacred precincts. The October 1956 inauguration of the Memorial to the Unknown Jewish Martyr on the rue Geoffroy l'Asnier in which ashes from the death camps and the Warsaw ghetto were entombed, was one of the few, if ironic, attempts to reclaim the neighborhood's complicated and darker memories. On the whole, however, the district gained an invented self-consciousness that in fact hollowed out the space of its public life and veiled the complexities of meaning written in its landscape. The Marais's preservation and abstraction could then be reiterated for all of the historic central districts bordering the Seine to create a dramatic historicist stage set deeply associated with Paris as a touristic imaginary.

CONCLUSION

Constructing the Paris of Tomorrow

In 1964 the architect Noël Boutet de Monvel published his *Les Demains de Paris*, a study of the capital's state of affairs financed by the Délégation général au district de la région de Paris. It began with the question of whether Paris was at a crossroads. Paris, he said, was "a living organism that energized the entire country." But underneath this appearance of vitality were signs of mortal illness that only a kind of medical resuscitation could reverse. "If," he warned, "we don't take steps now to ensure the survival and prosperity of this beautiful city . . . in thirty years, we will see a very rapid decline."[1] Boutet de Monvel's warning was part of a long lineage of dire predictions about the capital's imminent demise. His was a complete condemnation of the politically potent localism, the fragmented arrondissements, the quartiers and îlots that constituted Paris in the 1950s. The text was a clarion call for the reassertion of state power and authority. The capital was entering a new era under the Fifth Republic and the presidency of Charles de Gaulle.

Despite Boutet's assertions about dire ailment and dismal failure, a great deal of progress had already been made toward turning Paris into the symbol of a vigorous French nation. A series of grand-scale modernist redevelopment projects and monumental trophy buildings was radically reshaping the notion of urban place. Their uncompromising, vanguard designs made no concessions to the scale and particularities of the historic city. The first phase of the business complex at La Défense was under way, with a projected completion date of 1973. "The tourist of 1973," Boutet predicted, "will be able to stand in the courtyard of the Louvre and look

FIGURE 34. President Charles de Gaulle and Pierre Sudreau (on his right) visiting the exhibit "Demain . . . Paris" Exposition at the Grand Palais, before the scale model of the 15th arrondissement, April 17, 1961. © KEYSTONE-FRANCE

out through the arches of the Carousel and the Étoile to the heights of La Défense and a 250-meter high tower" designed by Bernard Zehrfuss that would complete the sight line. Just next to La Défense, at Nanterre, Le Corbusier was working on designs for a cultural complex that would include a museum, a new music conservatory, and an architecture school. The old railroad yards at Maine-Montparnasse were being transformed into a business center and commercial mall with a 185-meter high tower, to be completed by 1969. The UNESCO building, designed by Bernard Zehrfuss, Marcel Breuer, and Pier Nervi and located on the place de Fontenoy, was inaugurated in 1958 as a symbol of the city's role in international affairs, as was the NATO command center at the porte Dauphine. The headquarters of state media conglomerate ORTF, or the Maison de la Radio, was completed by 1963 by the French architect Henry Bernard in high-modernist idiom on the quai de Passy. Across the river at the Front de Seine, Raymond Lopez and Michel Holley were designing a project for a "true capital district" centered on 20 thirty-story towers (eventually cut back to 15 towers) and a six-hectare raised platform *dalle* that cascaded down five levels. For the redevelopment of Les Halles, also on the drawing board, the two imagined a colossal modernist "world trade complex" with a soaring office tower alongside Saint-Eustache Church. It was one of many futuristic visions for the old "guts" of Paris. All of these projects were emphatically internationalist in style. They were presented with enormous fanfare at the "Demain . . . Paris" Exposition organized by the Ministère de la construction at the Grand Palais in 1961. Theatrics and melodramatic display had shifted from *le peuple* to glamorous architecture. High-modernist designs were triumphs of technocratic planning, an expression of the instrumentality of state power and late twentieth-century capitalism. They were forms of political communication and propagandistic illusions of power. De Gaulle was remaking Paris into the de facto capital of Europe.

In 1961 de Gaulle appointed Paul Delouvrier as the head of the new far-flung district of Paris. Delouvrier's investiture heralded a radically new climate of regional planning. A strategic plan laid out a vast network of *grand ensemble* public housing projects, suburban "new towns," highways, and regional express trains. The entire emphasis in planning discourse shifted away from the venerated *zone cristalisée* of the historical districts to a far-reaching vision of the metropolitan region. Far from embracing the decentralization policy that threatened the lifeblood of the capital, Delouvrier anticipated the redistribution of a growing population, along with their housing and jobs, away from the central city and into an economically robust Île-de-France. Grand-scale modernism would go hand in hand with a new prosperity. Rather than a jumble of fragmented pieces, urban topography was now imagined as a broad, integrated, and rationalized *ensemble*. The state's understanding of urbanism was progressively configured around specific definitions of habitat norms, quantitative gauges of well-being, predictions about traffic flow, and the application of rational master-planning techniques. Data processing and a mountain of documents evidenced conditions and statistically measured patterns of activities and land use. These became the standard measures of quality of life in French cities and provided the rationale for an ongoing process of reform and regulation. This was an engineering-based systems approach in which planning was seen as a continuous process of control and monitoring. The spatial scale was monumental.

Private life was reified, social life continually supervised. The image of Paris began to depend less on what local residents produced than on what visitors consumed at the various sites developed for their pleasure. The ideal of the city's enchantment, its intimate scale, and its spatiality became fixed, stagnant concepts. Carefully selected historical imagery obscured existing social distinctions and the memory of recent political struggles while paving the way for a new kind of antidemocratic politics. Display began to eclipse debate as a staple of the public sphere. This had little to do with the loose urban textures, the jumble of neighborhoods and fluid sociability, once associated with public space. Instead, citywide events encouraged Parisians and tourists alike to participate in the public life of the city as an undifferentiated crowd and as consumers of a shared commercial culture.

However, from the late 1940s through the end of the 1950s, the city was the terrain of poetic humanism. It emerged as a cohesive intellectual ethos that attempted to mediate the transformation of the *trente glorieuses*. As a movement, it was powerful, wide-ranging, and porous. Concentrating on poetic humanism as a midcentury discourse provides the opportunity to rethink twentieth-century chronologies. It breaks down the boundary of 1945 as the traditional opening onto a distinctly new era. The origins of poetic humanism clearly lay in the prewar years. It was heavily influenced by the experience of war, and especially by the Resistance and Liberation, which it claimed as its own. It is my hope that this volume adds to a growing body of scholarship that reconceptualizes the mid-twentieth century as a significant period in its own right. Particularly in the case of Paris, focusing on humanism as a counterdiscourse moves us away from treatments of midcentury urban culture and spatiality as only a shadow of their former selves, as empty, as mesmerized and emaciated by capitalism's bewitching spell. It also turns away from notions of urban planning as feeble or defeated.

Instead, what we find is a rich public sphere, made even more dramatic by visual media. It was multiform, emotive, composed of a variety of publics and counterpublics. In no way was the public sphere politically and socially neutralized by media spectacle or commodified private ideals. The postwar reconstruction years were a transformative moment, a *theatrum mundi*. The streets overflowed with activity. Traditional uses of public space resurfaced alongside new forms of civic life. Street fairs, student processions, the fête de l'humanité, contended with endless commemoration ceremonies, with television and radio shows broadcast live as well as with riots, violent protests, and political marches. The phantasmagoria of the city's public atmosphere continued unabated and took on new, mediatized forms. There was never really a single, defined moment at which Paris turned into pure spectacle. Its public sphere has always been punctuated by multiple meanings, layers of action and counteraction, and creative materialization of urban life. Even as the city became a carefully controlled touristic dream in the 1960s, strikes and protests continued, culminating in the 1968 revolt. Entitlement to public space was transmittable and invigorating. Various social groups were successful in appropriating and adding to the endless vocabulary of image manipulation as effective civic engagement. These practices dramatized authentic conditions, real hopes, and, during the late 1940s and 1950s, the extraordinary collective power of liberation and postwar renewal.

In humanist discourse, Paris was imagined as a decidedly populist, working-class place. This idealization of the proletariat was immensely powerful, an expressive salve for the wounds that had torn France apart during the war and occupation. The place of action for this heroic *peuple* was the public spaces of the city. Space was imagined as decentered, spreading across the landscape in a jigsaw puzzle of localized places and lived experience. Rather than adhering to the systemic and centralizing practices of modern urbanism, the city broke apart. It became "humanized" and sensual, encrusted with the social practices that took place there. In humanist discourse, the neighborhood was a fragmented, autonomous zone where the spirit was free from centralizing control. It was a place of whimsy that created a mutable, fluid spatiality and temporality, what Michel de Certeau referred to as "spatial stories"—the everyday stories of moving through the city. For de Certeau, to practice space is to repeat the joyful activity of childhood and "a way of moving into something different."[2] Folk festival and celebration were noncompliant and subversive. Yet in this militant pedestrianism, tradition was evoked as much as change. The uses of the past were magnified and heightened, given mythic form. The urban fragments and objects that typify memory of place gained significance in the quotidian atmosphere of the everyday. Memory was an anchor in an environment of wrenching transformation.

Lastly, the destruction of the Second World War itself provoked a wide-ranging debate about the nature of the modern city, how it should be reformed and reconstructed, and what forms public space should take. It gave urban planning the quality of moral redemption. The charismatic high modernism offered by Le Corbusier and CIAM constituted the central referent in this discourse. Yet the production of urban space is always a battlefield of contending forces. The issue of city form is one of contradictions and spatial dissonance. The spaces of the city are always malleable. Its meanings are multiform and capable of being changed by the force of social and political events. In fact, Paris seethed in a long history of urbanistic visions and fantasies. In the field of struggle over the spaces of the city, counterdiscourses upset the pretense of dominant thinking and opened up perceptions.

As a counternarrative, the French conceived of the city as a geographic object—that is, they believed the basic unit of urban collective life had a spatial dimension. Even as recently as 1996, for example, the ethnologist Marc Augé argued that its village quality made Paris a place, or an agglomeration of places: "I call a 'place,'" he elucidated, "a space where individual and collective identities, as well as the relationship between people and the history they share, are so perceptible that anyone could read or decipher them." Augé went on to argue this orientation from an ethnographic point of view: the village is an ideal place for an ethnographer because "tradition is so deeply rooted that each and every individual plays his or her own part."[3] The robustness and durability of this thread of thinking about the way the French fashioned cities is striking. And it is certainly at odds with the utopian high modernism normally associated with postwar urban development. In general, then, the French perspective on urbanism was influenced not only by Haussmann and the beaux-arts tradition, but by social municipalism and the garden-city movement and by French interpretations of modernist architecture and design as much as by CIAM and American-style planning techniques. Urban observers and theorists drew on a rich theoretical and interpretive heritage. Paris was a monumental beacon of modernity, but also an assemblage of time-honored neighborhood-villages. The city's spatiality was imagined, invented, and produced by a multiplicity of actors and discourses, and poetic humanism was one of the most important of them. The idea that different aesthetics could be brought together without annihilating one another, and that such juxtaposition could create a new urban realm, offered an alternative ideal of modernity. It is also my hope, then, that this book adds to the scholarship on the varieties of modernism that traversed the twentieth century and the extraordinary richness of these visions.

By the late 1950s the great moment of poetic humanism was over. In many ways two films bookend this transitional era of extraordinary complexity in the city's public life and spaces: Marcel Carné's *Les Enfants du paradis* in 1944 and Pierre Prévert and Marcel Duchamps's *Paris la belle* in 1959. In *Paris la belle*, we meet the actress Arletty once again, this time reminiscing in her sultry voice about the streets and neighborhoods she once knew. Duchamps's black-and-white montages from the original 1928 version of the film are superimposed over charming scenes of Paris in the 1950s. The 1959 film was a demonstration of the humanist metamorphosis into nostalgia. Gone are the edgy debates about the nature of modernity and the *trente glorieuses*; gone are the social clashes that plunged the city into strikes and protests; gone are the magical urbanism and the subversive twists and turns of *la fête* and its political meaning. Instead, a dreamy reminiscence of life in simpler times pervades the visual imagery. A seamless narrative materializes on the screen: an eternal vision of place that came to represent the City of Light in the mid-twentieth century. Picturesque depictions of the city's street life, romanticized images of its space and culture invaded the imagination. Paris was a picture book of the past. The sighs of longing were audible.

Introduction

1. From Mario Preoth, *Le Boulevard du crime* (Paris: Balitout-Questroy, 1872).

2. Hugo Lacroix, "Notre paradis national," in *Mots de passe, 1945-1985: Petit abécédaire des modes de vie*, ed. Pascal Ory (Paris: Autrement, 1985), 103.

3. Jürgen Habermas, *The Structural Transformation of the Public Sphere: An Inquiry into a Category of Bourgeois Society*, trans. Thomas Burger (Cambridge, MA: MIT Press, 1991), 9.

4. See T. J. Clark's classic *The Painting of Modern Life* (Princeton, NJ: Princeton University Press, 1984); see also David Harvey, *Paris: Capital of Modernity* (New York: Routledge, 2003), and Vanessa Schwartz, *Spectacular Realities: Early Mass Culture in Fin-de-Siècle Paris* (Berkeley: University of California Press, 1998).

5. Recent urban histories of Paris are Patrice Higonnet, *Paris: Capital of the World* (Cambridge, MA: Belknap Press of Harvard University Press, 2002); Colin Jones, *Paris: Biography of a City* (New York: Viking, 2004); Pierre Pinon, *Paris: Biographie d'une capitale* (Paris: Hazan, 1999); and Bernard Marchand, *Paris: Histoire d'une ville* (Paris: Seuil, 1993).

6. The classic study of this period remains Jean Fourastié, *Les Trente glorieuses ou la révolution française, 1945-1975* (Paris: Fayard, 1979).

7. *Les Lettres françaises*, March 1-7, 1956.

8. See Henri Lefebvre, *The Production of Space*, trans. D. Nicholson-Smith (Oxford: Blackwell, 1991); David Harvey, *Spaces of Capital* (New York: Routledge, 2001); and Harvey, *Spaces of Hope* (Berkeley: University of California Press, 2000). Good recent overviews of the dynamics of "public space" vocabulary are given in Setha Low and Neil Smith, eds., *The Politics of Public Space* (New York: Routledge, 2005), and Don Mitchell, *The Right to the City: Social Justice and the Fight for Public Space* (New York: Guilford Press, 2003). See also Sharon Zukin, *The Culture of Cities* (London: Blackwell, 1996).

9. This point is made in Andrew Light and Jonathan M. Smith, eds., *The Production of Public Space* (Lanham, MD: Rowman & Littlefield, 1998), 2-3. See also Ken Hirschkop, *Mikhail Bakhtin: An Aesthetic for Democracy* (Oxford: Oxford University Press, 1999).

10. Michel Foucault, "Of Other Spaces (1967): Heterotopias," originally published as "Des espaces autres," *Architecture/Mouvement/Continuité* (October 1984): 46-49.

11. Richard Sennett, *The Fall of Public Man: On the Social Psychology of Capitalism* (New York: Vintage, 1978), 264.

12. Habermas, *Structural Transformation*, 159.

13. Guy Debord, *The Society of the Spectacle*, trans. Donald Nicholson-Smith (New York: Zone Books, 1994), 121.

14. Kristin Ross, *Fast Cars, Clean Bodies: Decolonization and the Reordering of French Culture* (Cambridge, MA: MIT Press, 1996), 4. See also David Harvey, *The Condition of Postmodernity: An Enquiry into the Origins of Cultural Change* (Cambridge, MA: Basil Blackwell, 1989).

15. This definition is given by Nancy Fraser, the most vocal proponent of the postmodern conception of the public sphere, in "Politics, Culture, and the Public Sphere," in *Social Postmodernism: Beyond Identity Politics*, ed. Linda Nicholson and Steven Seidman (Cambridge: Cambridge University Press, 1995), 291. A good entry into this literature is Nick Crossley and John Michael Roberts, eds., *After Habermas: New Perspectives on the Public Sphere* (Oxford and Malden, MA: Blackwell, 2004). See also Mike Hill and Warren Montag, eds., *Masses, Classes, and the Public Sphere* (London and New York: Verso, 2000). Also very useful is Robert Asen and Daniel C. Brouwer, eds., *Counterpublics and the State* (Albany: State University of New York Press, 2001).

16. Lacroix, "Notre paradis national," 103.

17. Particularly useful to this argument is Dilip Parameshwar Gaonkar, ed., *Alternative Modernities* (Durham, NC: Duke University Press, 2001). See also Sarah Williams Goldenhagen and Réjean Legault, eds., *Anxious Modernisms: Experimentation in Postwar Architectural Culture* (Montréal: Canadian Center for Architecture; Cambridge, MA: MIT Press, 2000).

18. Lefebvre, *Production of Space*, 31–33.

19. Walter Benjamin, *The Arcades Project*, trans. Howard Eiland and Kevin McLaughlin (Cambridge, MA: Belknap Press of Harvard University Press, 2002), 421, 23.

20. Michel de Certeau, *The Practice of Everyday Life*, trans. Steven Rendall (Berkeley: University of California Press, 1984), 97–100.

21. On the role of historical memory in contemporary France, see Pierre Nora, "Between Memory and History: Les Lieux de Mémoire," *Representations* 26 (Spring 1989): 17–24. His work has also been translated as *Realms of Memory: The Construction of the French Past*, ed. Pierre Nora and Lawrence D. Kritzman, trans. Arthur Goldhammer (New York: Columbia University Press, 1996).

22. Andreas Huyssen, *Present Pasts: Urban Palimpsests and the Politics of Memory* (Stanford, CA: Stanford University Press, 2003), 7.

23. Terry Eagleton, foreword to Kristin Ross, *The Emergence of Social Space: Rimbaud and the Paris Commune* (Minneapolis: University of Minnesota Press, 1988), x.

24. On the scenographic dimension of urban space, see Isaac Joseph, ed., *Prendre place: Espace public et culture dramatique* (Paris: Recherches, 1995), especially the series of articles grouped under the heading "La Règle du visible." On civic life and urban space, see Richard Sennett, *The Conscience of the Eye: The Design and Social Life of Cities* (New York: Norton, 1990).

25. Among others, see Susan Sontag, *On Photography* (New York: Picador, 2001), and Roland Barthes, *Camera lucida: Reflections on Photography* (New York: Hill and Wang, 1982).

26. See Michael E. Gardiner, "Wild Publics and Grotesque Symposiums: Habermas and Bakhtin on Dialogue, Everyday Life and the Public Sphere," in Crossley and Roberts, *After Habermas*, 28–48.

Chapter One

1. Léon-Paul Fargue, *La Flânerie à Paris* (Paris: Commissariat général au Tourisme, 1946), n.p.

2. Ibid.

3. Olivier Merlin, *Une belle époque, 1945–1950* (Paris: Olivier Orban, 1986), 12.

4. Claude Aveline, *Dans Paris retrouvé* (Paris: Émile-Paul Frères, 1945), 18. On the historic development of Paris and its identifiable spaces and landscape, see the interesting cartographic history by Jean-Robert Pitte, *Paris: Histoire d'une ville* (Paris: Hachette, 1993).

5. There are a myriad of histories and memoirs of Paris under the Nazi occupation. In English, David Pryce-Jones, *Paris in the Third Reich: A History of the German Occupation, 1940–1944* (New York: Holt, Rinehart & Winston, 1981); Gilles Perrault and Pierre Azema, *Paris under the Occupation*, trans. Allison Carter and Maximilian Vos (New York: Vendome Press, 1989). The classic studies in French are Henri Michel, *Paris allemand* (Paris: Albin Michel, 1981), and Hervé Le Boterf, *La Vie parisienne sous l'occupation*, 2 vols. (Paris: France-Empire, 1975).

6. Cited in Christine Levisse-Touzé, "Le Rôle particulier de Paris pendant la seconde guerre mondiale," in *La Résistance et les français: Villes, centres et logiques de décisions*, Actes du Colloque international, ed. Bette Husser and Gabrielle Drigeard Desgarnier (Cachan: Institut d'histoire du temps présent, 1995), 198.

7. The destruction caused by the German invasion in May–June 1940 surpassed that done during the entire four years of the First World War. The Île-de-France, Normandy, Nord-Pas-de-Calais, Val-de-Loire, Lorraine, and Bretagne were the regions that suffered the most damage.

8. C. de Saint-Pierre, *Des ténèbres à l'aube: Journal d'une française* (Paris: B. Arthaud, 1945), 54.

9. Benoîte Groult and Flora Groult, *Diary in Duo*, trans. Humphrey Hare (New York: Appleton-Century, 1965), 351.

10. *Le Figaro*, August 26, 1944.

11. Alain Brossat, *Libération: Fête folle*, Série Mémoires 30 (Paris: Autrement, 1994), 20.

12. Jean Galtier-Boissière, *Journal, 1940–1950* (Paris: Quai Voltaire, 1993), quoted in Pryce-Jones, *Paris in the Third Reich*, 204.

13. See in particular Brossat, *Libération: Fête folle*, 123–25.

14. On the decisions about how to film the Liberation in various locations throughout the city, see *L'Écran français*, August 15, 1945.

15. *Paris libéré*, Office national du film canadien (August 1944).

16. In particular see the photographs of Robert Doisneau in "La Libération de Paris de Robert Doisneau," Bibliothèque historique de la ville de Paris, NA Album 4.45.

17. *Combat*, August 28 and September 2, 1944.

18. Julian Jackson, *France: The Dark Years, 1940–1944* (Oxford and New York: Oxford University Press, 2001). See chapter 24 for a discussion of purge types.

19. "1946 à Paris vue par l'armée américaine," National Archives footage (1946).

20. Saul Bellow, *It All Adds Up: From the Dim Past to the Uncertain Future* (New York: Viking, 1994), quoted in Richard Pells, *Not Like Us: How Europeans Have Loved, Hated, and Transformed American Culture since World War II* (New York: Basic Books, 1997), 140.

21. These testimonials are given by Madeleine Louradour and Monique Bazous, as related in Mairie de Paris, *C'était Paris dans les années 50* (Paris: Ville de Paris, 1997), 14.

22. Jean-Louis Babelay, *Un an* (Paris: Raymond Schall, 1946), 76.

23. Henry Rousso, *The Vichy Syndrome: History and Memory in France since 1944*, trans. Arthur Goldhammer (Cambridge, MA: Harvard University Press, 1991), 23–25.

24. Huyssen, *Present Pasts*, 146.

25. Janet Flanner, *Paris Journal, 1944–1965* (London: Gollancz, 1966), 26–27.

26. *Combat*, May 9, 1945.

27. See the photographs of Serge de Sazo, "De la libération à la paix: des Alliés à Paris," Bibliothèque historique de la ville de Paris, NA Album 40.176.

28. Stanley Karnow, *Paris in the Fifties* (New York: Random House, 1997), 3.

29. Patrice Higonnet, *Paris: Capital of the World* (Cambridge, MA: Belknap Press of Harvard University Press, 2002), 434.

30. *BMO Débats*, July 2, 1950, 639.

31. *Le Parisien Libéré*, July 9, 1951.

32. *Combat*, July 9, 1951.

33. *Le Parisien libéré*, July 9, 1951.

34. Jean Giraudoux, *Pleins pouvoirs* (Paris: Gallimard, 1939), quoted in Noël Boutet de Monvel, *Les Demains de Paris* (Paris: Denoël, 1964), 95.

35. These figures are given in "Paris et huit métropoles mondiales," *Cahiers de l'Institut d'aménagement et d'urbanisme de la région parisienne* 2 (June 1965): 46.

36. Marcel Flouret, *Communication de M. le Préfet de la Seine au Conseil municipal et au Conseil général sur le problème du logement et le plan d'aménagement de Paris et de la banlieue* (Paris: Préfecture du département de la Seine, 1946), 97.

37. Jean Lobry, *Construction et urbanisme dans la région parisienne* (Paris: Commissaire à la construction et à l'urbanisme pour la région parisienne, 1958), 4.

38. See statistics in *France-soir*, May 15, 1956; and Jean Bastié, *Nouvelle histoire de Paris: Paris de 1945 à 2000* (Paris: Hachette, 2000), 401.

39. *Le Figaro*, January 12, 1951.

40. See Mathieu Flonneau, *Paris et l'automobile: Un siècle de passions* (Paris: Hachette, 2005).

41. André Siegfried, *Géographie humoristique de Paris* (Paris: La Passerelle, 1951), 10–11, 42–45.

42. Henri Calet, *Les Grands largeurs: Balades parisiennes* (Paris: Vineta, 1951), 27–28.

43. A description of the annual festival is given in Alain Duchemin, *Paris en fêtes* (Paris: France-Empire, 1985). See also *Les Actualités françaises*, June 28, 1951, and *Journal télévisée*, June 29, 1949.

44. *Paris Match*, June 20–27, 1953.

45. Duchemin, *Paris en fêtes*, 49.

46. Lobry, *Construction et urbanisme*, 11.

47. Siegfried, *Géographie humoristique de Paris*, 45.

48. After the Second World War, *vélo* was a metaphorical nickname for a worker, as *blouse* had been a century before. In the same sense, the boys (*gars*) of La Villette and the metalworkers (*métallos*) of Saint-Denis were given local monikers.

49. Albert Demangeon, *Paris: La Ville et sa banlieue* (Paris: Bourrelier, 1933), 46.

50. Jeanne Singer-Kérel, *La Coût de la vie à Paris de 1840 à 1954* (Paris: Armand Colin, 1961), 163–64.

51. "Inspection générale des services techniques de topographie et d'urbanisme," *Revue urbanisme* 92–93 (July–August 1943): 169.

52. The documentation on the postwar housing problem is legion. A good introduction is given by Roger-Henri Guerrand, "Paris-Quartiers, 1945–1955," *Revue urbanisme* 285 (November–December 1995): 48–52. See also the history of Paris housing in Jacques Lucan, ed., *Eau et gaz à tous les étages: Paris, 100 ans de logement* (Paris: Édition du Pavillon de l'Arsenal and Picard Éditeur, 1992). Issues of the journal *Logez-vous* for the 1950s are also an important source of information.

53. See Yankel Fijalkow, *La Construction des îlots insalubres: Paris, 1850–1945* (Paris: L'Harmattan, 1998).

54. Marcel Croze, "L'Origine des parisiens," in Société statistique de Paris, *Paris 1960* (Paris: Imprimerie municipale, 1961), 51; and Jean Lavedan, *Histoire de l'urbanisme à Paris* (Paris: Hachette, 1993), 525. On the evolution of the population in the Paris region, see also Jean Bastié, *Géographie du grand Paris* (Paris: Masson, 1984).

55. For a postwar analysis of the Paris suburbs, see Georges Chabot, "Faubourgs, banlieues et zones d'influence," *La Vie urbaine (Urbanisme et habitation)* 3–4 (July–December 1954): 161–66.

56. Quoted in Evelyne Cohen, *Paris dans l'imaginaire national de l'entre-deux-guerres* (Paris: Publications de la Sorbonne, 1999), 338.

57. Comité des Zoniers, "La Zône," pamphlet (Paris: Chartes Guyet, 1945). On the history and planning of the fortifications and the zone more generally, see "La Ceinture de Paris," *Revue urbanisme* 35–36 (1954): 5–15; and Jean-Louis Cohen and André Lortie, *Des fortifs au périf: Paris, les seuils de la ville* (Paris: Édition du Pavillon de l'Arsenal and Picard Éditeur, 1991).

58. See the outstanding work of Tyler Stovall, *The Rise of the Paris Red Belt* (Berkeley: University of California Press, 1990), and Annie Fourcaut, *La Banlieue en morceaux: La Crise des lotissements défectueux en France dans l'entre-deux-guerres* (Grâne: Créaphis, 2000).

59. On the Paris suburbs after the Second World War, see André Guillerme, Anne-Cécile Lefort, and Gérard Jigaudon, *Dangereux, insalubres et incommodes: Paysages industriels en banlieue parisienne, XIX–XXe siècles* (Paris: Champ Vallon, 2004), and Jean Bastié, *La Croissance de la banlieue parisienne* (Paris: Presses universitaires de la France, 1964). See also Françoise Soulignac, *La Banlieue parisienne: Cent cinquante ans de transformation* (Paris: La Documentation française, 1993).

60. These two particular communes sustained the most building damage and were the sites of numerous temporary barracks. In the case of Noisy-le-Sec, 142 barracks were established, while in Ivry-sur-Seine, 83 barracks were built. See Préfecture de la Seine, Mémoires du préfet de la Seine au Conseil municipal, Communication au Conseil municipal et au Conseil général sur la "Reconstruction," 1946, BAVP 19059, 9. More generally, see Danièle Voldman, *La Reconstruction des villes françaises de 1940 à 1954: Histoire d'une politique* (Paris: L'Harmattan, 1997).

61. These statistics and analysis on the Paris suburbs are given in Jean Legaret, ed., *L'Agglomération parisienne*, vol. 2 of *Le Statut de Paris* (Paris: R. Pichon and R. Durand-Auzias, 1959), especially 23–24.

62. Babelay, *Un an*, 75–76.

63. Armand Lanoux, "'Physiologie des grands boulevards,'" *Les Œuvres libres* 96 (May 1954): 140.

64. Bastié, *Nouvelle histoire de Paris*, 157.

65. Ibid., 152; and Pierre George, "Place de Paris dans l'économie française," in Société Statistique de Paris, *Paris 1960*, 135–43.

66. Steven Zdatny, *The Politics of Survival: Artisans in Twentieth-Century France* (New York: Oxford University Press, 1990), 155.

67. Pierre Bénaerts, "Le Commerce," in Société Statistique de Paris, *Paris 1960*, 103–10.

68. Jean-Paul Clébert, *Paris insolite* (Paris: Denoël, 1954), 79–80.

69. These statistics and more are given in Jean Prévot, "L'Industrie à Paris," in Société Statistique de Paris, *Paris 1960*, 91–101. See also Bernard Rouleau, *Villages et faubourgs de l'ancien Paris: Histoire d'un espace urbain* (Paris: Seuil, 1985), 312.

70. Paris was home to 51 percent of workers in the automobile industry and 58 percent of workers in the aircraft industry. Lobry, *Construction et urbanisme*, 12.

71. Préfecture de la Seine, "Décentralisation industrielle," *La Conjoncture économique dans le département* 3 (1961): 339–43.

72. See the advertisement for this building in the *Revue urbanisme*, 62–63 (1959).

Chapter Two

1. Michael Kelly, *The Cultural and Intellectual Rebuilding of France after the Second World War* (New York: Palgrave Macmillan, 2004), 180.

2. On a discussion of Bakhtin see Michael Gardiner, *Critiques of Everyday Life* (London and New York: Routledge, 2000), especially chapter 3.

3. Cohen, *Paris dans l'imaginaire national*, 280; and Léon Paul Fargue, *Le Piéton de Paris* (Paris: Gallimard, 1939). See also Louis Aragon, *Le Paysan de Paris* (Paris: Folio, 1926); Robert Garric, *Belleville: Scènes de la vie populaire avec des "témoignages et souvenirs"* (Paris: Bernard Grasset, 1928); Daniel Halévy, *Pays parisiens* (Paris: Émile-Paul Frères, 1929); and Jules Romains, *Les Hommes de bonne volonté*, vol. 4, *Eros de Paris* (Paris: Flammarion, 1932).

4. On the influence of folkloric images on French identity, see Herman Lebovics, *True France: The Wars over Cultural Identity, 1900–1945* (Ithaca, NY: Cornell University Press, 1992).

5. Lanoux, "'Physiologie des grands boulevards,'" 139–40.

6. Armand Lanoux, *Physiologie de Paris* (Paris: Librairie Arthème Fayard, 1954), 196.

7. Jean El Gammal, *Les Hauts quartiers de l'est parisien d'un siècle à l'autre* (Paris: Publisud, 1998), 96–97.

8. Robert Garric, "Le Peuple de Paris," in *Portrait de Paris*, ed. Jules Romains (Paris: Perrin, 1951), 149. On Garric's work in social reform, see Rémi Baudouï, "Un technicien social du service public: Raoul Dautry," in *Les Chantiers de la paix sociale (1900–1940)*, ed.Yves Cohen and Rémi Baudouï (Fontenay/Saint-Cloud: ENS Editions, 1995). See also Garric, *Belleville*.

9. Garric, "Le Peuple de Paris," 149.

10. *Les Lettres françaises*, January 10, 1952.

11. Garric, "Le Peuple de Paris," 150.

12. Clébert, *Paris insolite*, 37.

13. Henri Calet, *Le Tout sur le tout* (Paris: Gallimard, 1948), 235.

14. Benjamin, *Arcades Project*, 516–17.

15. For more specific detail, see Robert Doisneau, *Les Parisiens tels qu'ils sont* (Paris: Robert Delpire, 1954); Blaise Cendrars, *La Banlieue de Paris*, with 130 photos by Robert Doisneau (Paris: Pierre Seghers, 1949); Henri Guérard, *Le Regard d'un photographe sur Belleville, Ménilmontant, Charonne (1944–1999)* (Paris: Éditions de l'Amandier, 1998); and Brigitte Ollier, ed., *Robert Doisneau*, 4th ed. (Paris: Hazan, 2000).

16. The best biographies of Jacques Prévert are Yves Courrière, *Jacques Prévert: En vérité* (Paris: Gallimard, 2000), and, especially on Paris, Jean-Paul Caracalla, *Le Paris de Jacques Prévert* (Paris: Flammarion, 2000). See also Bernard Chardère, *Jacques Prévert: Inventaire d'une vie* (Paris: Gallimard, 1997).

17. *Les Lettres françaises*, April 12–18, 1956.

18. "La Rue de Buci maintenant," in Jacques Prévert, *Œuvres complètes* (Paris: Gallimard, 1992), 133; translation mine.

19. "Et la fête continue," ibid., 126; translation from Jacques Prévert, *Paroles: Selected Poems*, trans. Lawrence Ferlinghetti, bilingual ed., Pocket Poets 9 (San Francisco: City Lights Books, 1990), 103.

20. On the life and art of Willy Ronis, see Willy Ronis, *Autoportrait* (Cognac: Chez Fata Morgana, 1996), and Paul Ryan, *Willy Ronis* (London: Phaidon, 2002).

21. In 1951, the "Paris vu par le Groupe des XV" exposition gathered together the poetic images of everyday urban space by Ronis, Doisneau, and a host of the city's foremost photographers. This humanist photographic genre was also honored at the 1955–56 photographic exposition "The Family of Man," created by Edward Steichen for the Museum of Modern Art in NewYork, to which Ronis and Doisneau both contributed. See Marie de Thézy, *La Photographie humaniste 1930–1960: Histoire d'un mouvement en France* (Paris: Contrejour, 1992).

22. Collections of Ronis's photographs include Centre national de la photographie, *Willy Ronis*, introd. Betrand Eveno (Paris: Centre national de la photographie, 1991); Association française pour la diffusion du patrimoine photographique, *Willy Ronis par Willy Ronis: Exposition rétrospective* (Plessis-Robinson: Blanchard, 1985); and Willy Ronis, *Mon Paris*, preface by Henri Raczymow (Paris: Denoël, 1985). Ronis's shared vision with Prévert found expression in 1946 with the publication by the review *Quadrige* of Prévert's "The Mysteries of the Dark Room," with photographs by Ronis.

23. Pierre Mac Orlan, introduction to Willy Ronis, *Belleville Ménilmontant* (Paris: Arthaud, 1954), unpaginated.

24. Ibid.

25. *Les Lettres françaises*, April 12–18, 1956.

26. Mikhail Bakhtin, *Rabelais and His World*, trans. H. Isowolsky (Cambridge, MA: MIT Press, 1984), especially the introduction.

27. Ibid., 255. For a critical review of Bakhtin's concept of carnival, see Chris Humphrey, "Bakhtin and the Study of Popular Culture: Re-Thinking Carnival as a Historical and Analytical Concept," in *Materializing Bakhtin*, ed. Craig Brandist (London: Palgrave, 2000).

28. See the analysis in Michael Bishop, *Jacques Prévert: From Film and Theater to Poetry, Art and Song* (Amsterdam and New York: Rodopi, 2002), 59. See also Brian Rigby, *Popular Culture in Modern France: A Study of Cultural Discourse* (London: Routledge, 1991).

29. Ken Hirschkop describes this as the uneven structuring of language in the public sphere; it depends on the speaker and the audience, the social context. See Hirschkop, *Mikhail Bakhtin*, 251–54.

30. See Paul Rodaway, *Sensuous Geographies: Body, Sense and Place* (London and New York: Routledge, 1994).

31. See in particular Laura Mason, *Singing the French Revolution: Popular Culture and Politics, 1789–1799* (Ithaca, NY: Cornell University Press, 1996), and Regina Sweeney, *Singing Our Way to Victory: French Cultural Politics and Music during the Great War* (Middletown, CT: Wesleyan University Press, 2001). See also Philippe Gumplowicz, *Les Travaux d'Orphée: 150 ans de vie musicale amateur en France; Harmonies, chorales, fanfares* (Paris: Autier, 1987).

32. On the evolution of popular music, see Charles Rearick, *The French in Love and War: Popular Culture in the Era of the World Wars* (New Haven, CT: Yale University Press, 1997).

33. Certeau, *Practice of Everyday Life*, 97–99.

34. Lionel Mouraux, *Je me souviens du 11e arrondissement* (Paris: Parigramme/CPL, 1998), 25; and Lily Lian, *Lily Panam: Mémoires de la dernière chanteuse des rues* (Paris: Olivier Orban, 1981), 104. See also R. Carré, "Chanteurs et chansons des rues," *Gavroche: Revue d'histoire populaire* 69–70 (May–August 1993): 27–30; and Doisneau's photographs in Cendrars, *La Banlieue de Paris*, 55.

35. The "Chant des partisans," written in London by Joseph Kessel and Maurice Druon, became the quasi-official anthem of national liberation. The sheet music for "Le Petit Vin blanc" sold 1.5 million copies in 1943 (the year it was released), making it among the most popular songs of the war era. "Le Petit vin blanc" and songs such as "On boit l'café au lait au lit" and "Fleur de Paris" represented a more nostalgic genre of popular favorites sung throughout Paris as part of the resurrection of public culture. See Pierre Saka, *La Chanson française à travers ses succès* (Paris: Larousse, 1988), 152.

36. *Notre Xème*, Bulletin, Mairie du Xe arrondissement, no. 6 (December 1947). See also the schedule of programs listed by the Comité municipal des fêtes et des œuvres de solidarité du Xe in *Notre Xème*, nos. 1-6 (1947).

37. *L'Humanité*, January 9, 1946. See also Serge Dillaz, *La Chanson française de contestation de la Commune à Mai 68* (Paris: Seghers, 1973).

38. *L'Humanité*, January 16, 1946. Saint-Granier was a French singer and songwriter of the 1930s most well-known for "Ramona" and "C'est jeune et ça ne sait pas."

39. Jean-Louis Robert, "Paris enchanté: Le Peuple en chansons (1870–1990)," in *Paris le peuple, XVIIIe–XXe siècle*, ed. Jean-Louis Robert and Danielle Tartakowsky (Paris: Publications de la Sorbonne, 1999).

40. See Christian Marcadet, "Un chanteur populaire: Yves Montand," in "Le Peuple et tous ses états," ed. Jean-Louis Robert and Danielle Tartakowsky, special issue, *Sociétés et représentations* 8 (December 1999): 187–216. Originally booked for a three-week run, Montand's show at L'Étoile continued for six months and also became a best-selling live album.

41. On the history of the *bals populaires*, see, among others, Georges Pillement, *Paris en fête* (Paris: Bernard Grasset, 1972).

42. Marie-Claude Blanc-Chaléard, "Les Trois Temps du bal-musette ou la place des étrangers (1880–1960)," cited in Robert and Tartakowsky, "Le Peuple et tous ses états," 87.

43. Cendrars, *La Banlieue de Paris*, 26. See also Pierre Milza and Marie-Claude Blanc-Chaléard, *Le Nogent des Italiens*, Série monde/Français d'ailleurs, peuple d'ici, HS 80 (Paris: Autrement, 1995).

44. Mairie de Paris, *C'était Paris*, 116.

45. Michel Déon, *Les Gens de la nuit* (Paris: Plon, 1958), 208.

46. Clarisse Francillon, *Les Gens du passage* (Paris: Pierre Horay, 1959), 169.

47. Jean-Pierre A. Bernard, *Paris rouge, 1944–1964: Les Communistes français dans la capitale* (Seyssel: Champs Vallon, 1991), 47.

48. *L'Aube*, July 14, 1948.

49. *L'Humanité*, July 17, 1945.

50. *BMO Débats*, July 22, 1949, 510.

51. *L'Humanité*, July 17, 1945.

52. *Les Lettres françaises*, July 13, 1950.

53. Bakhtin, *Rabelais and His World*, 255–56.

54. The examples that follow are taken from the March–June numbers of *L'Avenir de la banlieue de Paris* in 1954, 1955, and 1956.

55. André Warnod, *Les Plaisirs de la rue* (Paris: Française illustrée, 1920), 40.

56. Préfecture de la Seine, Inspection générale et études service d'études et de recherche, "Les Fêtes foraines dans la région parisienne," Étude réalisée sous la direction de Edith Falque, September 1967, manuscript, BAVP 34 143/E38505, 11.

57. For these statistics on the *fêtes foraines*, see Préfecture de la Seine, Recueil des actes administratifs de la Préfecture de police, no. 16, August 31, 1948, BAVP 1758, 218–19; and Préfecture de la Seine, Inspection générale et études service d'études et de recherche, "Les Fêtes foraines." See also Michel-P. Hamelet, "Faut-il supprimer les fêtes foraines à Paris?" *Le Figaro*, March 20, 1951.

58. Agnès Rosolen and Lionel Mouraux, *De la foire au pain d'épice à la foire du Trône* (Charenton-le-Pont: L. M., 1985).

59. Robert Legrand, dir., *Fête foraine 1954* (1954).

60. See Hamelet, "Faut-il supprimer les fêtes foraines à Paris?"

61. "Fête foraine," in Prévert, *Paroles: Selected Poems*, trans. Ferlinghetti, 97.

62. Calet, *Le Tout sur le tout*, 173–75. Also useful are the oral histories gathered in Sylvie Bonin, *Je me souviens du 14e arrondissement* (Paris: Parigramme, 1993).

63. Jacques Baratier and Jean Valère, dirs., *Paris la nuit* (Argos Films, 1956).

64. *Les Actualités françaises*, March 15, 1951.

65. Henri Lefebvre, introduction to *Critique of Everyday Life*, trans. John Moore (London and New York: Verso, 2000), 1:40–41.

66. *L'Humanité*, September 4, 1945.

67. *Fête de L'Humanité 1946* (Cinéfrance, 1946).

68. *L'Humanité*, September 4–5, 1945; and *Fête de l'Humanité 1946*.

69. On Constant and New Babylon, see Simon Sadler, *The Situationist City* (Cambridge, MA: MIT Press, 1998), 132–38.

70. Guy-Ernest Debord, "L'Architecture et le jeu," *Potlatch* 20 (May 20, 1955), reprinted in *Guy Debord présente Potlatch, 1954–1957* (Paris: Gallimard, 1996), 158. See also Libero Andreotti, "Architecture and Play," in *Guy Debord and the Situationist International: Texts and Documents*, ed. Tom McDonough (Cambridge, MA: MIT Press, 2002), 213–40.

71. Certeau, *Practice of Everyday Life*, 105–7.

72. Recounted in Philippe Nivet and Yvan Combeau, *Histoire politique de Paris au XXe siècle* (Paris: Presses universitaires de France, 2000), 183.

73. *Cobra* 4 (Brussels, 1948), quoted in Sadler, *Situationist City*, 97.

74. Recounted in Bernard, *Paris rouge*, 35–36.

75. The rue de l'Entrepôt was renamed Yves Toudic; the rue Albouy, Lucien Sempaix; the rue de Bondy, René Boulanger; the rue des Vinaigriers, Jean Poulmarch; and the place Lancry, Jacques Bonsergent.

76. See *L'Humanité*, August 21, 1945; and Gérard Namer, *La Commémoration en France de 1945 à nos jours* (Paris: L'Harmattan, 1987), 119. See also the municipal council debates in *BMO Débats*, July 5, 1945.

77. *BMO Débats*, November 24, 1946, 527.

78. *BMO Débats*, July 5, 1945, 83.
79. Benjamin, *Arcades Project*, 519. On the importance of street names, see also Daniel Milo, "Le Nom des rues," in *Les Lieux de mémoire*, ed. Pierre Nora (Paris: Gallimard, 1984), 1:281–315.
80. *BMO Débats*, March 30, 1945, 45.
81. Ibid., 85–86.
82. *La Vie ouvrière*, May 10, 1945. See also Préfecture de Paris, *Les Plaques commémoratives des rues de Paris* (Paris: La Documentation française, 1984). Some 345 marble plaques eventually graced the capital's landscape.
83. Danielle Tartakowsky, "Manifestations en banlieue 1918–1969," in Jacques Girault, *Ouvriers en banlieue, XIXe–XXe siècle* (Paris: Éditions Ouvrières, 1998), 343.
84. *BMO Débats*, July 11–12, 1946, 438.
85. Namer, *La Commémoration en France*, 122–23.

Chapter Three

1. *Syndicalisme*, January 5, 1946.
2. On Habermas's recourse to the metonymy of the street, see Warren Montag, "The Pressure of the Street: Habermas's Fear of the Masses," in *Masses, Classes, and the Public Sphere*, ed. Mike Hill and Warren Montag (London and New York: Verso, 2000), 132–45. See also Bruno Latour, *Reassembling the Social: An Introduction to Actor-Network-Theory* (Oxford: Oxford University Press, 2005), as well as Mikhail Bakhtin, *The Dialectic Imagination: Four Essays by M. M. Bakhtin*, ed. M. Holquist (Austin, Texas University Press, 1981).
3. See Laurent Douzou, *La Résistance française: une histoire périlleuse* (Paris: Seuil, 2005).
4. Nivet and Combeau, *Histoire politique de Paris au XXe siècle*, 218. See also Annie Fourcaut, Emmanuel Bellanger, and Mathieu Flonneau, eds., *Paris/Banlieues: Conflits et solidarités* (Paris: Créaphis, 2007).
5. Jacques Girault, "Vers la banlieue rouge: Du social au politique," in *Immigration, vie politique et populisme en banlieue parisienne (fin XIXe–XXe siècles)*, ed. Jean-Paul Brunet (Paris: L'Harmattan, 1995), 260–61. In 1935, the communists controlled twenty-seven suburban communes in the department of the Seine. See also Annie Fourcaut, ed., *Banlieue Rouge, 1920–1960: Années Thorez, années Gabin: archétype du populaire, banc d'essai des modernités*, Série Mémoires 18 (Paris: Autrement, 1992).
6. On the party's principles and the idea of revolution, see Sunil Khilnani, *Arguing Revolution. The Intellectual Left in Postwar France* (New Haven and London: Yale University Press, 1993).
7. *Le Figaro*, March 19, 1951.
8. *Syndicalisme*, December 30, 1944.
9. Singer-Kérel, *La Coût de la vie à Paris*, 164.
10. "Les Ouvriers français," *Réalités* 121 (February 1956): 38–47.
11. Jean-Pierre Rioux, *The Fourth Republic, 1944–1958* (Cambridge: Cambridge University Press, 1987), 365–66.
12. Pierre Nora, "Gaullists and Communists," in Nora, *Realms of Memory*, 1:222. This communist topography in Paris is laid out in detail in Bernard, *Paris rouge*.
13. The incident in Ménilmontant is described in Michel Pigenet, *Au coeur de l'activisme communiste des années de guerre froide* (Paris: L'Harmattan, 1992). On the spatial enclaves of counterpublics, see Nancy Fraser, "Rethinking the Public Sphere: A Contribution to the Critique of Actually Existing Democracy," in Craig Calhoun, *Habermas and the Public Sphere* (Cambridge, MA: MIT Press, 1992).
14. *L'Avant-garde*, April 3, 1956, quoted in Bernard, *Paris rouge*, 213.
15. See Nivet and Combeau, *Histoire politique*, 170–71.
16. This proposal is recounted in Philippe Nivet, *Le Conseil municipal de Paris de 1944 à 1977* (Paris: Publications de la Sorbonne, 1994), 63–66.

17. *Paris centre*, October 1947, Fonds Pivert.

18. Marc Maurette, dir., *À la conquête de bonheur* (Communist Party Documentary, 1947). See also Girault, *Ouvriers en banlieue, XIXe–XXe siècle*, 261.

19. Bulletin municipal de Malakoff, September 1947, Fonds Pivert.

20. On the uses of film sources in understanding street protests, see Danielle Tartakowsky, "Les Manifestations de rues dans les actualités cinématographiques Éclair et Gaumont 1918–1968," *Les Cahiers de la cinémathèque: Revue d'histoire du cinéma*, 66 (July 1997): 27–32.

21. *L'Humanité*, October 7, 1944.

22. Quoted in Namer, *La Commémoration en France*, 74. On the history of May Day, see Danielle Tartakowsky, *La Part du rêve: Histoire du 1er Mai en France* (Paris: Hachette, 2005.

23. *La Vie ouvrière*, May 31, 1945. The funerals of such well-known communists as Ambroise Croizat in 1951 and Marcel Cachin in 1958 were also occasions for public displays of working-class power.

24. *Les Actualités françaises*, May 9, 1946.

25. *Les Actualités françaises*, July 17, 1946, and May 8, 1947.

26. *Combat*, May 2, 1947.

27. These dismissals were annulled in 1957. See Bernard, *Paris rouge*, 23.

28. Danielle Tartakowsky, *Les Manifestations de rue en France, 1918–1968* (Paris: Publications de la Sorbonne, 1997), 540, as well as her more recent *La Manif en éclats* (Paris: La Dispute, 2004).

29. David Glassberg, *Sense of History: The Place of the Past in American Life* (Amherst: University of Massachusetts Press, 2001), 79.

30. On the history of protests, demonstrations and marches in France, see the magisterial work of Tartakowsky, *Les Manifestations de rue en France, 1918–1968*, 531–32. See also her analysis of early postwar Parisian protests, "Les Manifestations parisiennes pendant la guerre froide," *Historiens et géographes* 358 (July–August 1997): 107–16.

31. See *Paris Match*, August 15 and August 22–29, 1953.

32. Alfred Sauvy, *La Vie économique des français de 1939 à 1945* (Paris: Flammarion, 1978), quoted in Philippe Buton, "L'Eviction des ministres communistes," in *L'Année 1947*, ed. Serge Berstein and Pierre Milza (Paris: Presses de Sciences Po, 2000), 340–41.

33. *L'Humanité*, November 22, 1947.

34. *Les Actualités françaises*, April 13, 1950.

35. *L'Humanité*, November 10, 1951. See Yves Santamaria, *Le Parti de l'ennemi? Le Parti communiste français dans la lutte pour la paix (1947–1958)* (Paris: Armand Colin, 2006).

36. Dossier MP36, File PCF, Fonds Pivert.

37. Bernard, *Paris rouge*, 216.

38. *L'Humanité*, May 29, 1952. On the Ridgway riots, see Richard Kuisel, *Seducing the French: The Dilemma of Americanization* (Berkeley: University of California Press, 1993), 48–50.

39. See *Le Parisien libéré*, May 29, 1952, for a description of the events.

40. *L'Humanité*, May 29, 1952.

41. *L'Humanité*, January 4, 1953.

42. *L'Humanité*, July 14 and July 15, 1954.

43. Report, "Cérémonie du 8 mai 1954, place de l'Étoile, XI Heures," Instructions, généralités, Fêtes de la victoire, 8 mai 1954, Archives de Police, FA/CO, Carton no. 2.

44. *Paris Match*, April 10–17, 1954.

45. Report, May 9, 1954, "Dépôt de gerbe à l'Arc de Triomphe par le Général De Gaulle," Instructions, Archives de Police, FA/CO, Carton no. 2.

46. See *Paris Match*, May 15–22, 1954.

47. Correspondence, "Lettre de la Fédération nationale des amicales d'anciens de la 9ème Division d'infanterie coloniale à Monsieur A. Quinson, Maire de Vincennes, Député de la Seine, Correspondances, Fêtes de la victoire, 8 Mai 1954, Archives de Police, FA/CO, Carton no. 2.

48. See, for example, *Les Actualitiés françaises*, November 14, 1956.

49. Daniel Roche, *The People of Paris: An Essay in Popular Culture in the 18th Century* (Berkeley: University of California Press, 1987), 97.

50. See Alain Faure and Claire Lévy-Vroelant, *Une chambre en ville: Hôtels meublés et garnis à Paris 1860–1990* (Paris: Créaphis, 2007).

51. "Inspection générale des services techniques de topographie et d'urbanisme," *Revue urbanisme* 92–93 (July–August 1943): 168–71. The MRU, the INSEE, and the Seine prefecture all published extensive statistical reports on conditions in Paris at the war's end.

52. La Documentation française, *La Lutte contre les taudis et l'amélioration de l'habitat*, Notes et études documentaires 305–6 (Paris: La Documentation française, 1946), 1:2; Préfecture de la Seine, Mémoires du préfet de la Seine au Conseil municipal, "Communication au Conseil municipal et au Conseil général sur le problème de logement et le plan d'aménagement de Paris et de sa banlieue," 1946, BAVP 19059.

53. Max Dravet, "Le Logement et l'action du mouvement de libération ouvrière," *Pour la vie: Revue d'études familiales* 52 (1st trimester 1952): 52. On social housing in France, see also Thibault Tellier, *Le Temps des HLM, 1945–1975: La saga urbaine des trente glorieuses* (Paris: Autrement, 2008) and Marie-Jeanne Dumont, *Le Logement social à Paris, 1850–1930: Les habitations à bon marché* (Liège: Mardaga, 1991).

54. Ministère de l'équipement, du logement, des transports, et de l'espace, Île-de-France, Enquête sociologique, Pantin (Seine) 1953, Archives nationales, F^{14} 18363.

55. These numbers are given in *BMO Débats*, July 24, 1952, 556; and in Lobry, *Construction et urbanisme*, 77–80.

56. Among the many outcries, see J. Desforges, "Le Problème du logement à Paris," *Pour la vie* 10 (April 1947): 3–13; Jean Lemoine, "La Crise du logement," *La Vie urbaine* 57 (July–September 1950): 5–12; "Nos maisons et nos villes," ed. Jean-Marie Domenach, special issue, *Esprit* 10–11 (October–November 1953); and *Quelques données sur le logement dans la région parisienne*, Notes et études documentaires 1823 (Paris: La Documentation française, 1954). For discussions of the state's postwar housing policy, see Danièle Voldman, *La Reconstruction des villes françaises*, and F. Boucher, "Abriter vaille que vaille, se loger coûte que coûte," in "Image, discours et enjeux de la reconstruction des villes françaises après 1945," ed. Danièle Voldman, special issue, *Les Cahiers de l'IHTP* 5 (1987): 117–39.

57. *BMO Débats*, December 27, 1954, 918.

58. Un groupe de Montreuil, "Les 'Castors': Issue provisoire," *Esprit* 10–11 (October–November 1953): 522.

59. *Syndicalisme*, February 23, 1946.

60. *La Vie ouvrière*, January 3, 1946.

61. *La Vie ouvrière*, September 27, 1945.

62. Pigenet, *Au cœur de l'activisme communiste*, 76.

63. PCF election material, MP36, File PCF, Fonds Pivert.

64. *BMO Débats*, July 24, 1952, 553. The PCF was active in both the Confédération nationale des locataires (National Renters' Association, or CNL) and in the new Confédération générale du logement (National Housing Association, or CGL), organized around Abbé Pierre's campaign.

65. *L'Humanité*, November 16, 1951.

66. *L'Humanité*, January 22, 1953.

67. *BMO Débats*, July 24, 1952, 560–61.

68. Editorial by Édouard Depreux, mayor of Sceaux, "Pour défendre la liberté: les logements valent mieux que les discours communistes," *L'Avenir de la banlieue de Paris*, March 25–31, 1954.

69. Paul-Henry Chombart de Lauwe, "Scandale du logement et espoirs de l'urbanisme," in "Nos maisons et nos villes," special issue, *Esprit* 21 (October–November 1953): 572.

70. Jean-Paul Flamand, *Loger le peuple: Essai sur l'histoire du logement social en France* (Paris: La Découverte, 1989), 251.

71. See Boris Simon, *Abbé Pierre and the Ragpickers of Emmaüs* (New York: P. J. Kennedy, 1955).

72. *Le Figaro*, January 6, 1954.

73. *Les Actualités françaises*, February 4, 1954. See also *Journal télévisée*, February 2, 1954.

74. Roland Barthes, *Mythologies*, trans. Annette Lavers (New York: Noonday Press, 1972), 48.

75. *Paris Match*, February 6–13 and February 13–20, 1954.

76. *Le Monde*, March 2, 1954.

77. *Abbé Pierre*, documentary (1954).

78. Roger Quilliot and Roger-Henri Guerrand, *Cent ans d'habitat social: Une utopie réaliste* (Paris: Albin Michel, 1989).

79. *Journal télévisée*, August 3, 1955; and *Les Actualités françaises*, August 5, 1955.

80. *Paris Match*, January 16–23, 1954, and December 11–18, 1954.

81. *Le Parisien libéré*, September 20, 1949.

82. *L'Aurore*, November 5, 1948.

83. *Ce Matin*, August 15, 1949, and August 23, 1951.

84. 1949 Statistics. Institut national d'études démographiques, *Les Algériens en France: Étude démographique et sociale*, Travaux et Documents 24 (Paris: Presses Universitaires de France, 1955), 44. Statistics on the North African population vary widely. The official Ministry of the Interior 1954 census numbers are 29,163 for the city of Paris, plus 46,046 for the Paris suburbs.

85. *L'Humanité*, February 19, 1953.

86. Service des affaires musulmanes et de l'action sociale, Ministère de l'intérieur, "Physionomie de l'implantation des migrants à Paris," *Étude sociologique de la migration des travailleurs musulmans d'Algérie en métropole*, cahier no. 9 (1959): 191.

87. Jean-François Gravier, *Paris et le désert français*, revised ed. (Paris: Flammarion, 1972), 191.

88. Préfecture de police, Direction de la police judiciare, "Étude de la population nord-africaine à Paris et dans le département de la Seine, Année 1955," manuscript, BAVP Br. 1455/E.1611, 49–52. See also Service des affaires musulmanes, "Physionomie de l'implantation," 191. Although suffering the bias of official records, these studies are invaluable for understanding the character of North African immigration in the 1950s. See also Clifford Rosenberg, *Policing Paris: The Origins of Modern Immigration Control between the Wars* (Ithaca, NY: Cornell University Press, 2006), and Vincent Viet, *La France immigrée* (Paris: Fayard, 1998), as well as Françoise de Barros, "Des 'Français musulmans d'Algérie' aux 'immigrés,'" *Actes de la recherche en sciences sociales* 159 (September 2005): 26–45.

89. *L'Humanité*, October 15, 1957.

90. Henri Calet, *Les Deux bouts*, 7th ed. (Paris: Gallimard, 1954), 133–38.

91. Prefecture de police "Étude de la population nord-africaine," 56–57.

92. Clébert, *Paris insolite*, 251–52.

93. See, for example, *Libération*, August 2, 1955.

94. Clébert, *Paris insolite*, 250.

95. Préfecture de police, "Étude de la population nord-africaine," 56–57.

96. Described in Alain Rustenholz, *Paris ouvrier: des sublimes aux camarades* (Paris: Parigramme, 2003), 326.

97. Prefecture de police "Étude de la population nord-africaine," 62–63.

98. *Franc-tireur*, December 10, 1951. The article quotes the police as identifying six thousand arrests, while the various Algerian political organizations put the total arrests at fifteen thousand. On the Algerian War and its impact on France, see, among many, Todd Shepard, *The Invention of Decolonization: The Algerian War and the Remaking of France* (Ithaca, NY: Cornell University Press, 2008).

99. This history of confrontation was catalogued in *France-soir*, July 15, 1953.

100. These economic pressures are described in Peggy Derder, *L'Immigration algérienne et les pouvoirs publics dans le département de la Seine, 1954–1962* (Paris: L'Harmattan, 2001).

101. *Le Parisien libéré*, July 15, 1953. See also the articles in *Combat*, July 15, 1953. On the July 14, 1953, riots and deaths, see Maurice Rajsfus, *1953, un 14 juillet sanglant* (Paris: Agnès Viénoet Editions, 2003).

102. The quote is from *L'Humanité*, June 22, 1953. See the series of headlines and articles in *L'Humanité*, June 15–22, 1953.

103. On these early protests by Algerians, see Danielle Tartakowsky, "Le Manifestations de rue," in *La Guerre d'Algérie et les français*, ed. Jean-Pierre Rioux (Paris: Fayard, 1990).

104. This sectarian battle, won by the FLN by 1959, is recounted in Pascal Blanchard, Eric Deroo, Driss El-Yazami, Pierre Fournié, and Gilles Manceron, *Le Paris arabe: Deux siècles de présence des Orientaux et de Maghrébins* (Paris: La Découverte, 2003), 155; and Derder, *L'Immigration algérienne*.

105. *Le Parisien libéré*, March 10, 1956.

106. *BMO Débats*, March 12, 1956, 227–34.

107. Alberto Arbasino, *Paris, Ô Paris*, trans. Dominique Férault (Paris: Gallimard, 1997), 110–12.

108. *L'Humanité*, October 18, 1957.

109. *Le Figaro*, May 8, 1958.

110. *Le Figaro*, May 14 and May 30, 1958.

111. *Le Figaro*, May 29, 1958.

112. *L'Humanité*, May 29, 1958.

Chapter Four

1. The best book in English on French postwar intellectual life is Tony Judt, *Past Imperfect: French Intellectuals, 1944–1956* (Berkeley: University of California Press, 1992). See also David Drake, *Intellectuals and Politics in Post-War France* (Basingstoke and New York: Palgrave, 2002), and Khilnani, *Arguing Revolution*. See also the interesting analysis of intellectual stardom in John Gaffney and Diana Holmes, eds., *Stardom in Postwar France* (New York: Berghahn, 2008).

2. Kelly, *Cultural and Intellectual Rebuilding*, 127–28. See also François Dosse, *L'Empire du sens: L'Humanisation des sciences humaines* (Paris: La Découverte, 1995).

3. Georges Friedmann, *Villes et campagnes: Civilisation urbaine et civilisation rurale en France*, Deuxième semaine sociologique organisé par le Centre d'études sociologiques du Centre national de la recherche scientifique (Paris: Armand Colin, 1953), xvi–xxii.

4. Lucien Febvre, in ibid., 32–33.

5. Alain Touraine, "Sociologies et sociologues," in *L'État des sciences sociales en France*, ed. Marc Guillaume (Paris: La Découverte, 1986), 134–35.

6. On the development of postwar urban sociology in France see Michel Amiot, *Contre l'état, les sociologues: Éléments pour une histoire de la sociologie urbaine en France (1900–1980)* (Paris: Éditions de l'École des hautes études en sciences sociales, 1986), and Pierre Lassave, *Les Sociologues et la recherche urbaine dans la France contemporaine* (Toulouse: Presses Universitaires du Mirail, 1997).

7. Judt, *Past Imperfect*, 211.

8. Quoted in Bernard Valade, "Le Destin de Paris dans la science sociale," in *Mélanges d'histoire de Paris à la mémoire de Michel Fleury*, ed. Laure Beaumont-Maillet, Bernard Billaud, Jean Dérens, and Guy-Michel Leproux (Paris: Maisonneuve, 2004), 200.

9. Louis Chevalier, "Le Problème de la sociologie des villes," in *Traité de sociologie*, ed. Georges Gurvitch (Paris: Presses universitaires de France, 1958), quoted in Maïté Clavel, *Sociologie de l'urbain* (Paris: Anthropos, 2002), 12.

10. Louis Chevalier, "La Statistique et la description sociale de Paris," *Population* 4, no. 11 (October–December 1956): 644.

11. These points are made in Paul-André Rosental and Isabelle Couzon, "Le Paris dangereux de Louis Chevalier: un projet d'histoire utile," in *La Ville des sciences sociales*, ed. Bernard Lepetit and Christian Topalov (Paris: Éditions Belin, 2001), 191–226. See also Louis Chevalier, "Préambule démographique aux projets d'aménagement de Paris," *Population* 2, no. 19 (April–May 1964): 335–48.

12. On the influence of Teilhard de Chardin and left-wing Catholic reform movements, see Paul-Henry Chombart de Lauwe, *Un anthropologue dans le siècle; Entretiens avec Thierry Paquot* (Paris: Descartes & Cie, 1996).

13. Paul-Henry Chombart de Lauwe, *Pour retrouver la France: Enquêtes sociales en équipes*, Le Chef et ses Jeunes 6 (Grenoble: École nationale des cadres d'uriage, 1943), 5–7.

14. Paul-Henry Chombart de Lauwe, S. Antoine, L. Couvreur, J. Bertin, L. Chauvet, and J. Gauthier, *Paris et l'agglomération parisienne*, 2 vols. (Paris: Presses universitaires de France, 1952).

15. Paul-Henry Chombart de Lauwe, *La Vie quotidienne des familles ouvrières*, 3rd ed. (Paris: CNRS, 1977).

16. Chombart de Lauwe, Antoine, Couvreur, Bertin, Chauvet, and Gauthier, *Paris et l'agglomération parisienne*, 2:53–56.

17. See Jean-Pierre Frey, "Paul-Henry Chombart de Lauwe: La Sociologie urbaine française entre morphologies et structures," *Espaces et sociétés* 103 (2000): 27–55.

18. La Documentation française, *La Lutte contre les taudis*, 1:2.

19. Clébert, *Paris insolite*, 239. The "A.S. skyscraper" refers to Le Corbusier's Salvation Army Refuge, built in 1933 on the rue Cantagrel.

20. Chombart de Lauwe, Antoine, Couvreur, Bertin, Chauvet, and Gauthier, *Paris et l'agglomération parisienne*, 1:10.

21. Chombart de Lauwe, "Scandale du logement et espoirs de l'urbanisme," 571–79.

22. On Lefebvre's life and work see Rob Shields, *Lefebvre, Love & Struggle: Spatial Dialectics* (London and New York: Routledge, 1999); Remi Hess, *Henri Lefebvre et l'aventure du siècle* (Paris: Éditions A. M. Métailié, 1988); and Henri Lefebvre, *Writings on Cities: Henri Lefebvre*, trans. and ed. Eleonore Kofman and Elizabeth Lebas (Oxford: Blackwell, 1996). See also Lefebvre's intellectual autobiography, *La Somme et le reste* (Paris: Méridiens Klincksieck, 1989).

23. Henri Lefebvre, introduction to *Critique of Everyday Life*, trans. John Moore (London and New York: Verso, 2000), 1:6.

24. Gardiner, *Critiques*, 80–81.

25. Lefebvre, *Critique of Everyday Life*, 1:134–39.

26. Kristin Ross, "Lefebvre on the Situationists: An Interview," in McDonogh, *Guy Debord and the Situationist International*, 279–80.

27. See Marcel Poëte, *Paris: Son évolution créatrice* (Paris: Vincent et Fréal, 1938). On Poëte, see Donatella Calabi, *Marcel Poëte et le Paris des années vingt: Aux origines de "l'histoire des villes,"* trans. P. Savy (Paris: L'Harmattan, 1998), and Cohen, *Paris dans l'imaginaire national*.

28. Pierre Lavedan, *Qu'est-ce que l'urbanisme?* (Paris: Henri Laurens, 1926), introduction.

29. Quoted in Pierre Pinon, "Pierre Lavedan: De l'histoire de l'art à l'architecture urbaine," *Le Visiteur: Ville, territoire, paysage, architecture* 2 (Spring 1996): 119.

30. Pierre Lavedan, *Géographie des villes*, 2nd ed. (Paris: Gallimard, 1959), 213. On Lavedan's conception of planning and the built environment, see Jean-Louis Cohen, "L'Architecture urbaine' selon Pierre Lavedan," *Les Cahiers de la recherche architecturale* 32–33 (1959): 157–68.

31. Jean-Louis Cohen, "Le 'nouvel urbanisme' de Gaston Bardet," *Le Visiteur: Ville, territoire, paysage, architecture* 2 (Spring 1996): 134–47. See also Jean-Pierre Frey, "Gaston Bardet, théoricien de l'urbanisme 'culturaliste,'" *Revue urbanisme* 319 (July–August 2001): 32–36.

32. Gaston Bardet, "Concordance entre les méthodes anglo-américaines d'aménagement et les méthodes de topographie sociale," *L'Architecture française* 50 (September 1945): 3–10; and Gaston Bardet, *Le Nouvel urbanisme* (Paris: Vincent et Fréal, 1948). On progressive social Catholicism, see Gerd-Rainer Horn and Emmanuel Gerard, eds., *Left Catholicism, 1943–1955: Catholics and Society in Western Europe at the Point of Liberation* (Leuven: Leuven University Press, 2001).

33. Gaston Bardet, "Incarnation de l'urbanisme: Des quelques conditions essentielles pour éviter une nouvelle faillite," *Esprit* 113 (1945): 342–62.

34. Chombart de Lauwe, Antoine, Couvreur, Bertin, Chauvet, and Gauthier, *Paris et l'agglomération parisienne*, 2:57.

35. Marcel Raval, "Pour un nouvel humanisme français," *L'Architecture française* 46 (May 1945): 12–13.

36. Auzelle, "La Rénovation des quartiers insalubres," in *Destinée de Paris*, ed. Bernard Champigneulle (Paris: Éditions du Chêne, 1943), 109, 12. See also Robert Auzelle, "Tendencies in French Town Planning," *Town Planning Review* (April 1949): 57. A good introduction to Auzelle's work can be found in Frédéric Bertrand, "Robert Auzelle et l'urbanisme français des années cinquante," *Revue urbanisme* 307 (1999): 42–49.

37. Chombart de Lauwe, *Anthropologue*, 181–82.

38. For descriptions of these proposals, see Robert Auzelle, "La Rénovation des quartiers insalubres," in Champigneulle, *Destinée de Paris*, 109–21.

39. Auzelle's own publications are the best source of information on his methods. See, for example, Auzelle, *Recherche d'une méthode d'enquête sur l'habitat défectueux* (Paris: Vincent et Fréal, 1950); and Auzelle, *Techniques de l'urbanisme* (Paris: Presses universitaires de France, 1953).

40. Robert Auzelle, "Secteur no. 7 de la porte de Pantin à la porte des Lilas" and "L'Enquête préalable à l'aménagement du secteur no. 7," *Revue urbanisme* 35–36 (1954): 15–20.

41. An outstanding resource on French literature in the 1950s is Marie-Claire Bancquart, *Paris dans la littérature française après 1945* (Paris: La Différence, 2006).

42. Pascal Ory, *L'Aventure culturelle française, 1945–1989* (Paris: Flammarion, 1989), 134–35.

43. See the discussion of surrealist perceptions of urban space in Michael Sheringham, "City Space, Mental Space, Poetic Space: Paris in Breton, Benjamin, and Réda," in *Parisian Fields*, ed. Michael Sheringham (London: Reaktion Books, 1996), 85–114. See also Marie-Claire Bancquart, *Paris des surréalistes* (Paris: Seghers, 1972).

44. Laurent Chollet, *Les Situationnistes: L'Utopie incarnée* (Paris: Gallimard, 2004), 12; and Greil Marcus, *Lipstick Traces: A Secret History of the Twentieth Century* (Cambridge, MA: Harvard University Press, 1989), 251.

45. Collected in Gérard Berréby, ed., *Documents relatifs à la fondation de l'internationale situationniste, 1948–1957* (Paris: Éditions Allia, 1985), 264.

46. Jean-Michel Mension, *The Tribe: Conversations with Gérard Berréby and Francesco Milo*, trans. D. Nicholson-Smith (San Francisco: City Lights Books, 2001), 102–5.

47. Many of these drifts were reported in *Les Lèvres nues* 9 (November 1956). See also "On détruit la rue Sauvage," *Potlatch* 7 (3 August 1954), reprinted in Debord, ed., *Guy Debord présente Potlatch*, 54–55.

48. Gilles Ivain, "Formulaire pour un urbanisme nouveau," *Internationale situationniste* 1 (October 1953): 15–20.

49. Quoted in Marcus, *Lipstick Traces*, 253.

50. Tom McDonough, "Situationist Space," in McDonogh, *Guy Debord and the Situationist International*, 261. See also McDonough, *"The Beautiful Language of My Century": Reinventing the Language of Contestation in Postwar France, 1945–1968* (Cambridge, MA: MIT Press, 2007).

51. Jean Vilar, "Enquête du théâtre," *Esprit* 5 (May 1949): 591–633, reprinted in Jean Vilar, *Le théâtre: Service public et autres textes* (Paris: Gallimard, 1975), 49.

52. Clébert, *Paris insolite*, 35.

53. See the analysis of *The Naked City*, the detective film, and urban space in Edward Dimendberg, *Film Noir and the Spaces of Modernity* (Cambridge, MA: Harvard University Press, 2004).

54. Guy Debord, "Introduction à un critique de la géographie urbaine," *Les Lèvres nues* 6 (September 1955), in Berréby, *Documents relatifs à la fondation de l'internationale situationniste*, 290. See also Sadler, *The Situationist City*, 82–84.

55. For a literary biography of Malet, see Alain (Alfu) Fuzellier, *Léo Malet: Parcours d'une œuvre* (Amiens: Alfu & Encrage, 1998). More recent is Laurent Bourdelas, *Le Paris de Nestor Burma: L'Occupation et les "trente glorieuses" de Léo Malet* (Paris: L'Harmattan, 2007). See also Robin Walz, *Pulp Surrealism: Insolent Popular Culture in Early Twentieth-Century Paris* (Berkeley: University of California Press, 2000).

56. Benjamin, *Arcades Project*, 442.

57. Abdelhafid Khatib, "Essai de description psychogéographique des Halles," *Internationale situationniste* 2 (December 1958): 13–17.

58. "Projet d'embellissements rationnels de la ville de Paris," *Potlatch* 23 (October 13, 1955), reprinted in Debord, *Guy Debord présente Potlatch*, 203–7.

59. Ralph Rumney, *Le Consul: Entretiens avec Gérard Berréby* (Paris: Allia, 1999), 71.

60. Léo Malet, *Brouillard au pont de Tolbiac: Les Nouveaux mystères de Paris* (Paris: Fleuve Noir, 1999).

61. Calet, *Le Tout sur le tout*, 124.

62. Michel P. Schmitt, "Le Septième arrondissement," *Europe* 883–84 (November–December 2002): 130–35.

63. Calet, *Les Deux bouts*, 165–67.

64. On this "fiction of the everyday" and Calet's relationship to Baudelaire and Poe, see Pierre Vilar, "Son epingle du jeu," *Europe* 883–84 (November–December 2002): 53–61.

65. Calet, *Les Deux bouts*, 5.

66. Henri Coing, *Rénovation urbaine et changement social (L'Îlot no. 4, Paris 13e)* (Paris: Éditions Ouvrières, 1966).

67. Norma Evenson, *Paris: A Century of Change, 1878–1978* (New Haven, CT: Yale University Press, 1979); see especially "The Passing of the Rue Nationale," 255–64.

Chapter Five

1. François Fleury, "Les Cinémas parisiens, un aspect de la vie urbaine," *Urbanisme et habitation (La Vie urbaine)*, n.s. (January–March 1953): 30–56.

2. Virginie Champion, Bertrand Lemoine, and Claude Terraux, *Les Cinémas de Paris, 1945–1995* (Paris: Délégation à l'action artistique de la ville de Paris, 1995), 29.

3. Catherine Gaston-Mathé, *La Société française au miroir de son cinéma: De la débâcle à la décolonisation* (Condé-sur-Noireau: Arléa-Corlet, 1996). See also N. T. Binh, *Paris au cinéma: La Vie rêvée de la capitale de Méliès à Amélie Poulain* (Paris: Parigramme, 2003), and Jean Douchet and Gilles Nadeau, *Paris cinéma: Une ville vue par le cinéma de 1895 à nos jours* (Paris: Éditions Du May, 1987).

4. On the city and film see Thierry Jousse and Thierry Paquot, eds., *La Ville au cinéma* (Paris: Cahiers du cinéma, 2005), and Stephen Barber, *Projected Cities: Cinema and Urban Space* (London: Reaktion Books, 2002).

5. On the history of French television, see, among many others, Jérôme Bourdon, ed., *La Grande aventure du petit écran: La Télévision française, 1935–1975* (Paris: Musée d'histoire contemporaine–BDIC et INA, 1997). On the 1950s see Evelyne Cohen and Marie-Françoise Lévy, eds., *La Télévision des trente glorieuses: Culture et politique* (Paris: CNRS, 2007); Michèle de Bussierre, *Les Années cinquante à la radio et à la télévision* (Paris: Comité d'histoire de la radio and Comité d'histoire de la télévision, 1991); and Marie-Françoise Lévy, ed., *La Télévision dans la République: Les Années 50* (Brussels: Complexe, 1999).

6. *Le Figaro*, January 1, 1951.

7. *Paris Match*, June 13–20, 1953, 38.

8. *Télé Magazine*, November 2–8, 1958, and August 9–15, 1959.

9. See the excellent analysis in Myriam Chimènes, ed., *La Vie musicale sous Vichy* (Paris: Complexe, 2001).

10. For a recent analysis of French film culture and its influences, see Schwartz, *It's So French: Hollywood, Paris, and the Making of Cosmopolitan Film Culture* (Chicago: University of Chicago Press, 2007).

11. A good discussion of the techniques and designs of poetic realist cinema can be found in Ginette Vincendeau, "Forms: The Art of Spectacle: The Aesthetics of Classical French Cinema," in *The French Cinema Book*, ed. Michael Temple and Michael Witt (London: British Film Institute, 2004). Also useful is Keith Reader, "Representations, 1930–1960: The Geography and Topography of French Cinema," ibid.

12. Marcel Carné, "Quand le cinéma descendra-t-il dans la rue?" *Cinémagazine* 13 (November 1933), quoted in Richard Abel, *French Film Theory and Criticism: A History/Anthology* (Princeton, NJ: Princeton University Press, 1988), 2:127–29.

13. Jacques Becker, dir., *Antoine et Antoinette* (S.N.E. Gaumont, 1947).

14. *Action*, November 5, 1947.

15. *Action*, November 12, 1947.

16. Julien Duvivier, dir., *Sous le ciel de Paris* (Regina Films, Filmsonor S.A., 1951).

17. Dimendberg, *Film Noir and the Spaces of Modernity*, 89.

18. Nezar AlSayyad, *Cinematic Urbanism: A History of the Modern from Reel to Real* (New York and London: Routledge, 2006), 148–49.

19. *L'Écran français*, April 17–23, 1951.

20. Jean-Paul Le Chanois, dir., *Sans laisser d'adresse* (Films Raoul Ploquin, Hoche Productions, Silver Films, 1951).

21. For a biography of Le Chanois, see Philippe Renard, *Un Cinéaste français des années cinquante: Jean-Paul Le Chanois* (Paris: Dreamland éditeur, 2000).

22. "Papa, maman, la bonne et moi," in *Libération*, December 3, 1954 (review of *Papa, maman, la bonne et moi*, dir. Jean-Paul Le Chanois [Champs-Élysées Productions, Lambor Films, Cocinex, 1954]).

23. Fargue, *La Flânerie*, 2.

24. *Les Lettres françaises*, January 17–23, 1951.

25. François Cazenave, ed., *Pionnier et visionaire de la télévision: Jean D'Arcy parle* (Paris: La Documentation française, 1984), 43.

26. *Les Lettres françaises*, August 7, 1952.

27. See, for example, *Télé Magazine*, November 27–December 3, 1955; May 5–11, 1957; June 2–8, 1957; and February 8–14, 1959. See also *Les Actualités françaises*, January 3, 1952, and November 21, 1956.

28. *Paris Presse*, January 29, 1951.

29. Quoted in Michèle de Bussièrre, Caroline Mauriat, and Cécile Méadel, *Histoire des programmes: Histoire des jeux à la radio et à la télévision*, (Paris: Comité d'histoire de la télévision, Groupe d'études historiques sur la radiodiffusion, and Comité d'histoire de la radio, 1986), 170.

30. *Télé Magazine*, September 28–October 4, 1958, and November 23–29, 1958.

31. *Télé Magazine*, July 12–18, 1959, and August 9–15, 1959.

32. Interview with Jacques Krier, December 15, 1994, in Bourdon, *La Grande Aventure du petit écran*, 158–59. See also Marie-Françoise Levy, "Paul-Henry Chombart de Lauwe: Un sociologue à la télévision," *Espaces et sociétés* 103 (2000): 85–95.

33. "Rue du Moulin de la pointe," episode of *À la découverte des français* [television series], dir. Jean-Claude Bergeret and Jacques Krier with the Groupe d'ethnologie sociale du CNRS; Paul-Henry Chombart de Lauwe, consultant (ORTF, broadcast April 5, 1957).

34. Commissariat à la construction et à l'urbanisme pour la région parisienne, *Construction et urbanisme dans la région parisienne* (Paris: Imprimerie municipale, 1957), 47.

35. Chombart de Lauwe, *Anthropologue*, 91.

36. "La Butte à la Reine," episode of *À la découverte des français* [television series], dir. Jean-Claude Bergeret and Jacques Krier, with the Groupe d'ethnologie sociale du CNRS; Paul-Henry Chombart de Lauwe, consultant (ORTF, broadcast April 12, 1957).

37. See in particular the publications of the Commissariat à la construction et à l'urbanisation on building projects in the Paris region, and Jacques Fresnais, ed., *Une politique du logement: Ministère de la reconstruction et de l'urbanisme, 1944–1954* (Paris: IFA-PCA, 1997), 99–105.

38. Levy, Chombart de Lauwe: Un sociologue," 92.

39. Bergeret and Krier, "La Butte à la Reine."

40. The term *film noir* first surfaced in France to describe American detective films produced between 1940 and the late 1950s. On this genre, see Robin Buss, *French Film Noir* (London and New York: Marion Boyars, 1994).

41. Marcel Carné, dir., *Les Portes de la nuit*, (Pathé Consortium Cinéma, 1946).

42. See Marcel Carné, *Ma vie à belles dentes* (Paris: Archipel, 1996), 13.

43. Quoted in Jean-Claude Klein, *La Chanson à l'affiche: Histoire de la chanson française du café concert à nos jours* (Paris: DuMay, 1991), 101.

44. Quoted in Bernard Chardère, *Le Cinéma de Jacques Prévert* (Bordeaux: Castor Astral, 2001), 229–30.

45. *Résistance*, December 8, 1946. See also *La France au combat*, December 19, 1946, and *Le Cinéma*, December 13, 1946.

46. Vincendeau, "The Art of Spectacle: The Aesthetics of Classical French Cinema," in Temple and Wit, *The French Cinema Book*, 149.

47. Marcel Carné, dir., *L'Air de Paris* (Del Duca Films–Galatea, 1954). See also Michel Perez, *Les Films de Carné* (Paris: Ramsey, 1986).

48. "Le Monde de Jacques Prévert," *Positif: Revue périodique de cinéma* 2 (1953–54): 76–77.

49. *Arts*, September 15, 1954.

50. René Clair, dir., *Porte des Lilas* (Filmsonor and Cinétel, 1956).

51. *Les Lettres françaises*, October 5, 1957.

52. *Les Lettres françaises*, September 9, 1957.

53. *L'Humanité*, September 28, 1957, and *Esprit*, December 1, 1957. The term "cinematic pantomime" is used by Joël Magny in "Paris et la nouvelle vague," quoted in Annie Fourcaut, "Aux origines du film de banlieue: Les Banlieusards au cinéma (1930–1980)," in Robert and Tartakowsky, "Le Peuple et tous ses états," 120.

54. Eli Lotar, dir., *Aubervilliers* (1945).

55. On the roots of this poetic realist vision in the prewar avant-garde, see Ian Walker, *City Gorged with Dreams: Surrealism and Documentary Photography in Interwar Paris* (Manchester and New York: Manchester University Press, 2002).

56. Clébert, *Paris insolite*, 49.

57. See *Combat*, March 30, 1946. *Aubervilliers* was usually shown in Paris theaters along with René Clément's *La Bataille du rail*, a heroic celebration of Resistance and reconstruction lionized by the Communist Party, as well as Prévert and Grimault's *Le Voleur de paratonnerres*.

58. Jean Dewever, dir., *La Crise du logement*, (Oka Films, 1956).

59. See, for example, Marcel Ranchal's review of *La Crise du logement* in *Positif: Revue périodique de cinéma* 27 (April 1958): 52–53.

60. Roland Bernard, dir., *Problèmes de la construction* [television series], "Entretien avec Monsieur Pierre Sudreau, Ministère de la reconstruction" (ORTF, broadcast November 6, 1958). On this television series, see Evelyne Cohen, "Expliquer Paris à la télévision: Pierre Sudreau et les problèmes de la construction (1958)," *Sociétés et représentations* 17 (2004): 117–27.

61. Jacques Tati, dir., *Mon oncle* (Specta Films, 1958).

62. *Les Lettres françaises*, May 2, 1958.

63. *L'Humanité*, May 10, 1958. On Tati's films see David Bellos, *The Cinema of Jacques Tati* (London: Harvill Press, 1999), and Michel Chion, *The Films of Jacques Tati* (Toronto: Guernica, 2003).

64. See Iain Borden, "Playtime: 'Tativille' and Paris," in *The Hierogloyphics of Space: Understanding the City*, ed. Neil Leach (New York: Routledge, 2002). See also Laurent Marie, "Jacques Tati's *Play Time* as New Babylon," in *Cinema and the City: Film and Urban Societies in a Global Context*, ed. Mark Shiel and Tony Fitzmaurice (Oxford: Blackwell, 2001).

65. *La Vie ouvrière*, June 14, 1958.

Chapter Six

1. *L'Humanité*, August 27, 1946.

2. See the series of early postwar articles "Mouvements et institutions de jeunesse," *Esprit* 11 (October 1, 1945).

3. *La Jeunesse*, December 28, 1941, cited in Gerard Walter, *Paris under the Occupation*, trans. Tony White (New York: Orion Press, 1960), 126.

4. Archives de police, Étudiants, manifestations, partis, groupes, 1946–1957, BA2134.

5. Paul Yonnet, *Jeux, modes et masses: La Société française et le moderne, 1945–1985* (Paris: Gallimard, 1986), 349–50.

6. See Jean-Claude Loiseau, *Les Zazous* (Paris: Éditions Grasset, 1990), and Rearick, *The French in Love and War*. See also Ginette Martz and Georges Martz, "La Chanson sous l'Occupation et à la Libération," *Histoire & sociétés* 51 (May–June 1994): 5–34.

7. Mairie de Paris, *C'était Paris*, 12. See also Jean-Pierre Dorian, *Jours et nuits de Paris* (Paris: Mondiale, 1953), and Antony Beevor and Artemis Cooper, *Paris after the Liberation, 1944–1949* (New York: Doubleday, 1994).

8. Fargue, *Le Piéton*, 148–49. Nicholas Hewitt, "Shifting Cultural Centres in Twentieth-Century Paris," in Sheringham, *Parisian Fields*, 30–45, provides a history of the relationship between Montmartre, Montparnasse, and Saint-Germain-des-Prés.

9. On the Left Bank during the occupation, see Herbert Lottman, *The Left Bank: Writers, Artists, and Politics from the Popular Front to the Cold War* (San Francisco: Halo Books, 1991).

10. Boris Vian, *Manuel de Saint-Germain-des-Prés* (1950; Paris: Chêne, 1974), 24–26.

11. Merlin, *Une belle époque*, 14.

12. La Rose Rouge was located first on the rue de la Harpe and then on the rue de Rennes, Le Quod Libet on the rue Pré-aux-Clercs, and L'Échelle de Jacob on the rue Jacob. The best look at the clubs and bistros of Saint-Germain-des-Prés is Geneviève Latour, *Le "Cabaret théâtre" 1945–1965* (Paris: Bibliothèque historique de la Ville de Paris, 1996).

13. Anne-Marie Deschodt, "Variétés," in *Les Années 40 d'Anne Bony*, ed. Anne Bony (Paris: Regard, 1985), 275.

14. Simone de Beauvoir, *The Prime of Life: The Autobiography of Simone de Beauvoir*, trans. Peter Green (Cleveland: World, 1962).

15. Claude Roy, "Le Monde de Jacques Prévert," *Positif: Revue périodique de cinéma* 2 (1953–54): 76–77.

16. Translation mine. For Lemarque's career and a history of song and popular culture in the contemporary period, see Serge Dillaz, *Vivre et chanter en France*, vol. 1, *1945–1980* (Paris: Fayard/Chorus, 2005).

17. On Saint-Germain-de-Prés and the postwar jazz era, see the works of Boris Vian, such as *Chroniques de jazz* (Paris: Pauvert, 1998), or *Jazz in Paris* (Paris: Pauvert, 1997). The revue *Jazz Hot* of the late 1940s provides excellent material on jazz. See also Colin Nettelbeck, *Dancing with de Beauvoir: Jazz and the French* (Melbourne: Melbourne University Publishing, 2005).

18. Roland Barthes, *Mythologies*, trans. Annette Lavers (New York: Noonday, 1972), 86. On

the Saint-Germain-des-Prés scene, see Guillaume Hanoteau, *L'Âge d'or de Saint-Germain-des-Prés* (Paris: Denoël, 1965), and Jean-Paul Caracalla, *Saint-Germain-des-Prés* (Paris: Flammarion, 1993).

19. In the mid-1950s there were some fifty thousand Americans in Paris, many of them living on the Left Bank.

20. "L'Existentialisme à Saint-Germain-des-Prés," *Les Actualités françaises*, October 20, 1951.

21. Jacques Becker, dir., *Rendez-vous de juillet* (U.G.C., Société nouvelle des établissements Gaumont, 1949). See *L'Écran français* 178 (23 November1948): 3.

22. *Combat*, August 20, 1949.

23. Beevor and Cooper, *Paris after the Liberation*, 344. See also Susan Weiner, *Enfants Terribles: Youth and Femininity in the Mass Media in France, 1945–1968* (Baltimore, MD: John Hopkins University Press, 2001).

24. Léo Malet, *La Nuit de Saint-Germain-des-Prés: Les Nouveaux mystères de Paris* (Paris: Livre de Poche, 1973), 32–33. *La Nuit de Saint-Germain-des-Prés* was adapted to film in 1976. Nestor Burma is one of the longest-running detective series of all time, with twenty-nine books and several short stories. The cartoonist Jacques Tardi adapted the novels to a series of superb graphic novels, and they were eventually adapted to both film and television. Under the pseudonym Frank Harding, Malet also created the character of the reporter Johnny Metal. See Francis Lacassin, *Sous le masque de Léo Malet: Nestor Burma* (Amiens: Encrage, 1993).

25. Léo Malet, *Micmac moche au Boul'Mich: Les Nouveaux mystères de Paris* (Paris: Presses de la Cité, 1957), 48–51. On the representation of Malet's arrondissements, see Lucette Le Van-Lemesle, "Léo Malet et ses 'nouveaux mystères,'" *Sociétés et représentations* 17 (2004): 171–82.

26. *L'Avant-garde*, January 4, 1949.

27. *L'Humanité*, January 2, 1953.

28. Bernard, *Paris rouge*, chapter 2.

29. *Clarté*, December 9, 1947. On the cold war and anti-Americanism in France, see Richard Kuisel, *Seducing the French*; Philippe Roger, *Rêves et cauchemars américains: Les États-Unis au miroir de l'opinion publique française (1945–1953)* (Paris: Presses universitaires du Septentrion, 1996); Jean-Philippe Mathy, *French Resistance: The French-American Culture Wars* (St. Paul: University of Minnesota Press, 2000); and Volker Berghahn, *America and the Intellectual Cold Wars in Europe* (Princeton, NJ: Princeton University Press, 2001).

30. Bernard, *Paris rouge*, 71.

31. Mension, *Tribe*, 11–12.

32. Karnow, *Paris in the Fifties*, 242.

33. *Télé Magazine*, November 30–December 6, 1958.

34. Marcel Carné, dir., *Les Tricheurs* (Silver-Films, Cinétel, 1958), and Eric Rohmer, dir., *Le Signe du lion* (Ajym Films, 1959).

35. *Le Monde*, October 14, 1958.

36. Stephen Barber makes this point in relation to Louis Malle's *Zazie dans le métro* (1960) and the French New Wave in *Projected Cities*, chapter 2.

37. *Les Lettres françaises*, October 16, 1958.

38. *Radio, cinéma, télévision*, October 26, 1958.

39. *Combat*, December 11, 1958.

40. *L'Express*, October 16, 1958.

41. "Le Dossier de la classe montante 18–23 ans," special issue, *Réalités femina-illustration* 167 (December 1959): 81.

42. Ibid., 68, and Émile Copfermann, *La Génération des blousons noirs: Problèmes de la jeunesse française*, 2nd ed. (Paris: La Découverte, 2003), 26, 33–34.

43. "Le Rock and Roll français, 1956," part 1, *Jukebox Magazine* 78 (February 1994): 57–65. See also Christian Victor and Julien Regoli, *Vingt ans de rock français* (Paris: Albin Michel, 1978),

16. The biography of Johnny Halliday is also very useful for details on early French rock: Alain Dister, *D'ou viens-tu Johnny?* (Paris: Plume, 1993).

44. *Paris Match* reported these scenes along with photographs. See, for example, *Paris Match*, October 3–10, 1953, and "Le Rock and Roll français, 1957–59," part 2, *Jukebox Magazine* 79 (March 1994): 53–58.

45. François Tétard makes the point that the *blousons noirs* of 1958–60 were still the generation of war children who dominated the 1950s. They were the older siblings of the baby boomers. For this reason, Tétard sees little relationship between the image and the arrival of rock and roll in France, at least in the first years after the *blousons noirs* appeared. François Tétard, "Le Phénomène 'blousons noirs' en France, fin des années 1950–début des années 1960," in *Révolte et société: Actes du IVe Colloque d'histoire au présent, May 1988*, ed. Fabienne Gambrelle and Michel Trebitsch, 2 vols. (Paris: Publications de la Sorbonne, 1989), 2:212.

46. Déon, *Les Gens*, 42.

47. Jean Chazal, *L'Enfance délinquante* (Paris: Presses universitaires de France, 1953), 20.

48. Préfecture de police, "Délinquance et prédélinquance juvénile," Report, 1959, 4–12. See also the summary of the report by the prefect of police to the municipal council, *BMO Débats*, December 7, 1959, 792–95.

49. Ibid., 782.

50. Copfermann, *Génération*, 26. Copfermann was in part motivated by his own difficult youth. His sociological study of the *blousons noirs* was originally published in 1962 by François Maspero Press. Copfermann was a writer and editor for the review *Partisans* and for François Maspero Press as well as Hachette. See Aurélie Cardin-Daeninckx, review of *La Génération des blousons noirs*, *Sociétés et représentations* 17 (2004): 374–75.

51. *Aux Écoutes du monde*, July 31, 1959.

52. Préfecture de police, "Délinquance et prédélinquance juvénile," 1959, 11.

53. *Aux Écoutes du monde*, 31 July 1959, 20.

54. Copfermann, *Génération*, 43.

55. *BMO Débats*, December 7, 1959, 788. Marcel Carné's film *Terrain vague* (1960) depicted a stark suburban void terrorized by a dangerous adolescent gang. Their leader is a violent bully who cruelly intimidates the film's young heroes and eventually drives one of them to his death.

56. Déon, *Gens de la nuit*, 136–37.

57. Flanner, *Paris Journal*, 386.

58. Pierre Bourdieu and Jean-Claude Passeron, *Les Héritiers: Les Étudiants et la culture* (Paris: Minuit, 1985), 120–21. Bourdieu and Passeron make the point that the proportion of French university students in Paris actually declined from 44 percent in 1950 to 32.5 percent by 1962.

59. These figures are given in the 1956 municipal council debates on the quality of higher education in Paris. *BMO Débats*, November 26, 1956, 835–36.

60. *Combat*, November 1, 1950. Student conditions are described in Didier Fischer, *L'Histoire des étudiants en France de 1945 à nos jours* (Paris: Flammarion, 2000), 35–36.

61. *France-soir*, November 17, 1949, cited in Didier Fischer, "Les Étudiants en France (1945–1968)" (Ph.D. diss., Université de Paris X-Nanterre, 1998), 65.

62. *Clarté* 14 (October–November 1958): 6.

63. Calet, *Les Deux bouts*, 101; and *Clarté* 14 (October–November 1958): 6.

64. Comité parisien des œuvres en faveur de la jeunesse scolaire et universitaire, "Assemblée générale du 5 juillet 1956," report; Kreigel, *Ce que j'ai cru comprendre* (Paris: Robert Laffont, 1991), quoted in Fischer, *L'Histoire des étudiants en France*, 36.

65. *Réalités*, December 1959, 114.

66. Hervé Hamon and Patrick Rotman, *Génération* (Paris: Seuil, 1987), 1:165.

67. Archives de Police, Étudiants, Manifestations, partis, groupes, 1946–1957, BA2134.

68. Bakhtin, *Rabelais and His World*, 260, 69.

69. See Jean-Paul Sartre, *L'Affaire Henri Martin* (Paris: Gallimard, 1953). See also the work of

the historian Alain Ruscio, especially *L'Affaire Henri Martin et la lutte contre la guerre d'Indochine* (Pantin: Le Temps des Cerises, 2005).

70. *Clarté* 1–9 (December 1947): 8; and *Clarté* 12 (March 1958): 1.

71. On the history of the UNEF, see Alain Monchablon, *Histoire de l'UNEF de 1956 à 1968* (Paris: Presses universitaires de France, 1983).

72. On the geography of protest in the Latin Quarter, see André Coutin, *Huit siècles de violence au Quartier Latin* (Paris: Stock, 1969), 354–55.

73. Cited in Eric Kocher-Marbœuf, "Le Maintien de l'ordre public lors des grèves de 1947," in *L'Année 1947*, ed. Serge Berstein and Pierre Milza (Paris: Presses de Sciences Po, 2000), 373–87. On the 1957 protests, see *Clarté* 4 (March 1957): 11.

74. See the collection of articles in Geneviève Dreyfus-Armand, Robert Frank, Marie-Françoise Lévy, and M. Zancarini-Fournel, *Les Années 68: Le Temps de la contestation* (Paris: Complexe, 2000). See also Joe Austin and Michael Nevin, *Generations of Youth: Youth Cultures and History in Twentieth-Century America* (New York: New York University Press, 1998), and Neil Smith, "Homeless/Global: Scaling Places," in *Mapping the Futures. Local Cultures, Global Change*, ed. Jon Bird, Barry Curtis, Tim Putnam, George Robertson, and Lisa Tickner (London and New York: Routledge, 1993), 87–121.

75. *Clarté*, special edition, November 12, 1948.

76. *Combat*, March 16, 1951; *Aurora*, March 16, 1951; *À Matin*, March 16, 1951; and Archives de Police, Grèves et manifestations étudiants 1951–1957, DB 553.

77. *Lutte pour une monde meilleur: Organe de combat des Jeunesses Socialistes (SFIO)*, January 10, 1954; and *Le Parisian libéré*, December 16, 1953.

78. *Libération*, December 16, 1953. See also *La Voix dentaire*, no. 57 bis, December 1954.

79. See *Le Parisian libéré*, June 30, 1954; and *Paris Match*, July 10–17, 1954.

80. *BMO Débats*, July 17, 1954, 601–4.

81. *L'Humanité*, March 3, 1956.

82. *France-soir*, May 25, 1956.

83. Jean-Yves Sabot, *Le Syndicalisme étudiant et la guerre d'Algérie: L'Entrée d'une génération en politique et la formation d'une élite* (Paris: L'Harmattan, 1995), 124–27. See also the introduction and chapter 1 of Michael Seidman, *The Imaginary Revolution: Parisian Students and Workers in 1968* (New York: Berghahn, 2004).

84. In response, the Ministry of Education cut off public funding for the UNEF. On the evolution of student attitudes and involvement in the Algerian crisis, see Michel de la Fournière, "Les Étudiants face à la guerre (1954–1957)," in *La Guerre d'Algérie et les français*, ed. Jean-Pierre Rioux (Paris: Fayard, 1990).

85. Jean Legaret, a member of the moderate RGR, was elected to the municipal council with heavy support from Gaullist voters. *BMO Débats*, March 17, 1956, 228 and 231–33.

86. Philippe Robrieux, *Notre génération communiste* (Paris: Laffont, 1977), cited in Bernard, *Paris rouge*, 94.

87. *Le Figaro*, May 12, 29, and 30, 1958.

Chapter Seven

1. There is extensive documentation on these expositions at the Centre des archives contemporaines de Fontainebleau (CAC) and the Archives nationales. Among the most interesting is the collection of "Albums photographiques" at the Archives nationales listed under numbers F14: 18267 and 18281–82. See also "L'Exposition des Techniques Américaines de l'Habitation et de l'Urbanisme," *L'Architecture d'aujourd'hui* 6 (May–June 1946): 84–88, and "L'Exposition internationale de l'Urbanisme et de l'Habitation," *L'Architecture d'aujourd'hui* 13–14 (September 1947): 120–32, as well as the special issue on the Exposition Internationale de l'Urbanisme et de l'Habitation, *L'Architecture française* 71–72 (1947).

2. Catalog of the Exposition internationale "L'Urbanisme et l'habitation," Paris, Grand

Palais and Cours la Reine, July 10–August 17, 1947, quoted in *Reconstructions et modernisation: La France après les ruines, 1918 . . . 1945*, ed. Direction des archives de France and Ministère de la culture de la communication et des grands travaux (Paris: Archives nationales, 1991).

3. For an analysis of Haussmann's work see David P. Jordan, *Transforming Paris: The Life and Labors of Baron Haussmann* (Chicago: University of Chicago Press, 1995). See also Michel Carmona, *Haussmann: His Life and Times, and the Making of Modern Paris* (Chicago: Ivan R. Dee, 2002).

4. C. Eyraud, "Ville de Paris," Exposition internationale de l'urbanisme et de l'habitation, *Revue urbanisme* 116 (June 1947): 160–61.

5. Christine M. Boyer, *The City of Collective Memory: Its Historical Imagery and Architectural Entertainments* (Cambridge, MA: MIT Press, 1994), 46. On the history of CIAM, see Eric Paul Mumford, *The CIAM Discourse on Urbanism, 1928–1960* (Cambridge, MA: MIT Press, 2000).

6. C. Eyraud, "Ville de Paris," 160–61.

7. Marcel Raval, "Haussmann contre Paris," in Champigneulle, *Destinée de Paris*.

8. Le Corbusier, *Destin de Paris* (Paris: Fernand Sorlot, 1941), 10. On Le Corbusier's vision of Paris, see also Rémy Baudouï, "LaVille et ses anti-modèles," *Revue urbanisme* 282 (May–June 1995): 46–50, and Bernard Rouleau, *Paris: Histoire d'un espace* (Paris: Seuil, 1997).

9. Le Corbusier, *The Radiant City: Elements of a Doctrine of Urbanism to be Used as the Basis of Our Machine-Age Civilization* (NewYork: Orion, 1967), 101.

10. Champigneulle, *Destinée de Paris*, 21.

11. For example, Gaston Bardet, "Incarnation de l'urbanisme," *Esprit* 9 (August 1, 1945): 342.

12. Conseil national, 7ème Commission, Commission d'étude de la région parisienne, Séance inaugurale de la Commission d'étude de la région parisienne, 5 Février 1942, Vœux adoptés par la Commission dans ses séances du mardi 10 Février 1942, CAC, Archives du Ministère de l'équipement, Documentation sur l'aménagement de la région parisienne, 1924–1945, 770784, AT 280.

13. Robert Paxton, *Vichy France: Old Guard and New Order, 1940–1944* (NewYork: Columbia University Press, 1972), 352.

14. The Comité supérieur de l'aménagement et de l'organisation générale de la région parisienne (CSAORP), created by President Raymond Poincaré in 1928, was transfigured into a consultive Comité d'Aménagement de la Région Parisienne (CARP), with a planning arm, the Service d'aménagement et d'urbanisme de la région parisienne (SARP), and technical services, the Services techniques de topographie et d'urbanisme. These new agencies were charged with studying conditions in the capital and its surrounding region and then creating a new plan.

15. Among the most important members of the DGEN was Henri Giraud, the director of public works for the city of Paris. Frédéric Surleau, an engineer who had worked for Raoul Dautry in railroad administration and in the ministry of armaments, took his place as head of the organization. André Prothin was initially an engineer with the Direction générale des travaux de Paris, then chief engineer with the Services techniques de la préfecture de la Seine where he worked under Henri Giraud. Prothin was a member of the DGEN from its inception and became the director of CARP. Pierre Gibel was as well an engineer with the Services techniques de la préfecture de la Seine during the 1930s, working directly under Henri Giraud, before joining the DGEN. Gibel became the director of SARP. On these administrative changes and the government policy on the reconstruction of French cities in general, see Voldman, *La Reconstruction des villes françaises*.

16. Conseil national, 7ème Commission, Commission d'étude de la région parisienne.

17. Louis Hourticq, "Paris d'hier et de demain," *L'Architecture française* 41 (March 1944): 3.

18. "L'inspection générale des services techniques de topographique et d'urbanisme de la préfecture de la Seine," IX Salon des urbanistes, *Revue urbanisme* 92–93 (July–August 1943): 168–71.

19. Maurice Baudot, "Le Problème du relogement à l'occasion des opérations d'urbanisme de Paris," *L'Architecture française* 34 (August 1943): 5.

20. Loi du 4 juin 1941 autorisant l'exécution d'un programme de travaux d'équipement et d'urbanisme à réaliser dans la région parisienne. No. 2379, Journal Officiel du 8 juin 1941, p. 2374, CAC, Archives du Ministère de l'équipement, Documentation sur l'aménagement de la région parisienne, 1924–1945, 770784, AT 280.

21. See "La 'Ceinture verte' de Paris," *Revue urbanisme* 86 (January 1943): 20–25.

22. L'Inspecteur général, Chef des Services techniques de topographie et d'urbanisme, Projet d'aménagement de la ville de Paris (1943), quoted in Cohen and Lortie, *Des fortifs au périf*, 46.

23. René Mestais, "Commentaires sur l'envoi des services de topographie et d'urbanisme de la Seine," *L'Architecture française* 34 (August 1943): 14.

24. Baudot, "Le Problème du relogement," 5.

25. Conseil national, 7ème Commission, Commission d'étude de la région parisienne.

26. Baudot, "Le Problème du relogement," 8. This reconceptualization of the Paris region initially took place in August 1941 with the Loi relative à l'aménagement de la région parisienne, in which the Prost Plan was officially approved by Vichy and then expanded. The Paris region was also described in detail in the 1941 Charte de l'urbanisme written largely by André Gutton; see Gutton, *La Charte de l'urbanisme* (Paris: Dunod, 1941). The plan was approved once again in June 1943 as part of the new Law on Urbanism.

27. Maurice Baudot and Ch.-J. Reverdy, "Le programme d'équipement sportif dans le département de la Seine," *Techniques et Architecture* 1 (September–October 1941), 32, quoted in Cohen and Lortie, *Des fortifs au périf*, 236. On Vichy policy, see Rémi Baudouï, *À l'assaut de la région parisienne: Les Conditions de naissance d'une politique d'aménagement régional, 1919–1945* (Paris: École d'architecture Paris-Villemin, 1990), and Jean-Pierre Rioux, *La Vie culturelle sous Vichy* (Paris: Complexe, 1990).

28. Maurice Baudot, "Paris 1942," *L'Architecture française* 17–18 (March–April 1942): 3.

29. Flouret, *Communication sur le problème du logement*, 3.

30. Pierre Lavedan, "Paris et l'urbanisme," in Romains, *Portrait de Paris*, 55.

31. Anatole Kopp, Frédérique Boucher, and Danièle Pauly, *L'Architecture de la reconstruction en France, 1945–1953* (Paris: Moniteur, 1982), 272–74.

32. Flouret, *Communication sur le problème du logement*, 55–56.

33. Ibid., 99.

34. The phrase *culture parisienne* is used in particular in Rémi Baudouï, "Institut d'urbanisme de Paris et le problème parisien (1919–1939)," in "Région parisienne: Approches d'une notion, 1860–1980," ed. Danièle Voldman, special issue, *Les Cahiers de l'IHTP* 12 (October 1989): 119–27.

35. André Prothin, "Urbanisme et reconstruction," *L'Architecture d'aujourd'hui* 7–8 (September–October 1946): 2.

36. Pierre Gibel, "La Région parisienne," *L'Architecture d'aujourd'hui* 7–8 (September–October 1946): 75.

37. Ibid., 72–75. See also the longer analysis in "La région parisienne," *La Vie urbaine* 56 (April–June 1950), the periodical associated with the Institut d'urbanisme de Paris.

38. Jean Lojkine, *La Politique urbaine dans la région parisienne, 1945–1971* (Paris: École Pratique des Hautes Études and Mouton, 1972), 50.

39. Eugène Claudius (Claudius-Petit), "Renaissance," *L'architecture d'aujourd'hui* 1 (1945). See Benoît Pouvreau, Danièle Voldman, and Dominique Claudius-Petit, *Un Politique en architecture: Eugène Claudius-Petit (1907–1989)* (Paris: Le Moniteur, 2004).

40. Gravier, *Paris et le désert français*, 192–93. Gravier taught at the University of Belgrade and worked at the Secrétariat général à la jeunesse (1941–42) and then the Alexis-Carrel Foundation (1943–44).

41. Nivet, *Le Conseil municipal de Paris de 1944 à 1977*, 287. Nivet cites a litany of examples of the budgetary and financial battles between the municipality and the state.

42. Zone A: Habitation et commerce de détail; Zone B: Résidence; Zone C: Centre des affaires; Zone D: Centre d'échanges commerciaux; Zone E: Entrepôts et transit; Zone F: Activités industrielles.

43. *BMO Débats*, July 5, 1956, 489–91.

44. Conseil municipal de Paris, Commission d'aménagement de Paris, Rapport présenté par M. André Thirion sur les opérations générales et locales de voirie et la répartition des espaces vertes, Décembre 1951, BAVP, 200801, 6.

45. *BMO Débats*, April 8, 1953, 103.

46. *BMO Débats*, 1950, 299, quoted in Philippe Nivet, "Le Conseil municipal face aux rénovations (1945–1977)," in Lucan, *Eau et gaz*, 122.

47. *BMO Débats*, April 8, 1953, 105.

48. This debate is described in Nivet, "Le Conseil municipal," in Lucan, *Eau et gaz*, 118–35. The negotiations over the regional highway system are recounted in Cohen and Lortie, *Des fortifs au périf*, 250–58.

49. Prothin, "Urbanisme et reconstruction," 2, and Comité d'aménagement de la région parisienne, Séance plénière du 17 mars 1952, CAC, Archives du Ministère de l'équipement, Documentation sur l'aménagement de la région parisienne, 1924–1945, 770784, AT 280.

50. *BMO Débats*, April 8, 1953, 107.

51. Préfecture de la Seine, Commissariat à la construction et à l'urbanisme pour la région parisienne, Direction de l'urbanisme, *Plan d'urbanisme directeur de Paris* (Paris: Imprimerie municipale, 1960), 3:37. The MRU's interpretation of these negotiations can be found in *Projet d'aménagement de la région parisienne, 1945–1956*, September 23, 1956 (1), Archives de l'Équipement, CAC 770784, AT 280.

52. Édouard Frédéric-Dupont, introduction to Legaret, *Le Statut de Paris*, 2:5–7. Frédéric-Dupont was president of the municipal council.

53. *Paris Match*, January 23–30, 1954.

54. Conseil municipal de Paris, "Solutions aux problèmes de Paris" (Paris: Comité du nouveau Paris, 1954), 85, brochure.

55. Bernard Lafay, "Problèmes de Paris: Contribution aux travaux du Conseil municipal; Esquisse d'un plan directeur et d'un programme d'action," Rapports et documents du Conseil municipal 11 (Paris: Conseil municipal, 1954). Published in brochure format as Conseil municipal de Paris, "Solutions aux problèmes de Paris" (Paris: Comité du nouveau Paris, 1954).

56. Raymond Lopez, "Problèmes de Paris," *L'Architecture d'aujourd'hui* 63 (December 1955–January 1956): 34–35. See also his master study, *L'Avenir des villes* (Paris: Robert Laffont, 1964).

57. This remark by the municipal councilor Édouard Frédéric-Dupont as well as a discussion on the Lafay plan are given in Nivet, "Le Conseil municipal," in Lucan, *Eau et gaz*, 124.

58. Raymond Lopez, "Paris se meurt: Vive Paris!," *Le Nef* 7 (June 1957): 84.

59. Maria Gravari-Barbas, "Patrimoine et modernité: Les Monuments historiques dans les deux Chartes d'Athènes, 1931–1933," in *Aux débuts de l'urbanisme français*, ed. Vincent Berdoulay and Paul Claval (Paris: L'Harmattan, 2001).

60. Albert Guérard, "Urbanisme parisien: Servitude de beauté," *Revue urbanisme* 55 (1957): 146–47.

61. Ibid., 157.

62. This term is used in, for example, "Le Nouveau Projet d'aménagement," *Revue urbanisme* 51 (1957): 51.

63. Bernard Lafay, *Problèmes de Paris*, 114.

64. See "L'Aménagement de la ceinture vert à Paris," *Revue urbanisme* 35–36 (1954): 11–20.

65. Evenson, *Paris*, 285.
66. Pierre Sudreau, "Reconquête de Paris," *Revue urbanisme* 49–50 (1956): 300–301.
67. Pierre Sudreau, "À l'heure de l'Europe," *Revue urbanisme* 55 (1957): 140–41.
68. Communication de M. le Préfet de la Seine (Émile Pelletier) au Conseil municipal, Activité du Centre de documentation et d'urbanisme, November 12, 1957.
69. See "Mémoire de M. le préfet de la Seine (Jean Benedetti) sur la plan d'urbanisme directeur de la ville de Paris," 1958; and Préfecture de la Seine, Commissariat à la construction et à l'urbanisme pour la région parisienne, *Plan d'urbanisme*, 3:13–14.
70. Roland Bernard, dir., *Problèmes de la construction* [television series], "La France de Demain" (ORTF, broadcast November 27, 1958).
71. Roland Bernard, dir., *Problèmes de la construction* [television series], "Aménagement du Territoire" (ORTF, broadcast November 20, 1958).
72. Préfecture de la Seine, "Décentralisation industrielle."
73. Sudreau, "A l'heure de l'Europe," 140.
74. Préfecture de la Seine, Commissariat à la construction et à l'urbanisme pour la région parisienne, *Plan d'urbanisme*, 2:95.
75. James C. Scott, *Seeing like a State: How Certain Schemes to Improve the Human Condition Have Failed* (New Haven, CT:Yale University Press, 1998), 102.
76. Léo Malet, *Fièvre au Marais: Les Nouveaux mystères de Paris* (Paris: Presses de la Cité, 1955), 84–85; translation mine.
77. Fargue, *Le Piéton de Paris*, 95, 99-100; translation mine.
78. Henri Laborde, quoted in B. Cacérès, *Regards neufs sur Paris* (Paris: Seuil, 1952), 161–63.
79. Clébert, *Paris insolite*, 41.
80. Mestais, "Commentaires sur l'envoi des services de topographie de d'urbanisme de la Seine," 10; translation mine.
81. Georges Pillement, *Destruction de Paris* (Paris: Grasset, 1941). Again in 1944, a group of intellectuals and writers, including Jean Giranduoux and Jean Cocteau, wrote a letter of protest to Marshal Pétain against the demolition of the Marais.
82. In 1942–43 well over two thousand dwellings in Paris were cleared out. La Documentation française, *La Lutte contre les taudis*, 1:15.
83. Guy Périer de Féral, "Aménagement de l'îlot XVI," *L'Architecture française* 41 (1944): 6.
84. Ibid.
85. Pierre Pinon, *Paris: Biographie d'une capitale* (Paris: Hazan, 1999), 265.The 1887 preservation law specifically protected any classified monument, and a new national preservation law in 1913 provided for the landmarking of private buildings. The 1930 law further protected historic, artistic, scientific, or picturesque sites (especially around monuments).Various preservation groups succeeded in classifying the Esplanade des Invalides, the Champs-Élysées from the place de la Concorde to the Rond-Point, and the Île de la Folie in the Bois de Boulogne as historic, protected areas.The Commission des perspectives monumentales (1909), the Commission du vieux Paris (1897), and the Commission départementale des sites (1930) were the most important preservationist organizations.The Ligue nationale contre le taudis (1925) and the Ligue urbaine (1928), created by Raoul Dautry and Jean Giraudoux, were also newer entries into the field.
86. Recounted in SimonTexier, *Paris contemporain de Haussmann à nos jours: Une capitale à l'ère des métropoles* (Paris: Parigramme, 2005), 172.
87. Élie Debidour, *La Conservation de vieux-Paris et l'urbanisme* (Paris: Musée Social, 1945), 29.
88. Georges Pillement, "Démolitions présentes et futures," in Champigneulle, *Destinée de Paris*, 92.
89. RogerVerlomme, *L'Œuvre de relèvement dans le département de la Seine depuis la Libération: Exposé présenté au Conseil municipal de Paris et au Conseil général de la Seine lors de leur session de mars 1950* (Paris: Imprimerie Municipale, 1950), 75.

90. Jean-Marc Campagne, "Renaissance d'un vieux quartier," *L'Architecture française* 41 (March 1944): 7–17.

91. Louis Chevalier, *Les Parisiens* (Paris: Hachette, 1967), 151–52.

92. Henri Vergnolle, "L'Œuvre de l'Office public d'habitations à loyer modéré de la ville de Paris," *Bulletin de l'Union nationale des fédérations d'organismes d'habitations à loyer modéré* 17 (January–February 1952), recounted in Jacques Lucan, "Mille cinq cents hectares à reconquérir," in Lucan, *Eau et gaz*, 138.

93. Comité d'aménagement de la région parisienne, Séance plénière du 17 mars 1952, CAC, Archives du Ministère de l'équipement, Documentation sur l'aménagement de la région parisienne, 1924–1945, 770784, AT 280, 6–8.

94. Albert Laprade, "Aménagement des quartiers historiques," *Revue urbanisme* 55 (1957):156–60.

95. Centre de documentation et d'urbanisme et la préfecture de la Seine, *Le Marais*, Étude présentée par M. Mayère, Ingénieur divisionnaire, STUVP, 3 vols. (1961–62).

Conclusion

1. Boutet de Monvel, *Les Demains de Paris*, 7. See also Michel Ragon, *Paris, hier, aujourd'hui, demain* (Paris: Hachette, 1965).

2. De Certeau, *Practice of Everyday Life*, 109.

3. Marc Augé, "Paris and the Ethnography of the Contemporary World," in Sheringham, *Parisian Fields*, 176.

Libraries and Archives

Archives du Ministère de l'équipement, Centre des archives contemporaines (CAC)
Archives nationales
Archives de Paris
Archives de la Préfecture de police
Bibliothèque administrative de la ville de Paris (BAVP)
Bibliothèque de l'Arsenal
Bibliothèque du film
Bibliothèque historique de la ville de Paris (BHVP)
Bibliothèque nationale
CEDIAS-Musée social
Centre de documentation France-Europe-Monde
Fonds Pivert, Centre d'histoire sociale du XXe siècle
Forum des Images
Institut national de l'audiovisuel (INA)
Médiathèque musicale de Paris
Pavillon de l'Arsenal

Government Documents

Bulletin municipal officiel (BMO), Débats
Centre de documentation et d'urbanisme
Commissariat à la construction et à l'urbanisme pour la région parisienne
Commission d'étude de la région parisienne
Conseil général de la Seine
Conseil municipal de Paris
La Documentation française
Institut national d'études démographiques
Ministère de l'équipement
Ministère de l'intérieur
Ministère de la reconstruction et de l'urbanisme (MRU)
Préfecture du département de la Seine

Periodicals

Action
L'Architecture d'aujourd'hui
L'Architecture française
L'Aube
L'Aurore
Aux Écoutes du monde
L'Avenir de la banlieue de Paris
Cahiers de l'Institut d'aménagement et d'urbanisme de la région parisienne
Ce Matin
Clarté
Combat
La Conjoncture économique dans le département
L'Écran français
Esprit
L'Express
Le Figaro
France-soir
Franc-tireur
L'Humanité
Jukebox Magazine
Les Lettres françaises
Le Monde
Lutte pour un monde meilleur
Paris Match
Le Parisien libéré
Population
Positif: Revue périodique de cinéma
Radio, cinéma, télévision
Réalités femina-illustration
Revue urbanisme
Syndicalisme
Télé Magazine
La Vie ouvrière
La Vie urbaine

Published Sources

Abram, Joseph. *Du Chaos à la croissance, 1940–1966.* Vol. 2 of *L'Architecture moderne en France*, edited by Gérard Monnier. Paris: Picard Éditeur, 1999.
Alary, Eric, Bénédicte Vergez-Chaignon, and Gilles Gauvin. *Les Français au quotidien, 1939–1949.* Paris: Perrin, 2006.
AlSayyad, Nezar. *Cinematic Urbanism: A History of the Modern from Reel to Real.* New York London: Routledge, 2006.
Amiot, Michel. *Contre l'état, les sociologues: Éléments pour une histoire de la sociologie urbaine en France (1900–1980).* Paris: Éditions de l'école des hautes études en sciences sociales, 1986.
Aragon, Louis. *Le Paysan de Paris.* Paris: Folio, 1926.
Arbasino, Alberto. *Paris, Ô Paris.* Translated by Dominique Férault. Paris: Gallimard, 1997.
Asen, Robert, and Daniel C. Brouwer, eds. *Counterpublics and the State.* Albany: State University of New York Press, 2001.

Association française pour la diffusion du patrimoine photographique. *Willy Ronis par Willy Ronis: Exposition rétrospective.* Plessis-Robinson: Blanchard, 1985.
Austin, Joe, and Michael Nevin. *Generations of Youth: Youth Cultures and History in Twentieth-Century America.* New York: New York University Press, 1998.
Auzelle, Robert. *Plaidoyer pour une organisation consciente de l'espace.* Paris: Vincent et Fréal, 1962.
———. *Recherche d'une méthode d'enquête sur l'habitat défecteux.* Paris: Vincent et Fréal, 1950.
———. *Techniques de l'urbanisme.* Paris: Presses universitaires de France, 1953.
Aveline, Claude. *Dans Paris retrouvé.* Paris: Émile-Paul Fréres, 1945.
Babelay, Jean-Louis. *Un an.* Paris: Raymond Schall, 1946.
Bachelard, Gaston. *La Poétique de l'espace.* Paris: Presses universitaires de France, 1957.
Bakhtin, Michael. *The Dialectic Imagination: Four Essays by M. M. Bakhtin.* Edited by M. Holquist. Austin: University of Texas Press, 1981.
———. *Rabelais and His World.* Translated by H. Isowolsky. Cambridge, MA: MIT Press, 1984.
Bancquart, Marie-Claire. *Paris dans la littérature française après 1945.* Paris: La Différence, 2006.
———. *Paris des surréalistes.* Paris: Seghers, 1972.
Barber, Stephen. *Projected Cities: Cinema and Urban Space.* London: Reaktion Books, 2002.
Bardet, Gaston. "Incarnation de l'urbanisme." *Esprit* 9 (August 1, 1945): 342–62.
———. *Le Nouvel urbanisme.* Paris: Vincent et Fréal, 1948.
———. *Pierre sur pierre: Construction du nouvel urbanisme.* Paris: L.C.B., 1946.
Barthes, Roland. *Camera lucida: Reflections on Photography.* New York: Hill and Wang, 1982.
———. *Mythologies.* Translated by Annette Lavers. New York: Noonday, 1972.
Bastié, Jean. *La Croissance de la banlieue parisienne.* Paris: Presses Universitaires de France, 1964.
———. *Géographie du grand Paris.* Paris: Masson, 1984.
———. *Nouvelle histoire de Paris: Paris de 1945 à 2000.* Paris: Hachette, 2000.
———. *Paris en l'an 2000.* Paris: Sedimo, 1964.
Baudouï, Rémi. *À l'assaut de la région parisienne: Les Conditions de naissance d'une politique d'aménagement régional, 1919–1945.* Paris: École d'architecture Paris-Villemin, 1990.
Baudry, Patrick, and Thierry Pacquot, eds. *L'urbain et ses imaginaires.* Pessac: Maison des sciences de l'homme d'Aquitaine, 2003.
Beaumont-Maillet, Laure, Bernard Billaud, Jean Dérens, and Guy-Michel Leproux, eds. *Mélanges d'histoire de Paris à la mémoire de Michel Fleury.* Paris: Maisonneuve, 2004.
Beauvoir, Simone de. *The Prime of Life: The Autobiography of Simone de Beauvoir.* Translated by Peter Green. Cleveland: World, 1962.
Beevor, Anthony, and Artemis Cooper. *Paris after the Liberation, 1944–1949.* New York: Doubleday, 1994.
Bellow, Saul. *It All Adds Up: From the Dim Past to the Uncertain Future.* New York: Viking, 1994.
Benjamin, Walter. *The Arcades Project.* Translated by Howard Eiland and Kevin McLaughlin. Cambridge, MA: Belknap Press of Harvard University Press, 2002.
Berdoulay, Vincent, and Paul Claval, eds. *Aux débuts de l'urbanisme français.* Paris: L'Harmattan, 2001.
Berghahn, Volker. *America and the Intellectual Cold Wars in Europe.* Princeton, NJ: Princeton University Press, 2001.
Bernard, Jean-Pierre A. *Paris rouge, 1944–1964: Les Communistes français dans la capitale.* Seyssel: Champs Vallon, 1991.
Berréby, Gérard. *Documents relatifs à la fondation de l'internationale situationniste, 1948–1957.* Paris: Éditions Allia, 1985.
Berstein, Serge, and Pierre Milza, eds. *L'Année 1947.* Paris: Presses de Sciences Po, 2000.

Bidermanas, Izis. *Paris Enchanted*. London: Harvill, 1951.
Binh, N. T. *Paris au cinéma: La Vie rêvée de la capitale de Méliès à Amélie Poulain*. Paris: Parigramme, 2003.
Bird, Jon, Barry Curtis, Tim Putnam, George Robertson, and Lisa Tickner, eds. *Mapping the Futures. Local Cultures, Global Change*. London and New York: Routledge, 1993.
Bishop, Michael. *Jacques Prévert: From Film and Theater to Poetry, Art and Song*. Amsterdam and New York: Rodopi, 2002.
Blanchard, Pascal, Eric Deroo, Driss El Yazami, Pierre Fournié, and Gilles Manseron. *Le Paris arabe*. Paris: La Découverte, 2003.
Blasquez, Adélaïde, ed,. *Gaston Lucas, serrurier: Chronique de l'anti-héros*. Paris: Plon, 1976.
Bloch-Lainé, François, and Jean Bouvier. *La France restaurée, 1944–1954*. Paris: Fayard, 1986.
Bonin, Sylvie. *Je me souviens du 14e arrondissement*. Paris: Parigramme, 1993.
Bony, Anne, ed. *Les Années 40 d'Anne Bony*. Paris: Regard, 1985.
———, ed. *Les Années 50 d'Anne Bony*. 2 vols. Paris: Regard, 1982.
Bourdelas, Laurent. *Le Paris de Nestor Burma: L'Occupation et les "trente glorieuses" de Léo Malet*. Paris: L'Harmattan, 2007.
Bourdieu, Pierre, and Jean-Claude Passeron. *Les Héritiers: Les Étudiants et la culture*. Paris: Minuit, 1985.
Bourdon, Jérôme, ed. *La Grande aventure du petit écran: La Télévision française, 1935–1975*. Paris: Musée d'histoire contemporaine–BDIC et INA, 1997.
Boutet de Monvel, Noël. *Les Demains de Paris*. Paris: Éditions Denoël, 1964.
Boyer, Christine M. *The City of Collective Memory: Its Historical Imagery and Architectural Entertainments*. Cambridge, MA: MIT Press, 1994.
Brandist, Craig, ed. *Materializing Bakhtin*. London: Palgrave, 2000.
Brossat, Alain. *Libération: Fête folle*. Série Mémoires 30. Paris: Autrement, 1994.
Brunet, Jean-Paul, ed. *Immigration, vie politique et populisme en banlieue parisienne (fin XIXe–XXe siècles)*. Paris: L'Harmattan, 1995.
Bullock, Nicholas. *Building the Post-war World: Modern Architecture and Reconstruction in Britain*. London: Routledge, 2002.
Buss, Robin. *French Film Noir*. London and New York: Marion Boyars, 1994.
Bussierre, Michèle de, and Caroline Mauriat, eds. *Les Années cinquante à la radio et à la télévision*. Paris: Comité d'histoire de la radio and Comité d'histoire de la télévision, 1991.
Bussierre, Michèle de, Caroline Mauriat, and Cécile Méadel. *Histoire des programmes: Histoire des jeux à la radio et à la télévision*. Paris: Comité d'histoire de la télévision, Group d'études historiques sur la radiodiffusion, Comité d'histoire de la radio, 1986.
Cacérès, B. *Regards neufs sur Paris*. Paris: Seuil, 1952.
Calabi, Donatella. *Marcel Poëte et le Paris des années vingt: Aux origines de "l'histoire des villes."* Translated by P. Savy. Paris: L'Harmattan, 1998.
Calet, Henri. *Les Deux bouts*. 7th ed. Paris: Gallimard, 1954.
———. *Les Grands largeurs: Balades parisiennes*. Paris: Vineta, 1951.
———. *Le Tout sur le tout*. Paris: Gallimard, 1948.
Calhoun, Craig. *Habermas and the Public Sphere*. Cambridge, MA: MIT Press, 1992.
Caracalla, Jean-Paul. *Le Paris de Jacques Prévert*. Paris: Flammarion, 2000.
———. *Saint-Germain-des-Prés*. Paris: Flammarion, 1993.
Carmona, Michel. *Le Grand Paris: L'Évolution de l'idée d'aménagement de la région parisienne*. 2 vols. Bagneux: Girotypo, 1979.
———. *Haussmann: His Life and Times, and the Making of Modern Paris*. Chicago: Ivan R. Dee, 2002.
Carné, Marcel. *Ma vie à belles dentes*. Paris: Archipel, 1996.
Carré, R. "Chanteurs et chansons des rues." *Gavroche: Revue d'histoire populaire* 69–70 (May–August 1993): 27–30.

Castells, Manuel, ed. *Crise du logement et mouvements sociaux urbains: Enquête sur la région parisienne*. Paris: Mouton, 1978.

Cazenave, François, ed. *Pionnier et visionaire de la télévision: Jean D'Arcy parle*. Paris: La Documentation française, 1984.

Célati, Jean-Louis, and Pierre Cavillon. *Chronique de la rue parisienne: Les Années 50*. Paris: Parigramme, 2005.

Cendrars, Blaise. *La Banlieue de Paris*. With 130 photographs by Robert Doisneau. Paris: Pierre Seghers, 1949.

Centre Georges Pompidou, ed. *Paris 1937–Paris 1957*. 2nd ed. Paris: Centre Georges Pompidou/ Gallimard, 1992.

Centre national de la photographie. *Willy Ronis*. Introduction by Betrand Eveno. Paris: Centre national de la photographie, 1991.

Certeau, Michel de. *The Practice of Everyday Life*. Translated by Steven Rendall. Berkeley: University of California Press, 1984.

Chabot, Georges. "Faubourgs, banlieues et zones d'influence." *La Vie urbaine (Urbanisme et habitation)* 3–4 (July–December 1954): 161–66.

Chadych, Danièle, and Dominique Leborgne. *Atlas de Paris : Évolution d'un paysage urbain*. Paris: Parigramme, 2007.

Champigneulle, Bernard, ed. *Destinée de Paris*. Paris: Éditions du Chêne, 1943.

Champion, Virginie, Bertrand Lemoine, and Claude Terraux. *Les Cinémas de Paris, 1945–1995*. Paris: Délégation à l'action artistique de la ville de Paris, 1995.

Chardère, Bernard. *Le Cinéma de Jacques Prévert*. Bordeaux: Castor Astral, 2001.

———. *Jacques Prévert: Inventaire d'une vie*. Paris: Gallimard, 1997.

Chaslin, François. *Les Paris de François Mitterrand*. Paris: Gallimard, 1989.

Chazal, Jean. *L'Enfance délinquante*. Paris: Presses universitaires de France, 1953.

Chevalier, Louis. *The Assassination of Paris*. Translated by David Jordan. Chicago: University of Chicago Press, 1994.

———. *Les Parisiens*. Paris: Hachette, 1967.

Chion, Michel. *The Films of Jacques Tati*. Toronto: Guernica, 2003.

Choay, Françoise. *L'Allégorie du patrimoine*. Paris: Seuil, 1992.

———. *Le Régle et le modèle*. Paris: Seuil, 1998.

Chollet, Laurent. *Les Situationnistes: L'Utopie incarnée*. Paris: Découvertes Gallimard, 2004.

Chombart de Lauwe, Paul-Henry. *Un anthropologue dans le siècle; Entretiens avec Thierry Paquot*. Paris: Descartes & Cie, 1996.

———. *Paris: Essais de sociologie, 1952–1964*. Paris: Éditions Ouvrières, 1965.

———. *Pour retrouver la France: Enquêtes sociales en équipes*. Grenoble: École nationale des Cadres d'Uriage, 1943.

———. "Scandale du logement et espoirs de l'urbanisme." *Esprit* 206 (September 1953): 571–79.

———. *La Vie quotidienne des familles ouvrières*. 3rd ed. Paris: CNRS, 1977.

———, Serge Antoine, Jacques Bertin, Louis Chauvet, Louis Couvreur, and Jacqueline Gauthier. *Paris et l'agglomération parisienne*. 2 vols. Paris: Presses universitaires de France, 1952.

Christ, Yvan. *Paris des utopies*. Paris: André Balland, 1970.

Clark, T. J. *The Painting of Modern Life*. Princeton, NJ: Princeton University Press, 1984.

Clavel, Maïté. *Sociologie de l'urbain*. Paris: Anthropos, 2002.

Clébert, Jean-Paul. *Paris insolite*. Paris: Denoël, 1954.

Coing, Henri. *Rénovation urbaine et changement social (L'Îlot no. 4, Paris 13e)*. Paris: Éditions Ouvrières, 1966.

Comité des Zoniers. "La Zône." Pamphlet. Paris: Chartes Guyet, 1945.

Cohen, Evelyne. "Expliquer Paris à la télévision: Pierre Sudreau et les problèmes de la construction (1958)." *Sociétés & Représentations* 17 (2004): 117–27.

———. *Paris dans l'imaginaire national de l'entre-deux-guerres*. Paris: Publications de la Sorbonne, 1999.
Cohen, Evelyne, and Marie-Françoise Lévy, eds. *La Télévision des trente glorieuses: Culture et politique*. Paris: CNRS, 2007.
Cohen, Jean-Louis. "L''architecture urbaine' selon Pierre Lavedan." *Les Cahiers de la recherche architecturale* 32–33 (1959): 157–68.
———. "Le 'nouvel urbanisme' de Gaston Bardet." *Le Visiteur: Ville, territoire, paysage, architecture* 2 (Spring 1996): 134–47.
———. *Scenes of the World to Come: European Architecture and the American Challenge, 1893–1960*. Paris: Flammarion; Montreal: Canadian Center for Architecture, 1995.
———, and André Lortie. *Des fortifs au périf: Paris, les seuils de la ville*. Paris: Édition du Pavillon de l'Arsenal and Picard Éditeur, 1991.
———, and Bruno Fortier, eds. *Paris: La Ville et ses projets*. Paris: Babylone/Pavillon de l'Arsenal, 1988.
Cohen, Yves, and Rémi Baudouï, eds. *Les Chantiers de la paix sociale (1900–1940)*. Fontenay/Saint-Cloud: ENS Editions, 1995.
Coornaert, Monique, and Jean-Pierre Garnier, eds. "Actualités de Henri Lefebvre." Special issue, *Espaces et sociétés* 76 (1994).
Copfermann, Emile. *La Génération des blousons noirs: Problèmes de la jeunesse française*. 2nd ed. Paris: La Découverte, 2003.
Corbin, Alain, Noëlle Gérome, and Danielle Tartakowsky, eds. *Les Usages politiques des fêtes aux XIXe–XXe siècles*. Paris: Publications de la Sorbonne, 1994.
Cornu, Marcel. *La Conquête de Paris*. Paris: Mercure de France, 1972.
Courand, Claude. *Je me souviens du 12e arrondissement*. Paris: Parigramme/CPL, 1997.
Courrière, Yves. *Jacques Prévert: En vérité*. Paris: Gallimard, 2000.
Coutin, André. *Huit siècles de violence au Quartier Latin*. Paris: Stock, 1969.
Crossley, Nick, and John Michael Roberts, eds. *After Habermas: New Perspectives on the Public Sphere*. Oxford and Malden, MA: Blackwell, 2004.
Dansette, Adrien. *Histoire de la libération de Paris*. Paris: Fayard, 1946.
Debidour, Élie. *La Conservation de vieux-Paris et l'urbanisme*. Paris: Musée Social, 1945.
Debord, Guy. *The Society of the Spectacle*. Translated by Donald Nicholson-Smith. New York: Zone Books, 1994.
———, ed. *Guy Debord présente Potlatch (1954–1957)*. Paris: Gallimard, 1996.
Decker, Sylviane, ed. *Paris, capitale de la photographie*. Paris: Hazan, 1998.
Demangeon, Albert. *Paris: La Ville et sa banlieue*. Paris: Bourrelier, 1933.
Dening, Greg. *Performances*. Chicago: University of Chicago Press, 1996.
Déon, Michel. *Les Gens de la nuit*. Paris: Plon, 1958.
Derder, Peggy. *L'Immigration algérienne et les pouvoirs publics dans le département de la Seine, 1954–1962*. Paris: L'Harmattan, 2001.
Desforges, J. "Le Problème du logement à Paris." *Pour la vie* 10 (April 1947): 3–13.
Dillaz, Serge. *La Chanson française de contestation de la Commune à Mai 68*. Paris: Seghers, 1973.
———. *Vivre et chanter en France*. Vol. 1, *1945–1980*. Paris: Fayard/Chorus, 2005.
Dimendberg, Edward. *Film Noir and the Spaces of Modernity*. Cambridge, MA: Harvard University Press, 2004.
Direction des archives de France and Ministère de la culture de la communication et des grands travaux, eds. *Reconstructions et modernisation: La France après les ruines, 1918 . . . 1945*. Paris: Archives nationales, 1991.
Dister, Alain. *D'où viens-tu Johnny?* Paris: Plume, 1993.
La Documentation française. *La Lutte contre les taudis et l'amélioration de l'habitat*. 2 vols. Notes et études documentaires 305–6. Paris: La Documentation française, 1946.
Doisneau, Robert. *Instantanés de Paris: 148 photographies en noir*. Paris: Arthaud, 1955.

———. *Les Parisiens tels qu'ils sont*. Paris: Robert Delpire, 1954.
Domenach, Jean-Marie, ed. "Nos maisons et nos villes." Special issue, *Esprit* 10–11(October–November 1953).
Dorian, Jean-Pierre. *Jours et nuits de Paris*. Paris: Mondiale, 1953.
Dosse, François. *L'Empire du sens: L'Humanisation des sciences humaines*. Paris: La Découverte, 1995.
Douchet, Jean, and Gilles Nadeau. *Paris cinéma: Une ville vue par le cinéma de 1895 à nos jours*. Paris: Éditions Du May, 1987.
Drake, David. *Intellectuals and Politics in Post-War France*. Basingstoke and NewYork: Palgrave, 2002.
Dreyfus-Armand, Geneviève, Robert Frank, Marie-Françoise Lévy, and Michelle Zancarini-Fournel. *Les Années 68: Le Temps de la contestation*. Paris: Complexe, 2000.
Duchemin, Alain. *Paris en fêtes*. Paris: France-Empire, 1985.
Dumont, Marie-Jeanne. *Le Logement social à Paris, 1850–1930: Les Habitations à bon marché*. Liège: Mardaga, 1991.
El Gammal, Jean. *Les Hauts quartiers de l'est parisien d'un siècle à l'autre*. Paris: Publisud, 1998.
———. *Parcourir Paris du Second Empire à nos jours*. Paris: Publications de la Sorbonne, 2001.
Eveno, Claude, ed. *Paris perdu: Quarante ans de bouleversements de la ville*. Paris: Carré, 1995.
Evenson, Norma. *Paris: A Century of Change, 1878–1978*. New Haven, CT: Yale University Press, 1979.
Fargue, Léon-Paul. *La Flânerie à Paris*. Paris: Commissariat général auTourisme, 1946.
———. *Lanterne magique*. Marseille: R. Laffont, 1944.
———. *Le Piéton de Paris*. Paris: Gallimard, 1939.
Faure, Alain, and Claire Lévy-Vroelant. *Une chambre en ville: Hôtels meublés et garnis à Paris, 1860–1990*. Grâne: Créaphis, 2007.
Fierro, Alfred. *Histoire et mémoire du nom des rues de Paris*. Paris: Parigramme, 1999.
Fierro, Annette. *The Glass State: The Technology of the Spectacle, Paris, 1981–1998*. Cambridge, MA: MIT Press, 2006.
Fijalkow, Yankel. *La Construction des îlots insalubres: Paris, 1850–1945*. Paris: L'Harmattan, 1998.
Fischer, Didier. "Les Étudiants en France (1945–1968)." Ph.D. diss., Université de Paris X–Nanterre, 1998.
———. *L'Histoire des étudiants en France de 1945 à nos jours*. Paris: Flammarion, 2000.
Flamand, Jean-Paul. *Loger le peuple: Essai sur l'histoire du logement social en France*. Paris: La Découverte, 1989.
Flanner, Janet. *Paris Journal, 1944–1965*. London: Gollancz, 1966.
Flonneau, Mathieu. *Paris et l'automobile: Un siècle de passions*. Paris: Hachette, 2005.
Flouret, Marcel. *Communication de M. le Préfet de la Seine au Conseil Municipal et au Conseil Général sur le problème du logement et le plan d'aménagement de Paris et de la banlieue*. Paris: Préfecture du département de la Seine, 1946.
Foucault, Michel, "Of Other Spaces (1967): Heterotopias." Originally published as "Des Espaces autres," *Architecture/Mouvement/Continuité* 5 (October 1984): 46–49.
Fourastié, Jean. *Les Trente glorieuses ou la révolution française, 1945–1975*. Paris: Fayard, 1979.
Fourcaut, Annie. *La Banlieue en morceaux: La Crise des lotissements défectueux en France dans l'entre-deux-guerres*. Grâne: Créaphis, 2000.
———, ed. *Banlieue Rouge, 1920–1960: Années Thorez, années Gabin: Archétype du populaire, banc d'essai des modernités*. Série Mémoires 18. Paris: Autrement, 1992.
———, Emmanuel Bellanger, and Mathieu Flonneau, eds. *Paris/Banlieues: Conflits et solidarités*. Grâne: Créaphis, 2007.
Francillon, Clarisse. *Les Gens du passage*. Paris: Pierre Horay, 1959.
Frank, Bernard. *Les Rats: Roman*. Paris: LaTable ronde, 1953.
Fresnais, Jacques, ed. *Une politique du logement: Ministère de la reconstruction et de l'urbanisme*. Paris: IFA-PCA, 1997.

Friedmann, Georges. *Villes et campagnes: Civilisation urbaine et civilisation rurale en France.* Paris: Armand Colin, 1953.
Gaffney, John, and Diana Holmes, eds. *Stardom in Postwar France.* New York: Berghahn, 2008.
Gaillard, Marc. *Paris: Les Trente glorieuses au temps de Malraux.* Paris: Presses du Village, 2006.
Galtier-Boissière, Jean. *Journal, 1940–1950.* Paris: Quai Voltaire, 1993.
———. *Mémoires d'un Parisien.* Paris: La Table ronde, 1960.
Gaonkar, Dilip Parameshwar, ed. *Alternative Modernities.* Durham, NC: Duke University Press, 2001.
Gardiner, Michael. *Critiques of Everyday Life.* London and New York: Routledge, 2000.
Garric, Robert. *Belleville: Scènes de la vie populaire avec des "témoignages et souvenirs."* Paris: Bernard Grasset, 1928.
Gaston-Mathé, Catherine. *La Société française au miroir de son cinéma: De la débâcle à la décolonisation.* Condé-sur-Noireau: Arléa-Corlet, 1996.
George, Pierre. *Études sur la banlieue de Paris: Essais méthodologiques.* Fondation nationale des sciences politiques, Cahiers 12. Paris: Armand Colin, 1950.
Gérome, Noëlle, Danielle Tartakowsky, and Claude Willard, eds. *La Banlieue en fête: De la marginalité urbaine à l'identité culturelle.* Saint-Denis: Presses Universitaires de Vincennes, 1988.
Gilpin, Robert. *France in the Age of the Scientific State.* Princeton, NJ: Princeton University Press, 1968.
Giraudoux, Jean. *Pleins pouvoirs.* Paris: Gallimard, 1939.
———. *Pour une politique urbaine.* Paris: Arts et Métiers graphiques, 1947.
Girault, Jacques. *Ouvriers en banlieue, XIXe–XXe siècle.* Paris: Éditions Ouvrières, 1998.
Godard, Francis, ed. *La Rénovation urbaine à Paris: Structure urbaine et logique de classe.* Paris: Mouton, 1973.
Goldenhagen, Sarah Williams, and Réjean Legault, eds. *Anxious Modernisms: Experimentation in Postwar Architectural Culture.* Montreal: Canadian Center for Architecture; Cambridge, MA: MIT Press, 2000.
Goujon, Jean-Pierre. *Léon-Paul Fargue.* Paris: Gallimard, 1997.
Granet, Marie, Claude Lévy, Ginette Gros, and Pierre Mermet. *Les Jeunes dans la Résistance.* 2nd ed. Paris: France Empire, 1999.
Gravier, Jean-François. *Paris et le désert français.* Revised ed. Paris: Flammarion, 1972.
Griotteray, Alain. *L'État contre Paris.* Paris: Hachette, 1962.
Groult, Benoîte, and Flora Groult. *Diary in Duo.* Translated by Humphrey Hare. New York: Appleton-Century, 1965.
Guérard, Albert Léon. *L'Avenir de Paris: Urbanisme français et urbanisme américain.* Paris: Payot, 1929.
Guérard, Henri. *Le Regard d'un photographe sur Belleville, Ménilmontant, Charonne (1944–1999).* Paris: Éditions de l'Amandier, 1998.
Guillaume, Marc, ed. *L'État des sciences sociales en France.* Paris: La Découverte, 1986.
Guillerme, André, Anne-Cécile Lefort, and Gérard Jigaudon. *Dangereux, insalubres et incommodes: Paysages industriels en banlieue parisienne, XIX–XXe siècles.* Paris: Champ Vallon, 2004.
Gumplowicz, Philippe. *Les Travaux d'Orphée: 150 ans de vie musicale amateur en France; Harmonies, chorales, fanfares.* Paris: Aubier, 1987.
———, and Jean-Claude Klein, eds. *Paris 1944–1954: Artistes, intellectuels, publics: La Culture comme enjeu.* Série Mémoires 38. Paris: Autrement, 1995.
Gutton, André. *La Charte de l'urbanisme.* Paris: Dunod, 1941.
Habermas, Jürgen. *The Structural Transformation of the Public Sphere: An Inquiry into a Category of Bourgeois Society.* Translated by Thomas Burger. Cambridge, MA: MIT Press, 1991.
Halbwachs, Maurice. *Morphologie sociale.* Paris: Armand Colin, 1938.
———. *La Population et les tracés de voies à Paris depuis un siècle.* Paris: Presses universitaires de France, 1928.

Hall, Peter. *Cities of Tomorrow: An Intellectual history of Urban Design in the Twentieth Century.* New York: Blackwell, 1996.
Hamon, Hervé, and Patrick Rotman. *Génération.* 2 vols. Paris: Seuil, 1987.
Hanoteau, Guillaume. *L'Âge d'or de Saint-Germain-des-Prés.* Paris: Denoël, 1965.
Harvey, David. *Paris: Capital of Modernity.* New York: Routledge, 2003.
———. *The Condition of Postmodernity: An Enquiry into the Origins of Cultural Change.* Cambridge, MA: Basil Blackwell, 1989.
———. *Spaces of Capital.* New York: Routledge, 2001.
———. *Spaces of Hope.* Berkeley: University of California Press, 2000.
———. *The Urban Experience.* Baltimore, MD: John Hopkins University, 1989.
Hervo, Monique. *Chroniques du bidonville: Nanterre en guerre d'Algérie, 1959–1962.* Paris: Seuil, 2001.
Hess, Remi. *Henri Lefebvre et l'aventure du siècle.* Paris: Éditions A. M. Métailié, 1988.
Hetherington, Kevin. *The Badlands of Modernity: Heterotopia and Social Ordering.* London: Routledge, 1997.
Higonnet, Patrice. *Paris: Capital of the World.* Cambridge, MA: Belknap Press of Harvard University Press, 2002.
Hill, Mike, and Warren Montag, eds. *Masses, Classes, and the Public Sphere.* London and New York: Verso, 2000.
Hillairet, Jacques. *Connaissance du vieux Paris.* 3 vols. Paris: Gonthier, 1954. Reprint, Paris: Payot & Rivages, 1993.
———. *Dictionnaire historique des rues de Paris.* 2 vols. Paris: Minuit, 1963.
———. *Évocation du vieux Paris.* Paris: Minuit, 1951.
Hirschkop, Ken. *Mikhail Bakhtin: An Aesthetic for Democracy.* Oxford: Oxford University Press, 1999.
Holley, Michel. *L'Espace parisien.* Paris: Centre de documentation et d'urbanisme, 1960.
Horn, Gerd-Rainer, and Emmanuel Gerard, eds. *Left Catholicism, 1943–1955: Catholics and Society in Western Europe at the Point of Liberation.* Leuven: Leuven University Press, 2001.
Horne, Janet R. *A Social Laboratory for Modern France: The Musée Social and the Rise of the Welfare State.* Durham, NC: Duke University Press, 2002.
Huyssen, Andreas. *Present Pasts: Urban Palimpsests and the Politics of Memory.* Stanford, CA: Stanford University Press, 2003.
Institut national d'études démographiques. *Les Algériens en France: Étude démographique et sociale.* Travaux et Documents, cahier 24. Paris: Presses universitaires de France, 1955.
Jackson, Julian. *France: The Dark Years, 1940–1944.* Oxford and New York: Oxford University Press, 2001.
Jones, Colin. *Paris: Biography of a City.* New York: Viking, 2004.
Jordan, David. *Transforming Paris: The Life and Labors of Baron Haussmann.* Chicago: University of Chicago Press, 1995.
Joseph, Isaac. *Prendre place: Espace public et culture dramatique.* Paris: Recherches, 1995.
Jousse, Thierry, and Thierry Paquot, eds. *La Ville au cinéma.* Paris: Cahiers du cinéma, 2005.
Judt, Tony. *Past Imperfect: French Intellectuals, 1944–1956.* Berkeley: University of California Press, 1992.
Karnow, Stanley. *Paris in the Fifties.* New York: Random House, 1997.
Kaspi, André, and Antoine Marès, eds. *Paris des étrangers depuis un siècle.* Paris: Imprimerie Nationale, 1989.
Kelly, Michael. *The Cultural and Intellectual Rebuilding of France after the Second World War.* New York: Palgrave Macmillan, 2004.
———. *Modern French Marxism.* Baltimore, MD: John Hopkins University Press, 1982.
Khilnani, Sunil. *Arguing Revolution: The Intellectual Left in Postwar France.* New Haven, CT: Yale University Press, 1993.

Klein, Jean-Claude. *La Chanson à l'affiche: Histoire de la chanson française du café concert à nos jours.* Paris: DuMay, 1991.
Kopp, Anatole, Frédérique Boucher, and Danièle Pauly. *L'Architecture de la reconstruction en France, 1945–1953.* Paris: Moniteur, 1982.
Kuhn, Annette, and Kirsten Emiko McAllister, eds. *Locating Memory: Photographic Acts.* New York: Berghahn, 2006.
Kuisel, Richard F. *Capitalism and the State in Modern France: Renovation and Economic Management in the Twentieth Century.* Cambridge: Cambridge University Press, 1981.
———. *Seducing the French: The Dilemma of Americanization.* Berkeley: University of California Press, 1993.
Kupferman, Fred. *Les Premiers beaux jours, 1944–1946.* Paris: Calmann-Levy, 1985; reprint, Paris: Tallandier, 2007.
Lacassin, Francis. *Sous le masque de Léo Malet: Nestor Burma.* Amiens: Encrage, 1993.
Lacaze, Jean-Paul. *Paris: Urbanisme d'état et destin d'une ville.* Paris: Flammarion, 1994.
Lafay, Bernard. *Problèmes de Paris: Contribution aux travaux du Conseil municipal; Esquisse d'un plan directeur et d'un programme d'action.* Rapports et documents du Conseil municipal 11. Paris: Conseil Municipal, 1954.
Lanoux, Armand. *Physiologie de Paris.* Paris: Arthème Fayard, 1954.
———. "Physiologie des grands boulevards." *Les Œuvres libres* 96 (May 1954): 139–78.
Lassave, Pierre. *Les Sociologues et la recherche urbaine dans la France contemporaine.* Toulouse: Presses Universitaires du Mirail, 1997.
Latour, François. *Paris 1937 et le grand Paris.* Paris: Hôtel de Ville, 1936.
Latour, Geneviève. *Le "Cabaret théâtre" 1945–1965.* Paris: Bibliothèque historique de la Ville de Paris, 1996.
Lavedan, Jean. *Géographie des villes.* 2nd ed. Paris: Gallimard, 1959.
———. *Histoire de l'urbanisme à Paris.* Paris: Hachette, 1993.
———. *Qu'est-ce que l'urbanisme?* Paris: Henri Laurens, 1926.
Leach, Neil, ed. *Hieroglyophics of Space: Understanding the City.* New York: Routledge, 2002.
Le Boterf, Hervé. *La Vie parisienne sous l'occupation.* 2 vols. Paris: France-Empire, 1975.
Lebovics, Herman. *True France: The Wars over Cultural Identity, 1900–1945.* Ithaca, NY: Cornell University Press, 1992.
Le Corbusier. *La Charte d'Athènes.* First published 1941. 2nd ed., Paris: Minuit, 1957.
———. *Destin de Paris.* Paris: Fernand Sorlot, 1941.
———. *The Radiant City: Elements of a Doctrine of Urbanism to Be Used as the Basis of Our Machine-Age Civilization.* New York: Orion, 1967.
———. *La Ville radieuse.* Paris: Vincent, Fréal et Cie, 1933.
Lefebvre, Henri. *Critique of Everyday Life.* Translated by John Moore. 2 vols. London and New York: Verso, 1991, 2002.
———. *The Production of Space.* Translated by D. Nicholson-Smith. Oxford: Blackwell, 1991.
———. *La Somme et le reste.* Paris: Méridiens Klincksieck, 1989.
———. *Writings on Cities: Henri Lefebvre.* Translated and edited by Eleonore Kofman and Elizabeth Lebas. Oxford: Blackwell, 1996.
Lefebvre, Virginie. *Paris-ville moderne: Maine-Montparnasse et La Défense, 1950–1975.* Paris: Norma, 2003.
Legaret, Jean, ed. *Le Statut de Paris.* 3 vols. Paris: R. Pichon and R. Durand-Auzias, 1959.
Lehning, James. The *Melodramatic Thread: Spectacle and Political Culture in Modern France* Bloomington: Indiana University Press, 2007.
Lépidis, Clément. *Belleville au cœur.* Paris: Vermet, 1980.
———. *Je me souviens du 20e arrondissement.* Paris: Parigramme, 1997.
Lemoine, Jean. "La Crise du logement." *La Vie urbaine* 57 (July–September 1950): 5–12.
Lepetit, Bernard, and Christian Topalov, eds. *La Ville des sciences sociales.* Paris: Éditions Belin, 2001.

Le Van-Lemesle, Lucette. "Léo Malet et ses 'nouveaux mystères.'" *Sociétés et représentations* 17 (2004): 171–82.

Levisse-Touzé, Christine. "Le Rôle particulier de Paris pendant la seconde guerre mondiale." In *La Résistance et les français:Villes, centres et logiques de décisions*. Cachan: Institut d'histoire du temps présent, 1995.

Lévy, Marie-Françoise, ed. *La Télévision dans la république: Les Années 50*. Brussels: Complexe, 1999.

Lian, Lily. *Lily Panam: Mémoires de la dernière chanteuse des rues*. Paris: Olivier Orban, 1981.

Light, Andrew, and Jonathan M. Smith, eds. *The Production of Public Space*. Lanham, MD: Rowman & Littlefield, 1998.

Lobry, Jean. *Construction et urbanisme dans la région parisienne*. Paris: Commissaire à la construction et à l'urbanisme pour la région parisienne, 1958.

Loiseau, Jean-Claude. *Les Zazous*. Paris: Grasset, 1990.

Lojkine, Jean. *La Politique urbaine dans la région parisienne, 1945–1971*. Paris: École Pratique des Hautes Études and Mouton, 1972.

Lopez, Raymond. *L'Avenir des villes*. Paris: Laffont, 1964.

———. "Paris se meurt:Vive Paris!" *Le Nef* 7 (June 1957): 78–85.

Lottman, Herbert. *The Left Bank:Writers, Artists, and Politics from the Popular Front to the Cold War*. San Francisco: Halo Books, 1991.

Loyer, Emmanuelle. *Le Théâtre citoyen de Jean Vilar: Une utopie d'après-guerre*. Paris: Presses universitaires de France, 1997.

Low, Setha, and Neil Smith, eds. *The Politics of Public Space*. NewYork: Routledge, 2005.

Lucan, Jacques. *Architecture en France (1940–2000): Histoire et théories*. Paris: Moniteur, 2001.

———, ed. *Eau et gaz à tous les étages: Paris, 100 ans de logement*. Paris: Édition du Pavillon de l'Arsenal and Picard Éditeur, 1992.

Mairie de Paris. *C'était Paris dans les années 50*. Paris:Ville de Paris, 1997.

Malet, Léo. *Brouillard au pont de Tolbiac: Les Nouveaux mystères de Paris*. Paris: Fleuve Noir, 1999.

———. *Fièvre au Marais: Les Nouveaux mystères de Paris*. Paris: Presses de la Cité, 1955.

———. *Micmac moche au Boul' Mich': Les Nouveaux mystères de Paris*. Paris: Presses de la Cité, 1957.

———. *La Nuit de Saint-Germain-des-Prés*. *Les Nouveaux mystères de Paris*. Paris: Livre de Poche, 1973.

Marchand, Bernard. *Paris: Histoire d'une ville*. Paris: Seuil, 1993.

Marcus, Greil. *Lipstick Traces:A Secret History of the Twentieth Century*. Cambridge, MA: Harvard University Press, 1989.

Martz, Ginette, and Georges Martz. "La Chanson sous l'occupation et à la libération." *Histoire & sociétés* 51 (May–June 1994): 5–34.

Mason, Laura. *Singing the French Revolution: Popular Culture and Politics, 1789–1799*. Ithaca, NY: Cornell University Press, 1996.

Mathy, Jean-Philippe. *French Resistance:The French-American Culture Wars*. St. Paul: University of Minnesota Press, 2000.

McDonough,Tom. *"The Beautiful Language of My Century": Reinventing the Language of Contestation in Postwar France, 1945–1968*. Cambridge, MA: MIT Press, 2007.

———, ed. *Guy Debord and the Situationist International:Texts and Documents*. Cambridge, MA: MIT Press, 2002.

Mencherini, Robert. *Guerre froide, grèves rouges: Parti communiste, stalinisme et luttes sociales en France; Les Grèves "insurrectionnelles" de 1947–1948*. Paris: Syllepse, 1998.

Mension, Jean-Michel. *The Tribe: Conversations with Gérard Berréby and Francesco Milo*.Translated by D. Nicholson-Smith. San Francisco: City Lights Books, 2001.

Merlin, Olivier. *Une belle époque, 1945–1950*. Paris: Olivier Orban, 1986.

Michel, Henri. *Paris allemand*. Paris: Albin Michel, 1981.

Milza, Pierre, and Marie-Claude Blanc-Chaléard. *Le Nogent des Italiens*. Série monde/Français d'ailleurs, peuple d'ici 80. Paris: Autrement, 1995.
Mitchell, Don. *The Right to the City: Social Justice and the Fight for Public Space*. New York: Guilford Press, 2003.
Monchablon, Alain. *Histoire de l'UNEF de 1956 à 1968*. Paris: Presses universitaires de France, 1983.
Monnier, Gérard, and Richard Klein, eds. *Les années ZUP: Architectures de la croissance, 1960–1973*. Paris: Picard Éditeur, 2002.
Mouraux, Lionel. *Je me souviens du 11e arrondissement*. Paris: Parigramme/CPL, 1998.
Mumford, Eric Paul. *The CIAM Discourse on Urbanism, 1928–1960*. Cambridge, MA: MIT Press, 2000.
Namer, Gérard. *La Commémoration en France de 1945 à nos jours*. Paris: L'Harmattan, 1987.
Nettelbeck, Colin. *Dancing with de Beauvoir: Jazz and the French*. Melbourne: Melbourne University Publishing, 2005.
Nicholson, Linda, and Steven Seidman, eds. *Social Postmodernism: Beyond Identity Politics*, Cambridge: Cambridge University Press, 1995.
Nivet, Philippe. *Le Conseil municipal de Paris de 1944 à 1977*. Paris: Publications de la Sorbonne, 1994.
———, and Yvan Combeau. *Histoire politique de Paris au XXe siècle*. Paris: Presses universitaires de France, 2000.
Nora, Pierre, and Lawrence D. Kritzman, eds. *Realms of Memory: The Construction of the French Past*. Translated by Arthur Goldhammer. 2 vols. New York: Columbia University Press, 1996.
Ollier, Brigitte, ed. *Robert Doisneau*. 4th ed. Paris: Hazan, 2000.
Ory, Pascal. *L'Aventure culturelle française, 1945–1989*. Paris: Flammarion, 1989.
———, ed. *Mots de passe, 1945–1985: Petit abécédaire des modes de vie*. Paris: Autrement, 1985.
"Paris et huit métropoles mondiales." *Cahiers de l'Institut d'aménagement et d'urbanisme de la région parisienne* 2 (June 1965): 1–74.
Paxton, Robert. *Vichy France: Old Guard and New Order, 1940–1944*. New York: Columbia University Press, 1972.
Pells, Richard. *Not Like Us: How Europeans Have Loved, Hated, and Transformed American Culture since World War II*. New York: Basic Books, 1997.
Perrault, Gilles, and Pierre Azema. *Paris under the Occupation*. Translated by Allison Carter and Maximilian Vos. New York: Vendome Press, 1989.
Picon-Lefebvre, Virginie, ed. *Les Espaces publics modernes*. Paris: Moniteur, 1997
Pigenet, Michel. *Au cœur de l'activisme communiste des années de guerre froide*. Paris: L'Harmattan, 1992.
Pillement, Georges. *Destruction de Paris*. Paris: Bernard Grasset, 1941.
———. *Paris disparu*. Paris: Bernard Grasset, 1966.
———. *Paris en fête*. Paris: Bernard Grasset, 1972.
Pilliet, Georges, *L'Avenir de Paris*. Paris: Hachette, 1961.
Pinol, Jean-Luc, ed. *Histoire de l'Europe urbaine*. Vol. 2. *De l'ancien régime à nos jours*. Paris: Seuil, 2003.
Pinon, Pierre. *Paris: Biographie d'une capitale*. Paris: Hazan, 1999.
———. "Pierre Lavedan: De l'histoire de l'art à l'architecture urbaine." *Le Visiteur: Ville, territoire, paysage, architecture* 2 (Spring 1996): 112–27.
Pitte, Jean-Robert. *Paris: Histoire d'une ville*. Paris: Hachette, 1993.
Poëte, Marcel. *Paris: Son évolution créatrice*. Paris: Vincent, Fréal et Cie, 1938.
Pouvreau, Benoît, Danièle Voldman, and Dominique Claudius-Petit. *Un politique en architecture: Eugène Claudius-Petit (1907–1989)*. Paris: Le Moniteur, 2004.
Préfecture de la Seine. "Décentralisation industrielle." *La Conjoncture économique dans le département* 3 (1961): 339–43.

BIBLIOGRAPHY | 389

Préfecture de Paris. *Les Plaques commémoratives des rues de Paris.* Paris: La Documentation française, 1984.
Prévert, Jacques. *Œuvres complètes.* Paris: Gallimard, 1992.
———. *Paroles: Selected Poems.* Translated by Lawrence Ferlinghetti. Bilingual ed. Pocket Poets 9. San Francisco: City Lights Books, 1990.
———, and Izis Bidermanas. *Grand bal du printemps.* Lausanne: Clairefontaine, 1951.
Pryce-Jones, David. *Paris in the Third Reich: A History of the German Occupation, 1940–1944.* New York: Holt, Rinehart & Winston, 1981.
Quelques données sur le logement dans la région parisienne. Notes et études documentaires 1823. Paris: La Documentation française, 1954.
Quilliot, Roger, and Roger-Henri Guerrand. *Cent ans d'habitat social: Une utopie réaliste.* Paris: Albin Michel, 1989.
Rabinow, Paul. *French Modern: Norms and Forms of the Social Environment.* Cambridge, MA: MIT Press, 1989.
Ragon, Michel. *Paris, hier, aujourd'hui, demain.* Paris: Hachette, 1965.
Rajsfus, Maurice. *1953: Un 14 juillet sanglant.* Paris: Agnès Viénoet Éditions, 2003.
Rearick, Charles. *The French in Love and War: Popular Culture in the Era of the World Wars.* New Haven, CT: Yale University Press, 1997.
———, and Rosemary Wakeman, eds. "New Perspectives on Modern Paris." Special issue, *French Historical Studies* 27 (Winter 2004).
Remy, Jean, ed. "Paul-Henry Chombart de Lauwe et l'histoire des études urbaines en France." Special issue, *Espaces et sociétés* 103 (2001).
Rigby, Brian. *Popular Culture in Modern France: A Study of Cultural Discourse.* London: Routledge, 1991.
Rioux, Jean-Pierre. *The Fourth Republic, 1944–1958.* Cambridge: Cambridge University Press, 1987.
———. *La Vie culturelle sous Vichy.* Paris: Complexe, 1990.
———, ed. *La Guerre d'Algérie et les français.* Paris: Fayard, 1990.
———, and Jean-François Sirinelli. *Histoire culturelle de la France.* 4 vols. Paris: Seuil, 1997.
———, eds. "Le Peuple et tous ses états." Special issue, *Sociétés et représentations* 8 (December 1999).
Robert, Jean-Louis, and Danielle Tartakowsky, eds. *Paris le peuple, XVIIIe–XXe siècle.* Paris: Publications de la Sorbonne, 1999.
———, eds. "Le Peuple et tout ses états." Special issue, *Sociétés et représentations* 8 (December 1999).
Robert, Jean-Louis, and Myriam Tsikounas, eds. "Imaginaires parisiens." Special issue, *Sociétés et représentations* 17 (March 2004).
Rodaway, Paul. *Sensuous Geographies: Body, Sense and Place.* London and New York: Routledge, 1994.
Roger, Philippe. *Rêves et cauchemars américains: Les États-Unis au miroir de l'opinion publique française (1945–1953).* Paris: Presses Universitaires du Septentrion, 1996.
Romains, Jules, ed. *Portrait de Paris.* Paris: Perrin, 1951.
Roncayolo, Marcel. *La Ville et ses territories.* Paris: Gallimard, 1990.
———, and Guy Burgel, eds. *La Ville aujourd'hui: Mutations urbaines, décentralisation et crise du citadin.* 2nd ed. Vol. 5, *Histoire de la France urbaine,* edited by Georges Duby. Paris: Seuil, 2001.
———, and Thierry Paquot. *Villes & civilisation urbaine, XVIIIe–XXe siècle.* Paris: Larousse, 1992.
Ronis, Willy. *Autoportrait.* Cognac: Chez Fata Morgana, 1996.
———. *Belleville Ménilmontant.* Introduction by Pierre Mac Orlan. Paris: Arthaud, 1954.
———. *Mon Paris.* Preface by Henri Raczymow. Paris: Denoël, 1985.

Rosenberg, Clifford. *Policing Paris: The Origins of Modern Immigration Control between the Wars.* Ithaca, NY: Cornell University Press, 2006.
Ross, Kristin. *The Emergence of Social Space: Rimbaud and the Paris Commune.* Minneapolis: University of Minnesota Press, 1988.
———. *Fast Cars, Clean Bodies: Decolonization and the Reordering of French Culture.* Cambridge, MA: MIT Press, 1996.
Rouleau, Bernard. *Paris: Histoire d'un espace.* Paris: Seuil, 1997.
———. *Villages et faubourgs de l'ancien Paris: Histoire d'un espace urbain.* Paris: Seuil, 1985.
Roumajon, Yves. *Enfants perdus, enfants punis: Histoire de la jeunesse délinquante en France: Huit siècles de controverses.* Paris: R. Laffont, 1989.
Rousso, Henry. *The Vichy Syndrome: History and Memory in France since 1944.* Translated by Arthur Goldhammer. Cambridge, MA: Harvard University Press, 1991.
Roy, Claude. "Le Monde de Jacques Prévert." *Positif: Revue périodique de cinéma* 2 (1953–54): 76–77.
———. *Nous.* Paris: Gallimard, 1972.
Rumney, Ralph. *Le Consul: Entretiens avec Gérard Berréby.* Paris: Allia, 1999.
Ruscio, Alain. *L'Affaire Henri Martin et la lutte contre la guerre d'Indochine.* Pantin: Le Temps des Cerises, 2005.
Rustenholz, Alain. *Paris ouvrier: Des sublimes aux camarades.* Paris: Parigramme, 2003.
Ryan, Paul. *Willy Ronis.* London: Phaidon, 2002.
Sabot, Jean-Yves. *Le Syndicalisme étudiant et la guerre d'Algérie: L'Entrée d'une génération en politique et la formation d'une élite.* Paris: L'Harmattan, 1995.
Sadler, Simon. *The Situationist City.* Cambridge, MA: MIT Press, 1998.
Sadoul, Georges. "Les Films de Carné: Expression de notre époque." *Les Lettres françaises,* March 1–7, 1956.
Saint-Pierre, C. de. *Des ténèbres à l'aube: Journal d'une française.* Paris: B. Arthaud, 1945.
Saka, Pierre. *La Chanson française à travers ses succès.* Paris: Larousse, 1988.
Sanson, Rosemonde. *Le 14 juillet: Fête et conscience nationale, 1789–1975.* Paris: Flammarion, 1976.
Sansot, Pierre. *Poétique de la ville.* Paris: Armand Colin, 1996.
Santamaria, Yves. *Le Parti de l'ennemi? Le Parti communiste français dans la lutte pour la paix (1947–1958).* Paris: Armand Colin, 2006.
Sayad, Abdelmalek, and Eliane Dupuy. *Un Nanterre algérien, terre de bidonvilles.* Série Monde/ Français d'ailleurs, peuple d'ici, H5 85. Paris: Éditions Autrement, 2008.
Schwartz, Vanessa. *It's So French! Hollywood, Paris, and the Making of Cosmopolitan Film Culture.* Chicago: University of Chicago Press, 2007.
———. *Spectacular Realities: Early Mass Culture in Fin-de-Siècle Paris.* Berkeley: University of California Press, 1998.
Scott, James C. *Seeing like a State: How Certain Schemes to Improve the Human Condition Have Failed.* New Haven, CT: Yale University Press, 1998.
Seidman, Michael. *The Imaginary Revolution: Parisian Students and Workers in 1968.* New York: Berghahn, 2004.
Sennett, Richard. *The Conscience of the Eye: The Design and Social Life of Cities.* New York: Norton, 1990.
———. *The Fall of Public Man: On the Social Psychology of Capitalism.* New York: Vintage, 1978.
Shepard, Todd. *The Invention of Decolonization: The Algerian War and the Remaking of France.* Ithaca, NY: Cornell University Press, 2008.
Sheringham, Michael, ed. *Parisian Fields.* London: Reaktion, 1996.
Shiel, Mark, and Tony Fitzmaurice, eds. *Cinema and the City: Film and Urban Societies in a Global Context.* Oxford: Blackwell, 2001.
Shields, Rob. *Lefebvre, Love & Struggle: Spatial Dialectics.* London and New York: Routledge, 1999.

Siegfried, André. *Géographie humoristique de Paris*. Paris: La Passerelle, 1951.
Simon, Boris. *Abbé Pierre and the Ragpickers of Emmaüs*. NewYork: P. J. Kennedy, 1955.
Singer-Kérel, Jeanne. *La Coût de la vie à Paris de 1840 à 1954*. Paris: Armand Colin, 1961.
Sirinelli, Jean-François. *Les Baby-boomers: Une génération, 1945–1969*. Paris: Fayard, 2003.
Société statistique de Paris. *Paris 1960*. Paris: Imprimerie municipale, 1961.
Sontag, Susan. *On Photography*. NewYork: Picador, 2001.
Soulignac, Françoise. *La Banlieue parisienne: Cent cinquante ans de transformations*. Paris: La Documentation française, 1993.
Stierle, Karlheinz. *La Capitale des signes: Paris et son discours*. Paris: Éditions de la Maison des sciences de l'homme, 2001.
Stovall, Tyler. *The Rise of the Paris Red Belt*. Berkeley: University of California Press, 1990.
Sutcliffe, Anthony. *TheAutumn of Central Paris:The Defeat ofTown Planning, 1850–1970*. London: Edward Arnold, 1970.
———. *Paris: An Architectural History*. New Haven, CT:Yale University Press, 1993.
Sweeney, Regina. *Singing OurWay toVictory: French Cultural Politics and Music during the Great War*. Middletown, CT:Wesleyan University Press, 2001.
Tafuri, Manfredo. *Architecture and Utopia: Design and Capitalist Development*. Cambridge, MA: MIT, 1996.
Tartakowsky, Danielle. *La Manif en éclats*. Paris: La Dispute, 2004.
———. *Les Manifestations de rue en France, 1918–1968*. Paris: Publications de la Sorbonne, 1997.
———. *La Part du rêve: Histoire du 1er mai en France*. Paris: Hachette, 2005.
———. *Le Pouvoir est dans la rue*. Paris: Aubier, 1998.
Tellier,Thibault. *LeTemps des HLM, 1945–1975: La Saga urbaine des trente glorieuses*. Paris: Autrement, 2008.
Temple, Michael, and MichaelWitt, eds. *The French Cinema Book*. London: British Film Institute, 2004.
Texier, Simon. *Paris contemporain de Haussmann à nos jours: Une capitale à l'ère des métropoles*. Paris: Parigramme, 2005.
Thézy, Marie de. *La Photographie humaniste 1930–1960: Histoire d'un mouvement en France*. Paris: Contrejour, 1992.
Topalov, Christian. *Le Logement en France: Histoire d'une marchandise impossible*. Paris: Presses de la Fondation des sciences politiques, 1987.
Turk, Edward. *Child of Paradise: Marcel Carné and the Golden Age of French Cinema*. Cambridge, MA: Harvard University Press, 1989.
Vayssière, Bruno. *Reconstruction, deconstruction: Le Hard French ou l'architecture française des trente glorieuses*. Paris: Picard, 1988.
Verlomme, Roger. *L'Œuvre de relèvement dans le département de la Seine depuis la Libération: Exposé présenté au Conseil municipal de Paris et au Conseil général de la Seine lors de leur session de mars 1950*. Paris: Imprimerie Municipale, 1950.
Vialle, Catherine. *Je me souviens du 13e arrondissement*. Paris: Parigramme, 1995.
Vian, Boris. *Chroniques de jazz*. Paris: Pauvert, 1998.
———. *Jazz in Paris*. Translated by Gilbert Pestureau. Paris: Pauvert, 1997.
———. *Manuel de Saint-Germain-des-Prés*. 1950; Paris: Chêne, 1974.
Victor, Christian, and Julien Regoli. *Vingt ans de rock français*. Paris: Albin Michel, 1978.
Viet,Vincent. *La France immigrée*. Paris: Fayard, 1998.
Vilar, Jean. *Le théâtre: Service public et autres textes*. Paris: Gallimard, 1975.
Voldman, Danièle. *La Reconstruction des villes françaises de 1940 à 1954: Histoire d'une politique*. Paris: L'Harmattan, 1997.
———, ed. "Image, discours et enjeux de la reconstruction des villes françaises après 1945." Special issue, *Les Cahiers de l'IHTP* 5 (1987).

———, ed. "Région parisienne: Approches d'une notion, 1860–1980." Special issue, *Les Cahiers de l'IHTP* 12 (1989).

Wagenaar, Cor, ed. *Happy Cities and Public Happiness in Post-war Europe.* Rotterdam: NAi Publishers/Architecturalia, 2004.

Walker, Ian. *City Gorged with Dreams: Surrealism and Documentary Photography in Interwar Paris.* Manchester and New York: Manchester University Press, 2002.

Walter, Gerard. *Paris under the Occupation.* Translated by Tony White. New York: Orion Press, 1960.

Walz, Robin. *Pulp Surrealism: Insolent Popular Culture in Early Twentieth-Century Paris.* Berkeley: University of California Press, 2000.

Ward, Stephen V. *Planning the Twentieth-Century City: The Advanced Capitalist World.* West Sussex: John Wiley & Sons, 2002.

Warner, Michael. *Publics and Counterpublics.* New York: Zone, 2002.

Warnod, André. *Les Plaisirs de la rue.* Paris: Française illustrée, 1920.

Weiner, Susan. *Enfants Terribles: Youth and Femininity in the Mass Media in France, 1945–1968.* Baltimore, MD: John Hopkins University Press, 2001.

Yonnet, Paul. *Jeux, modes et masses: La Société française et le moderne, 1945–1985.* Paris: Gallimard, 1986.

Zdatny, Steven. *The Politics of Survival: Artisans in Twentieth-Century France.* New York: Oxford University Press, 1990.

Zukin, Sharon. *The Culture of Cities.* London: Blackwell, 1996.

Abbé Pierre: background, 138; celebrity, 140–42; housing campaign, 44, 108, 139–44, 238, 311, 313; housing designs, 143, 145
Actualités françaises, Les, 96, 118–19, 220; Abbé Pierre, 139; existentialism, 253 aerial photography, 186, 209, 214–15
A la découverte des français (1957–60), 222; *La Butte à la Reine*, 224–26; *La Rue du Moulin de la Pointe*, 223–25, 238. *See also* Chombart de Lauwe, Paul-Henry
Algerians, 42, 145–49, 151–54, 218, 268, 270, 285, 360n88; Algerian independence movement, 152, 284–87; marches and protests, 152–57, 160. *See also* North African, population
Algerian War, 43, 45, 108, 131, 147, 268; protests, 152–61; student protests, 276, 278, 286, 288
aménagement du territoire, 59, 237, 289, 301, 306–7, 323–24. *See also* decentralization anniversary commemorations, 32, 34, 87, 104, 128, 216, 288; Armistice Day, 128, 243; Bi-millénaire, 34–36, 66, 294; November 1940 protest, 279; Second World War victory, 127, 158
Antoine et Antoinette (1947), 205, 210–12, 258. *See also* Becker, Jacques
Aragon, Louis, 108, 163, 194
Architecture française, L', 298, 334, 337–38
Arletty, 2, 5, 207, 231, 336, 346
artisans, 2, 43, 71, 84, 295, 297, 317, 325, 335–36, 338–39; artisanal economy, 51–52

Athens Charter, 185, 291, 313, 315, 322
Aubervilliers, 24, 57–58, 63, 147, 229, 235–36; and communist party, 109, 113, 125, 136; film *Aubervilliers* (1945), 235–36, 249; lettrists, 189, 201
Auzelle, Robert, 167–68, 179, 193; Centre d'études de la Direction générale de l'urbanisme, 175; design for îlot 16 (Marais), 182, 333–34; design for *zone vert*, 232, 318; *Plaidoyer pour une organisation consciente de l'espace*, 185; La Plaine at Clamart, 186–87; social thought and urbanism, 185–87, 196, 333, 337, 339; *Technique de l'urbanisme*, 186

Bakhtin, Mikhail, 6, 64, 79, 81, 90, 107, 276
bals populaires, 35–36, 80, 85–88, 95, 98, 144, 157, 250; youth, 245, 258, 264, 266, 269
Bardet, Gaston, 179, 181, 185–86, 203, 295, 314, 333; background, 182; and Catholic reformism, 182–84; social thought and *Le Nouvel urbanisme*, 173, 182–84, 196
Bastille, place de la, 31, 35, 63, 84–85, 88, 92; description, 56; in film, 215, 217; street marches and parades, 30, 94, 118–19, 126, 138, 153, 182; urban planning, 314–15, 322; youth, 245, 267
Baylot, Jean, 125, 127–28, 281–82
"beauty of Paris," 65, 67, 162, 184, 293, 295, 297, 312, 316, 318, 333, 340. *See also* preservationism
Beauvoir, Simone de, 160, 164, 246, 249, 252–53, 260, 273

393

Becker, Jacques, 205, 222, 268; *Antoine et Antoinette*, 210–13, 224; background, 210; *Rendez-vous de juillet*, 253–54, 256, 258
Belleville, 43, 51, 63, 65–67, 75, 77–78, 84, 86, 170, 182, 200, 287, 322; and communist party, 112–13
Benedetti, Jean, 322–23
Benjamin, Walter, 4, 10, 68, 102, 195
Bercy, 54, 59, 63, 66, 272, 310; in television and film, 200, 215–16, 218
bidonvilles, 49, 134, 219, 237; definition, 148–49. See also slums
boulevard périphérique, 299, 309, 318–19, 324
Boulogne-Billancourt, 24, 49, 58, 144–45, 147

Cachin, Marcel, 113, 154, 358
cafés, 35, 48, 69, 71, 86, 191, 206, 216, 255, 259–63, 269, 273–74, 328; Arab, 42, 146–50, 274, 328; Bonaparte, 261; Brasserie Lipp, 246, 251, 270; Café de Flore, 164, 246, 249, 251, 253, 274; Capoulade, 274; Le Champo, 274; Chop Gauloise, 251; Chez Georges, 251; Deux Magots, 246, 251–52, 253, 274; Dupont-Latin, 259; Mahieu, 274; Moineau, 190
Calet, Henri, 39, 75, 188, 203, 234, 364n64; background, 199; *Les Deux bouts*, 149, 200–201, 273; *Les Grandes largeurs*, 65, 199; radio and television, 200; *Le Tout sur le tout*, 65, 68, 75, 95, 199; urban perspective, 199–201
canal de l'Ourcq, 24, 54, 57, 70, 132, 227
canal Saint-Martin, 5, 54, 57, 63, 70–71, 82, 227, 315, 336; and street naming, 101
Carné, Marcel, 16, 71–72, 77, 163, 208–9, 232, 268; and *L'Air de Paris*, 231; background, 227, 246; and *Les Enfants du paradis*, 1–2, 6, 228–31, 345; and *Les Portes de la Nuit*, 192, 198, 226, 228, 230–31; *Les Tricheurs*, 260–65
Catholic social reformism, 66–67, 164, 171, 175–77, 182–85, 278
Centre de documentation et d'urbanisme (CDU), 320–21, 339
Centre national de la recherche scientifique (CNRS), 163–64, 167, 177, 196
Certeau, Michel de, 10, 18, 82, 99, 164, 345
Champigneulle, Bernard, 163, 295. See also *Destinée de Paris* (1943)

Château-des-Rentiers, rue du, 148, 174–75, 197–98, 202, 319
Chevalier, Louis, 167; *Classes laborieuses et classes dangereuses*, 170; urban exploration, 188, 195; urban sociology, 169–70, 182, 196, 333, 337
Chevalier, Maurice, 31, 40, 84, 206–7
Chombart de Lauwe, Paul-Henry, 16, 137–38, 167, 203; background, 170–71; *A la découverte des français*, 222–26; relationship with state planning agencies, 175–76, 186, 188, 190, 193; social geography and urbanism, 171–73, 176–78, 182–84, 196, 201, 304; urban exploration, 195, 198. See also *Paris et l'agglomération parisienne* (1952)
CIAM (Congrès internationaux d'architecture moderne), 17, 115, 166, 291–92, 303, 308, 326, 338, 345–46; Exposition Internationale des Arts et Techniques, 162, 298; and Raymond Lopez, 313–14
Ciné-Clubs, 189, 241, 252
cité Jeanne-d'Arc, 47, 147, 174, 198, 202
Citroën: automobile, 38, 58; automobile plant, 58, 82, 98, 308, 310; strikes and protests, 122
Clair, René, 16, 208, 239; *Porte des Lilas*, 232–35
Clarté, 258–59, 273–74, 276–77
Claudius-Petit, Eugène, 133, 136, 144, 300, 306
Clébert, Jean-Paul, 54, 65, 68, 150, 175, 192, 235, 330
cold war, 11, 15, 44, 96, 248, 261, 283–84; in housing debates, 137; protests against, 108–9, 119, 122–23, 129, 259, 278
collaboration, 24, 28, 40, 101, 113, 163, 171, 207, 229, 236, 246, 301
Combat, 27, 31, 36, 106, 119, 164, 199, 253–54, 272
Comité national des écrivains (CNE), 163–64
Commission du vieux Paris, 103, 181, 333, 335, 374n85
Communist Party (PCF), 71, 75, 328; Algerian population, 153–55; Algerian War, 157, 159, 286; anti-Americanism, 122–23, 135, 137, 259, 277; and avant-garde, 163, 166, 216, 250; expulsion from government (1947), 119, 122, 278; film, 108, 114–15, 210, 213; founding myths, 116–17, 125; housing crisis, 135–37,

158, 273, 309; Latin Quarter, 276–77; municipal power, 108–9, 111–15, 130, 268, 301–2, 307, 312; music, 83, 250–51, 258; peace movement, 123–24; street marches, 117, 119–20; street naming, 99–100; strikes and protests, 122–26, 130, 153–55, 159, 281, 283, 286; student organizations, 273, 275, 277–78; urban planning, 309, 315, 338; youth culture, 258–59, 264
Confédération générale du travail (CGT), 100, 117, 126, 159, 209, 213, 216
Conseil général de la Seine, 281, 305
counterdiscourse, 8, 17, 292, 326, 344, 346
counterpublics, 8, 18, 107, 324, 344

D'Arcy, Jean, 219, 221–22. *See also* television
Dautry, Raoul, 184, 289, 300, 306, 371, 374n81
Debord, Guy, 99, 164, 179, 203; *dérive*, 190–92; influence of Chombart, 190; influence of Tati, 240; and Lettrists, 189–90; urban thought, 193, 195, 200
decentralization, 7, 59, 111, 271, 300, 305–8, 324–25, 343. *See* also *aménagement du territoire*
decolonization, 11, 15–16, 43–44, 129, 131, 151, 226, 260, 278, 284
de Gaulle, Charles, 27, 98, 103–4, 109, 117, 260, 322, 324, 342–43; Algerian War, 159, 161, 288; Fifth Republic, 341; May 8 1954 commemoration ceremonies, 127–28
Délégation générale de l'équipement national (DGEN), 296, 300, 306
Delouvrier, Paul, 343
Demangeon, Albert, 43, 45, 169
demonstrations. *See* protests
Denfert-Rochereau, place, 92, 95, 225, 315
Déon, Michel: background, 270; *Les Gens de la Nuit*, 86, 265, 270, 277
Destinée de Paris (1943), 185, 294–95, 334, 336
Dewever, Jean, 16, 238–39; *La Crise du logement* (1956), 236–37
Dien Bien Phu, 44, 128–29
Doisneau, Robert, 16, 27, 65, 69, 72, 74–75, 354
Duvivier, Julien, 208; *Sous le ciel de Paris* (1951), 213–15

École des beaux-arts, 181, 271, 274, 321, 338; brass band, 274, 281, 288. *See* also *mônome du bac* (rag parade)
Économie et Humanisme, 171, 182
employment (jobs, unemployment), 47, 49–51, 60, 134–35, 145, 147, 153–54, 193–94, 223, 254, 321, 324, 343
Enfants du paradis, Les (1944), 1–3, 5, 8, 20, 75, 228–30, 233, 235, 249, 346. *See also* Carné, Marcel
Esprit, 137, 163, 184, 192, 234, 252, 277. *See also* Mounier, Emmanuel
existentialism, 189, 192, 248, 251, 259–60, 276; and youth culture, 252–53, 262
Exposition de la reconstruction, Première (1945), 134–35, 289
Exposition des Techniques Américaines de l'Habitation et de l'Urbanisme (1946), 289–90
Exposition internationale de l'urbanisme et de l'habitation (1947), 110, 290, 302

Fargue, Léon Paul, 19–20, 64–65, 163, 217, 246, 329
Fête de l'Humanité, 97–99, 130, 138, 344
fête nationale (July 14), 14, 23, 28, 30, 92, 144, 218, 221; in film, 233, 269; protests, 121, 153–54, 157; *quatorze juillet*, 70, 81, 87–89; street marches, 32, 116, 118, 126
fêtes foraines (fun fairs), 56, 70, 75, 77, 79, 86, 266–67; description, 91–97, 120; Foire du Trône, 92–94
Figaro, Le, 25, 123; Algerian War, 158–59, 286; housing crisis, 139
film noir, 193, 198, 214, 226, 232
Flouret, Marcel, 302–4
fortifs (fortifications), 48, 60, 299, 318
Fourastié, Jean, 167
Fourth Republic, 14–15, 17, 28, 43, 107, 109, 157–58, 238, 241, 260, 287, 304, 312
France-soir, 34, 38, 74
Front de libération nationale (FLN), 151, 156–57, 361

Gabin, Jean, 40–41, 71–72, 227, 231
Gallimard, 164, 199–200, 246, 252
Gare, La, 58, 63, 173–75, 198, 202–3
Garric, Robert, 64, 66–68, 171; background, 371
Gibel, Pierre, 296, 304–6
Giraudoux, Jean, 37, 163, 184, 374

grands ensembles (housing projects), 7, 61, 186, 268, 318–20, 323, 327, 343
Grasset, 177, 246
Gravier, Jean, 147, 306–7, 372; *Paris et le désert français*, 180, 306–7
Gréco, Juliette, 41, 217, 248, 252–53, 260
Groupe Octobre, 71, 209, 216, 249

habitations à loyer modéré (HLM), 133, 224, 239
Hadj, Messali, 152–54, 156
Halles, Les, 38, 51, 63, 69, 161; description, 54–56; in film and television, 220–21, 231, 269; and lettrists, 189, 191, 196; urban planning, 114, 298–99, 308–11, 321, 342–43
Halles aux Vins, 38, 59, 272, 310
haussmannisme (*haussmannisation*), 17, 180, 291, 293, 299
historic district, 335, 339–40
Holley, Michel, 315, 321, 342
housing crisis, 15, 17, 37, 45, 106, 110, 131–39, 141–42, 144–45, 293, 309, 312, 327; in film and television, 131, 140, 143, 236–38; housing studies, 297, 339; Marais, 330–32, 337; student housing, 272–73
humanism, 165–66, 168, 176–78, 185, 202, 344–46; and poetic realism, 208; urban planning, 303, 311, 333, 337–39
Humanité, L', 83–84, 88–89, 100, 108, 117, 234, 239, 241, 258; Algerian Crisis, 161; and Fête de l'Humanité, 97–98; housing crisis, 136; North African population, 147–48; and strikes, 122, 126, 130

îlots insalubres, 46–47, 173, 237, 321, 334, 336–37; îlot 1 Saint-Merri, 46, 327; îlot 2 rue Mouffetard, 46–47, 290; îlot 3 Saint-Michel, 47; îlot 4 cité Jeanne-d'Arc, 47, 198, 203; îlot 5 porte de Clichy, 47; îlot 6 faubourg Saint-Antoine, 47; îlot 9 Clignancourt, 47; îlot 11 Ménilmontant, 290; îlot 13 Moulin de la Pointe, 223; îlot 16 Marais, 186, 290, 327, 330–31, 333, 338–39
Indochinese War, 42, 44, 122, 128, 276, 278
industries, 24, 49, 146, 310, 325, 328–29; automobile, 51; chemical, 57; construction, 133, 137; fashion, 40; film, 40, 204, 207–9; food, 57; leather, 223; luxury, 40, 51; mechanical, 51, 57, 122; music, 40, 81; publishing, 40, 51
Institut d'urbanisme (IUUP), 181–82, 184–85, 297, 304
Italie, place d', 42, 47, 221, 315

jazz clubs, 253–54, 259, 272; Le Bar Vert, 247; Caveau de la Huchette, 251, 259–60, 262, 264; Club Saint-Germain, 217, 247, 253; L'Échelle de Jacob, 248–49; Kentucky, 259, 264; Lorient, 247; Quod Libet, 248; Rose Rouge, 190, 248–49, 251; Rôtisserie de l'Abbaye, 220; Tabou, 190, 251; Vieux-Colomier, 248, 259
Jewish population, 2, 22, 52, 74, 216, 243–44, 329–30, 334, 340; round up (*rafle*), 22, 28, 329, 334
July 14. See *fête nationale* (July 14)
Jussieu, 38, 59, 61, 201, 272, 283, 310

kermesse, 70, 90, 266; Kermesses aux Étoiles (Festival of the stars), 40–41, 218; Kermesse des Écoles, 90
Kosma, Joseph, 2, 71, 73, 85, 217, 227–28; background, 209; film scores, 229, 235; music, 248–49; social thought, 229
Krier, Jacques, 218, 222, 226

La Courneuve, 57, 92
La Défense, 42, 61, 311, 316, 341–42
Lafay, Bernard, 180, 239, 314; background, 312
Lafay Law, 145, 187, 318
Lafay Plan, 313–15, 318, 322
La Goutte d'Or, 42, 154; Algerian War, 155; and communist party, 113; North African population, 145, 147–50; violence and raids, 151–52
Laprade, Albert, 316, 333–34, 338–39
Latin Quarter, 16, 21, 28, 35, 338; Algerian War, 158, 161; as center of student activism, 277–88; communists, 276–77; description, 242, 270–74; in film, 215; music and dance, 245; wartime resistance, 243–44; youth culture, 259–61, 263
Lavedan, Pierre, 179; social thought and urbanism, 181–82, 303
Le Chanois, Jean-Paul Dreyfus-, 209–10, 218; background, 216; *Sans laisser d'adresse*, 216–18, 229
Le Corbusier, 162, 175, 181–82, 185, 292,

294, 297, 303, 312, 314–16, 333, 342, 345; *Destin de Paris*, 295, 309
Lefebvre, Henri, 9, 15, 96, 165, 167; background, 176–77; *Critique of Everyday Life*, 177–79, 188; social thought, 177–79
Lemarque, Francis, 40, 248; background, 250; music, 84–85, 231, 249–50
Lettres françaises, Les, 6, 67, 71, 79, 108, 163, 213, 234; avant-garde, 252; origins, 164
lettrist movement, 188–92, 201, 251, 282; *dérive*, 190–93, 196; *The Naked City*, 193, 196; *Naked Lips*, 191; *Potlatch*, 196; psychogeography and urbanism, 193, 196, 198. See also situationism
Liberation, 9–11, 13–15, 21, 32, 37, 79, 183, 205, 207; and avant-garde, 162–63, 188, 192, 209, 228; commemoration and street naming, 98–105, 130; and communist party, 108, 116, 243; description of, 5, 25–27, 30, 35, 43–44, 80, 86, 89; in film and television, 209–10, 220, 222, 227–28, 237; and humanism, 165–66, 169, 176–77, 184, 227, 344; memory of, 62, 106, 154, 161, 261; municipal power, 112–14; street marches, 115–19, 129; urbanism, 300–301, 304, 309, 336; youth, 241, 243, 245, 247, 271
Lopez, Raymond, 239, 312, 314–15, 321, 323, 342; background, 313; *rocade Lopez*, 317–18
Lotar, Eli, 235, 238

magical urbanism, 97, 103, 105, 112, 142, 145, 313, 340, 347
Malet, Léo, 188, 202–3, 217, 234, 328; background, 193–94, 256; Saint-Germain-des-Prés, 256; urban thought, 195–96, 198, 200. See also *Nouveaux mystères de Paris, Les* (1953–59)
Marais, 37, 56, 63, 173, 182, 191, 308, 327–40; Festival of the Marais, 339
Marshall Plan, 44, 50, 122, 138, 290
Marxism, 15, 164–65, 192; and humanism, 176–78
May Day, 14, 30, 77, 81, 87; street marches, 116–19, 126, 138, 153, 288
Ménilmontant, 2, 43, 51, 53, 63, 66, 70, 77, 84, 322; and communist party, 112–13; in film, 215, 238
Mestais, René, 180, 298–99, 302–3, 330
Métro, 3, 6, 9–10, 71, 82, 86, 99, 101, 140, 196, 201, 204, 244–45, 266, 309; in film, 211, 228, 230; housing crisis, 140; protests, 161; and Ridgway riots, 124–25; symbolism, 39, 42, 125, 211
Ministère de la Reconstruction et de l'Urbanisme (MRU), 59, 175, 184, 289–90; housing crisis, 131, 133–34, 137–38, 143; origins, 292, 300–301; planning Paris, 302, 305–6, 309–10
Monde, Le, 20, 41, 140, 260, 268
mônome du bac (rag parade), 116, 192; origins, 274; as student protest, 275–76, 281–83; and wartime resistance, 244, 275
Montand, Yves, 34, 40, 88, 96, 108, 227, 259; background, 229, 249–50; music, 73, 84–85, 229, 231, 286; *Les Portes de la Nuit*, 228–30
Montmartre, 42, 52, 66, 74, 77, 86, 92, 146, 170, 182, 215, 247, 249
Montparnasse, 28, 42, 61, 71, 89–90, 161, 163, 242, 246, 313, 316, 342
Mouffetard, rue ("la Mouff"), 47, 53, 63, 173, 272, 290; in film, 215–16, 269; protests, 158, 161, 288; on television, 219, 223
Mounier, Emmanuel, 164, 184, 252. See also *Esprit*
Mouvement pour le triomphe des libertés démocratiques (MTLD), 152–54, 156
Mouvement républicain populaire (MRP), 138, 301–2
municipal council: communists, 115, 268, 301–2, 307, 309, 338; conflict with state, 34, 135, 301, 305, 307–8, 311, 313, 320–21, 324–25; housing, 145, 318; planning debates, 184, 241, 308–12, 314–15, 324–25, 338; powers, 22, 101, 113–14, 301; urban policy, 38, 46, 88–89, 101, 103–4, 130, 156; youth, 243, 267, 282, 286
Mur des Fédérés, 30, 82, 117
music, 274; accordion, 28, 82, 84–86, 89, 91, 98, 228, 258; amateur, 81–82, 84–86, 90–92, 220, 258; *bals musettes* and *guinguettes*, 85–86, 150; bebop, 86, 245, 248, 251, 253; jazz, 31, 86, 245, 247–48, 251, 253–54, 257, 259–61, 265, 272; meaning of, 36, 68, 81, 83, 85, 88; musical festivities, 34–36, 81–82, 88–92, 98, 103–4, 218, 245; rock 'n' roll, 220, 248, 265; street singers, 19, 81–83; swing, 86, 135, 244–45; yé-yé, 248–49

Nanterre, 109, 137, 269, 342; North African population, 147–48
Nation, place de la, 30–31, 88; Algerian War, 159, 161; and *fêtes foraines*, 92–94; in film, 218; July 14, 1953 riots, 153–54; street marches, 118–20, 126, 159, 288
Noisy-le-Sec, 24, 49, 115, 289
North African, population, 42–43, 145–47, 175, 267, 322; employment, 51, 125, 146–47, 154, 247; and La Goutte d'Or, 149–51; housing crisis, 147–49; July 14, 1953 riots, 153–54; perceptions of, 145–46, 149–50, 154, 231; raids, 151–52, 155
Nouveaux mystères de Paris, Les (1953–59), 193–95; *Brouillard au Pont de Tolbiac*, 198–99; *Fièvre au Marais*, 328–29; *Micmac moche au Boul'Mich'*, 257–58; *La Nuit de Saint-Germain-des-Prés*, 256–57. *See also* Malet, Léo

Opération Million, 145
ouvriérisme, 40, 115, 131, 154, 209, 212

Panthéon, 28, 117, 139, 220, 244, 272, 274, 277
Pantin, 51, 57, 59, 132, 187, 232, 327
Papon, Maurice, 28, 155
Paris et l'agglomération parisienne (1952), 172–75, 186, 190, 196, 238. *See also* Chombart de Lauwe, Paul-Henry
Parisien libéré, Le, 35, 145, 154, 156, 200, 281
Paris la belle (1959), 346–47
Paris-Match, 74, 116, 127–28, 206, 282, 311–12; Abbé Pierre, 140, 142, 144
Paris region: description, 50–51, 53, 150, 153, 179; planning, 294, 296, 300–301, 305–6, 313–14, 319–20, 323–24, 326, 343; politics, 114, 126, 156, 277, 292; population, 42, 47–50, 109, 146, 306, 324, 343; television sets in, 206; wartime damage, 24, 50. *See also* suburbs
Paris school of urban planning, 296–97, 304. *See also* Institut d'urbanisme (IUUP)
Périer de Féral, Guy, 290, 298–99, 334
Pétain, Marshal, 24, 296, 335, 374; *pétainistes*, 244
Philippe, Gérard, 40–41, 108, 160, 207, 259
Plan d'aménagement et d'organisation générale de la région parisienne (PADOG), 324
Plan d'urbanisme directeur, 297, 316, 322, 324–26

Poëte, Marcel, 163, 179–82, 185, 333
poetic humanism, 13, 15, 17, 65, 70, 77, 144, 165, 167, 188, 201, 203, 205, 214, 238, 261, 293–94, 326, 328, 344–46; in film, 210, 212–13; in urban planning, 293–94, 317, 326, 335, 339
poetic realism, 40, 201, 205, 207–9, 216, 228, 234, 268
population: city of Paris, 37, 306; density, 37–38, 300, 330; Jewish, 329; North African, 42, 146–49; Paris region, 42, 47–50, 109, 306, 324, 343; in planning policy, 132, 319–20, 324, 330, 337; population studies, 169–70, 172, 187
populism (populist), 3; festivals of, 36, 79, 88–89, 92, 94, 96–97, 118, 127–28, 130; in film and media, 143–44, 205–6, 209, 212, 216–17, 219–21, 224, 227, 231, 234, 240; image, 13, 43, 67, 79, 84, 166–67, 196, 200, 247–48, 266, 288, 328; landscape of, 43, 62, 65, 69–70, 99–100, 105, 112, 188–89, 199, 201, 204, 265, 317, 322; meaning, 14, 17, 121, 238; politics of, 123, 126, 130, 328, 345; Resistance and Liberation origins, 25, 32, 100, 161, 261
porte des Lilas, 187, 232, 272
Porte des Lilas (1957), 232–35. *See also* Clair, René
Portes de la Nuit, Les (1946), 192, 198, 226, 228–31, 255. *See also* Carné, Marcel
preservationism, 17, 162–63, 184–85, 196, 293–94, 296–98, 311, 315–16, 335–36; *Destruction de Paris* (1941), 333; *façadisme*, 339; legislation, 335, 340, 374; Marais, 327, 333, 335–40; *triangle sacré*, 315. *See also* historic district
Prévert, Jacques, 1, 112, 163, 188, 208, 260–61; *Aubervilliers*, 235–36, 249; background, 70–71, 209, 216, 246, 249; ballet *Le Rendez-vous*, 249; *Les Enfant du Paradis*, 249; films, 77, 227, 231, 235, 249; lyrics, 85, 229; *Paroles*, 72–74, 94–95, 228, 248; plays, 249; poetry, 77–80, 229, 248; *Les Portes de la Nuit*, 228, 230; *Spectacle*, 73, 75
protests, 121–23; Algerian War, 157–61, 284–88; anticommunist, 121, 130, 131; July 14, 1953 riots, 153–54; student, 278–88. *See also* strikes
Prothin, André, 296, 304, 310–11, 338; background, 371n14

psychogeography, 193, 200, 210, 215
purges, 28, 44, 62, 68, 113, 163, 207, 228, 336

Radiodiffusion télévision française (RTF/ORTF), 116, 205–6, 219, 237, 322, 342
Rassemblement du peuple français (RPF), 98, 109, 128, 307–9
Renault, 58, 82, 91, 98, 308; automobile, 253; and strikes, 121–22, 144
Rendez-vous de juillet (1949), 253–54, 258. See also Becker, Jacques
République, place de la, 40, 63, 88, 94, 138; Algerian War, 159, 161; Ridgway riots, 124; and street marches, strikes, 119, 121, 123, 159, 288; and street naming, 101; urban planning, 309
Resistance, 32, 43–44, 106, 108, 171, 176, 178, 213; and avant-garde, 209, 216, 228; commemoration and street naming, 99–105; and communist party, 116, 163, 275; in film, 229; and humanism, 165–66, 169, 344; municipal power, 113, 293, 301–2; as youth movement, 242–45, 255, 277, 284
Revue urbanisme, 289, 316, 320
Ridgway, General Matthew, 44, 124, 153
Ridgway riots, 121, 124–26, 277
Rohmer, Eric. See *Signe de Lion, Le* (1959)
Romains, Jules, 64, 66
Ronis, Willy, 16, 65, 112, 188; background, 74–75; *Belleville-Ménilmontant*, 77; photography 74–77, 218
Roux-Spitz, Michel, 185, 334, 336–37; City of Paris design, 336–37

Saint-Antoine, faubourg, 43, 47, 51, 53, 56, 63, 94, 126, 227, 298
Saint-Denis, 24, 43, 49, 57–59, 63, 104; Algerian War, 158; and communist party, 109, 113, 115, 147
Saint-Germain-des-Prés, 16, 35, 72–73, 164, 274; avant-garde, 246, 252–53; decline, 260–62, 265–66, 269–70; description, 242, 246–47; existentialism, 192, 253; jazz clubs, 220, 247–48, 252; and lettrists, 189, 191, 251; music, 86, 245, 247–48, 251; prewar, 70–71, 216; youth culture, 251, 255, 258–59, 261–65
Saint-Germain-des-Prés, boulevard, 244, 257, 271, 308; avant-garde, 246, 249; as boundary, 246, 259, 287; student marches and protests, 279–82
Saint-Gervais, 337, 339
Saint-Michel, boulevard (Boul' Mich'), 47, 152, 201, 246, 257, 271; as boundary, 259, 279, 287; fairs and festivals, 35, 92; Liberation, 243–44; student marches and protests, 242, 275, 277–83
Saint-Michel, place, 35, 281; and street naming, 102–4
Saint-Paul, 161, 189–90, 330
salaries (wages), 44, 110–11, 120–22
Salon des Urbanistes (1943), 162, 298–99, 332. See also Vichy Regime: urban planning
Sans laisser d'adresse (1951), 216–18, 229. See also Le Chanois, Jean-Paul Dreyfus-
Sarcelles, 61, 327. See also *grands ensembles* (housing projects)
Sartre, Jean-Paul, 27, 31, 160, 246, 253, 260; *Le Temps modernes*, 252–53, 277
Sauvage, rue, 190, 196, 201–2
Schéma directeur d'aménagement et d'urbanisme, 325
Sébille, Georges, 37; social thought and urbanism, 185–86, 333, 337
Services des affaires indigènes nord-africaines, 151
Services techniques de topographie et d'urbanisme, Inspection général de, 45, 132, 290, 298. See also, Mestais, René
Siegfried, André, 39, 42–43
Signe de lion, Le (1959), 260, 268–70
situationism, 79, 99, 179, 188, 192, 196, 201, 282; and Calet, 200; film, 189, 191, 210; and Tati, 240. See also lettrist movement
slum clearance, 47, 173–74, 202, 224, 290, 296, 299, 306, 312, 320–21, 332–33, 336, 338. See also *îlots insalubres*
slums, 42, 46–47, 50, 59, 83, 132–37, 139, 158, 178–80, 184, 196, 198, 232, 299–300, 310, 325, 327, 330, 332; definition of, 46, 70, 131, 173, 317, 334; in film and television, 223–38; North African, 145, 147–48
Socialist Party, 30, 117–19, 123, 159, 278, 281, 301
social segregation, 39, 148, 172, 180, 231, 255
Solutions aux problèmes de Paris. See Lafay Plan

song: festivals and recitals, 90, 235; military, 104; "Paris" songs, 84–85, 199; political meaning, 25, 32, 81–83, 161, 277, 285–86, 355n35; popular, 70, 73, 207, 229, 231, 233, 248–49; vernacular tradition, 36, 66, 68, 77, 79, 81, 84, 122, 142, 220, 244, 249

Sorbonne, 28, 164, 243; description, 270–72, 274; student protests, 278–79, 280

Soufflot, rue, 272, 274–75, 277–78, 280, 282

Sous le ciel de Paris (1951), 205, 213–15. *See also* Duvivier, Julien

street names, 57, 77, 112, 200, 209, 232, 258, 356n75; ceremonies, 100, 102–4; debates, 101, 103–5, 130; Henri Martin, 277; lettrists, 191, 198; Malet, 198; meaning, 99–103, 105, 191

strikes, 14–16, 37, 75, 116, 121, 123, 131, 137, 166, 218, 226, 345, 347; November 1947, 119, 121, 279; September 1948, 121; August 1953, 121; March 1956, 286; October 1957, 157–58; student strikes, 277–81. *See also* protests

students: colonial students, 273; conditions, 272–75, 278, 283–84; number of, 271–72; organizations, 273, 276–78; protests, 278–85, 287–88; wartime resistance, 242–45, 275

suburbs, 17, 120, 138, 153, 271; communists, 109, 113–15, 130, 309; description, 38, 43–45, 49, 57, 59, 82, 85–86, 133, 147–48, 169, 180, 236, 326; fairs and festivals, 92, 97, 126; image of, 48, 200, 223–24, 263, 268, 294, 305–6; planning, 188, 289–90, 297, 299, 305–6, 309–10, 318–20, 323–24, 327, 337; population, 42, 48–49, 146; street naming, 105; wartime destruction, 16, 24, 49. *See also* Paris region

Sudreau, Pierre, 223, 239, 319, 324–25, 342; background, 320; *Problèmes de la construction* (1958), 237–38, 322–23

surrealism, 71, 74, 163–64, 178, 188–89, 194, 235, 242

Syndicalisme, 107, 110, 134

Tati, Jacques: *Mon oncle* (1958), 238–40; urban perspective, 238

teenagers, 263, 265, 267; *blousons noirs*, 265–68, 288; hoodlums, 250; *les jeunes*, 264; juvenile delinquents, 260, 263; teddy boys, 265; *tricheurs*, 261–62, 264–65

television, 11–13, 15–16, 74, 96, 199, 205–8, 225–26, 264, 344; *36 Chandelles*, 265; coverage, 61, 80, 116, 121, 128, 131, 140, 143, 200, 218, 237, 263, 281; *À la découverte des français*, 222–26; Jean D'Arcy, 219, 221–22; live broadcasts, 218–22; *Problèmes de la construction*, 237–38, 322–23; sets, 50, 116, 206, 221, 223; *Télé-Match*, 92, 221; *Télé-Paris*, 92, 206

theaters, 1–4, 40, 204, 213, 235, 247, 252, 254–55, 260, 266–67, 271; ABC, 40, 265; Alhambra, 40; Athénée, 249; Champs-Elysées, 206; Étoile, de l', 40; Gaumont, 29, 40, 139; Huchette, 252; Noctumbules, 252; Olympia, 40, 251, 265; Pathé, 5, 40; Pleyel, 249; Rex, 206; Sarah Bernhardt, 249; Théâtre de l'Humour, 249; Théâtre de Poche, 249, 252; Vieux-Colombier, 189, 246, 252

Thirion, André, 180, 308–9, 311, 317

Thorez, Maurice, 98, 108, 122

tourism (touristic), 17, 19–20, 35–36, 189, 220, 294, 316, 326, 330, 338–41, 345

traffic, 22, 28, 32, 34, 89, 94, 143; description, 36, 38–39; in film, 215, 268; and protests, 123, 156, 280–81, 283; urban planning, 183, 187, 315, 323, 338, 343

Trauner, Alexander, 2, 71, 75, 209, 227–28, 230

trente glorieuses, 5, 7, 11, 109–11, 140, 142, 167, 182, 222, 239, 260, 316, 327, 344, 347

Tricheurs, Les (1958), 260–64, 270. *See also* Carné, Marcel

Union de la jeunesse républicaine française (UJRF), 123, 241

Union des étudiants communistes (UEC), 274, 276

Union des jeunesses communistes (UJC), 273, 276, 278, 287

Union national des étudiants de France (UNEF), 277–78, 280, 282–85

Vél' d'Hiv' (Vélodrome d'hiver), 22, 28–29, 122, 152–53, 164, 258

Verlomme, Roger, 148, 307–8, 336

Vian, Boris, 247–48, 252, 255, 285

Vichy Regime, 1, 40, 163, 182–83, 248; administration of Paris, 22–23, 113, 292–

93; Law on Urbanism, 296, 298, 335; urban planning, 47, 54, 167, 296–300, 326, 334–36; Uriage Leadership School, 171, 175
Vie Ouvrière, La, 103, 117, 135, 240
Vilar, Jean, 18, 192, 228
Villes et campagnes conference (1951), 167–69
Villette, La, 38, 43, 54, 57–59, 63, 66, 70, 86, 200, 310; in film, 235; North African population, 147–48; and protests, 121

wages. *See* salaries (wages)

youth, as generational category, 254, 287–88. *See also* teenagers

zazous, 135, 192, 244–45, 248, 253–54, 265
zone, 17, 138; description, 48–49, 232, 235, 267; urban renewal, 59, 144–45, 187, 299, 318
zone à urbaniser en priorité (ZUP), 322
zone cristallisé, 294, 316, 321–22, 326, 343
zoning, 295, 308, 310–11, 316, 318, 324, 338